Lecture Notes in Computer Science   8709

Commenced Publication in 1973
Founding and Former Series Editors:
Gerhard Goos, Juris Hartmanis, and Jan van Leeuwen

Lei Chen   Yan Jia   Timos Sellis
Guanfeng Liu (Eds.)

Web Technologies and Applications

16th Asia-Pacific Web Conference, APWeb 2014
Changsha, China, September 5-7, 2014
Proceedings

 Springer

Volume Editors

Lei Chen
Hong Kong University of Science and Technology
Hong Kong, China
E-mail: leichen@cse.ust.hk

Yan Jia
National University of Defense Technology
Changsha, China
E-mail: jiayanjy@vip.sina.com

Timos Sellis
RMIT University
Melbourne, VIC, Australia
E-mail: timos.sellis@rmit.edu.au

Guanfeng Liu
Soochow University
Suzhou, China
E-mail: gfliu@suda.edu.cn

ISSN 0302-9743   e-ISSN 1611-3349
ISBN 978-3-319-11115-5   e-ISBN 978-3-319-11116-2
DOI 10.1007/978-3-319-11116-2
Springer Cham Heidelberg New York Dordrecht London

Library of Congress Control Number: Applied for

LNCS Sublibrary: SL 3 – Information Systems and Application, incl. Internet/Web
and HCI

Typesetting: Camera-ready by author, data conversion by Scientific Publishing Services, Chennai, India

Printed on acid-free paper

Springer is part of Springer Science+Business Media (www.springer.com)

Message from the General Chairs and Program Committee Chairs

Welcome to the proceedings of APWeb 2014! This was the 16th edition of the Asia Pacific Web Conference. Since the first APWeb conference started in 1998, APWeb has evolved with the time to lead the frontier of data-driven information technology research. It has now firmly established itself as a leading Asia Pacific-focused international conference on research, development, and advanced applications on large-scale data management, Web and search technologies, and information processing. Previous APWeb conferences were held in Sydney (2013), Kunming (2012), Beijing (2011), Busan (2010), Suzhou (2009), Shenyang (2008), Huangshan (2007), Harbin (2006), Shanghai (2005), Hangzhou (2004), Xi'an (2003), Changsha (2001), Xi'an (2000), Hong Kong (1999), and Beijing (1998).

APWeb 2014 was held during September 5–7 in the beautiful city of Changsha, China, a city proud of its history of 3,000 years. The conference moved from its usual spring slot to be held with the VLDB conference this year, which took place immediately before APWeb in Hangzhou, China. That was the third time that APWeb was synchronized with a major database conference held in China (i.e., SIGMOD 2007 in Beijing, and ICDE 2009 in Shanghai). The host organization of APWeb 2014 was the National University of Defence Technology, a leading university in China best known for developing the currently fastest supercomputer in the world, Tianhe-2.

As in the previous years, the APWeb 2014 program featured the main conference with research papers, an industry track, tutorials, demos, and a panel. APWeb this year received 134 paper submissions to the main conference from North America, South America, Europe, Asia, and Africa. Each submitted paper underwent a rigorous review process by at least three independent members of the Program Committee, with detailed review reports. Finally, 34 full research papers and 23 short research papers were accepted and included in these proceedings, from Australia, Canada, China, Italy, Luxembourg, Japan, New Zealand, and Tunisia. The conference this year also had three satellite workshops.

- First International Workshop on Social Network Analysis (SNA 2014)
- First International Workshop on Network and Information Security (NIS 2014)
- First International Workshop on Internet of Things Search (IoTS 2014)

We were fortunate to have three world-leading scientists as our keynote speakers: Binxing Fang (Beijing University of Posts and Telecommunications, China), Christian Jensen (Aalborg University, Denmark) and Divesh Srivastava (AT&T, USA). The two tutorial presenters were Xin Luna Dong (Google, USA) and Feifei Li (University of Utah, USA). Starting from this edition, APWeb included a new exciting program, the Distinguished Lecture Series, co-chaired this year by Xin

Luna Dong (Google, USA) and Jiaheng Lu (Renmin University of China), to invite active, high-achieving, and mostly pre-tenture researchers to discuss their work at APWeb. The four speakers this year are Fabian Suchanek (Telecom ParisTech, France), Nan Tang (QCRI, Qatar), Steven Whang (Google, USA), and Xiaokui Xiao (Nanyang Technological University, Singapore).

The success of APWeb 2014 would not have been possible without the hard work by a great team of people, including Workshop Chairs Weihong Han (NUDT, China) and Zi Huang (The University of Queensland, Australia), Panel Chair Jianmin Wang (Tsinghua University, China), Industrial Chairs Hoyoung Jeung (SAP, Australia) and Yu Zheng (Microsoft Research Asia, China), Demo Chairs Toshiyuki Amagasa (University of Tsukuba, Japan) and Feida Zhu (SMU, Singapore), Research Students Symposium Chairs Guoliang Li (Tsinghua University, China) and Wen-Chih Peng (National Chiao Tung University, Taiwan), Publication Chair Guangfeng Liu (Soochow University, China), Publicity Chair Reynold Cheng (University of Hong Kong, China), and our webmaster, Chen Zhao (HKUST, China). We would also like to take this opportunity to extend our sincere gratitude to the Program Committee members and external reviewers. A special thank you goes to the local organization chair, Bin Zhou (NUDT, China), and his team of organizers and volunteers!

Last but not least, we would like to thank all the sponsors, the APWeb Steering Committee led by Jeffrey Yu, and the host organization, National University of Defence Technology, for their support, help, and assistance in organizing this conference.

June 2014

Changjie Tang
Xiaofang Zhou
Lei Chen
Yan Jia
Timos Sellis

Organization

General Co-chairs

Changjie Tang   Sichuan University, China
Xiaofang Zhou   The University of Queensland, Australia

Program Committee Co-chairs

Lei Chen   Hong Kong University of Science and Technology, SAR China
Yan Jia   National University of Defense Technology, China
Timos Sellis   RMIT, Australia

Workshop Co-chairs

Weihong Han   National University of Defense Technology, China
Zi Huang   University of Queensland, Australia

Tutorial Chair

Kyuseok Shim   Seoul National University, Korea

Panel Chair

Jianmin Wang   Tsinghua University

Industrial Co-chairs

Hoyoung Jeung   SAP Research, Australia
Yu Zheng   Microsoft Research Asia, China

Demo Co-chairs

Toshiyuki Amagasa   University of Tsukuba, Japan
Feida Zhu   SMU, Singapore

Distinguished Lecture Series Co-chairs

Jiaheng Lu   Renmin University of China
Luna Xin Dong   Google, USA

Research Students Symposium Co-chairs

Guoliang Li   Tsinghua University, China
Wen-Chih Peng   National Chiao Tung University, Taiwan

Publication Chair

Guanfeng Liu   Soochow University, China

Publicity Chair

Reynold Cheng   University of Hong Kong, China

Local Organization Chair

Bin Zhou   National University of Defense Technology,
                                         China

APWeb Steering Committee Liaison

Xuemin Lin   University of New South Wales, Australia

WISE Society Liaison

Yanchun Zhang   Victoria University, Australia

WAIM Steering Committee Liaison

Weiyi Meng   State University of New York at Binghamton,
                                         USA

Webmaster

Chen Zhao   Hong Kong University of Science and
                                         Technology, SAR China

Program Committee

Adam Jatowt   Kyoto University, Japan
Aixin Sun   Nanyang Technological University, Singapore
Alex Thomo   University of Victoria, Canada
Anastasios Kementsietsidis   IBM T.J. Watson Research Center, USA
Apostolos Papadopoulos   Aristotle University, Greece
Aviv Segev   KAIST, South Korea

Baihua Zheng	Singapore Management University, Singapore
Bin Shao	Microsoft Research Asia, China
Bin Cui	Beijing University, China
Bo Luo	University of Kansas, USA
Byung Lee	Vermont University, USA
Carson K. Leung	University of Manitoba, Canada
Chaokun Wang	Tsinghua University, China
Chaoyi Pang	CSIRO, Australia
Cheqing Jin	East China Normal University, China
Claudia Szabo	University of Adelaide, Australia
Daling Wang	Northeastern University, China
David Taniar	Monash University, Australia
Derong Shen	Northeastern University, China
Djamal Benslimane	University of Lyon, France
Eric Pardede	Latrobe University, Australia
Guimei Liu	National University of Singapore, Singapore
Guoren Wang	Northeastern University, China
Haiming Chen	Chinese Academy of Sciences, China
Haruo Yokota	Tokyo Institute of Technology, Japan
Helen Paik	University of New South Wales, Australia
Hong Gao	Harbin Institute of Technology, China
Hongzhi Wang	Harbin Institute of Technology, China
Hua Wang	University of Southern Queensland, Australia
Jae-Gil Lee	KAIST, South Korea
Jef Wijsen	University of Mons-Hainaut, Belgium
Jeong-Hyon Hwang	State University of New York at Albany, USA
Jian Yin	Sun Yat-Sen University, China
Jian Yu	Swinburne University of Technology, Australia
Jiangang Ma	University of Adelaide, Australia
Jianliang Xu	Hong Kong Baptist University, SAR China
Jianlin Feng	Sun Yat-Sen University, China
Jianyong Wang	Tsinghua University, China
Jinchuan Chen	Renmin University of China, China
Jin-Ho Kim	Kangwon National University, South Korea
Joao Rocha-Junior	Universidade Estadual de Feira de Santana, Brazil
Jun Hong	Queen's University Belfast, UK
Kazutoshi Sumiya	University of Hyogo, Japan
KeunHo Ryu	Chungbuk National University, South Korea
Kostas Stefanidis	ICS-FORTH, Greece
Lidan Shou	Zhejiang University, China
Markus Schneider	University of Florida, USA
Markus Kirchberg	Institute for Infocomm Research, Singapore

Table of Contents

Distinguished Lecture

Invited Paper

Full Paper

Short Paper

Demo

Recent Topics of Research
around the YAGO Knowledge Base

Antoine Amarilli[1], Luis Galárraga[1], Nicoleta Preda[2], and Fabian M. Suchanek[1]

[1] Télécom ParisTech, Paris, France
[2] University of Versailles, France

Abstract. A knowledge base (KB) is a formal collection of knowledge about the world. In this paper, we explain how the YAGO KB is constructed. We also summarize our contributions to different aspects of KB management in general. One of these aspects is rule mining, i.e., the identification of patterns such as $spouse(x,y) \wedge livesIn(x,z) \Rightarrow livesIn(y,z)$. Another aspect is the incompleteness of KBs. We propose to integrate data from Web Services into the KB in order to fill the gaps. Further, we show how the overlap between existing KBs can be used to align them, both in terms of instances and in terms of the schema. Finally, we show how KBs can be protected by watermarking.

1 Introduction

Recent advances in information extraction have led to the creation of large knowledge bases (KBs). These KBs provide information about a great variety of entities, such as people, countries, rivers, cities, universities, movies, animals, etc. Among the most prominent academic projects are Cyc [12], DBpedia [2], Freebase[1], and our own YAGO [21]. Most of these projects are linked together in the Semantic Web [5]. KBs find numerous applications in the industry. The Knowledge Graph released by Google is an example of a large commercial KB project. It contains linked information about millions of people, places, and organizations, and helps Google deliver more semantic search results. Facebook is also building a KB from the information of its users and their interests, and Microsoft, too, is experimenting with a KB to enhance its search results. These projects show not just the advances in technology and the growth of semantic data, but also the rising commercial interest in KBs.

Our work investigates models and algorithms for the automated construction, maintenance, and application of large-scale KBs. The main project is the YAGO knowledge base, which we develop jointly at the Télécom ParisTech Institute in Paris and the Max Planck Institute for Informatics in Germany. YAGO was extracted automatically from Web sources, and contains around 10 million entities and 120 million facts. We use YAGO as an example to study different aspects of KB management in general: how new information can be added automatically

---

[1] http://freebase.com

L. Chen et al. (Eds.): APWeb 2014, LNCS 8709, pp. 1–12, 2014.
© Springer International Publishing Switzerland 2014

to a KB, how we can protect KBs from plagiarism, how KBs can be integrated with other KBs, and how we can mine patterns from KBs.

In this paper, we summarize 5 main directions of research. Section 2 describes our latest efforts in the construction of the YAGO KB. In Section 3, we discuss our work on automated matching of one KB to another KB. Our system matches not just instances, but also classes and relations at the same time. In Section 4 we introduce AMIE, a system for mining semantic rules in KBs. Section 5 shows models and algorithms for the integration of Web services into KBs. Section 6 discusses algorithms to protect KBs against plagiarism. We conclude in Section 7 with an outlook.

2   YAGO: Knowledge à la Carte

The YAGO KB. YAGO [21,10,3] is one of the largest public knowledge bases. It contains more than 10 million entities (such as people, cities, rivers, or movies), and more than 120 million facts about them. YAGO knows, e.g., which actors acted in which movies, which cities are located in which countries, and which person is married to which other person. YAGO is constructed by extracting information automatically from Web sources such as Wikipedia. Unlike other such projects, YAGO has a manually confirmed accuracy of 95%.

Achieving such accuracy is no simple task, because YAGO draws from few, but very different sources. The system extracts and merges information from Wikipedia, WordNet, Geonames, the Universal WordNet, and WordNet Domains. Facts have to be extracted from the infoboxes, the categories, and the full text of Wikipedia, and reconciled with conflicting, duplicate, or complementary facts from the other sources. Entities have to be mapped and deduplicated, and class hierarchies have to be merged and combined. In addition, we have to apply a suite of verifications to make sure that domain and range constraints are respected, that functional relations have no more than one object for any given subject, and that the types of an entity are consistent with each other. This entire process takes several days to run. Furthermore, the YAGO team has steadily grown, which requires a careful distribution of responsibilities. Apart from this, more than a dozen researchers work directly or indirectly on the knowledge base. To adapt to these conditions, we have recently taken a radical step, and refactored the YAGO system from scratch into a transparent and modular architecture [3].

The YAGO2s Architecture. The refactored version of YAGO is called YAGO2s. The main ingredients of the new architecture are *themes* and *extractors*. A theme is a collection of facts, such as all facts extracted from Wikipedia infoboxes, all facts derived from WordNet, or all facts that concern people. A theme is stored in a file in the RDF Turtle format.

An extractor is a module of code, which takes a number of themes as input, and produces a number of themes as output. For example, one extractor is the *deduplicator*, which takes a number of themes as input, and produces one theme with the deduplicated facts as output. Other extractors check types, verify functional constraints, or merge information. Some extractors also extract information from an external data source. These extractors take a raw data file as an additional input. The *Wikipedia category extractor*, e.g., takes as input the XML dump of Wikipedia and produces a theme with facts extracted from Wikipedia categories. Similar extractors exist for WordNet [13], UWN [6], and Geonames[2]. We also added an extractor for WordNet domains [11]. The WordNet domains give YAGO a thematic structure of topics, such as "music", "law", and "emotions". Therefore, it is now possible to ask for all entities related to, e.g., "music". An extractor can only be run once its input themes have been produced. This constraint yields a dependency graph, in which some extractors have to run before others, and some can run in parallel.

We have designed a scheduler that respects the dependencies of extractors and themes. Of the 40 extractors, up to 16 run in parallel, producing around 80 themes in 4 days on a 8-core machine. The interplay of data extractors and verification extractors ensures that all facts that make it into the final layer of the architecture have been checked for consistency and uniqueness. Together, the themes of the final layer constitute the YAGO KB.

Applications. The new architecture allows us to add new extractors easily. To exemplify this, we have added a new module to YAGO, which extracts flight information from Wikipedia. Thanks to this module, YAGO now knows which airports are connected by direct flights to which other airports. Since YAGO also has vast data on geographic entities, users can now ask YAGO for flights between any two cities. Our interface will determine all airports in the vicinity of the departure city, all airports in the vicinity of the arrival city, and all direct flights between them [20]. YAGO also finds applications elsewhere. Two of the most prominent applications are the DBpedia KB [2] and the IBM Watson system [7]. DBpedia uses the taxonomy of YAGO to structure its entities into a hierarchy of classes. The IBM Watson system uses YAGO (and other KBs) to answer natural language questions. It has recently beaten the human champion at the US quizz show *Jeopardy!*.

YAGO can be downloaded for free from the Web site[3]. Thanks to the new architecture, facts about entities, literals, or multilingual labels all appear in different themes. The themes can be downloaded separately, so that users can download just what they need. With this concept, called "YAGO à la carte", we hope to facilitate further applications of our KB.

3   PARIS: Aligning Instances and Schemas

KB Alignment. The Semantic Web is a large collection of publicly available knowledge bases (KBs). YAGO is only one of them: there are other KBs, such as DBpedia, Freebase, or domain-specific KBs, which cover music, movies,

---

[2] http://geonames.org
[3] http://yago-knowledge.org

geographical data, scientific publications, and medical or government data. Many of these KBs are complementary. For instance, a general KB may know who discovered a certain enzyme, whereas a biological database may know its function and properties. However, since the KBs often use different identifiers for an entity, their information cannot be joined or queried across KBs. In the example, we cannot ask who discovered which enzyme with which properties. In addition, the KBs generally use different relations. For example, YAGO will say that Elvis Presley *wasBornIn* Tupelo, whereas another KB could say that Tupelo is the *placeOfBirth* of Elvis.

We propose an approach, PARIS [17], that solves both of these alignment problems. PARIS can match not just the equivalent entities, but also equivalent classes and relations across two KBs. Since PARIS considers all problems at the same time, we can benefit from a fruitful interplay between schema and instance matching, where the alignment of relations helps the alignment of instances, and the alignment of instances may lead to the alignment of relations.

Model. Our insight is that equalities between instances and relations determine each other. This link is achieved by using *functional relations*. A functional relation is a relation that has at most one second argument for each first argument, and conversely an inverse functional relation has at most one first argument for each second argument. Thus, if two instances x and x' share the same second argument of an inverse functional relation, then they must be equal:

$$\exists r, y, y' : r(x, y) \land r(x', y') \land y \equiv y' \land r \text{ inv. functional} \Rightarrow x \equiv x'$$

For example, if two instances share an email address, and if each email address can belong to only one instance, then the two instances must be equal.

However, real-world KBs are never free from noise. They may contain erroneous statements, and functional constraints may not always be respected. This is why we designed a *probabilistic model* to relax the hard logical rules. We call an *alignment fact* a statement of the form $x \equiv x'$, where x and x' are two entities in the first and second ontology, respectively. We also consider alignment facts of the form $r \subseteq r'$, where r and r' are two relations, and likewise $c \subseteq c'$, where c and c' are classes. For the purposes of our model, we also consider the statement $invfun(r)$ an alignment fact. It states that r is an inverse functional relation. A possible world is a set of alignment facts, and we call it simply an *alignment*. Our universe Ω is the set of all possible alignments.

The probability function of our model associates a probability $P(A)$ to each alignment $A \in \Omega$, with the constraint that $\sum_{A \in \Omega} P(A) = 1$. We do not know what this probability distribution is, but we will never try to manipulate it directly. Instead, we will study it through the *marginal probabilities* of the various alignment facts. Formally, for each alignment fact a, we define a random variable X_a such that $X_a(A) = 1$ if $a \in A$, and $X_a(A) = 0$ otherwise. The *marginal probability* of X_a is the total probability of the alignments of Ω where a holds: $P(X_a) = \sum_{A \in \Omega} X_a(A)P(A)$. For brevity we will write the marginal probability of X_a as $P(a)$. We impose constraints on the marginal probabilities, for instance $P(x \equiv x) = 1$ for every entity x. With the *product measure*, we can always construct a probability distribution that respects these constraints: $P(A) = \prod_{a \in A} P(a) \prod_{a \notin A} (1 - P(a))$. The product measure results in de-facto independence between the events of all alignment facts. Therefore, we make the assumption that all the X_a are independent. We can now replace the hard implication rule above by an equation which relates the marginal probabilities for various alignment facts. Namely, for every two instances x and x':

$$P(x \equiv x') = 1 - \prod_{r(r,x),r(x',y')} (1 - P(invfun(r))) \times P(y \equiv y')$$

The equality of instances can help us determine whether a class c of one KB is a subclass of a class c' of the other KB. We estimate this probability as the ratio of instances of c that are instances of c'. Since the instances of c belong to one KB, and the instances of c' belong to the other KB, we must count the overlap of the classes by taking into account the equality of instances that we have already estimated:

$$P(c \subseteq c') = \frac{\sum_{x \in c} (1 - \prod_{y \in c'} (1 - P(x \equiv y)))}{|c|}$$

The probability that one relation subsumes another relation can be estimated in a similar manner. This probability is then factored back into the probability for the equality of instances. This yields a system of equations in which the probability for the equality of instances, the subsumption of relations, and the subsumption of classes depend on each other.

Implementation. To bootstrap the dependencies of the probabilities, we make use of literals. Literals are strings, numbers, and dates. Two identical literals are always considered equal, so the probability that they are aligned is always 1. Starting from these probabilities, we implemented an iterative algorithm, which computes the equalities and relation subsumptions of the current step from the values of the previous step. Once this process has converged, we output the marginal probability scores as estimations for the equalities of instances, subsumptions of classes, and subsumptions of relations.

The large number of instances in today's KBs implies a prohibitively high number of potential matches. A naive implementation would need a quadratic number of comparisons per iteration, which would be practically infeasible. We therefore impose more conditions on the alignment, such as requiring that each entity is matched to at most one other entity. Since the original publication of PARIS [17], we have considerably improved the implementation of the system. We store the KB facts in main memory, and we use a new method to update probability scores: We simultaneously compute entity and relation alignments, and run this in parallel across multiple threads. To match YAGO [21] and DBpedia [2], two of the largest public KBs on the Semantic Web with several dozen million facts each, PARIS needs less than 30 minutes.

We have also experimented with refinements of the approach. For instance, we can align a single relation of one KB with a join of two relations in the other one, or we can use approximate matches between literals rather than exact matches. These additional features may help in specific situations. However, for the scenarios that we considered, our experiments show that the default approach of PARIS is both simpler and more efficient. What is more, it is parameter-free: Unlike its competitors, the system has no thresholds to tune, no similarity functions to design, and no settings to be tried out. In our experiments, the system was run on all different datasets with the default settings.

Results. To show the practical viability of our approach, we have run PARIS on the benchmark matching problems of the Ontology Alignment Evaluation Initiative (OAEI). PARIS outperformed the previously leading system on the instance alignment test data. In addition, it also computed the alignment between relations and classes, which was not even requested by the task.

We also conducted large-scale experiments with real KBs on the Semantic Web. PARIS is able to align YAGO and DBpedia with a precision of 94% on the instances, 84 % on the classes, and 100% on the relations (weighted by their number of occurrences). This alignment revealed interesting correspondences between the KBs, such as different naming policies, different design decisions, or redundancies within one KB. PARIS was also able to align YAGO with an ontology built from IMDb (the Internet Movie Database).

All data, alignments, and results, as well as our implementation, are available on the Web site of the project[4]. Our alignments have become part of the Semantic Web, and thus contribute to the vision of a large Web of linked data, where the KBs truly complement each other.

4   AMIE: Mining Logical Rules

Rules. Knowledge bases can show us which facts are typically true about entities. For example, we could find:

$$motherOf(m, c) \land marriedTo(m, f) \Rightarrow fatherOf(f, c)$$

This rule says that the husband of a mother is often the father of her children. Such a rule does not always hold. Still, such rules can be interesting for several reasons. First, by applying such rules on the data, new facts can be derived that make the KB more complete. For example, if we know the mother of a child and her husband, we can infer the father. Second, such rules can identify potential errors in the knowledge base. If, for instance, the KB claims that a totally unrelated person is the father of a child, then maybe this statement is wrong. Finally, rules about general tendencies can help us understand the data better. We can, e.g., find out that countries often trade with countries speaking the same language, that marriage is a symmetric relationship, that musicians who influence each other often play the same instrument, and so on.

While mining logical rules has been well studied in the Inductive Logic Programming (ILP) community, mining logical rules in KBs is different in two aspects: First, current rule mining systems are easily overwhelmed by the amount

---

[4] http://webdam.inria.fr/paris

of data (state-of-the art systems cannot even run on today's KBs). Second, ILP usually requires counterexamples. KBs, however, implement the open world assumption (OWA), meaning that absent data cannot be used as counterexamples. On that ground, we developed the AMIE approach [9]. AMIE learns a set of meaningful logical rules from a KB. She uses a new mining model and a confidence metric, suitable for potentially incomplete KBs under the OWA.

Model. Technically, a Horn rule takes the form

$$r_1(x_1, y_1) \wedge ... \wedge r_n(x_n, y_n) \Rightarrow r(x, y)$$

Here, all $r_i(x_i, y_i)$ and $r(x, y)$ are binary atoms, each containing a relation name r_i, and constants or variables x_i, y_i. The left hand side is called the *body* and we abbreviate it by $\mathcal{B}$. $r(x, y)$ is called the *head*. AMIE mines only closed rules, i.e., each variable must appear at least twice in the rule. This constraint ensures the rule can make concrete predictions as follows: Whenever some facts of the KB match the body of the rule, the rule predicts the instantiated head atom as a new fact. For instance, if the KB knows *motherOf(Priscilla,Lisa)* and *marriedTo(Priscilla,Elvis)*, then our example rule will predict *fatherOf(Elvis,Lisa)*. Our goal is to find rules that are true for many instances in the KB. We measure this by the *support* of the rule:

$$supp(\mathcal{B} \Rightarrow r(x, y)) := \#(x, y) : \exists z_1, ..., z_m : \mathcal{B} \wedge r(x, y)$$

Here, $\#(x, y)$ is the number of pairs x, y that fulfill the condition, and the $z_1, ..., z_n$ are the variables of $\mathcal{B}$. We want to count not just the cases where the rule makes a correct prediction, but also where it makes a wrong prediction. However, KBs usually do not contain negative information, and so we cannot say that a prediction is wrong. We can only count the predictions that are not in the KB. The *standard confidence* is a measure borrowed from association rule mining [1], which computes the ratio of predictions that are in the KB:

$$conf(\mathcal{B} \Rightarrow r(x, y)) := \frac{supp(\mathcal{B} \Rightarrow r(x, y))}{\#(x, y) : \exists z_1, ..., z_m : \mathcal{B}}$$

This measure punishes a rule if it makes many predictions that are not in the KB. However, due to the Open World Assumption, not all absent facts are wrong. Furthermore, such punishment is even counter-productive, because we want to use the rule to predict new facts.

To address this problem, AMIE resorts to the *Partial Completeness Assumption* (PCA). The PCA is the assumption that if the database knows $r(x, y)$ for some x and r, then it knows all facts $r(x, y')$. This assumption is sound for functional relations (such as *wasBornOnDate*, *hasCapital*). If we reverse all inverse functional relations (such as *creates* and *owns*), the assumption holds also for them. Even for non-functional relations, the PCA is still reasonable for KBs that have been extracted from a single source (such as DBpedia and YAGO). These usually contain either all objects or none for a given entity and a given relation.

The PCA can be used to infer negative information. For instance, if the database knows the citizenship of a person, then any other statement about her citizenship is assumed to be false. The *PCA confidence* normalizes the support of the rule only against the facts that are known to be true or false according to the PCA.

$$pcaconf(\mathcal{B} \Rightarrow r(x,y)) := \frac{supp(\mathcal{B} \Rightarrow r(x,y))}{\#(x,y) : \exists z_1, ..., z_m, y' : \mathcal{B} \wedge r(x,y')}$$

The denominator of the PCA confidence expression includes all pairs x, y for which the r values of x are in the KB. If the relation is incomplete, those gaps are not used as counter-evidence.

Results. Our experiments compare the usability and running times of AMIE against two state-of-the-art systems: WARMR and ALEPH[5]. Since these approaches are designed to serve more general purposes, they require additional input such as a language bias and, in some cases, output post-processing. In contrast, AMIE runs out of the box with her default setting. Furthermore, AMIE runs several orders of magnitude faster. For example, AMIE can mine rules on the entity-entity facts of the YAGO2 KB (approx. 1M facts) in only 4 minutes. The other systems did not terminate or failed to start on this KB due to its size. Since the original publication [9], we have further improved our implementation by means of fine-grained optimizations such as query rewriting and smarter query plans. This has improved the running time significantly. The latest version can run on YAGO2 in approximately 30 seconds.

We used the rules mined by AMIE on YAGO2 to predict new facts, and evaluated the facts by comparing to the newer version of the KB (YAGO2s), or by manually comparing to Wikipedia. Our results show that the PCA confidence outperforms the standard confidence in terms of precision and recall. The top rules ranked by PCA confidence produce many more predictions than the top rules ranked by standard confidence, while at the same time the aggregated precision of the results is higher. Our predictions beyond YAGO2 have an overall precision of 40%. While the rules cannot be used directly to infer new facts for KBs, they still provide a signal that can be used, e.g., in conjunction with other rules or with other prediction mechanisms. Furthermore, we show that the PCA confidence is a better estimate of the actual precision of rules. All results are available on the Web site of the project[6].

Ontology Alignment. Rule mining can be used not just to mine Horn rules, but also to align two KBs. In Section 3, we have already seen an approach that can align the instances, classes, and relations of two KBs. Unfortunately, there are cases where a simple 1:1 alignment of relations is not enough. For instance, KB $\mathcal{K}$ may express the relation between a person and their native land by the relationship $k:wasBornInCountry$, while $\mathcal{K}'$ may require a join of the relationships $k':wasBornInCity$ and $k':locatedInCountry$. Here, a "one-hop"

---

[5] http://www.cs.ox.ac.uk/activities/machlearn/Aleph/aleph_toc.html
[6] http://mpi-inf.mpg.de/departments/ontologies/projects/amie

relation of one KB has to be aligned with a "two-hop" relation in the other. In [8], we propose to discover such alignments by rule mining. As input, the approach requires two KBs whose instances have already been aligned. We coalesce the KBs into a single KB, where facts about the same entity use the same entity identifier. This coalesced KB mixes the facts from one KB with the facts of the other. Then we use AMIE to mine rules in which the body atoms are restricted to relation names from the first KB, and the head atom must use a relation from the second KB. In the example, we could mine

$$k':wasBornInCity(x, z) \land k':locatedInCountry(y, z) \Rightarrow k:wasBornInCountry(x, z)$$

We call these expressions *rules for ontological schema alignment*, ROSA rules for short. They express common structural mappings between two ontologies, such as relation subsumptions, class subsumptions, relation equivalences, two-hop subsumptions, and predicate-object translations, among others. However, ROSA rules define just a subset of all the possible mappings required for the alignment of ontologies in the Semantic Web, and thus give us room for further research.

5   SUSIE: Integrating Web Services

Web Services. A growing number of data providers let us access their data through Web services. There are Web services about books (`isbndb.org`, `librarything.com`, Amazon, AbeBooks), about movies (`api.internetvideoarchive.com`), about music (`musicbrainz.org`, `lastfm.com`), and about a large variety of other topics. We have studied Web services under a variety of aspects [14,4,16].

The API of a Web service restricts the types of queries that the service can answer. For example, a Web service might provide a method that returns the songs of a given singer, but it might not provide a method that returns the singers of a given song. If the user asks for the singer of some specific song, then the Web service cannot be called – even though the underlying database might have the desired piece of information. This problem is particularly pronounced if multiple Web services have to be combined in order to deliver the answer to the user query. In this case, it may happen that the API restrictions force the query answering system into an infinite series of attempts to orchestrate the services to no avail.

The Web as an Oracle. With the SUSIE project [15], we propose to use Web-based information extraction (IE) on the fly to determine the right input values for asymmetric Web services. For example, assume that we have a Web service *getSongsBySinger*, which returns the songs of a given singer. Now assume that the user wishes to find the singer of the song *Hallelujah*. This query cannot be answered directly with the service *getSongsBySinger*. Therefore, we issue a keyword query "singers Hallelujah" to a search engine. We extract promising candidates from the result pages, say, *Leonard Cohen, Lady Gaga,* and *Elvis Presley.* Next, we use the existing Web service to validate these candidates. In the example, we would call *getSongsBySinger* for every candidate, and see whether the result contains *Hallelujah*. This confirms the first singer and discards the others. This way, we can use an asymmetric Web service as if it allowed querying for an argument that its API does not support.

We show how such functions can be integrated into a Web orchestration system, and how they can be prioritized over infinite chains of calls. For this purpose, we define the notion of *smart service calls*. These are those calls for which we can guarantee an answer under certain conditions. We have implemented our system, and shown in experiments with real-world Web services that SUSIE can answer queries on which standard approaches fail.

With SUSIE, we have opened the door to an interesting suite of research questions: How can promising calls be prioritized over less promising calls? Under which assumptions can we give guarantees that a call composition will be successful? We plan to investigate these questions in future work.

6   Watermarking

Licensing. Most KBs on the Internet are available for free. However, in most cases, their use is governed by a license: If a user re-publishes the data or part of the data, he has to give credit to the creators of the original KB. If he does not, then this constitutes plagiarism. In some cases, re-publication may be prohibited completely (e.g., for commercially licensed KBs).

This raises the question of how we can prove if someone re-published the data. Since ontological statements are usually world knowledge, there is no way we can show that someone took the data from us. The other person might as well have taken the data from a different source. He might even claim that we took the data from him. We propose to address this problem through watermarking. We developed two approaches: Additive Watermarking and Subtractive Watermarking.

Additive Watermarking. Additive Watermarking works by adding a small number of wrong statements to the KB ("fake facts"). If these fake facts appear in another KB, then the other KB most likely took the data from our KB. The fake facts have to be plausible enough in order not to be spotted by a machine or by a human. At the same time, they may not be so plausible that they are correct. We provide a theoretical analysis of how many facts we have to add in order to ensure plausibility and security at the same time.

The main objection to this approach is that it compromises the data quality of the KB. It is true that watermarking is always a trade-off between data quality and the ability to prove provenance. However, our technique has to add only very few fake facts, usually a handful or a dozen. Large, automatically constructed KBs contain anyway several thousands of wrong facts. YAGO, for example, one of the KBs with a particularly rigorous quality assessment, has a guaranteed correctness of 95%. Since YAGO contains millions of facts, thousands are wrong. Adding a few more might be a valuable trade-off.

We show in a system demonstration of our approach how fake facts can be generated in such a way that most of them go undetected by a human [18].

Subtractive Watermarking. Subtractive Watermarking works by removing a small number of statements from the KB. The KB is then published without these statements. This creates a pattern of "holes" in the KB, which we can imagine like holes in a cheese. If this pattern of holes appears in another KB, then the data has likely been taken from the source KB.

The main advantage of this approach is that it does not compromise the precision of the data. It just removes statements. The Semantic Web is governed by the Open World Assumption, which states that the absence of a statement implies neither its truth nor its falsehood. Thus, the removal of a statement does not influence the correctness of the data. It does influence its completeness, though. As always, watermarking remains a trade-off between the quality of the data and the ability to prove provenance.

We show in theoretical analyses that only a few hundred facts have to be removed in order to protect the KB effectively from plagiarism. If this number is slightly increased, then the method can work even if only part of the KB is plagiarized [19]. Further information on watermarking KBs can be found on the Web page of our project[7].

7   Outlook

In this paper, we have summarized approaches that address challenges in the mining, linking, and extension of knowledge bases (KBs). Research in these areas has made huge progress during the last decade. However, many challenges remain. One issue is making those methods run at Web scale. Computers become ever more powerful, but we also produce ever more data. Currently, the growth rate of data outpaces the advancement rate of computers. Therefore, new methods will have to be developed to extract information at scale, to integrate it with existing information, and also to make use of large-scale semantic data. It is not just the size of the data that poses a challenge, but also the different types of information that we encounter. Social media, such as Twitter, Blogs, or Facebook, have seen a rise in recent years. The public parts of these sources could be harvested for KBs. Finally, new applications for semantic data will be explored. This includes its use in search, translation, decision making, or education. Ultimately, our goal is to make computers ever more useful for mankind.

References

1. Agrawal, R., Imieliński, T., Swami, A.: Mining association rules between sets of items in large databases. SIGMOD Rec. 22(2) (June 1993)
2. Auer, S., Bizer, C., Kobilarov, G., Lehmann, J., Cyganiak, R., Ives, Z.G.: DBpedia: A Nucleus for a Web of Open Data. In: Aberer, K., et al. (eds.) ISWC/ASWC 2007. LNCS, vol. 4825, pp. 722–735. Springer, Heidelberg (2007)

---

[7] http://mpi-inf.mpg.de/departments/ontologies/projects/watermarking

3. Biega, J., Kuzey, E., Suchanek, F.M.: Inside YAGO2s: A transparent information extraction architecture. In: Proc. WWW (Companion volume) (2013)
4. Bienvenu, M., Deutch, D., Martinenghi, D., Senellart, P., Suchanek, F.: Dealing with the deep web and all its quirks. In: VLDS Workshop (2012)
5. Bizer, C., Heath, T., Idehen, K., Berners-Lee, T.: Linked data on the Web. In: WWW (2008)
6. de Melo, G., Weikum, G.: Towards a universal wordnet by learning from combined evidence. In: CIKM. ACM (2009)
7. Ferrucci, D.A., Brown, E.W., Chu-Carroll, J., Fan, J., Gondek, D., Kalyanpur, A., Lally, A., William Murdock, J., Nyberg, E., Prager, J.M., Schlaefer, N., Welty, C.A.: Building Watson: An Overview of the DeepQA Project. AI Magazine 31(3) (2010)
8. Galárraga, L., Preda, N., Suchanek, F.M.: Mining rules to align knowledge bases. In: AKBC Workshop (2013)
9. Galárraga, L., Teflioudi, C., Hose, K., Suchanek, F.M.: AMIE: Association Rule Mining under Incomplete Evidence in Ontological Knowledge Bases. In: WWW (2013)
10. Hoffart, J., Suchanek, F.M., Berberich, K., Weikum, G.: Yago2: A spatially and temporally enhanced knowledge base from wikipedia. Artif. Intell. 194 (2013)
11. Magnini, B., Cavaglia, G.: Integrating subject field codes into wordnet. In: LREC (2000)
12. Matuszek, C., Cabral, J., Witbrock, M., Deoliveira, J.: An introduction to the syntax and content of cyc. In: AAAI Spring Symposium (2006)
13. Miller, G.A.: WordNet: An Electronic Lexical Database. MIT Press (1998)
14. Preda, N., Kasneci, G., Suchanek, F.M., Neumann, T., Yuan, W., Weikum, G.: Active Knowledge: Dynamically Enriching RDF Knowledge Bases by Web Services (ANGIE). In: SIGMOD (2010)
15. Preda, N., Suchanek, F.M., Yuan, W., Weikum, G.: Susie: Search using services and information extraction. In: ICDE (2013)
16. Suchanek, F., Bozzon, A., Della Valle, E., Campi, A., Ronchi, S.: Towards an Ontological Representation of Services in Search Computing. In: Ceri, S., Brambilla, M. (eds.) Search Computing II. LNCS, vol. 6585, pp. 101–112. Springer, Heidelberg (2011)
17. Suchanek, F.M., Abiteboul, S., Senellart, P.: PARIS: Probabilistic Alignment of Relations, Instances, and Schema. PVLDB 5(3) (2011)
18. Suchanek, F.M., Gross-Amblard, D.: Adding fake facts to ontologies. In: WWW (Companion volume) (2010)
19. Suchanek, F.M., Gross-Amblard, D., Abiteboul, S.: Watermarking for ontologies. In: Aroyo, L., Welty, C., Alani, H., Taylor, J., Bernstein, A., Kagal, L., Noy, N., Blomqvist, E. (eds.) ISWC 2011, Part I. LNCS, vol. 7031, pp. 697–713. Springer, Heidelberg (2011)
20. Suchanek, F.M., Hoffart, J., Kuzey, E., Lewis-Kelham, E.: YAGO2s: Modular High-Quality Information Extraction with an Application to Flight Planning. In: German Database Symposium, BTW 2013 (2013)
21. Suchanek, F.M., Kasneci, G., Weikum, G.: YAGO: A core of semantic knowledge - unifying WordNet and Wikipedia. In: WWW (2007)

Big Data Cleaning

Nan Tang

Qatar Computing Research Institute, Doha, Qatar
ntang@qf.org.qa

Abstract. Data cleaning is, in fact, a lively subject that has played an important part in the history of data management and data analytics, and it still is undergoing rapid development. Moreover, data cleaning is considered as a main challenge in the era of big data, due to the increasing volume, velocity and variety of data in many applications. This paper aims to provide an overview of recent work in different aspects of data cleaning: error detection methods, data repairing algorithms, and a generalized data cleaning system. It also includes some discussion about our efforts of data cleaning methods from the perspective of big data, in terms of volume, velocity and variety.

1 Introduction

Real-life data is often dirty: Up to 30% of an organization's data could be dirty [2]. Dirty data is costly: It costs the US economy $3 trillion+ per year [1]. These highlight the importance of data quality management in businesses.

Data cleaning is the process of identifying and (possibly) fixing data errors. In this paper, we will focus on discussing dependency based data cleaning techniques, and our research attempts in each direction [5].

Error Detection. There has been a remarkable series of work to capture data errors as violations using integrity constraints (ICs) [3, 9, 10, 18, 20, 21, 25, 27] (see [17] for a survey). A violation is a set of data values such that when putting together, they violate some ICs, thus considered to be wrong. However, ICs cannot tell, in a violation, which values are correct or wrong, thus fall short of guiding dependable data repairing. Fixing rules [30] are proposed recently that can precisely capture which values are wrong, when enough evidence is given.

Data Repairing. Data repairing algorithms have been proposed [7,8,12–15,23,24, 26,28,31]. Heuristic methods are developed in [6,8,13,26], based on FDs [6,27], FDs and INDs [8], CFDs [18], CFDs and MDs [23] and denial constraints [12]. Some works employ confidence values placed by users to guide a repairing process [8,13,23] or use master data [24]. Statistical inference is studied in [28] to derive missing values, and in [7] to find possible repairs. To ensure the accuracy of generated repairs, [24,28,31] require to consult users. Efficient data repairing algorithms using fixing rules have also been studied [30].

Data Cleaning Systems. Despite the increasing importance of data quality and the rich theoretical and practical contributions in all aspects of data cleaning,

L. Chen et al. (Eds.): APWeb 2014, LNCS 8709, pp. 13–24, 2014.

	name	country	capital	city	conf
r_1:	George	China	Beijing	Beijing	SIGMOD
r_2:	Ian	China	Shanghai (Beijing)	Hongkong (Shanghai)	ICDE
r_3:	Peter	China (Japan)	Tokyo	Tokyo	ICDE
r_4:	Mike	Canada	Toronto (Ottawa)	Toronto	VLDB

Fig. 1. Database D: an instance of schema Travel

there is a lack of *end-to-end* off-the-shelf solution to (semi-)automate the detection and the repairing of violations *w.r.t.* a set of heterogeneous and ad-hoc quality constraints. NADEEF [14, 15] was presented as an extensible, generalized and easy-to-deploy data cleaning platform. NADEEF distinguishes between a *programming interface* and a *core* to achieve generality and extensibility. The programming interface allows the users to specify multiple types of data quality rules, which uniformly define *what* is wrong with the data and (possibly) *how* to repair it through writing code that implements predefined classes.

Organization. We describe error detection techniques in Section 2. We discuss data repairing algorithms in Section 3. We present a commodity data cleaning system, NADEEF, in Section 4, followed by open research issues in Section 5.

2 Dependency-Based Error Detection

In this section, we start by illustrating how integrity constraints work for error detection. We then introduce fixing rules.

Example 1. Consider a database D of travel records for a research institute, specified by the following schema:

$$\text{Travel (name, country, capital, city, conf)},$$

where a Travel tuple specifies a person, identified by name, who has traveled to conference (conf), held at the city of the country with capital. One Travel instance is shown in Fig. 1. All errors are highlighted and their correct values are given between brackets. For instance, $r_2[\text{capital}] = \text{Shanghai}$ is wrong, whose correct value is Beijing.

A variety of ICs have been used to capture errors in data, from traditional constraints (*e.g.,* functional and inclusion dependencies [8,10]) to their extensions (*e.g.,* conditional functional dependencies [18]).

Example 2. Suppose that a functional dependency (FD) is specified for the Travel table as:

$$\phi_1: \text{Travel ([country]} \rightarrow \text{[capital])}$$

	country	{capital⁻}	capital⁺
φ_1:	China	Shanghai	Beijing
		Hongkong	

	country	{capital⁻}	capital⁺
φ_2:	Canada	Toronto	Ottawa

Fig. 2. Example fixing rules

which states that country uniquely determines capital. One can verify that in Fig. 1, the two tuples (r_1, r_2) violate ϕ_1, since they have the same country but carry different capital values, so do (r_1, r_3) and (r_2, r_3).

Example 2 shows that although ICs can detect errors (*i.e.*, there must exist errors in detected violations), it reveals two shortcomings of IC based error detection: (*i*) it can neither judge which value is correct (*e.g.*, t_1[country] is correct), nor which value is wrong (*e.g.*, t_2[capital] is wrong) in detected violations; and (*ii*) it cannot ensure that *consistent* data is correct. For instance, t_4 is consistent with any tuple *w.r.t.* ϕ_1, but t_4 cannot be considered as correct.

Fixing Rules. Data cleaning is not magic; it cannot guess something from nothing. What it does is to make decisions from evidence. Certain *data patterns* of semantically related values can provide evidence to precisely capture and rectify data errors. For example, when values (China, Shanghai) for attributes (country, capital) appear in a tuple, it suffices to judge that the tuple is about China, and Shanghai should be Beijing, the capital of China. In contrast, the values (China, Tokyo) are not enough to decide which value is wrong.

Motivated by the observation above, fixing rules were introduced [30]. A fixing rule contains an *evidence pattern*, a set of *negative patterns*, and a *fact* value. Given a tuple, the evidence pattern and the negative patterns of a fixing rule are combined to precisely tell which attribute is wrong, and the fact indicates how to correct it.

Example 3. Figure 2 shows two fixing rules. The brackets mean that the corresponding cell is multivalued.

For the first fixing rule φ_1, its evidence pattern, negative patterns and the fact are China, {Shanghai, Hongkong}, and Beijing, respectively. It states that for a tuple t, if its country is China and its capital is either Shanghai or Hongkong, capital should be updated to Beijing. For instance, consider the database in Fig. 1. Rule φ_1 detects that r_2[capital] is wrong, since r_2[country] is China, but r_2[capital] is Shanghai. It will then update r_2[capital] to Beijing.

Similarly, the second fixing rule φ_2 states that for a tuple t, if its country is Canada, but its capital is Toronto, then its capital is wrong and should be Ottawa. It detects that r_4[capital] is wrong, and then will correct it to Ottawa.

After applying φ_1 and φ_2, two errors, r_2[capital] and r_4[capital], can be repaired.

Notation. Consider a schema R defined over a set of attributes, denoted by attr(R). We use $A \in R$ to denote that A is an attribute in attr(R). For each attribute $A \in R$, its domain is specified in R, denoted as dom(A).

Syntax. A *fixing rule* φ defined on a schema R is formalized as $((X, t_p[X]), (B, T_p^-[B])) \to t_p^+[B]$ where

1. X is a set of attributes in $\mathsf{attr}(R)$, and B is an attribute in $\mathsf{attr}(R) \setminus X$ (*i.e.*, B is not in X);
2. $t_p[X]$ is a pattern with attributes in X, referred to as the *evidence pattern* on X, and for each $A \in X$, $t_p[A]$ is a constant value in $\mathsf{dom}(A)$;
3. $T_p^-[B]$ is a finite set of constants in $\mathsf{dom}(B)$, referred to as the *negative patterns* of B; and
4. $t_p^+[B]$ is a constant value in $\mathsf{dom}(B) \setminus T_p^-[B]$, referred to as the *fact* of B.

Intuitively, the evidence pattern $t_p[X]$ of X, together with the negative patterns $T_p^-[B]$ impose the condition to determine whether a tuple contains an error on B. The fact $t_p^+[B]$ in turn indicates how to correct this error.

Note that condition (4) enforces that the correct value (*i.e.*, the fact) is different from known wrong values (*i.e.*, negative patterns) relative to a specific evidence pattern.

We say that a tuple t of R *matches* a rule $\varphi : ((X, t_p[X]), (B, T_p^-[B])) \to t_p^+[B]$, denoted by $t \vdash \varphi$, if (i) $t[X] = t_p[X]$ and (ii) $t[B] \in T_p^-[B]$. In other words, tuple t matches rule φ indicates that φ can identify errors in t.

Example 4. Consider the fixing rules in Fig. 2. They can be formally expressed as follows:

φ_1: (([country], [China]), (capital, {Shanghai, Hongkong})) $\to$ Beijing
φ_2: (([country], [Canada]), (capital, {Toronto})) $\to$ Ottawa

In both φ_1 and φ_2, X consists of country and B is capital. Here, φ_1 states that, if the country of a tuple is China and its capital value is in {Shanghai, Hongkong}, its capital value is wrong and should be updated to Beijing. Similarly for φ_2.

Consider D in Fig. 1. Tuple r_1 does not match rule φ_1, since $r_1[\text{country}] = \text{China}$ but $r_1[\text{capital}] \notin \{\text{Shanghai}, \text{Hongkong}\}$. As another example, tuple r_2 matches rule φ_1, since $r_2[\text{country}] = \text{China}$, and $r_2[\text{capital}] \in \{\text{Shanghai}, \text{Hongkong}\}$. Similarly, we have r_4 matches φ_2.

Semantics. We next give the semantics of fixing rules.

We say that a fixing rule φ is *applied* to a tuple t, denoted by $t \to_\varphi t'$, if (i) t matches φ (*i.e.*, $t \vdash \varphi$), and (ii) t' is obtained by the update $t[B] := t_p^+[B]$.

That is, if $t[X]$ agrees with $t_p[X]$, and $t[B]$ appears in the set $T_p^-[B]$, then we assign $t_p^+[B]$ to $t[B]$. Intuitively, if $t[X]$ matches $t_p[X]$ and $t[B]$ matches some value in $T_p^-[B]$, it is evident to judge that $t[B]$ is wrong and we can use the fact $t_p^+[B]$ to update $t[B]$. This yields an updated tuple t' with $t'[B] = t_p^+[B]$ and $t'[R \setminus \{B\}] = t[R \setminus \{B\}]$.

Example 5. As shown in Example 3, we can correct r_2 by applying rule φ_1. As a result, $r_2[\text{capital}]$ is changed from Shanghai to Beijing, *i.e.*, $r_2 \to_{\varphi_1} r_2'$ where $r_2'[\text{capital}] = \text{Beijing}$ and the other attributes of r_2' remain unchanged.

Similarly, we have $r_4 \to_{\varphi_2} r_4'$ where the only updated attribute value is $r_4'[\text{capital}] = \text{Ottawa}$.

Fundamental problems associated with fixing rules have been studied [30].

Termination. The *termination problem* is to determine whether a rule-based process will stop. We have verified that applying fixing rules can ensure the process will terminate.

Consistency. The *consistency problem* is to determine, given a set Σ of fixing rules defined on R, whether Σ is consistent.

Theorem 1. *The consistency problem of fixing rules is* PTIME.

We prove Theorem 1 by providing a PTIME algorithm for determining if a set of fixing rules is consistent in [30].

Implication. The *implication problem* is to decide, given a set Σ of consistent fixing rules, and another fixing rule φ, whether Σ implies φ.

Theorem 2. *The implication problem of fixing rules is* coNP-complete. *It is down to* PTIME *when the relation schema R is fixed.*

Please refer to [30] for a proof.

Determinism. The *determinism problem* asks whether all terminating cleaning processes end up with the same repair.

From the definition of consistency of fixing rules, it is trivial to get that, if a set Σ of fixing rules is consistent, for any t of R, applying Σ to t will terminate, and the updated t' is deterministic (*i.e.*, a unique result).

3   Data Repairing Algorithms

In this section, we will discuss several classes of data repairing solutions. We will start by the most-studied problem: computing a consistent database (Sectioin 3.1). We then discuss user guided repairing (Section 3.2) and repairing data with precomputed confidence values (Section 3.3). We will end up this section with introducing the data repairing with fixing rules (Section 3.4).

3.1   Heuristic Algorithms

A number of recent research [4,8,12] have investigated the data cleaning problem introduced in [3]: repairing is to find another database that is consistent and minimally differs from the original database. They compute a consistent database by using different cost functions for value updates and various heuristics to guide data repairing.

For instance, consider Example 2. They can change r_2[capital] from Shanghai to Beijing, and r_3[capital] from Tokyo to Beijing, which requires two changes. One may verify that this is a repair with the *minimum* cost of two updates. Though these changes correct the error in r_2[capital], they do not rectify r_3[country]. Worse still, they mess up the correct value in r_3[capital].

	country	capital
s_1:	China	Beijing
s_2:	Canada	Ottawa
s_3:	Japan	Tokyo

Fig. 3. Data D_m of schema Cap

3.2   User Guidance

It is known that heuristic based solutions might introduce data errors [22]. In order to ensure that a repair is dependable, users are involved in the process of data repairing [22, 29, 31].

Consider a recent work [24] that uses editing rules and master data. Figure 3 shows a master data D_m of schema Cap (country, capital), which is considered to be correct. An editing rule eR$_1$ defined on two relations (Travel, Cap) is:

eR$_1$: ((country, country) → (capital, capital), t_{p1}[country] = ())

Rule eR$_1$ states that: for any tuple r in a Travel table, if r[country] is correct and it matches s[country] from a Cap table, we can update r[capital] with the value s[capital] from Cap. For instance, to repair r_2 in Fig. 1, the users need to ensure that r_2[country] is correct, and then match r_2[country] and s_1[country] in the master data, so as to update r_2[capital] to s_1[capital]. It proceeds similarly for the other tuples.

3.3   Value Confidence

Instead of interacting with users to ensure the correctness of some values or to rectify some data, some work employs pre-computed or placed confidence values to guide a repairing process [8, 13, 23]. The intuition is that the values with high confidence values should not be changed, and the values with low confidence values are mostly probably to be wrong and thus should be changed. These information about confidence values will be taken into consideration by modifying algorithms *e.g.*, those in Section 3.1.

3.4   Fixing Rules

There are two data repairing algorithms using fixing rules that are introduced in Section 2. Readers can find the details of these algorithms in [30]. In this paper, we will give an example about how they work.

Example 6. Consider Travel data D in Fig. 1, rules φ_1, φ_2 in Fig 2, and the following two rules.

φ_3: (([capital, city, conf], [Tokyo, Tokyo, ICDE]), (country, {China})) → Japan
φ_4: (([capital, conf], [Beijing, ICDE]), (city, {Hongkong})) → Shanghai

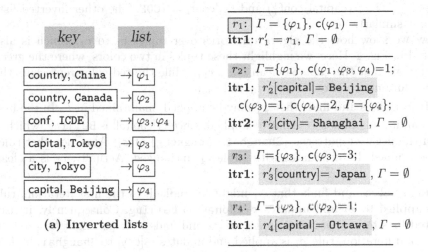

Fig. 4. A running example

Rule φ_3 states that: for t in relation Travel, if the conf is ICDE, held at city Tokyo and capital Tokyo, but the country is China, its country should be updated to Japan.

Rule φ_4 states that: for t in relation Travel, if the conf is ICDE, held at some country whose capital is Beijing, but the city is Hongkong, its city should be Shanghai. This holds since ICDE was held in China only once at 2009, in Shanghai but never in Hongkong.

Before giving a running example, we shall pause and introduce some indices, which is important to understand the algorithm.

Inverted Lists. Each inverted list is a mapping from a *key* to a set Υ of fixing rules. Each key is a pair (A, a) where A is an attribute and a is a constant value. Each fixing rule φ in the set Υ satisfies $A \in X_\varphi$ and $t_p[A] = a$.

For example, an inverted list *w.r.t.* φ_1 in Example 4 is as:

$$\boxed{\text{country, China}} \rightarrow \boxed{\varphi_1}$$

Intuitively, when the country of some tuple is China, this inverted list will help to identify that φ_1 might be applicable.

Hash Counters. It uses a hash map to maintain a counter for each rule. More concretely, for each rule φ, the counter $c(\varphi)$ is a nonnegative integer, denoting the number of attributes that a tuple agrees with $t_p[X_\varphi]$.

For example, consider φ_1 in Example 4 and r_2 in Fig. 1. We have $c(\varphi_1) = 1$ *w.r.t.* tuple r_2, since both $r_2[\text{country}]$ and $t_{p_1}[\text{country}]$ are China. As another example, consider r_4 in Fig. 1, we have $c(\varphi_1) = 0$ *w.r.t.* tuple r_4, since $r_4[\text{country}] = $ Canada but $t_{p_1}[\text{country}] = $ China.

Given the four fixing rules φ_1–φ_4, the corresponding inverted lists are given in Fig. 4(a). For instance, the third key (conf, ICDE) links to rules φ_3 and φ_4, since conf $\in X_{\varphi_3}$ (*i.e.*, $\{\text{capital}, \text{city}, \text{conf}\}$) and $t_{p_3}[\text{conf}] = $ ICDE; and moreover, conf $\in X_{\varphi_4}$ (*i.e.*, {capital, conf}) and t_{p_4}[conf] = ICDE. The other inverted lists are built similarly.

Now we show how the algorithm works over tuples r_1 to r_4, which is also depicted in Fig. 4. Here, we highlight these tuples in two colors, where the green color means that the tuple is clean (*i.e.*, r_1), while the red color represents the tuples containing errors (*i.e.*, r_2, r_3 and r_4).

$\boxed{r_1:}$ It initializes and finds that φ_1 may be applied, maintained in Γ. In the first iteration, it finds that φ_1 cannot be applied, since r_1[capital] is Beijing, which is not in the negative patterns {Shanghai, Hongkong} of φ_1. Also, no other rules can be applied. It terminates with tuple r_1 unchanged. Actually, r_1 is a clean tuple.

$\boxed{r_2:}$ It initializes and finds that φ_1 might be applied. In the first iteration, rule φ_1 is applied to r_2 and updates r_2[capital] to Beijing. Consequently, it uses inverted lists to increase the counter of φ_4 and finds that φ_4 might be used. In the second iteration, rule φ_1 is applied and updates r_2[city] to Shanghai. It then terminates since no other rules can be applied.

$\boxed{r_3:}$ It initializes and finds that φ_3 might be applied. In the first iteration, rule φ_3 is applied and updates r_3[coutry] to Japan. It then terminates, since no more applicable rules.

$\boxed{r_4:}$ It initializes and finds that φ_2 might be applied. In the first iteration, rule φ_2 is applied and updates r_4[capital] to Ottawa. It will then terminate.

At this point, we see that all the fours errors shown in Fig. 1 have been corrected, as highlighted in Fig. 4.

4   NADEEF: A Commodity Data Cleaning Systems

Despite the need of high quality data, there is no *end-to-end off-the-shelf* solution to (semi-)automate error detection and correction *w.r.t.* a set of *heterogeneous* and *ad-hoc* quality rules. In particular, there is no commodity platform similar to general purpose DBMSs that can be easily customized and deployed to solve application-specific data quality problems. Although there exist more expressive logical forms (*e.g.*, first-order logic) to cover a large group of quality rules, *e.g.*, CFDs, MDs or denial constraints, the main problem for designing an effective holistic algorithm for these rules is the lack of *dynamic semantics*, *i.e.*, alternative ways about *how* to repair data errors. Most of these existing rules only have *static semantics*, *i.e.*, *what* data is erroneous.

Emerging data quality applications place the following challenges in building a commodity data cleaning system.

Heterogeneity: Business and dependency theory based quality rules are expressed in a large variety of formats and languages from rigorous expressions (*e.g.*, functional dependencies), to plain natural language rules enforced by code embedded in the application logic itself (as in many practical scenarios). Such diversified semantics hinders the creation of one uniform system to accept

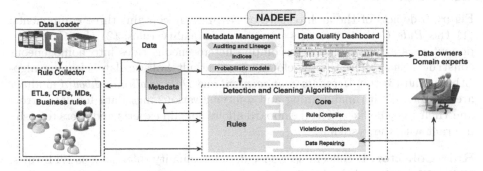

Fig. 5. Architecture of NADEEF

heterogeneous quality rules and to enforce them on the data within the same framework.

Interdependency: Data cleaning algorithms are normally designed for one specific type of rules. [23] shows that interacting two types of quality rules (CFDs and MDs) may produce higher quality repairs than treating them independently. However, the problem related to the interaction of more diversified types of rules is far from being solved. One promising way to help solve this problem is to provide unified formats to represent not only the static semantics of various rules (*i.e.,* what is wrong), but also their dynamic semantics (*i.e.,* alternative ways to fix the wrong data).

Deployment and Extensibility: Although many algorithms and techniques have been proposed for data cleaning [8,23,31], it is difficult to download one of them and run it on the data at hand without tedious customization. Adding to this difficulty is when users define new types of quality rules, or want to extend an existing system with their own implementation of cleaning solutions.

Metadata Management and Data Custodians: Data is not born an orphan. Real customers have little trust in the machines to mess with the data without human consultation. Several attempts have tackled the problem of including humans in the loop (*e.g.,* [24,29,31]). However, they only provide users with information in restrictive formats. In practice, the users need to understand much more meta-information *e.g.,* summarization or samples of data errors, lineage of data changes, and possible data repairs, before they can effectively guide any data cleaning process.

NADEEF[1] is a prototype for an extensible and easy-to-deploy cleaning system that leverages the separability of two main tasks: (1) isolating rule specification that uniformly defines *what* is wrong and (possibly) *how* to fix it; and (2) developing a core that holistically applies these routines to handle the detection and cleaning of data errors.

---

[1] https://github.com/Qatar-Computing-Research-Institute/NADEEF

4.1   Architecture Overview

Figure 5 depicts of the architecture of NADEEF. It contains three components: (1) the *Rule Collector* gathers user-specified quality rules; (2) the *Core* component uses a rule compiler to compile heterogeneous rules into homogeneous constructs that allow the development of default holistic data cleaning algorithms; and (3) the *Metadata management* and *Data quality dashboard* modules are concerned with maintaining and querying various metadata for data errors and their possible fixes. The dashboard allows domain experts and users to easily interact with the system.

Rule Collector. It collects user-specified data quality rules such as ETL rules, CFDs (FDs), MDs, deduplication rules, and other customized rules.

Core. The core contains three components: *rule compiler, violation detection* and *data repairing*.

(i) Rule Compiler. This module compiles all heterogeneous rules and manages them in a unified format.

(ii) Violation Detection. This module takes the data and the compiled rules as input, and computes a set of data errors.

(iii) Data Repairing. This module encapsulates holistic repairing algorithms that take violations as input, and computes a set of data repairs, while (by default) targeting the minimization of some pre-defined cost metric. This module may interact with domain experts through the *data quality dashboard* to achieve higher quality repairs.

For more details of NADEEF, please refer to the work [14].

4.2   Entity Resolution Extension

Entity resolution (ER), the process of identifying and eventually merging records that refer to the same real-world entities, is an important and long-standing problem. NADEEF/ER [16] was an extension of NADEEF as a generic and interactive entity resolution system, which is built as an extension over NADEEF. NADEEF/ER provides a rich programming interface for manipulating entities, which allows generic, efficient and extensible ER. NADEEF/ER offers the following features: (1) *Easy specification* – Users can easily define ER rules with a browser-based specification, which will then be automatically transformed to various functions, treated as *black-boxes* by NADEEF; (2) *Generality and extensibility* – Users can customize their ER rules by refining and fine-tuning the above functions to achieve both effective and efficient ER solutions; (3) *Interactivity* – NADEEF/ER [16] extends the existing NADEEF [15] dashboard with summarization and clustering techniques to facilitate understanding problems faced by the ER process as well as to allow users to influence resolution decisions.

4.3   High-Volume Data

In order to be scalable, NADEEF has native support for three databases, PostgreSQL, mySQL, and DerbyDB. However, to achieve high performance for high-volume data, a single machine is not enough. To this purpose, we have also built NADEEF on top of Spark[2], which is transparent to end users. In other words, users only need to implement NADEEF programming interfaces in logical level. NADEEF will be responsible to translate and execute user provided functions on top of Spark.

4.4 High-Velocity Data

In order to deal with high-velocity data, we have also designed new NADEEF interfaces for incremental processing of streaming data. By implementing these new functions, NADEEF can maximally avoid repeated comparison of existing data, hence is able to process data in high-velocity.

5 Open Issues

Data cleaning is, in general, a hard problem. There are many issues to be addressed or improved to meet practical needs.

Tool Selection. Given a database and a wide range of data cleaning tools (*e.g.,* FD-, DC- or statistical-based methods), the first challenging question is which tool to pick for the given specific task.

Rule Discovery. Although several discovery algorithms [11, 19] have been developed for *e.g.,* CFDs or DCs, rules discovered by automatic algorithms are far from clean themselves. Hence, often times, manually selecting/cleaning thousands of discovered rules is a must, yet a difficult process.

Usability. In fact, usability has been identified as an important feature of data management, since it is challenging for humans to interact with machines. This problem is harder when comes to the specific topic of data cleaning, since given detected errors, there is normally no evidence that which values are correct and which are wrong, even for humans. Hence, more efforts should be put to usability of data cleaning systems so as to effectively involve users as first-class citizens.

References

1. Dirty data costs the U.S. economy $3 trillion+ per year,
   http://www.ringlead.com/dirty-data-costs-economy-3-trillion/
2. Firms full of dirty data,
   http://www.itpro.co.uk/609057/firms-full-of-dirty-data
3. Arenas, M., Bertossi, L.E., Chomicki, J.: Consistent query answers in inconsistent databases. TPLP (2003)
4. Bertossi, L.E., Kolahi, S., Lakshmanan, L.V.S.: Data cleaning and query answering with matching dependencies and matching functions. In: ICDT (2011)
5. Beskales, G., Das, G., Elmagarmid, A.K., Ilyas, I.F., Naumann, F., Ouzzani, M., Papotti, P., Quiané-Ruiz, J.-A., Tang, N.: The data analytics group at the qatar computing research institute. SIGMOD Record 41(4), 33–38 (2012)

---

[2] http://spark.apache.org

6. Beskales, G., Ilyas, I.F., Golab, L.: Sampling the repairs of functional dependency violations under hard constraints. PVLDB (2010)
7. Beskales, G., Soliman, M.A., Ilyas, I.F., Ben-David, S.: Modeling and querying possible repairs in duplicate detection. In: VLDB (2009)
8. Bohannon, P., Fan, W., Flaster, M., Rastogi, R.: A cost-based model and effective heuristic for repairing constraints by value modification. In: SIGMOD (2005)
9. Bravo, L., Fan, W., Ma, S.: Extending dependencies with conditions. In: VLDB (2007)
10. Chomicki, J., Marcinkowski, J.: Minimal-change integrity maintenance using tuple deletions. Inf. Comput. (2005)
11. Chu, X., Ilyas, I.F., Papotti, P.: Discovering denial constraints. PVLDB 6(13) (2013)
12. Chu, X., Papotti, P., Ilyas, I.F.: Holistic data cleaning: Put violations into context. In: ICDE (2013)
13. Cong, G., Fan, W., Geerts, F., Jia, X., Ma, S.: Improving data quality: Consistency and accuracy. In: VLDB (2007)
14. Dallachiesa, M., Ebaid, A., Eldawy, A., Elmagarmid, A.K., Ilyas, I.F., Ouzzani, M., Tang, N.: Nadeef: a commodity data cleaning system. In: SIGMOD (2013)
15. Ebaid, A., Elmagarmid, A.K., Ilyas, I.F., Ouzzani, M., Quiané-Ruiz, J.-A., Tang, N., Yin, S.: Nadeef: A generalized data cleaning system. PVLDB (2013)
16. Elmagarmid, A., Ilyas, I.F., Ouzzani, M., Quiane-Ruiz, J., Tang, N., Yin, S.: NADEEF/ER: Generic and interactive entity resolution. In: SIGMOD (2014)
17. Fan, W.: Dependencies revisited for improving data quality. In: PODS (2008)
18. Fan, W., Geerts, F., Jia, X., Kementsietsidis, A.: Conditional functional dependencies for capturing data inconsistencies. TODS (2008)
19. Fan, W., Geerts, F., Li, J., Xiong, M.: Discovering conditional functional dependencies. IEEE Trans. Knowl. Data Eng. 23(5), 683–698 (2011)
20. Fan, W., Geerts, F., Tang, N., Yu, W.: Inferring data currency and consistency for conflict resolution. In: ICDE (2013)
21. Fan, W., Geerts, F., Wijsen, J.: Determining the currency of data. In: PODS (2011)
22. Fan, W., Li, J., Ma, S., Tang, N., Yu, W.: Towards certain fixes with editing rules and master data. PVLDB 3(1), 173–184 (2010)
23. Fan, W., Li, J., Ma, S., Tang, N., Yu, W.: Interaction between record matching and data repairing. In: SIGMOD (2011)
24. Fan, W., Li, J., Ma, S., Tang, N., Yu, W.: Towards certain fixes with editing rules and master data. VLDB J. (2012)
25. Fan, W., Li, J., Tang, N., Yu, W.: Incremental detection of inconsistencies in distributed data. In: ICDE, pp. 318–329 (2012)
26. Fellegi, I., Holt, D.: A systematic approach to automatic edit and imputation. J. American Statistical Association (1976)
27. Kolahi, S., Lakshmanan, L.: On approximating optimum repairs for functional dependency violations. In: ICDT (2009)
28. Mayfield, C., Neville, J., Prabhakar, S.: ERACER: a database approach for statistical inference and data cleaning. In: SIGMOD (2010)
29. Raman, V., Hellerstein, J.M.: Potter's Wheel: An interactive data cleaning system. In: VLDB (2001)
30. Wang, J., Tang, N.: Towards dependable data with fixing rules. In: SIGMOD (2014)
31. Yakout, M., Elmagarmid, A.K., Neville, J., Ouzzani, M., Ilyas, I.F.: Guided data repair. PVLDB (2011)

Differentially Private Data Release: Improving Utility with Wavelets and Bayesian Networks *

Xiaokui Xiao

Nanyang Technological University, Singapore
xkxiao@ntu.edu.sg

Abstract. Privacy-preserving data publishing is an important problem that has been the focus of extensive study. The state-of-the-art privacy model for this problem is *differential privacy*, which offers a strong degree of privacy protection without making restrictive assumptions about the adversary. In this paper, we review two methods, *Privelet* and *PrivBayes*, for improving utility in differentially private data publishing. *Privelet* utilizes wavelet transforms to ensure that any range-count query can be answered with noise variance that is polylogarithmic to the size of the input data domain. Meanwhile, *PrivBayes* employs Bayesian networks to publish high-dimensional datasets without incurring prohibitive computation overheads or excessive noise injection.

Keywords: Data publishing, Differential privacy, Wavelet, Bayesian network.

1 Introduction

The advancement of information technologies has made it never easier for various organizations (e.g., hospitals, bus companies, census bureaus) to create large repositories of user data (e.g., patient data, passenger commute data, census data). Such data repositories are of tremendous research value. For example, statistical analysis of patient data can help evaluate health risks and develop new treatments; passenger commute data provides invaluable insights into the effectiveness of transportation systems; census data is an essential source of information for demographic research. Despite of the research value of data, they are seldom available for public accesses, due to concerns over individual privacy. A common practice to address this issue is to *anonymize* the data by removing all personal identifiers (such as names and IDs). Nevertheless, recent research [2–4, 11–14, 16] has shown that eliminating personal identifiers alone is insufficient for privacy protection, since the remaining attributes in the data may still be exploited to re-identify an individual. This has motivated numerous data publishing techniques (see [1, 7, 9] for surveys) that aim to provide better privacy protection based on formal models of privacy requirements.

Differential privacy [8] is the state-of-the-art privacy model for data publishing. Informally, it requires that a sensitive dataset T should be modified using a randomized algorithm G with the following property: Even if we arbitrarily change one tuple in T and then feed the modified data as input to G, the output of G should still be more or

---

* Material based on [17] and [18] appearing in TKDE and SIGMOD'14, respectively.

L. Chen et al. (Eds.): APWeb 2014, LNCS 8709, pp. 25–35, 2014.
© Springer International Publishing Switzerland 2014

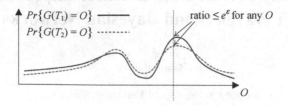

Fig. 1. Illustration of Definition 1

less the same with the case when the original T is the input. In other words, the output of G should only rely on the general properties of the input data, and should not be very sensitive to any particular tuple. This ensures that, when an adversary observes the data modified by G, he would not be able to infer much about any individual tuple in the original data, i.e., privacy is preserved.

Meanwhile, the data generated from G can still be useful, as long as the modification imposed by G does not significantly change the statistical properties of the original data. The design of such an algorithm G, however, is often highly non-trivial due to stringent requirements of differential privacy and the inherent complexity of the input/output data. In what follows, we first formalize the concept of differential privacy, and then demonstrate how we may utilize wavelet transforms and Bayesian networks to improve the utility of data released under differential privacy.

2 Differential Privacy

We say that two datasets are *neighboring*, if they have the same cardinality and they differ in only one tuple. The formal definition of differential privacy is as follows:

Definition 1 (ε-Differential Privacy [8]). A randomized algorithm G satisfies ε-differential privacy, if for any two neighboring datasets T_1 and T_2 and for any output O of G, we have

$$Pr\left\{G(T_1) = O\right\} \leq e^{\varepsilon} \cdot Pr\left\{G(T_2) = O\right\}. \qquad \square$$

Note that ε is a user-specified parameter that controls the degree of privacy protection; a smaller ε leads to stronger privacy assurance. Figure 1 illustrates Definition 1.

The *Laplace mechanism* [8] is the most fundamental mechanism for achieving differential privacy. To explain, consider that we have a non-private algorithm F whose output is a set of numeric values. Given F, the Laplace mechanism can transform F into a differentially private algorithm, by adding i.i.d. noise (denoted as η) into each output value of F. The noise η is sampled from a *Laplace distribution* $Lap(\lambda)$ with the following pdf: $\Pr[\eta = x] = \frac{1}{2\lambda}e^{-|x|/\lambda}$. We refer to λ as the *magnitude* of the Laplace noise.

Dwork et al. [8] prove that the Laplace mechanism ensures ε-differential privacy if $\lambda \geq S(F)/\varepsilon$, where $S(F)$ is the *sensitivity* of F:

Definition 2 (Sensitivity [8]). *Let F be a function that maps a dataset into a fixed-size vector of real numbers. The sensitivity of F is defined as*

$$S(F) = \max_{T_1, T_2} \|F(T_1) - F(T_2)\|_1, \tag{1}$$

where $\|\cdot\|_1$ denotes the L_1 norm, and T_1 and T_2 are any two neighboring datasets.

Intuitively, $S(F)$ measures the maximum possible change in F's output when we modify one arbitrary tuple in $\mathcal{F}$'s input. A large $S(\mathcal{F})$ indicates that F may reveal significant information about a certain tuple, in which case we should inject a large amount of noise into F's output to protect privacy. This explains why the Laplace mechanism sets the standard deviation of the noise proportional to $S(F)/\varepsilon$.

3 Differentially Private Data Publishing: A First-Cut Solution

Suppose that we are to publish a relational table T that contains d attributes $A_1, A_2, \ldots, A_d$, each of which is discrete and ordered. We define n as the number of tuples in T, and m as the size of the multi-dimensional domain on which T is defined, i.e., $m = \prod_{i=1}^{d} |A_i|$.

To release T under ε-differential privacy, we can first transform T into a d-dimensional *frequency matrix* M with m entries, such that (i) the i-th ($i \in [1, d]$) dimension of M is indexed by the values of A_i, and (ii) the entry in M with a coordinate vector $\langle x_1, x_2, \ldots, x_d \rangle$ stores the number of tuples t in T such that $t = \langle x_1, x_2, \ldots, x_d \rangle$. (Note: M can be regarded as the lowest level of the data cube of T.)

Notice that if we modify a tuple in T, then (i) at most two entries in the frequency matrix M will change, and (ii) each of those two entries will change by 1. Therefore, if we regard M as the output of a function, then by Definition 2, the sensitivity of the function equals 2. Hence, using the Laplace mechanism, we can ensure ε-differential privacy by adding Laplace noise $Lap(2/\varepsilon)$ into each entry of M.

The above noise injection approach is simple, but it fails to provide accurate results for aggregate queries. Specifically, if we answer a range-count query using a noisy frequency matrix M^* generated with the aforementioned approach, then the noise in the query result has a variance $\Theta(m/\varepsilon^2)$ in the worst case. This is because (i) each entry in M^* has a noise variance $8/\epsilon^2$ (by the pdf of $Lap(2/\varepsilon)$), and (ii) a range-count query may cover up to m entries in M^*. Note that m is typically an enormous number, as practical datasets often contain multiple attributes with large domains. Hence, a $\Theta(m/\varepsilon^2)$ noise variance can render the query result meaningless, especially when the original result is small. In Section 4, we address this problem by utilizing wavelet transforms [5, 15].

4 Differential Privacy via Wavelets

This section introduces *Privelet* (privacy preserving wavelet), a data publishing technique that not only ensures ϵ-differential privacy, but also provides accurate results for all *range-count queries*. In particular, *Privelet* guarantees that any range-count query

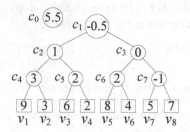

Fig. 2. One-Dimensional Haar Wavelet Transform

can be answered with a noise whose variance is polylogarithmic in m. This significantly improves over the $O(m)$ noise variance bound provided by the first-cut solution in Section 3.

Overview. At a high level, *Privelet* works in two steps as follows. First, it derives the frequency matrix M of the input table T, and then applies a *wavelet transform* on the frequency matrix M. Generally speaking, a wavelet transform is an invertible linear function, i.e., it maps M to another matrix C, such that (i) each entry in C is a linear combination of the entries in M, and (ii) M can be losslessly reconstructed from C. The entries in C are referred to as the *wavelet coefficients*. Second, *Privelet* adds an independent Laplace noise to each wavelet coefficient in a way that ensures ϵ-differential privacy. This results in a new matrix C^* with noisy coefficients. Finally, *Privelet* maps C^* back to a noisy frequency matrix M^*, which is returned as the output.

In the following, we clarify the details of *Privelet*. We first focus on the case when T has only one attribute (i.e., M is a one-dimensional matrix), and introduce the one-dimensional *Haar wavelet transform (HWT)*. After that, we explain how this wavelet transform can be incorporated in *Privelet*. Finally, we clarify how our solution can be extended to the case when T is multi-dimensional.

One-Dimensional HWT. For ease of exposition, we assume that the number m of entries in M equals 2^l ($l \in \mathbb{N}$) – this can be ensured by inserting dummy values into M [15]. Given M, the one-dimensional HWT converts it into 2^l wavelet coefficients as follows. First, it constructs a full binary tree R with 2^l leaves, such that the i-th leaf of R equals the i-th entry in M ($i \in [1, 2^l]$). It then generates a wavelet coefficient c for each internal node N in R, such that $c = (a_1 - a_2)/2$, where a_1 (a_2) is the average value of the leaves in the left (right) subtree of N. After all internal nodes in R are processed, an additional coefficient (referred to as the *base coefficient*) is produced by taking the mean of all leaves in R. For convenience, we refer to R as the *decomposition tree* of M, and slightly abuse notation by not distinguishing between an internal node in R and the wavelet coefficient generated for the node.

Example 1. Figure 2 illustrates an HWT on a one-dimensional frequency matrix M with 8 entries $v_1, \ldots, v_8$. Each number in a circle (square) shows the value of a wavelet coefficient (an entry in M). The base coefficient c_0 equals the mean 5.5 of the entries in M. The coefficient c_1 has a value -0.5, because (i) the average value of the leaves in its left (right) subtree equals 5 (6), and (ii) $(5 - 6)/2 = -0.5$. □

Given the Haar wavelet coefficients of M, any entry v in M can be easily reconstructed. Let c_0 be the base coefficient, and c_i ($i \in [1, l]$) be the ancestor of v at level i of the decomposition tree R (we regard the root of R as level 1). We have

$$v = c_0 + \sum_{i=1}^{l} (g_i \cdot c_i), \tag{2}$$

where g_i equals 1 (-1) if v is in the left (right) subtree of c_i.

Example 2. In the decomposition tree in Figure 2, the leaf v_2 has three ancestors $c_1 = -0.5$, $c_2 = 1$, and $c_4 = 3$. Note that v_2 is in the right (left) subtree of c_4 (c_1 and c_2), and the base coefficient c_0 equals 5.5. We have $v_2 = 3 = c_0 + c_1 + c_2 - c_4$. □

Privelet with 1D HWT. *Privelet* with the one-dimensional HWT follows the three-step paradigm mentioned previously. Given a parameter λ and a table T with a single ordinal attribute, *Privelet* first computes the Haar wavelet coefficients of the frequency matrix M of T. It then adds to each coefficient c a random Laplace noise with magnitude $\lambda / \mathcal{W}_{Haar}(c)$, where $\mathcal{W}_{Haar}$ is a weight function defined as follows: For the base coefficient c, $\mathcal{W}_{Haar}(c) = m$; for a coefficient c_i at level i of the decomposition tree, $\mathcal{W}_{Haar}(c_i) = 2^{l-i+1}$. For example, given the wavelet coefficients in Figure 2, $\mathcal{W}_{Haar}$ would assign weights 8, 8, 4, 2 to c_0, c_1, c_2, and c_4, respectively. After the noisy wavelet coefficients are computed, *Privelet* converts them back to a noisy frequency matrix M^* based on Equation 2, and then terminates by returning M^*.

By the properties of the Laplace mechanism [8], it can be proved that the above version of *Privelet* ensures ε-differential privacy with $\epsilon = 2(1 + \log_2 m)/\lambda$, where λ is the input parameter [17]. In addition, it also provides strong utility guarantee for range-count queries, as shown in the following lemma.

Lemma 1 ([17]). *Let C be a set of one-dimensional Haar wavelet coefficients such that each coefficient $c \in C$ is injected independent noise with a variance at most $(\sigma/\mathcal{W}_{Haar}(c))^2$. Let M^* be the noisy frequency matrix reconstructed from C. For any range-count query answered using M^*, the variance of noise in the answer is at most $(2 + \log_2 |M^*|)/2 \cdot \sigma^2$.*

By Lemma 1, *Privelet* achieves ϵ-differential privacy while ensuring that the result of any range-count query has a noise variance bounded by

$$(2 + \log_2 m) \cdot (2 + 2\log_2 m)^2/\epsilon^2 = O\big((\log_2 m)^3/\epsilon^2\big) \tag{3}$$

In contrast, under the same privacy requirement, the first-cut solution in Section 3 incurs a noise variance of $O(m/\epsilon^2)$ in query answers.

Finally, we point out that *Privelet* with the one-dimensional HWT has an $O(n + m)$ time complexity for construction. This follows from the facts that (i) mapping T to M takes $O(m + n)$ time, (ii) converting M to and from the Haar wavelet coefficients incur $O(m)$ overhead [15], and (iii) adding Laplace noise to the coefficients takes $O(m)$ time.

Extension to Multi-dimensional Datasets. For the case when M is a multi-dimensional matrix, we apply the multi-dimensional Haar wavelet transform [15] on

M, and then inject noise into the wavelet coefficients in a manner similar to the one-dimensional case [17]. After that, we obtain a noisy matrix M^* from the noisy coefficients, by applying the inverse multi-dimensional Haar wavelet transform. It can be proved that, by any range-count query answered using M^*, its noise variance is at most $O((\log m)^d/\varepsilon^2)$. In addition, the time complexity of the solution is $O(n + m)$.

5   Differential Privacy via Bayesian Networks

The *Privelet* approach in Section 4 suffers from the curse of dimensionality. In particular, it requires converting the input table T into a frequency matrix M whose number of entries is exponential to the number d of attributes in T – this incurs prohibitive overheads even when d is moderate. In addition, its noise variance bound (for range-count query results) is $O((\log m)^d/\varepsilon^2)$, which also increases exponentially with d. In fact, these deficiencies are not unique to *Privelet*: most existing techniques for differentially private data publishing require materializing M, and they provide poor data utility when d is large.

We propose to circumvent the curse of dimensionality as follows: We first approximate the high-dimensional data distribution in T with a set of low-dimensional distributions, and then inject noise into the low-dimensional distributions for privacy protection; after that, we use the modified distributions to reconstruct a high-dimensional dataset T^*, and then publish T^*. This approach improves data utility since it performs noise injection on low-dimensional data (instead of T), which is much less susceptible to noise injection. The core of our approach is an algorithm that utilizes *Bayesian networks* [10] to obtain low-dimensional approximations of high-dimensional data. In the following, we first introduce Bayesian networks, and then clarify our approach.

Bayesian Networks. Let $\mathcal{A}$ be the set of attributes in T, and d be the size of $\mathcal{A}$. A *Bayesian network* on $\mathcal{A}$ is a way to compactly describe the (probability) distribution of the attributes in terms of other attributes. Formally, a Bayesian network is a directed acyclic graph (DAG) that (i) represents each attribute in $\mathcal{A}$ as a node, and (ii) models conditional independence among attributes in $\mathcal{A}$ using directed edges. As an example, Figure 3 shows a Bayesian network over a set $\mathcal{A}$ of five attributes, namely, *age*, *education*, *workclass*, *title*, and *income*. For any two attributes $X, Y \in \mathcal{A}$, there exist three possibilities for the relationship between X and Y:

Case 1: Direct Dependence. There is an edge between X and Y, say, from Y to X. This indicates that for any tuple in T, its distribution on X is determined (in part) by its value on Y. We define Y as a *parent* of X, and refer to the set of all parents of X as its *parent set*. For example, in Figure 3, the edge from *workclass* to *income* indicates that the income distribution depends on the type of job (and also on title).

Case 2: Weak Conditional Independence. There is a path (but no edge) between Y and X. Assume without loss of generality that the path goes from Y to X. Then, X and Y are *conditionally independent* given X's parent set. For instance, in Figure 3, there is a two-hop path from *age* to *income*, and the parent set of *income* is $\{workclass, title\}$. This indicates that, given workclass and job title of an individual, her income and age are conditionally independent.

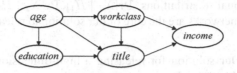

Fig. 3. A Bayesian network $\mathcal{N}_1$ over five attributes

Table 1. The attribute-parent pairs in $\mathcal{N}_1$

i	X_i	Π_i
1	age	$\emptyset$
2	education	{age}
3	workclass	{age}
4	title	{age, education, workclass}
5	income	{workclass, title}

Case 3: Strong Conditional Independence. There is no path between Y and X. Then, X and Y are conditionally independent given any of X's and Y's parent sets.

Formally, a Bayesian network $\mathcal{N}$ over $\mathcal{A}$ is defined as a set of d *attribute-parent (AP)* pairs, $(X_1, \Pi_1), \dots, (X_d, \Pi_d)$, such that

1. Each X_i is a unique attribute in $\mathcal{A}$;
2. Each Π_i is a subset of the attributes in $\mathcal{A} \setminus \{X_i\}$. We say that Π_i is the parent set of X_i in $\mathcal{N}$;
3. For any $1 \le i < j \le d$, we have $X_j \notin \Pi_i$, i.e., there is no edge from X_j to X_i in $\mathcal{N}$. This ensures that the network is acyclic, namely, it is a DAG.

We define the *degree* of $\mathcal{N}$ as the maximum size of any parent set Π_i in $\mathcal{N}$. For example, Table 1 shows the AP pairs in the Bayesian network $\mathcal{N}_1$ in Figure 3; $\mathcal{N}_1$'s degree equals 3, since the parent set of any attribute in $\mathcal{N}_1$ has a size at most three.

Let $\Pr[\mathcal{A}]$ denote the full distribution of tuples in database $\mathcal{T}$. The d AP pairs in $\mathcal{N}$ essentially define a way to approximate $\Pr[\mathcal{A}]$ with d conditional distributions $\Pr[X_1 \mid \Pi_1], \Pr[X_2 \mid \Pi_2], \dots, \Pr[X_d \mid \Pi_d]$. In particular, under the assumption that any X_i and any $X_j \notin \Pi_i$ are conditionally independent given Π_i, we have

$$
\begin{aligned}
\Pr[\mathcal{A}] &= \Pr[X_1, X_2, \dots, X_d] \\
&= \Pr[X_1] \cdot \Pr[X_2 \mid X_1] \cdot \Pr[X_3 \mid X_1, X_2] \dots \Pr[X_d \mid X_1, \dots X_{d-1}] \\
&= \prod_{i=1}^{d} \Pr[X_i \mid \Pi_i].
\end{aligned}
\tag{4}
$$

Let $\Pr_{\mathcal{N}}[\mathcal{A}] = \prod_{i=1}^{d} \Pr[X_i \mid \Pi_i]$ be the above approximation of $\Pr[\mathcal{A}]$ defined by $\mathcal{N}$. Intuitively, if $\mathcal{N}$ accurately captures the conditional independence among the attributes in $\mathcal{A}$, then $\Pr_{\mathcal{N}}[\mathcal{A}]$ would be a good approximation of $\Pr[\mathcal{A}]$. In addition, if the degree of $\mathcal{N}$ is small, then the computation of $\Pr_{\mathcal{N}}[\mathcal{A}]$ is relatively simple as it requires only d low-dimensional distributions $\Pr[X_1 \mid \Pi_1], \Pr[X_2 \mid \Pi_2], \ldots, \Pr[X_d \mid \Pi_d]$. Low-degree Bayesian networks are the core of our solution to release high-dimensional data.

Solution Overview. Our solution for releasing a high-dimensional data T under ε-differential privacy, dubbed *PrivBayes*, runs in three phases:

1. Construct a k-degree Bayesian network $\mathcal{N}$ over the attributes in T, using an $(\varepsilon/2)$-differentially private method. (k is a small value that can be chosen automatically by *PrivBayes*.)
2. Use an $(\varepsilon/2)$-differentially private algorithm to generate a set of *conditional distributions* of T, such that for each AP pair (X_i, Π_i) in $\mathcal{N}$, we have a noisy version of the conditional distribution $\Pr[X_i \mid \Pi_i]$. (We denote this noisy distribution as $\Pr^*[X_i \mid \Pi_i]$.)
3. Use the Bayesian network $\mathcal{N}$ (constructed in the first phase) and the d noisy conditional distributions (constructed in the second phase) to derive an approximate distribution of the tuples in T, and then sample tuples from the approximate distribution to generate a synthetic dataset T^*.

In short, *PrivBayes* utilizes a low-degree Bayesian network $\mathcal{N}$ to generate a synthetic dataset T^* that approximates the high dimensional input data T. The construction of $\mathcal{N}$ is highly non-trivial, as it requires carefully selecting AP pairs and the value of k to derive a close approximation of T without violating differential privacy. Interested readers are refer to [18] for the details of the algorithm for *PrivBayes*'s first phase. In the following, we provide the details of the second and third phases of *PrivBayes*.

Generation of Noisy Conditional Distributions. Suppose that we are given a k-degree Bayesian network $\mathcal{N}$. To construct the approximate distribution $\Pr_{\mathcal{N}}[\mathcal{A}]$, we need d conditional distributions $\Pr[X_i \mid \Pi_i]$ ($i \in [1, d]$), as shown in Equation (4). Algorithm 1 illustrates how the distributions specified by our algorithm can be derived in a differentially private manner. In particular, for any $i \in [k+1, d]$, the algorithm first materializes the joint distribution $\Pr[X_i, \Pi_i]$ (Line 3), and then injects Laplace noise into $\Pr[X_i, \Pi_i]$ to obtain a noisy distribution $\Pr^*[X_i, \Pi_i]$ (Line 4-5). To enforce the fact that these are probability distributions, all negative numbers in $\Pr^*[X_i, \Pi_i]$ are set to zero, then all values are normalized to maintain a total probability mass of 1 (Line 5). After that, based on $\Pr^*[X_i, \Pi_i]$, the algorithm derives a noisy version of the conditional distribution $\Pr[X_i \mid \Pi_i]$, denoted as $\Pr^*[X_i \mid \Pi_i]$ (Line 6). The scale of the Laplace noise added to $\Pr[X_i, \Pi_i]$ is set to $4(d-k)/n\varepsilon$, which ensures that the generation of $\Pr^*[X_i, \Pi_i]$ satisfies $(\varepsilon/2(d-k))$-differential privacy, since $\Pr[X_i, \Pi_i]$ has sensitivity $2/n$. Meanwhile, the derivation of $\Pr^*[X_i \mid \Pi_i]$ from $\Pr^*[X_i, \Pi_i]$ does not incur any privacy cost, as it only relies on $\Pr^*[X_i, \Pi_i]$ instead of the input data T.

Overall, Lines 2-6 of Algorithm 1 construct $(d-k)$ noisy conditional distributions $\Pr^*[X_i \mid \Pi_i]$ ($i \in [k+1, d]$), and they satisfy $(\varepsilon/2)$-differential privacy, since each $\Pr^*[X_i \mid \Pi_i]$ is $(\varepsilon/2(d-k))$-differentially private. This is due to the composability property of differential privacy [6]. In particular, composability indicates that when a set of k algorithms satisfy differential privacy with parameters $\varepsilon_1, \varepsilon_2, \ldots, \varepsilon_k$, respectively, the set of algorithms as a whole satisfies $(\sum_i \varepsilon_i)$-differential privacy.

Algorithm 1. NoisyConditionals $(T, \mathcal{N}, k)$: returns $\mathcal{P}^*$

1: Initialize $\mathcal{P}^* = \emptyset$
2: **for** $i = k + 1$ to d **do**
3:   Materialize the joint distribution $\Pr[X_i, \Pi_i]$
4:   Generate differentially private $\Pr^*[X_i, \Pi_i]$ by adding Laplace noise $Lap\left(\frac{4 \cdot (d-k)}{n \cdot \varepsilon}\right)$
5:   Set negative values in $\Pr^*[X_i, \Pi_i]$ to 0 and normalize;
6:   Derive $\Pr^*[X_i \mid \Pi_i]$ from $\Pr^*[X_i, \Pi_i]$; add it to $\mathcal{P}^*$
7: **for** $i = 1$ to k **do**
8:   Derive $\Pr^*[X_i \mid \Pi_i]$ from $\Pr^*[X_{k+1}, \Pi_{k+1}]$; add it to $\mathcal{P}^*$
9: **return** $\mathcal{P}^*$

After $\Pr^*[X_{k+1} \mid \Pi_{k+1}], \ldots, \Pr^*[X_d \mid \Pi_d]$ are constructed, Algorithm 1 proceeds to generate $\Pr^*[X_i \mid \Pi_i]$ ($i \in [1, k]$). This generation, however, does not require any additional information from the input data T. Instead, we derive $\Pr^*[X_i \mid \Pi_i]$ ($i \in [1, k]$) directly from $\Pr^*[X_{k+1}, \Pi_{k+1}]$, which has been computed in Lines 2-7 of Algorithm 1. Such derivation is feasible, since our algorithm [18] for constructing the Bayesian network $\mathcal{N}$ ensures that $X_i \in \Pi_{k+1}$ and $\Pi_i \subset \Pi_{k+1}$ for any $i \in [1, k]$. Since each $\Pr^*[X_i \mid \Pi_i]$ ($i \in [1, k]$) is derived from $\Pr^*[X_{k+1}, \Pi_{k+1}]$ without inspecting T, the construction of $\Pr^*[X_i \mid \Pi_i]$ does not incur any privacy overhead. Therefore, Algorithm 1 as a whole is $(\varepsilon/2)$-differentially private. Example 3 illustrates Algorithm 1.

Example 3. Suppose that we are given a 2-degree Bayesian network $\mathcal{N}$ over a set of four attributes $\{A, B, C, D\}$, with 4 AP pairs: $(A, \emptyset), (B, \{A\}), (C, \{A, B\})$, and $(D, \{A, C\})$. Given $\mathcal{N}$, Algorithm 1 constructs two noisy joint distributions $\Pr^*[A, B, C]$ and $\Pr^*[A, C, D]$. Based on $\Pr^*[A, C, D]$, Algorithm 1 derives a noisy conditional distribution $\Pr^*[D \mid A, C]$. In addition, the algorithm uses $\Pr^*[A, B, C]$ to derive three other conditional distributions $\Pr^*[A]$, $\Pr^*[B \mid A]$, and $\Pr^*[C \mid A, B]$. Given these four conditional distributions, the input tuple distribution is approximated as

$$\Pr_{\mathcal{N}}^*[A, B, C, D] = \Pr^*[A] \cdot \Pr^*[B \mid A] \cdot \Pr^*[C \mid A, B] \cdot \Pr^*[D \mid A, C].$$

Generation of Synthetic Data. Even with the simple closed-form expression in Equation 4, it is still time and space consuming to directly sample from $\Pr_{\mathcal{N}}^*[\mathcal{A}]$ by computing the probability for each element in the domain of $\mathcal{A}$. Fortunately, the Bayesian network $\mathcal{N}$ provides a means to perform sampling efficiently without materializing $\Pr_{\mathcal{N}}^*[\mathcal{A}]$. As shown in Equation 4, we can sample each X_i from the conditional distribution $\Pr^*[X_i \mid \Pi_i]$ independently, without considering any attribute not in $\Pi_i \cup \{X_i\}$. Furthermore, the properties of $\mathcal{N}$ ensure that $X_j \notin \Pi_i$ for any $j > i$. Therefore, if we sample X_i ($i \in [1, d]$) in increasing order of i, then by the time X_j ($j \in [2, d]$) is to be sampled, we must have sampled all attributes in Π_j, i.e., we will be able to sample X_j from $\Pr^*[X_j \mid \Pi_j]$ given the previously sampled attributes. That is to say, the sampling of X_j does not require the full distribution $\Pr_{\mathcal{N}}^*[\mathcal{A}]$.

With the above sampling approach, we can generate an arbitrary number of tuples from $\Pr_{\mathcal{N}}^*[\mathcal{A}]$ to construct a synthetic database T^*. In this paper, we consider the size of T^* is set to n, i.e., the same as the number of tuples in the input data T.

Privacy Guarantee. The correctness of *PrivBayes* directly follows the composability property of differential privacy [6]. In particular, the first and second phases of *PrivBayes* require direct access to the input database, and each of them consumes $\varepsilon/2$ privacy budget. No access to the original database is invoked during the third (sampling) phase. The results of first two steps, i.e., the Bayesian network $\mathcal{N}$ and the set of noisy conditional distributions, are sufficient to generate the synthetic database T^*. Therefore, we have the following theorem.

Theorem 1 ([18]). PrivBayes *satisfies ε-differential privacy.*

6   Conclusion

This paper reviews the concept of differential privacy as well as two methods, *Privelet* and *PrivBayes*, for improving utility in differentially private data publishing. *Privelet* utilizes wavelet transforms to ensure that any range-count query can be answered with noise variance that is polylogarithmic to the size of the input data domain. Meanwhile, *PrivBayes* employs Bayesian networks to publish high-dimensional datasets without incurring prohibitive computation overheads or excessive noise injection.

References

1. Sarwate, A.D., Chaudhuri, K.: Signal processing and machine learning with differential privacy: theory, algorithms, and challenges (September 2013)
2. Backstrom, L., Dwork, C., Kleinberg, J.M.: Wherefore art thou r3579x?: anonymized social networks, hidden patterns, and structural steganography, pp. 181–190 (2007)
3. Barbaro, M., Zeller, T.: A face is exposed for AOL searcher no. 4417749. New York Times, August 9 (2006)
4. Calandrino, J.A., Kilzer, A., Narayanan, A., Felten, E.W., Shmatikov, V.: "You might also like:" privacy risks of collaborative filtering. In: IEEE Symposium on Security and Privacy, pp. 231–246 (2011)
5. Chakrabarti, K., Garofalakis, M.N., Rastogi, R., Shim, K.: Approximate query processing using wavelets 10(2-3), 199–223 (2001)
6. Dwork, C.: Differential privacy. In: Bugliesi, M., Preneel, B., Sassone, V., Wegener, I. (eds.) ICALP 2006. LNCS, vol. 4052, pp. 1–12. Springer, Heidelberg (2006)
7. Dwork, C.: Differential privacy in new settings. In: SODA, pp. 174–183 (2010)
8. Dwork, C., McSherry, F., Nissim, K., Smith, A.: Calibrating noise to sensitivity in private data analysis. In: Halevi, S., Rabin, T. (eds.) TCC 2006. LNCS, vol. 3876, pp. 265–284. Springer, Heidelberg (2006)
9. Fung, B.C.M., Wang, K., Chen, R., Yu, P.S.: Privacy-preserving data publishing: A survey of recent developments. ACM Comput. Surv. 42(4) (2010)
10. Koller, D., Friedman, N.: Probabilistic Graphical Models: Principles and Techniques. MIT Press (2009)
11. Narayanan, A., Paskov, H., Gong, N.Z., Bethencourt, J., Stefanov, E., Shin, E.C.R., Song, D.: On the feasibility of internet-scale author identification. In: IEEE Symposium on Security and Privacy, pp. 300–314 (2012)
12. Narayanan, A., Shmatikov, V.: Robust de-anonymization of large sparse datasets. In: IEEE Symposium on Security and Privacy, pp. 111–125 (2008)

13. Narayanan, A., Shmatikov, V.: De-anonymizing social networks. In: IEEE Symposium on Security and Privacy, pp. 173–187 (2009)
14. Srivatsa, M., Hicks, M.: Deanonymizing mobility traces: using social network as a side-channel. In: ACM Conference on Computer and Communications Security, pp. 628–637 (2012)
15. Stollnitz, E.J., Derose, T.D., Salesin, D.H.: Wavelets for computer graphics: theory and applications. Morgan Kaufmann Publishers Inc. (1996)
16. Sweeney, L.: k-anonymity: A model for protecting privacy. International Journal of Uncertainty, Fuzziness and Knowledge-Based Systems 10(5), 557–570 (2002)
17. Xiao, X., Wang, G., Gehrke, J.: Differential privacy via wavelet transforms. TKDE 23(8), 1200–1214 (2011)
18. Zhang, J., Cormode, G., Procopiuc, C.M., Srivastava, D., Xiao, X.: Privbayes: Private data release via bayesian networks. In: SIGMOD (2014)

A Top K Relative Outlier Detection Algorithm in Uncertain Datasets

Fei Liu, Hong Yin, and Weihong Han

College of Computer, National University of Defense Technology,
410073, Changsha, Hunan, China
fliu@cse.unsw.edu.au, huiseguiji0521@yahoo.com.cn,
hanweihong@gmail.com

Abstract. Focusing on outlier detection in uncertain datasets, we combine distance-based outlier detection techniques with classic uncertainty models. Both variety of data's value and incompleteness of data's probability distribution are considered. In our research, all data objects in an uncertain dataset are described using x-tuple model with their respective probabilities. We find that outliers in uncertain datasets are probabilistic. Neighbors of a data object are different in distinct possible worlds. Based on possible world and x-tuple models, we propose a new definition of top K relative outliers and the $RPOS$ algorithm. In $RPOS$ algorithm, all data objects are compared with each other to find the most probable outliers. Two pruning strategies are utilized to improve efficiency. Besides that we construct some data structures for acceleration. We evaluate our research in both synthetic and real datasets. Experimental results demonstrate that our method can detect outliers more effectively than existing algorithms in uncertain environment. Our method is also in superior efficiency.[1]

Keywords: outlier detection, uncertain dataset, relative, x-tuple.

1 Introduction

In recent years, outlier detection has been widely used, specially in network intrusion detection [1], credit card abuse analysis [2], measurement result analysis of abnormal data [2] and so on. Lots of outlier detection algorithms in deterministic dataset have been proposed, such as model-based [3], index-based [4], distance-based [5], density-based algorithms [6] and so on. In these years, research has turned into uncertain datasets. Uncertainty is inherent in data collected in various applications, such as sensor networks, marketing research, and social science [7]. Sensors in a wireless network can be at different positions at different times with different probabilities. Many datasets published are deformed to hide information for privacy protection. In this case, distance

---

[1] The authors work is sponsored by the National High Technology Research and Development Program (863) of China (2012AA01A401 and 2012AA01A402), the Nature Science Foundation of China (61303265).

L. Chen et al. (Eds.): APWeb 2014, LNCS 8709, pp. 36–47, 2014.

among data objects, region density and many other metric are uncertain. These properties prevent classic outlier detection methods in deterministic datasets to be used in uncertain datasets directly.

In order to detect outliers in uncertain datasets, C. C. Aggarwal et al. [8] propose a density-based δ-η algorithm to detect outliers in uncertain datasets. They estimate the density of regions. For any data object, with lower probability to be in a high density region, more likely it would be an outlier. They propose the definition of η-probability of a data object. That is defined as the probability that the uncertain data object lies in a region with (overall data) density at least η [8]. An uncertain data object X_i would be a (δ,η)-outlier, if the η-probability of X_i in some subspace is less than δ. For η-probability estimation, authors use a sampling procedure to generate values according to some distribution. For this intention, a value is obtained from uniform distribution as the input of the inverse function of some cumulative density function. However, there are some limitations. First, the data must be in some determinate distribution. But its distribution would usually be unknown in real application. In some application, users can not get complete data distribution. Besides that, the method assumes that the inverse of the distribution can be calculated efficiently. It is difficult too. Although the data is assumed to be in normal distribution in their experiments, the sampling procedure is with heavy time cost. Similarly B. Jian et al. [7] use kernel density estimation to get densities of uncertain objects and their instances. In that model, value of uncertain data is dominated by conditioning attributes. They use kernel density estimation with Gaussian kernels to estimate the probability density of a distribution. In this method, obvious conditioning attributes must be determined first. This limits its application. Wang et al. [9] introduce distance-based outlier detection into uncertain dataset for the first time. They utilize x-tuple model to describe data objects. The method enlightens our research. Nonetheless, they don't take into account data variety.

<table>
<tr><td colspan="3">Table 1. x-tuple Model</td></tr>
<tr><th>x-tuple</th><th>tuple</th><th>probability</th></tr>
<tr><td rowspan="2">T_1</td><td>t_1</td><td>p_1</td></tr>
<tr><td>t_2</td><td>p_2</td></tr>
<tr><td>T_2</td><td>t_3</td><td>p_3</td></tr>
</table>

<table>
<tr><td colspan="3">Table 2. Possible Worlds</td></tr>
<tr><th>ID</th><th>possible world</th><th>probability</th></tr>
<tr><td>1</td><td>{}</td><td>$(1\text{-}p_1\text{-}p_2)(1\text{-}p_3)$</td></tr>
<tr><td>2</td><td>$\{t_1\}$</td><td>$p_1(1\text{-}p_3)$</td></tr>
<tr><td>3</td><td>$\{t_2\}$</td><td>$p_2(1\text{-}p_3)$</td></tr>
<tr><td>4</td><td>$\{t_3\}$</td><td>$(1\text{-}p_1\text{-}p_2)(p_3)$</td></tr>
<tr><td>5</td><td>$\{t_1 t_3\}$</td><td>$p_1 p_3$</td></tr>
<tr><td>6</td><td>$\{t_2 t_3\}$</td><td>$p_2 p_3$</td></tr>
</table>

In order to overcome above problems, we propose the concept of relative outlier and a novel distance-based outlier detection algorithm, $RPOS$ algorithm, focusing on top K outlier detection in uncertain datasets. In our research, all data objects exist with independent probabilities. A data object could show various values with different probabilities. We compare every pair of data objects to find the one more like to be an outlier relative to the other one. Global distribution of data value is unnecessary in our research.

2   Outlier in Uncertain Datasets

2.1   Possible World and x-tuple Model

We describe uncertain datasets using possible world semantics [10] and x-tuple model [11]. An x-tuple containing several tuples denotes a data object. A tuple containing several attributes denotes an instance. Every tuple has its own probability. Tuples in different x-tuples are independent. Tuples in the same x-tuple are mutually exclusive. Probability of an x-tuple is the product of probabilities of tuples in the x-tuple. An x-tuple may not exist if no its tuple exists. A subset of tuples from different x-tuples construct a possible world. Probability of a possible world is the product of probabilities of tuples in the possible world. An example of tuples, x-tuples, possible worlds and their probabilities can be shown in Table 1 and 2.

2.2   Relative Outlier

Based on possible world semantics and x-tuple model, we introduce the concept of distance-based outlier into uncertain datasets. In a possible world, every tuple has an outlier score as defined in Definition 1. K tuples ranked at most k according to their outlier scores in descending order are top K outliers in the possible world. If a tuple is a top K outlier in a possible world, the x-tuple containing the tuple would be a top K outlier in the possible world. The tuple's outlier score is also the x-tuple's outlier score. Since there would be many different possible worlds for data variety, top K outliers are uncertain.

Intuitively expected rank of an x-tuple in different possible worlds could be used to detect outlier. But expected rank would be easily influenced by sparse noise. For example, an x-tuple A is ranked $k+1$ in every possible world, another x-tuple B is ranked $10k$ in a possible world but k in others. x-tuple B is more like to be an outlier since it's ranked in front of A in most possible world. However, the expected rank of B may be smaller than that of A. So A would be considered as outlier in error. Besides that, the concept of uncertain top-k query [12], that is returning a list of k records which has the highest probability to be the top-k list in all possible worlds, is similar with our problem. But it can also be influenced by sparse data. For example, an x-tuple A is ranked $k+1$ in every possible world, another x-tuple B is ranked k in a possible world but $10k$ in others. Although A is not a top K outliers in any possible world, it's more like to be an outlier than B, since it's ranked in front of B in most cases.

In this paper, We propose the concept of relative outlier based on multiple comparisons. All x-tuples are compared with each other to evaluate their possibilities to be outliers. Above problems can be overcome in our method since outliers detected are more likely to have higher outlier scores than other x-tuples. Definition 2 defines the relative outlier between two x-tuples. Definition 3 defines top K relative outliers in an uncertain dataset.

Definition 1. Outlier score of a tuple is the mean distance to its n nearest neighbors [13,1,14].

Definition 2: For two x-tuples A and B in an uncertain dataset, if A is with higher probability to has higher outlier score than B, A is an outlier relative to B. Outlier score in a possible world is computed based on Definition 1.

For example, x-tuple A has higher outlier score than B with probability 0.5, x-tuple B has higher outlier score than A with probability 0.4 and A or B does not exit with probability 0.1. A would be an outlier relative to B.

Definition 3: Top K relative outliers in an uncertain dataset are those x-tuples. They are ranked top K according to the amount of x-tuples relative to which they are outliers based on Definition 2.

For example, x-tuple A is an outlier relative to another 5 x-tuples and x-tuple B is an outlier relative to another 6 x-tuple. B is more likely to be a top K outlier than A. If there are just K x-tuples who are outliers relative to at least another 6 x-tuples, B would be included in top K outliers, but A would be excluded. If there are K x-tuples who are outliers relative to at least another 7 x-tuples, both A and B would not be top K outliers.

3   Basic RPOS Algorithm

In this section, we propose the basic $RPOS$(Relative Probability Outlier Score) algorithm to detect the top K x-tuples most likely to be outliers. For x-tuples A and B, we compute the probability $P(A{>}B)$ meaning that A's outlier score is higher than B's and $P(B{>}A)$ meaning that B's outlier score is higher than A's. If $P(A{>}B){>}P(B{>}A)$, A is considered as an outlier relative to B, and vice versa. Relative Probability Outlier Score($RPOS$) of x-tuple A relative to B is 1 in this case. It's noted as $RPOS(A{\rightarrow}B){=}1$. At the same time, $RPOS(B{\rightarrow}A){=}{-}1$. The sum of A's $RPOS$s relative to other x-tuples is $all\text{-}RPOS(A) = \sum_{X \in S, X \neq A} RPOS(A{\rightarrow}X)$. S is the dataset. x-tuples with top K highest $all\text{-}RPOS$s would be outliers.

Algorithm 1 gives details of $RPOS$ algorithm. It compares all x-tuples with others to calculate their $all\text{-}RPOS$s and sort all x-tuples in descending order(lines 2-7). $OutlierScore$ algorithm computes an x-tuple's relative probability outlier score with another x-tuple. $sgn(x) = {-}1$,if $x{<}0$; 0,if $x{=}0$; 1,if $x{>}0$.

Algorithm 2 gives details of $OutlierScore$ algorithm. Because an x-tuple consists of several distinct tuples, comparison between two x-tuples is actually comparison among tuples from distinct x-tuples(lines 2-10). Unfortunately Definition 1 can not be used to compute a tuple's outlier score directly. Because all tuples' existence are uncertain, a tuple would exist in several possible worlds with distinct probabilities. So a tuple would have different neighbors in different possible worlds. In order to overcome this problem, we propose relative probability outlier score of a tuple, that is a tuple's outlier score relative

---

Algorithm 1. RPOS

```
Input: dataset S; outlier amount K
Output: queue of x-tuples Q
1: Q := ∅;
2: for each x-tuple Ti in S do
3:    all-RPOS(Ti) := 0;
4:    for each x-tuple Tj in S, Tj ≠Ti do
5:       all-RPOS(Ti)+=sgn(OutlierScore(Ti,Tj)-OutlierScore(Tj,Ti));
6:    end for
7:    insert Ti into Q according to all-RPOS in descending order;
8: end for
9: return  Q
```

Algorithm 2. OutlierScore

```
Input: x-tuple T1, T2
Output: P(T1 > T2)
1: P(T1 > T2) := 0;
2: for each tuple ti in T1 do
3:    P := 0;
4:    for each tuple tj in T2 do
5:       if RelativeOutlierScore_Tuple(ti,tj) = 1 then
6:          P := P + Probability(tj);
7:       end if
8:    end for
9:    P(T1 > T2) += Probability(ti)·P;
10: end for
11: return  P(T1 > T2)
```

---

to another tuple. *RelativeOutlierScore_Tuple* algorithm is used to calculate it. If *RelativeOutlierScore_Tuple* returns 1, the first tuple would has higher probability to get larger outlier score than the second tuple.

3.1   Relative Probability Outlier Score of a Tuple

We show details of *RelativeOutlierScore_Tuple* algorithm in this subsection. Supposing t_{1i} and t_{2j} are respective tuples of x-tuples T_1 and T_2, $score[t_{1i}]$ and $score[t_{2j}]$ are their deterministic outlier scores in a possible world and $score[t_{1i}, t_{2j}]$ is t_{1i}'s relative probability outlier score toward t_{2j}. We compute $score[t_{1i}]$ and $score[t_{2j}]$ in every possible world first. Then $score[t_{1i}, t_{2j}]$ can be computed as follows:

$score[t_{1i}, t_{2j}] \leftarrow 1$, if $P(score[t_{1i}] > score[t_{2j}]) > P(score[t_{2j}] > score[t_{1i}])$.

$P(score[t_{1i}] > score[t_{2j}])$ is the probability that t_{1i}'s deterministic outlier score is greater than that of t_{2j}. $P(score[t_{2j}] > score[t_{1i}])$ is the probability that t_{2j}'s deterministic outlier score is greater than that of t_{1i}. $score[t_{2j}, t_{1i}] = -1$ at the same time;

$score[t_{1i}, t_{2j}] = -1$, if $P(score[t_{1i}] > score[t_{2j}]) < P(score[t_{2j}] > score[t_{1i}])$. $score[t_{2j}, t_{1i}] = 1$ at the same time.

In a large uncertain dataset, the probability that two tuples have same deterministic outlier score is near 0. $score[t_{1i}, t_{2j}]$ can be computed as follows:

$score[t_{1i}, t_{2j}] = 1$, if $P(score[t_{1i}] > score[t_{2j}]) > 0.5$; $score[t_{1i}, t_{2j}] = -1$, if $P(score[t_{1i}] > score[t_{2j}]) < 0.5$.

The intuitive method to compute $score[t_{1i}, t_{2j}]$ is to traverse all possible worlds, compute $score[t_{1i}]$ and $score[t_{2j}]$ and accumulate the probability of $score[t_{1i}] > score[t_{2j}]$. However, this is unavailable in a real application. Traversing all possible worlds would cost exponential time overhead. Suppose S is the dataset, $|S| = N$ and every x-tuple includes N_x tuples. For any tuple t, the amount of possible worlds containing t's n nearest neighbor tuples would be at least $C_N^n N_x{}^n$. In order to lower time cost, we use sampling technique to get an approximate $P(score[t_{1i}] > score[t_{2j}])$.

Tuples in an x-tuple are sampled according to their probabilities. All tuples sampled from different x-tuples composed a possible world. X_k is a random variable in the kth sampling. In the possible world produced by the kth sampling, if both t_{1i} and t_{2j} exist and $score[t_{1i}] \geq score[t_{2j}]$, we set $X_k = 1$. Or else $X_k = 0$. When all tuples' probabilities are determined, $P(score[t_{1i}] \geq score[t_{2j}])$ is determined. $P(score[t_{1i}] \geq score[t_{2j}])$ is named as p in short. We can get $P(X_k = 1) = p$, $P(X_k = 0) = 1-p$ and $E[X_k] = 1 \cdot p + 0 \cdot (1-p) = p$. $X_1, X_2, \cdots, X_m$ are independent identical distribution random variables. m is sampling number. Variable $X = \sum X_k$, $1 \leq k \leq m$. So we can get $E[X] = E(\sum X_k) = \sum E(X_k) = mp$. That means $p = E[X]/m$. We use X to estimate $E[X]$ and estimate p using X/m. In order to ensure the accuracy of estimation, sampling must satisfy some conditions.

When $p \leq 0.5$, the probability of a wrong estimation, namely $X/m > 0.5$, is that:

$$P(X > 0.5m) = P(X > 0.5mp/p) = P(X > (1 + (0.5 - p)/p)mp). \quad (1)$$

According to *Chernoff bound*:

$$P(X > (1 + (0.5 - p)/p)mp) \leq exp\{-((0.5 - p)/p)^2 mp/3\}$$
$$= exp\{-(0.5 - p)^2 m/3p\}. \quad (2)$$

If m is determined, $1 - exp\{-(0.5-p)^2 m/3p\}$ is the accuracy of the estimation. It's only dominated by p.

Similarly, when $p > 0.5$, the probability of a wrong estimation is that:

$$P(X < 0.5m) = P(X < (1 - (p - 0.5)/p)mp)$$
$$< exp\{-(p - 0.5)^2 m/2p\}. \quad (3)$$

$1 - exp\{-(p-0.5)^2 m/2p\}$ is the accuracy of estimation. In summary, the confidence of the estimate is no less than $1 - exp\{-(0.5-p)^2 m/3p\}$. For example, when $p = 0.7$ and $m = 100$, accuracy of the estimation is no less than 0.94.

Algorithm 3. RelativeOutlierScore_Tuple

Input: tuples t_{1i} and t_{2j}; sampling time m
Output: outlier score of t_{1i} relative to t_{2j}, $score[t_{1i}, t_{2j}]$
1: $score[t_{1i}, t_{2j}] := 0$;
2: **for** the kth sampling, $1 \leq k \leq m$ **do**
3:     $score[t_{1i}, t_{2j}] \mathrel{+}= sgn(\textbf{DistanceOutlierScore}(t_{1i})_k -$
     $\textbf{DistanceOutlierScore}(t_{2j})_k)$;
4: **end for**
5: $score[t_{1i}, t_{2j}] := sgn(score[t_{1i}, t_{2j}])$;
6: **return** $score[t_{1i}, t_{2j}]$

$DistanceOutlierScore(t)_k$ the deterministic outlier score of t in the possible world produced by the kth sampling. In $DistanceOutlierScore(t)_k$, outlier score of the target tuple in a possible world is computed as Definition 1. However, it's in high time cost to detect a tuple's n nearest neighbors like classic methods e.g. *RBRP* algorithm [15] in each sampling. In order to reduce time cost, we construct a neighbor list L_t for every tuple t. The node of L_t is a novel *Neighbor* structure:

$Neighbor\langle t_{neighbor}, d_{neighbor}, tag \rangle$
$t_{neighbor}$: a neighbor tuple of t;
$d_{neighbor}$: distance from $t_{neighbor}$ to t;
tag: it is used to state whether $t_{neighbor}$ is selected in the sampling.

All *Neighbor*s in L_t are sorted according to $d_{neighbor}$ in ascending order. Tuples in the same x-tuple with t will not be in L_t. Let $|L_t|=L$. In each sampling, we traverse L_t in order and get n nearest selected tuples noted by tags. The mean distance of these n $d_{neighbor}$s is t's outlier score. When L is large enough, L_t could contain almost all n nearest neighbors of t in each sampling. While n nearest neighbors may exist in the latter part of the list with a low probability. Too large L leads to redundant memory consumption. Proper value of L should be set.

4   Pruning Strategies

In basic *RPOS* algorithm above, every x-tuple has to be compared with all others. Its time cost is proportional to the square of a dataset's cardinality. In order to improve running speed of basic *RPOS* algorithm, we introduce two pruning strategies.

4.1   Strategy 1

In order to detect outlier in high efficiency, we must find every tuple's neighbors quickly. Neighbors of a tuple should be close to each other. These neighbors could construct in a cluster. Using for reference from existing methods [15,16], we cluster all tuples in a dataset. Usually distances among tuples in a cluster are much less than those among tuples in different clusters. n nearest neighbors of a tuple t would be in the same cluster with t or t's neighboring clusters. In order to construct L_t, we check tuples in the cluster containing t first, and then tuples in neighboring clusters. Other clusters would be in the end. The distance from the Lth tuple in L_t to t will be a threshold in following process. We name the threshold as h. When we check a following neighbor tuple, if its distance to t is larger than h, it would not be inserted into L_t. On the contrary, it would be a candidate tuple and inserted into L_t in ascending order. h is then updated. Because we check tuples near with t first, h will always be small. Tuples far away from t will be pruned soon. In order to accelerate clustering process, we first partition the dataset into several large clusters and then partition every cluster into some sub-clusters recursively.

When we check t's neighbor t', if $L_{t'}$ has be constructed with threshold h', the distance from one of t''s n nearest neighbor tuples to t would be less than $D(t,t')+h'$. $D(t,t')$ is the distance from t to t'. So that $h<D(t,t')+h'$. h is updated by $min\{h, D(t,t')+h'\}$.

Further, before checking a neighbor cluster C' of t, we compute the maximum and minimum distances from t to C' first. The maximum distance from t to C' is $MaxD(t,C')=D(t,o')+r'$, where o' is the center of C' and r' is the radius of C'. The minimum distance from t to C' is $MinD(t,C')=D(t,o')-r'$. If $MinD(t,C')>h$, distance from t to any tuple in C' can not be less than h. All tuples in C' would not be inserted into L_t. C' will be jumped over. If $MinD(t,C')\leq h$, we will check its sub-clusters. In this way, we only need to check a few tuples to construct L_t. Smaller search space leads to lower time cost.

4.2   Strategy 2

When we compute all-$RPOS$ of an x-tuple, the x-tuple has to be compared with all other x-tuples. When we compare two x-tuples, we have to compare all tuples from two x-tuples respectively. Time complexity in this process is $O(N_x^2N^2)$. N is the cardinality of the dataset. N_x is the amount of tuples in an x-tuple. But in real application outliers are in minority of the entire dataset. It's wasteful to compare all pairs of x-tuples. Suppose there are K outliers in a dataset and X x-tuples have been checked in $RPOS$ algorithm. If $X>K$, we sort these X x-tuples based on their all-$RPOS$s and use the Kth all-$RPOS$ as the threshold namely H. If expected value of an x-tuple's all-$RPOS$ is less than H, it can not be an outlier. When new top K candidate outliers are detected, H is updated. In above process, expected all-$RPOS$ value of an x-tuple can be computed using existed all-$RPOS$ value (as that in line 5 of $RPOS$ algorithm) of the x-tuple plus the number of x-tuples will be compared with it.

Further Acceleration 1: Efficiency of pruning process above would be influenced by H. Quickly H increases, more x-tuples could be pruned early. We sort all x-tuples according to expected all-$RPOS$ in descending order.

Further Acceleration 2: In order to avoid redundant comparison in pairs of x-tuples, we record all x-tuples have been compared with and the intermediate result of every x-tuple's all-$RPOS$.

5   Experiments

In this section, we evaluate our *RPOS* algorithm in synthetic and real datasets. All algorithms are implemented in Java. Our experiments are ran on a machine with 2 Intel Core 2 Duo E8400 3GHZ CPUs and 8.1GB RAM running Linux 3.8 Ubuntu 13.04. In our research, all attributes of data are numerical and the value of each attribute is a real number. We compare *RPOS* algorithm with *RBRP* [15] and δ-η [8] algorithms. B.Jiang's work [7] focuses on condition attributes and B. Wang's work [9] neglects data diversity. It's hard to compare them with our work. In order to use *RBRP* algorithm to detect outliers in uncertain datasets, we pretreat uncertain data for experiments. All tuples in an x-tuple are transformed into a tuple. The value of the new tuple in every dimension is the weighted mean value of all tuples of the x-tuple in the dimension. Weight of a tuple is its probability.

5.1   Dataset

Synthetic Dataset. In order to test the effectiveness and efficiency of different outlier detection algorithms, we construct several synthetic datasets. The synthetic data includes N_d attributes. Every data entity is an x-tuple including several tuples. A tuple's value in every attribute is numeric. We produce some normal regions in the N_d-dimension space. Normal tuples are allocated in these regions. On the contrary, outliers will not be in normal regions. Besides synthetic data values, we also produce the probability for every tuple. We define N_R normal regions in N_d dimensions respectively. R_i is the normal region in dimension i. $R_i=[LOW(R_i),UP(R_i)]$. R'_{i*} is a sub-region of R_i. $R'_{i*} \subset R_i$. N_d sub-regions construct a N_d-dimension normal region $\langle R'_{1*}, R'_{2*} \cdots R'_{N_d*} \rangle$. $r=R'_{i*}/R_i$ determines the size of sub-region R'_{i*}. We produce N_R N_d-dimension normal regions in this way. Data objects outside of these N_R regions is abnormal. First we produce normal x-tuples in normal regions produced above. Then we produce outlier x-tuples with at least N'_x abnormal tuples in each x-tuple. In order to evaluate performance of *RPOS* algorithm, we insert some counterfeit outliers into the dataset as disturbance. A counterfeit outlier x-tuple contains several abnormal tuples. The tuples may be allocated far away from normal regions. But their quantity is small and their probabilities are smaller than those of abnormal tuples in real outliers x-tuples.

Real Dataset. We choose the real MiniBooNE dataset[2] provided by UCI. Number of entities in this dataset is 130000. Number of attributes is 50. Attribute characteristics are real. We transform the original dataset into an uncertain dataset for our experiments. Every entity in the original dataset is an x-tuple containing one tuple in the uncertain dataset. We fluctuate the value of a tuple to produce other tuples in the x-tuple. The value of a tuple in every dimension fluctuates with probability p_f. Fluctuation range is controlled by r_f. There are at most N_x tuples in an x-tuple. We add every tuple's probability as in synthetic dataset.

---

[2] http://archive.ics.uci.edu/ml/datasets

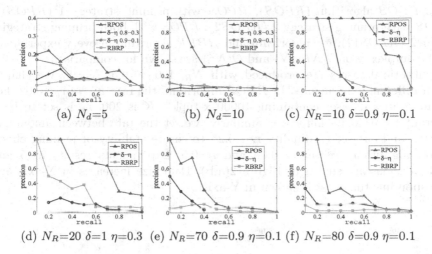

(a) $N_d=5$ (b) $N_d=10$ (c) $N_R=10$ $\delta=0.9$ $\eta=0.1$

(d) $N_R=20$ $\delta=1$ $\eta=0.3$ (e) $N_R=70$ $\delta=0.9$ $\eta=0.1$ (f) $N_R=80$ $\delta=0.9$ $\eta=0.1$

Fig. 1. Effectiveness of different algorithms

5.2 Effectiveness Evaluation

In this sub-section, we show the evaluation result of different algorithms'
effectiveness to detect outliers. Because no instance in real datasets is labeled as
an outlier, effectiveness evaluation is performed only in synthetic datasets. Some
parameters are modified to produce different datasets.

In order to test the influence of the data dimensionality, we perform
experiments in 5 and 10 dimensions respectively. We set $N_R=100$,
$N_x=5$. Amount of outliers $N_{outlier}=0.01N$. Amount of counterfeiters
$N_{counterfeiter}=0.05N$. N is the cardinality of a dataset. For $RPOS$ algorithm
we set parameters $L=200$ and $m=100$ (see section 3). For δ-η algorithm we
do experiments in two situations. First, parameter δ is set to be 0.8 and η is
set to be 0.3, and then δ is set to be 0.9 and η is set to be 0.1. Space lack
for more parameter setting. But they do not influence experimental results. In
Figure 1(a), dimensions amount is $N_d=5$. $N_d=10$ in Figure 1(b). Precision and
recall ratio are two test indexes. As shown in these figures, in various amount
of dimensions, $RPOS$ algorithm always performs best in three algorithms. With
same recall rate, $RPOS$ algorithm detects outliers in high precision.

We then change parameter N_R to produce different uncertain synthetic
datasets to evaluate the effectiveness of different algorithms. Data is processed
in these experiments with $N_d=5$. N_R is set to be different values with $r=0.5$.
δ and η are set arbitrarily. Results can be found in Figure 1(c-f). As shown in
above figures, $RPOS$ algorithm performs best in almost all experiments.

5.3 Efficiency Evaluation

In this sub-section, we show evaluation results of different algorithms' time cost.
Our experiments perform in both synthetic and real datasets. We implement

basic $RPOS$ algorithm ($RPOS$), $RPOS$ with pruning strategy 1 ($RPOS1$), $RPOS$ with pruning strategy 2 ($RPOS2$), $RPOS$ with both pruning strategies 1 and 2 ($RPOS12$), δ-η algorithm and $RBRP$ algorithm in every experiment. Time complexity of $O(NlogN)$ and $O(N^2)$ are shown for comparison.

Synthetic datasets are produced with N_R=100, r=0.5, N_x=5. We change N_d in different experiments. In $RPOS$ algorithm, the rate K/N=r_k=0.02. For instance, in a dataset containing 10000 x-tuples, K is 200. r_k is set to be a constant to avoid its influence. Similarly, we set the rate between amount of clusters and dataset cardinality r_C=0.25 to ensure stability of pruning effect. In δ-η algorithm, we set δ=0.06 and η=0.5. Experiments results in 5 and 20 dimensions are shown in Figure 2(a,b). Data size increases in X-axis and corresponding time cost is shown in Y-axis.

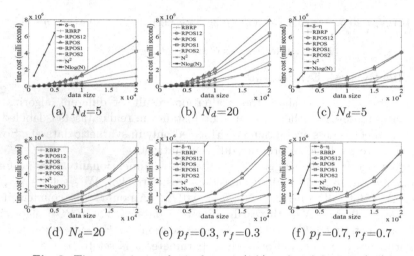

Fig. 2. Time cost in synthetic datasets(a,b) and real datasets(c-f)

As shown in Figure 2(a), pruning strategies 1 and 2, especially strategy 2 can accelerate $RPOS$ algorithm. Time cost of basic $RPOS$ algorithm and $RPOS1$ are higher than $O(N^2)$. The main time consumption is from comparison among tuples and x-tuples. Time cost of $RPOS2$ and $RPOS12$ are lower than $O(N^2)$ but higher than $O(NlogN)$. Pruning strategies can improve basic $RPOS$ algorithm obviously. Speedup using pruning strategies in 20 dimensions is similar as in 5 dimensions.

Time cost are also evaluated in real datasets. First we set parameters p_f=0.5, r_f=0.5. Other parameters keep consistent with those in synthetic datasets. Experiments are implemented in 5 and 20 dimensions respectively. Results of time cost can be shown in Figure 2(c,d). Basic $RPOS$ algorithm runs with higher time complexity than $O(N^2)$. pruning strategy 2 can improve $RPOS$ algorithm greatly.

We then change p_f and r_f to produce different uncertainty with N_d=20. Time cost is shown in Figure 2(e,f). We can find that results are similar in different experiments. With various values of p_f and r_f, $RPOS12$ performs better than others in time cost.

References

1. Eskin, E., Arnold, A., Prerau, M., Portnoy, L., Stolfo, S.: A geometric framework for unsupervised anomaly detection. In: Applications of Data Mining in Computer Security, pp. 77–101. Springer (2002)
2. Kriegel, H.P., Kroger, P., Schubert, E., Zimek, A.: Outlier detection in arbitrarily oriented subspaces. In: 12th International Conference on Data Mining (ICDM), pp. 379–388. IEEE (2012)
3. Rousseeuw, P.J., Leroy, A.M.: Robust regression and outlier detection, vol. 589. Wiley.com (2005)
4. Han, J., Kamber, M., Pei, J.: Data mining: concepts and techniques. Morgan Kaufmann (2006)
5. Aggarwal, C.C., Yu, P.: An effective and efficient algorithm for high-dimensional outlier detection. The VLDB Journal 14(2), 211–221 (2005)
6. Breunig, M.M., Kriegel, H.P., Ng, R.T., Sander, J.: Lof: identifying density-based local outliers. ACM Sigmod Record, 93–104 (2000)
7. Jiang, B., Pei, J.: Outlier detection on uncertain data: Objects, instances, and inferences. In: ICDE, pp. 422–433. IEEE (2011)
8. Aggarwal, C.C., Yu, P.: Outlier detection with uncertain data. In: SDM, pp. 483–493 (2008)
9. Wang, B., Xiao, G., Yu, H., Yang, X.C.: Distance-based outlier detection on uncertain data. In: CIT, pp. 293–298. IEEE (2009)
10. Dalvi, N., Suciu, D.: Efficient query evaluation on probabilistic databases. The VLDB Journal 16(4), 523–544 (2007)
11. Parag, A., Benjelloun, O., Sarma, A.D., Hayworth, C., Nabar, S., Sugihara, T., Widom, J.: Trio: A system for data uncertainty and lineage. In: VLDB (2006)
12. Hua, M., Pei, J., Zhang, W.J., Lin, X.M.: Efficiently answering probabilistic threshold top-k queries on uncertain data. In: ICDE, vol. 8, pp. 1403–1405 (2008)
13. Angiulli, F., Pizzuti, C.: Outlier mining in large high-dimensional data sets. IEEE Transactions on Knowledge and Data Engineering 17(2), 203–215 (2005)
14. Bay, S.D., Schwabacher, M.: Mining distance-based outliers in near linear time with randomization and a simple pruning rule. In: Proceedings of the Ninth ACM SIGKDD, pp. 29–38. ACM (2003)
15. Ghoting, A., Parthasarathy, S., Otey, M.E.: Fast mining of distance-based outliers in high-dimensional datasets. Data Mining and Knowledge Discovery 16(3), 349–364 (2008)
16. Vu, N.H., Gopalkrishnan, V.: Efficient pruning schemes for distance-based outlier detection. In: Buntine, W., Grobelnik, M., Mladenić, D., Shawe-Taylor, J. (eds.) ECML PKDD 2009, Part II. LNCS, vol. 5782, pp. 160–175. Springer, Heidelberg (2009)

Identifying Users Based on Behavioral-Modeling across Social Media Sites[*]

Yuanping Nie, Jiuming Huang, Aiping Li, and Bin Zhou

College of Computer, National University of Defense Technology, China
{yuanpingnie,naicky,apli1974,bin.zhou.cn}@gmail.com

Abstract. Social media is playing an important role in our daily life. People usually hold various identities on different social media sites. User-contributed Web data contains diverse information which reflects individual interests, political opinions and other behaviors. To integrate these behaviors information, it is of value to identify users across social media sites. This paper focuses on the challenge of identifying unknown users across different social media sites. A method to relate user's identities across social media sites by mining users' behavior information and features is introduced. The method has two key components. The first component distinguishes different users by analyzing their common social network behaviors and finding strong opposing characters. The second component constructs a model of behavior features that helps to obtain the difference of users across social media sites. The method is evaluated through two experiments on Twitter and Sina Weibo. The results of experiments show that the method is effective.

Keywords: Identification, Behavioral model, Cross media analysis.

1 Introduction

Online social media sites such as Facebook, Twitter, Youtube and Sina Weibo own thousands of millions users. The recent investigation shows that Facebook, the most popular social media site, has more than 1 billion users. Also, those users create huge information: over 500 million tweets are posted on Twitter [2]. It is a very convenient platform for a large amount of users to share their interests and emotions at anytime and anywhere. Obviously, every social media site has their own specificity and people use various social media sites for different purposes [1]. Identification of users across social media sites will support the Internet crime tracking. Many Internet swindlers and terrorists have their own social network accounts, which provide a great opportunity to collect their information on the Internet. However, some of the accounts did not use their true names. Identification of users across social media sites will help to find their hidden accounts.

---

[*] Sponsored by National Key Technology Research and Development Program No.2012BAH38B04, National Key fundamental Research and Development Program No.2013CB329601.

L. Chen et al. (Eds.): APWeb 2014, LNCS 8709, pp. 48–55, 2014.
© Springer International Publishing Switzerland 2014

Identifying across social media sites is a challenging problem due to the heterogeneity and uncertainty of data. The information provided by users like usernames, profession and gender may not verified. The primary obstacle is that the connection relationships between user identities across social media sites are usually unavailable. It is not a straightforward task to find a mapping between two users among huge information redundancy.

In this paper, we introduce a behavior-modeling identification method to detect users in different sites. It is said "Old habits, die hard" and we focus on those behavior patterns that have been reflected on different platforms. Our contributions and main ideas are as follow: 1) Build a behavior-modeling. 2) Propose a fast exclusion method and provide an algorithm to determine the difference of two users.

2   Related Work

Some existing work focusing on identification has been presented. We summarized research related to identifying individuals across social media sites. There is a related research about identifying contents produced by an individual on the web. In [3] the authors take eyes on the contents generation behavior of the same individuals' for the collections of documents. A method for detecting pages is created by the same individual across different documents. They use a method based on Normalized Compression Distance (NCD) [4] to compare the similarity between the documents. There are some machine learning techniques employed to determine authors in online messages [6]. The content based on textual is also has been studied [9,10]. The paper [7] considered the determination by the content of E-mails. The paper [1] introduced a methodology to identify users by detecting their usernames based on behavior features. They considered human being's limitations in times, memory and knowledge. They constructed features by the information of human behavioral patterns and employed a machine learning method for users' identification across social media sites. Paper [5,11] contributed to identify the contents for events in different social media sites. They analyzed the user-contributed web data and constructed the information ranges from event features on event aggregation platforms. Sakaki ct al. [12] developed techniques for identifying earthquake events. In this paper, we focus on the similarity of behaviors that individuals performed in different social media sites, which is important to avoid making mistakes on identity determination.

3   Problem Definition

Identifying and relating users across social network are hard tasks since most sites maintain anonymity of users by allowing them to pick usernames at will instead of their real identities and social media sites rarely have identity authentication systems. A large amount of users provide false information such as incorrect names, age, profession and even incorrect gender to hide their privacy.

Although users have various identities in different social media sites, they exhibit consistent behavioral patterns. It is necessary that an individual will keep their reality behavioral patterns [8] in the virtual life on the internet. The behavioral information can contribute to identify individuals across social media sites. We analyze the information available on all social media sites.

There are some public figures that hold accounts authenticated by social media sites. Those famous figures include actors, athletes, politicians and entrepreneurs. The remarks from famous accounts are much more widely spread than the regular users. Obviously most of the famous users have certain labels. It is easier to identify a regular user by analysis of the public figures they follow since public figures have clear labels. We can determine a user's interests, political view and other behaviors features. There is an example if a user follows Kobe Bryant (e.g. his label is basketball player, Los Angles Lakers) and re-posts his tweets, we will give the user such labels, interests on basketball and maybe a supporter of Kobe Bryant and Los Angles Lakers.

A regular user will follow a number of public accounts and connect them. Connection includes all the information transformations between two users. It includes re-posts action, comments and mentions (like @ function in Twitter). From those connections, we can give a behavioral-modeling for regular user.

We define the users behavioral-modeling of individual I as a set of famous users $U = \{u_1, u_2, u_3, \ldots u_n\}$ followed by individual I. U is behavioral-modeling of users and u_i ($1 < i < n$) is a factor of U.

When considering behavioral-modeling, two general problems need to be solved for user identification. The first problem is: Given two users and all their media action information (U_1 and U_2), how to determine whether they belong to the same individual? The second problem is: Given one user's behavior features, can we find a user from other platform belonging to the same individual. To the first problem, we provide behavior similarity S to measure the similarity between I_1 and I_2. Behavior similarity S is decided by function about U_1 and U_2.

$$S = f(U_1, U_2) \tag{1}$$

We can identify users across media sits by determination of their similarity. There is a threshold l. So we can get:

$$R(S, l) = \begin{cases} 1(S > l) \\ 0(S \leq l) \end{cases} \tag{2}$$

To the second problem, obviously, it is much easier to detect different users than to determine the users belonging to the same individual since there are huge redundant information on the across media sites. We provide a fast exclusion method. The method firstly excludes the obvious different users and then determines whether the two users belong to one individual.

4   Identification Method: Behavior Patterns

4.1   Fast Exclusion Method

As human beings, we have some behavior limitations. Behavior limitations include:
1) If an event has two antagonistic attitudes, people will often choose one side, positive or negative. There are a kind of events that are strongly antagonistic, such as political opinions, religions and some athletic projects. 2) People are not willing to receive information from the sources doesn't like. 3) Because of the energy limitation, the interests of people are also limited. And among those interests, the core interests are more stable than the periphery interests. In other words, the core interests won't change no matter which social network platforms the individual uses. Based on the behavior limitations, the Exclusion Method consist two components.

The first component aims to find the antagonistic factors of two users.

We firstly build a library to list the antagonistic factors, e.g., {Los Angeles Lakers supporter and Los Angeles clippers supporters, the fans of Real Madrid and Barcelona, Republican surrounded and Democrats surrounded, Jewish believers and Muslims}

We can put those events' antagonistic factors into two pools: P and N. $P= \{p_1, p_2,..., p_n\}$ and $N= \{n_1, n_2,..., n_n\}$. There are behaviors features of two users U_1 and U_2. We can get: If $p_i \in U_1$, $p_i \in P$ and $n_i \in U_2$, $n_i \in N$, we will know U_1 and U_2 are not the same individual.

The second component is based on limitation 3. We believe that if two users in different social media sites belong to the same individual, there must be core interests that they both have. It means: there are behaviors features of two users U_1 and U_2, if they belong to the same individual, we can know: $U_1 \cap U_2 \neq \varnothing$ and $(U_1 \cap U_2)/(U_1 \cup U_2) \geq \rho$. $(U_1 \cap U_2)$ is the common interests of two users and $(U_1 \cup U_2)$ is the complete interests of two users. The ρ is the minimum common probability of identification. The value of ρ is picked by experience. The false alarm will increase when ρ is higher or otherwise, the undetected value will increase.

4.2   Behavior-Modeling Identification Algorithm

The fast exclusion method can exclude apparent different users. But it is hard to identify whether the users have the same hobby circle since the exclusion method only consider the users they connect. The exclusion method doesn't consider how many times the users connect. As we know that there are core and periphery interests. We define the connected users as nodes and the time of connections are edge weights. It forms a network its structure shown in Fig.1. The core nodes (with high weight edges) represent the core interests which have closer relationship with the user.

If the two users belong to the same individual, they will have analogous core nodes and the structure of relation network will be similar. The structure can be expressed by vector $P = \{p_1, p_2, ..., p_n\}$, p_i is the value of edges. Because the two networks have

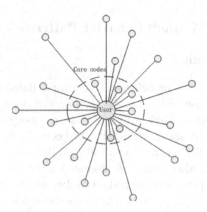

Fig. 1. The structure of a user

the same nodes and edges (the edge weights are different), the two vectors have identical length. The difference of two network structure can be measured by Kullback-Liebler divergence (KL). KL is a non-symmetric measure of the difference between two probability distributions.

For two vectors $P = \{p_1, p_2, ..., p_n\}$ and $Q = \{q_1, q_2, ..., q_n\}$, we can get:

$$\text{Difference}: D(\text{P} \parallel \text{Q}) = \sum_i \ln(\frac{p(i)}{q(i)})p(i) \tag{3}$$

It is the expectation of the logarithmic difference between the probabilities P and Q, where the expectation is taken using the probability P.

When two probability distributions are completely same $P(x) = Q(x)$, the $D(\text{P} \parallel \text{Q})$ is zero. So it means the value of D is smaller and the two probability distributions are more similar. Using the algorithm, we can obtain a measurement to compare the two accounts between users' behavior across social network. Also, it is possible to find the most similar user from other group of users.

5   Experiments

We evaluate our behavior-modeling identification method using data from several popular social media sites. Table 1 shows the selected social media sites. To protect the privacy of users, the private information like usernames and ids has been hidden. We did two different experiments:

1. Comparing the similarity of one user behavior similarity with different periods of time.
2. Evaluating the similarity between two given users across the social media sites.

5.1   The First Experiment

In the first experiment, we want to ensure users on social media sites have stable behavior performance. We can compare the similarity of one user behavior with different periods of time. We choose one user from twitter and we collected data posted
between November 26, 2013 and March 15, 2014 on Twitter. We divided the data
into 8 periods and each period is 10 days. Each period length is one month. We used
the Twitter API to collect the user behaviors information including: Tweets and retweets, mentions users and their connection times. We calculate the difference value
between one period and the previous period. The similarity result is shown in Table1.

Table 1. The Difference Value One User In Different Period Of Time

Period	1	2	3	4	5	6	7	8
Tweets /Re-tweets	475	761	599	757	543	612	703	563
Mentioned users	31	37	29	42	33	35	38	31
Difference value	0.0702	0.0849	0.0724	0.0821	0.0712	0.0759	0.0827	0.0904

As Table 1 shows, all of the similarity results are lower than 0.1. It indicates that
one user's behavior is very similar in different priod of time.

5.2   The Second Experiment

A simple method for identifying usernames across sites is by finding users manually.
Users sometimes provide some personal information such as their real names, E-mail
addresses, and profile photos on the social media websites. The information can be
employed to map users on different sites to the same individual. And we choose some
volunteers to share their accounts on different social network.

We finally collected 240 pairs that are belonging to the same individual. The 213
pairs' accounts include volunteers' accounts and accounts confirmed by artificial. The
dataset is from Twitter and Sina Weibo, which called dataset 1. We also pick another
1000 pairs that is belonging to different users from Twitter and Sina Weibo to be a
comparative dataset 2.

We firstly use the fast exclusion method to exclude the different users and the results are shown below.

Table 2. The Result Of Using Fast Exclusion Method

	Dataset 1	Dataset 2
Pairs of accounts	240	1000
Different pairs of accounts	27	795

We can calculate the recall rate is: 79.5% and accurate rate is 96.7%. It proves the
accuracy of the fast exclusion method is high and the method is effective.

After the fast exclusion method, dataset 1 left 213 pairs of accounts and dataset 2 left 205 pairs of accounts. We secondly use the behavior-modeling identification algorithm to acquire the difference values of those pairs.

Table 3. The Results Of Experiments Using The Behavior-modeling Identification Algorithm

Difference	Dataset 1	Dataset 2
$0.1 \leqq$	11	0
$0.3 \leqq$	124	0
$0.6 \leqq$	69	4
$0.9 \leqq$	7	12
$1.2 \leqq$	2	43
>1.2	0	146
Total	213	205

Table 3 illustrates that the difference values of dataset 1 are much lower than values of dataset 2. The threshold to determine whether the two accounts belong to the same individual is picked by experience. If we set the threshold at 0.6, we can acquire the final results that we judged whether the pairs belong to same individual.

Table 4. The Final Results Of Experiment 2

	Dataset 1	Dataset 2
Original values	240	1000
Result values	213	4

From Table 4, we can calculate the recall rate is: 88.7% and accurate rate is 98.1%. It illustrates the behavior-modeling identification algorithm is effective.

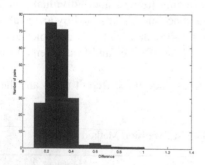
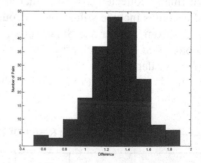

Fig. 2. (a) Histogram of Dataset 1   **Fig. 2.** (b) Histogram of Dataset 2

Fig.2(a) shows the histogram of dataset 1. The difference of users belong to same individuals is much lower than the difference of different users (Fig.2(b) illustrated). The experiments illustrate three conclusions: 1) The first experiment result shows that it is very similar for the behavior-modeling of one individual on the same platform.

2) The fast exclusion method can effectively exclude different users across social media sites. 3) The behavior-modeling identification algorithm do well in identifying the users across the social media sites.

6   Conclusion and Future Work

In this paper, we have demonstrated a method for identifying users in different social media sites. The method is based on behavioral modeling approach. The information employed by our method is available on social media sites. Users will keep their exhibits and behavioral patterns no matter what platform they choose. We used a fast exclusion method and provide a similarity to determine whether the users are belong to the same individual. The two experiments demonstrate that our method is effective.

There are other studies on users' behavior patterns; we can do the research on user's action model analysis. Future work includes analyzing those models' possibility and studying the multiple methods proved mutually.

References

1. Zafarani, R., Liu, H.: Connecting users across social media sites: a behavioral-modeling approach. In: Proceedings of the 19th ACM SIGKDD International Conference on Knowledge Discovery and Data Mining. ACM (2013)
2. Ahmed, A., Xing, E.P.: Staying informed: supervised and semi-supervised multi-view topical analysis of ideological perspective. In: EMNLP, pp. 1140–1150 (2010)
3. Amitay, E., Yogev, S., Yom-Tov, E.: Serial Sharers: Detecting Split Identities of Web Authors. In: SIGIR PAN Workshop (2007)
4. Cilibrasi, R., Vitanyi, P.M.B.: Clustering by Compression. IEEE Transactions on Information Theory 51(4), 1523–1545 (2005)
5. Albakour, M.-D., Macdonald, C., Ounis, I.: Identifying Local Events by Using Microblogs as Social Sensors. In: OAIR 2013, May 22-24 (2013)
6. Zheng, R., Li, J., Chen, H., Huang, Z.: A Framework for Authorship Identification of Online Messages: Writing-style Features and Classification Techniques. JASIST 57(3), 378–393 (2006)
7. De Vel, O., Anderson, A., Corney, M., Mohay, G.: Mining E-mail Content for Author Identification forensics. ACM Sigmod Record 30(4), 55–64 (2001)
8. Albakour, M.D., Macdonald, C., Ounis, I., Pnevmatikakis, A., Soldatos, J.: SMART: An open source framework for searching the physical world. In: OSIR at SIGIR 2012 (2012)
9. Bache, K., Newman, D., Smyth, P.: Text-based measures of document diversity. In: Proceedings of the 19th ACM SIGKDD International Conference on Knowledge Discovery and Data Mining. ACM (2013)
10. Tang, J., Zhang, M., Mei, Q.: One theme in all views: modeling consensus topics in multiple contexts. In: Proceedings of the 19th ACM SIGKDD International Conference on Knowledge Discovery and Data Mining. ACM (2013)
11. Becker, H., et al.: Identifying content for planned events across social media sites. In: Proceedings of the Fifth ACM International Conference on Web Search and Data Mining. ACM (2012)
12. Sakaki, T., Okazaki, M., Matsuo, Y.: Earthquake shakes Twitter users: Real-time event detection by social sensors. In: Proceedings of the 19th International World Wide Web Conference, WWW 2010 (2010)

An Effective Approach
on Overlapping Structures Discovery
for Co-clustering

Wangqun Lin[1], Yuchen Zhao[2], Philip S. Yu[2], and Bo Deng[1]

[1] Beijing Institute of System Engineering, Beijing, China
{linwangqun,bodeng}@nudt.edu.cn
[2] University of Illinois, Chicago, USA
{yzhao,psyu}@cs.uic.edu

Abstract. Co-clustering, which explores the inter-connected structures between objects and features simultaneously, has drawn much attention in the past decade. Most existing methods for co-clustering focus on partition-based approaches, which assume that each entry of the data matrix can only be assigned to one cluster. However, in the real world applications, the cluster structures can potential be overlapping. In this paper, we propose a novel overlapping co-clustering method by introducing the density guided principle for discriminative features (objects) identification. This is done by simultaneously finding the non-overlapping blocks. Based on the discovered blocks, an effective strategy is utilized to select the features (objects), which can discriminate the specified object (feature) cluster from other object (feature) clusters. Finally, according to the discriminative features (objects), a novel overlapping method, OPS, is proposed. Experimental studies on both synthetic and real-world data sets demonstrate the effectiveness and efficiency of the proposed OPS method.

1 Introduction

Co-clustering attracted much attentions during the past decade, where the task is to perform clustering on two types of inter-connected entities (i.e., rows and columns of a data matrix) simultaneously. Usually, each row of the data matrix represents an object, and each column of the data matrix represents a feature. For example, in the document analysis, the rows and columns of the data matrix correspond to the documents and words. Co-clustering on documents and words simultaneously can achieve better quality than clustering on documents alone. However, most existing co-clustering methods [1] [4] [8] are mainly partition-based, which usually assume that each entry in a data matrix can only be assigned to one cluster. Some cases of such application scenarios are as follows:

- **Row/Object Overlapping:** In many clustering applications, each individual object should be assigned to more than one cluster. For example, news articles can belong to multiple categories; Movies can have more than one genre; Chemical compounds can be associated with multiple types of efficacy.

L. Chen et al. (Eds.): APWeb 2014, LNCS 8709, pp. 56–67, 2014.

- **Column/Feature Overlapping:** For the scientific paper clustering problem, it is desirable that the clustering algorithm can automatically put papers from the same discipline into the same cluster. In the co-clustering setting, each paper is represented as one row while the term features are represented in columns. It is natural that some terms (columns) can be significant features for multiple clusters. For example, the term "matrix" can be important for both Math and Computer Science, and the term "molecule" can be frequently used in both Biology and Chemistry.

Such overlapping structures can often appear in a variety of clustering applications. The clustering quality can be greatly improved if the real overlapping structures of both rows and columns are captured. However, the overlapping scenarios make the problem very challenging from a number of aspects:

- Most existing works [5] [7] [14] on overlapping structures discovery focus on traditional clustering environment. The new challenge is on how to simultaneously find overlapping structures on both rows and columns. Discovered overlapping structures on rows will actively reinforce to discover the overlapping structures on columns and vice versa.
- Another challenge is on how to effectively define the overlapping criteria? If the criteria are set too strict, few overlapping structures will be discovered. However, if the criteria are too loose, many objects will be incorrectly identified to have overlapping structures, which will lead to poor clustering quality.
- Traditional co-clustering approaches usually require users to specify how many row clusters and column groups to cluster. Nonetheless, these two parameters are often difficult to obtain In reality. Designing an efficient and effective approach which requires no user specified parameter is quite challenging yet much desired.

In this paper, we will study the problem of overlapping structures discovery in the context of co-clustering. This is done by first finding the blocks, which have either dense or sparse connections, by non-overlapping co-clustering. Then based on the discovered blocks, we propose a density guided strategy to select the features (objects), which can discriminate the specified object (feature) clusters from other object (feature) clusters. Finally, according to the discriminative features (objects), a novel overlapping strategy (OPS), which can work with any non-overlapped co-clustering methods, is developed.

The rest of the paper is organized as follows. In Section 2, we introduce the related work. The strategy of overlapping co-clustering is elaborated in Section 3. Then, in Section 4 we introduce the co-clustering methods based on MDL, followed by the experimental evaluation in section 5. Finally, we conclude in Section 6.

2   Related Work

Co-clustering focuses on simultaneously clustering both dimensions of a matrix by exploiting the clear duality between rows and columns [13] [6]. Most works in co-clustering attempt to discover non-overlapping structures. Chakrabarti et al. [1] assumed the process of co-clustering as the problem of how to transfer the matrix with the least bits. By minimizing the total bits used to describe the matrix, the homogeneous blocks, whose densities are either very high or very low, are discovered. The denser blocks are used as co-clusters. Later, Papadimitriou et al. [15] further extended this method to the hierarchical situation. Long [12] proposed a Spectral Relational Clustering (SRC) approach, which iteratively embeds each type of data objects into low dimensional spaces. Since SRC needs to calculate eigenvectors, it is very time-consuming for large data set. Cheng et al.[2] devised the sequential bi-clustering model that finds one co-cluster, which has low mean squared residue scores in expression data at each time. Later, Lazzeroni et al. [10] proposed a plaid model for directly finding the overlapping co-clusters, but still can not identify multiple co-clusters simultaneously. Deodhar et al. [3] proposed a robust co-clustering algorithm called ROCC, which can work with various distance measures and different co-cluster definitions. However, in order to handle noisy or incoherent data, where a large fraction of the data points and features is irrelevant and needs to be discarded, ROCC focuses more on pruning. But in this paper, our assumption is that all of the objects and features are useful. In addition, approaches in [2] [3] [10] only focus on the overlapping structures between co-clusters but not among the row clusters and column clusters. Hence, their goals are quite different from our problem. Wang et al. [16] proposed a method similar to k-means by making use of the correlations between users and tags in social media. However, this method is only tailored for social media domain and is ineffective for the general case of overlapping structures.

3   The Framework of Discovering Overlapping Structures for Co-clustering

An un-weighted bipartite graph G is described by a binary matrix D of $m \times n$, in which each element $e_{i,j}(1 \le i \le m, 1 \le j \le n)$ indicates whether the i-th object has a link relation with the j-th feature or not. R represents the set of rows and C represents the set of columns in D. $\mathcal{A}$ is the set of co-clustering algorithms which aim at co-clustering the set of rows, i.e., R into k row clusters and the set of columns, i.e., C into l column clusters. We use $\mathcal{I}$ denoting the set of row clusters, i.e., $\mathcal{I} = \{\mathcal{I}_i\}_{i=1}^k$, and $\mathcal{J}$ denoting the set of column clusters, i.e., $\mathcal{J} = \{\mathcal{J}_j\}_{j=1}^l$. Since each row r stands for an object and each column c stands for a feature in matrix D, we use r to represent both row and object and c to represent both column and feature in this paper.

Definition 1 (Pattern). *Given an object-feature matrix D of size $m \times n$, assume matrix D is to be co-clustered into k row clusters and l column clusters. A pattern $\mathcal{M}_i = (Q_X^i, Q_Y^i)$ is a mapping of rows and columns of matrix D respectively, where Q_X^i denotes the mapping of rows and Q_Y^i denotes the mapping of columns, i.e., $Q_X^i : \{1, 2, \cdots, m\} \to \{1, 2, \cdots, k\}; Q_Y^i : \{1, 2, \cdots, n\} \to \{1, 2, \cdots, l\}$. $\mathcal{M}$ denotes the set of the patterns in D, i.e., $\mathcal{M}_i \in \mathcal{M}$.*

In order to gather the similar objects into the same row clusters and the similar features into the same column clusters, co-clustering approach $\mathcal{A}_i \in \mathcal{A}$ searches the appropriate optimal pattern $\mathcal{M}^* \in \mathcal{M}$ for optimizing a specified objective function as shown in [1] [13]. A regular co-clustering process is given from Figure 1(a) to 1(b). All the discussion in this section is under the assumption that we have already computed a co-clustered matrix D. In other words, given an object-feature matrix D, the co-clustering approach $\mathcal{A}_i \in \mathcal{A}$ has already co-clustered different objects into different row clusters and different features into different column clusters.

We notice that, any row (column) cluster becomes an independent row (column) cluster because it has some discriminative feature (object) sets. Before we give the detailed description of discriminative feature (object) set, we give the observations of co-clustering process in Figures 1(a) and 1(b). It is clear that there are four row clusters and four column clusters in this example. From Figure 1(b), we notice that, for each row cluster, it certainly has some features that distinguish the row cluster itself from other row clusters. Otherwise, this row cluster will be merged into other row clusters. As shown in Figure 1(c), the first row cluster and the second row cluster are separated from each other because they have different features. In details, in the first row cluster, features in block $P3$ and $P5$ are most important features. In addition, features in $P5$ can be more discriminative than those features in $P3$ since other row clusters have much lower densities for features in $P5$. Similarly, features in $P1$ are more discriminative than features in $P2$ for the second row cluster in terms of separating from other row clusters. Symmetrically, for column clusters, objects located in $P1$ are more important than objects located in $P3$ to discriminate the first column cluster from other column clusters. Compared to objects located in $P3$, objects located in $P4$ contribute more for discriminating the second column cluster from other column clusters.

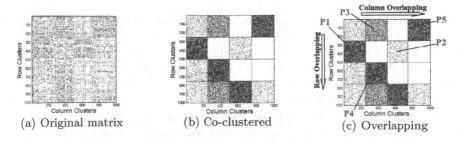

(a) Original matrix   (b) Co-clustered   (c) Overlapping

Fig. 1. The process of overlapping co-clustering

For any row cluster $\mathcal{I}_p \in \mathcal{I}(1 \leq p \leq k)$, in order to measure the importance of the features in column cluster $\mathcal{J}_s \in \mathcal{J}(1 \leq s \leq l)$ for distinguishing row cluster $\mathcal{I}_p$ from other row clusters, the difference of density between the block $D_{p,s}$ and average density of all blocks in the s-th column group of matrix D should be considered. This is referred to as the *density guided principle* for discriminative features (objects) identification. We give the *Discriminative Feature Function* $w(p, s)$ to evaluate the contribution of column cluster $\mathcal{J}_s$ for separating row cluster $\mathcal{I}_p$ from other row clusters as follow:

$$w(p, s) = N(D_{p,s}) - \frac{1}{|\mathcal{I}|} \sum_{i=1}^{|\mathcal{I}|} N(D_{i,s}) \tag{1}$$

where $N(D_{p,s})$ is the density function which measures the percentage of "1"s in block $D_{p,s}$. Obviously, the larger value of $w(p, s)$, the more contribution of features in $\mathcal{J}_s$ for discriminating row cluster $\mathcal{I}_p$ from other row clusters. Symmetrically, we further define the *Discriminative Object Function* $w'(s, p)$ to evaluate the contribution of row cluster $\mathcal{I}_p$ for distinguishing column cluster $\mathcal{J}_s$ from other column clusters below.

$$w'(s, p) = N(D_{p,s}) - \frac{1}{|\mathcal{J}|} \sum_{j=1}^{|\mathcal{J}|} N(D_{p,j}) \tag{2}$$

Definition 2 (Discriminative Feature Set). *Given the row cluster $\mathcal{I}_p \in \mathcal{I}$ and the column cluster $\mathcal{J}_s \in \mathcal{J}$, the group of features located in the column cluster $\mathcal{J}_s$ is the discriminative feature set for the row cluster $\mathcal{I}_p$ iff $\mathcal{J}_s$ contributes to the distinction of row cluster $\mathcal{I}_p$ from other row cluster $\mathcal{I}_q \in \mathcal{I}(p \neq q)$, i.e., $w(p, s) \geq 0$.*

Definition 3 (Discriminative Object Set). *Given the column cluster $\mathcal{J}_s \in \mathcal{J}$ and the row cluster $\mathcal{I}_p \in \mathcal{I}$, the group of objects located in the row cluster $\mathcal{I}_p$ is the discriminative object set for the column cluster $\mathcal{J}_s$ iff $\mathcal{I}_p$ contributes to the distinction of column cluster $\mathcal{J}_s$ from other column cluster $\mathcal{J}_t \in \mathcal{J}(s \neq t)$, i.e., $w'(s, p) \geq 0$.*

Given an object $r \in \mathcal{I}_q$, when we consider its relation with row cluster $\mathcal{I}_p(p \neq q)$, we examine its features shared with the objects in $\mathcal{I}_p$. Concretely, the more discriminative feature sets they shared, the closer relation they are. Moreover, for a specified discriminative feature set in $\mathcal{I}_p$, if an object r has a higher feature density in this discriminative feature set, it indicates the closer relation between object r and objects in $\mathcal{I}_p$. Consequently, for any row $r \in \mathcal{I}_q$, in order to test whether row r should also be placed into row cluster $\mathcal{I}_p$ $(p \neq q)$ or not, all the discriminative feature sets in p-th row group are considered by Equation (3).

$$E_{or}(r, p) = \sum_{f \in F} w(p, f)(N(r_f) - N(D_{p,f})) - \alpha \tag{3}$$

where r_f is the set of elements from row r located in column cluster $\mathcal{J}_f$; F is index set of discriminative feature set of column cluster, i.e., $F = \{f | w(p, f) \geq 0, \mathcal{J}_f \in \mathcal{J}\}$; α is a parameter used to control the extent of the row overlap. On the right hand side of Equation (3), the first term in the summation indicates the significance of the discriminative feature set to the p-th row group, while the second term measures the density difference of row r relative to the p-th row group. Intuitively, the larger of their product, the more likely that row r will be related to the p-th row group. We take the sum of the products over all discriminative feature sets of the p-th row group as the measure. If $E_{or}(r,p) \geq 0$, row r will not only be placed into its original row cluster $\mathcal{I}_q$ but also to row cluster $\mathcal{I}_p$. We notice that, it is possible for $(N(r_f) - N(D_{p,f}))$ to be negative. If in this case, it means row r has a lower feature density located in column cluster $\mathcal{J}_s$ than $\mathcal{I}_p$. Consequently, the possibility of placing row r into row cluster $\mathcal{I}_p$ is penalized.

Similarly, we have Equation (4) for evaluating any column $c \in \mathcal{J}_t$ whether should also be placed into column cluster $\mathcal{J}_s$ $(s \neq t)$.

$$E_{oc}(c,s) = \sum_{b \in B} w'(s,b)(N(c_b) - N(D_{b,s})) - \beta \tag{4}$$

where c_b is the set of elements from column c located in row cluster $\mathcal{I}_b$; B is the index set of discriminative object set of row cluster, i.e., $B = \{b | w'(s,b) \geq 0, \mathcal{I}_b \in \mathcal{I}\}$; β is a parameter used to control the extent of the column overlap. The description of Overlapping Pattern Search (OPS) for overlapping co-clustering is given in Algorithm 1. We note that the order of step 2 and step 3 does not matter, since going through the rows and columns are solely based on the appropriate optimal non-overlapping patterns. In other words, step 2 and step 3 are independent. Besides, $\alpha = \beta = 0$ is used in this paper.

Algorithm 1. $OPS(\mathcal{A}_i, D)$

---

1. Call co-clustering algorithm $\mathcal{A}_i$ to find the approximate optimal non-overlapping pattern (Q_X^*, Q_Y^*) of D.
2. Based on (Q_X^*, Q_Y^*), for each row $r \in R$ and each row cluster $\mathcal{I}_p \in \mathcal{I}$ $(r \notin \mathcal{I}_p)$, compute $E_{or}(r,p)$ according to Equation (3). If $E_{or}(r,p) \geq 0$, copy row r to row cluster $\mathcal{I}_p$, i.e., $\mathcal{I}_p \leftarrow \mathcal{I}_p \cup r$.
3. Based on (Q_X^*, Q_Y^*), for each column $c \in C$ and each column cluster $\mathcal{J}_s \in \mathcal{J}$ $(c \notin \mathcal{J}_s)$, compute $E_{oc}(c,s)$ according to Equation (4). If $E_{oc}(c,s) \geq 0$, copy column c to column cluster $\mathcal{J}_s$, i.e., $\mathcal{J}_s \leftarrow \mathcal{J}_s \cup c$.
4. Return overlapping row clusters and column clusters $(\mathcal{I}_o^*, \mathcal{J}_o^*) = (\mathcal{I}, \mathcal{J})$.

---

4   Co-clustering Approach Based on Information Compression

We have presented a general framework for overlapping co-clustering based on non-overlapping co-clustering in the last section. In this section, we give the co-clustering approach used in this paper for generating the non-overlapping row clusters and column clusters. Although the overlapping framework described in Section 3 can work with any non-overlapping co-clustering method, here we further extend FACA [1] to generate the non-overlapping co-clusters because it can be parameter free and generate good quality results. Due to the space limit, we first briefly introduce the process of FACA. Then we explain how we extend it further to be more efficient and effective. Finding the optimal co-clustering pattern is NP-hard [1]. In order to find the appropriate optimal pattern $\mathcal{M}^*$, FACA makes use of Minimum Description Length (MDL) theory to encode matrix without information loss. Assume a matrix D with $m \times n$ is divided into k row clusters and l column clusters. Compressing matrix D includes two parts which are *description complexity* $T_m(D)$ and *code length* $T_c(D)$. Therefore, the total bits used for condensing matrix D is

$$
\begin{aligned}
&T(D) \\
=&T_m(D) + T_c(D) \\
=& \log^* m + \log^* n + m\lceil \log m \rceil + n\lceil \log n \rceil + \log^* k + \log^* l \\
&+ \lceil \log\binom{m}{m_1,\cdots,m_k} \rceil + \lceil \log\binom{n}{n_1,\cdots,n_l} \rceil + \sum_{i=1}^{|\mathcal{I}|}\sum_{j=1}^{|\mathcal{J}|} \lceil \log(m_i n_j + 1) \rceil \\
&+ \sum_{i=1}^{|\mathcal{I}|}\sum_{j=1}^{|\mathcal{J}|}\sum_{h=0}^{1} N_h(D_{ij}) \log\left(\frac{N(D_{ij})}{N_h(D_{ij})}\right)
\end{aligned}
\tag{5}
$$

where $N_h(D_{ij})$ denotes the number of "h"s (h=0 or 1) in block D_{ij}, m_i denotes the number of objects in row cluster $\mathcal{I}_i$, and n_j denotes the number of features in column cluster $\mathcal{J}_j$. All the logarithms are based 2 in Equation (5). Besides, in Equation (5), the first term to the ninth term represents the *description complexity*, and the tenth term represents the *code length*. The original algorithms only used the tenth term as the objective function. The detailed description of FACA can be found in [1]. As we will see in the experimental section, by retaining all these terms to capture the effect of both description complexity and code length, we can achieve better clustering quality.

5   Experiments

In this section, we test our method on both synthetic and real-world data sets. Each experiment is repeated 10 times and the average is reported. We use two metrics to measure the performance. The first metric used in this paper is *Purity* and the second one is *Normalized Mutual Information* (NMI) [9].

5.1   Data Set Description

Synthetic Data Set. We generate the synthetic data based on Classic3[1]. Classic3 data set contains three types of non-overlapping documents, which are MEDLINE (medical journals), CISI (information retrieval) and CRANFIELD

---

[1] http://www.dataminingresearch.com/index.php/2010/09/classic3-classic4-datasets

(aero-dynamics). The documents and words form a bipartite graph described by a binary matrix of 3891×5896. In order to get the overlapping documents, firstly, we randomly select 1000 documents from each type of documents. Secondly, we randomly choose two documents d_i and d_j, which belong to two different types T_i, T_j ($i \neq j$), from the total 3000 documents. Thirdly, we merge documents d_j and d_i together to form a new document d_{ij}, which is tagged with two types T_i and T_j. The above processes repeat until the total specified overlapping percentage $OV\%$ of new documents are generated.

Real-World Data Sets. In addition to the synthetic data set, we use two real-world data sets to test the proposed method. The first real data set is *Reuter* data set[2] , which contains 294 documents. Each document records a story happened from February 2009 to April 2009. Among these stories, 40 stories are tagged more than one type of the total six types, which are *business, entertainment, health, politics, sport* and *technology*. The second real data set is *BBC* data set[3] , which also contains six types of documents as the Reuter data set. BBC data set contains the total number of 352 documents and 40 documents are annotated with more than one type.

We notice that the standard text preprocessing approaches such as stemming, stop words removal have already been applied to all of these data sets.

5.2   Experiment Results

We compare our method with four state-of-the-art methods. The first one is FACA [1]. The second compared method is NMF [11], which is a co-clustering method based on non-negative matrix factorization. The third compared method is SRC [12] and the fourth one is DOGSM [16]. We note that FACA, NMF and SAC can detect effective row clusters and column clusters but cannot discover the overlapping structures. While DOGSM can detect the overlapping structures of row clusters and column clusters, but the number of row clusters and column clusters are limited to be exactly the same because DOGSM is a k-means based method.

We first consider the case that the number of row clusters and column clusters are presumably given. In Classic3 data set, the number of row cluster $k = 3$ is given and the number of column cluster l is unknown. Hence, different values of $l = 15, 20, 25$ are provided to all of these compared methods. In this situation, OPS calls extended FACA for non-overlapping co-clustering. Besides, DOGSM is a clustering method similar to k-means, it has no parameter l. The metrical scores on Purity and NMI on Classic3 data set are given in Tables 1 and 2 respectively. We observe that, generally speaking, FACA, NMF, SRC and OPS achieve comparative scores over two metrics on Classic3 data set. In detail, OPS outperforms all of the compared methods. Especially, OPS takes more advantage than the other compared methods as the number of overlapping percentage

---

[2] http://mlg.ucd.ie/datasets
[3] http://mlg.ucd.ie/datasets

$OV\%$ increases. This is because, compared to FACA, NMF and SRC, OPS can discover the overlapping structures which can further reveal the cluster structure of the data set. Even though DOGSM can also discover the overlapping clusters, its performance is not as good as OPS. This is because it can not distinguish the different number of row clusters and column clusters. Besides, compared to other three methods, DOGSM can not make use of the relations between objects and features when performing clustering. This is critical for the performance of clustering when the data is very sparse and noisy. Therefore, OPS gains much better scores on two metrics than DOGSM at different overlapping levels.

Another observation of Tables 1 ~ 2 is that the metrical scores of two metrics on the compared methods decrease as the percentage of overlapping $OV\%$ increasing. The probable reasons for this phenomenon are as follows. Firstly, the higher overlapping percentage of the documents makes the data set more complicated and challenging to all of the compared methods. Secondly, the number of hybrid objects, which belong to two clusters, are increasing as the overlapping percentage getting higher. This makes the number of hybrid objects of the same type, such as hybrid objects of LINE and CISI, enough to form new independent clusters. In other words, the ground truth of the number of the row clusters is moving from 3 to 6 as the number of overlapping documents increasing. However, OPS still performs very well even the overlapping percentage $OV\% = 20\%$.

Table 1. Purity scores on Classic3 data set

OV%	k	l	FACA [1]	NMF [11]	SRC [12]	OPS	DOGSM [16]
		15	0.9387	0.8971	0.85778	**0.9632**	
5%	3	20	0.9397	0.9107	0.84571	**0.9613**	0.3931
		25	0.9444	0.91175	0.8565	**0.9698**	
		15	0.8882	0.8684	0.8200	**0.9294**	
10%	3	20	0.8870	0.8724	0.7781	**0.9312**	0.3681
		25	0.8945	0.8666	0.6857	**0.9367**	
		15	0.8412	0.8379	0.61014	**0.9113**	
15%	3	20	0.8478	0.8310	0.59362	**0.9136**	0.4052
		25	0.8475	0.8307	0.61014	**0.9168**	
		15	0.7981	0.7933	0.6908	**0.8894**	
20%	3	20	0.8036	0.7936	0.5927	**0.8814**	0.4157
		25	0.8067	0.7930	0.5536	**0.8825**	

In the real data sets of Reuter and BBC, the number of row clusters $k = 6$ is given, but the number of column clusters is unknown. In order to test the ability of automatically finding the number of row clusters k and column clusters l, we run OPS without given the number of row clusters and column clusters. Since FACA can also automatically detect the number of row clusters and column clusters when searching for the optimal pattern, we use FACA(Auto) to denote this situation. While for the other compared methods, we provide exactly the number of row clusters and different parameters for the number of column clusters.

Table 2. NMI scores on Classic3 data set

OV%	k	l	FACA [1]	NMF [11]	SRC [12]	OPS	DOGSM [16]
		15	0.8284	0.6995	0.4567	**0.8693**	
5%	3	20	0.8309	0.6060	0.7359	**0.8697**	0.0501
		25	0.8506	0.7331	0.5874	**0.8891**	
		15	0.7345	0.6674	0.4651	**0.7875**	
10%	3	20	0.7296	0.5300	0.6596	**0.7895**	0.0208
		25	0.7567	0.6674	0.4850	**0.8009**	
		15	0.6503	0.6331	0.4375	**0.7270**	
15%	3	20	0.6724	0.4434	0.6146	**0.7526**	0.0615
		25	0.6694	0.6118	0.3128	**0.7503**	
		15	0.5866	0.5562	0.3038	**0.6499**	
20%	3	20	0.6013	0.4190	0.5587	**0.6706**	0.0411
		25	0.6077	0.5558	0.3611	**0.6790**	

The results of the different methods on Reuter data set are presented in Figures 2(a)-2(b). Since the results of OPS and FACA(Auto) are not affected by the number of column clusters, their results are horizontal lines over different values of l. Despite without any information of the number of row clusters and column clusters, OPS still gains the highest scores over all of the three metrics. It is evident that OPS has better advantage than other compared methods for finding the most appropriate row clusters and column clusters. Though FACA(Auto) can also detect the number of row clusters and column clusters automatically, its performance is not as good as OPS. That is because of the following reasons. Firstly, OPS can discover the overlapping structures hidden among the clusters. Secondly, OPS uses the total bits used to describe the whole matrix as the objective function, which can get an appropriate balance between model description complexity and code length, and improve the co-clustering quality. We keep in mind that OPS automatically detects the number of row clusters and column clusters. We also notice that FACA(Auto) performs better than FACA in this data set. Besides, SRC outperforms NMF in most of the cases. Though DOGSM can also discover the overlapping structure, it seems very sensitive to the sparsity and noise of the data set. Hence, the performance of DOGSM is relative poor in our tests.

In Figures 2(c)-2(d), we illustrate the results of the compared methods on BBC data set. Once again, OPS gains the highest scores on two different metrics. We note that FACA(Auto) does much poorly on NMI compared to OPS. Moreover, NMF and SRC do poorly on Purity. We observe that the NMI scores of all of the compared methods are not very high. We carefully analyze this phenomenon and find BBC data set is very unbalanced. For example, the number of document annotated as *sports* is 44, while the number of documents annotated as *business* is 102, which is more than two times the number of documents annotated as *sports*. Besides, compared to the Classic3 data set, the number of documents is relatively small, but the number of document clusters is relatively large in this data set. Both of which make the co-clustering in BBC data set a non-trivial

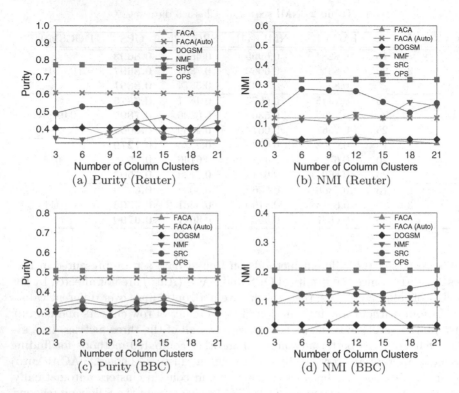

Fig. 2. The results of two metrics with different methods on the data sets of Reuter and BBC

challenge for all of these compared methods. However, even in this case, OPS still gains a comparative performance.

6   Conclusion

Discovering the overlapping structures of objects and features simultaneously is significant in many real-world applications. However, this problem is neglected by many existing works. In this paper, a novel parameter-free algorithm OPS, which utilize a density guided principle to discover the overlapping structures among row clusters and column clusters simultaneously, is proposed. Experiments including real-world and synthetic data sets demonstrate our method is effective and efficient. Further works will focus on non-binary matric co-clustering.

Acknowledgements. This work is supported in part by National Natural Science Foundation of China through grants 61271252, NSF through grants CNS-1115234, DBI-0960443, and OISE-1129076.

References

1. Chakrabarti, D., Papadimitriou, S., Modha, D.S., Faloutsos, C.: Fully automatic cross-associations. In: KDD, pp. 79–88 (2004)
2. Cheng, Y., Church, G.M.: Biclustering of expression data. In: ISMB, pp. 93–103 (2000)
3. Deodhar, M., Cho, H., Gupta, G., Ghosh, J., Dhillon, I.: Robust overlapping co-clustering. In: IDEAL-TR (2008)
4. Dhillon, I.S., Guan, Y.: Information theoretic clustering of sparse co-occurrence data. In: ICDM, pp. 517–528 (2003)
5. Evans, T.S., Lambiotte, R.: Line graphs, link partitions and overlapping communities. Physical Review E 80, 016105 (2009)
6. Gossen, T., Kotzyba, M., Nürnberger, A.: Graph clusterings with overlaps: Adapted quality indices and a generation model. Neurocomputing 123, 13–22 (2014)
7. Huang, J., Sun, H., Han, J., Deng, H., Sun, Y., Liu, Y.: Shrink: a structural clustering algorithm for detecting hierarchical communities in networks. In: CIKM, pp. 219–228 (2010)
8. Huh, Y., Kim, J., Lee, J., Yu, K., Shi, W.: Identification of multi-scale corresponding object-set pairs between two polygon datasets with hierarchical co-clustering. ISPRS Journal of Photogrammetry and Remote Sensing 88, 60–68 (2014)
9. Lancichinetti, A., Fortunato, S., Kertész, J.: Detecting the overlapping and hierarchical community structure in complex networks. New Journal of Physics 11(3), 033015 (2009)
10. Lazzeroni, L., Owen, A.: Plaid models for gene expression data. Statistica Sinica 12, 61–86 (2000)
11. Lee, D.D., Seung, H.S.: Algorithms for non-negative matrix factorization. In: NIPS, pp. 556–562. MIT Press (2000)
12. Long, B., Zhang, Z., Wu, X., Yu, P.S.: Spectral clustering for multi-type relational data. In: ICML, pp. 585–592 (2006)
13. Long, B., Zhang, Z., Yu, P.S.: Co-clustering by block value decomposition. In: KDD, pp. 635–640 (2005)
14. Palla, G., Derenyi, I., Farkas, I., Vicsek, T.: Uncovering the overlapping community structure of complex networks in nature and society. Nature 435, 814–818 (2005)
15. Papadimitriou, S., Sun, J., Faloutsos, C., Yu, P.S.: Hierarchical, parameter-free community discovery. In: Daelemans, W., Goethals, B., Morik, K. (eds.) ECML PKDD 2008, Part II. LNCS (LNAI), vol. 5212, pp. 170–187. Springer, Heidelberg (2008)
16. Wang, X., Tang, L., Gao, H., Liu, H.: Discovering overlapping groups in social media. In: ICDM, pp. 569–578 (December 2010)

Group-Based Personalized Location Recommendation on Social Networks

Henan Wang, Guoliang Li, and Jianhua Feng

Department of Computer Science and Technology,
Tsinghua University, Beijing 100084, China
whn13@mails.thu.edu.cn, {liguoliang,fengjh}@tsinghua.edu.cn

Abstract. Location-based social networks (LBSNs) have attracted significant attention recently, thanks to modern smartphones and Mobile Internet, which make it convenient to capture a user's location and share users' locations. LBSNs generate large amount of user generated content (UGC), including both location histories and social relationships, and provide us with opportunities to enable location-aware recommendation. Existing methods focus either on recommendation efficiency at the expense of low quality or on recommendation quality at the cost of low efficiency. To address these limitations, in this paper we propose a group-based personalized location recommendation system, which can provide users with most interested locations, based on their personal preferences and social connections. We adopt a two-step method to make a trade-off between recommendation efficiency and quality. We first construct a hierarchy for locations based on their categories and group users based on their locations and the hierarchy. Then for each user, we identify her most relevant group and use the users in the group to recommend interested locations for the user. We have implemented our method and compared with existing approaches. Experimental results on real-world datasets show that our method achieves good quality and high performance and outperforms existing approaches.

1 Introduction

The rapid development of Mobile Internet enables users to share their information on mobile phones. As modern smartphones are equipped with GPS, we can easily obtain users' locations. Thanks to modern smartphones and Mobile Internet, location-based social networks (LBSNs) are becoming more and more popular and widely accepted by mobile-phone users [3,14]. There are many real LBSN systems, e.g., Foursquare (foursquare.com) and Jiepang (jiepang.com). Moreover, there are many studies on identifying users' locations from traditional social networks, e.g., Twitter (twitter.com) [10,11]. Thus we have many ways to obtain real-world LBSNs.

LBSNs generate large amount of user generated content (UGC), including both location histories and social relationships, and provide us with opportunities to enable location-aware recommendation, which has many real applications [2,15].

L. Chen et al. (Eds.): APWeb 2014, LNCS 8709, pp. 68–80, 2014.

For example, a new tourist visits a city and we want to recommend her some interested scenic spots.

To build a personalized location recommendation system on LBSNs, we should consider both the recommendation quality and efficiency. Existing methods focus either on recommendation efficiency at the expense of low quality or on recommendation quality at the cost of low efficiency [1,17]. To achieve high performance, it requires to devise effective structures and efficient algorithms. To achieve high quality, it needs to consider the following factors. First, user preferences are very important. For example, if a user often goes to cinemas, she may like movies, and thus we can recommend her locations related to movies. It is worth noting that a user may have multiple interests, and we should analyze the importance of these interests. Second, it is important to consider users' comments on locations, e.g., user ratings or visited times. Third, social connections are also important. A user may be more interested in the locations their friends are also interested in. [9] solves the location-aware influence maximization problem, which reflects the importance of social connections for location recommendation.

To utilize these information, we need to address the following challenges. The first one is the data-sparseness problem. A user's location histories are limited, which leads to the user-location matrix very large but sparse. The second one is the cold-start problem. For a new user, we do not know her preferences and it is hard to recommend relevant locations.

To address these limitations, in this paper we propose a group-based personalized location recommendation system, which can provide users with most interested locations, based on their personal preferences and social connections.

The main contribution of this paper is as follows.

- We develop a group-based personalized location recommendation system to do real-time location recommendation on LBSNs, emphasizing on both efficiency and quality.
- We propose a hierarchical clustering method to cluster locations and build a hierarchy for the locations. We group the users based on their interested locations and the location hierarchy.
- We devise a two-step method to recommend users with interested locations. For each user, we first identify her relevant group based on user-group similarity. Then from the identified group, we recommend interested locations based on user-location similarity.
- We have implemented our method and compared with existing approaches. Experimental results on real-world datasets show that our method achieves good quality and high performance and outperforms existing approaches.

The rest of the paper is organized as follows. Section 2 gives the problem formulation and the system overview. We introduce how to generate the groups in Section 3 and discuss how to do personalized location recommendation in Section 4. Section 5 shows the experiment results. We review related works in Section 6. Finally, Section 7 concludes the paper.

2 System Overview

In this section, we first introduce the problem formulation, and then present the overview of our proposed location recommendation system.

2.1 Problem Formulation

We use a graph to model an LBSN where nodes are all users and edges are relationships between users (e.g., follower/followee relationships). In addition, for each node, it includes a set of locations that the use has visited (e.g., checked in). For each user, when she comes to a new place, denoted by a minimum bounding rectangle (MBR) r, we want to recommend her n new locations within the region r that the user has never visited. Next we use an example to illustrate our problem, as shown in Fig 1.

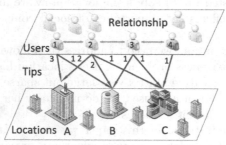

Fig. 1. Example of Problem Definition

Assuming locations L_A, L_B and L_C are within search range r, the possible recommended results are: L_C is recommended to user U_1, L_A is recommended to user U_3, L_A and L_B are recommended to user U_4 (since U_3 and U_4 are friends, L_B may have higher rating than L_A).

2.2 System Architecture

As shown in Fig.2, the system can be divided into two parts: offline clustering and online recommendation.

Location-Aware and Preference-Aware Clustering. The lower part of Fig. 2 is the clustering part. First, we extract locations users have visited. From existing POIs or knowledge base [13], we can obtain the categories of locations (e.g., KFC belongs to 'Fast Food' which in turn belongs to 'Food') and build a category hierarchy, where nodes on the hierarchy are categories and the parent-child edges denote the category-subcategory relationships. Then, for each user, we can get her category hierarchy based on her locations, which is a subtree of the category tree. In addition, we evaluate the user preferences by her visited locations and the number of visited times using the term frequency * inverse document frequency (TF*IDF) method, and incorporate the weight into her location hierarchy, called weighted category hierarchy (WCH) [1]. Next we cluster

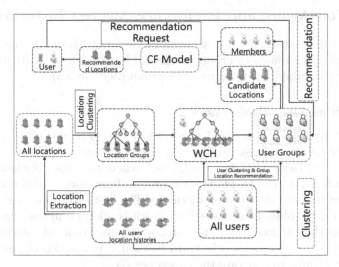

Fig. 2. System Architecture

users into different groups according to their WCHs using the K-Means algorithm. Finally for each group, we use all locations that the users in the group have visited and some popular locations as the candidate locations. Section 3 gives the details of offline clustering.

Personalized Location Recommendation. The upper part of Fig.2 is the recommendation part. First, we find the group that the user belongs to (or most relevant group if the user is a new user) and get the members of the group. Second, we get candidate locations in a specified geospatial range using the group's R-tree index. Third, we calculate the similarity between the user and candidate locations. Finally, we devise recommendation algorithms to recommend the top-k locations to the user.

System Features. The proposed system is designed to provide real-time location recommendation for the users, and we focus on improving the efficiency while achieving high quality. The system has the following characteristics. First, we can address the data-sparseness problem using the group-based method since we use the locations in the group to support recommendation. Second, we can address the cold-start problem as we use the users in the relevant group to recommend locations. Third, our method has high performance, since the user-location matrix (user-user matrix) is replaced by the user-category (user-group) matrix and the computation overhead is significantly reduced.

Research Challenges. Generating high-quality groups is very important and challenging in our method since it affects the recommendation quality. We devise effective techniques to address this issue in Section 3. Second, identifying relevant groups and locations for each user is also very challenging and we propose some similarity functions to calculate the user-group and user-location similarities and devise efficient recommendation algorithms in Section 4.

3   Location-Aware and Preference-Aware Clustering

In this section we first discuss how to analyze user preferences (Section 3.1) and then utilize the preferences to group the users (Section 3.2). Finally we present how to select candidate locations for each group (Section 3.3).

3.1   Analyzing User Preferences

We study how to capture user's preference, which is very important to do personalized recommendation. First, to describe the locations, we propose a location category hierarchy (e.g., KFC, fast food, food), where each node is a location category and each parent-child edge is a category-subcategory relationship. There are many ways to build the location hierarchy. The first method is to use existing knowledge bases to obtain the hierarchy, which is adopted in our experiments. The second method is to extract the categories from Points of Interest (POIs) as POIs contain the categories. The third method is to use existing hierarchical clustering algorithms to generate the categories [7].

Then based on the category hierarchy, we construct a weighted category hierarchy (WCH) for each user. WCH is a subtree of the category tree. For each user, we insert her locations to the leaf nodes if the locations belong to the corresponding categories. Then the minimum subtree that contains all the locations is the WCH of the user. To capture user preference, for each category, we add the user's preference on the category (i.e., whether the user likes the category). To this end, we use the term frequency * inverse document frequency (TF*IDF) method to calculate the value using Eq. 1.

$$u.w_c = TF * IDF = \frac{|\{u.l_i : l_i.c = c\}|}{|u.L|} * lg \frac{|U|}{|\{u_j : c \in u_j.C\}|} \tag{1}$$

where $|\{u.l_i : l_i.c = c\}|$ is the times that user u visits category c, $|u.L|$ is the size of the u's location histories, $|\{u_j : c \in u_j.C\}|$ is the number of users who have visited c, and $|U|$ is the number of users.

WCH in our system has the following advantages. First, it can help to solve the data-sparseness problem, because the WCH can effectively reduce the dimensions of the user-location matrix by replacing it with the user-category matrix, and the data is not sparse any more. Second, it can solve the cold-start problem. Although a user may not visit any location in a new city, we can infer her preferences from her WCH and recommend interesting locations to her. Third, two categories may not exact match and WCH can tolerate the category mismatching problem using the hierarchy.

3.2   Constructing User Groups

To group the users into different groups based on their preferences, we use the K-means algorithm to do user clustering, based on the following four steps.

- **Data Preparation.** We utilize all users' WCHs to group the users. In some others studies, relationships, tags, or location histories can be used as the data source, compared with WCHs, they are large-scale and inefficient.

- **Feature Selection and Extraction.** There are many possible ways to select features from WCHs, e.g., only using the first, second, or third level nodes on the WCHs, or using the mixed level nodes. If we use lower level nodes, there will be larger number of groups and the relationships between categories in the different groups will be neglected. If we use higher level nodes, there will be less number of groups and we can use more relationships between categories. For example, we use the first level nodes as the features. The features can reflect the diversity of user preference and the users will be classified into $2^9 = 512$ groups.
- **Similarity Computing.** For each user, we create a vector for her, and the dimension is the number of nodes on the first level of her WCH, and the value of each item is the value of corresponding node. We use cosine distance to calculate the similarity of two users' vectors.
- **Clustering.** We apply the K-Means algorithm to cluster users, and all users are classified into K groups and one user only belongs to one group.

3.3 Generating Group Candidate Locations

For each group, we use locations the group members have visited and some highly rated locations as the candidate locations. The following part describes how to generate the highly rated locations.

We use an iterative method to rate locations, where a location's rating is called the authority score, represented by $l.a$, and a user's rating is called the hub score, represented by $u.h$. Through iterative computing we can pick out high-quality locations and users. Eq. 2 is used to calculate the authority and hub score, while $l.a$ is initialized as the times that l is visited, and $u.h$ is initialized as the size of u's location histories:

$$l.a = \sum_{u \in U_l} u.h, \quad u.h = \sum_{l \in L_u} l.a \quad (2)$$

In order to get the candidate locations efficiently within a geospatial range, we use the R-tree to index all locations, which is proposed by Guttman [4] as a spatial index structure. Searching on the R-tree is quite efficient, and we construct an R-tree for each group to further accelerate the search speed.

4 Personalized Location Recommendation

In this section, we introduce how to support online personalized location recommendation. After a user submits a location recommendation request, we first find which group the user belongs to by calculating the user-group similarity (Section 4.1). Then, we search candidate locations within the query search region. We use the R-tree to index candidate locations, and thus we only need to search on the corresponding group's R-tree nodes and efficiently get the candidate locations. Next we calculate the user-location similarity and recommend high rating locations to the user (Section 4.2).

4.1   Identifying User's Group

Consider a user submits a recommendation request. It is rather important to determine the group that the user belongs to because a user group reflects the preferences of users in the group. If the user belongs to a group, we can easily get the corresponding group. On the contrary, we need to find the most relevant group to the user. Since we use the K-Means algorithm to cluster users, each group has a virtual center user. Given a group, we use the similarity between the user and the center to compute the similarity between the user and the group. In this way, we can calculate the similarity between the user and all groups, and select the highest one as the user's group.

4.2   Recommending Locations

From the identified group, we find the candidate locations using the R-tree. Here we introduce how to recommend top-k locations from the candidate locations. One big challenge is to calculate the user-location similarity. We can use Eq. 3 or Eq. 4 to measure the user-location similarity.

$$\textbf{User-based: } Sim(u,l) = \sum_{u' \in U_u} Sim(u,u') * v(u',l) \tag{3}$$

where u' is the user in the same group with u, $Sim(u,u')$ is the similarity between users u and u', and $v(u',l)$ represents the times that u' visits location l.

$$\textbf{Item-based: } Sim(u,l) = \sum_{l' \in L_u} Sim(l,l') * l(l',u) \tag{4}$$

where l' is the location that user u has visited, $Sim(l,l')$ indicates the similarity between locations l and l', and $l(l',u)$ indicates the times that the user u has visited location l'.

To efficiently compute the user-location similarity, we can convert calculating the user-location similarity to computing user-user (Eq. 3) and location-location (Eq. 4) similarity. We propose several metrics to measure the similarity between users: user relationship similarity ($Sim1$), location histories similarity ($Sim2$), common words similarity ($Sim3$), and WCH similarity ($Sim4$). Our method uses a weighted sum combination of the above similarity scores as the final similarity. $Sim1$ between two users is the ratio of the intersection size of their friends to the union size of their friends. Similarly $Sim2$ ($Sim3$) is the ratio of the intersection size of their visited locations (rating words) to the union size of their visited locations (rating words). For $Sim4$, we use the cosine similarity on the categories of the first level to evaluate the WCH similarity, similar to the feature selection step in Section 3.3.

Computing the similarity between two locations is simple, we only need to get the user vector and calculate the cosine similarity of the vectors, where user vector is a vector that stores the users who have ever visited the location, e.g., in Fig.1, L_A's user vector is $[U_1, U_2]$.

To identify the relevant group, we use the user-group similarity. To rate a location, user-location similarity is calculated, and the similarity can reflect the user's preference on the location. User-user and location-location similarity are used to calculate user-location similarity using Eq.3 and Eq.4, while the former one measures how close two users are in terms of user preferences, and the later one reflects two locations attract how many same users, and the more same users, the higher similarity. Based on the user-user and location-location similarity we can use the CF algorithm to recommend locations for users.

To sum up, our proposed system enables high quality personalized location recommendation through calculating the similarity between the user and candidate locations online, while using group to prune the candidate locations offline and improve the computing efficiency.

5   Experiment

We conduct experiments to evaluate our proposed method. Our experimental goal is to evaluate the recommendation efficiency and quality.

5.1   Experiment Settings

Dataset. We use a large-scale real-world dataset collected from Foursquare [1]. The users are mostly from two main cities in the United States: New York (NYC) and Los Angeles (LA). Table 1 shows the statistics of the dataset. As we can see from the table, the dataset is large-scale but sparse.

Table 1. Statistics of the dataset

	LA	NYC
# of users	501,940	717,382
# of users (with tips)	31,537	49,005
# of relationship	2,923,486	5,109,420
# of locations	215,614	206,416
# of tips	268,091	425,692

We selected users with home city of New Jersey (NJ) as our test dataset. In order to ensure the accuracy of the experimental results, we further selected users whose number of tips is greater than 7, and tips around LA and NYC. Hence we select 992 test users and 7,242 tips as the test dataset.

Comparison Algorithms. We implemented two algorithms of our method: group-based personalized location-based recommendation (GPLR) and user-based recommendation (GPUR). We compared with three existing algorithms. (1) Location-based collaborative filtering (LCF) [5], which is based on the item-based CF. It utilizes all of the users' location histories to build a user-location matrix, and applies location-based CF on the matrix (Eq.4). The similarity of two locations is computed by cosine similarity, and higher rating locations are recommended to the user [12]; (2) User-based collaborative filtering (UCF) [5], which is based on the user-based CF, and applies user-based CF on the matrix (Eq.3); (3) Preference-aware (PA) [1], which uses location classification and user preferences extraction method in the offline part, and employs candidate selection algorithm and CF algorithms for online recommendation.

Evaluation. To evaluate a recommendation method, we used cross validations. We divided the location histories of a user into two parts. One is the training set, which is used to learn user preferences and the other is the test set. Fig.3 explains our evaluation method.

Fig. 3. Evaluation Method

In Fig.3, the black filled circles indicate the test set, and we draw a minimum boundary rectangle (MBR, the dotted line in the figure) as the recommendation range; the slash circles present the recommended locations. Through the evaluation method we can calculate the quality of the recommendation.

Experiment Environment. All of our experiments ran on an HP server with a 3.47GHz 6-core Intel Xeon CPU, and gcc-4.3.4.

5.2   Recommendation Quality

We compare quality with existing algorithms, by varying the number of recommended answers N (default 20), the average size of location histories of users (default 7), and the density (the number of locations per square mile). Fig.4 shows the results by varying the number of recommended answers (the size of location histories is set to 7).

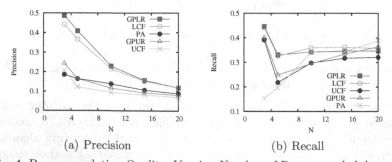

(a) Precision   (b) Recall

Fig. 4. Recommendation Quality: Varying Number of Recommended Answers

Fig.4 shows that our proposed GPLR achieves the best precision, while LCF and GPLR have the best recall. This is because LCF is based on all locations, and GPLR is based on the candidate locations of the group, and thus LCF has slightly advantages in recall. Our proposed GPUR, outperformed UCF in terms of both precision and recall, proving our user-user similarity method is effective. LCF and GPLR are better in quality than UCF and GPUR, which indicates location-based method is better than user-based method for the dataset, for location-based recommendation. Finally, PA performs better than the user-based method but worse than location-based method.

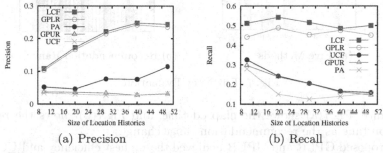

(a) Precision   (b) Recall

Fig. 5. Recommendation Quality: Varying Size of Location Histories

Fig.5 shows the results by varying the number of location histories with N=20. With the size of location histories grows, the precision of the five methods increases. Particularly, GPLR and LCF have a significant increase. This is because the five methods are all based on the user location histories. The recall decreases as the size of location histories grows in all five methods. This seems unreasonable because the size of the dataset is fixed, and as the size of training set grows, the size of test set decreases, the recall should increase. However in fact, since the number of correct recommendations decreases faster than the size of test set decreases, the recall decreases.

Fig.6 shows the result by varying the location density, with N=10. In general, the precision decreases as the location density grows, while the recall increases. Intuitively, while there are more locations in the same range, the probability to recommend correct locations is lower, and the result proves the intuitive inference.

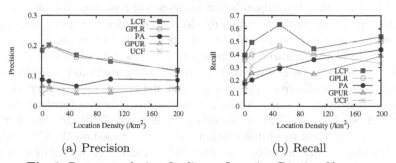

(a) Precision   (b) Recall

Fig. 6. Recommendation Quality as Location Density Changes

5.3   Efficiency

The main factors affecting the efficiency are the recommendation number and query range. We compare the five methods' average recommendation

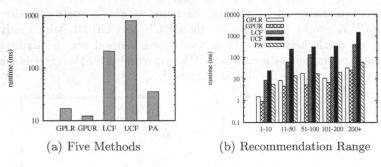

(a) Five Methods   (b) Recommendation Range

Fig. 7. Efficiency Evaluation

performance. Fig.7(a) shows the elapsed time, and Fig.7(b) shows the recommendation time as the recommendation range changes.

The proposed GPLR and GPUR achieved the highest efficiency and UCF algorithm had the worst perforamnce. The main reason is as follows. Our proposed recommendation algorithms are based on groups and can effectively filter out irrelevant locations for personalized recommendation part, while LCF and UCF algorithm are not based on groups. As a result, the candidate location set is very large. PA algorithm adopts a candidate selection algorithm, and uses local experts to filter candidate locations, but the efficiency is not as good as ours.

From Fig.7(b), we can see the larger the recommendation range, the more candidate locations, causing worse efficiency. Moreover, although the time that GPLR and GPUR algorithm consume increases with the range, the average growth rate is slower than the other three methods, reflecting the proposed methods have better scalability.

6   Related Work

Most existing location recommendation systems are based on distance and ratings [2,15,18]. These methods typically do not consider the user's preferences and for every user the recommended locations are almost the same.

There are some personalized methods [1,6,16]. Personalized methods typically use tags to identify the user's interests, and they allow users to manually specify their own tags. The disadvantage of such systems is that they do not consider the location histories of other users. Some systems take the location histories into account, such as [8,17], but the efficiency is a big challenge. Another type of personalized location recommendation systems are based on the CF model by considering other users' location histories and can infer the rating of a location that the user has not visited. However, the disadvantage of such systems is all locations are computed independently, resulting in the user-location matrix too large to be computed efficiently.

7   Conclusion

This paper presents a group-based personalized location recommendation system with the following characteristics. First it can address the data-sparseness and cold-start problems. Second, it achieves high efficiency and scalability by utilizing group-based information. Third, it achieves high quality by utilizing user preferences, social relations, user ratings and distances. The experiment results on a real-world dataset show that the proposed methods have significant advantages in quality and efficiency than baselines.

Acknowledgements. This work was partly supported by the National Natural Science Foundation of China under Grant No. 61272090 and 61373024, National Grand Fundamental Research 973 Program of China under Grant No. 2011CB302206, Beijing Higher Education Young Elite Teacher Project under grant No. YETP0105, Tsinghua-Tencent Joint Laboratory for Internet Innovation Technology, the "NExT Research Center" funded by MDA, Singapore, under Grant No. WBS:R-252-300-001-490, and the FDCT/106/2012/A3.

References

1. Bao, J., Zheng, Y., Mokbel, M.F.: Location-based and preference-aware recommendation using sparse geo-social networking data. In: SIGSPATIAL/GIS, pp. 199–208 (2012)
2. Berjani, B., Strufe, T.: A recommendation system for spots in location-based online social networks. In: SNS, p. 4 (2011)
3. Chow, C.-Y., Bao, J., Mokbel, M.F.: Towards location-based social networking services. In: GIS-LBSN, pp. 31–38 (2010)
4. Guttman, A.: R-trees: A dynamic index structure for spatial searching, vol. 14 (1984)
5. Herlocker, J.L., Konstan, J.A., Borchers, A., Riedl, J.: An algorithmic framework for performing collaborative filtering. In: SIGIR, pp. 230–237 (1999)
6. Jin, Z., Shi, D., Wu, Q., Yan, H., Fan, H.: Lbsnrank: personalized pagerank on location-based social networks. In: UbiComp, pp. 980–987 (2012)
7. Johnson, S.C.: Hierarchical clustering schemes. Psychometrika 32(3), 241–254 (1967)
8. Kodama, K., Iijima, Y., Guo, X., Ishikawa, Y.: Skyline queries based on user locations and preferences for making location-based recommendations. In: GIS-LBSN, pp. 9–16 (2009)
9. Li, G., Chen, S., Feng, J., Tan, K.-l., Li, W.-S.: Efficient location-aware influence maximization (2014)
10. Li, G., Hu, J., Lee Tan, K., Bao, Z., Feng, J.: Effective location identification from microblogs. In: ICDE (2014)
11. Li, R., Wang, S., Deng, H., Wang, R., Chang, K.C.-C.: Towards social user profiling: unified and discriminative influence model for inferring home locations. In: KDD, pp. 1023–1031 (2012)
12. Sarwar, B.M., Karypis, G., Konstan, J.A., Riedl, J.: Item-based collaborative filtering recommendation algorithms. In: WWW, pp. 285–295 (2001)
13. Xiao, X., Zheng, Y., Luo, Q., Xie, X.: Finding similar users using category-based location history. In: GIS, pp. 442–445 (2010)

14. Yang, D.-N., Shen, C.-Y., Lee, W.-C., Chen, M.-S.: On socio-spatial group query for location-based social networks. In: KDD, pp. 949–957 (2012)
15. Ye, M., Yin, P., Lee, W.-C.: Location recommendation for location-based social networks. In: GIS, pp. 458–461 (2010)
16. Zheng, V.W., Zheng, Y., Xie, X., Yang, Q.: Collaborative location and activity recommendations with gps history data. In: WWW, pp. 1029–1038 (2010)
17. Zheng, Y., Zhang, L., Xie, X., Ma, W.-Y.: Mining interesting locations and travel sequences from gps trajectories. In: WWW, pp. 791–800 (2009)
18. Zheng, Y., Zhou, X. (eds.): Computing with Spatial Trajectories. Springer (2011)

A Lexicon-Based Multi-class Semantic Orientation Analysis for Microblogs

Yuqing Li[1], Xin Li[1,*], Fan Li[1,**], and Xiaofeng Zhang[2,***]

[1] School of Computer Science, Beijing Institute of Technology, China
[2] School of Computer Science and Technology, Harbin Institute of Technology
Shenzhen Graduate School, China

Abstract. In the literature, most of existing works of semantic orientation analysis focus on the distinguishment of two polarities (positive and negative). In this paper, we propose a lexicon-based multi-class semantic orientation analysis for microblogs. To better capture the social attention on public events, we introduce *Concern* into the conventional psychological classes of sentiments and build up a sentiment lexicon with five categories(*Concern, Joy, Blue, Anger, Fear*). The seed words of the lexicon are extracted from HowNet, NTUSD, and catchwords of the Sina Weibo posts. The semantic similarity in HowNet is adopted to detect more sentiment words to enrich the lexicon. Accordingly, each Weibo post is represented as a multi-dimensional numerical vector in feature space. Then we adopt the Semi-Supervised Gaussian Mixture Model (Semi-GMM) and an adaptive K-nearst neighbour (KNN) with symmetric Kullback-Leibler divergence (KL-divergence) as similarity measurements to classify the posts. We compare our proposed methodologies with a few competitive baseline methods e.g., majority vote, KNN by using Cosine similarity, and SVM. The experimental evaluation shows that our proposed methods outperform other approaches by a large margin in terms of the accuracy and F1 score.

Keywords: Semantic Orientation Analysis, Semi-supervised Gaussian mixture model (Semi-GMM), Kullback-Leibler divergence.

1 Introduction

Online social services such as Twitter, Quora have been heavily used in recent years, the data produced by which is ever growing and has inspired many researchers to invest their efforts into text mining related tasks. Sentiment analysis of online texts has recently become a hot research topic. Detecting the emotional

* The work of X. Li is partially supported by National Program on Key Basic Research Project under Grant No. 2013CB329605 and NSFC under Grant No. 61300178. X. Li is the corresponding author.
** The work of F. Li is partially supported in part by NSFC under Grant No. 61370192 and 60903151.
*** The work of X. Zhang is supported in part by NSFC under Grant No. 61370213, Shenzhen Science and Technology Program under Grant No. JCYJ20120613150552967.

L. Chen et al. (Eds.): APWeb 2014, LNCS 8709, pp. 81–92, 2014.

tendencies could help ones better understand the public opinions and social behaviors, thus to conduct corresponding financial and political decision making for enterprise and government [1].

The classification of semantic orientation has shown its effectiveness for sentiment analysis. In the literature, previous works mainly focus on two-class classification (positive and negative emotion). However, the sentiments of human beings are complex in a variety of forms. In this paper, we propose a lexicon-based multi-class semantic orientation analysis for Sina Weibo posts. Sina Weibo is a popular Twitter-like micro-blogging service in China with more than 600 million users. Firstly, based on the conventional classes(*Joy, Blue, Anger, Fear*) in psychology study [2], we build up a sentiment lexicon with five categories(*Concern, Joy, Blue, Anger, Fear*) for online texts sentiment detection. We argue that the adoption of new class *Concern* helps better capture the social behaviors and public concerns for the public events. The lexicon is based on the words extracted from the amount of randomly grabbed Sina Weibo posts and the semantic similarity presented in HowNet [3] - a WordNet-like lexical resource in Chinese. Accordingly, each post is represented as a multi-dimensional numerical vector in feature space. Then we adopt a Semi-Supervised Gaussian Mixture Model (Semi-GMM) and a K-nearst neighbor (KNN) by using symmetric Kullback-Leibler divergence (KL-divergence) as the similarity measurement to classify the posts. We compare our proposed methodologies with the competitive baseline methods e.g., majority vote, KNN by using Cosine similarity and Support Vector Machine (SVM). The experimental evaluation validates the effectiveness of our proposed methods. Semi-GMM is rather robust to noises and the small data set as compared with other approaches.

The remainder of the paper is organized as follows. Section 2 discusses the related work of semantic orientation analysis. Section 3 presents the details of the sentiment lexicon construction. Section 4 introduces why we divide the posts into 5 categories and the adaptive classification methods. The experimental results and performance evaluation are reported in Section 5. The conclusion and future work are presented in Section 6.

2   Related Work

Semantic orientation analysis of online texts has been attracting increasing attentions from researchers and widely adopted in many applications. Recent advances in research often fall into two categories, lexicon-based approach and text classification-based approach. In general, lexicon-based approach achieves better performance than the text classification-based one [4] due to the leverage of typical sentiment words in lexicon. In this paper, other than developing a multi-class lexicon for Chinese Weibo posts, we adapt different learning approaches to classify the lexicon-based semantic vectors so that the accuracy of the semantic orientation detection can be further enhanced.

Lexicon is a pre-built and classified list of labeled words and emoticons. The sentiment lexicons are usually derived from thesaurus or knowledge base. Recently, the learning techniques are introduced to enrich the lexicon due to the emerging of out-of-vacabulary words from online social media. And most of the existing sentiment lexicons are built for the polarity classification (positive and negative sentiment) e.g., NRC hashtag sentiment lexicon and Sentiment140 lexicon [5]. The NRC hashtag sentiment lexicon is created according to the positive and negative hashtags in the tweets such as *#good*, *#bad*. While Sentiment140 lexicon is built according to the positive and negative emoticons. In addition to manually labeling the lexicon, researchers exploit various ways of automatically collecting the training data to build the lexicon with larger size and more accurate category assignment. In this paper, we develop a sophisticated Chinese sentiment lexicon by manually labeling the seed words. Then we adopt the semantic similarity between words defined in HowNet to detect more words "similar" to the seed words from the amount of corpus to extend the dictionary.

In the literature, there exist lots of related works for the sentiment orientation detection. In [6], the authors demonstrate that a learning approach performs better than simply counting the positive and negative sentimental terms using a handcrafted dictionary. P. Melville *et al.* [4] propose to combine background lexical information with supervised learning to achieve higher classification accuracy.

In [7], the authors adopt semi-Naive Bayes learning to classify the emotional intensity such as, *very negative, negative, neutral, positive, very positive* opinions towards a specific subject on the long texts. However, Naive Bayes is sensitive to the problem with sparse data and not suitable for the short texts classification such as Tweets, Microblogs and Weibo posts etc. In [8], the authors study a bayesian modeling approach to classify the sentiments with incorporation of a document-level multi-dimensional sentiment distributions prediction. However, the prediction of sentiment distribution over documents is time consuming and the document-level approach can not be applied directly for the short texts mining. Moreover, most of the existing works focus on the polarities classification. Intuitively, recognizing the texts as fine-grained emotions such as happiness, anger, sadness, fear, etc. could offer much delicate financial or political insights. In [9], the authors group the Weibo posts into 4-category sentiments (*Joy, Blue, Anger, Disgusting*) according to 95 emoticons among the texts instead of using the semantics of words and sentences. And the new set of categories in [9] is a variation of the conventional psychological category(*Joy, Blue, Anger, Fear*). We argue that the aforementioned categories are unable to perceive the public concern and support to special events which will be further discussed in Sec. 4.1. From the above observations, we propose to adopt semi-GMM supervised learning and supervised learning to a Multi-class emotion classification to further improve the performance of semantic orientation classification for microblogs.

3   Sentiment Lexicon

In this section, we propose to generate a comprehensive Chinese sentiment lexicon by using the Chinese affective words and phases from Sina Weibo posts. And we evaluate the lexicon coverage by adopting the approach in [10].

3.1 Sentiment Lexicon Generation

First, we conduct a serial of statistical analysis methods over a large amount of online posts. We take the highly frequent terms of the existing corpus dictionary (HowNet and NTU Sentiment Dictionary (NTUSD) [11]) and the manually annotated words as the seed words. Based on the set of seed words and the semantic similarity defined in HowNet [3], a set of new sentiment words are obtained accordingly to further enrich the lexicon. In HowNet, each vocabulary v_k has many items expressing different concepts, and each item S_k composes several primitives $p_{k1}, \cdots, p_{kn}$ to describe its characteristics. The semantic similarity between different items v_k is defined as follows:

$$sim(v_1, v_2) = \max_{i=1\cdots n, j=1\cdots m} sim(S_{1i}, S_{2j}) \tag{1}$$

$$sim(S_1, S_2) = \frac{1}{t_1 t_2} \sum_{i=1}^{t_1} \sum_{j=1}^{t_2} \frac{1}{2^{t_1-i+1}} sim(p_{1i}, p_{2j}) \tag{2}$$

where t_1, t_2 is the number of primitive for S_1 and S_2. $\frac{1}{2^{t_1-i+1}}$ is the weight of the primitive p_{1i} for item S_1. And the similarity between words is denoted as $sim(p_{1i}, p_{2j}) = \frac{\alpha}{\alpha+d}$, where d is the distance of the path from p_{1i} to p_{2j} in HowNet's well-constructed semantic tree, α is an empirical constant to guarantee the denominator is non-zero [12]. We also extract the catchwords from Sina Weibo posts which are popularly used by Chinese young generation and have gradually become the mainstream languages and the items of modern Chinese vocabularies. In this paper, we obtain 8204 sentiment words including 613 catchwords and 101 commonly used emoticons.

3.2 Lexicon Coverage Evaluation

To verify the effectiveness of our constructed lexicon, we adopt the approach proposed in [10] to observe whether the average emotional values E_{avg} follow a consistent trend for the daily posts and social events. E_{avg} is defined as:

$$E_{avg}(d) = \frac{\sum_{i=1}^{N} SO - IR(v_i) f_i}{\sum_{i=1}^{N} f_i} \tag{3}$$

$$SO - IR(v) = \frac{\sum_{i=1}^{M} sim(Key_p i, v)}{M} - \frac{\sum_{i=1}^{N} sim(Key_n i, v)}{N} \tag{4}$$

where d stands for the Weibo post, f_i is the frequency of the ith word v_i, Key_p and Key_n refer to the predefined positive and negative seed lexicons. M and N are the number of positive and negative seed lexicons respectively. And for those catchwords which do not exist in HowNet, we conduct the majority vote on the manually scores to determine their emotional value.

Fig. 1 shows the average emotional value of daily Sina Weibo posts from $March.23^{th}, 2013$ to $April.26^{th}, 2013$ based on our newly created lexicon. It is obvious that the value is correlated with the catastrophic events and holidays. The consistency of the emotion tendency with the real world events illustrates the effectiveness and the coverage of the lexicon.

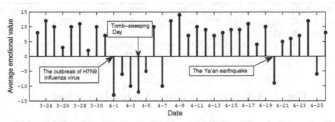

Fig. 1. The average emotional value of daily Sina Weibo posts from $March.23^{th}$, 2013 to $April.26^{th}$, 2013

4 Multi-class Sentiment Classification

In this section, we present the motivation of our newly designed category of the sentiments and the details of the adaptive learning approach for semantic orientation classification.

4.1 Sentiment Categories

The conventional psychology study [13] suggests a four-class identification for human sentiments, namely, *Joy, Blue, Anger*, and *Fear*. Our observation from daily online posts is that people resort to the online services e.g., Twitter, Sina Weibo as the portal to convey their concern and support to some special groups and events. Fig. 2 shows a post published on Sina Weibo after the Malaysia Airlines (MAS) flight MH370 was confirmed lost. The post mainly expresses the social concern and support for the victims and their next of kin. And this kind of emotion often breaks out shortly after some public events happen e.g., the disaster like earthquake and the crimes of causing death. With investigation of vocabulary frequency in numerous emotional posts, we find that numbers of words and emoticons such as *Pray, Peace, [candle]* (shown in Fig. 2)... tend to express such feelings. While in the conventional four-class orientation detection, it's highly likely the post will be identified as a *Joy* post. For words like "condolence" also express the concern while it will be identified as a blue word in four-class sentiment scale.

To further highlight the need of *Concern* category, Fig. 3 presents the proportion of the *Concern* posts in the daily posts from $March.23^{th}$, 2013 to $April.26^{th}$, 2013 according to the sentiment lexicon we built in Sec. 3 and the lexicon vector introduced in Sec. 4.2. We could observe that the number of *concern* posts is increasing sharply when some vital social event happens which illustrates the importance of the *Concern* category. Thus, we introduce the 5th emotional identification *Concern* into the conventional four-class sentiment classifications. Accordingly, the sentiment categories in this paper are *Concern, Joy, Blue, Anger* and *Fear*.

4.2 Lexical Vectors

Based on the constructed sentiment lexicon in Sec. 3, we build a seed set composed of the manually labeled representative words for five categories. The seed set is denoted as $seedset = \{PC, PJ, PB, PA, PF\}$, where PC, PJ, PB, PA, PF stands for the subset of (*Concern, Joy, Blue, Anger, Fear*) respectively. For each *non-seedset* vocabulary v, we propose to detect its tendency based on Eq.(5) defined as follow:

离马航MH370航班失联已超过54个小时了。飞机上，有才华横溢的少数民族画家；有热爱旅行的老年驴友；有幸福一家五口；有事业刚起步的80后年轻职员，尚在襁褓中的婴儿…他们的人生，不该这样画上句点。我们不会放弃，全中国都在祈祷：平安，回家！🕯
(It has been more than 54 hours since the Flight MH307 lost. On the plane, there are talented minority artists, elderly travel enthusiasts, happy families, post-80s whose careers are just begun, and infants. Their lives should not end in this way. Everybody will never give up hope. The whole country is praying for their peace and return. [candle])

Fig. 2. A Weibo post about Flight MH370 lost

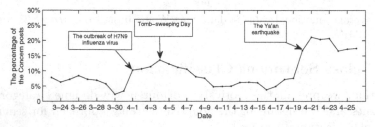

Fig. 3. The proportion of the *Concern* posts in the daily sentiment-oriented posts from $March.23^{th}, 2013$ to $April.26^{th}, 2013$

$$\theta(v) = \underset{\{PC,PJ,PB,PA,PF\}}{argmax} \ (\frac{1}{K_1} \sum_{k_1=1}^{K_1} sim(v, PC_{k_1}), \frac{1}{K_2} \sum_{k_2=1}^{K_2} sim(v, PJ_{k_2}), \quad (5)$$

$$\frac{1}{K_3} \sum_{k_3=1}^{K_3} sim(v, PB_{k_3}), \frac{1}{K_4} \sum_{k_4=1}^{K_4} sim(v, PA_{k_4}), \frac{1}{K_5} \sum_{k_5=1}^{K_5} sim(v, PF_{k_5}))$$

where K_1, K_2, K_3, K_4, K_5 is the number of vocabularies in the set of PC, PJ, PB, PA, PF respectively. $\theta(v)$ is the category for which the above argument attains its maximum value. And for those catchwords which do not exist in HowNet, we conduct the majority vote on the manually marked labels to determine its sentiment category. So far the sentiment lexicon is a list of vocabularies with sentiment labels indicating their assigned category and there is no overlap between categories. Eventually, in our derived lexicon, there are 816, 2618, 2189, 1382 and 1199 words for the five categories respectively.

To address the issue of sentence segmentation, we adopt NLPIR [14]- a popular Chinese words segmentation system (also known as ICTCLAS2013) to segment the Weibo posts into the vocabularies, as it's well-known that unlike English there is no spaces between Chinese characters. To further clean the data, we remove the obviously useless vocabularies and interpunctions e.g., "De","," .

Then we determine the sentiment category of each segmented vocabulary in the Weibo post and convert the post into a vector-based numerical expression by using the generated five-class sentiment lexicon. Let $D = \{d_1, d_2, \cdots, d_N\}$ be a set of posts, where d_i is the i-th post. $d_i = [w_{iC}, w_{iJ}, w_{iB}, w_{iA}, w_{iF}]^T$ where $w_{iC}, w_{iJ}, w_{iB}, w_{iA}, w_{iF}$ is the number of vocabularies belonging to the category of *Concern, Joy, Blue, Anger* and *Fear* respectively. Then all the posts can be represented as 5-dimensional vectors accordingly.

For those non-lexicon-based sentiment analysis [15], the researchers usually set up a relatively large training set and use TF-IDF (term frequency-inverse document frequency) to select a number of sentiment words to form a high-dimensional vector. It will lead to the incomplete expression, high-dimensionality suffering and over-fitting for the sentiment{ learning. With the generated lexicon and defined lexical vectors, we reduced the information loss and made the data more suitable for further classification.

4.3 Adaptive Classification Approaches

In this section we present the details of the adaptive Semi-GMM and KNN algorithm to classify the lexical vectors.

Semi-GMM Sentiment Classifier. Gaussian mixture model (GMM) adapted with the optimization method - Expectation Maximization algorithm (EM) is a classy unsupervised learning combo for the data classification. GMM leverages the latent variables to estimate each Gaussian density and the weight (π_i) of each Gaussian, with the assumption that the data is produced according to a set of multivariate Gaussian component. Semi-supervised learning has shown its effectiveness for the problem with a small set of labeled training data. To further improve the classification performance, we propose to adopt a semi-supervised GMM for the sentiment clustering by leveraging the prior knowledge of the labeled data, the hidden structure among the unlabeled data and the effectiveness of GMM as a probability clustering method.

We incorporate the labeled data into the standard GMM to influence the clustering preferences. Then the Semi-supervised GMM performs as a self-training method. In each iteration of the training process, the positive result from the classification is added to the set of labeled sample set L. The newly updated L in turn helps to maximize the distribution likelihood. With the results of E-step, M-step will be the intermediate classifier on the training set under the new training. And the unlabeled sample set U continues shrinking during each iteration. The pseudo codes for the Semi-GMM is illustrated as follow:

Algorithm of Semi-GMM

	Input:	A small set of labeled samples, Gauss mixture model.
	Output:	$\Theta^{(i)}$
1		$i \leftarrow 0$
2		$\Theta^{(0)} \leftarrow arg\ \max_{\theta} P(\theta \mid L)$
3		while $U! = NULL$ or $\| Q(\theta^{(i+1)}, \theta^{(i)}) - Q(\theta^{(i)}, \theta^{(i)}) \| > \epsilon$
4		E-step:
5		do $\gamma_{jk} \leftarrow \frac{\alpha_k \phi(u_j \mid \theta_k)}{\sum_{k=1}^{K} \alpha_k \phi(u_j \mid \theta_k)}$
6		$(j, k) \leftarrow arg\ \max_{(j,k)} \{\gamma_{jk} \mid u_j \in U\}$
7		$L \leftarrow L \cup u_j$
8		$U \leftarrow U - u_j$
9		M-step:
10		$\Theta^{(i+1)} \leftarrow arg\ \max_{\theta} P(\theta \mid \Gamma^{(i)}; L)$
11		$i \leftarrow i + 1$

where L is the labeled sample set, U is the unlabeled sample set, K indicates the number of categories. $\phi(u_j \mid \theta_k)$ is Gaussian distribution density, $\theta_k = (\mu_k, \sigma_k^2)$.

KNN by Symmetric KL-Divergence. k-nearest neighbors algorithm (KNN) [16] classifies the objects based on the majority vote of its k "closest" training examples in the feature space. The "closeness" is measured by the similarity between the clustering center and the other nodes. KNN usually adopts the cosine of the angle between two vectors of an inner product space as the similarity. However cosine similarity is not a proper metric for measuring the "closeness" between the probabilities.

In this paper we adopt Kullback-Leibler divergence (KL-divergence) as the similarity measurement between the normalized lexical vectors for the semantic orientation analysis. KL-divergence is a rigorous non-symmetric measure of the difference between two probability distributions P and Q, denoted as $D_{KL}(P \parallel Q)$. Recall that the lexical vector d_i is defined in Section 4.2, here we convert the vector space into a set of probability distributions via normalization. And the normalized vector T_i is denoted as follows:

$$T_i = < w_{iC}/W, w_{iJ}/W, w_{iB}/W, w_{iA}/W, w_{iF}/W > \tag{6}$$
$$W = w_{iC} + w_{iJ} + w_{iB} + w_{iA} + w_{iF}$$

The KL-divergence between T_i and T_j is defined as follow:

$$D_{KL}(T_i \parallel T_j) = \sum_k t_{ik} log_2 \frac{t_{ik}}{t_{jk}} \tag{7}$$

As KL-divergence is a non-symmetric measurement which represents the information loss of using Q to approximate P, where P usually represents the precise distribution. In sentiment analysis, we use the labeled lexical vectors as T_i, the unlabeled vectors as T_j to indicate the "distance" from the unknown data to the determined data. In order to alleviate the asymmetry of the conventional KL-divergence, a symmetric formula [17] is given as follows

$$\frac{1}{D_{KL}(T_i \parallel T_j)} = \frac{1}{\sum_k t_{ik} log_2 \frac{t_{ik}}{t_{jk}}} + \frac{1}{\sum_k t_{jk} log_2 \frac{t_{jk}}{t_{ik}}} \tag{8}$$

5   Experimental Evaluation

In this section, we compare the experimental results of the adaptive classification algorithms (Semi-GMM and KNN by Symmetric KL-divergence) with the conventional baseline approaches (Majority Vote, KNN by Cosine similarity, SVM). We randomly selected 7170 Sina Weibo posts to evaluate our proposed methodology. We invited 25 students working on Natural Language Processing to manually classify the posts into 5 groups. Thus each post gets 25 votes. And then the majority vote was conducted to determine its sentiment category. Among these posts, there are 1300 posts for *Concern*, 2100 posts for *Joy*, 1340 posts for *Blue*, 1310 posts for *Anger* and 1120 posts for *Fear*.

Firstly, we adopt two different measurements Eq. (7) and Eq. (8) as similarities for KNN-based sentiment classification. Table 1 shows that the accuracy achieved by using the symmetric KL-divergence is higher than that of using non-symmetric conventional KL-divergence. Hereinafter, we only put KNN by using symmetric KL-divergence (KNN-KL) into the comparison. The size of training sets ranges from 1000 to 4000. And we randomly selected 3170 posts as the test set. There are 500 posts for *Concern*, 1300 posts for *Joy*, 540 posts for *Blue*, 510 posts for *Anger* and 320 posts for *Fear*.

Table 1. The accuracy achieved by KNN by using different similarities under different training set size settings

Training Set Size	non-symmetric KL-Div.	symmetric KL-Div.
4000	84.7%	85.1%
1000	76.1%	76.2%

Fig. 4 shows the detailed performance of the adopted classification algorithms over different training sets. When the size of training set is 4000, KNN by symmetric KL-divergence outperforms other algorithms and the accuracy reaches 85.1%. It is obvious that KNN-KL outperforms KNN-Cosine for all the training sets, which illustrates the effectiveness of using symmetric KL-divergence as the measurement to define its k neighbors. KNN now captures the lexical vectors' relations better than that of using cosine similarity.

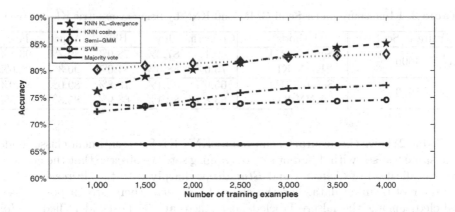

Fig. 4. Accuracy comparison of the adaptive approaches for multi-class sentiment classification

When the size of training set is smaller than 3000, Semi-GMM outperforms all the algorithms. We can observe that the performance of Semi-GMM is more stable than that of KNN-Cosine and KNN-KL when the size of training set fluctuates. After removing 3000 samples from the training set of 4000 labeled data, the accuracy of KNN-KL based classification has declined by 8.9%, while Semi-GMM has merely declined by 2.9%, which demonstrates the effectiveness of the semi-supervised learning on the small training set. While the performance of the supervised learning methods such as KNN is sensitive to the size of training set and the number of neighbors k.

With respect to SVM, it is usually adopted for two-class classification. Although there are a lot of variations of SVM for multi-classification, the competitive advantage over other multi-classification algorithms is far less than that of the conventional SVM. And its classification performance also depends on the high quality of the training data. Besides, SVM is also not favored for large-scale data mining tasks due to its high complexity. Thus we argue that Semi-GMM is more suitable for the sentiment classification with smaller training set. And in practice, obtaining training labels is expensive in sentiment analysis and many other text classification problems, while large quantities of unlabeled texts are ready-made [18].

Table 2. Classification accuracy achieved by Semi-GMM and KNN-KL for 5 sentiment classes with different sizes of training sets

Methods	Training Set Size	Concern	Joy	Blue	Anger	Fear
KNN-KL	4000	90.6%	82.1%	80.7%	83.3%	98.8%
	1000	74.8%	76.5%	69.6%	76.3%	88.1%
Semi-GMM	4000	85.8%	81.1%	77.4%	81.8%	99.1%
	1000	84.4%	78.1%	74.4%	80.6%	91.6%

Table 3. F1-measure under Semi-GMM and KNN by using symmetric KL-divergence

Training Set Size	Methods	Concern	Joy	Blue	Anger	Fear
4000	Semi-GMM	69.1%	87.2%	78.0%	89.7%	93.1%
	KNN-KL	73.0%	88.6%	81.0%	90.3%	96.6%
1000	Semi-GMM	65.9%	85.1%	73.8%	89.0%	88.9%
	KNN-KL	63.8%	82.1%	68.9%	85.3%	89.8%

Table 2 shows the accuracy achieved by KNN-KL for 5 sentiment classes under the same test set with different size of training set. We observe that the accuracy of classification of *Concern* and *Blue* drops sharply with the decreasing of the number of training data. For the class of *Concern*, there are 79 posts falsely labeled, among the falsely labeled posts there are 64 posts identified as *Joy*, 11 posts identified as *Blue* and 4 posts identified as *Anger*. For the class of *Blue*, there are 60 posts falsely classified, among them 8 posts are identified as *Concern*, 28 posts are identified as *Joy*, 13 posts are identified as *Anger*, 11 posts are identified as *Fear*. As *Concern* and *Blue* are not intense emotional feelings as *Fear* and *Joy*, the clustering for the *Concern* and *Blue* is quite sensitive to the training set. While Table 2 also shows the accuracy achieved by Semi-GMM for 5 sentiment classes and Table 3 shows the F1-score by Semi-GMM and KNN-KL on different size of training set, which further illustrates the advantages of Semi-GMM on the small training set. We also conducted the experiments with unsupervised learning approach GMM and k-means to determine the sentiment orientation by classifying the Sina Weibo posts. The accuracy of the GMM algorithm is ranging from 58.6% to 64.4%. For another popular unsupervised learning algorithm k-means, the accuracy is around 54.6% which is slightly worse than GMM. The unsupervised learning achieves relatively poor performance comparing with our proposed adaptive approaches as it is lack of the utilization of the prior knowledge from the labels.

6   Conclusion and Future Work

In this paper, we propose to generate a five-class sentiment lexicon by using Sina Weibo posts, HowNet and NTUSD. The *Concern* class is introduced into the lexicon to better capture the public attention, concern and support for the public event. Based on the lexicon , the posts are then represented as the lexical vectors. The adaptive Semi-GMM and KNN by symmetric KL-divergence are proposed to classify the lexical vectors to further enhance the performance of semantic orientation classification. Extensive experiments have been conducted and the results show that our classification methods outperform the conventional approaches in terms of the learning accuracy and F1 score. Especially, the proposed Semi-GMM shows its advantages over other approaches when the training set is relatively small.

In the future work, we will further modify the proposed methodologies. One potential modification is to build the sentiment lexicon via the soft clustering and assign the proper weights for each sentiment vocabulary. A more sophisticated sentiment lexicon and lexical vector will be further investigated to enhance the classification performance for the semantic orientation analysis.

References

1. Zhou, L., He, Y., Wang, J.: Survey on research of sentiment analysis. Journal of Computer Applications 28(11), 2725–2728 (2008)
2. Cornelius, R.R.: The science of emotion: Research and tradition in the psychology of emotions. Prentice-Hall, Inc. (1996)
3. HowNet[EBOL] (2007), http://www.keenage.com
4. Melville, P., Gryc, W., Lawrence, R.D.: Sentiment analysis of blogs by combining lexical knowledge with text classification. In: Proceedings of the 15th ACM SIGKDD International Conference on Knowledge Discovery and Data Mining, pp. 1275–1284. ACM (2009)
5. Mohammad, S.M., Kiritchenko, S., Zhu, X.: Nrc-canada: Building the state-of-the-art in sentiment analysis of tweets. arXiv preprint arXiv:1308.6242 (2013)
6. Pang, B., Lee, L.: Opinion mining and sentiment analysis. Foundations and Trends in Information Retrieval 2(1-2), 1–135 (2008)
7. Ortigosa-Hernández, J., Rodríguez, J.D., Alzate, L., Lucania, M., Inza, I., Lozano, J.A.: Approaching sentiment analysis by using semi-supervised learning of multi-dimensional classifiers. Neurocomputing 92, 98–115 (2012)

8. He, Y.: A bayesian modeling approach to multi-dimensional sentiment distributions prediction. In: Proceedings of the First International Workshop on Issues of Sentiment Discovery and Opinion Mining, p. 1. ACM (2012)
9. Zhao, J., Dong, L., Wu, J., Xu, K.: Moodlens: an emoticon-based sentiment analysis system for chinese tweets. In: Proceedings of the 18th ACM SIGKDD International Conference on Knowledge Discovery and Data Mining, pp. 1528–1531. ACM (2012)
10. Dodds, P.S., Harris, K.D., Kloumann, I.M., Bliss, C.A., Danforth, C.M.: Temporal patterns of happiness and information in a global social network: Hedonometrics and twitter. PloS One 6(12), e26752 (2011)
11. Ku, L.-W., Liang, Y.-T., Chen, H.-H.: Opinion extraction, summarization and tracking in news and blog corpora. In: AAAI Spring Symposium: Computational Approaches to Analyzing Weblogs, vol. 100107 (2006)
12. Zhu, Y.-L., Min, J., Zhou, Y.-Q., Huang, X.-J., Wu, L.-D.: Semantic orientation computing based on hownet. Journal of Chinese Information Processing 20(1), 14–20 (2006)
13. Parrott, W.: Emotions in social psychology: Essential readings. Psychology Press (2001)
14. http://ictclas.nlpir.org/
15. Ye, Q., Zhang, Z., Law, R.: Sentiment classification of online reviews to travel destinations by supervised machine learning approaches. Expert Systems with Applications 36(3), 6527–6535 (2009)
16. Ronglu, L., Jianhui, W., Xiaoyun, C., Xiaopeng, T., Yunfa, H.: Using maximum entropy model for chinese text categorization. Journal of Computer Research and Development 1, 22–29 (2005)
17. Johnson, D.H., Sinanovic, S., et al.: Symmetrizing the kullback-leibler distance. Technical report, Rice University (2001)
18. Nguyen-Dinh, L.-V., Rossi, M., Blanke, U., Tröster, G.: Combining crowd-generated media and personal data: semi-supervised learning for context recognition. In: Proceedings of the 1st ACM International Workshop on Personal Data Meets Distributed Multimedia, pp. 35–38. ACM (2013)

Discovering Urban Spatio-temporal Structure from Time-Evolving Traffic Networks

Jingyuan Wang[1], Fei Gao[1], Peng Cui[2], Chao Li[1,3], and Zhang Xiong[1]

[1] School of Computer Science and Engineering, Beihang University, Beijing, China
gf0109@gmail.com, {jywang,licc,xiongz}@buaa.edu.cn
[2] Department of Computer Science and Technology, Tsinghua University,
Beijing, China
cuip@tsinghua.edu.cn
[3] Research Institute of Beihang University, ShenZhen, China

Abstract. The traffic networks reflect the pulse and structure of a city and shows some dynamic characteristic. Previous research in mining structure from networks mostly focus on static networks and fail to exploit the temporal patterns. In this paper, we aim to solve the problem of discovering the urban spatio-temporal structure from time-evolving traffic networks. We model the time-evolving traffic networks into a 3-order tensor, each element of which indicates the volume of traffic from i-th origin area to j-th destination area in k-th time domain. Considering traffic data and urban contextual knowledge together, we propose a regularized Non-negative Tucker Decomposition (rNTD) method, which discovers the spatial clusters, temporal patterns and relations among them simultaneously. Abundant experiments are conducted in a large dataset collected from Beijing. Results show that our method outperforms the baseline method.

Keywords: urban computing, pattern discovery.

1 Introduction

Understanding the urban structure is important for urban planning, transportation management, epidemic prevention, and location based business. However, our knowledge in this area is limited. Nowadays, the rapid growth of information infrastructure collect huge volumes of trajectory data, such as GPS trajectories, mobiles and IC card records, from which we can build a "from-where-to-where" traffic network that indicates time volume of traffic from one origin area to another destination area. The traffic networks give us a great chance to study the detail of urban structures [2]. In this paper, we consider the problem of discovering urban spatio-temporal structure from time-evolving traffic networks. The goal is to discover spatial clusters of urban areas, temporal patterns of urban traffic and their correlations simultaneously, which we refer to urban spatio-temporal structure.

Significant progresses have been made on the problem about finding interesting structures from networks in the field of community detection [1]. For example, researchers have found protein clusters that have same specific function

L. Chen et al. (Eds.): APWeb 2014, LNCS 8709, pp. 93–104, 2014.

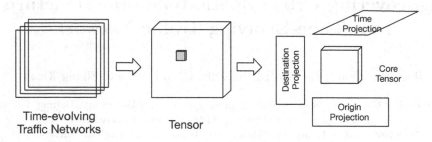

Fig. 1. Framework of rNTD

within the cell from protein-protein interaction networks [3]. Social circles can be mined from social networks [7]. The basic intuition shared by this methods is to find community that have more edges "inside"the community than edges "outside". However, in urban situation, challenges arise because the traffic network is different from network in previous research. First, the traffic network is time-evolving and dynamic. Traffic in the morning is apparently different from that in the evening. Second, the structure is also related with urban contextual information. A working area owns different structure from a residential area. Then, the structure we want to find need to consider not only edge information, but also the time and urban contexture attribution.

To solve these challenges, in this paper we model the time-evolving traffic networks into a 3-order *origin-destination-time* tensor [10], each element (i, j, k) of which represents the volume of traffic from the i-th origin area to the j-th destination area in the k-th time domain. Considering traffic data and urban contextual information together, we propose a regularized Non-negative Tucker Decomposition (rNTD) method to solve the problem, which decomposes the original tensor to three projection matrix and a core tensor. The projection matrix in *origin* and *destination* mode indicate which cluster an area belongs to. The projection matrix in *time* mode shows temporal patterns. And the core tensor gives the correlation between spatial clusters and temporal patterns. The framework of rNTD is shown in Fig. 1. We apply Alternating Proximal Gradient to optimize the rNTD problem, and carry out intensive experiments to demonstrate the effectiveness of our proposed method.

It's worthwhile to highlight the key contribution of this paper.

- We formulate the urban spatio-temporal structure discovery problem formally with rNTD, and devise an efficient proximal gradient method to solve it.
- The discovered urban spatio-temporal structure is easy to understand and well explained, which can support to solve some urban problem, such as urban planning, traffic jam and so on.
- We conducted intensive experiments on a real dataset collected from Beijing, and the results show that the rNTD can achieve a better performance compared with other competitors.

The rest of the paper is organized as follow: Section 2 summarizes related work. Section 3 gives the formulation of our problem and the method we propose. We give experimental results in Section 4 and conclude in Section 5.

2 Related Work

The research of urban computing have recently received much attention. Yuan *et al.* [14] discover regions of different functions in a city using human mobility data and POI. Zheng *et al.* [17] design an algorithm to detect flawed urban planning with GPS trajectories of taxicabs traveling in urban areas. Zhang *et al.* [15] propose an context-aware collaborative filtering method to sense the pulse of urban refueling behavior. Zheng *et al.* [16] give a novel method to infer the real-time air quality information throughout a city. Different from these study, we explore urban spatio-temporal structure from time-evolving traffic networks.

A great deal of work has been devoted to mining community structure from network [1]. Recently, Wang et al. [11] use Non-negative Matrix Factorization to discover community from undirected, directed and compound networks. Yang *et al.* [13] develop CESNA for detecting communities in networks with node attribution. Kim *et al.* [4] propose a nonparametric multi-group membership model for dynamic networks. Different from the above mentioned work, we mine time-evolving traffic networks by considering node attribution (*urban contextual information*) and temporal dynamic (*time-evolving*) together.

3 Regularized Non-negative Tucker Decomposition

3.1 Problem Formulation

In this section, we will introduce details of our model. First, we formally define the problem of urban spatio-temporal structure discovery. Suppose we have M areas in city with i-th origin area denoted as o_i and j-th destination area denoted as d_j. We split the day time uniformly to K time domain with k-th domain denoted as t_k.

We denote the time-evolving traffic networks data as a 3-order tensor $\hat{\mathcal{X}} \in \mathbb{R}^{M \times M \times N}$, whose (i, j, k)-th entry $\mathcal{X}_{ijk}$ represents the volume of traffic from i-th origin area to j-th destination area in k-th time domain. Since the distribution of the value in tensor $\hat{\mathcal{X}}$ is severely skewed, to reduce the impact of high value, we use the *log* function for scaling the tensor data:

$$\mathcal{X}_{ijk} = log_2 \left(1 + \hat{\mathcal{X}}_{ijk} \right) \tag{1}$$

Then given the time-evolving traffic networks, the spatial and temporal structure discovery problem is converted to finding latent projection matrix in every mode and the correlation core tensor between them simultaneously from the traffic tensor. The projections of mode $\mathbf{O}$ and $\mathbf{D}$ summarize the spatial clusters on urban areas, and projection on $\mathbf{T}$ shows the temporal patterns, and correlation between $\mathbf{O}$, $\mathbf{D}$ and $\mathbf{T}$ give the a compact view of urban traffic. As show in Fig. 1. From the result, we can get the urban spatio-temporal structure.

3.2 Basic Tucker Decomposition

Let $\mathbf{O} \in \mathbb{R}^{M \times m}$ be the latent origin projection matrix, $\mathbf{D} \in \mathbb{R}^{M \times m}$ be the latent destination projection matrix, and $\mathbf{T} \in \mathbb{R}^{N \times n}$ be the latent time projection matrix. Let $\mathcal{C} \in \mathbb{R}^{m \times m \times n}$ be the latent core tensor. We have $\mathbf{O} = \{\mathbf{o}_1, \mathbf{o}_2, ..., \mathbf{o}_m\}$, $\mathbf{D} = \{\mathbf{d}_1, \mathbf{d}_2, ..., \mathbf{d}_m\}$, and $\mathbf{T} = \{\mathbf{t}_1, \mathbf{t}_2, ..., \mathbf{t}_n\}$, where every column vector in projection matrix present the weight of every factor for each area or time accordingly and $\mathcal{C}_{ijk}$ represents the correlation between latent factor $\mathbf{o}_i$, $\mathbf{d}_j$, and $\mathbf{t}_k$.

According to the Tucker Decomposition[5], we can factorize the tensor approximately based on the factor matrix and core tensor as

$$\mathcal{X} \approx \mathcal{C} \times_o \mathbf{O} \times_d \mathbf{D} \times_t \mathbf{T} \tag{2}$$

where $\times_n$ represents the tensor-matrix multiplication on mode n.

Then, given the observed origin-destination-time tensor $\mathcal{X}$, the objective of this paper is to find the optimal latent projection matrix $\mathbf{O}$, $\mathbf{D}$, $\mathbf{T}$ and core tensor $\mathcal{C}$ by minimizing the following objectives

$$\mathcal{J}_1 = \|\mathcal{X} - \mathcal{C} \times_o \mathbf{O} \times_d \mathbf{D} \times_t \mathbf{T}\|_F^2 \tag{3}$$

The objective function can be seen as the quality of approximation of tensor $\mathcal{X}$ by the projection matrix $\mathbf{O}$, $\mathbf{D}$, $\mathbf{T}$ and core tensor $\mathcal{C}$. However, as mentioned above, urban structure is also strongly related with urban contextual information, and the sparsity of X makes it very challenging to directly learn the structure from only observed urban traffic network. That's the reason why we need to make full use of the urban contextual information.

3.3 Urban Contextual Regularization

A point of interest(POI), is a specific point location that someone may find useful or interesting. A POI is associated with a geo-position (latitude, longitude) and a POI category, which implies the urban contextual information . Table 1 shows the information of POI category used in this paper. For each area, the number of POI in each POI category can be counted. Then the POI feature vector in area i can be denoted by $v_i = (c_1, c_2, ..., c_P)$, where the P is the number of POI categories, and c_k is the number of k-th category POI. Based on the POI feature vectors, we consider the *consin* distance of POI vectors to measure similarity of two areas.

$$W_{ij} = \frac{v_i \cdot v_j}{\|v_i\| \cdot \|v_j\|} \tag{4}$$

In this way, we can construct the area-area similarity matrix $\mathbf{W} \in \mathbb{R}^{M \times M}$. We further assume that $\mathbf{W}$ can be approximated by the inner product of the latent origin projection matrix and latent destination projection matrix respectively, thus we need to minimize the following objective

$$\mathcal{J}_2 = \|\mathbf{W} - \mathbf{O}\mathbf{O}^\top\|_F^2 \tag{5}$$

Table 1. Information of POI category

id	POI category	id	POI category
1	food & beverage Service	8	education and culture
2	hotel	9	business building
3	scenic spot	10	residence
4	finance & insurance	11	living service
5	corporate business	12	sports & entertainments
6	shopping service	13	medical care
7	transportation facilities	14	government agencies

$$\mathcal{J}_3 = \|\mathbf{W} - \mathbf{DD}^\top\|_F^2 \tag{6}$$

We also use non-negativity constraints and sparsity regularizer on the core tensor and/or factor matrices. Non-negativity allows only additivity, so the solutions are often intuitive to understand and explain[6]. Promoting the sparsity of the core tensor aims at improving the interpretability of the solutions. Roughly speaking, the core tensor interacts with all the projection matrices, and a simple one is often preferred. Forcing the core tensor to be sparse can often keep strong interactions between the projection matrices and remove the weak ones. Sparse projection matrices make the decomposed parts more meaningful and can enhance uniqueness, as explained in [8].

Finally, by combining $\mathcal{J}_1$, $\mathcal{J}_2$, $\mathcal{J}_3$, together, we can get the latent projection matrix $\mathbf{O}$, $\mathbf{D}$, $\mathbf{T}$ and latent core tensor $\mathcal{C}$ by minimizing the following objective function.

$$\mathcal{J} = \|\mathcal{X} - \mathcal{C} \times_o \mathbf{O} \times_d \mathbf{D} \times_t \mathbf{T}\|_F^2 + \alpha\|\mathbf{W} - \mathbf{OO}^\top\|_F^2$$
$$+ \beta\|\mathbf{W} - \mathbf{DD}^\top\|_F^2 + \gamma\|\mathcal{C}\|_1 + \delta\|\mathbf{O}\|_1 + \epsilon\|\mathbf{D}\|_1 + \varepsilon\|\mathbf{T}\|_1 \tag{7}$$
$$s.t. \quad \mathcal{C} \geq 0, \mathbf{O} \geq 0, \mathbf{D} \geq 0, \mathbf{T} \geq 0$$

3.4 Optimization

In this section, we will introduce an Alternating Proximal Gradient(APG)[12] method to solve the optimization problem.

For convenience of description, We first introduce the basic APG method to solve the problem

$$\min_x F(\mathbf{x}_1, \cdots, \mathbf{x}_s) = f(\mathbf{x}_1, \cdots, \mathbf{x}_s) + \sum_{i=1}^s r_i(\mathbf{x}_i) \tag{8}$$

where variable $\mathbf{x}$ is partitioned into s blocks $\mathbf{x}_1, \cdots, \mathbf{x}_s$, f is a differentiable and for each i, it is a convex function of $\mathbf{x}_i$ while all the other blocks are fixed. Each $r_i(\mathbf{x}_i)$ is the regularization item on $\mathbf{x}_i$.

Then at the k-th iteration of APG, $\mathbf{x}_1, \cdots, \mathbf{x}_s$ are updated alternatively from $i = 1$ to s by

$$\mathbf{x}_i^k = \arg\min_{\mathbf{x}_i} \langle \mathbf{g}_i^k, \mathbf{x}_i - \mathbf{x}_i^{k-1} \rangle + \frac{L_i^k}{2}\|\mathbf{x}_i - \mathbf{x}_i^{k-1}\|_2^2 + r_i(\mathbf{x}_i) \tag{9}$$

where $\mathbf{g}_i^k = \nabla f_i^k \left(\mathbf{x}_i^{k-1}\right)$ is the block-patial gradient of f at $\mathbf{x}_i^{k-1}$, L_i is a Lipschitz constant of $\nabla f_i\left(\mathbf{x}_i\right)$, namely,

$$\|\nabla f_i\left(\mathbf{x}_{i_1}\right) - \nabla f_i\left(\mathbf{x}_{i_2}\right)\|_F \leq L_i \|\mathbf{x}_{i_1} - \mathbf{x}_{i_2}\|_F, \forall \mathbf{x}_{i_1}, \mathbf{x}_{i_2} \qquad (10)$$

In this paper, we consider the non-negative and sparse regularization. Then the Equation 9 has closed form

$$\mathbf{x}_i^k = \max\left(0, \mathbf{x}_i^{k-1} - \frac{1}{L_i^k}\nabla f_i\left(\mathbf{x}_i^{k-1}\right) - \frac{\lambda_i}{L_i^k}\right) \qquad (11)$$

Then we return to our problem. Although the objective function is not jointly convex with respect to $\mathcal{C}$, $\mathbf{O}$, $\mathbf{D}$, and $\mathbf{T}$, it is convex with each of them with the other three fixed. We can adopt a block coordinate descent scheme to solve the problem. That is, starting from some random initialization on $\mathcal{C}$, $\mathbf{O}$, $\mathbf{D}$, and $\mathbf{T}$, we solve each of them alternatively with the other three fixed, and proceed step by step until convergence. Specifically, the gradients of the objective $\mathcal{J}$ with respect to the variables are

$$\frac{\partial \mathcal{J}}{\partial \mathcal{C}} = 2\left(\mathcal{C} \times_o \left(\mathbf{O}^\top \mathbf{O}\right) \times_d \left(\mathbf{D}^\top \mathbf{D}\right) \times_t \left(\mathbf{T}^\top \mathbf{T}\right) - \mathcal{X} \times_o \mathbf{O}^\top \times_d \mathbf{D}^\top \times_t \mathbf{T}^\top\right)$$

$$\frac{\partial \mathcal{J}}{\partial \mathbf{O}} = 2\left(\mathbf{O}\left(\mathcal{C} \times_d \left(\mathbf{D}^\top \mathbf{D}\right) \times_t \left(\mathbf{T}^\top \mathbf{T}\right)\right)_{(o)} \mathcal{C}_{(o)}^\top - \left(\mathcal{X} \times_d \mathbf{D}^\top \times_t \mathbf{T}^\top\right)_{(o)} \mathcal{C}_{(o)}^\top\right.$$
$$\left. - \alpha\left(\mathbf{W} - \mathbf{O}\mathbf{O}^\top\right)\mathbf{O}\right)$$

$$\frac{\partial \mathcal{J}}{\partial \mathbf{D}} = 2\left(\mathbf{D}\left(\mathcal{C} \times_o \left(\mathbf{O}^\top \mathbf{O}\right) \times_t \left(\mathbf{T}^\top \mathbf{T}\right)\right)_{(d)} \mathcal{C}_{(d)}^\top - \left(\mathcal{X} \times_o \mathbf{O}^\top \times_t \mathbf{T}^\top\right)_{(d)} \mathcal{C}_{(d)}^\top\right.$$
$$\left. - \beta\left(\mathbf{W} - \mathbf{D}\mathbf{D}^\top\right)\mathbf{D}\right)$$

$$\frac{\partial \mathcal{J}}{\partial \mathbf{T}} = 2\left(\mathbf{T}\left(\mathcal{C} \times_o \left(\mathbf{O}^\top \mathbf{O}\right) \times_d \left(\mathbf{D}^\top \mathbf{D}\right)\right)_{(t)} \mathcal{C}_{(t)}^\top - \left(\mathcal{X} \times_o \mathbf{O}^\top \times_d \mathbf{D}^\top\right)_{(t)} \mathcal{C}_{(t)}^\top\right)$$
$$(12)$$

where $\mathcal{X}_{(k)}$ denotes the mode-k matricization of tensor $\mathcal{X}$.

4   Experiment

4.1   Data Sets

In this section, we conduct extensive experiments to evaluate the effectiveness and show insight of our proposed method based on a real taxi trajectory dataset, which contains more than 3 millions occupied trips generated by taxis of Beijing in one month (November, 2011). According to the report of Beijing Transportation Bureau, the taxi trips occupy over 12 percent of traffic flows on road surface[14]. We split the Beijing map within 5-th Ring Road into 651 areas according to the traffic analysis zone, as shown in Fig. 2(a), which is the most commonly used unit of geography. We also split 24 time domains according to

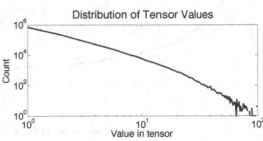

(a) Areas in 5-th Ring Road of
Beijing split by traffic analysis
zone

(b) Distribution of values in tensor

Fig. 2. Description of datasets

hours. After the data preprocessing, we built a $(651 \times 651 \times 24)$ traffic tensor. Statistics about tensor data distribution shown in Fig. 2(b) reflects severe skewness. Our datasets also include a POI dataset in year 2011, which contains more than 30 thousands POI records.

4.2 Comparative Method

Besides the proposed rNTD method, we also implement the following methods for comparison.

- **Basic Non-negative Tensor Factorization** (bNTF): As an extension to non-negative matrix factorization, this method suppose a joint latent space for each mode by solving the objective function:

$$\min_{O,D,T} \|\mathcal{X} - \sum_r o_r \odot d_r \odot t_r\|^2 \tag{13}$$

  where $\odot$ represents the vector outer product. This method can be also seen as the special case of NTD when the core tensor is super diagonal, also known as PARAFAC.

- **Regularized Non-negative Tensor Factorization** (rNTF): By incorporating the urban contextual regularization, this method consider the following objective function

$$\min_{O,D,T} \|\mathcal{X} - \sum_r o_r \odot d_r \odot t_r\|^2 + \alpha\|W - OO^\top\|_F^2 + \beta\|W - DD^\top\|_F^2 \tag{14}$$

- **Basic Non-negative Tucker Decomposition** (bNTD): This is a variant of our method, but with no consideration about regularization terms by solving:

$$\min_{\mathcal{C},O,D,T} \|\mathcal{X} - \mathcal{C} \times_o O \times_d D \times_t T\|_F^2 \tag{15}$$

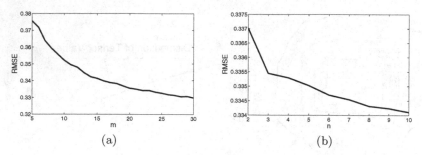

Fig. 3. Dimensionality of hidden space

We evaluate the quality of structures we discover by tensor reconstructed error using the *Root Mean Square Error*(RMSE)

$$RMSE = \sqrt{\frac{\sum_{ijk \in \mathcal{H}} \mathcal{X}_{ijk} - \hat{\mathcal{X}}_{ijk}}{|\mathcal{H}|}} \tag{16}$$

where $\mathcal{H}$ is the set of hidden elements in our experiment and $|\mathcal{H}|$ is its size, $\hat{\mathcal{X}}$ is the reconstructed tensor.

4.3 Parameter Settings

In this section, we report the sensitivity of parameters our method involves, the dimensionality of hidden space m, n, and the tradeoff parameter for urban contextual regularization α, β.

Dimensionality of Hidden Space. The goal of our model is to find a $m \times m \times n$-dimensional space for origin areas, destination areas and time. How to set m and n is important for our problem. If m, n are too small, the cluster can not be well represented and discriminated in the latent space. If m, n are too large, the low-rank structure would not capture the relations between different dimensions and the computational complexity will be greatly increased. Thus, we conduct 10 experiments with m ranging from 5 to 30 and n ranging from 2 to 10 on the dataset. The result are shown in Fig. 3, from which we can see that with the increase on the dimension m, n, $RMSE$ will reduce gradually. When $m \geq 20, n \geq 3$, the $RMSE$ reduces rather slow. For the concern of the tradeoff between precision and explaination, we choose $m = 20$ and $n = 3$ as latent space dimension in our experiments.

Tradeoff Parameters. The tradeoff parameters α, β in our method play the role of adjusting the strength of different terms in the objective function. Fig. 4 shows the $RMSE$ when α, β changes from 10^{-5} to 1. When α, β are small, the performance is close to that of bNTD, as we will see in Table 2. However, when

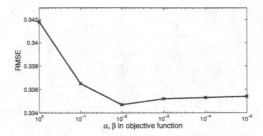

Fig. 4. Varing the city context regularization coefficient α, β

Table 2. Experiment performance

	bNTF	rNTF	bNTD	rNTD
50%	0.3974	0.3952	0.3366	**0.3359**
70%	0.3970	0.3950	0.3361	**0.3352**
90%	0.3963	0.3943	0.3354	**0.3347**

α, β are relatively large, the optimization in Equation 7 may be dominated by the urban contextual regularization term, therefore the reconstructed loss term is not properly optimized. The result in Fig. 4 shows that the parameter set $\alpha = \beta = 0.01$ produce the best performance. In our following, we just use this parameter setting. Moreover, we also find the best configurations in every comparative methods on our datasets to make sure comparisons are fair.

4.4   Experimental Performance

To do the comparision, We randomly select 50% 70% and 90% of the observed entries in tensor as training dataset and compute the reconstruction error of the hidden entries, where we obtain the $RMSE$. We repeat the experiments 10 times and report the average performance of all methods in Table 2,

From the Table 2, we can observed that:

- The comparison between bNTF v.s. bNTD and rNTF v.s. rNTD reveals the advantage of the tensor Tucker decomposition as a method to capture relation from high dimensions data and get stable and compact representation.
- The advantage of rNTD over bNTD, as well as the advantage of rNTF over bNTF, shows the importance of urban contextual in our problem.
- Finally, our proposed method, rNTD, which incorporates the spatio-temporal interaction data and urban contextual information together, achieves the best performance in all experimental trials.

4.5   Insights

In this section, we will give the empirical study to show the insights that founded by our method. As shown in Fig. 1, the goal of urban spatio-temporal structure

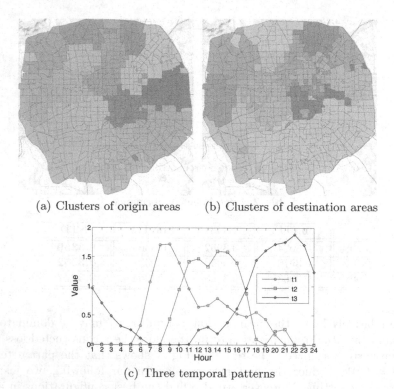

(a) Clusters of origin areas   (b) Clusters of destination areas

(c) Three temporal patterns

Fig. 5. Spatial clusters of Beijing areas and temporal patterns of Beijing traffic

discovery is to find a low-rank tensor, from which we can not only identify cluster behaviors on the *origin, destination, time* modes, but can also detect the cross-mode association.

The projection on **O** and/or **D** gives the spatial correlation information among the areas in city. The entries with high values in a columns of **O** and/or **D** imply which cluster an area belongs to. The result is visualized in Fig. 5(a) and Fig. 5(b). Surprisingly, we see that although our method make no use of geography information, spatial cluster are geographically close. In Fig. 5(c), we plot the three columns of projection matrix **T**. Along the time mode, three temporal patterns are found. This result is similar with the work in [9], where three patterns are explained as home to workspace, workspace to workspace, workspace to others. Although the patterns are similar, our method can find also the corresponding spatial patterns and the correlation between them, thus the better understanding of spatio-temporal structure of city.

We choose the Central Business District (CBD) of Beijing as a destination cluster for case study, which is shown within the black line in Fig. 6. We visualize the origin cluster that have non-zero value with CBD destination cluster in core tensor in three temporal patterns accordingly. From Fig. 6(a), we see that most traffic to CBD, as a typical workplace, reach peak in the morning and fade down soon. In the daytime, most traffic occur in the nearby area. Since CBD is one

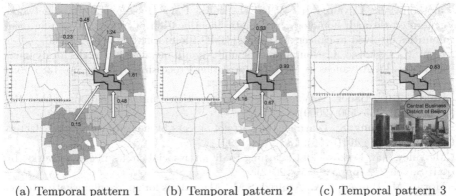

(a) Temporal pattern 1   (b) Temporal pattern 2   (c) Temporal pattern 3

Fig. 6. Visualization of core tensor: within the black line is the a destination cluster for case study, which is Central Business District (CBD) of Beijing. Three subfigures represent three temporal patterns respectively. Each subfigure gives the origin cluster that have correlations with CBD. Values are from the core tensor.

of the most congested place in Beijing, Fig. 6 give an intuitional guidance for urban planning to solve traffic jam.

5   Conclusion and Future Work

In this paper we investigate the problem of discovering urban spatio-temporal structure from time-evolving traffic network. We model the time-evolving traffic network into a 3-order origin-destination-time tensor. We propose a regularized Non-negative Tucker Decomposition (rNTD) method to solve this problem, which consider traffic data and urban contextual knowledge together. We also propose an alternating proximal gradient algorithm for optimization. Experimental results on a real-world dataset show that our method can significantly outperform the baseline methods.There are many potential directions of this work. It would be interesting to investigate how the POI affect urban traffic, which will give us more guideline for urban planning.

Acknowledgement. This work is supported by National High Technology Research and Development Program of China (No. 2013AA01A601), NSFC (No. 61370022, No. 61202426, No. 61303075), and International Science and Technology Cooperation Program of China, (No. 2013DFG12870).

References

1. Fortunato, S.: Community detection in graphs. Physics Reports 486(3), 75–174 (2010)
2. Gonzalez, M.C., Hidalgo, C.A., Barabasi, A.-L.: Understanding individual human mobility patterns. Nature 453(7196), 779–782 (2008)

3. Jonsson, P.F., Cavanna, T., Zicha, D., Bates, P.A.: Cluster analysis of networks generated through homology: automatic identification of important protein communities involved in cancer metastasis. BMC Bioinformatics 7(1), 2 (2006)
4. Kim, M., Leskovec, J.: Nonparametric multi-group membership model for dynamic networks. In: Advances in Neural Information Processing Systems, pp. 1385–1393 (2013)
5. Kolda, T.G., Bader, B.W.: Tensor decompositions and applications. SIAM Review 51(3), 455–500 (2009)
6. Lee, D.D., Seung, S.: Learning the parts of objects by non-negative matrix factorization. Nature 401(6755), 788–791 (1999)
7. McAuley, J.J., Leskovec, J.: Learning to discover social circles in ego networks. In: NIPS, vol. 272, pp. 548–556 (2012)
8. Mørup, M., Hansen, L.K., Arnfred, S.M.: Algorithms for sparse nonnegative tucker decompositions. Neural Computation 20(8), 2112–2131 (2008)
9. Peng, C., Jin, X., Wong, K.-C., Shi, M., Liò, P.: Collective human mobility pattern from taxi trips in urban area. PloS One 7(4), e34487 (2012)
10. Sun, J., Tao, D., Faloutsos, C.: Beyond streams and graphs: dynamic tensor analysis. In: Proceedings of the 12th ACM SIGKDD International Conference on Knowledge Discovery and Data Mining, pp. 374–383. ACM (2006)
11. Wang, F., Li, T., Wang, X., Zhu, S., Ding, C.: Community discovery using nonnegative matrix factorization. Data Mining and Knowledge Discovery 22(3), 493–521 (2011)
12. Xu, Y., Yin, W.: A block coordinate descent method for regularized multiconvex optimization with applications to nonnegative tensor factorization and completion. SIAM Journal on Imaging Sciences 6(3), 1758–1789 (2013)
13. Yang, J., McAuley, J., Leskovec, J.: Community detection in networks with node attributes. In: 2013 IEEE 13th International Conference on Data Mining, pp. 1151–1156 (2013)
14. Yuan, J., Zheng, Y., Xie, X.: Discovering regions of different functions in a city using human mobility and pois. In: Proceedings of the 18th ACM SIGKDD International Conference on Knowledge Discovery and Data Mining, pp. 186–194. ACM (2012)
15. Zhang, F., Wilkie, D., Zheng, Y., Xie, X.: Sensing the pulse of urban refueling behavior. In: Proceedings of the 2013 ACM International Joint Conference on Pervasive and Ubiquitous Computing, pp. 13–22. ACM (2013)
16. Zheng, Y., Liu, F., Hsieh, H.-P.: U-air: when urban air quality inference meets big data. In: Proceedings of the 19th ACM SIGKDD International Conference on Knowledge Discovery and Data Mining, pp. 1436–1444. ACM (2013)
17. Zheng, Y., Liu, Y., Yuan, J., Xie, X.: Urban computing with taxicabs. In: Proceedings of the 13th International Conference on Ubiquitous Computing, pp. 89–98. ACM (2011)

A Novel Topical Authority-Based Microblog Ranking

Yanmei Zhai[1], Xin Li[1,*,**], Jialiang Chen[1], Xiumei Fan[1,***],
and William K. Cheung[2]

[1] School of Computer Science, Beijing Institute of Technology, Beijing, China
[2] Department of Computer Science, Hong Kong Baptist University, Hong Kong

Abstract. The high volume of microblogs produced daily together with
their rich social structure makes microblogs' better query and filtering
ever challenging. In the literature, most of the existing ranking methods are based on the overall popularity of the authors and the tweets
without considering author's expertise. In this paper, we propose the
topical authority-based ranking methods for social networks like Twitter and investigate how the underlying topical feature modeling can be
optimized for performance boosting. In particular, we present a detailed
study on the empirical distributions of the topical features. We propose
the use of specific parametric forms for different features, which we believe to be crucial as the value of the cumulative distribution function
is explicitly used for topical authority ranking. We applied the extended
topical authority-based ranking method to a Twitter dataset for ranking
keyword-matched microblogs. The experimental results show that our
proposed approach outperforms a number of existing approaches by a
large margin which verify the effectiveness of our proposed features and
the importance of the topical authority for ranking microblogs.

Keywords: Topical Authority, Feature Distribution, Microblog Ranking.

1 Introduction

The recent proliferation of micro-blogging causes tens of thousands of microblogs produced daily. The availability of the large amount of microblog data,
often together with the user profiles, allows a number of data mining tasks
possible, e.g., hot topic detection [1], opinion leader detection [2], etc. Yet, this
also brings new challenges to microblog search engines like Twitter, in particular
the high demand of billions of daily search queries and the need to provide

* Corresponding author.
** The work of Xin Li is partially supported by National Program on Key Basic Research Project under Grant No. 2013CB329605 and the NSFC Grant under Grant
No. 61300178.
*** The work of X. Fan is supported in part by NFSC under Grant No. 61272509 and
61120106010, BNSF under Grant No. 4132049, and Specialized Research Fund for
the Doctoral Program of Higher Education under grant No. 20136118110002.

L. Chen et al. (Eds.): APWeb 2014, LNCS 8709, pp. 105–116, 2014.

high quality microblogs for users. Microblogs are known to be fragmental and ephemeral, making accurate content filtering and retrieval non-trivial and also a hot research area. Various ranking strategies for microblogs have been proposed in the literature. The approaches adopted include the use of the content and specific features (e.g., tags) of the microblogs, as well as the bloggers' social structure (e.g, the author's popularity).

In general, the content-based strategies adopt variations of TFIDF-based cosine similarity to measure the content popularity [3]. And for those strategies based on microblog specific features [4], the number of hashtags, the length of tweet, the presence of URLs, and the number of retweets, etc., have been proposed for ranking tweet data. For the authority-based approach, the basic idea is to rank the tweets of the authors with more followers or more retweets higher. Intuitively, each author has his/her own expertise of some specific areas. For example, Alex J. Smola - the prestigious machine learning researcher has high authority in machine learning related domains, his twitter account "@smolix" distributes lots of useful resources related to ML research but few posts discussing food, trips etc. Thus treating author authority with no topical difference might not be appropriate in microblog ranking.

In [5], the Gaussian ranking algorithm for microblogs topical authority identification was proposed based on a set of so-called topical features which indicate the topical signals over tweets and authors. The use of the approach is mainly for the influential author detection. And its optimality is pretty much relying on the assumption that each feature follows a Gaussian distribution with their parameters estimated from the data.

In this paper, we propose to incorporate author's topical authority to enhance the performance of microblog ranking, with the conjecture that the topical authorities of the authors are good and robust signals to indicate the degree of relevancy with the query keywords. And we develop topical authority-based methodologies and conduct experiments in a Twitter dataset. Detailedly speaking, other than extending the set of topical features proposed in [5], we also adopt different parametric forms of probability distribution for the feature modeling so that the accuracy of our proposed cumulative distribution functions (CDFs) based approaches can be further optimized. The experimental results showed that our proposed approaches can significantly improve the ranking performance measured based on normalized discounted cumulative gain (NDCG) by over 20% when compared to both Gaussian-based and conventional ranking approaches. To the best of our knowledge, we are the first to incorporate topical authority into microblog ranking.

The remainder of the paper is organized as follows. Section 2 discusses the related work of microblog ranking and identification of topical authorities. Section 3 presents the feature extraction of all topical and conventional features, followed by several novel authority-based ranking methods. The details of the feature distribution modelling are described in Section 4. Section 5 reports the experimental results and performance evaluation. The conclusion and future work are presented in Section 6.

2   Related Work

In the literature, there exist lots of work on microblog ranking. The importance of considering author authority in Twitter author ranking was first demonstrated in [6]. *TweetRank* and *FollowerRank* [7] were proposed to rank tweets by considering the number of tweets posted by an author and the proportion of the followers in his networks, respectively. Different hybrid approaches that incorporate content relevance, user authority and tweet-specific features have also been considered to support real-time search and ranking [8,4]. In the literature, the existing works have validated the contribution of publishing authority to the microblog ranking approaches. However, the author authority is based on the conventional popularity instead of being evaluated in topics. And ranking the microblogs in consideration of author's topical authority is rarely discussed.

In domains other than microblog ranking, identification of topical author authority was first investigated by Jianshu *et al.* [9]. *TwitterRank* was proposed to identify author authority, which is a PageRank [10] similar approach by adopting both topical similarity and link structure. The topical distribution is constructed using the Latent Dirichlet Allocation (LDA) algorithm [11], and then a weighted user graph is derived accordingly with its edge weight indicating the topical similarity between authors. However the high complexity of the approach can not meet the requirement of real-time ranking. Aditya *et al.* [5] emphasized on real-time performance and first proposed a set of features for characterizing the topical authorities. They performed a probabilistic clustering over the feature space and computed a final list of top k authors for a given topic by Gaussian-based inner-cluster ranking.

In this paper, we aim to enhance the ranking performance by identifying and incorporating topical authority into microblog ranking scheme. Detailedly, we i) propose two new features based on [5] as the author's topical follower signal and the conventional popularity signal respectively, and ii) adopt different parametric distributions for feature modeling so as to relax the Gaussian distribution assumption. This relaxation is particularly crucial as the cumulative distribution function values are explicitly used to compute the the ranking. Also, we evaluate the effectiveness of topical author authority in microblog ranking.

3   Topical Authority-Based Microblog Ranking

In this section we will present the feature extraction of all topical and conventional features as well as several novel authority-based ranking methods.

3.1   Topical Authority Feature Construction

We adopt and extend the topical authority metrics and features proposed in [5] to further enhance microblog ranking performance. And to make this paper self-contained we include some details of [5].

Topical Metrics in Microblogs. Following the setup of [5], we also utilize a list of metrics extracted and computed for each potential authority. Table 1 tabulates the metrics proposed in [5], where OT, CT, RT, M and G stand for metrics associated with the original tweets, conventional tweets, repeated tweets, mentions and graph-based characteristics, respectively. All the features indicate the morphology of tweets (the number of embedded URLs, hashtags, etc.), the way they are used (re-tweeting, mentions or conventional tweets), or the signal of author's topical interests. We here propose two additional metrics, $F1$ and $F2$, to indicate author popularity as people tend to have strong interests in celebrities. We then use these two metrics to define new features.

Table 1. List of Metrics of Potential Authority [5]

ID	Metric
OT1	Number of original tweets
OT2	Number of links shared
OT3	Self-similarity score in the words of tweets
OT4	Number of keyword hashtags used
CT1	Number of conversational tweets
CT2	Number of conversational tweets initiated by the author
RT1	Number of retweets of others'
RT2	Number of unique tweets (OT1) retweeted by other users
RT3	Number of unique users who retweeted authors tweets
M1	Number of mentions of other users by the author
M2	Number of unique users mentioned by the author
M3	Number of mentions by others of the author
M4	Number of unique users mentioning the author
G1	Number of topically active followers
G2	Number of topically active friends
G3	Number of followers tweeting on topic after the author
G4	Number of friends tweeting on topic before the author
F1	Number of followers
F2	Number of friends

Topical Features in Microblogs. Most of the topical features adopted in this paper are again based on [5] as shown in Table 2. Among them, TS indicates how much an author is involved with a specific topic. SS estimates the originality of author's topical tweets which also indicates author's topical signal. Additionally, $\overline{C}S$ estimates how much an author posts on a topic and how far he wanders from the topic into casual conversations. $\overline{C}S$ is proposed to distinguish real people from the agents or organizations, since people incline to fall into conversations out of courtesy. Referring to λ in $\overline{C}S$, it is used to discount the fact that the author did not initiate the conversation but simply replied back out of politeness. Intuitively, $\overline{C}S$ is less than $\frac{OT1}{OT1+CT2}$, and thus we can solve for λ with this constraint. Empirically, we solve λ to satisfy over 90% of users in our dataset. RI considers how many times the author's tweets have been retweeted by others so as to measure the content impact of author. MI is used to estimate the mention impact. Feature ID is to estimate the diffused influence by the author in his own networks. And *NS* is to estimate the raw number of topical active users around the author. For *OT21* and *OT41*, they indicate the rate of link and keyword hashtag in original tweets respectively. *OT3* reflects the portion of words an author borrows from his previous posts including both on and off topics, where $S(s_i, s_j) = \frac{|s_i \cap s_j|}{|s_i|}$ is the similarity function defined over the set of words s_i and s_j which are extracted from the author's i^{th} and j^{th} tweets repectively. Moreover, before computing the scores, we should make author's tweets in time order, and apply stemming and stop-word removal.

Intuitively, for a specific area, the more followers an author has, the more influential he is; and the more attention an author receives, the more authoritative he is. Thus, we propose to include feature $F12$ as the conventional popularity signal considering that people tend to have great interests in celebrities' opinions, and also feature $GF1$ to indicate the author's topical follower signal. Both newly added features are found to be effective ones based on our empirical results.

Table 2. List of Features for Each User

	Feature	Description
TS	$\frac{OT1+CT1+RT1}{|\#tweets|}$	Topic Involvement Signal
SS	$\frac{OT1}{OT1+RT1}$	Topical Signal Strength
$\overline{CS}$	$\frac{OT1}{OT1+CT1} + \lambda\frac{CT1-CT2}{CT1+1}$	Non-Chat Signal
RI	$RT2 * log(RT3)$	Retweet Impact
MI	$M3 * log(M4) - M1 * log(M2)$	Mention Impact
ID	$log(G3+1) - log(G4+1)$	Information Diffusion
NS	$log(G1+1) - log(G2+1)$	Network Score
OT21	$\frac{OT2}{OT1}$	Link Rate
OT41	$\frac{OT4}{OT1}$	Keyword Hashtag Rate
OT3	$\frac{2*\sum_{i=1}^{n}\sum_{j=1}^{i-1} S(s_i,s_j)}{(n-1)*n}$	Word Self Similarity
GF1	$\frac{G1}{F1}$	Topical Follower Signal
F12	$\frac{F1}{F2}$	Follower Signal

3.2 Cumulative Distribution-Based Ranking

Since all the topical authority features are assumed to follow Gaussian distribution in [5], which however may not be true as to be discussed in Sec. 4.2. We adopt the feature distribution modelling approach in this paper and compute the cumulative distribution functions (CDF) of the topical authority features to calculate the author's *Authority Score (AS)*. For author x_i, *AS* is defined as:

$$AS(x_i) = \prod_{f=1}^{m} F_f(x_i^f; \Theta_f) \tag{1}$$

where F_f denotes the CDF of feature f with parameter Θ_f and m is the number of features (similarly hereinafter). With the conjecture that the conventional authority features and topical authority features may carry different weights, one can explore a weighted version of the Authority Score, given as:

$$AS(x_i) = [\prod_{f=1}^{11} F_f(x_i^f; \Theta_f)]^\beta [F_{12}(x_i^{12}; \Theta_{12})]^{(1-\beta)} \tag{2}$$

where $\beta \in (0, 1)$ denotes the trade-off parameter between topical authority and conventional authority. In our experiments, the empirical settings of β are over 0.7.

Other than the proposed CDF-based ranking approaches, there exist a number of other possibilities (Seen in Table 3). *Conv_based* corresponds to the ranking method based on conventional author popularity with only feature $F12$ used as the authority score. *Gaus-10* refers to the Gaussian-based ranking method with AS defined as $\prod_{f=1}^{m} \int_{-\infty}^{x_i^f} \mathcal{N}(x; \mu_f, \sigma_f) dx$, where μ_f and σ_f denote the mean and standard deviation of feature f. *SUM-based* defines the AS as $\sum_{f=1}^{m} x_i^f$, and *SUM-12* corresponds to summation over all 12 features shown in Table 2. Similarly, *MUL-based* method defines AS as $\prod_{f=1}^{m} x_i^f$.

Table 3. List of Authority Ranking Methods

Ranking Methods	Description
Conv_based	Conventional authority-based ranking by feature $F12$ only
Gaus-10	Gaussian-based over top 10 features in table 2
SUM-12	Summation-based over all 12 features in table 2
MUL-12	Multiplication-based over all 12 features in table 2
CDF-10	CDF-based over top 10 features in table 2
CDF-12	CDF-based over all 12 features in table 2
CDF_weighted	Weighted version of *CDF-12*

4   Optimizing Feature Modeling

In this section, we first present the statistics of the Twitter dataset we used and then suggest better design of the probability distribution for each feature to achieve the model optimality.

4.1   DataSet

We use a Twitter dataset which was collected from June 11st 2009 to October 8th 2009. All collected tweets together with their relationship profiles takes up about $65.8G$ storage space. We select five hot hastags as the keywords. They are *google, healthcare, iran, music* and *twitter*. For each keyword, we collect thousands of most recent and best matched tweets via substring matching and obtain the corresponding authors' relationship.

The statistics of our dataset are shown in Table 4, where |MTN| means the number of matched tweets by keywords, |UTN| indicates the number of unique authors. |UFoN| and |UTFoN| represent the number of unique followers and that of unique topical followers respectively. Similarly, |UFrN| and |UTFrN| indicate the number of unique friends and that of unique topical friends respectively.

Table 4. Dataset Statistics

keywords	google	healthcare	iran	music	twitter
|MTN|	5,371	2,919	4,162	5,175	5,208
|UTN|	4,221	1,949	1,953	4,446	4,651
|UFoN|	788,149	600,355	917,983	634,016	832,140
|UTFoN|	131,281	34,292	57,197	143,870	321,804
|UFrN|	550,980	347,651	388,208	426,138	604,472
|UTFrN|	114,565	30,401	39,763	121,119	272,095

4.2 Feature Distributions of Different Parametric Forms

We first group the features into four categories based on the form of their underlying distributions. The groupings are {*ID, GF1*}, {*TS, F12*}, {*MI, RI, OT41*}, and {*NS, OT3, OT21, CS, SS*}. For each category, they fit the corresponding features with distribution functions of same parametric form. Due to the page limit, we only present some of the features in detail here.

Fig.1 shows the probability distributions of different features. It can be easily noted that features *ID, GF1* and *MI* can be fitted well by Gaussian distribution, and features *TS* and *NS* are unlikely Gaussian. Fig.2 gives the Q-Q plots (where "Q" stands for quantile) of some features based on the Gaussian assumption. It is obvious that only features *ID* and *GF1* end up with good fitting as indicated by having not too many points deviated from the straight line $y = x$. For features *TS* and *NS*, they are found to be better fitted with Lognormal and Gaussian mixture model respectively, as evidenced in Fig.3, compared to Gaussian fitting result shown in Fig.2. For feature *RI*, we can hardly find an appropriate distribution to fit it since its values are too concentrated around zero. And we adopt the method that divides its range into n equal parts first and then turns the discrete probability mass function into a continuous one to calculate its CDF.

For the distributions we adopted, we apply the Maximum Likelihood Estimation to obtain their model parameters. For the sake of brevity, we only present the parameter estimation steps for Gaussian Mixture Model (GMM). GMM is a probabilistic model that assumes all the data points to be generated from a linear superposition of Gaussian components which provides a richer class of density models than the single Gaussian.

Considering that we have n data points $x = \{x_1, x_2, ..., x_n\}$ in d-dimensional space (in our case, $d = 1$), the log likelihood with respect to a GMM can be denoted as:

$$log(p(x|\Theta)) = \sum_{i=1}^{n} log \sum_{k=1}^{K} \pi_k * \mathcal{N}(x_i|\mu_k, \Sigma_k) \tag{3}$$

where $\{\pi_k, s.t. \sum_{k=1}^{K} \pi_k = 1\}$ is the prior probability over the K Gaussian components, and (μ_k, Σ_k) are mean and standard deviation (model parameters) of the kth Gaussian component. Then we use the Expectation Maximization (EM) algorithm to maximize the log likelihood to estimate the unknown parameters. Due to the page limits, we skip the details of EM process.

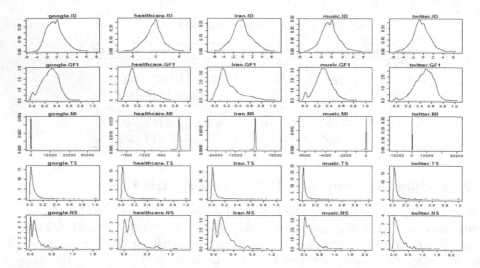

Fig. 1. Probability distributions of feature $ID, GF1, MI, TS, NS$ under different topics

Recall that we have proposed Authority Score(AS) based on the features' CDF in Sec.3.2. For feature f fitted by GMM, its CDF value of author x_i is defined as,

$$F_f(x_i) = \sum_{k=1}^{K} \int_{-\infty}^{x_i^f} \pi_k \mathcal{N}(x|\mu_k, \Sigma_k) \, dx \qquad (4)$$

Figs.4-6 give the plots of the empirical densities of some features together with their fitting results of "google" dataset based on different models. We can observe that univariate Gaussian and Lognormal fitting have achieved good performance for feature ID and TS respectively. Fig.6 shows the GMM-based fitting and Gaussian-based fitting of feature NS. Obviously, GMM-based approach achieves more accurate fit than the univariate Gaussian-based one.

5   Experimental Evaluation

While preparing for the evaluation of our proposed ranking approaches, we manually labelled each tuple <query keyword, tweet> with a method which is similar to 3-point Likert scale, considering how relevant the tweet is to the query keyword and the amount of information it carries.

5.1   Evaluation Metric

To evaluate the ranking results, we adopt Normalized Discounted Cumulative Gain (NDCG) as the metric which is based on DCG [12]. NDCG measures the effectiveness of the ranking methods by penalizing the position from the result list with normalization. It is defined as:

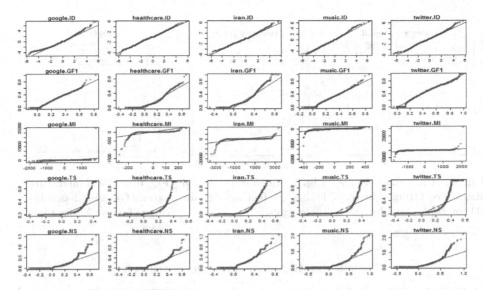

Fig. 2. Q-Q plots of features with Gaussian Fitting

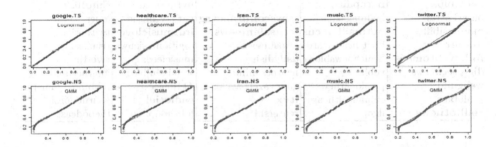

Fig. 3. Q-Q plots of features TS and NS with Lognormal and GMM Fitting

$$NDCG_n = Z_n \sum_{i=1}^{n} \frac{2^{G_i} - 1}{\log_2(i + 1)} \tag{5}$$

where G_i is the label of ith tweet in the final ranked list, and Z_n is a normalization factor, which is used to make the value of NDCG of the ideal list to be 1.

5.2 Evaluating Author Ranking Results

In Table 5, we present the top 10 authors of each dataset selected by *CDF-12* approach. With careful manual effort checking with Twitter, we find that the top-10 list is dominated by celebrities, popular bloggers and organizations. Besides, our method also discovers those authors who focus on certain areas and have a small number of followers (denoted in bold font).

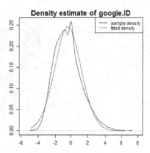
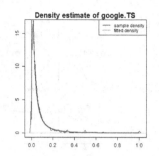
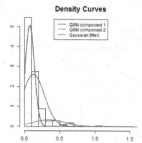

Fig. 4. Univariate Gaussian based fitting of feature ID for topic "google"

Fig. 5. Lognormal based fitting of feature TS for topic "google"

Fig. 6. GMM and Univariate Gaussian based fitting of feature NS for topic "google"

Table 5. Top 10 Authors From Query Datasets

google	healthcare	iran	music	twitter
programmableweb	healthcareintl	iranhr	showhype	dehboss
paulkbiba	**hcrepair**	jricole	nytimesmusic	chito1029
omarkattan	hcdmagazine	**newscomirancvrg**	variety_music	louer_voiture
morevisibility	**notmaxbaucus**	**jerusalemnews**	**im_musiclover**	twithority
wormreport	bnet_healthcare	jewishnews	digitalmusicnws	trueflashwear
followchromeos	healthnewsblogs	dailydish	musicfeeds	**twedir**
digg_technews	vcbh	haaretzonline	wemissmjblog	jointhetrain
webguild	presidentnews	guneyazerbaycan	411music	robbmontgomery
junlabao	chinahealthcare	**ltvx**	**radioriel**	youtubeprofits
redhotnews	ilgop	reuterskl	jobsinhiphop	thepodcast

5.3   Evaluating Microblog Ranking Results

We re-rank our dataset according to author Authority Score(AS) which is calculated by the methods described in Sec.3.2. In this section, we present the results of only two of the five topics ("google" and "healthcare") due to the page limit. Figs. 7 and 8 show the top-k ranking performance in terms of $NDCG_k$ (seen in Sec.5.1), where k varies from 5 to 1, 000.

It is obvious that the *CDF_weighted* approach outperforms the others. According to Fig.7, we observe that the performance of *Conv_based* ranking method drops sharply with the increasing value of k in general. For another topic ("healthcare") that corresponds to Fig.8, the *Conv_based* method also underperforms our proposed approaches by a large margin. The phenomenon further demonstrates the effectiveness of the adoption of the topical authority in microblog ranking.

Figs. 7 and 8 show that *CDF-10* performs much better than its Gaussian version (i.e., *Gaus-10*), which verifies the benefit brought by the more accurate feature modeling in the CDF-based method. Also, we can observe that *CDF-12* outperforms *CDF-10* except for the top-5 case of the topic "google". This demonstrates the benefit brought by the two newly proposed authority features.

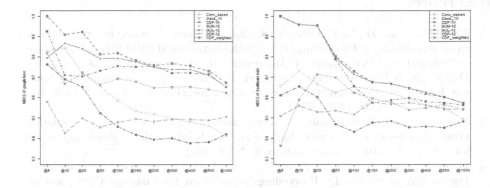

Fig. 7. A Plot of NDCG of the Top-k Results for the topic "google"

Fig. 8. A Plot of NDCG of the Top-k Results for the topic "healthcare"

Furthermore, the *CDF_weighted* approach further boosts the ranking quality by making an appropriate trade-off between the conventional popularity feature and the topical authority features. In addition, we adopt *SUM-based* and *MUL-based* approaches for benchmarking. And the *CDF-based* ones perform much better than the *non-CDF-based* approaches.

To summarize, our proposed *CDF_weighted* approach enhances the ranking performance significantly and perform best among all the proposed approaches. Quantitative analysis over the performance of the approaches show that *CDF_weighted* achieves more than 20% enhancement as compared to the conventional method as well as the Gaussian-based ranking method.

6   Conclusion and Future Work

In this paper, we first proposed to adopt the topical authority in microblog ranking and investigated to what extent the topical feature modeling can be optimized for boosting the performance of topical authority-based microblog ranking. Our attempts include extending the set of features considered and improving the feature modelling step. We applied the proposed extensions to a Twitter data set and compared the corresponding tweet ranking results with a number of existing methods for benchmarking. The experimental results validated the effectiveness of our proposed approaches and showed that the weighted version of CDF-based method outperforms other ones.

For future work, we will further investigate how the trade-off weight can be optimized for enhancing the microblog ranking quality. In addition, we are also interested in incorporating more features, e.g., content-based features, to further improve the microblog ranking quality.

References

1. Chen, Y., Amiri, H., Li, Z., Chua, T.-S.: Emerging topic detection for organizations from microblogs. In: Proceedings of the 36th International ACM SIGIR Conference on Research and Development in Information Retrieval, pp. 43–52. ACM (2013)
2. Dalrymple, K.E., Shaw, B.R., Brossard, D.: Following the leader: Using opinion leaders in environmental strategic communication. Society & Natural Resources 26(12), 1438–1453 (2013)
3. Ravikumar, S., Balakrishnan, R., Kambhampati, S.: Ranking tweets considering trust and relevance. In: Proceedings of the Ninth International Workshop on Information Integration on the Web, p. 4. ACM (2012)
4. Duan, Y., Jiang, L., Qin, T., Zhou, M., Shum, H.-Y.: An empirical study on learning to rank of tweets. In: Proceedings of the 23rd International Conference on Computational Linguistics, pp. 295–303. Association for Computational Linguistics (2010)
5. Pal, A., Counts, S.: Identifying topical authorities in microblogs. In: Proceedings of the Fourth ACM International Conference on Web Search and Data Mining, pp. 45–54. ACM (2011)
6. Kwak, H., Lee, C., Park, H., Moon, S.: What is twitter, a social network or a news media? In: Proceedings of the 19th International Conference on World Wide Web, pp. 591–600. ACM (2010)
7. Nagmoti, R., Teredesai, A., De Cock, M.: Ranking approaches for microblog search. In: 2010 IEEE/WIC/ACM International Conference on Web Intelligence and Intelligent Agent Technology (WI-IAT), vol. 1, pp. 153–157. IEEE (2010)
8. Cheng, F., Zhang, X., He, B., Luo, T., Wang, W.: A survey of learning to rank for real-time twitter search. In: Zu, Q., Hu, B., Elçi, A. (eds.) ICPCA 2012 and SWS 2012. LNCS, vol. 7719, pp. 150–164. Springer, Heidelberg (2013)
9. Weng, J., Lim, E.-P., Jiang, J., He, Q.: Twitterrank: finding topic-sensitive influential twitterers. In: Proceedings of the Third ACM International Conference on Web Search and Data Mining, pp. 261–270. ACM (2010)
10. Page, L., Brin, S., Motwani, R., Winograd, T.: The pagerank citation ranking: bringing order to the web (1999)
11. Blei, D.M., Ng, A.Y., Jordan, M.I.: Latent dirichlet allocation. The Journal of Machine Learning Research 3, 993–1022 (2003)
12. Järvelin, K., Kekäläinen, J.: Cumulated gain-based evaluation of ir techniques. ACM Transactions on Information Systems (TOIS) 20(4), 422–446 (2002)

A Time-Based Group Key Management Algorithm Based on Proxy Re-encryption for Cloud Storage

Yihui Cui, Zhiyong Peng, Wei Song[*,**], Xiaojuan Li,
Fangquan Cheng, and Luxiao Ding

Computer School, Wuhan University, Wuhan, China
{cuiyihui,peng,songwei,lxj,cheng,dingluxiao}@whu.edu.cn

Abstract. Users are motivated to outsource their data into the cloud for its great flexibility and economic saving. However, outsourcingdata to cloud also increases the risk of privacy leak.A straightforward method to protect the users'privacy is to encrypt the files before outsourcing.The existing group key management methods always presume that the server is trustworthy, but cloud storage applications do not meet this condition. Therefore, how to manage the group key to enable authenticated usersto access the files securely and efficientlyis still a challenging problem.In our paper, wepropose a Time-basedGroup Key Management (TGKM)algorithmforcryptographiccloud storage applications, which uses the proxy re-encryption algorithm to transfermajorcomputingtask of the group key management to the cloud server.So, the proposed TGKM scheme greatly reduces the user's computation and storage overhead and makes full use of cloud server to achieve an efficient group key management for the cryptographic cloud storage applications.Moreover, we introduce a key seed mechanism to generate a time-based dynamic group key which effectively strengthens the cloud data security. Our security analysis and performance evaluations both show that the proposed TGKM scheme is a secure and efficient group key management protocol for the cloud storage applications with low overheads of computation and communication.

Keywords: cryptographic cloud storage,proxy re-encryption,group key management.

1 Introduction

Cloud storage is a typical service model of online outsourcing storage where data is stored in virtualized pools which are generally hosted by third parties. Companies need only pay for the storage they actually use. But when data is stored into cloud, user simultaneously loses the control of his data. It makes that the unauthorized accesses from hackers even cloud service providers is inevitable. Security is one of the most important problems that should be addressed in cloud storage applications [1].

---

[*] Corresponding author.
[**] This work is partially supported by National Natural Science Foundation of China No. 61202034, 61232002 and Program for Innovative Research Team of Wuhan(2014070504020237).

L. Chen et al. (Eds.): APWeb 2014, LNCS 8709, pp. 117–128, 2014.

In recent years, many scholars have proposed the use of encryption methods to protect users' privacy in cloud storage applications [2-6]. In cryptographic cloud storage application framework data owner encrypts files before outsourcing to protect his privacy. Because the authorized users have the key, they could decrypt the files after downloading. Obviously, unauthorized users, attackers, even the cloud service provider can't breach user's privacy without authentication. In cryptographic cloud storage, data owner need not only store files on the cloud but also shares these files to some group users. Therefore, group key management is an important problem in cloud storage, and it is also the main motivation of our paper.

The problem of group key management in cryptographic cloud storage environment is different from the traditional one. In a cryptographic cloud storage model, computing tasks should be transferred to the cloud as much as possible and ensure user privacy at the same time. The main contributions of our work are:

— We propose a suitable group key management method of cloud storage, which transfers calculations to the cloud computing service providers, who can't get the group key.
— The data owner and authorized group users compute different group keys in different phases with the same seed, rather than always using the same group key, so our method is safer. Besides, because group key in a phase is computed by key seed, the distribute group key number of times is less than traditional method

The remainder of this paper is organized as follows: in Section 2, we discuss the related work. Then we introduce several cryptographic primitives in Section 3. Section 4 details the TGKM. Security analyses of TGKM will be given in Section 5. Finally, we evaluate the performance of our mechanism in Section 6, and conclude this paper in Section 7.

2   Related Work

There are many group key management algorithms to address the problem of group key management in the network environments, some are depended on a trusted group key server, and others don't need any trusted group key servers.

Xiao proposes a cryptographic file system called CKS-CFS based on the security assumption that the CKS-CFS is trusted [7]. A trusted Group Key Server (GKS) is introduced to manage file encryption keys in a centralized manner and to enable the employment of flexible access control policies. But if GKS is invaded, hacker can get all the private files.

Goh proposes the SiRiUS which doesn't need a trusted group key server usually let each user has a public and private key pairs to obtain the group key [8]. When a data owner wants to share data, he uses the group key to encrypt the file and uses the authorized user's public keys to encrypt the group key, and then he uploads the encrypted file and encrypted keys to the cloud. The authorized user uses his private key to decrypt the group key by which the authorized user decrypts the encrypted file. This method is one of the simplest group key managements, but it requires that the data owner encrypts the group key for each user using his public key, which will generate a great overhead of computing at the data owner. Kim proposes a secure protocol called Tree-based Group Diffie–Hellman (TGDH) that is both simple and fault-tolerant[9]. In order to protect the security of data, different files are encrypted by different keys. But the processes of key negotiation in TGDH need to replace the user's private key, so the algorithm is not suitable for group key management in cloud storage.

3   Preliminaries

3.1   Proxy Re-encryption

Proxy re-encryption schemes are cryptosystems which allow third-parties (proxies) to alter a ciphertext which has been encrypted for one party, so that it may be decrypted by another. However the third-parties can't get the secret value [10]. Blaze presents the BBS, Elgamal-based scheme operating over two group G_1, G_2 of prime order q with a bilinear map $e: G_1 \times G_1 \rightarrow G_2$. The system parameters are random generators $g \in G_1$ and $Z = e(g, g) \in G_2$.

- Key Generation(KG). The user A select random $x \in Z_q$. A's key pair is the form $pk_a = g^a$, $sk_a = a$.
- Re-Encryption Key Generation(RG). A user A delegates to B by publishing the re-encryption key $rk_{A \rightarrow B} = g^{b/a} \in G_1$, computed from B's public key.
- First-Level Encryption(E_1). to encrypt a message $m \in G_2$ under pk_a in such a way that it can only be the holder of sk_a, output c=(Z^{ak}, mZ^k) .
- Second-level Encryption(E_2). to encrypt a message $m \in G_2$ under pk_a in such a way it can be decrypted by user A and   his delegates, output c=(g^{ak}, mZ^k).
- Re-Encryption(R). Anyone can change a second-level ciphertext for A into a first-level ciphertext for B with $rk_{A \rightarrow B}$. From $c_a = (g^{ak}, mZ^k)$, compute $e(g^{ak}, g^{b/a}) = Z^{bk}$ and publish $c_b = (Z^{bk}, mZ^k)$.
- Decryption(D_1, D_2) . To decrypt a first-level ciphertext $c_a = (\alpha, \beta)$ with secret key sk =a, compute $m = \beta / \alpha^{1/a}$. To decrypt a second-level ciphertext $c_a = (\alpha, \beta)$ with secret key sk=a, compute m=$\beta / e(\alpha, g)^{1/a}$.

3.2   Chinese Remainder Theorem

Suppose $m_1, m_2, ..., m_k$ are positive integers that are pairwise coprime. Then, for any given sequence of integers $a_1, a_2, ..., a_k$, there exists an integer x solving the following system of simultaneous congruences[11].

$$\left. \begin{array}{l} x \equiv a_1 \ (mod \ m_1) \\ x \equiv a_2 \ (mod \ m_2) \\ \vdots \\ x \equiv a_k \ (mod \ m_k) \end{array} \right\} \tag{1}$$

Furthermore, all solutions x of this system are congruent modulo the product $N=m_1 m_2 \ldots m_k$, so the value of $x \bmod N$ is unique.

4   TGKM: A Time-Based Group Key Management Algorithm

Table 1 shows the notations in the following of this paper.

Table 1. Notations

Notations	Description
$GK_{file(j)}$	Files which upload in T_j is encrypted by $GK_{file(j)}$
S_{key}	Key seed S_{key}
$S_{forward(i)}$	Forward key seed in T_i is used to compute $K_{forward}$ in one phase
$S_{backward(i)}$	Backward key seed in T_i is used to compute $K_{backward}$ in one
$K_{forward(j)}$	phase
$K_{backward(j)}$	Forward assistant key in T_j is used to compute GK_{file} in T_j
$\{file\}_{GK_{file}}$	Backward assistant key in T_j is used to compute GK_{file} in T_j
$\{S_{key}\}PK_A$	The file is encrypted by GK_{file}
$RK_{A \to B}$	The S_{key} is encrypted by user A's public key
T_j	The re-encryption key from A to B
g	The time phase in T_j
	The system parameters are random generators $g \in G_1$

We design TGKM to implement an efficient and scalable group key management service for the cloud storage applications. The TGKM system model has three parties as follows:

(1) **Data Owner:** data owner encrypts his data and stores data in the cryptographic cloud storage system, and he not only uses data but also authorizes data to other user groups to access his data.

(2) **Authorized Group Users:** users who have the permission to access the encrypted data after authorized by the data owner to the group which the users belong to.

(3) **Cloud Service Provider:** the cloud offers data storage and sharing services to users. It follows our proposed protocol in general, but also tries to find out as much secret information as possible.

TGKM uses two steps to share the GK_{file} in the authenticated group users. GK_{file} is not fixed in various phases, so even GK_{file} is disclosed during any period, other GK_{file} is still secure.

In the first step, TGKM shares the key seed S_{key} based on proxy re-encryption mechanism in the authorized group users. We use the S_{key} to represent the key seed which consists of $S_{forward}$ and $S_{backward}$. The pair $\{S_{forward}, S_{backward}\}$ can compute file encryption group key. Then data owner and authorized users further compute time-based group keys from S_{key} to enable forward security and back ward security. Fig.1 describes TGKM for cryptographic cloud storage applications, and it is composed of three parts: data owner domain, cloud domain, and authorized user domain. Data owner domain is a full trusted service domain in which data owner generates key seed S_{key} and uploads it to the cloud after encryption. The cloud domain is an untrusted service domain with powerful computing capability, TGKM introduces a proxy re-encryption tree structure to efficiently share key in the authorized group users by transferring data owner encrypted S_{key} to the key seed encrypted by authorized group users. In TGKM structure, the authorized users in the authorized group user domain could download the transferred encrypted S_{key} and decrypts it by his private key.

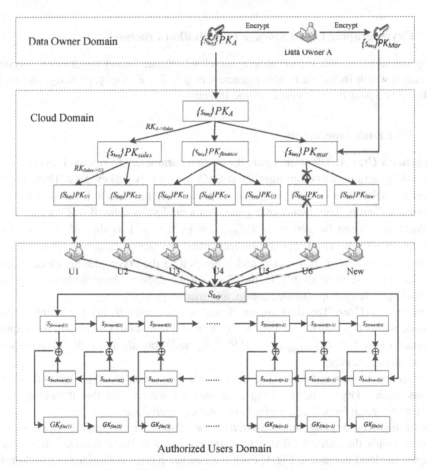

Fig. 1. Time-based Group Key Management for Cryptographic Cloud Storage (TGKM)

In the second step, as shown in the Fig. 1, the authorized group users get a set of keys $S_{forward(1)}$ and $S_{backward(n)}$ from the key seed S_{key}. In TGKM model, every authorized user group builds a hash function link to compute the GK_{file}. For example in Fig. 1, U_1 gets S_{key} which includes $S_{forward(1)}$ and $S_{backward(k)}$ from cloud, and U_1 can compute $S_{forward(i+1)}$ from $S_{forward(i)}$ and compute $S_{backward(i-1)}$ from $S_{backward(i)}$. And then

U_1 can get all the pair keys $S_{forward(i)}$ and $S_{backward(i)}$ $(1 \leq i \leq n)$ based on which further to get $GK_{file(i)}$ through $GK_{file(i)} = S_{forward(i)} \oplus S_{backward(i)}$. So, by this mechanism the key GK_{file} in any period is determined and enable a time-based key shared to achieve the forward security and backward security. For the data owner and the authorized group users can compute the same $S_{forward(i)}$ and $S_{backward(i)}$, they can share the same $GK_{file(i)}$ of any phase.

In this work, we just consider honest but curious cloud servers as [2] does. That is to say, cloud servers will follow our proposed protocol in general, but try to find out as much secret information as possible based on their inputs.

4.1 Cryptographic Cloud Storage Initialization Processes

During initial processes, the cryptographic cloud storage server generates the system parameters which include a random generators $g \in G_1$, $Z = e(g,g) \in G_2$, and m_1, m_2 which are two positive pairwise coprime integers.

4.2 User Basic Operations

- **Register a User A.** The user A gets the system parameters from cloud server first of all, and generates a random number $\alpha \in Z_P^*$ as A's private key SK_A. Then A generates his public key $PK_A=[g, h=g^\alpha]$ and uploads PK_A to cloud to finish registration.
- **Create a Group.** The data owner generates a random number $\beta \in Z_P^*$ as the group private key. Then he generates $PK_{group} = [g, h = g^\beta]$ as the public key of the group. Finally, he computes the re-encryption key $RK_{A \to group} = \beta/\alpha$ in which α is the private key of data owner and uploads it to the cryptographic cloud storage server. For example in Fig.1, the data owner creates three authorized groups including: sales group, finance group, and market group.
- **Authorize a User.** The data owner A authorizes a user B and put it into certain group. A gets B's public key $PK_B = [g, h = g^\gamma]$ from cloud. And then A computes re-encryption key $RK_{group \to B} = g^{\gamma/\beta} \in G_1$ and uploads it to the cryptographic cloud storage server.
- **Revoke an Authorized User.** The data owner A requests cloud server to delete the re-encryption key of the revoking user. In Fig.1 we can see that the cloud server deletes the edge from PK_{mar} to U_6 to revoke U_6's privilege.
- **Build the Key Management Structure in Cloud.** Cryptographic cloud storage server builds the authorized tree to share resources in the authorized users. As is shown in cloud domain in Fig.1, each data owner has an authorized tree to describe the shared relationship of his resources. In the authorized tree, the root node stores key seed which is encrypted by the data owner's public key, each the child node presents a user group which stores key seed encrypted by the group public key, and every leaf node presents an authorized user stores the key seed encrypted by user's public key. And the edges describe the re-encryption operations and store the proxy re-encryption key.

4.3   The First Step of TGKM: Key Seed Distribution

The main motivation of our paper is to enable a time-based access control for the cloud storage applications. We introduce a key seed mechanism to achieve it. In this section, we introduce the key seed distribution.

The data owner A encrypts a key seed S_{key} under PK_A in such a way it can be decrypted by A and his delegates. A uploads $\{S_{key}\}PK_A$ to the cloud server.

$$\{S_{key}\}PK_A = (g^{\alpha k}, S_{key}Z^k), \tag{2}$$

The TGKM cloud server masters proxy re-encryption key $RK_{A\rightarrow group} = \beta/\alpha$ and $RK_{group\rightarrow B} = g^{\gamma/\beta}$ to distribute key seeds in all the authorized groups and their users, so that the cryptographic cloud server can transfer the key seed encrypted by data owner to the key seed encrypted by authorized group public key. The re-encryption from A to a group is described in equation (3) and (4) in which g^{β} is the group's public key. The transfer from a group to a user is shown in (5) and (6).

$$g^{\beta k} = (g^{\alpha k})^{\beta/\alpha} \tag{3}$$
$$\{S_{key}\}PK_{group} = (g^{\beta k}, S_{key}Z^k), \tag{4}$$
$$e(g^{\beta k}, g^{\gamma/\beta}) = Z^{\gamma k} \tag{5}$$
$$\{S_{key}\}PK_{user} = (Z^{\gamma k}, S_{key}Z^k) . \tag{6}$$

Through the above re-encryption, the authorized group user can decrypt key seed from key seed encrypted by the data owner. The decryption is illustrated in equation (7) in which γ is authorized user's private key.

$$S_{key} = S_{key}Z^k / (Z^{\gamma k})^{1/\gamma}, \tag{7}$$

After getting the key seed, the user can compute GK_{file} by $K_{forward}$ and $K_{backward}$ which is generated by the key seed. For example in Fig.1, the data owner generates $\{S_{key}\}PK_A$ and uploads it to the cloud server. The cloud server transfers $\{S_{key}\}PK_A$ to $\{S_{key}\}PK_{sales}$ by $RK_{A\rightarrow sales}$, then transfers $\{S_{key}\}PK_{sales}$ to $\{S_{key}\}PK_{U1}$ by $RK_{sales\rightarrow U1}$. As a result, the user U_1 can decrypt $\{S_{key}\}PK_{U1}$ to get S_{key}.

If the data owner just grants an encrypted file's accessing privilege to a group, he encrypts the key seed S_{key} by the group public key. Such as in the Fig.1, the data owner only allows the market group to access an encrypted file, and then he encrypts the seed by the market group public key, and uploads $\{S_{key}\}PK_{Mar}$ in which PK_{Mar} is the public key of group market to the cloud.

4.4   The Second Step of TGKM: Computing GK_{file} by Key Seed

In our TGKM scheme, we introduce key seed S_{key} to enable the efficient and flexible time-based access control. The file encryption key management in TGKM is a time-based dynamic key which uses different key to encrypt files in different period.

The data owner generates Key seed S_{key} which consists of a forward seed $S_{forward}$ and a backward seed $S_{backward}$. The prior $S_{forward}$ can compute the next

$S_{forward}$ by a hash function. For the same reason, the behind $S_{backward}$ can compute the prior $S_{backward}$ by another hash function.

$$\left. \begin{array}{l} S_{forward(i+1)} = f_{forwardhash}\ (S_{forward(i)}) \\ S_{backward(i)} = f_{backwardhash}\ (S_{backward(i+1)}) \end{array} \right\} \tag{8}$$

For example, in Fig.2 If data owner wants to limit a group user accessing the uploaded files from T_1 to T_3, The key seed he distributed is $\{S_{forward(i)},\ S_{backward(i)}\}$. If data owner wants to limit a group accessing to the uploaded files from T_1 to T_6, The key seed he distributed is $\{\ S_{forward(i)},\ S_{backward(i+1)}\}$.

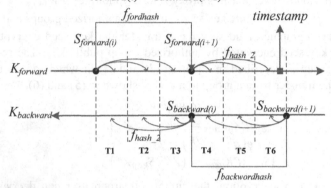

Fig. 2. Key seed mechanism to enable time-based data access control

Data owner and authorized group users use $S_{forward(i)}$ and $S_{backward(i)}$ to compute $K_{forward(j)}$ and $K_{backward(j)}$ separately by hash function (9). Every $S_{forward(i)}$ and $S_{backward(i)}$ can compute $K_{forward(j)}$ or $K_{backward(j)}$ of one time period. T_j is the time phase.

$$\left. \begin{array}{l} K_{forward(j)} = f_{hash\_2}\ (S_{forward(i)}, T_j) \\ K_{backward(j)} = f_{hash\_2}(S_{backward(i)}, T_j) \end{array} \right\} \tag{9}$$

In Fig.2, $S_{forward(i)}$ can compute $K_{forward}$ from T_1 to T_3. $S_{backward(i)}$ can compute $K_{backward}$ from T_1 to T_3. The data owner and authorized group users shared m1 and m2 which meets $gcd(m_i, m_j) = 1$ in formula (10). When they have the same $K_{forward(j)}$ and $K_{backward(j)}$, they can generate the same $GK_{file(j)}$ based on Chinese remainder theorem.

$$\left. \begin{array}{l} GK_{file(j)} \equiv K_{forward(j)}\ (mod\ m_1) \\ GK_{file(j)} \equiv K_{backward(j)}(\ mod\ m_2) \end{array} \right\} \tag{10}$$

Data owner and authorized group users can get the same $\{\ S_{forward(i)},\ S_{backward(i)}\}$, so they can compute the same file encrypted group key. In Fig.2 user can generate $K_{forward(j)}$ in every phases by the forward seed $S_{forward(i)}$, and back forward seed $S_{backward(i)}$ can generate $K_{backward(j)}$, and then generate the $GK_{file(j)}$ at a certain period.

Algorithm 1. Compute file encryption group key $GK_{file(j)}$ by S_{key}

Input: $m_1, m_2, S_{forward(i)}, S_{backward(i)}, T_j$

Output: File encryption key $GK_{file(j)}$

1. $K_{forward(j)} = f_{hash\_2}(S_{forward(i)}, T_j)$
2. $K_{backward(j)} = f_{hash\_2}(S_{backward(i)}, T_j)$
3. $C \leftarrow 1.$
4. $u \leftarrow m_1^{-1} \bmod m_2.$
5. $C \leftarrow u \times C \bmod m_2.$
6. $u \leftarrow K_{forward(j)}, x \leftarrow u.$
7. $u \leftarrow (K_{backward(j)} - x)C \bmod m_2, x \leftarrow x + um_1, GK_{file(j)} = x$
8.   Return $GK_{file(j)}$

4.5   Data Sharing to Group Users

When the data owner wants to upload a shared file, he gets the current time as the *timestamp* and computes encrypted file group key $GK_{file(j)}$ in the time phase by key seed, and encrypts file by $GK_{file(j)}$. Finally, the data owner uploads the encrypted file and the timestamp to the cloud server.

$$Files_{upload} = [\{file\}_{GK_{file(j)}}, timestamp] \tag{11}$$

When an authorized group user attempts to access a file, he firstly downloads $[\{file\}_{GK_{file(j)}}, timestamp]$. After downloaded, he computes encrypted file key $GK_{file(j)}$ by the algorithm 1 and decrypts $\{file\}_{GK_{file(j)}}$.

For example in Fig. 2, when data owner uploads a file, he gets the current time as timestamp. Then the data owner determines that accessing time phase is T_6. Finally, he computes the $GK_{file(6)}$ by $S_{forward(i+1)}$ and $S_{backward(i+1)}$. The authorized user can get the timestamp from $Files_{upload}$, and he determines that time phase is T_6. Consequently, he can get the $GK_{file(6)}$ by $S_{forward(i+1)}$ and $S_{backward(i+1)}$ to achieve the time-based accessing.

5   Security and Performance Analysis

5.1   TGKM Correctness Guarantee

Because the data owner and the authorized group share the same timestamp, they can determine the time phase which the timestamp is belonged to. They also get the same pair $\{S_{forward(i)}, S_{backward(i)}\}$, so they can compute the same pair $\{K_{forward(j)}, K_{backward(j)}\}$. According to Chinese remainder theorem, the data owner and authorized group users can get the consistent $GK_{file(j)}$ by formula (10). By the TGKM mechanism, authorized user can only get the corresponding seed key which is generated by the data owner according to his own will. By the seed key mechanism, we achieve a time-based access control to limit all the authorized users accessing data in the period of time defined by the data owner.

5.2   Forward Security and Backward Security Guarantee

There are two types of security requirements on a secure group key management system: the **forward security** and the **backward security**. The former refers to a newly joined user cannot gain access to the past group keys. And the latter refers to after a user has left the secure group, he should not be able to gain access to the future group keys [14]. The proposed TGKM can fully meet the forward security and the backward security. The forward security requires that the authorized group user can't access any file encryption group key $GK_{file(j)}$ before start time of key seed. This notion was first proposed by Günther[15]. The backward security requires that a revoked user can't access file encryption group key $GK_{file(j)}$ after end time of key seed. In our key seed structure, the authorized user only knows $\{S_{forward(i)}, S_{backward(k)}\}$ $(i<=k)$, so he can only obtain $K_{forward}$ and $K_{backward}$ from phase i to k, that is to say he just can compute file encryption group key GK_{file} from phase i to k. Because the front forward key seed $S_{forward(i)}$ can compute the back forward key seed $S_{forward(i+1)}$ by hash function, but a posterior forward key seed $S_{forward(i+1)}$ can't compute the prior forward key seed $S_{forward(i)}$. It is as the same to the backward key's computation.

5.3   Computing Overhead Analysis

In TGKM, most of group key management computing operations is transferred to cloud. For computing $GK_{file(j)}$ by key seed, the main computing overhead is to compute $GK_{file(j)}$ by Chinese remainder theorem, so the time complexity is almost linear. And the computing overhear of cloud sever is $O(h)$ in which h is the number of authorized users. As the TGKM algorithm mentioned above, the computing overhead at the user is related to the time of computing GK_{file} by forward and backward seed keys, so it is $O(1)$. In the experimental section, we will carry out experiments to evaluate the performance of TGKM's efficiency.

6   Experiments

In this section, we carry out experiments to evaluate the performance of proposed TGKM. All the experiments are executed under Ubuntu with an Inter Pentium 2.1GHz Processor and 1GB memory. The re-encryption algorithm is used JHU-MIT Proxy Re-cryptography Library [12]. We evaluate the efficiency of TGKM including: cost of distribution the keys at the data owner, computing overhead on the cloud server and cost of getting the keys at the client.

In the time cost experiments of data owner distributing the keys, we compare TGKM to SiRiUS, TGDH, and ABE. The experimental results are illustrated in the Fig. 3. As the results shown in the Fig.3 (a), the distributing group key cost on the data owner of SiRiUS and TGDH both rise with users' size increasing, while TGKM's time cost is almost not changed. Analyzing this phenomenon, we find that TGDH is a tree-based group key management algorithm which makes the tree layer increasing with the number of users increasing, so that key negotiation time increases as well. It is also in agreement with the experimental results in Fig. 3(a). However, TGKM data owner only encrypts key seed once based on the group, so the time cost of TGKM will not rise with user increasing. ABE is an

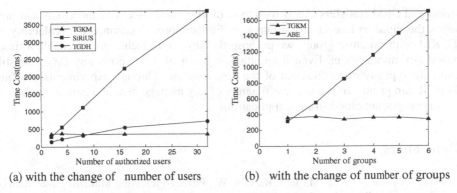

(a) with the change of number of users   (b) with the change of number of groups

Fig. 3. Time cost of data owner distribution group key

efficient find-grained authentication method which can be a method of group key management by treating a group as an attribute [13]. The experiments in Fig.3(b) shows the time overhead of TGKM and ABE. With the number of user group increasing, our proposed TGKM achieve a better computing performance than ABE.

Fig.4 shows the time cost of authorized user' computing the group key. The time cost of TGKM and SiRiUS is approximately equal. The time cost is decrypt group key by authorized user private key. And the time cost of TGKM is almost not changed with authorized user number increasing. But the time cost of TGDH is increase with authorized user number increase. The authorized user needs to negotiate with other group user.

Fig.5 shows cloud computing time cost. The overload is transfer from data owner to cloud. To the first group user, cloud has two proxy re-encryption operations. To the other users of the same group, cloud just has one proxy re-encryption operation.

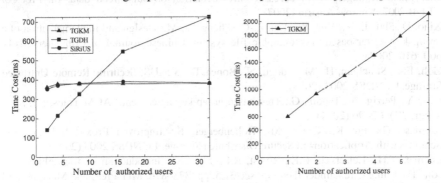

Fig. 4. Time cost for a user to get his key   **Fig. 5.** Cloud computing time

7   Conclusion

When enterprises or individuals use cryptographic cloud storage applications to outsource their sensitive data, how to efficiently share data in the authorized group users without privacy leak is still one of the most challenging tasks. In this paper, we propose a novel time-based group key management (TGKM) in cryptographic cloud storage. TGKM transfers much workload of key management to the cloud and prevents the cloud to master any group key. Furthermore, to enhance the scalability of TGKM with dynamic group, we propose the key seed mechanism to enable a time-based key management. Even if an attacker gets a file encryption key GK_{file}, he still can't decrypt any other files out of the time window. Through experiments, we find TGKM can greatly improve the efficiency of key management and can be applied to the cryptographic cloud storage applications.

References

1. Cao, N., Wang, C., Li, M., Ren, K., Lou, W.: Privacy-Preserving Multi-Keyword Ranked Search over Encrypted Cloud Data. IEEE Trans. Parallel Distrib. Syst. 25(1), 222–233 (2014)
2. Yu, S., Wang, C., Ren, K., Lou, W.: Achieving secure, scalable and fine-grained data access control in cloud computing. In: Proceedings of IEEE INFOCOM 2010, pp. 15–19 (2010)
3. Wang, Q., Wang, C., Ren, K., Lou, W., Li, J.: Enabling Public Auditability and Data Dynamics for Storage Security in Cloud Computing. IEEE Trans. Parallel Distrib. Syst. 22(5), 847–859 (2011)
4. Kamara, S., Lauter, K.: Cryptographic Cloud Storage. In: Sion, R., Curtmola, R., Dietrich, S., Kiayias, A., Miret, J.M., Sako, K., Sebé, F. (eds.) FC 2010 Workshops. LNCS, vol. 6054, pp. 136–149. Springer, Heidelberg (2010)
5. Hong, C., lv, Z., Zhang, M., Feng, D.: A Secure and Efficient Role-Based Access Policy towards Cryptographic Cloud Storage. In: Wang, H., Li, S., Oyama, S., Hu, X., Qian, T. (eds.) WAIM 2011. LNCS, vol. 6897, pp. 264–276. Springer, Heidelberg (2011)
6. De Capitani di Vimercati, S., Foresti, S., Jajodia, S., Paraboschi, S., Samarati, P.: Over-encryption: Management of access control evolution on outsourced data. In: Proc. of VLDB 2007, Vienna, Austria (2007)
7. Xiao, D., Shu, J.-W., Xue, W., Liu, Z.-C., Zheng, W.-M.: Design and implementation of a group key server-based cryptographic file system. Chinese Journal of Computers 31(4), 600–610 (2008)
8. Goh, E.-J., Shacham, H., Modadugu, N., Boneh, D.: SiRiUS: Securing Remote Untrusted Storage. In: NDSS 2003 (2003)
9. Kim, Y., Perrig, A., Tsudik, G.: Tree-based group key agreement. ACM Trans. Inf. Syst. Secur. 7(1), 60–96 (2004)
10. Ateniese, G., Fu, K., Green, M., Hohenberger, S.: Improved Proxy Re-Encryption Schemes with Applications to Secure Distributed Storage. In: NDSS 2005 (2005)
11. Cormen, T.H., Leiserson, C.E., Rivest, R.L., Stein, C.: Introduction to Algorithms, 2nd edn. The Chinese remainder theorem, sec.31.5, pp. 873–876. MIT Press and McGraw-Hill (2001) ISBN 0-262-03293-7
12. http://spar.isi.jhu.edu/~mgreen/prl/
13. Bethencourt, J., Sahai, A., Waters, B.: Ciphertext-Policy Attribute-Based Encryption. In: 28th IEEE Symposium on Security and Privacy 2007, pp. 321–334 (2007)
14. Yang, Y.R., Lam, S.S.: A Secure Group Key Management Communication Lower Bound, University of Texas at Austin, Austin, TX (2000)
15. Günther, C.G.: An identity-based key-exchange protocol. In: Quisquater, J.-J., Vandewalle, J. (eds.) EUROCRYPT 1989. LNCS, vol. 434, pp. 29–37. Springer, Heidelberg (1990)

A Fragile Watermarking Scheme
for Modification Type Characterization
in 2D Vector Maps

Mingliang Yue, Zhiyong Peng, and Yuwei Peng*

Computer School, Wuhan University, Wuhan, Hubei, 430072, China
ywpeng@whu.edu.cn

Abstract. As the most important geographical data, 2D vector maps have been widely used in various areas. Meanwhile, the increasingly simplified data access and manipulation methods in geographical data related applications make it important to verify data truthfulness. In this paper, we propose a fragile watermarking scheme for the content authentication of 2D vector maps. The scheme embeds (detects) two kinds of watermarks, i.e., group watermark and object watermark, into (from) each object. Based on the patterns extracted from the detection results, the scheme can not only detect and locate data modifications, but also characterize modification types. Both theoretical analysis and experimental evaluation are carried out to verify the fragility of the proposed scheme.

Keywords: Vector maps, Content authentication, Fragile watermarking, Modification characterization.

1 Introduction

Geographical data have long been incorporated in various applications for more convenient information visualization and sharing [1]. Due to the nature of data sharing, the digital data of GIS related applications is easy to be duplicated and tampered with. Therefore, the content authentication methods are in need to verify data truthfulness.

Watermarking is one of the most important techniques for the security consideration of digital data [2]. Basically, watermarking means slightly modifying the host data and forcing it to imply certain secret information. The information (i.e., watermark) can then be detected from the watermarked data for ownership assertion [3], content authentication [4], etc. The watermarking scheme for content authentication is called fragile watermarking scheme. In a fragile watermarking scheme, the embedded watermark should be sensitive to modifications so as to detect and locate modifications.

In fact, fragile watermarking has been predominantly used for the content authentication of digital contents, and large amounts of fragile watermarking

---

* Corresponding author.

L. Chen et al. (Eds.): APWeb 2014, LNCS 8709, pp. 129–140, 2014.
© Springer International Publishing Switzerland 2014

schemes have been proposed for various types of digital data, e.g., images [5], audios [6], videos [7] and databases [8]. Recently, researchers recognized the importance of authenticating 2D vector maps [9], the most widely used geographical data [10]. By borrowing experiences from multimedia watermarking, a few fragile watermarking schemes have been proposed for vector maps. The schemes first divide the underlying map into blocks [11][12] or groups of vertices/objects [13][14][15]. Then, a fragile watermark is generated from and embedded into each block (group). During the detection, the data modifications are located by comparing the generated and detected block (group) fragile watermarks: a block (group) is considered integrated only if the generated and detected fragile watermarks are the same.

The above schemes for vector maps are effective and can properly detect and locate illegal modifications. However, those schemes share two common problems. First, the authentication can only be carried out on block (group) level. Namely, if any vertices or objects in a block or a group are modified, then the whole block or group will be considered tampered. This means certain (possibly quite a lot of) un-modified vertices and objects that can be legally used may be negatively considered tampered. This relatively rough detection granularity may result in extra time for reacquiring the original legal data. Second, the types of modifications (i.e., object addition, deletion and modification) cannot be characterized from the detection results. As noted in [8], modification type characterization is important for distinguishing usable data elements from unusable ones, and can guide a more effective data recovery.

In accordance with the aforementioned problems, in this paper, for 2D vector maps, we propose a fragile watermarking scheme that can detect, locate and characterize data modifications on object level. The main idea is to embed two kinds of watermarks, i.e., group watermark and object watermark, into each object. Consequently, if the watermarked map is modified, the scheme can acquire different detection patterns based on the detection results of the two kinds of watermarks. The detection patterns are localizable and distinguishable to locate modifications and characterize modification types. Our contributions include (1) developing a fragile watermarking scheme that competes the state of art in (a) guaranteeing a more precise detection granularity and (b) having the ability of modification type characterization; (2) analyzing the fragility of the scheme theoretically in a probabilistic way; and (3) verifying the fragility of the scheme empirically.

The remainder of this paper is organized as follows. In Section 2, we introduce some preliminaries. Then, the proposed fragile watermarking scheme is described and the fragility of the scheme is analyzed in Section 3. Finally, performance study and conclusions are given in Sections 4 and 5 respectively.

2   Preliminaries

This section introduces the framework (and a detail technique) that will be adopted in the paper, and discusses the data modifications a fragile watermarking scheme proposed for vector map should detect and characterize.

2.1 Generate-and-Embed/Detect Framework

Generally, almost all the existing fragile watermarking schemes are subject to generate-and-embed/detect framework [4]. Namely, the schemes first generate a data summary, i.e., fragile watermark, from the host data, and then embed this summary into the data. Further, during watermark detection, the fragile watermark is again generated and then compared with the fragile watermark detected from the data. If the data is integrated, then the two watermarks should be exactly the same, otherwise, they should be different.

Two important requirements should be fulfilled in the afore-process. First, there should be an obligated change on the generated watermark if any modification is made to the data used for watermark generation. This is achieved by adopting cryptographic hash function for watermark generation. A cryptographic hash function, $H()$, has two important properties: (1) one-wayness, it is computationally infeasible, for a given value V' to find a V such that $H(V) = V'$; (2) randomness, changing even one bit of the hash input causes random changes to the output bits. The first property guarantees the overall security of a watermarking scheme, while the second is the foundation of fragility. Potential cryptographic hash functions include MD5 and SHA hash [16]. The second requirement is induced by the first one: to avoid false positive (i.e., the reporting of the data modifications caused by watermark embedding), the watermark embedding should not interfere the watermark generation.

In this paper, we also adopt the generate-and-embed/detect framework, in which cryptographic hash function is used for watermark generation.

2.2 Data Modifications

General data modifications include data element addition, deletion and modification [5][6][7][8]. The data element may be pixel block, frame, motion vector and tuple for image, audio, vedio and relational database. Since a vector map is commonly modeled as a set of objects, denoted as $VM = \{O_1, O_2, \ldots, O_n\}$, where each $O_i = \langle p_0, p_1, \ldots, p_{l_i-1} \rangle$ is composed of a sequence of ordered vertices, and each $p_j = (x_j, y_j)$ is a vertex represented by a pair of coordinates. In this paper, we regard object as data element.

The meaning of object deletion and addition are obvious. In geographical field, object modification means altering an object with general structure preserved [2]. We adopt turning function to qualitatively model the concept. Turning function is one of the most effective ways that can be used to qualitatively describe an object's geometry [17]. It measures the angle φ of tangent as a function of arc length ℓ. From the function, an unique integral value, $Area_T$, can always be calculated to describe an object's geometry. Therefore, we link an $Area_T$-based identity to every object (i.e., using geometry to identify object), and regard the tampered object with identity (i.e., general structure) preserved as modified object [1]. For more information about turning function, please consult [17].

---

[1] We hold the assumption that $Area_T$ is identifiable, since a more distinguishable description can always be achieved by employing more detailed descriptions [17].

3   The Proposed Watermarking Scheme

On an overview level, our watermarking scheme embeds two kinds of fragile watermarks into every object by the following process: (1) extract an identity for each object based on its $Area_T$, and partition it into an object group; for each object in every group, (2) generate a group fragile watermark based on all the identities of the objects in the group, and embed it into the object; (3) generate an object fragile watermark based on all the vertices in the object, and embed it into the object. When the vector map needs to be verified, (4) the identities are extracted and the objects are partitioned into groups; for every object group, (5) the two kinds of fragile watermarks are detected from the objects, and the detection grid is constructed; (6) according to the detection pattern revealed in the grid, the tampered objects are located and the modification types are determined.

In the following we first introduce the proposed watermark embedding and detection methods in Sections 3.1 and 3.2. Then, the tamper locating and characterization method is introduced in Section 3.3. Finally, the fragility analysis is given in Section 3.4.

3.1   Watermark Embedding

Let $bs(a)$, $hb(a, b)$ and $bit(a, b)$ return the bit-size, the bits higher than b, and the b-th bit of $(a)_2$ respectively, where $(a)_2$ signifies the binary representation of a. For example, since $2.25 = (10.01)_2$, we have $bs(2.25) = 4$, $hb(2.25, -2) = 100$, $bit(2.25, -2) = 1$ ('-' signifies decimal place). Furthermore, we define $msb(a, b)$ as the function returns the most significant b bits of $(a)_2$ if $b \leq bs(a)$, otherwise, the function returns $(a)_2 || msb(a, b - bs(a))$, where $||$ signifies string concatenation, e.g., $msb(2.25, 3) = 100$, $msb(2.75, 5) = 10011$.

Based on the notations, in the **first step** of our embedding process we calculate for each object O_i an identity $id_i = hb(Area_{T_i}, \gamma)$, and partition the object into an object group $G_j = H(id_i || K) \bmod g$, where g and K are two parameters given by data owner representing the number of groups and secret key. We use the higher bits of $Area_T$ as object identity so that it can remain unchanged when only small perturbation is made to the object's structure - which is required by object modification defined in Section 2.2.

After group partition, for every group G_i with m_i objects, in the **second step**, we generate a *seed* $S_i = H(id_1 || id_2 || \ldots || id_{m_i} || K)$, $\forall j \in \{1, \ldots, m_i - 1\}$, $id_j \leq id_{j+1}$. Then, for every $O_j \in G_i$, in the **third step**, we generate and embed the group fragile watermark and object fragile watermark as follows. (1) Generate group fragile watermark as $W_j^g = msb(H(id_j || S_i || K), l_j)$, where l_j is the number of vertices in O_j. (2) Embed the kth ($0 \leq k \leq l_j - 1$) bit of W_j^g into the kth vertex's x-coordinate of O_j, by replacing the ζ-th bit of $(x_k)_2$ as the watermark bit, i.e., $bit(x_k, \zeta) = bit(W_j^g, k)$. The embedding position ζ should be determined in accordance with the map's precision tolerance τ to ensure data fidelity. (3) Generate object fragile watermark as $W_j^o = msb(H((\hat{x}_0 || \hat{y}_0) || \ldots || (\hat{x}_{l_j-1} || \hat{y}_{l_j-1}) || K), l_j)$, $\forall k \in \{0, \ldots, l_j - 1\}$, $\hat{x}_k = hb(x_k, \zeta -$

1), $\hat{y}_k = hb(y_k, \zeta)$. (4) Embed the kth bit of W_j^o into the kth vertex's y-coordinate, i.e., $bit(y_k, \zeta) = bit(W_j^o, k)$. We only use the bits higher than ζ of $(y_k)_2$ in object watermark generation to avoid the influence of watermark embedding (i.e., modifying $bit(y_k, \zeta)$) on the watermark generation. It is also to be noted that the group and object watermark embedding as a whole only makes negligible perturbations to objects' structures. The embedding rarely influences object identities, group seeds or the generated group watermarks (Actually, in our algorithm implementation, we avoid this influence by omitting $bit(x, \zeta)$ and $bit(y, \zeta)$ when calculating $Area_T$). However, any modification made to the watermarked map will cause change on either the generated or the detected values of the two kinds of watermarks.

3.2 Watermark Detection

During the watermark detection, all the objects in a suspicious map are divided into groups by the identification-and-partition method used in the watermark embedding, and each group is verified independently. Since each object covers two fragile watermarks, for every group G_i with m_i objects, a *detection grid* composed of two m_i-element vectors $V_i^o = \{v_1^o, v_2^o, \ldots, v_{m_i}^o\}$ and $V_i^g = \{v_1^g, v_2^g, \ldots, v_{m_i}^g\}$ is constructed to hold the detection results of object fragile watermarks and group fragile watermarks. Then, for every object $O_j \in G_i$, the object fragile watermark and group fragile watermark are generated and detected. The watermark generation is the same as in the watermark embedding. While for watermark detection, we have $bit(W_j^{gd}, k) = bit(x_k, \zeta)$, $bit(W_j^{od}, k) = bit(y_k, \zeta)$, where $0 \le k \le l_j - 1$, l_j is the number of vertices in O_j, W_j^{gd} and W_j^{od} are the detected group fragile watermark and object fragile watermark of O_j respectively. At last, to get v_j^g, the generated and detected group fragile watermarks are compared. If the two watermarks are exactly the same, v_j^g is true, otherwise, v_j^g is false. Likewise, v_j^o is acquired by comparing the generated and detected object fragile watermarks. Fig. 1 (a) shows the detection grid of an unmodified group with five objects (i.e., $m_i = 5$).

	O_1	O_2	O_3	O_4	O_5		O_1	O_2	O_3	O_4	O_5	O_6
V_i^g	T	T	T	T	T		F	F	F	F		
V_i^o	T	T	T	T	T		T	T	T	T		
	(a) an unmodified group						(b) a deleted group					
V_i^g	T	T	F	T	T		F	F	F	F	F	F
V_i^o	T	T	F	T	T		T	T	T	T	T	F
	(c) a modified group						(d) an added group					

Fig. 1. Detection grid for various modification types

3.3   Tamper Locating and Characterization

We demonstrate how the modifications can be located and the modification types can be characterized in this section.

Object Deletion. According to Fig. 1 (*b*), suppose O_1 is deleted, theoretically the group seed (see Section 3.1) will change due to the randomness property of the cryptographic hash function, which will in turn cause considerable change on all the relevant generated group watermarks. However, since the remaining objects themselves in the group are unmodified, the detected group watermarks remain unchanged, which means these detected watermarks will very likely be different from the generated ones, i.e., every $v_j^g \in V_i^g$ will very likely be false. We will model the expression *very likely* in a probabilistic way in Section 3.4. On the other hand, for object fragile watermarks that only depend on individual objects, the corresponding detection results are naively true. Consequently, we can get the detection grid shown in Fig. 1 (*b*) (Some of the "F" in V_i^g could probabilistically be "T"). Apparently, the locating of object deletions can only be done on group level. Let deleted-group convey the meaning that an object group has suffered at least one object deletion, then the *detection pattern* for an deleted-group can be defined as:

$$\bigwedge_{O_j \in G_i} v_j^o = True, \quad \bigwedge_{O_j \in G_i} v_j^g = False$$

The set of deleted-group(s) can be located as $G_{del} = \{G_i | \exists O_j \in G_i, \forall O_k \in G_i, v_j^g = False, v_k^o = True\}$.

Object Modification. According to Fig. 1 (*c*), suppose an object O_3 is modified to O_3'. By the definition of object modification, the modification does not influence the object's identity. Namely, the generated group watermarks of all the objects (including O_3') remain unchanged. Since the objects except O_3' are exactly the original ones, their detected group watermarks, generated and detected object watermarks remain unchanged. The detection results of their group watermarks and object watermarks will all be true. For O_3', its generated object watermark changes (due to the randomness property of the cryptographic hash function). Its detected object watermark and group watermark also change due to modification. Therefore, its detection result of group watermark and object watermark will very likely be false. Then, the detection grid for this situation is shown in Fig. 1 (*c*). The detection pattern for a modified-group (group suffers at least one object modification) can be defined as:

$$\bigwedge_{O_j \in G_i} v_j^o = False, \quad \bigwedge_{O_j \in G_i^T} v_j^g = True$$

where $G_i^T = \{O_j | O_j \in G_i, v_j^o = True\}$ is the subset of objects in G_i whose object watermark detection results are *True*. The set of modified object(s) can be located as $O_{mod} = \{O_i | v_i^o = False, G_j = argG(O_i), \forall O_k \in G_j^T, v_k^g = True\}$, where $argG(O_i)$ signifies the group O_i rests in. It is to be noted that the detection pattern does not include the group watermark detection result(s) of the modified object(s) (O_3' in this example), since both object addition (see 3.3) and object modification can lead to the detection of 'False' of an object's group watermark. Namely, this (these) result(s) does (do) not contribute to the modification type characterization.

Object Addition. As to object addition, according to Fig. 1 (d), suppose an object O_6 is added into the group. For the same reason as for object deletion, all the detection results of group fragile watermarks of the originally existing objects will every likely be false, and the results of their object fragile water-marks are true. As to O_6, since both the generated and detected values of its group and object fragile watermarks are random, the detection results of the two watermarks are very likely false. Therefore, the detection gird shown in Fig. 1 (d) can be acquired. The detection pattern for an added-group (group suffers at least one object addition) can be defined as:

$$\bigwedge_{O_j \in G_i} v_j^o = False, \quad \bigwedge_{O_j \in G_i^T} v_j^g = False$$

The set of added object(s) can be located as $O_{add} = \{O_i | v_i^o = False, G_j = argG(O_i), \exists O_k \in G_j^T, v_k^g = False\}$.

It is to be noted that if the identity of an object is modified due to a large magnitude object modification, then, two situations may occur. The first is that the object shifts into another group, then, the original group will follow the detection pattern of object deletion, and the destination group will follow the pattern of object addition. The second is that the object remains in the original group, and the detection results of the group will follow the pattern of object addition. No matter which situation occurs, the detection results agree with the intuition that a large magnitude modification can be considered as an addition along with a deletion.

3.4 Fragility Analysis

In this section, we aim to estimate how likely the modifications can be located and characterized in a probabilistic way. Since both the generation of object identity and fragile watermarks are secure-hash-based, without loss of generality, we take the following hypothesis during the analysis: 1) objects distribute uniformly in g object groups, every group contains m objects, and every object has l points (i.e., the length of object and group fragile watermarks are all l); 2) a data modification has equal probability to fall on any object in any group; 3) after data modification, every pair of the corresponding bits in the corresponding detected and generated watermarks has equal probability to be either the same as or different from each other, i.e., the probability that the two watermarks are exactly the same is $\frac{1}{2^l}$.

Object Addition. During the detection, an added object can be located and characterized if: the detection result of its object fragile watermark is false (p_1); while for the originally existing objects, the detection results of their group fragile watermarks have at least one false (p_2). That is, the probability that single object addition can be located and characterized is $p = p_1 * p_2 = (1 - \frac{1}{2^l})(1 - (\frac{1}{2^l})^m)$. For multiple object additions, since any object may fall into any group, suppose ω objects are inserted into the watermarked map, and the insertions cause k $(1 \leq k \leq min(\omega, g))$ added-groups, with ω_i $(1 \leq i \leq k, \sum_{i=1}^{k} \omega_i = \omega)$ objects inserted into group G_i. Then, the probability that all these added objects can be located and characterized is

$$p = \prod_{i=1}^{k}(1 - \frac{1}{2^l})^{\omega_i}(1 - (\frac{1}{2^l})^m) = (1 - \frac{1}{2^l})^\omega(1 - (\frac{1}{2^l})^m)^k$$

Apparently, the probability depends on the value of k. For a more explicit understanding, we give a lower bound of the probability in terms of m and ω as follows.

$$p = (1 - \frac{1}{2^l})^\omega(1 - (\frac{1}{2^l})^m)^k \geq (1 - \frac{1}{2^l})^\omega(1 - (\frac{1}{2^l})^m)^\omega \tag{1}$$

Object Deletion. As we have stated, object deletion can only be located and characterized on group level. For single object deletion, it can be located and characterized if: for all the remaining objects, their detection results of object fragile watermarks are true (p_1), while the results of the group fragile watermarks have at least one false (p_2). Since the results of the object fragile watermarks are naively true, we have $p_1 = 1$. The probability that single object deletion can be located and characterized is $p = p_2 = 1 - (\frac{1}{2^l})^{m-1}$. For multiple object deletions, suppose ω objects are deleted from the watermarked map, and the deletions cause k $(1 \leq k \leq min(\omega, g))$ deleted-groups, with w_i $(1 \leq i \leq k, 1 \leq \omega_i \leq m, \sum_{i=1}^{k} \omega_i = w)$ objects deleted from group G_i. Then, the probability that all these deleted objects can be located and characterized is $p = \prod_{i=1}^{k}(1 - (\frac{1}{2^l})^{m-\omega_i})$. Again, for a more explicit understanding, let us suppose every group has at least one object left after deletions, then the lower bound of the probability can be represented as

$$p = \prod_{i=1}^{k}(1 - (\frac{1}{2^l})^{m-\omega_i}) > (1 - \frac{1}{2^l})^k > (1 - \frac{1}{2^l})^\omega \tag{2}$$

Note that it is impossible to detect the deletion of a group if the entire group is deleted. However, the probability of an entire group deletion is very low [8]. This conclusion was also verified by our experimental results presented in Section 4.

Object Modification. A modified object can be located and characterized if: the detection result of its object fragile watermark is false (p_1); while for the unmodified objects (i.e., the objects with $v_i^o = True$), the detection results of their group fragile watermarks are true (p_2). Since the detection results of those group fragile watermarks are naively true, we have $p_2 = 1$. The probability that single object modification can be located and characterized is $p = p_1 = 1 - \frac{1}{2^l}$. For multiple object modifications, suppose ω objects has been modified, the probability that all the modified objects can be located and characterized is shown in Eq. 3.

$$p = (1 - \frac{1}{2^l})^\omega \tag{3}$$

According to the afore-analysis, it is easily to be noted that the larger l is, the more fragile our scheme will be. To highlight the importance of l, we give an even looser lower bound of Eq. 1, 2 and 3 as $p = (1 - \frac{1}{2^l})^{2\omega}$. This means that the fragility of the scheme can be guaranteed if objects have sufficient points. According to our experimental results in Section 4, most objects have adequate points. For objects whose points are inadequate, since the vertex coordinates are usually represented in 64-bit double-precision format, there are always large amount of meaningless *mantissa* bits in a coordinate [18]. We can embed more bits (instead of one bit) into each coordinate so that the reasonable length of fragile watermark can be fulfilled, in the expense of introducing some extra but negligible noise to the cover map.

An other fact is that, on one hand, the larger m is, the harder for an entire-group to be deleted by massive object deletions [8]. On the other hand, better locating precision for object deletions can be achieved with smaller m. We can make trade-offs between security and locating precision when choosing g, since m is roughly decided by the group number g.

4 Experimental Results

To evaluate the performance of the proposed watermarking scheme, we performed our experiments based on 16 vector maps provided by the National Administration of Surveying, Mapping and Geoinformation of China. The watermarking algorithm was implemented in C and run on a computer with Intel Core i5 CPU (2.9GHz) and 4G RAM. We focus on demonstrating the influence of watermark length l and group number g on the fragility of the proposed scheme. In the following, we take the county administrative boundary map of China as example for demonstration. The map contains 3207 objects and 1128242 vertices, with precision tolerance $\tau = 10^{-5}$. Correspondingly, the embedding position ζ was set as -16 so that the embedding caused an approximately 0.00001 variation on each coordinate. We set γ as 7 so that for an modified object the allowed variation on $Area_T$ was approximately 1% (which is a reasonable assumption [10][17]). *It is to be noted that according to our experimental results the embedding never influence the object identities*, i.e., all the objects can be correctly authenticated if the map is not modified after watermark embedding.

4.1   Evaluation on l

To show the influence of l on the fragility of the scheme, we slightly modified our scheme so that for every object O_i, we generated and embedded a l-bit object and group fragile watermark. Since the numbers of vertices in objects are different, during the embedding, if the number of vertices of O_i is less than l, then the vertices were used recurrently for embedding. Otherwise, the l-bit fragile watermark was embedded repeatedly into the vertices. The detection process was also amended to generate and detect l-bit watermarks. After embedding, we applied modifications on the watermarked maps and recorded the detection results. All the three modification types were considered in different processes. The modification magnitude (the ratio of added, modified or deleted object) was set to 50%. That is, data modification influenced approximately 1600 objects in each run (i.e., $\omega \simeq 1600$). *The experiment showed that with fixed g (e.g., 300 and 150 in this experiment), both the objects and the modifications fall averagely into each group (i.e., $m_i \simeq 3207/g$, $\omega_i \simeq 1600/g$).*

Table 1. Detection Results of Various l

$g = 300$, $m_i \simeq 10$, $\omega_i \simeq 5$				$g = 150$, $m_i \simeq 20$, $\omega_i \simeq 10$			
l	Mod	Add	Del	l	Mod	Add	Del
4	72.42	72.31	99.35	4	52.45	52.44	100
8	98.06	98.05	99.39	8	96.16	96.16	100
16	100	100	99.37	16	100	100	100

We varied l as 4, 8 and 16 for evaluation, and we repeated the experiment 65 times for each modification type so that more than 10^5 modifications of that type were applied to the watermarked map. The results are showed in Table 1, where the value in each cell represents the percents of modifications (out of 10^5 modifications) that were successfully characterized in the experiment. Form the results, the following conclusions can be drawn: 1) When l is small, the fragility (quantitatively measured by the percentage of successfully characterized modifications) of the scheme is relatively low and it is influenceable by g. This is because that, according to Eq. 1, 2 and 3, whether a modification in a specific group can be characterized is related to both the watermark length and the number of modifications applied to the group. 2) The scheme is comparatively more fragile against object deletion than object addition and modification. Actually, this conclusion is true only when g is relatively small, since according to Eq. 2, the more objects left in a deleted group, the larger probability is for these deletions to be characterized. 3) The scheme gets more fragile with larger l. When l is large enough (e.g., $l = 16$), the influence of g on the scheme's fragility decreases to a negligible level, and all the modifications can be correctly characterized with proper g (e.g., $g = 150$). This is also consistent with our analysis in Section 3.4. In real world application, an additional parameter, l, can be added to our scheme to make sure the objects with inadequate vertices can have long enough watermarks (by recurrent embedding).

Please pay attention to the detection results of object deletion for $g = 300$: (1) the percents of characterized deletions are approximately the same; (2) none of the percents reaches 100. The reason is that the objects in every group are too few. Consequently, the groups are at the risk of being entirely deleted, which makes the deletions undetectable. Next, we demonstrate the evaluation on g.

4.2 Evaluation on g

Since m is roughly determined by g, in this experiment, we fixed l as 16, and varied g as 256, 512 and 1024 for evaluation (correspondingly, m was approximately 12, 6, 3). In each run, we carried out data modifications with magnitude 10%, 20%, 30%, 40% and 50% before detection. According to our experimental results, *all the object additions and object modifications were characterized*. However, for object deletion, the experimental results presented in Table 2 show that, (*a*) when only a small portion of objects were deleted, in general all deletions can be correctly characterized; (*b*) the deletions can be characterized decrease with increasing deletion rate for larger g. This is because that certain groups were deleted entirely thus can not be detected. However, if g is relatively small, the probability of an entire group deletion is very low. Consequently, all deletions can still be detected even with high deletion rates, e.g., when $g = 256$ and deletion rate is 50%. This fact gives us a very concrete clue on how to select a proper g.

Table 2. Detection Results of Various g

Deleted (%) g	10	20	30	40	50
256	100	100	100	100	100
512	100	100	100	98.68	89.45
1024	100	95.22	82.33	66.85	57.73

5 Conclusion

In this paper, we investigated the problem of authenticating 2D vector maps on object level. We proposed a fragile watermarking scheme that can not only detect and locate modifications, but also characterize modification types. We analyzed the scheme's fragility theoretically in a probabilistic way, and verified it experimentally on real data. Both the analysis and evaluation show the fragility of the scheme.

Acknowledgments. This work is supported by the National Natural Science Foundations of China under grant (No.61100019 and No. 61262021).

References

1. Lin, C.E., Kao, C.M., Lai, Y.C., Shan, W.L., Wu, C.Y.: Application of Integrated GIS and Multimedia Modeling on NPS Pollution Evaluation. Environmental Monitoring and Assessment 158(11), 319–331 (2009)
2. Petitcolas, F.A.P., Anderson, R.J., Kuhn, M.G.: Information Hiding: A Survey. Proceedings of the IEEE 87(7), 1062–1078 (1999)
3. Guo, J.M., Liu, Y.F.: Continuous-tone Watermark Hiding in Halftone Images. In: Proceedings of the 16th International Asia-Pacific Web Conference on Web Technologies and Applications, pp. 411–414 (2010)
4. Wu, C.-C., Chang, C.-C., Yang, S.-R.: An Efficient Fragile Watermarking for Web Pages Tamper-Proof. In: Chang, K.C.-C., Wang, W., Chen, L., Ellis, C.A., Hsu, C.-H., Tsoi, A.C., Wang, H. (eds.) APWeb/WAIM 2007. LNCS, vol. 4537, pp. 654–663. Springer, Heidelberg (2007)
5. Kee, E., Johnson, M.K., Farid, H.: Digital Image Authentication from JPEG Headers. IEEE Transactions on Information Forensics and Security 6(3), 1066–1075 (2011)
6. Li, W., Zhu, B., Wang, Z.: On the music content authentication. In: Proc. of ACM International Conference on Multimedia, pp. 1101–1104 (2012)
7. Upadhyay, S., Singh, S.K.: Video Authentication: Issues and Challenges. International Journal of Computer Science 9(1-3), 409–418 (2012)
8. Guo, H., Li, Y., Liu, A., Jajodia, S.: A Fragile Watermarking Scheme for Detecting Malicious Modifications of Database Relations. Information Sciences 176, 1350–1378 (2006)
9. Niu, X.M., Shao, C.Y., Wang, X.T.: A Survey of Digital Vector Map Watermarking. International Journal of Innovative Computing, Information and Control 2(6), 1301–1316 (2006)
10. Guting, R.H.: An Introduction to Spatial Database Systems. The VLDBJ 3(4), 357–399 (1994)
11. Zheng, L., You, F.: A Fragile Digital Watermark Used to Verify the Integrity of Vector Map. In: Proc. of IEEE International Conference on E-Business and Information System Security, pp. 1–4 (2009)
12. Wang, N., Men, C.: Reversible Fragile Watermarking for Locating Tampered Blocks in 2D Vector Maps. In: Multimedia Tools and Applications, pp. 1–31 (2013)
13. Zhang, H., Gao, M.: A Semi-fragile Digital Watermarking Algorithm for 2D Vector Graphics Tamper Localization. In: Proc. of IEEE International Conference on Multimedia Information Networking and Security, vol. 1, pp. 549–552 (2009)
14. Zheng, L., Li, Y., Feng, L., Liu, H.: Research and Implementation of Fragile Watermark for Vector Graphics. In: Proc. of IEEE International Conference on Computer Engineering and Technology, vol. 1, pp. V1-522–V1-525 (2010)
15. Wang, N., Men, C.: Reversible Fragile Watermarking for 2-D Vector Map Authentication with Localization. Computer-Aided Design 44(4), 320–330 (2012)
16. Schneier, B.: Applied Cryptography. John Wiley and Sons (1996)
17. Cohen, S.D., Guibas, L.J.: Partial Matching of Planar Polylines under Similarity Transformations. In: Proc. of the ACM-SIAM Symposium on Discrete Algorithms, pp. 777–786 (1997)
18. IEEE Standard for Binary Floating-point Arithmetic. ANSI/IEEE Standard 754-1985

Technology Effect Phrase Extraction
in Chinese Patent Abstracts

Dacheng Liu, Zhiyong Peng, Bin Liu[*], Xu Chen, and Yuqi Guo

School of Computer, Wuhan University 129 Luoyu Road Wuhan, China
{dacheng.liu,peng,binliu,chenxu,yuqi.guo}@whu.edu.cn

Abstract. Patents are the greatest source of technical information in the world. High-efficient patent mining technologies are of great help to technical innovations and protection of intellectual property right. The extraction of technology effect clauses or phrases is an important research area in patent mining. Due to the specialty and uniqueness of patent data, traditional keyword extraction algorithms cannot properly apply to the extraction of technology effect phrases, leaving it dependent on high-cost manual processing. We propose a semi-automatic method based on partitioning corpus to extract technology effect phrases in Chinese patent abstracts. Experiments show that this method achieves satisfying precision and recall while involving little human labor.

Keywords: Patent mining, information retrieval, technology effect clause, technology effect phrase, partitioning corpus.

1   Introduction

Patents are the greatest source of technical information in the world. Statistics show that patents contain 90%-95% of the information in today's scientific and technological innovations. For any enterprise, patents are the key technical information that must be made public. By analyzing patent data, people can obtain valuable information to avoid wasting money on redundant research and to prevent property rights violations. Before any technical innovations, researchers must thoroughly learn about the existing patents in the targeted domain[1].

The extraction of technology effect clauses (**TEC**) is an important research area in patent mining. Patent technology effect matrix analysis has attracted much attention these years for its ability to reveal important hidden information in patent data[2]. TEC's point out technologies used in patents and effects they achieve. They are good raw materials for in-depth analysis of the patent data in a given domain. The extraction of TEC's with high precision and recall is the foundation of this technology. Patent abstracts contain most useful information in patent data[2], and there are many tools to help patent analyzers to download patent abstracts in bulk. Therefore, we focus our extraction mainly on patent abstracts. Note that patent data

---

[*] Corresponding author.

L. Chen et al. (Eds.): APWeb 2014, LNCS 8709, pp. 141–152, 2014.

of different domains differ much in content. To guarantee high recall, we execute the extraction in one domain each time.

At present, TEC extraction depends on technology effect phrases (**TEP**). In the domain of Chinese patent mining, few algorithms are able to effectively extract TEP's without much human assistance. To ensure high precision and recall, patent mining algorithms invariably rely on manual extraction, rather than traditional keyword extraction algorithms. Most of these algorithms consider word frequency as a decisive component in determining keywords. However, the uniqueness of patents makes word frequency in patent abstracts fairly low. Therefore, we propose a novel method that is independent of word frequency and that requires little human involvement.

This paper is organized as follows: Section 2 discusses related works. Section 3 presents our algorithm and its improvements. Section 4 shows our experiment results. Section 5 summarizes this paper and discusses future work.

2   Related Works

2.1   Technology Effect Annotation in Patent Data

The number of patents has greatly increased in recent decades, and patent retrieval technologies are also developing fast. Current researches mainly focus on the annotation of patent function, technology, and composition parts[3]. In English and Japanese patent processing, large amount of manually annotated patent data have provided good corpora for some machine learning algorithms, such as the rule-based method by Peter Parapaics[5] and many supervised training methods proposed on NTCIR Workshops[4]. Using these algorithms, people have achieved remarkable results in technology effect annotation. Due to the lack of annotated Chinese patent data, Xu Chen[3] proposes a semi-supervised co-training algorithm to annotate TEC's in Chinese patent abstracts without using a large corpus. By several times of iteration, the algorithm achieves an F-Measure over 80%. However, in each iteration, manual processing is needed to extract TEP's from newly identified TEC's. Too much human labor prevents this method from practical use.

2.2   Keyword Extraction and Technology Effect Phrase Extraction

Many state-of-the-art algorithms are available for extracting keywords from general text. Y. Matsuo[6] et al. propose a domain-independent keyword extraction algorithm that needs no corpus. The algorithm measures the distribution of the co-occurrence of frequent terms and other terms to determine the importance of words. It achieves good performance in experiments on general text, but the importance of TEP's is determined by their semantic meanings, rather than how important they seem according to the rules in [6]. Besides, traditional keyword extraction algorithms are dependent on word frequency, but TEP's are hard to distinguish from other phrases in this sense. Ni W.[7] et al. propose an under-sampling approach to extract imbalanced key phrases in general text. The algorithm is based on a training set represented by two views of the samples, i.e. the morphology view and occurrence view of the (non-)key phrases. In TEP extraction, however, the occurrence of TEP's are hard to distinguish from other phrases. Besides, we have tried various approaches to identify TEP's using their morphologies by an LVQ neural network as a classifier but none of them works well. The difficulty lies in isolating the morphologies belonging only to TEP's. Ying Chen[2] et al. propose a method based on patent structure-grammar-keyword feature to identify the TEP's in patent data. Because DII (Derwent Innovations Index) is an essential part of this algorithm, and the construction of DII demands much processing by patent experts, the algorithm is not successful in reducing human labor.

2.3 Parsing Chinese Patent Data

Roger Levy[8] et al. carefully investigate the errors that Stanford Parser[9] makes in parsing general Chinese text and provide some simple and targeted improvements for each case. These improvements enable the parser to achieve high accuracy in parsing general Chinese text. Unfortunately, after parsing some Chinese patent abstracts with Stanford Parser, we find it almost impossible to distinguish the subtrees containing a TEP from other subtrees. We even notice that a few subtrees containing a TEP are identical with other subtrees in both tree structure and part-of-speech tagging (See Figure 1), making it hard to extract TEP's by the parsing results. The Chinese Academy of Sciences develops a word-segmenting and part-of-speech tagging software ICTCLAS [10]. The software does well in general Chinese text such as news, magazine articles, and literature works. Though it is now the best Chinese text tokenizer, our experiment shows that it often segments terminologies in patent abstracts into separated parts(See Figure 2). It also wrongly tags a few words in almost every patent abstract.

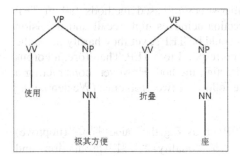

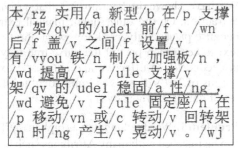

Fig. 1. Identical parse trees are generated for both a TEP ("convenient + usage") and an unexpected phrase ("fold + foundation")

Fig. 2. In a TEP "提高+稳固性" ("enhance + stability"), "稳固性"(stability) is wrongly segmented into "稳固"(stable) and "性"(sex) with wrong word tags

3   Proposed Method

3.1   Definitions

For convenience, we give definitions to some frequently used terms in this paper.

Definition 1. Technology Effect Clause (TEC) A technology effect clause (TEC) is a clause describing the technology and effect of a patent.

Definition 2. Technology Effect Phrase (TEP) A technology effect phrase (TEP) is a phrase that seldom appears in a non-TEC. Once it appears, the clause containing the phrase must be a TEC.

There are mainly two forms of TEP's: "verb + noun" and "adjective + noun". We unify the two forms by "Value + Attribute". E.g. "增加 + 产量" (increase + production) and "高 + 可靠性" (high + reliability) are effect phrases, and "使用 + 环保材料" (uses + green material) is a technology phrase.

Definition 3. Value and Attribute Value is the verb or adjective part in the above two common forms of TEP, and Attribute is the noun part.

Definition 4. Domain-Independent Corpus (DIC) A Domain-Independent Corpus (DIC) is a pre-constructed corpus consisting of Values and Attributes shared by most patent domains.

Definition 5. Domain-Dependent Corpus (DDC) A Domain-Dependent Corpus (DDC) is a corpus constructed using Values and Attributes in the targeted domain.

3.2   The Basic Idea of the Algorithm

We have shown in Section 2.3 that grammar-structure-based methods fail in TEP extraction. On the other hand, manual extraction achieves high recall and precision because patent analyzers know what phrases could be TEP's, yet they hardly parse the text to see which part of the parse tree may correspond to a TEP. Therefore, a corpus is needed for an effective and automatic extracting method. However, constructing a corpus of TEP's directly is impractical for the following two problems: (We denote the set of patent abstracts by A)

Problem 1. Word redundancy is high in the TEP corpus. E.g. the Value "提高" (improve) can be matched with many Attributes such as "质量" (quality), "产量" (production), and "效率" (efficiency). Including all these phrases into the corpus seems unnecessary.

Problem 2. If all TEP's in A have been manually extracted to construct the corpus, then the corpus is just the result of manual extraction. It is meaningless to use this corpus to extract the patent abstracts.

For Problem 1, we partition the corpus into a "Value corpus" and a "Attribute corpus". The algorithm first performs a Cartesian product of the Values and the Attributes. We denote this result set by R. Then for every patent abstract $P \in A$, the algorithm scans for every phrase $e_i \in R$ to see if it appears in P. If so, we consider e_i as a TEP candidate.

We address Problem 2 based on a fact we observe in our experiments: the content of patent data in a certain domain is highly domain-dependent. Let B be a subset of A

formed by random sampling. The number of elements in **B** is far less than that of **A**. This observation is presented as follow:

Observation 1. Let **A** be a set of patent abstracts. Let **B** be a subset of **A** where M<|B|<|A|. M is a small positive integer. The technologies and effects mentioned in **B** are also frequently mentioned in the set **A** – **B**, and those technologies and effects in **A** – **B** but not in **B** are very rare.

This observation indicates that we can construct a corpus C_B using only the patent abstracts in **B**. The key is that corpus C_B is able to generate new TEP's. There could be many different expressions for one technology or effect. E.g. let there be "提高+效率" (improve + efficiency) and "增加+稳定性" (increase + stability) in **B**, C_B has the potential to generate "提高+稳定性" (improve + stability) and "增加+效率" (increase + efficiency), which are quite likely to appear in set **A** – **B**.

Further observations show that there are domain-independent Values and Attributes. Values such as "提高"(improve) and "防止"(prevent) and Attributes such as "成本"(cost) and "质量"(quality) are likely to appear in most patent abstracts. Meanwhile, Values like "制动"(brake) and "燃烧"(burn) and Attributes like "油耗"(oil consumption) and "机械效率"(mechanical efficiency) are dependent to the domain of diesel engine. To further reduce human labor in corpus construction, we partition both the corpora of Values and Attributes into domain-independent corpus (**DIC**, Definition 4) and domain-dependent corpus (**DDC**, Definition 5). We have constructed DIC for both Values and Attributes according to our observation of large quantities of patent abstracts. When a patent analyzer wants to extract patent abstracts in a new domain, he only needs to manually extract domain-dependent Values and Attributes (especially Attributes) from a small number of patent abstracts. Then the algorithm will incorporates the DIC and DDC and eliminates duplicate elements during extraction process. We show the details of the partitioning in Figure 3.

3.3   Improving Precision and Recall

Though recall of the method in Section 3.2 is acceptable, its precision is only around 50%. This is due to some certain common Chinese language grammar structures. We accordingly propose the following rules to improve precision:

Rule 1. If the character "了" appears in a clause and there is a Value identified right before this "了", then this Value is considered to be the only Value of this clause.

The necessity of this rule is substantiated by the abundance of TEP's presented in the form "Value+了+Attribute". E.g. in clause "在生产过程中减小了成本" (decrease cost in production) we extract "减小" (decrease) as the only Value for the Attribute "成本" (cost), ignoring the verb "生产" (produce).

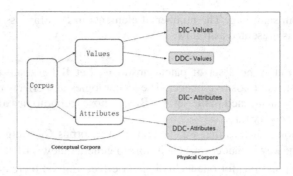

Fig. 3. Corpus partition. The three hollow boxes on the left represent the conceptual corpora in our analysis. The four solid boxes on the right are the physically existent corpora used in our algorithm. The sizes of the four solid corpora reflect their actual sizes in our experiment. The pre-constructed DIC-Values plays an important role in the extraction.

Rule 2. If a Value matches several Attributes in a clause, and none of these Attributes is a substring of another, we check if there is an Attribute right behind a character "的". If so, we match the Value with only this Attribute.

This rule is needed for a specific yet common case where an Attribute is embellished by another word before it. E.g. in clause "增加单位体积燃料的里程数" *(increase the mileage per unit fuel),* "里程数" *(mileage) rather than* "燃料" *(fuel) is the correct Attribute.*

Rule 3. If a Value matches several Attributes in a clause, and some of these Attributes are substrings of others, only the longest Attribute should be matched.

This rule is designed to eliminate obvious duplications. Still using the example of "增加单位体积燃料的里程数" *(increase the mileage per unit fuel), if* "单位体积燃料的里程数" *(mileage per unit fuel) appears so frequently that it is included in the DDC of Attribute, it is unnecessary to consider* "里程数" *(mileage) as an Attribute.*

Summarizing Section 3.2 and 3.3, we now give a formal description of our algorithm in Table 1. A flowchart of the entire method is shown in Figure 4.

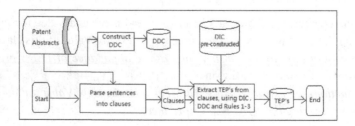

Fig. 4. The flowchart of the entire TPE extraction method

Table 1. Algorithm for Extracting TEP's from Chinese Patent Abstracts

Algorithm: Technology Effect Phrases Extraction Based on Partitioning Corpus **Input**: DIC (Domain Independent Corpus), DDC (Domain Dependent Corpus), m patent abstracts

Output: All technonogy effect phrases in the m patent abstracts

1. Load DIC and DDC, combine them with duplicate elimination. Put all Values in **Values[]**$_{n1}$, all Attributes in **Attributes[]**$_{n2}$;
2. Load patent abstract A$_i$, segment it by '，', '。' and '；', save the result in **Array[]**$_p$;
3. For each sub-sentence S$_j$ in **Array[]**$_p$
4.   Apply **Rule 1** and **Rule 2** (in order) to S$_j$;
5.   If either rule takes effect, then output the phrase(s) extracted by the rule, **GOTO** Step 3 ;
6.   Apply **Rule 3** to S$_j$;
7.   For each Value V$_x$ in **Values[]**$_{n1}$ and each Attribute A$_y$ in **Attributes[]**$_{n2}$
8.   IF V$_x$ and A$_y$ are found in S$_j$, then output "V$_x$ + A$_y$" as a TEP, **GOTO** Step 3 ;
9.   End For
10. End For
11. **GOTO** Step 2 until all patent abstracts are exhausted;

The main step of the algorithm may seem straightforward. However, we have made great efforts trying to come up with algorithms based on supervised learning, referring to methods mentioned in Section 2. All these approaches fail to properly adapt to the specific job of TEP extraction. Because they either show disappointing recall and precision or require too much manual processing. Compared with these methods, our method substantially reduces manual processing while achieving relatively high precision and recall. We also compare our method with two standard keyword extraction algorithms in Section 4.4. Our method achieves obviously higher recall and precision.

3.4   The Number of Manually Extracted Patent Abstracts

In Observation 1 a lower bound M is given for the number of manually extracted patent abstracts. It should be noted that M is not a fixed portion of the total patent abstract number. Suppose there are 100 patent abstracts in a domain, a patent analyzer may need to manually extract 20 abstracts to cover the domain-dependent Values and Attributes. But when the number rises to 1000, only about 60 abstracts should be pre-extracted. Since all these patents belong to one domain, the rest 940 patents are all focusing on what the 60 patents are doing. Therefore, the more patents in a domain, the less the portion for manual extraction, and the more cost-effective the method. We give the following function as a reference:

$$y = \lfloor 19ln(x) \rfloor - 66, (x \geq 100, x \in N) \tag{1}$$

Here y is the number of patent abstracts to manually extract, and x is the number of all patent abstracts in a domain. We use logarithm because we find the increment rate of y reduces significantly as x grows. The parameters in the function are determined using

Least Square Fit according to our experiment results. Further details will be given in Section 4.3.

4   Experiments

We download over 3000 patent abstracts from the website of State Intellectual Property Office of China. These patents are distributed in 7 domains, each consists of 102, 160, 263, 354, 459, 648, 1042 abstracts respectively. We first make a comparison between precisions of our method as Rule 1 to 3 are included to justify these rules. Then we show how precision and recall change as the number of manually extracted abstracts grows, and draw some interesting conclusions. Then we provide details on how the parameters in formula (1) are determined. Finally we compare our method with two standard keyword extraction algorithms.

4.1   Precision Increment by the Rules

We compare the precision before and after the introduction of each rule in Section 3.3 on the 7 domains respectively. We manually extract 20% abstracts in the first 4 domains and 10% abstracts in the following 3 domains[1]. The results are shown in Figure 5. A significant increase in precision occurs after each rule comes into play. We do not plot changes in recalls in Figure 5 because their decreases are negligible, and these rules are relatively conservative in this sense.

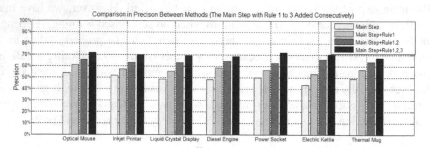

Fig. 5. Comparison in precision between methods with and without the rules

4.2   Precision and Recall

To test the overall precision and recall of our method, we run the algorithm on the 7 domains of abstracts respectively. For each domain, we start from zero manual extraction, then each time we manually extract a new 3% abstracts and add the Values and Attributes into DDC. We measure the precision and recall of TEP extraction based on Definition 2. Results are presented in Table 2 and Figure 6.

In Table 2, the underlined data represent the highest F-Measure achieved in that domain while precision is over 70%. The algorithm achieves F-Measures over 75% in all 7 domains, with recalls over 80% and precisions over 70%.

---

[1] Here the percentages of manual extraction are decided a little arbitrarily because we only intend to see if the rules work. To achieve the best F-Measure, one needs to follow the formula in Section 3.4.

Table 2. Changes in precision and recall as more abstracts are manually extracted. The first row is the domain name, including OM (Optical Mouse), IP (Inkjet Printer), LCD (Liquid Crystal Display), DE (Diesel Engine), PS (Power Socket), EK (Electric Kettle), and TM (Thermal Mug). The second row is the corresponding number of patents in each domain. In the first column, "M.E." stands for "Manually Extracted". In the second column, "P", "R", and "F" are "Precision", "Recall", and "F-Measure" respectively. A few cells are given by a "*", because the F-Measures have reached their peak before them, and testing them requires manually extracting over 100 abstracts.

Patent Domain		OM	IP	LCD	DE	PS	EK	TM
Num. of Patents		102	160	263	354	459	648	1042
0% M.E.	P%	67.0	68.1	65.3	66.7	64.5	68.2	66.4
	R%	15.1	18.2	13.4	12.0	14.9	16.6	17.8
	F%	24.6	28.7	22.2	20.3	24.2	26.7	28.1
3% M.E.	P%	69.1	73.1	76.7	75.8	77.4	76.3	73.2
	R%	34.5	37.6	40.0	45.5	51.7	59.7	72.1
	F%	46.0	49.7	52.6	56.9	62.0	67.0	72.6
6% M.E.	P%	75.9	74.4	74.2	72.1	73.8	73.8	71.3
	R%	51.8	55.3	58.3	68.1	72.5	74.7	82.0
	F%	61.6	63.4	65.3	70.0	73.1	74.2	76.3
9% M.E.	P%	73.7	73.6	72.6	70.4	71.2	71.4	67.9
	R%	60.3	69.6	73.5	78.3	78.0	81.5	83.1
	F%	66.3	71.5	73.0	74.1	74.4	76.1	74.7
12% M.E.	P%	72.0	71.9	71.5	70.5	70.3	69.0	
	R%	68.8	77.1	80.1	81.9	82.8	82.8	*
	F%	70.4	74.4	75.6	75.8	76.0	75.3	
15% M.E.	P%	72.5	71.0	71.2	69.6	69.2	68.8	
	R%	75.4	79.5	83.6	82.5	83.0	83.4	*
	F%	73.9	75.0	76.9	75.5	75.5	75.4	
18% M.E.	P%	71.9	70.2	70.3	68.5	68.3		
	R%	78.9	81.3	83.9	83.0	83.1	*	*
	F%	75.2	75.3	76.5	75.1	75.0		
21% M.E.	P%	71.4	69.9	68.9	68.6	67.0		
	R%	80.6	81.8	84.1	83.2	83.5	*	*
	F%	75.7	75.4	75.7	75.2	74.3		

Though precisions are obviously lower than full manual processing, patent retrieval is recall-oriented[12], and our recalls approximate manual performance. When a human is employed to do the extraction, things are quite on the contrary: Non-TEP's are easy to spot and exclude, yet he probably overlooks some real TEP's due to the variant grammatical structures or tiredness. Then we apply our method in Chen's solution to annotating Chinese patent data[3]. With a little human involvement in excluding obvious non-TEP's, our method is able to complete in a few seconds what takes a human several days.

When the algorithm runs without DDC, the recalls are extremely low. Once a 3% abstracts are included in DDC, an obvious increase is shown in all recalls. As more abstracts are included, the increment rates drop, and the growth basically stops when recalls reach over 80%. This indicates a lower bound for the amount of manual extraction. On the other hand, precisions increase only in the beginning[2]. Then they are on a steady decrease because manual extraction introduces "noises" to DDC. Thus an upper bound of manual extraction amount is expected. This relationship is better seen from the F-Measures. In each column there is a peak for F-Measure. The corresponding M.E. value is what we recommend as the ideal manual extraction amount in each domain. Interestingly, the more patents in a domain, the less the percentage of manual extraction is recommended, and our method is therefore more cost-effective.

---

[2] This increase is caused by the inclusion of more correct TEP's in the result set, not the exclusion of the wrong ones.

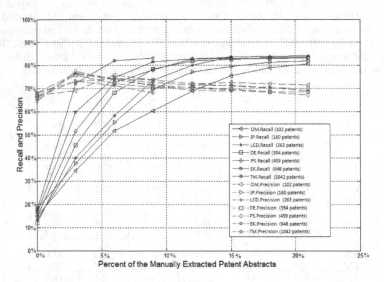

Fig. 6. Variance of precision and recall. The numbers in the brackets on the legend are the number of patents in the domains.

4.3   Determining the Number of Abstracts to Manually Extract

Formula (1) in Section 3.4 helps a patent analyzer to decide how many patent abstracts to manually extract in a certain domain. Now we discuss in detail how the function is determined.

In Table 2 we see that more patent abstracts in a domain means less *portion* to manually extract, but the *number* increases while the increment rate drops. Thus a logarithm function $y = a\ln(x) + b$ is a good approximation, where y is the number of manually extracted abstracts and x is the total patent number. Its parameters are determined as follow: Denote $ln(x)$ by t. For each domain in Table 2, take the natural logarithms of the total abstract number as a value of t, take the product of the "ideal portion" and total patent number as a value of y. Then we use Least Square Fit to determine a and b for function $y = at + b$. The result $y = 19ln(x)$ 66 is plotted in Figure 7.

4.4   Comparing with Other Methods

We compare our method with two standard keyword extraction algorithms: the TF-IDF algorithm and Matsuo's algorithm[6] for extracting keywords in a single document. We merge all abstracts of a domain into a single file as the input for Matsuo's statistical method, and segment all sentences into words by ICTCLAS[10]. Finally we choose the top 10 words extracted from each abstract by TF-IDF and top 4000 words extracted from the merged file by Matsuo's method. The result is shown in Figure 8. Our method outperforms the two algorithms in both precision and recall. The poor performance of the first two algorithms is mainly a result of their inherent ineligibility. Though they have

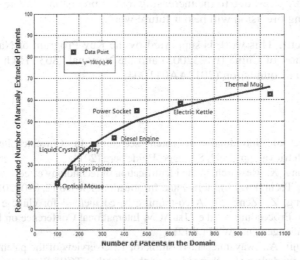

Fig. 7. Graph of $y = 19ln(x)$ 66. Domain names are given beside each data point.

been modified to adapt to TEP extraction, the targeted keywords are not necessarily TEP's. The two algorithms are also impaired by the inaccuracy in word-segmentation by ICTCLAS. In contrast, our method is free from such influences of word tokenizer.

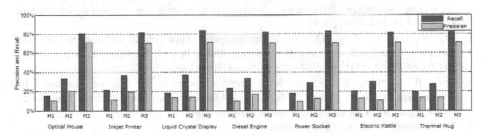

Fig. 8. Comparison in recall and precision. M1 is TF-IDF, M2 is Matsuo's algorithm[6], and M3 is our method.

5   Conclusions

Technology effect phrase (TEP) extraction is an indispensable part of many patent mining algorithms. To reduce human labor in the extraction, we propose a method based on partitioning corpus to extract TEP's from Chinese patent abstracts. To further increase precision, we propose 3 rules to deal with some specific yet common cases. We also find that the larger the patent domain, the more cost-effective the method. We give a formula to calculate the optimal number of patent abstracts to manually extract. The logarithm function indicates that human workload will be acceptable even when the number of patents is enormous.

In future, we will try to further increase the recall of our method. According to our experiments, adding more patent abstracts into DDC alone does not help, because the

F-Measure will drop fast due to the increasing loss of precision. How to increase recall without sacrificing precision will be our future work.

Acknowledgement. This work is supported by the Key Program of National Natural Science Foundation of China (61232002) and the National "863" High-tech Research Development Plan Foundation (2012AA011004).

References

1. Alberts, D., et al.: Introduction to patent searching. In: Currentchallenges in Patent Information Retrieval, pp. 3–43. Springer, Heidelberg (2011)
2. Chen, Y., Zhang, X.: Research on the identification of technology effect phrases in patents. Contemporary Technology in Library and Information Science 12, 010 (2011)
3. Chen, X., Peng, Z., Zeng, C.: A co-training based method for chinese patentsemantic annotation. In: Proceedings of the 21st ACM International Conference on Information and Knowledge Management. ACM (2012)
4. Nanba, H., Fujii, A., Iwayama, M., Hashimoto, T.: Overview of the patent mining task at the NTCIR-8 workshop. In: Proceeding of the Eighth NTCIR Workshop, Tokyo, Japan, June 15-18, pp. 293–302 (2010)
5. Parapatics, P., Dittenbach, M.: Patent claim decomposition for improvedinformation extraction. In: Current Challenges in Patent Information Retrieval, pp. 197–216. Springer, Heidelberg (2011)
6. Matsuo, Y., Ishizuka, M.: Keyword extraction from a single document using wordco-occurrence statistical information. International Journal on Artificial Intelligence Tools 13(01), 157–169 (2004)
7. Ni, W., Liu, T., Zeng, Q.: An Under-Sampling Approach to ImbalancedAutomatic Keyphrase Extraction. In: Gao, H., Lim, L., Wang, W., Li, C., Chen, L. (eds.) WAIM 2012. LNCS, vol. 7418, pp. 387–398. Springer, Heidelberg (2012)
8. Levy, R., Manning, C.: Is it harder to parse Chinese, or the Chinese Treebank? In: Proceedings of the 41st Annual Meeting on Association for Computational Linguistics, vol. 1. Association for Computational Linguistics (2003)
9. The Stanford Parser: A statistical parser, http://nlp.stanford.edu/software/lex-parser.shtml
10. Zhang, H.-P., et al.: HHMM-based Chinese lexical analyzer ICTCLAS. In: Proceedings of the Second SIGHAN Workshop on Chinese Language Processing, vol. 17. Association for Computational Linguistics (2003)
11. Yuuji, K.: Inkjet Printer: China, 02154598.7[P]. 2003-06-18
12. Xue, X., Bruce Croft, W.: Automatic query generation for patent search. In: Proceedings of the 18th ACM Conference on Information and Knowledge Management. ACM (2009)

Sharing-Aware Scheduling of Web Services[*]

Junyan Jiang[1], Zhiyong Peng[1], Xiaoying Wu[2,**] and Nan Liang[1]

[1] Computer School, Wuhan University, China
{Jiangjy,peng}@whu.edu.cn, Ln9312@gmail.com
[2] State Key Laboratory of Software Engineering, Wuhan University, China
xiaoying.wu@whu.edu.cn

Abstract. The increasing and widespread use of web services, usually represented by database queries, is putting a strain on web database systems behind them. In such systems web services are associated with soft-deadlines, and the success of these systems (i.e., the user satisfaction) is better measured in terms of minimizing the deviation from the deadline, that is, tardiness. Previous work on query scheduling focused on ordering the execution of independent queries while ignoring the commonality among queries, such that a same work will be computed multiple times which can impact user satisfaction negatively. This paper proposes a new query scheduling framework which incorporates semantic caching techniques into the query scheduling procedure. We develop a query splitting-based strategy to discover common sub-expressions among queries and design a sharing-aware query scheduling algorithm **GASA** which minimizes average tardiness while reducing redundant work at the same time. We experimentally compare our approach with state-of-the-art methods on TPC H workloads. Our experimental results show that our method can efficiently and effectively minimize average tardiness of a large number of data service requests.

Keywords: web services, query scheduling, semantic caching.

1   Introduction

The increasing and widespread use of web service is putting a strain on web databases systems behind them. These web services need to support SQL-style queries from form-based interface for strategic decision making in industries as varied as travel reservation, financial, insurance or even social networking. With the number of internet users and web services increasing, these systems are faced with loads that often involve hundreds or thousands of queries submitted at the same time [1]. In such highly interactive applications, user satisfaction or positive experience determines their success. Therefore it's crucial for such systems to prioritize execution of services as needed in order to keep users satisfied under varying workloads.

---

[*] This work is supported by National Natural Science Foundation of China under Grant No.61202035 and No. 61232002.

[**] Corresponding author.

L. Chen et al. (Eds.): APWeb 2014, LNCS 8709, pp. 153–164, 2014.
© Springer International Publishing Switzerland 2014

One way to quantify a user's satisfaction is to associate a service/query with a soft-deadline which defines an upper bound (i.e. deadline) on the latency perceived by the end user accessing the results. The assigned deadline is a mapping from the service level agreements (SLAs) provided by the service provider to the end user. Hence, the success of the system (i.e., the user satisfaction) is better measured in terms of minimizing the deviation from the deadline, that is, tardiness.

Previous work [4, 9, 10, 11, 12, 13] on query scheduling focused on ordering of the execution of independent queries while ignoring the commonality among queries. As a result, a same work will be computed multiple times which negatively impacts user satisfaction. Lots of techniques such as multi-query optimization [2] and semantic caching [3] can discover the query relevance by identifying commonality among queries and make use of intermediate results during the query execution to answer relevant queries. In this paper we propose a new query scheduling framework which takes into account of semantic caching techniques to improve user satisfaction. The intuition is that reducing evaluation cost of queries can help the minimization of tardiness of queries. Appropriately incorporating semantic caching into traditional scheduling methods brings us the following two challenges: First, we need a mechanism to model query relevance and develop a strategy to discover commonality among queries; second, we need to assess the impact of local query optimization on the global query scheduling. The following example illustrates the problem of traditional query scheduling method and the sharing opportunities among queries that can be exploited to minimize average tardiness.

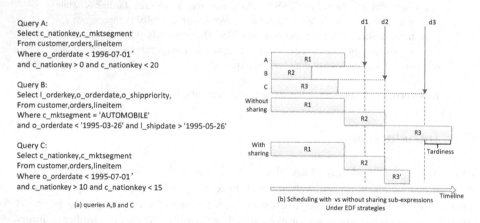

Query A:
Select c_nationkey,c_mktsegment
From customer,orders,lineitem
Where o_orderdate < 1996-07-01'
and c_nationkey > 0 and c_nationkey < 20

Query B:
Select l_orderkey,o_orderdate,o_shippriority,
From customer,orders,lineitem
Where c_mktsegment = 'AUTOMOBILE'
and o_orderdate < '1995-03-26' and l_shipdate > '1995-05-26'

Query C:
Select c_nationkey,c_mktsegment
From customer,orders,lineitem
Where o_orderdate < 1995-07-01'
and c_nationkey > 10 and c_nationkey < 15

(a) queries A,B and C

(b) Scheduling with vs without sharing sub-expressions Under EDF strategies

Fig. 1. (a) Query Examples; (b) Scheduling Example

EXAMPLE 1 . Consider three queries A, B, C shown in figure 1(a), each query has a arrival time, a deadline, and a processing time. By *EDF* (Earliest Deadline First) strategy [16] we'll run query A first followed by B and C in that order. In this case, C will miss its deadline (see figure 1(b). However we can analyze the three queries and discover their commonalities. For example, the common sub-expressions between A and C are: "*o_orderdata<'1995-07-01'*" and "*c_nation>10* and *c_nation <15*". We need to compute the common sub-expressions only once and cache their results.

The cached results can be used to evaluate C. This way, the evaluation cost of C is minimized and the tardiness of these three queries becomes 0.

Contributions. The main contributions of our paper are the followings:

- We propose a sharing-aware approach for query scheduling which exploits commonalities among queries.
- We develop a mechanism to model query relevance and design a strategy to discover commonalities among queries.
- We design a sharing-aware query scheduling algorithm **GASA** which minimizes average tardiness while reducing redundant work at the same time.
- We run extensive experiments to verify the efficiency and effectiveness of our proposed approach.
- To the best of our knowledge, our paper is the first one that combines classical query scheduling algorithms with semantic caching techniques.

Paper Organization. The rest of this paper is organized as follows: Section 2 presents related work. In Section 3, we describe preliminaries and our proposed problem. Section 4 illustrates our approach, and Section 5 presents the experiment. In Section 6 we discuss the conclusions.

2   Related Work

In this section, we introduce background information, including semantic caching and query scheduling. To our knowledge, no prior work considers both semantic caching and query scheduling in web databases system.

2.1   Semantic Caching

There are some related works on Semantic Caching. In a client-server system, a cache may be employed at the client-side in order to reduce the communication cost and improve query response time. A cache located at a client can only serve queries from the client itself, not from other clients. Such a cache is only beneficial for a query-intensive user. All techniques in this category adopt the dynamic caching approach. Semantic caching [3, 5] is a client-side caching model that associates cached results with valid ranges. Upon receiving a query Q, the relevant results in the cache are reported. A sub-query Q_0 is constructed from Q such that Q_0 covers the query region that cannot be answered by the cache. The sub-query Q_0 is then forwarded to the server in order to obtain the missing results of Q. Dar et al. [6] focuses on semantic caching of relational datasets. As an example, we assume that the dataset stores the age of each employee and that the cache contains the result of the query "find employees with age below 30." Now we assume that the client issues a query Q "find employees with age between 20 and 40." First, the employees with age between 20 and 30 can be obtained from the cache. Then, a sub-query Q_0 "find employees with age between 30 and 40" is submitted to the server for retrieving the remaining results.

The difference between our work and semantic cache is that we exploit intermediate results among queries while semantic cache reason queries based on pre-computed query results.

2.2   Query Scheduling

Scheduling is a well-studied research topic and is ubiquitous in many applications [7]. When per-query scheduling decisions are made where each query has a known execution time and deadlines, most problem instances become NP-complete [8]. Furthermore, the situation is not improved when the hard dead-lines are replaced by minimization of the number of deadline violations [9]. Therefore, most scheduling algorithms adopt certain heuristics. One family of such algorithms is cost-aware or value-based scheduling algorithms. In these algorithms, the decisions on scheduling are made so that certain costs are optimized. The costs could be defined in different ways: they could be fixed or time-varying values assigned to different queries [10, 11]; they could be about other metrics such as fairness [12] and result quality [13]. On minimizing average tardiness, [4] proposed an approach ASETS* efficiently minimizes query's tardiness integrating EDF and HDF/SRPT which highly relates our objective, the intuition is: at a given time t, we divide queries into two list, EDF list for those queries that can be finished before deadline and sorted by its deadline, and another list (SRPT) for queries that can't be finished before deadline sorted by its processing time. Each time we either (i) choose the first query from the EDF list or (ii) choose the first query from the SRPT list, the criterion to choose which query first is based on the impact of which order incurs less tardiness. However, none of these works considered sharing among queries during scheduling.

3   Preliminaries and Problem

In this section, we'll provide the query model and describe the system architecture. Finally we'll formally define our problem.

The query model is SQL queries associated with soft-deadline. We assume that a database D is given as a set of relations $\{R_1, R_2, \cdots, R_n\}$, each relation defined on a set of attributes. The expression of a SQL query only includes selection predicates which are called *tasks*. Given the query expression, we next define a partial order on tasks, including implication and satisfiability which characterize query relevance.

Definition 3.1(Query Relevance): We define query relevance in terms of *query predicate implication* and *query satisfiability*.

- *Query Implication*: A task ta_i implies task $ta_j(ta_i \Rightarrow ta_j)$ iff ta_i is a conjunction of selection predicates on attributes $A_1, A_2, A_3, \cdots, A_k$ of some relation R, and ta_j is a conjunction of selection predicates on the same relation R and on attributes $A_1, \cdots, A_l$ with $l \leq k$, and it is the case that for any instance of the relation R the result of evaluating ta_i is a subset of the result of evaluating ta_j.
- *Query Satisfiaiblity*: We call $ta_i \wedge ta_j$ is satisfiable, if that part of ta_i's answer is contained in ta_j.

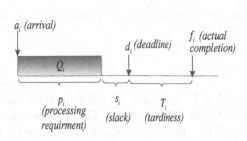

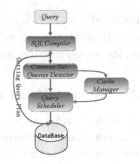

Fig. 2. Query Characteristics   **Fig. 3.** System Architecture

Definition 3.2: We define the characteristics of a query to be (see Fig.2):

- Arrival Time (a_i): The time when Q_i has arrived at the database system.
- Deadline (d_i): The ideal time by which Q_i should finish execution.
- Processing Time (p_i): The processing time needed to execute Q_i. We assume that if caching or materialization is utilized for fragments, then Q_i's processing time is adjusted accordingly.
- Slack Time (s_i): The slack time of Query Q_i is the amount of time Q_i can take to finish after the deadline d_i. If the query cannot finish before the deadline then the slack time of query Q_i is 0.
- Tardiness ($T(Q_i)$): The tardiness of a query Q_i is the extra amount of time Q_i can take to finish after the deadline d_i. Specifically, at any beginning time t, $T'(Q_i) = \max(f_i - d_i, 0)$, where $f_i = t + p_i$ is the actual completion time. Obviously, if the query is completed before the deadline, the tardiness of query Q_i is 0, otherwise the tardiness is larger than 0.

Given a set of queries, from the optimizer of the underlying database system, we can obtain the optimal plan of each query. From these plans, we can identify common sub-expressions among queries. Based on the common sub-expressions, a query can be split into two parts. One part is the common sub-expressions and the other is the non-common sub-expressions. Formally we provide a notion of query splitting as follows:

Definition 3.3(Query Splitting): Given two queries Q_i and Q_j, query splitting is the process of reducing the overlapped part of the two queries. Each query contains two parts: common sub-expression (we also call sub-queries) and non- common sub-expression. The overlapped part of queries (common sub-expression) is $C_{i,j}(Q_j, Q_i)$ (we may also use $C_{i,j}$ for simplicity) and the non-common sub-expressions of Q_i and Q_j are correspondingly $N_{i,j}$ and $N_{j,i}$. Note that if $C_{i,j}$ dose not exist, then $N_{i,j}$ equals to Q_i and $N_{j,i}$ equals to Q_j. The splitting strategies are presented in section 4.1. Once the query Q_i is split with Query Q_j, then the tardiness of the query Q_i is
$$T(Q_i) = \max \left(T(C_{i,j}), T(N_{i,j}) \right)$$

Definition 3.4(Query Processing Time Savings): Given two queries Q_i and Q_j, the query processing time saving is the extra time after the query splitting process.

Specifically we have $S_{i,j} = S(Q_i, Q_j) = \max(0, p(Q_i) + p(Q_j) - p(C_{i,j}) - p(N_{i,j}) - p(N_{j,i}))$, evidently we only do those splitting which yield positive savings among queries while excluding negative ones.

3.1   System Architecture

The system architecture is shown in Fig.3. It consists of three modules including Common Sub-Expressions Detector, Cache Manager and Query Scheduler. The Common Sub-Queries Detector finds all the common sub-expressions among queries. The Cache Manger decides which query results to be cached into or be discarded from memory. The Query Scheduler utilizes several scheduling strategies to schedule queries to minimize the average tardiness. The three modules work on top of a database system.

3.2   Problem Statement

Next we define the query scheduling problem. Given a set of queries with the characteristics defined above where common sub-expressions can be identified among the queries, we find an order to execute the queries with the goal of minimizing the average tardiness while reducing redundant computations as much as possible. From the optimizer of the underlying database system, we can obtain the optimal plan of each query. From these plans, we can identify common sub-expressions among queries. We need a way to: 1) decide the execution order of queries; 2) select a subset of the common sub-expressions whose results need to be cached; 3) determine a subset of the queries which can reuse the cached results. The problem is formally defined as follows:

(Sharing-Aware Query Scheduling Problem) Given a query set $\bar{S} = \{Q_i, 1 \leq i \leq n\}$ and their query splitting Strategies $C = \{C_{i,j}\}$. Then we want to minimize the average tardiness $\frac{1}{n}\sum_{i=1}^{n} T(Q_i)$ by ordering queries while reducing total query processing time $\sum_{i,j,i \neq j} S_{i,j}$ as much as possible by caching common sub-queries.

4   Sharing-Aware Scheduling Approach

In this section, we present in detail our approach which explicitly takes into account the sharing results among queries. At a high level, our approach makes use of the following insight: we consider the most important possible sharing opportunities among queries, together with their consequences in terms of average tardiness. First, we present our method to discover the relevance (i.e. the sub-expressions) among queries in section 4.1. Next we show our algorithm to schedule queries by reusing the common sub-expressions' results in section 4.2.

4.1   Discovering Common Sub-expressions among Queries

To discover common sub-expressions among queries, we need to determine whether a given pair of queries is relevant. We first use Table-Indicator to filter those queries which are definitely irrelevant, then we split queries based on their semantic relationship.

(a) Table-Indicator

Because most queries don't contain similar expressions, then we need to a fast filter with minimal overhead during the scheduling.

Definition 4.1: A table indicator TI_Q exists for a selection query Q iff Q represents SQL expression. If TI_s exists, it's a triple tuple $TI_Q = [C_Q, S_Q, A_Q]$ where

- C_Q is the set of output columns in the selection clause of Q,
- S_Q is the set of source tables (or views) in Q,
- A_Q is the set of attributes in the where clause of Q.

Using the Table-Indicator, we can quickly detect the relevance of two queries Q_i and Q_j by check the following conditions: 1) $S_{Q_i} = S_{Q_j}$;2) $C_{Q_i} \cap C_{Q_j} \neq \emptyset$ and $A_{Q_i} \cap A_{Q_j} \neq \emptyset$. If Q_i and Q_j satisfy the above two conditions, then we can make them a group.

(b) Query Splitting

Detecting commonality among queries based on queries' table indicators, we have groups whose queries may share common sub-expressions. Then we compute the common predicates between each two queries using semantic caching method [5].

Suppose query Q_1's *task* $ta_{Q_1} = P_1 \wedge P_2 \cdots \wedge P_n$, and Q_2's *task* $ta_{Q_2} = P'_1 \wedge P'_2 \wedge \cdots \wedge P'_m$ (P_i is comparison predicate with the form of "attribute operator value"). Hence there are three types of relationships between Q_1 and Q_2 (see Fig. 4).

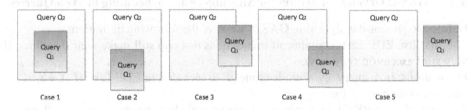

Fig. 4. Semantic relation between Query A and B

- The first type (case 1 in Fig.4) is query containment (i.e. implication): Q_2's result contain Q_1's or vice versa. Suppose Q_1 is contained by Q_2 (i.e. $ta_{Q_1} \Rightarrow ta_{Q_2}$, $C_{Q_1} \subseteq C_{Q_2}$), we have two splitting strategies: 1) we only evaluate Q_2 on database, and caching Q_2's result to evaluate Q_1; 2) we reformulate two queries to sub-expression $C_{1,2}(Q_1, Q_2) = Q_1$ and $N_{1,2}(Q_1, Q_2) = Q_2 \wedge \neg Q_1$.
- The second type (case2-4 in Fig.4) is query overlap: we process query overlap based on the relationships of query's output attributes and the range predicate. Suppose Q_1 and Q_2 are overlapped, we have three types of overlapping

relationship:1) vertically overlap (case 2, $C_{Q_1} \subseteq C_{Q_2}$, $ta_{Q_1} \wedge ta_{Q_2}$ is satisfiable); 2) horizontally overlap (case 3, $C_{Q_1} \cap C_{Q_2} \neq \emptyset$, $ta_{Q_1} \Rightarrow ta_{Q_2}$); 3) mixed overlap(case 3, $C_{Q_1} \cap C_{Q_2} \neq \emptyset$, $ta_{Q_1} \wedge ta_{Q_2}$ is satisfiable). To reduce overlap between queries, we have three parts: $C_{1,2}(Q_1, Q_2) = Q_2 \wedge Q_1$, $N_{1,2} = \neg Q_2 \wedge Q_1$ and $N_{2,1} = Q_2 \wedge \neg Q_1$.

- The last one (case 5) is no connection between two queries: we have already processed this type using our table-indicators.

To facilitate our processing of detecting sub-queries, we have the following two heuristics to pruning the improper ones.

- *Heuristics 1*(Containment size Check): Given two queries Q_1, Q_2, and $Q_1 \Rightarrow Q_2$, if $size(Q_1)/size(Q_2) < \alpha$ ($\alpha < 1$, here we take size of query as its result size in memory), then we will not cache Q_1's result, because sharing Q_1 doesn't greatly improve the total performance.
- *Heuristics 2*(Exclude Sub-expressions With Huge Results): Given two queries Q_1 and Q_2, $C_{i,j}$ is their common sub-expression, if $size(C_{i,j}) > C_1$ (where C_1 is some constant), then we'll not cache $C_{i,j}$'s result, because it doesn't fit in the cache.

(c) Estimating Processing Time of Queries

An important aspect of ordering queries is to estimate queries' processing time which is orthogonal to our work, and there are two method we can use to estimate it by sampling the database [14] or by machine learning (ML) based method [15].The sampling method is to sample a small corpus from the original database as an alternative for the candidate queries. ML-based method is to learn the time from the training dataset. Considering that querying databases is time-consuming work, we adopt the sampling method [14] to estimate the query's processing time due to its efficiency.

4.2   GASA: *Greedy Algorithm for Sharing-Aware Scheduling of Web Queries*

Before we present the algorithm **GASA**, we have the following definitions.

The first list, EDF-List, contains all transactions that can still make their deadlines, if they start execution right now.

De nition 4.2: A query Q_i with deadline d_i is included in EDF-List iff, $t + r_i \le d_i$, where t is the current time.

The second list, SRPT-List, contains all queries that already missed their deadlines.

De nition 4.3: A query Q_i with deadline d_i is included in SRPT-List iff, $t + r_i > d_i$, where t is the current time.

The main idea of the algorithm is to pick one query Q1 from the heads of the two lists and then choose another query Q2 from the remaining queries of the two lists such that the sharing of the sub-expressions' results of Q1 and Q2 can maximize the savings of the total query processing time for Q1 and Q2. We now describe the algorithm (The pseudo-code of Algorithm 1 is shown in figure 5) in detail as follows.

Algorithm 1. GASA(S̄,C)

Input: A set of queries with arrival time, estimated processing time and deadline.
Output: The id of the queries to run until next scheduling point and the id of common sub-expressions to cache.

1   Begin
2   for all newly arrived queries Q_i do
3   Place Q_i in the appropriate queue (*EDF*-List or *SPRT*-List)
4   end for
5   resort *EDF*-List & resort *SRPT*-List
6   while(*EDF*-List !=null and *SRPT*-List!=null)
7        $Q_{1,EDF}$ ←*Top (EDF-List)*
8        $Q_{1,SRPT}$ ←*Top (SRPT-List)*
9   if $r_{1,EDF} < (r_{1,SRPT} - s_{1,EDF})$ then $Q = Q_{1,EDF}$
10   else $Q = Q_{1,SRPT}$
11   end if
12
13       $S_Q = \{Q_j | Q_j \neq Q, Q_j$ and Q is disjoint$\}$
14   j'=argmax$_{Q_j \in S_Q}(savings(Q, Q_j)),$)
15   Return Q, run Q and cache $C(Q, Q_{j'})$'s result
16   refresh $Q_{j'}$' expression and re-estimate processing time
17   end while
18   End

Fig. 5. GASA: *Greedy Algorithm for Sharing-Aware Scheduling*

Step 1: (line 7-11 in figure 5) We consider the impact of tardiness on the total set of queries, and compare the total tardiness of running $Q_{1,EDF}$. first and $Q_{1,SRPT}$ second with running $Q_{1,SRPT}$ first and $Q_{1,EDF}$ second, we have that if $r_{1,EDF} < (r_{1,SRPT} - s_{1,EDF})$,then running $Q_{1,EDF}$ first will achieve lower tardiness, otherwise running $Q_{1,SRPT}$ will have a lower tardiness. By this checking, we then decide which query to run first.

Step 2: (line 12-14 in figure 5) To achieve sharing among queries, we need to decide which queries to share the picked queries' results. Suppose the picked query in the first step is Q, then we check which subset $S(Q)$ of queries shares common sub-expressions with Q, and then we pick the query $Q_{j'}$ out of $S(Q)$ as the sharing query where the processing time saving of Q and $Q_{j'}$ is the maximal one, then we do splitting between Q and $Q_{j'}$, run query Q and cache their common sub-expressions' result.

Step 3: (line 15 in figure5) We refresh $Q_{j'}$ after splitting and estimate its processing time, then return to step 1 until no more queries exist.

GASA needs to be invoked in response to two types of events, the arrival and the completion of queries. We can use the standard balanced binary search tree as the priority queue, which requires only a time $O(\log N)$ to insert and update the priority lists. For splitting queries, we need $O(N)$ to find common sub-expressions.

5   Experimental Evaluation

In this section, we describe our experimental settings and report our results.

5.1   Experimental Settings

Our experiments were conducted on the hardware configuration with 4-core 2.90GHz Intel CPU and 4GB memory running JVM 1.6.0 in Windows 7 Professional and data were stored in PostgreSQL 9.3.

We tested our method on TPC-H 1 GB databases. We chose 5 variant of TPC-H template queries without join predicates and aggregate predicates: #1,#4,#5 and #6.We generated 250 queries, according to a Zipf distribution over the range[1-100] time units with the default Zipf parameter for skewness (α) set to 0.5 which was skewed for short queries. We chose 50,100,150,200 queries from the original 250 queries as a workload respectively. Arrival times of queries are assigned according to a Poisson process. The arrival rate of the Poisson distribution is set to be the rate of normal processed query number divided by the average query processing time. Each query is assigned a deadline $d_i = a_i + p_i + k_i * p_i$ where k_i is a factor that determines the ration between the initial slack time of a query and its processing time. k_i is generated uniformly over the range $[0.0\text{-} k_{max}]$, where k_{max} is a simulation parameter with default value of 3.0.

We conduct the comparison in both the sharing and non-sharing cases. In the sharing case **GASA** is compared with ASETS*, EDF and SRPT [4], and also LS (least slack), under which the priority is $1/s_i$; in the non-sharing case, we compare **GASA** with EDF-Sharing, SRPT-Sharing LS-Sharing (which are EDF,SRPT and LS adapted with our greedy sharing strategies).

The performance of all the approaches is measured in terms of two metrics: (a) average tardiness which characterizes the total performance of our system, (b) total processing time savings of the whole workload.

5.2   Experimental Results

- **Comparison with Sharing-Nothing Polices**

In our first experiment, we measured the average tardiness for the four scheduling policies mentioned above as the number of queries increases from 0 to 250, with Zipf parameter $\alpha = 0.5$ and $k_{max} = 3.0$.

The experiment results for the average tardiness of the 4 scheduling policies on different query workload are shown in Figure 6. As we can see, when the number of queries is small, the system is able to meet most of the deadlines. In this case, the sharing opportunity for computing queries is small, however **GASA** still performs a little bit better than other policies. As the number of queries increases, the system cannot meet all the deadlines, whereas the sharing opportunity improves, and **GASA** substantially outperforms the other four polices. The maximum improvement by **GASA** is around 50.6% percent compared with ASETS* when the query number is 250.

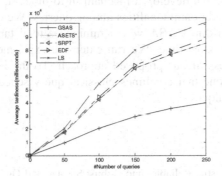

Fig. 6. Comparing GASA with state of art scheduling polices

- **Comparison with Baseline Sharing Polices**

We compare the performance of **GASA** with EDF-Sharing, SRPT-Sharing and LS-Sharing. Figure 7 shows the average tardiness comparison and figure 8 shows the average processing time savings.

In figure 7, **GASA** outperforms the other three polices in all the cases. LS-Sharing performs the worst, and the performance of SRPT-Sharing is comparable to **GASA** due to the high workload (in which most queries cannot meet their deadlines). In figure 8, the average processing time savings of all the approaches increase substantially when the number of queries increases from 0 to 50; when the number of queries is larger than 100, the savings begins to decrease. This can be explained by the fact that the rate of reduced processing time is smaller than the increasing rate of queries.

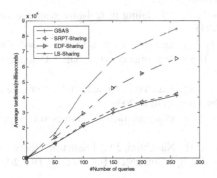 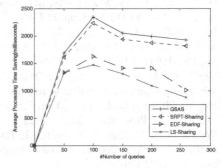

Fig. 7. Comparison of sharing-based polices   **Fig. 8.** Average Processing Time Savings

6   Conclusions

In this paper we proposed the problem of sharing-aware scheduling of web services. We propose a sharing-aware approach for query scheduling which exploits commonalities among queries. We develop a mechanism to model query relevance and design a strategy to discover commonalities among queries. We design a sharing-aware query scheduling algorithm **GASA** which minimizes total tardiness while reducing redundant work at the same time. We run extensive experiments to verify the efficiency and effectiveness of our proposed approach. To the best of our knowledge, our paper is the first one that combines classical query scheduling algorithms with semantic caching techniques.

References

1. Unterbrunner, P.: Elastic, Reliable, and Robust Storage and Query Processing with Crescando /RB. PhD thesis, ETH Zurich (2012)
2. Zhou, J., Larson, P.-A., Freytag, J.C., Lehner, W.: Efficient Exploitation of Similar Subexpression for Query Processing. In: Proc. SIGMOD 2007, pp. 533–544 (2007)
3. Chidlovskii, B., Borghoff, U.M.: Semantic Caching of Web Queries. The VLDB Journal 9(1), 2–17 (2000)
4. Guirguis, S., Sharaf, M.A., Chrysanthis, P.K., Labrinidis, A., Pruhs, K.: Adaptive scheduling of web transactions. In: Proc. ICDE, pp. 357–368 (2009)
5. Ren, Q., Dunham, M.H., Kumar, V.: Semantic Caching and Query Processing. IEEE Transactions on Knowledge and Data Engineering 15(1), 192–210 (2003)
6. Dar, S.,Franklin, M.J., Þór Jónsson, B., Srivastava, D., Tan, M. : Semantic Data Caching and Replacement. In Proc. VLDB 1996, pp.330–341(1996).
7. Brucker, P.: Scheduling algorithms, 5th edn. Springer (2007)
8. Ullman, J.D.: Np-complete scheduling problems. J. Computer. Syst. Sci. 10(3), 384–393 (1975)
9. Peha, J.M.: Scheduling and dropping algorithms to support integrated services in packet-switched networks. PhD thesis, Stanford University (1991)
10. Haritsa, J.R., Carey, M.J., Livny, M.: Value-based scheduling in real-time database systems. In: Proc. VLDB 1993, pp. 117–152 (1993)
11. Irwin, D.E., Grit, L.E., Chase, J.S.: Balancing Risk and Reward in a Market-Based Task Service. In: Proc. 13th IEEE Int'l Symp. High Performance Distributed Computing, pp. 160–169 (2004)
12. Gupta, C., Mehta, A., Wang, S., Dayal, U.: Fair, effective, efficient and differentiated scheduling in an enterprise data warehouse. In: Proc. EDBT (2009)
13. He, Y., Elnikety, S., Larus, J., Yan, C.: Zeta: Scheduling interactive services with partial execution. In: Proc. SOCC 2012 (2012)
14. Wu, W., Chi, Y., Zhu, S., Tatemura, J., Hakan, H., Naughton, J.F.: Predicting Query Execution Time:Are Optimizer Cost Models Really Unusable? In: Proc. ICDE 2013, pp. 1081–1092 (2013)
15. Malic, T., Rurns, R., Chawla, N.: A Black-Box Approach to Query Cardinality Estimation. In: Proc. CIDR 2007, pp. 56–67 (2007)
16. Schroeder, B., Harchol-Balter, M.: Web servers under overload: How scheduling can help. ACM Trans. Inter. Tech. 6(1), 20–52 (2006)

A Taxonomy of Hyperlink Hiding Techniques

Guang-Gang Geng[1], Xiu-Tao Yang[2], Wei Wang[1], and Chi-Jie Meng[1]

[1] China Internet Network Information Center, Computer Network Information
Center, Chinese Academy of Sciences, Beijing, China, 100180
{gengguanggang,wangwei,mengchijie}@cnnic.cn
[2] Beijing Institute of Electronic System Engineering, Beijing, China, 100854
xiutaoyang_temp@163.com

Abstract. Hidden links are designed solely for search engines rather
than visitors. To get high search engine rankings, link hiding techniques
are usually used for the profitability of underground economies, such
as illicit game servers, false medical services, illegal gambling, and less
attractive high-profit industry. This paper investigates hyperlink hiding
techniques on the Web, and gives a detailed taxonomy. We believe the
taxonomy can help develop appropriate countermeasures.

Statistical experimental results on real Web data indicate that link
hiding techniques are very prevalent. We also tried to explore the attitude
of Google towards link hiding spam by analyzing the PageRank values
of relative links. The results show that more should be done to punish
the hidden link spam.

Keywords: Web spam, link hiding, hidden spam, spam detection.

1 Introduction

Most Web surfers depend on search engines to locate information on the Web.
Link analysis algorithms [11], such as PageRank [12] and HITS [8], are usually
used for Search engines ranking. Link analysis algorithms assume that every link
represents a vote of support, in the sense that if there is a link from page x to
page y and these two pages are authored by different people, then the author of
page x is recommending page y. In particular, PageRank is the basis of Google's
search technology [1].

Web spammers try to mislead search engines to make a high rank in search
results [6]. In this context, hyperlink hiding techniques are often used to de-
ceive search engines. Spammers hope that many small endorsements from these
pages with hidden links result in a sizable PageRank for the target page. Several
questions naturally arise: what link hiding techniques are the spammers using;
and, how prevalent are hidden spam links on the Web? This paper attempts to
answer those questions.

The rest of sections are organized as follows. Section 2 presents a literature
review. Section 3 gives a comprehensive taxonomy of current hidden link spam
techniques. Section 4 describes the experimental analysis on 5,583,451 Chinese
Web sites. At last, section 5 draws the conclusion.

L. Chen et al. (Eds.): APWeb 2014, LNCS 8709, pp. 165–176, 2014.

2   Related Work

Hidden links are designed to increase link popularity, which are invisible for visitors [17]. Google considers hyperlinks hidden by small characters as deception [5]. Gyongyi etc al. point out that hidden links are often used in honey pot to boost the ranking of the spam pages [7]. They further present a comprehensive taxonomy of current spamming techniques and survey content hiding techniques, where spam links hidden by avoiding anchor texts or tiny anchor images are mentioned [6]. Link-hiding related features are not paid more attention to in statistical Web spam detection studies [3][9][14].

To the best of our knowledge, there is no previously published literature that directly studied how prevalent, successful, or varied hidden link spam techniques are on the Web. This paper attempts to study hidden link spam in detail. It is hoped that the findings can help in developing appropriate countermeasures.

3   Hyperlink Hiding Techniques

There are many different ways to hide links from visitors while leaving it perfectly viewable to search engines. In this section, we will examine current hyperlink hiding techniques used by spammers and attempt to categorize them based on their features. Just as the work on JavaScript redirection spam [2], we present short examples to show the hiding techniques really used by spammers. Simple techniques are presented first and are followed by more advanced ones.

3.1   A: Making Anchor Text Font Color the Same as Background Color

The simplest and oldest method that spammers use to create hidden links is to make the font of anchor text the same color as the background. Here is one example.

```
<span style="background:white;" >
    <a href="target.html" style="color:white"> invisible anchor text </a>
</span>
```

In this example, the color scheme is defined in the HTML document. Color schemes can also be defined in an attached cascading style sheet file (CSS). Sometimes, spammers also consider background images. They set the image color to be the same as the font color, which is relatively harder to detect.

3.2   B: Making Anchor Text Font Color Almost Match Background Color or Background Image

Instead of setting the font color to entirely match the background color, some spammers and web masters set their font colors to almost match the background color. The idea behind this method is that they believe that they are thwarting the search engines' software detection systems by slightly changing the color of the text.

```
<div style="background-color:white;" >
  <a href="target.html" style="color:#feffee"> text color similar to white </a>
</div>
```

3.3   C: Setting Tiny Anchor Text or Placing the hyperlinks in a Tiny Block

Making tiny anchor text is another hyperlink hiding method. This way, the hyperlink can be set small enough, such as 1 pixel high, even 0 pixel. Here's a simple example of that.

```
<a href="target.html" style="font-size:0px"> tiny text </a>
```

In HTML, the div element is often used for generic organizational or stylistic applications. Spammers can also use div to set the link size. The following is another example.

```
<div style="font-size:0px;"> <a href="target.html" >invisible text</a> </div>
```

Perhaps the most common use of div element is to carry class or id attributes in conjunction with CSS to apply layout, typographic, color, and other presentation attributes to parts of the content. In the previous example, the *font-size:0px* can also be defined in a CSS file. Besides, div block size can be set via width and height attributes. For example, <div style="width:1px;height:1px;">, where the div size is 1 pixel.

Another example of hiding a hyperlink via tiny scrolling block is presented below.

```
<marquee scrollAmount=1 width=1 height=1>
  <a href="target.html"> text in a tiny scrolling block </a>
</marquee>
```

In this example, *target.html* is put in a scrolling block with area 1 × 1 pixel, which is invisible to Web users.

3.4   D: Disguising Anchor Text as Plain Text

Sometimes, spammers insert hyperlinks into a paragraph, where the anchor text looks like plain text. Here's a paragraph of text on a site:

```
The SEO company follows strict rules to
insure the clients website reach the top of
search engines and stay there.
```

A user wouldn't see any hyperlinks, even if they moused over every word in the paragraph. But if you happened to click on just the right word, you'd get whisked away to a SEO site. Actually, there is a hidden link under the anchor text "SEO company". If you view the source of the page, here's what you'll see:

> The <a href="http://www.seomarketleaders.com" onMouseOver=
> "window.status='';return true;" style="cursor:text;color:black;
> text-decoration:none;"> SEO company</a> follows strict
> rules to insure the clients website reach the top of search engines and stay there.

3.5   E: Placing Hyperlinks in High-Speed Scrolling Blocks

The <marquee> tag is a non-standard HTML element which causes text to scroll up, down, left or right automatically [16]. Although the W3C advises against its use in HTML documents, it's still widely used. SCROLLAMOUNT attribute sets the speed of the scrolling. A bigger value for SCROLLAMOUNT makes the marquee scroll faster. If the SCROLLAMOUNT value is big enough, the scrolling block will be invisible to the naked eye. Here is a simple example.

> <marquee height=1 width=8 scrollamount=3000>
>   <a href="target.html"> *text in a high-speed scrolling block* </a>
> </marquee>

The default *scrollamount* value is 6. The value in the example is 3000, which is too fast to see.

Similar effects can also be achieved through the use of JavaScript or HTML <blink> element [16] [15].

3.6   F: Putting Links Outside the Screen

Using cascading style sheets, you have the option to absolutely or relatively position any division. Using absolute position, you can simply position the text you wish to hide any number of pixels off the screen to the left of the window. Here are some example codes:

> .hiddenclass { position : absolute;left : -977px; }

If you put that in your style sheet and then assign the class "hiddenclass" to your div, then the div will display 977 pixels to the left of the visible screen - i.e., it will not appear on the screen. Here is a example:

> <div id="hiddenclass"> <a href="target.html"> *invisible anchor text* </a> </div>

The absolute position can also be set in the div directly as follows:

> <div style="left: -977px; position: absolute; top: -977px">
>   <a href="target.html"> *invisible anchor text* </a>
> </div>

In the example above, $left : -977$ may be written in more complex formats, such as $left : expression(23 - 1000)$.

In addition to the methods described above, users can use CSS text-indent property or margin-left property to put hyperlinks outside the screen. A example is presented below.

```
<div style="text-indent:-999px;"><a href="target.html">hidden text</a> </div>
```

3.7 G: Using Visibility:Hidden or Display:None Style Commands

An alternative to the method above is to simply use the built in features of style sheets to hide hyperlinks:

```
.hiddenclass { visibility : hidden;}
```

Again, if you put that into a style sheet and then assign the class "hiddenclass" to your div, the hyperlinks in the div block will not appear in the browser window.

3.8 H: Hiding Hyperlinks via JavaScript

JavaScript is an open source programming language commonly implemented as part of a web browser in order to create enhanced user interfaces and dynamic websites [4]. Google claims that search engines have difficulty accessing JavaScript [5]. In 2011, labnol.org reported that Google indexes JavaScript based Facebook comments, but there is no clear report that Google parsers JavaScript codes on the whole Web. This fact encourages spammers to hide hyperlinks by the aid of JavaScript. Here is a simple example:

```
<script language="JavaScript" type="text/javascript">
    document.write( "<div style='visibility:hidden'>" );
</script>
<a href="target.html">keywords</a>
<script language="JavaScript" type="text/javascript">
    document.write( "</div>" );
</script>
```

The example is easy to understand, which is a packaging of the method described in section 3.7. In the above codes, <div> and </div> tags are embed in JavaScript codes separately, which may not be indexed by search engines. However, the hyperlink *target.html* is displayed in html codes, which is more likely to indexed by search engines. In a similar manner, almost all the link hiding techniques described in this section can be further disguised with JavaScript. Next, let's look into a more complex example.

```
<div id="ql1000">
  <a href="target.html" title="keyword">
    target keyword
  </a>
</div>
<script language="JavaScript">
var _xa= [
  "\x64\69\x73\x70\x6C\x61\x79", "\x6E\x6F\x6E\x65",
  "\x71\x6c\x31\x30\x30\x30", "\x73\x74\x79\x6C\x65",
  "\x67\x65\x74\x45\x6C\x65\x6D\x65\x6E\x74\x42\x79\x49\x64"];
  document[_xa[4]](_xa[2])[_xa[3]][_xa[0]]=_xa[1];
</script>
```

The above JavaScript codes are designed in rather vague terms. The elements of array _xa are written with ASCII characters. The last line of the above JavaScript codes is document['getElementById']('ql1000')['style']['display']='none', which makes all the content, including hyperlinks, in the div named ql1000 invisible. In order to avoid presenting the whole style assignment directly, script can build up the style assignment via string concatenation. One very straight forward example is presented below.

```
<script type="text/javascript">
  document.getElementById("q" + "l" + "1000").style.display="n" + "o" + "ne";
</script>
```

What is worse, JavaScript as a programming language, has many functions and operators, which throw off a human readers. The following codes show the flexibility of JavaScript.

```
<script language="javascript">function HexTostring(s){
  var r='';
  for(var i=0;i<s.length;i+=2){
    var sxx=parseInt(s.substring(i,i+2),16);
  r+=String.fromCharCode(sxx);}
  return r;}
  eval(HexTostring("646f63756d656e742e676574456c656d65
  6e74427949642822716c3130303022292e7374796c652e6469
  73706c6179203d20226e6f6e6522"));
</script>
```

These codes are essentially equivalent to the previous example, yet look completely different.

3.9 I: Hiding Hyperlinks via Cloaking or Redirection Techniques

Cloaking is a Web spam technique in which the page presented to the search engine spider is different from that presented to the user's browser [19]. Some spammers hide target hyperlinks using cloaking technique. Similarly, spammers also use redirection techniques to hide targeting hyperlinks. Among the redirection spam techniques, JavaScript based redirection is the most notorious and difficult to catch [2]. Wu et al. [19] and Chellapilla et al. [2] have conducted comprehensive studies of cloaking and redirection techniques respectively, so the techniques will not be repeated here. However, it's important to point out that we do not consider the redirected target URL, but the hyperlinks in the redirection page as hidden links. For example, A redirects to B, and C is a hyperlink in page A. In this paper, C is a hidden link, but B is not seen as a hidden link.

3.10 J: Hiding Hyperlinks in Pull-Down Menu

Pull-down menu is also called a drop-down menu, which is a menu of commands or options that appears when you select an item with a mouse. A drop down menu can make it easier to display a large list of choices - since only one choice is displayed initially, the remaining choices can be displayed when the user activates the dropbox. Some spammers insert the target hyperlinks into a long pull-down list, which are hard to find.

3.11 K: Inserting Links into Long Title or Meta Tags

Generally, web browsers show the preceding part of a long title. Thus, some spammers insert urls into long title. Similarly, meta tags provide structured meta data about a Web page and they are used for search engines. Although they have been the targets of spammers for a long time and search engines consider these data less and less, there are pages still using them.

3.12 L: Hiding Div "Below" the Visible Layer

Another sneaky way to hide a hyperlink from Web users while keeping it available to the search engines is to put the hyperlinks in a layer that is "behind" the visible layer. The CSS z-index property specifies the stack order of an element, which is supported in all major browsers. An element with a greater stack order is always in front of an element with a lower stack order. One example hiding hyperlinks via z-index is presented below.

```
<div id="front" style="position:absolute; z-index:1">
    <img src="image.gif" >
</div>
<div id="back" style="position:absolute; z-index:-1">
    <a href="target.html" target="_blank"> target keyword</a>
</div>
```

The codes show that the second div has a negative stack order, which determines the *target.html* is behind the *image.gif*. Besides z-index, "overflow:hidden" can also hide the hyperlinks below the visible layer. Here is a simple example.

```
<style type="text/css">
#spam{width:99px;height:20px;overflow:hidden;position:absolute;}
#spam a{display:block;line-height:20px;text-decoration:none;}
</style>
<div id="spam">
   <a href="/"> </a>
   <a href="target.html" title="keywords">
     target keyword
   </a>
</div>
```

In the example above, *target.html* is covered by a non-breaking space.

4   Prevalence of Link Hiding Techniques

Link-hiding can be considered an adversarial problem. As commercial search engines develop algorithms to detect and discard certain types of hidden links, new techniques for hiding links will be developed. In last section, we examined current hyperlink hiding techniques used by spammers and categorized them based on their features. In this section, we study the prevalence of hidden spam links, and how prevalence of the variety of techniques described in Section 3.

We carried out the analysis on 5,765,357 Chinese homepages (*http://www. + domain name*) in Sep. 2012, including .com, .net and .cn domain names. To detect the Web pages with hiding links, we first train a cost sensitive naive bayes classifier on 103 pages with hidden links and 271 normal pages. The cost sensitive model ensures a high recall of pages with hidden links. Then, we filtered the 5,765,357 pages with the trained model. The detection results contain quite a few false alarms, but it's enough for us to analyze the prevalence of hidden links. By random sampling from the suspicious set and carrying out manual verification, we approximately determined the number of pages with hidden links. Table 1 tabulates the statistics in detail.

Table 1. Percentage occurrence of hidden link spam among Chinese Web pages

URL Type	Count / Total	Percentage
.com/.net/.cn	81775/5765357 = 1/70.5	1.42%

It is noticed that a number of Chinese pages use hyperlink hiding techniques. To analyze the prevalence of the variety of techniques described in Section 3, we randomly sampled 4727 pages with hidden links from .com/.net/.cn set. Each sampled hidden link spam page was manually analyzed. All the 4727 samples were labeled with the types of techniques they used. Besides, all the hidden links are extracted for further analysis. In total, 16767 unique target hyperlinks are hidden in the 4727 pages.

Table 2 describes the prevalence of hidden link techniques in detail. The table shows that the 4727 pages contain 16767 unique hidden links. F, G and H are the most popular link hiding techniques, which account for 75.3% of that total. These three techniques can be easily used to hide multiple hyperlinks. It can be observed that some of the 4727 web pages contain more than one link hiding technique.

Table 2. Prevalence of different link hiding techniques

techniques	number (percentage)=>number of hidden links
A	102 (2.2%) => 661
B	51 (1.1%) => 493
C	137 (2.9%) => 561
D	322 (6.8%) => 357
E	136 (2.9%) => 1987
F	1157 (24.5%) => 68661
G	511 (10.8%) => 30192
H	1888 (39.9%) => 51570
I	86 (1.8%) => 2071
J	151 (3.2%) => 527
K	255 (5.4%) => 103
L	53 (1.1%) => 779
All	4849 (4849/4727=102.6%) => 157962(unique links: 16767)

Are the 16767 target pages punished by the search engines? We do not know the detailed ranking strategy of commercial search engines, but we can explore this problem from a side by analyzing the PageRank values of the target hyperlinks. Google provides a public interface, toolbarqueries.google.com, for querying the PageRank values. Table 3 shows the average PageRank values of target hidden links and randomly selected 39756 urls from DNS resolution logs.

Table 3. Comparison of average PageRank values

	hidden links	randomly selected urls
Number	16767	39756
Average PageRanks	1.340	1.137

Table 3 shows that the 16767 hidden links have an average PageRank value 1.34, which is higher than that of the randomly selected urls. To some extent, the result means that Google needs to establish a more effective punitive mechanism for the hidden links.

We further analyzed the high-frequency words in the anchor texts of the 16767 target hyperlinks. The top 20 high-frequency keywords and the corresponding types are described in figure 1. The statistics show that gambling sites, personal game servers and medical services are the main types of the hidden links. Most of the sites belong to shady or illegal industries.

Keywords	Type	Keywords	Type
百家乐	Gambling	皇冠现金网	Gambling
全讯网	Gambling	时时彩	Gambling
博彩通	Gambling	癫痫病	Medical service
太阳城	Gambling	世博	Gambling
皇冠网	Gambling	武动乾坤	Illicit game server
传奇私服	Illicit game server	金宝博	Gambling
办证	Fake certificates	盈丰国际	Gambling
牛皮癣	Medical service	神印王座	Online game
澳门赌场	Gambling	网通传奇	Online game
网址之家	Navigation site	足球比分	Gambling

Fig. 1. The high-frequency words in the anchor texts of the target hyperlinks

5   Conclusion and Future Work

In this paper we presented a variety of commonly used link hiding techniques, and organized them into a taxonomy. We analyzed the prevalence of common link hiding techniques on the web. Just as the previous work on Web spam [6] [2], we argue that such a structured discussion of the subject is important to raise the awareness of the research community. Given that most of the sites using link hiding techniques are shady or illegal industries, more should be done to punish the hidden link spam.

In the future, we should pay more attention to two things. The first is studying link hidden spam on a bigger data set, which includes multilingual samples. The second is developing a proper countermeasure to address the problem as a whole, despite the variety of different link hiding techniques. One possible solution draws support from maturing optical character recognition techniques (OCR) [10]. The motivation is that as a computer vision technique, OCR can only read the visible content on the Web page like humans. The snapshot of a Web page can be easily taken via some softwares, such as wkhtmltopdf [18] and snapshotter [13].

All the visual text on the snapshot image can be recognized via OCR techniques as *textVector*. If an anchor text does not exist in the *textVector*, the corresponding hyperlink is identified as hidden link. And, of course, the relative position of anchor text should also be taken into account.

Acknowledgment. This paper is supported by grants National Natural Science Foundation of China (Nos. 61375039, 61005029 & 61103138).

References

1. Brin, S., Page, L.: The anatomy of a large-scale hypertextual web search engine. Computer Networks and ISDN Systems 30(1), 107 117 (1998)
2. Chellapilla, K., Maykov, A.: A taxonomy of javascript redirection spam. In: Proceedings of the 3rd International Workshop on Adversarial Information Retrieval on the Web, pp. 81–88. ACM (2007)
3. Erdélyi, M., Garzó, A., Benczúr, A.A.: Web spam classification: a few features worth more. In: Proceedings of the 2011 Joint WICOW/AIRWeb Workshop on Web Quality, pp. 27–34. ACM (2011)
4. Flanagan, D.: JavaScript: the definitive guide. O'Reilly Media, Incorporated (2006)
5. Google: Webmaster guidelines - webmaster tools help (2013), http://www.google.com/webmasters/guidelines.html (accessed January 17, 2013)
6. Gyongyi, Z., Garcia-Molina, H.: Web spam taxonomy. In: First International Workshop on Adversarial Information Retrieval on the Web (AIRWeb 2005) (2005)
7. Gyöngyi, Z., Garcia-Molina, H., Pedersen, J.: Combating web spam with trustrank. In: Proceedings of the Thirtieth International Conference on Very Large Data Bases, vol. 30, pp. 576–587. VLDB Endowment (2004)
8. Kleinberg, J.: Authoritative sources in a hyperlinked environment. Journal of the ACM (JACM) 46(5), 604–632 (1999)
9. Liu, Y., Chen, F., Kong, W., Yu, H., Zhang, M., Ma, S., Ru, L.: Identifying web spam with the wisdom of the crowds. ACM Transactions on the Web (TWEB) 6(1), 2 (2012)
10. Mori, S., Nishida, H., Yamada, H.: Optical character recognition. John Wiley & Sons, Inc. (1999)
11. Ng, A., Zheng, A., Jordan, M.: Stable algorithms for link analysis. In: Proceedings of the 24th Annual International ACM SIGIR Conference on Research and Development in Information Retrieval, pp. 258–266. ACM (2001)
12. Page, L., Brin, S., Motwani, R., Winograd, T.: The pagerank citation ranking: bringing order to the web (1999)
13. Snapshotter (2013), http://www.mewsoft.com/Products/Snapshotter.html (accessed Febrary 20, 2013)
14. Spirin, N., Han, J.: Survey on web spam detection: principles and algorithms. ACM SIGKDD Explorations Newsletter 13(2), 50–64 (2012)
15. element Wikipedia, The Free Encyclopedia, B (2013), http://en.wikipedia.org/wiki/Blink_element (accessed January 20, 2013)

16. Wikipedia: Marquee element — Wikipedia, the free encyclopedia (2013),
    http://en.wikipedia.org/wiki/Marquee_element (accessed January 19, 2013)
17. Wikipedia: Spamdexing — Wikipedia, the free encyclopedia (2013),
    http://en.wikipedia.org/wiki/Spamdexing (accessed January 17, 2013)
18. Wkhtmltopdf (2013), http://code.google.com/p/wkhtmltopdf/ (accessed Febrary 20, 2013)
19. Wu, B., Davison, B.: Cloaking and redirection: A preliminary study. In: First International Workshop on Adversarial Information Retrieval on the Web (AIRWeb 2005) (2005)

Improving Recommendation Accuracy with Clustering-Based Social Regularization

Xiao Ma, Hongwei Lu, Zaobin Gan*, and Yao Ma

School of Computer Science and Technology,
Huazhong University of Science and Technology, Wuhan, China
{cindyma,luhw,zgan}@hust.edu.cn, mayaobox@qq.com

Abstract. Social network information has been proven to be beneficial to improve the recommendation accuracy. Some recent works show a user may trust different subsets of friends regarding different domains concerning the heterogeneity and diversity of social relationships. However, these works obtain the friends subsets mainly by dividing friendships depending on the item categories, which aggravate the sparsity problem of social relationships and limit the contribution of social recommendation. In order to solve the issue, in this paper, we propose a novel social recommendation model by incorporating the friendships from different clustering-based user groups. We first formalize the user-preference matrix which describes the preferences of users from multiple domains and obtain the user groups by using the PDSFCM (Partial Distance Strategy Fuzzy C-Means) algorithm. Then we define the clustering-specific friends subsets and design a clustering-based social regularization term to integrate these friendships into the traditional Matrix Factorization model. The comparison experiments on Epinions data set demonstrate that our approach outperforms other state-of-the-art methods in terms of RMSE and MAE.

Keywords: Social Recommendation, Fuzzy C-Means, Clustering-based Social Regularization, Matrix Factorization.

1 Introduction

With the explosion of information on the Internet, recommender systems as an indispensable type of Information Filtering technique have attracted lots of attention in the past decades. Typically, recommender systems are based on Collaborative Filtering, which is a technique that automatically predicts the interests of an active user by collecting rating information from other similar users or items[1,4,14].

Recent years, the fast development of online social network has provided new opportunities to increase recommendation accuracy beyond the capabilities of purely rating-driven recommender systems. Some social network based recommender systems [4,7,9]have been proposed. Generally, social recommendation

---

* Corresponding author.

L. Chen et al. (Eds.): APWeb 2014, LNCS 8709, pp. 177–188, 2014.

relies on the assumption that friends in the social network will always share similar tastes. However, the majority of these works neglect the phenomenon that people may declare similar interest with their friends in one domain, but different interest in another one. For example, Alice and Amy are friends, and they share similar interests in the aspect of clothing, but they have different taste about food. Therefore, we cannot simply consider that Alice and Amy are similar regardless of other information. Some recent works focus on this issue [6,8,11].

However, existing domain-specific social recommendation approaches obtain the friends subsets mainly by dividing friendships depending on the item categories, which may aggravate the social relationships sparsity problem. As we know that, the available friendships in online social network are extremely sparse [3] and the distribution of the number of social relations follow a power-law-like distribution [17]. A small portion of users have lots of social relations, while a large amount of users have a few relations. If we divide the friendships based on the item categories, the available friendships of users from each category will become even less. Actually, people are interested in 6.3 item categories on average [11] in the product review sites Epinions[1], which indicates that in most of the item categories, social recommendation may have few contributions.

In order to solve the issue, in this paper, we propose a novel social recommendation model by incorporating the friendships from different clustering-based user groups and try to improve the accuracy of social recommendation concerning the heterogeneity and diversity of the social relationships. The main contributions of our work are summarized as follows:(1) We formalize the user-preference matrix which describes the preferences of users from multiple domains and obtain the user groups by using the PDSFCM (Partial Distance Strategy Fuzzy C-Means) algorithm, which is a more reasonable method to divide users based on the similarity of users' preferences; (2) we define the clustering-specific friends subsets and design a clustering-based social regularization term to integrate these clustering-based friendships into the traditional Matrix Factorization model.

The remainder of this paper is organized as follows. In Section 2, we provide background information about recommender systems and review related social recommendation models. Section 3 gives the problem formulation and detailed our clustering-based social recommendation model. The experiment results and analysis are presented in section 4. Finally, Section 5 concludes this study with future work.

2   Related Work

Recommender systems play an important role in helping online users find potential items they like. Many techniques are used to build recommender systems, which can be generally classified into content-based methods[14], collaborative

---

[1] http://www.epinions.com/

filtering(CF) based methods[2,5,16], and hybrid methods[1]. Although recommender systems have been comprehensively analyzed in the past decades, the study of social-based recommender systems just started. Using social network information to recommend items has become a hot topic in the area of recommender systems. Traditional recommender systems [13,14] are based on the assumption that users are independent and identically distributed, and ignore the social relationships between users, which are not consistent with the reality that we usually turn to our friends for recommendations. Therefore, social recommendation is more reasonable.

Ma et al. [4] proposed a social recommendation model based on the matrix factorization model. Their method combines a basic matrix factorization approach and a social network based approach, which naturally fuses the users tastes and their trusted friends favors together. Jamali et al. [7] introduce SocialMF, which is one of the most popular social recommendation algorithms. The authors incorporate the mechanism of trust propagation into their probabilistic matrix factorization based model, which is a crucial phenomenon in social sciences and increases the rating accuracy to a large extent. An effective and efficient social regularization approach is proposed by Ma et al. [9] to constrain the taste between a user and his/her friends. The authors employed two type of regularization terms: (1) average-based regularization that targets to minimize the difference between a user's latent factors and the average of that of his/her friends; (2) individual-based regularization that focuses on latent factor difference between a user and each of his/her friends.

Most of the above methods assume that users and their friends will share similar tastes. However, they ignore the phenomenon that friends may share similar preferences in a domain, and different preferences in another one. Recently, some works focusing on this issue have been proposed. As far as we know, Yang et al. [8] is the first to argue that a user may trust different subsets of friends regarding different domains. They divided the social network of all trust relationships into several sub-networks, each of which concerning a single category of items. Based on the SocialMF model, they proposed a circle-based recommendation model to make prediction in each inferred circle. Guo et al. [6] proposed the mTrustMF model. They considered that a user may trust different people in different domains. They connected user-category (which can be derived from the categories of users interested items) and user-item rating matrix through a shared user latent feature space. A category-specific regularization term is proposed to make a user's latent feature vector to be close to the average of the latent feature vectors of his trusted friends in the same item categories.

However, these approaches divide friendships mainly depending on the item categories. Social recommendation can be done within certain category. Thus the social relationships can be used in each category are even less, which may aggravate the sparsity problem of social relationships and limit the contribution of social recommendation. Therefore, in our work, we divide the friendships by fuzzily partition the users with similar preferences from multiple domains and integrate these friendships into the traditional Matrix Factorization model to improve the prediction accuracy of recommendation.

3   Clustering-Based Social Recommendation Model

In this section, we discuss how to build our social recommendation model based on the fuzzy clustering of user preferences from multiple domains. We first define some notations and formalize the problem studied in Section 3.1. Then the definition of user preference vectors is detailed and the user-preference matrix is obtained in Section 3.2. By employing the PDSFCM algorithm, user groups are generated in Section 3.3 based on the fuzzily partitioning of the user-preference matrix produced in the previous section. Finally, we give the definition of the clustering-specific friends subsets and describe how to make social recommendation with the clustering-based social regularization term in Section 3.4.

3.1   Preliminaries

We denote the user set by $\mathcal{U} = \{u_1, u_2, ..., u_m\}$, the item set by $\mathcal{V} = \{v_1, v_2, ..., v_n\}$ and the item category set by $\mathcal{C} = \{C_1, C_2, ..., C_w\}$. m,n,and w is the total number of users, items and categories, respectively. A rating provided by user u_i to item v_j is denoted by $R_{i,j}$, and all the ratings $\mathcal{R} = \{R_{i,j} \in \{1,2,3,4,5\}| u_i \in \mathcal{U}, v_j \in \mathcal{V}\}$constructs an $m \times n$ user-item rating matrix. Regarding the social network, we define a directed graph $\mathcal{G} = (\mathcal{U}, \mathcal{E})$, where edge set $\mathcal{E}$ represents the relations between users $(\mathcal{U})$. The friends set of user u_i is denoted by $friends(i) \subset \mathcal{U}$.

Traditional recommender systems mainly consider the user-item rating matrix as shown in Figure 1(b) to make recommendation. In this paper, we also consider the item category information and social relationships of users as shown in Figure 1(a). The problems studied in this paper is to find the friends subsets with similar preferences from multiple domains in the social network and integrate these friendships into the traditional recommender systems to further improve the accuracy of social recommendation.

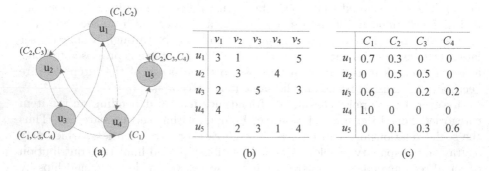

(a)   (b)   (c)

Fig. 1. A toy example: (a) Category-specific Social Network, each user is labeled with the categories in which she has ratings; (b) user-item rating matrix; (c) user-preference matrix

3.2   User Preference Matrix Construction

Definition 1. *(User Preference Vectors)*
Regarding each user, the preferences of user u_i from multiple domains can be represented by a vector. We formulate the user preference vectors as follows:
$Pre(i) = (\frac{r_i^{C_1}}{|R_i|}, \frac{r_i^{C_2}}{|R_i|}, ..., \frac{r_i^{C_w}}{|R_i|})$, *for* $i = 1, 2, ...m$

where $r_i^{C_k} (k = 1, 2, ...w)$ represents the total number of ratings by user u_i in category C_k. $|R_i|$ represents the total number of ratings issued by user u_i. $Pre(i)_k = \frac{r_i^{C_k}}{|R_i|} \in [0, 1]$ denotes the preference of user u_i to category C_k. If $|R_i|$ equals to zero, that is to say, user u_i has no ratings in all the categories, we assume that the preference of user u_i for each category is the same and equals to $\frac{1}{w}$.

Thus an $m \times w$ user-preference matrix is generated as shown in Figure 1(c). For example, suppose C_1, C_2, C_3 and C_4 represent the Fashion, Beauty, Computers and Cameras, respectively, then the preferences of user u_1 for Fashion and Beauty is 0.7 and 0.3, and she/he has no interest in the Computers and Cameras.

3.3   PDSFCM-Based Fuzzily Partitioning Algorithm

In this section, we cluster users with multiple similar preferences into different groups based on the partition of user-preference matrix generated in Section 3.2. Clustering algorithms partition users into different groups. Users in the same group are assumed to have similar preferences and those in different groups are assumed to have distinct preferences [10,12].

In real life, users often have diverse preferences. For example, one user may prefer both fashion and computers, or even more. Hence, it is more reasonable to allow a user to be assigned to more than one group. Therefore, we need a soft clustering method to design a fuzzily partitioning approach.

As we know that the data sparsity is a serious problem in recommender systems. One user may just issue a few ratings to a small amount of items. For most of the users, their preference vectors are filled with more than one zero elements as shown in Figure 1(c). Actually, the elements in the zero positions are the missing (or incomplete) data. If we simply regard them as zero, it may affect the results of clustering.

For these two reasons, we choose to use the PDSFCM algorithm[12] which is a useful tool for clustering incomplete data sets. The general formula for the partial distance calculation of $D(Pre(i), g_c)$ is given by Equation 1. l is the total number of groups, g_c denotes the group center of group $c(c = 1, 2, ...l)$. $g_{c,k}$ is the kth element of g_c.

$$D(Pre(i), g_c) = \frac{w}{\delta_i} \sum_{k=1}^{w} (Pre(i)_k - g_{c,k})^2 \delta_{i,k}, i = 1, 2...m \qquad (1)$$

where $\delta_{i,k} = \begin{cases} 0, & if \ Pre(i)_k = 0 \\ 1, & if \ Pre(i)_k = 1 \end{cases}$ and $\delta_i = \sum_{k=1}^{w} \delta_{i,k}$.

We define the objective function as follows:

$$F(P,G) = \sum_{c=1}^{l}\sum_{i=1}^{m} p_{c,i}^{m} D(Pre(i), g_c) \tag{2}$$

where $P = [p_{c,i}]_{l \times m}$ is the membership matrix and $p_{c,i} \in [0,1]$ is the probability that user u_i belongs to group c; $G = \{g_1, g_2, ..., g_l\}$ is the group center matrix; $\theta \in [1, \infty)$ is the fuzzification parameter and usually is set to 2 [10];

The goal of PDSFCM is to find the matrix P and G to minimize the objective function. We summarize the PDSFCM as follows:

1) select appropriate values for θ, l and a small positive number ε. Initialize the center matrix G randomly. Set step variable $t = 0$.

2) calculate (at $t = 0$) or update (at $t > 0$) the membership matrix P by

$$P_{c,i}^{(t+1)} = 1/(\sum_{s=1}^{l} (\frac{D(Pre(i), g_c)}{D(Pre(i), g_s)})^{\frac{1}{\theta-1}}), \quad i = 1, 2, ...m \tag{3}$$

3) update the center matrix G by

$$g_c^{(t+1)} = (\sum_{i=1}^{m} (p_{c,i}^{(t+1)})^{\theta} Pre(i))/(\sum_{i=1}^{m} (p_{c,i}^{(t+1)})^{\theta}), \quad i = 1, 2...m \tag{4}$$

4) repeat steps 2)-3) until $\|G^{(t+1)} - G^{(t)}\| < \varepsilon$.

After the fuzzily partitioning of users is performed, the membership matrix P which describes the group information of all the users is generated. For example: suppose $p_1 = \{0.2, 0.3, 0.4, 0.1\}$, it means the probabilities that user u_1 belongs to $group^1$, $group^2$, $group^3$ and $group^4$ are 0.2,0.3,0.4, and 0.1, respectively. By taking appropriate threshold T, for each row of P, the larger elements are remained and each row sums to one (normalized). Suppose the threshold T is set to be 0.25, then $p_1 = (0, 0.375, 0.625, 0)$. Thus the corresponding user groups are produced.

3.4   Clustering-Based Social Regularization

Social recommender systems usually assume that users are similar with their friends, and always turn to their friends for recommendation. In order to get the friends groups which contain the users with similar preferences from multiple domains, we define the clustering-specific friends subsets based on the user groups generated in Section 3.3 as follows:

Definition 2. (Clustering-specific Friends Subsets)
Regarding each group c, a user u_f is in the friends subset of user u_i, i.e., in the subset $\mathcal{F}^c(i)$, if and only if the following two conditions hold:
(1) $u_f \in friends(i)$ and (2) $u_f \in group^c$, f=1,2...m and c=1,2...l.

Users with multiple similar preferences are clustered into one group. The similarity between users within a group is higher than the similarity between users belonging to different groups. More specifically, if user u_i's outlink friends set in $group^c$ is $\mathcal{F}_+^c(i)$, then we could assume that u_i's taste U_i should be close to the average taste of all the friends in $\mathcal{F}_+^c(i)$, which is $\frac{1}{|\mathcal{F}_+^c(i)|} \sum_{f \in \mathcal{F}_+^c(i)} U_f$. Based on this intuition, following the approach proposed in[15], a clustering-based social regularization term is proposed in Equation 5 to constrain the user feature vectors in each group.

$$\alpha \sum_{i=1}^{m} \sum_{c=1}^{l} \|p_{c,i}(U_i - \frac{1}{|\mathcal{F}_+^c(i)|} \sum_{f \in \mathcal{F}_+^c(i)} U_f)\|_F^2 \tag{5}$$

where $\alpha > 0$ and α is a constant controlling the extent of social regularization. $p_{c,i}$ represents the probability user u_i belongs to $group^c$. Intuitively, if $p_{c,i}$ is large, say 0.75, it means user u_i has more preferences in $group^c$. Then the friendships of $group^c$ should contribute more in the whole model. $\mathcal{F}^c(i)$ denotes the friends subset of user u_i in $group^c$. $|\mathcal{F}^c(i)|$ is the number of friends in the set $\mathcal{F}^c(i)$. In some social networks, the relationship between users is directed. Therefore, we use notation $\mathcal{F}_+^c(i)$ to denote the outlink friends of u_i, and use notation $\mathcal{F}_-^c(i)$ to represent the inlink friends of u_i. Only when in undirected social networks, there exists $\mathcal{F}_+^c(i) = \mathcal{F}_-^c(i)$.

Hence, based on the matrix factorization model, we propose our CLUSR (Clustering-based Social Recommendation) model. The objective function can be formulated as:

$$\mathcal{L}(U,V) = \frac{1}{2} \sum_{i=1}^{m} \sum_{j=1}^{n} I_{ij}(R_{ij} - U_i^{\mathrm{T}} V_j)^2$$

$$+ \frac{\alpha}{2} \sum_{i=1}^{m} \sum_{c=1}^{l} \|p_{c,i}(U_i - \frac{1}{|\mathcal{F}_+^c(i)|} \sum_{f \in \mathcal{F}_+^c(i)} U_f)\|_F^2 \tag{6}$$

$$+ \frac{\lambda}{2} \|U\|_F^2 + \frac{\lambda}{2} \|V\|_F^2.$$

where $U \in \mathcal{R}^{f \times m}$ is a user-specific matrix, $V \in \mathcal{R}^{f \times n}$ is an item-specific matrix, $f(f \ll \min(m,n))$ is the dimension of a latent factor vector which characterizes a user or an item[13]. Since in the real world, each user only rates a very small portion of items, the matrix R is usually extremely sparse. I_{ij} is 1 if user u_i has rated item v_j, and 0 otherwise. $\frac{\lambda}{2}\|U\|_F^2$ and $\frac{\lambda}{2}\|V\|_F^2$ are regularization terms to avoid overfitting, where $\|\cdot\|_F^2$ denotes the Frobenius norm. The parameter $\lambda (\lambda > 0)$controls the extent of regularization.

The objective function can be minimized by the gradient decent approach. More formally, the gradients of the objective function with respect to the feature vectors U_i and V_j are shown as Equation 7 and Equation 8 respectively.

$$\frac{\partial \mathcal{L}}{\partial U_i} = \sum_{j=1}^{n} I_{ij}(U_i^{\mathrm{T}}V_j - R_{ij})V_j + \lambda U_i$$

$$+ \alpha \sum_{c=1}^{l} p_{c,i}(U_i - \frac{1}{|\mathcal{F}_+^c(i)|} \sum_{f \in \mathcal{F}_+^c(i)} U_f) \tag{7}$$

$$+ \alpha \sum_{c=1}^{l} \sum_{h \in \mathcal{F}^c(i)} \frac{p_{c,h}}{|\mathcal{F}_+^c(h)|}(\frac{1}{|\mathcal{F}_+^c(h)|} \sum_{f \in \mathcal{F}_+^c(h)} U_f - U_h)$$

$$\frac{\partial \mathcal{L}}{\partial V_j} = \sum_{i=1}^{m} I_{ij}(U_i^{\mathrm{T}}V_j - R_{ij})U_i + \lambda V_j \tag{8}$$

When model training is finished, the predicted rating $\hat{R}_{ij}$ of user u_i to item v_j can be generated by Equation 9,

$$\hat{R}_{ij} = \tilde{r} + U_i^{\mathrm{T}}V_j \tag{9}$$

where $\tilde{r}$ is the global bias term which can be obtained by the average value of the observed training ratings.

4   Experiment

In this section, we conduct some experiments to evaluate the performance of the proposed method CLUSR using the Epinions data set.

4.1   Dataset Description

Epinions is a well-known general consumer review site which consists of ratings and directed trust relations. We use the version of Epinions data set published in[11]. The data set consists of 22,164 users with 296,277 items from 27 different item categories. The total number of issued trust relations and ratings is 355,727 and 912,566, respectively. In this paper, we choose ten representative categories to verify the performance of our method. The statistical information of the chosen categories is shown in Table 1. In some categories, there are comparatively enough ratings and trust relations for studying social recommendation. However, in the categories of Education, Musical Instruments and Gifts, the ratings and social relations are few. Actually, in the Epinions dataset, there exist many categories like these three categories.

4.2   Methodology and Metrics

In our experiments, we perform 5-fold cross validation. In each fold, we use 80% of the data as the training set and the remaining 20% as the test set. Since the objective of our approach is to improve rating prediction accuracy, we use two standard metrics to measure the accuracy of various models: Mean Absolute

Table 1. Epinions Dataset: Statistics of the Chosen Categories

Name	Ratings	Users	Trust Relations	Rating Fraction	Trust Fraction
Online Stores & Service	40829	10672	94801	4.47%	26.65%
Movies	166554	14180	153951	18.25%	43.28%
Electronics	45162	11385	102990	4.95%	28.95%
Computer Hardware	32989	9198	66993	3.61%	18.83%
Hotels & Travel	57942	10660	100038	6.35%	28.12%
Restaurants & Gourmet	47827	8376	62753	5.24%	17.64%
Wellness & Beauty	54953	7209	51520	6.02%	14.48%
Education	4036	3114	7730	0.44%	2.17%
Musical Instruments	3266	747	502	0.36%	0.14%
Gifts	808	546	392	0.08%	0.11%

Error(MAE): $MAE = \frac{1}{N} \sum_{r=1}^{N} |R - \hat{R}|$ and Root Mean Square Error(RMSE):

$RMSE = \sqrt{\frac{1}{N} \sum_{r=1}^{N} (R - \hat{R})^2}$, where N denotes the number of tested ratings. R is the real rating of an item and $\hat{R}$ is the corresponding predicted rating.

In order to validate the superiority of our approach, we compare the recommendation results of the following methods:

BaseMF: This method is the baseline matrix factorization approach proposed in [13], which does not take into account the social network.

SoReg: This method is proposed in[9]. It improves the recommendation accuracy of BaseMF by adding a social regularization term to control friends taste difference. It uses all the social links available in the dataset.

mTrustMF: In this method, the author impose a category-based regularization term to constrain the user feature vectors. One user's feature vector should be close to the average of the feature vectors of his friends in the same categories[6].

CLUSR: In this method, a clustering-based social regularization term is added to the BaseMF to constrain the user feature vectors. One user's feature vector should be close to the average of the feature vectors of his friends in the same preferences groups.

4.3 Parameter Selection

Parameter selection plays a crucial role to many algorithms. In our experiment, we set the dimension of matrix factorization to be $f = 10$ and the regularization constant to be $\lambda = 0.01$. The social regularization parameter α of SoReg, mTrustMF, CLUSR approaches is 0.01, 0.1 and 0.01 respectively. For our CLUSR, there are two main parameters: α and l.

Parameter α controls how much our method should incorporate the information of the social network. Figure 2 shows the influence of parameter α to the

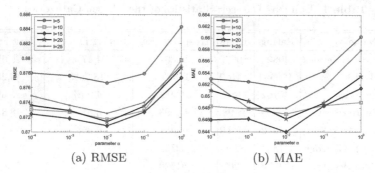

(a) RMSE   (b) MAE

Fig. 2. Impact of parameter α

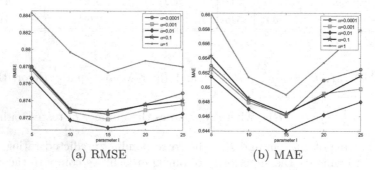

(a) RMSE   (b) MAE

Fig. 3. Impact of parameter l

results of RMSE and MAE. We observe that both the RMSE and MAE get the best when α reaches around 0.01. Intuitively, if we employ a small value of α, the social information may have little use to the prediction results. When α continues increasing, the results of RMSE and MAE increase at the same time, which can be explained that if the value of α is too large, the social information may dominate the learning processes.

Parameter l is the number of groups each user can belong to. The threshold T for retaining the elements of the membership matrix P is set to be $\frac{1}{l}$ .Figure 3 shows the influence of l to the results of RMSE and MAE. When l reaches around 15, both the RMSE and MAE get the best. When l is too small, i.e., around 5, or too large, i.e., around 25, the results get worse. In our consideration, small number of groups cannot clearly partition different user-preference groups. Therefore, the fuzzy weights are inaccurate to capture the users' preferences for different groups. As l increases, better groups are captured and the fuzzy weights become more meaningful. However, when l becomes too large, the results get worse, which can be explained that if too many groups are generated, the influence of fuzzy weight becomes too weak that cannot get better results.

Table 2. Performance Comparison (the smaller the better)

Method	RMSE	MAE
BaseMF	1.0281	0.7457
SoReg	0.9064	0.7151
mTrustMF	1.0186	0.7254
CLUSR	**0.8708**	**0.6440**

4.4 Results Analysis

Below we give a detailed breakdown of our experiment results. From Table 2, we can observe that our method CLUSR outperforms the other methods. BaseMF gets the worst result mainly because it was only based on the rating information and did not consider the social network information. The SoReg approach considered the social information, however, they regard all the friendships/trust relationships as the same. The mTrustMF method divided the trust relationships depending on the item categories. But the social information in some categories are extremely sparse as shown in Table 1, few trust relationships can be used to constrain users preferences in those categories, which limits the contribution of the social recommendation. From Table 2 we can see that mTrustMF performs worse than SoReg on the sampled data we use.

Our CLUSR method on the one hand considers both the rating information and social information; on the other hand, we let the feature vectors of user u_i to be close to the average of the feature vectors of his/her friends who share similarly preferences from multiple domains with u_i in each group and further improve the recommendation accuracy.

5   Conclusion and Future Work

In this paper, we proposed a novel clustering-based social recommendation model to improve the accuracy of recommendation. The clustering-specific friends subsets are obtained by partitioning users based on their similar preferences from multiple domains. A clustering-based social regularization term is designed to integrate the friendships from each group into the traditional Matrix Factorization model. Real dataset based experiments demonstrate that our approach outperforms the comparison approaches both in RMSE and MAE. In this work, the weights of friendships are ignored, in the future, we plan to estimate the friendships among users and incorporate the weighted friendships into our model. In addition, we will validate our model on some other data sets.

Acknowledgment. This research is funded by the National Natural Science Foundation of China under grant No.61272406 and the Fundamental Research Funds for the Central Universities, HUST:2013TS101.

References

1. Adomavicius, G., Tuzhilin, A.: Toward the next generation of recommender systems: A survey of the state-of-the-art and possible extensions. Knowledge and Data Engineering 17, 734–749 (2005)
2. Jamali, M., Ester, M.: TrustWalker: a random walk model for combining trust-based and item-based recommendation. In: Proceedings of the International Conference on Knowledge Discovery and Data Mining, KDD 2009, pp. 397–406. ACM (2009)
3. Tang, J., Hu, X., Liu, H.: Social recommendation: a review. Social Network Analysis and Mining 3, 1113–1133 (2013)
4. Ma, H., King, I., Lyu, M.R.: Learning to recommend with social trust ensemble. In: Proceedings of the International Conference on Research and Development in Information Retrieval, SIGIR 2009, pp. 203–210. ACM (2009)
5. Tang, J., Hu, X., Gao, H.: Exploiting local and global social context for recommendation. In: Proceedings of the International Joint Conference on Artificial Intelligence, AAAI 2013, pp. 2712–2718. ACM (2009)
6. Guo, L., Ma, J., Chén, Z.: Learning to recommend with multi-faceted trust in social networks. In: Proceedings of the International Conference on World Wide Web Companion, WWW 2013 Companion, pp. 205–206. ACM (2013)
7. Jamali, M., Ester, M.: A matrix factorization technique with trust propagation for recommendation in social networks. In: Proceedings of the ACM Conference on Recommender Systems, RecSys 2010, pp. 135–142. ACM (2010)
8. Yang, X., Steck, H., Liu, Y.: Circle-based recommendation in online social networks. In: Proceedings of the International Conference on Knowledge Discovery and Data Mining, KDD 2012, pp. 1267–1275. ACM (2012)
9. Ma, H., Zhou, D., Liu, C., Lyu, M.R., King, I.: Recommender systems with social regularization. In: Proceedings of ACM International Conference on Web Search and Data Mining, WSDM 2011, pp. 287–296. ACM (2011)
10. Xu, R., Wunsch, D.: Survey of clustering algorithms. IEEE Transactions on Neural Networks 16, 645–678 (2005)
11. Tang, J., Gao, H., Liu, H.: mTrust: discerning multi-faceteded trust in a connected world. In: Proceedings of the ACM International Conference on Web Search and Data Mining, WSDM 2012, pp. 93–102. ACM (2012)
12. Hathaway, R.J., Bezdek, J.C.: Fuzzy c-means clustering of incomplete data. IEEE Transactions on Systems, Man, and Cybernetics, Part B: Cybernetics 31, 735–744 (2001)
13. Koren, Y., Bell, R., Volinsky, C.: Matrix factorization techniques for recommender systems. Computer 42, 30–37 (2009)
14. Su, X., Khoshgoftaar, T.: A survey of collaborative filtering techniques. In: Advances in Artificial Intelligence 2009, p. 4 (2009)
15. Ma, H., Zhou, D., Liu, C.: Recommender systems with social regularization. In: Proceedings of the International Conference on Web Search and Data Mining, WSDM 2011, pp. 287–296. ACM (2011)
16. Sarwar, B., Karypis, G., Konstan, J., John, R.: Item-based collaborative filtering recommendation algorithms. In: Proceedings of the International Conference on World Wide Web, WWW 2001, pp. 285–295. ACM (2001)
17. Newman, M.E.J.: Power laws, Pareto distributions and Zipf's law. Contemporary Physics 46, 323–351 (2005)

TS-IDS Algorithm for Query Selection in the Deep Web Crawling

Yan Wang[1], Jianguo Lu[2,3], and Jessica Chen[2]

[1] School of Information, Central University of Finance and Economics, China
dayanking@gmail.com
[2] School of Computer Science, University of Windsor, Canada
{jlu,xjchen}@uwindsor.ca
[3] Key Lab of Novel Software Technology, Nanjing, China

Abstract. The deep web crawling is the process of collecting data items inside a data source hidden behind searchable interfaces. Since the only method to access the data is by sending queries, one of the research challenges is the selection of a set of queries such that they can retrieve most of the data with minimal network traffic. This is a set covering problem that is NP-hard. The large size of the problem, in terms of both large number of documents and terms involved, calls for new approximation algorithms for efficient deep web data crawling. Inspired by the TF-IDF weighting measure in information retrieval, this paper proposes the TS-IDS algorithm that assigns an importance value to each document proportional to term size (TS), and inversely proportional to document size (IDS). The algorithm is extensively tested on a variety of datasets, and compared with the traditional greedy algorithm and the more recent IDS algorithm. We demonstrate that TS-IDS outperforms the greedy algorithm and IDS algorithm up to 33% and 24%, respectively. Our work also makes a contribution to the classic set covering problem by leveraging the long-tail distributions of the terms and documents in natural languages. Since long-tail distribution is ubiquitous in real world, our approach can be applied in areas other than the deep web crawling.

Keywords: deep web crawling, query selection, set covering problem, greedy algorithm, Zipf's law.

1 Introduction

The deep web [1] is the content that is dynamically generated from data sources such as databases or file systems. Unlike the surface web, where pages are collected by following the hyperlinks embedded inside collected pages, data from the deep web are guarded by search interfaces such as HTML forms, web services, or programmable web API, and can be retrieved by queries only. The deep web contains a much bigger amount of data than the surface web [2,3]. This calls for deep web crawlers to collect the data so that they can be used, indexed, and searched in an integrated environment. With the proliferation of publicly available web services that provide programmable interfaces, where input and

L. Chen et al. (Eds.): APWeb 2014, LNCS 8709, pp. 189–200, 2014.
© Springer International Publishing Switzerland 2014

output data formats are explicitly specified, automated extraction of deep web data becomes more practical.

Deep web crawling is the process of collecting data from search interfaces by issuing queries. Sending queries and retrieving data are costly operations because they occupy network traffic. More importantly, many deep web data sources impose daily quota for the queries to be sent. In addition, most data sources paginate the matched results into many pages. All these restrictions call for the judicious selection of the queries.

The selection of queries can be modelled as a set covering problem. If we regard all the documents in a data source as the universe, each query is a subset of the documents it can match, the query selection problem is to find the subsets (the queries) to cover all the documents with minimal cost. Since the entire set of documents is not available, the queries have to be selected from a sample of partially downloaded documents [4,5,6,7]. In particular, [7,8] demonstrates that the queries selected from a sample set of documents can also work well for the entire data set. This paper will focus on the set covering algorithm on the sampled documents.

The set covering problem is NP-hard, and approximate algorithms have to be used. For large problems, the greedy algorithm is often recommended [9]. The greedy algorithm treats every document equally important. In deep web crawling, not every document is the same. A very large document containing virtually all possible terms is not an important document in the sense that it will be matched sooner or later by some terms. The query selection algorithm can almost neglect such documents since they can be covered by many terms. Therefore, the weight of a document is inversely proportional to the document size (IDS), or the distinct number of terms. In [10], we proposed and evaluated IDS approach.

This paper reveals that the document importance not only depends on the number of terms it contains, but also the sizes of these terms. The size of a term is the document it can cover, or its document frequency. A document that contains a small term can be covered with less redundancy, therefore they are of less importance in query selection. A document that is comprised of large terms only is costly to cover, since only large terms can be used. This kind of documents is more important, and the importance should be proportional to the minimal term size (TS) within the document.

Based on the above analysis, we propose the TS-IDS algorithm to select queries. It outperforms both greedy and IDS algorithms, and is extensively verified on a variety of datasets. We also exam the query selection process, and find that TS-IDS fundamentally differs from the other two approaches: both greedy and IDS methods prefer to use small terms (the terms with low document frequency) first, while TS-IDS tries to use frequent terms first even though it causes redundancy in the initial stage. In the final stage it uses the small terms to pick up remaining documents.

Our work also makes a contribution to the classic set covering problem by leveraging the distributions of the terms and documents in natural languages.

Most of the set covering research assumes that the data are of normal or uniform distribution. For instance, the classic benchmark for set covering algorithms is the famous Beasley data, all are of normal distribution. However, most real-world data follows power law, including natural language texts [11]. We are the first to use data distribution to improve optimization algorithms as far as we are aware of.

In the following we will first give an overview of the related work on deep web crawling, focusing on the query selection task. Then we describe the problem formally in the context of set covering and bipartite graph. After explaining the motivations for the TS-IDS method, we present the detailed algorithm and its comparison with the greedy algorithm. Section 4 compares the three approaches, i.e., greedy, IDS, TS-IDS on four corpora.

2   Related Work

In deep web crawling, the early work selects terms according to the frequencies of the terms [12], in the belief that high frequency terms will bring back more documents. Soon people realize that what is important is the number of new documents being retrieved, not the number of documents. If queries are not selected properly, most of the documents may be redundant. Therefore, query selection is modelled as a set covering [4] or dominating vertex [5] problem, so that the queries can return less redundancies. Since set covering problem or dominating vertex problem is NP-hard, the optimal solution can costly be found, especially because the problem size is very big that involves thousands or even more of documents and terms. Typically, a greedy method is employed to select the terms that maximize the new returns per cost unit. We realized that not every document is equal when selecting the queries to cover them. Large documents can be covered by many queries, no matter how the queries are selected. Therefore the importance of a document is inversely proportional to its size. We proposed IDS (inverse document size) algorithm in [10]. Our further exploration in this problem finds that the importance of the document depends not only on the number of the terms it contains, but also the sizes of those terms.

In addition to the optimization problem, query selection has also been modelled as reinforcement learning problem [13,14]. In this model, a crawler and a target data source are considered as an agent and the environment respectively. Then its selection strategy will be dynamically adjusted by learning previous querying results and takes account of at most two-step long reward.

Query selection may have goals other than exhaustive exploration of the deep web data. For instance, in Google deep web crawling, the goal is to harvest some documents of a data source, preferably 'good' ones. Their focus is to look into many data sources, instead of exhausting one data source. In this case they use the traditional TF-IDF weighting to select the most relevant queries from the retrieved documents [6]. For another instance, data sources may be ranked and only return the top-k matches per query. [15] studies the method to crawl the top ranked documents .

In addition to query selection, there are other deep web crawling challenges that are out of the scope of this paper. The challenges include locating the data sources [16,17], learning and understanding the interface and the returned results so that query submission and data extraction can be automated [18,17,19,20].

The set covering is an extensively studied problem [21,22,23]. The state of art commercial Cplex optimizer can find optimal solutions for small problems. When the matrix contains hundreds of elements, it often keeps on running for hours or days. The greedy algorithm is believed to be the better choice for large problems. Although many other heuristics are proposed, such as genetic algorithms[24], the improvements are very limited. The classic test cases are Beasley data [24]. Most of the data are synthesized from normal distribution, i.e., in the context of our document-term analogy, the document size and term size follow normal distributions. Some datasets even have uniform size for all the documents and terms. Such datasets cannot reflect the almost universal power-law in real world, and prohibit the discovery of the algorithms such as TS-IDS. We also tested the TS-IDS algorithm on the Beasley datasets. The result is almost the same as the greedy algorithm. The reason is obvious–there is little variation of TS and DS, therefore it reduces to the greedy algorithm.

The inception of TS-IDS algorithm is inspired by the classic TF-IDF weighting. TS-IDS can be regarded as dual concept of TF-IDF. TF-IDF measures the importance of terms in a document in the presence of a collection documents, while TS-IDS measures the importance of a document covered by a term among a set of terms.

3   The TS-IDS Algorithm

3.1   The Query Selection Problem

Given a set of documents $D = \{D_1, D_2, \ldots, D_m\}$ and a set of terms $T = \{T_1, T_2, \ldots, T_n\}$, each document contains a set of terms. In turn, each term covers a set of documents. Documents and terms form an undirected bipartite graph $G(D, T, E)$, where the nodes are D and T, E is the set of edges between T and D ($E \subseteq T \times D$). There is an edge between a document and a term iff the term occurs in the document. This graph can be represented by the document-term matrix $A = (a_{ij})$ where

$$a_{ij} = \begin{cases} 1, & \text{if } T_j \text{ occurs in } D_i; \\ 0, & otherwise. \end{cases} \tag{1}$$

Let d_i^D and d_j^T denote the degrees of the document D_i (the size of document) and term T_j (the size of term) respectively. Note that $d_i^D = \sum_{k=1}^{n} a_{ik}, d_j^T = \sum_{k=1}^{m} a_{kj}$. d_j^T is also called document frequency of the term in information retrieval. We call it term size to be consistent with document size. The query selection problem can be modelled as the set covering problem [25]. In our context, it is a set covering problem where the cost for each term is the term size d_j^T:

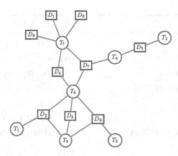

Fig. 1. A deep web data source is modelled as a bipartite graph

Definition 1. *(Set Covering Problem) Given an $m \times n$ binary matrix $A = (a_{ij})$. The set covering problem is to find a binary n-vector $X = (x_1, \ldots, x_n)$ that satisfies the objective function*

$$Z = min \sum_{j=1}^{n} x_j d_j^T, \qquad (2)$$

subject to

$$\begin{cases} \sum_{j=1}^{n} a_{ij}x_j \geq 1, & for \ all \ 1 \leq i \leq m, and \\ x_j \in \{0,1\}, & 1 \leq j \leq n. \end{cases} \qquad (3)$$

Here the first constraint requires that each document is covered at least once. The second constraint says that the solution is a binary vector consists of either one or zero, i.e., a term can be either selected or not selected. The solution cost ($\sum_{j=1}^{n} x_j d_j^T$) is the total number of documents retrieved by the selected queries.

One may wonder that the cost of retrieving documents over a network depends on the total size of the documents rather than their number. In fact, for a crawler, when its goal is to download documents instead of URLs, it would be efficient to separate the URLs collection from the document downloading itself. More importantly, the cost for downloading documents is constant, for example, downloading all documents inside the target data source. Thus, the cost for downloading can be ignored. However, the cost for retrieving URLs is different from method to method. The cost of a query can be measured by the number of matched documents by it because of pagination function, i.e., web sites paginate the matched URLs into many *query sessions* (usually 10 URLs per session) not returning a long list. Each session needs one additional query (ordinarily it is a 'next' link). So the number of queries grows linearly with the number of matched documents. Hence, the cost for retrieving documents can be measured by the total number of documents retrieved by the selected queries $\sum_{j=1}^{n} x_j d_j^T$.

The set covering is an NP-hard problem. The greedy method described in Fig. 2 is proved to be an effective approximation algorithm [9]. It iteratively

Fig. 2: The greedy algorithm	**Fig. 3:** The TS-IDS algorithm

$x_j = 0$, for $1 \le j \le n$;
 $\mu_j = \sum_{i=1}^{m} a_{ij}$, for $1 \le j \le n$;
 while *not all docs covered* **do**
     Find j that maximizes μ_j/d_j^T;
     $x_j = 1$;
     Remove column j;
     Remove all rows that contain T_j;
     $\mu_j = \sum_{i=1}^{m'} a_{ij}$ in the new matrix;
 end
	$x_j = 0$, for $1 \le j \le n$;
	 $\mu_j = \sum_{i=1}^{m} a_{ij}w_{ij}$, for $1 \le j \le n$;
	 while *not all docs covered* **do**
	     Find j that maximizes u_j/d_j^T;
	     $x_j = 1$;
	     Remove column j;
	     Remove all rows that contain T_j;
	     $\mu_j = \sum_{i=1}^{m'} a_{ij}w_i$ in the new
	     matrix.
	 end

Fig. 4. The greedy and the TS-IDS algorithms. The input is an $m \times n$ doc-term matrix. The output is an n-vector $X = (x_1, ..., x_n)$. $x_j = 1$ if term j is selected.

selects the best term that maximizes the new harvest per cost unit, as described in Fig. 3. Initially, all $x_j = 0$, meaning that no query is selected. Then it selects the next best query until all the documents are covered. The best term is the one that returns the most new documents per cost unit (μ_j/d_j^T). Note that m' is number of rows in the new matrix after the all covered documents are removed.

3.2   Motivation for the TS-IDS Algorithm

The greedy algorithm treats every document equally when it selects the best query using μ_j/d_j^T. Every document contributes unit one to μ_j, as long as it is a new document not being covered by other queries yet. However, not every document is of the same importance in the query selection process. This can be explained using the example in Fig. 1.

Document 7 and 6 have degrees 3 and 1, respectively, meaning that document 7 has more chances being captured than document 6. In this sense, D_6 is more important than D_7. If we include all the terms in the solution, D_7 is captured three times, while D_6 is captured only once. When we include a term, say T_4, in a solution, D_7 contributes only one third portion of the *new* document, because other terms could also be selected and D_7 will be covered again. Therefore, the importance of a document D_i is inversely proportional to document size d_i^D (*IDS*).

Furthermore, the document importance depends also on the term size (TS). Small (or rare) terms, whose degrees are small relative to other terms, are inherently better than large terms in achieving a good solution of set covering problem. Take the extreme case when all the terms have degree one. Every document will be covered only once without any redundancy. In general, when every term covers k documents, The greedy algorithm can approximate the optimal solution within a factor of $\sum_{i=1}^{k} \frac{1}{i} \approx ln(k)$[26]. Small terms result in good solutions, while large terms prone to cause high cost. Documents containing only large terms are costly to cover, thus they are more important in the query selection process.

Looking back at our example again in Fig. 1. Both document 5 and 4 have degree two. Document 5 has a query whose degree is 1, while document 4 has two queries whose degrees are both 5. This means that document 5 can be covered by query 2 without any redundancy, while document 4 has to be covered by either T_6 or T_7, either one of them will most probably resulting in some duplicates. Therefore, we say that D_4 is more important than D_5 in the query selection process, even though their degrees are the same.

3.3   The TS-IDS Algorithm

For each document D_i, we define its document weight as follows:

Definition 2 (Document weight). *The weight of document D_i, denoted by w_i, is proportional to the minimal term size of the terms connected to D_i, and inversely proportional to its document size, i.e.,*

$$w_i = \frac{1}{d_i^D} \min_{T_j \in D_i} d_j^T . \tag{4}$$

With this definition, we give the TS-IDS as described in Fig. 3. Note that m' is the number of documents in the new matrix after covered documents are removed. The weighted new documents of a term T_j, denoted by μ_j, is the sum of the document weights containing term T_j, i.e., $\mu_j = \sum_{i=1}^{m} a_{ij} w_i$. Compared with the μ_j in the greedy algorithm, where $\mu_j = \sum_{i=1}^{m'} a_{ij}$, the difference in TS-IDS algorithm is the weight w_i for each document. Compared with the IDS algorithm where the weight is $1/d_i^D$, TS-IDS weights a documents not only by its length $(1/d_i^D)$, but also by the terms it contains. It gives a higher priority to short documents $(1/d_i^D)$ that contain popular terms only $(\min_{T_j \in D_i} d_j^T)$.

4   Experiments

4.1   Data

To demonstrate the performance of our TS-IDS algorithm, the experiment was carried out on four data collections that cover a variety of forms of web data, including regular web pages (Gov), wikipedia articles (Wikipedia), newswires (Reuters), and newsgroup posts (Newsgroup). 10,000 documents are selected uniformly at random from the original corpora. Table 1 summarizes the statistics of the four datasets, including the numbers of documents (m), the number of terms (n), and the degree properties of the documents and terms. Figures 5 plots in log-log scale the distributions of the document size and term size respectively. As expected, document size follows log-normal distribution, while term size follows power-law [27]. The highly skewed data distribution is the basis of the

Table 1. Statistics of the four datasets

Data	n	Document size			Term size		
		max	min	avg	max	min	avg
Reuters	56,187	833	8	106.7	3722	1	19.0
Wikipedia	224,725	2670	15	222.2	3041	1	9.89
Gov	164,889	3797	1	327.9	3028	1	19.8
Newsgroup	193,653	3836	1	245.6	3532	1	12.7

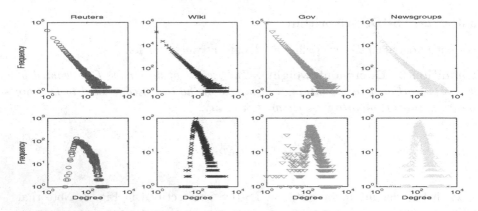

Fig. 5. Distributions of document sizes d_i^D and term sizes d_j^T of the four datasets. First row: term size distributions. Second row: document size distributions.

success of our algorithm. In traditional set covering studies, the benchmark test data, called Beasley data [28], are uniformly at random. For such data, term size (d_j^T) and document size (d_i^D) are mostly the same. We have also carried experiments on these data sets, and found that, as expected, TS-IDS and IDS algorithms perform very closely to the greedy algorithm. Due to space limitation, this paper focuses on the document-term matrix data only.

4.2   Results and Discussions

We run three algorithms, the Greedy (Fig. 2), the IDS algorithm in [10], and the TS-IDS algorithm (Fig. 3). Fig. 6 shows the comparison of these algorithms in terms of the solution quality, the average solution cost. The result is the average from running each algorithm 50 times for the same data. Each run may find a different solution because there may be a tie when selecting the best queries. When this happens, we select a random one from a set of equally good queries.

From Fig. 6, we can see that performance improvement differs from data to data. TS-IDS achieve better improvement for Reuters and Gov, but less for Wiki and Newsgroups, although all the four datasets have similar document size and term size distributions. For Reuters dataset, the TS-IDS outperforms the

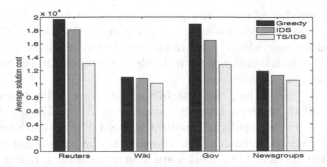

Fig. 6. Comparison between greedy, IDS, and TS-IDS algorithms on four datasets. The average solution costs are from 50 runs for each dataset.

IDS method around 24%, and outperforms the Greedy method around 33% in average. On the other hand, for Wiki and Newsgroup datasets, TS-IDS is better than IDS method and Greedy method around 6% and 10% respectively. This is because the solution costs for Wiki and Newsgroups are already close to one. Note that the best solution is one, whose redundancy is zero. Therefore there is little room for the TS-IDS algorithm to improve.

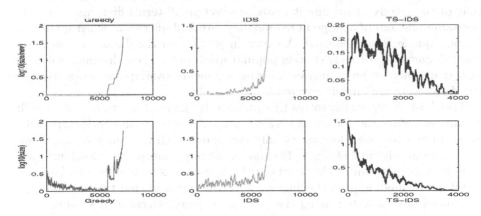

Fig. 7. Types of queries being selected in the process. First row: redundancy rate d_j^T/μ_j in the selection processes. Second row: corresponding query size d_j^T. Dataset is from Reuters corpus.

To gain the insight into these algorithms, we plot the *redundancy rate* (d_j^T/μ_j) for each query that is selected on Reuters data set in the first row of Figure 7. Note that the redundancy rate is the reciprocal of the new documents per returned document μ_j/d_j^T used in the greedy algorithm. Here the redundancy rate d_j^T/μ_j is used to analyse query selection process since we want to measure the quality of a query from the viewpoint of overlap. The x-axes are the number of queries selected. The y-axes are the redundancy rate of each query in log scale, i.e., the number of duplicates per new document in log10 scale. The redundancy rate is smoothed with moving window size 100. The second row shows the corresponding query size d_j^T, also in log10 scale and smoothed with the same window size. The data is obtained from the Reuters corpus. Other three datasets demonstrate similar patterns.

For the greedy algorithm, the first 5785 terms have redundancy rate one, meaning that all those terms have zero duplicates. After 5785 queries, the redundancy rate increases rapidly in exponential speed. For the last a few hundreds queries, the average redundancy rate is above 30. In the corresponding query size plot, we see that the first 5785 queries are mostly small ones. It starts with the average term size 3.2, then decreases because only smaller queries (i.e., small subsets) can be found that do not overlap with others already used. When overlapping occurs after first 5785 queries, the query size increases greatly, causing high redundancy rate. Because most of the small queries are already used in the first stage, it has to use large queries to cover the remaining documents.

The IDS algorithm improves the greedy algorithm by distinguishing documents according to their sizes. Long documents can be covered by many queries. Hence, in each iteration the IDS algorithm prefers the queries that cover smaller documents, even if the redundancy rate of the query is not the smallest. Thus, we can see that in the second column of Fig. 7 the redundancy rate is not always one for the first 5000 queries. However, the overall pattern is similar to that of the greedy algorithm: it tends to select small terms first, and it suffers the same problem of a surge in redundancy rate and query size when small and "good" queries are exhausted. A closer inspection on the dataset reveals that short documents normally contain popular words only. These documents can be picked up only by large queries, causing significant overlapping when most of the documents are already covered.

The TS-IDS algorithm solves this problem by giving higher priority to such documents. Since the document weight is proportional to term size, it starts with large queries to cover documents only containing high frequency terms, as we can see from column 3 of Fig. 7. Because of the large query, the redundancy rate is high at the beginning. The benefit of this approach is to save the small queries to fill in the small gaps in the final stage. These terms are not the best in terms of redundancy rate, but along the process of query selection, the redundancy rate decreases, and the overall performance is better. Surprisingly enough, the process is the inverse of the greedy algorithm: instead of selecting the best for the current stage, its current selection is in average worse than later selections.

The greedy algorithm not only has the highest redundancy rate here (1.94 compared with 1.81 for IDS and 1.31 for TS-IDS), but also uses more queries than other two methods. It selects 7256 queries, while IDS uses 6738 queries, and TS-IDS uses 4051 queries.

5   Conclusions

This paper presents the TS-IDS method to address the query selection problem in deep web crawling. It is extensively tested on textual deep web data sources whose document sizes and document frequencies follow the log-normal and power law distribution. By utilizing the distributions, TS-IDS method consistently outperforms the greedy and IDS algorithms. The success of the method is due to the highly skewed distributions of term size (Zipf's law) and document size (log-normal).

Without loss of generality, this paper discuss the set covering problem assuming each query is a single term. Our bipartite graph model can be extended to allow nodes representing multiple terms. Although this will greatly increase the graph size, such queries of multiple terms also follow power-law distribution. Therefore, our result can be extended to such queries as well.

In real deep web crawling scenario, usually it is impossible to directly apply a set covering algorithm to all the documents. Those documents are not known yet by the algorithm. Besides, a data source is usually so large that even approximate algorithms such as the ones discussed in this paper cannot handle it. The only option is to run the set covering algorithm on a sample subset of the data source. In [7], we showed that a solution that works well on a sample is also a good solution for the entire data source.

Our method is restricted to textual data sources that returns all the matched documents. Many data sources, especially large ones such Google, rank the matched documents and return only the top-k matches. This kind of data sources demand a different query selection strategy. One approach is to select and construct the low frequency queries, so that the number of matched documents is within the k limit.

Acknowledgements. This work is supported by NSERC, BSSF(No.14JGA001) and the 111 Project under Grant Number B14020.

References

1. Bergman, M.K.: The deepweb: Surfacing hidden value. The Journal of Electronic Publishing 7(1) (2001)
2. He, B., Patel, M., Zhang, Z., Chang, K.C.: Accessing the deep web: A survey. Communications of the ACM 50(5), 94–101 (2007)
3. Madhavan, J., Cohen, S., Dong, X., Halevy, A., Jeffery, S., Ko, D., Yu, C.: Web-scale data integration: You can afford to pay as you go. In: Proc. of CIDR, pp. 342–350 (2007)
4. Ntoulas, A., Zerfos, P., Cho, J.: Downloading textual hidden web content through keyword queries. In: Proc. of the Joint Conference on Digital Libraries (JCDL), pp. 100–109 (2005)
5. Wu, P., Wen, J.R., Liu, H., Ma, W.Y.: Query selection techniques for efficient crawling of structured web sources. In: Proc. of ICDE, pp. 47–56 (2006)
6. Madhavan, J., Ko, D., Kot, L., Ganapathy, V., Rasmussen, A., Halevy, A.: Google's deep-web crawl. In: Proc. of VLDB, pp. 1241–1252 (2008)
7. Lu, J., Wang, Y., Liang, J., Chen, J., Liu, J.: An approach to deep web crawling by sampling. In: Proc. of Web Intelligence, pp. 718–724 (2008)

8. Wang, Y., Lu, J., Liang, J., Chen, J., Liu, J.: Selecting queries from sample to crawl deep web data sources. Web Intelligence and Agent Systems 10(1), 75–88 (2012)
9. Caprara, A., Toth, P., Fishetti, M.: Algorithms for the set covering problem. Annals of Operations Research 98, 353–371 (2000)
10. Wang, Y., Lu, J., Chen, J.: Crawling deep web using a new set covering algorithm. In: Huang, R., Yang, Q., Pei, J., Gama, J., Meng, X., Li, X. (eds.) ADMA 2009. LNCS, vol. 5678, pp. 326–337. Springer, Heidelberg (2009)
11. Barabási, A., Albert, R.: Emergence of scaling in random networks. Science 286(5439), 509–512 (1999)
12. Barbosa, L., Freire, J.: Siphoning hidden-web data through keyword-based interfaces. In: Proc. of SBBD (2004)
13. Zheng, Q., Wu, Z., Cheng, X., Jiang, L., Liu, J.: Learning to crawl deep web. Information Systems (2013)
14. Jiang, L., Wu, Z., Feng, Q., Liu, J., Zheng, Q.: Efficient deep web crawling using reinforcement learning. In: Zaki, M.J., Yu, J.X., Ravindran, B., Pudi, V. (eds.) PAKDD 2010, Part I. LNCS, vol. 6118, pp. 428–439. Springer, Heidelberg (2010)
15. Valkanas, G., Ntoulas, A., Gunopulos, D.: Rank-aware crawling of hidden web sites. In: Proc. of In WebDB (2011)
16. Sizov, S., Biwer, M., Graupmann, J., Siersdorfer, S., Theobald, M., Weikum, G., Zimmer, P.: The bingo! system for information portal generation and expert web search. In: Proc. of CIDR (2003)
17. Barbosa, L., Freire, J.: An adaptive crawler for locating hidden-web entry points. In: Proc. of WWW, pp. 441–450 (2007)
18. Alvarez, M., Pan, A., Raposo, J., Bellas, F., Cacheda, F.: Extracting lists of data records from semi-structured web pages. Data Knowl. Eng. 64(2), 491–509 (2008)
19. Knoblock, C.A., Lerman, K., Minton, S., Muslea, I.: Accurately and reliably extracting data from the web: a machine learning approach. IEEE Data Engineering Bulletin 23(4), 33–41 (2000)
20. Lu, J., Li, D.: Estimating deep web data source size by capture-recapture method. Informatoin Retrieval 13(1), 70–95 (2010)
21. Feo, T.A., Resende, M.G.: Greedy randomized adaptive search procedures. Journal of Global Optimization, 109–133 (1995)
22. Lorena, L.W., Lopes, F.B.: A surrogate heuristic for set covering problems. European Journal of Operational Research 1994(79), 138–150 (1994)
23. Caprara, A., Fishetti, M., Toth, P.: A heuristic method for the set covering problem. Operations Research (1995)
24. Beasley, J.E., Chu, P.C.: Theory and methodology. a genetic algorithm for the set covering problem. European Journal of Operational Research 94, 392–404 (1996)
25. Cormen, T.H., Leiserson, C.E., Rivest, R.L., Stein, C.: Introduction to Algorithms, 2nd edn. MIT Press and McGraw-Hill (2001)
26. Chvatal, V.: A greedy heuristic for the set-covering problem. Mathematics of Operations Research 4(3), 233–235 (1979)
27. Zipf, G.K.: Human Behavior and the Principle of Least Effort: An Introduction to Human Ecology. Addison-Wesley Press (1949)
28. Beasley, J.E., Jornsten, K.: Enhancing an algorithm for set covering problems. European Journal of Operational Research 58, 293–300 (1992)

A Method for Fine-Grained Document Alignment Using Structural Information

Naoki Tsujio, Toshiyuki Shimizu, and Masatoshi Yoshikawa

Graduate School of Informatics, Kyoto University, Kyoto 606-8501, Japan
tsujio@db.soc.i.kyoto-u.ac.jp, {tshimizu,yoshikawa}@i.kyoto-u.ac.jp

Abstract. It is useful to understand the corresponding relationships between each part of related documents, such as a conference paper and its modified version published as a journal paper, or documents in different versions. However, it is hard to associate corresponding parts which have been heavily modified only using similarity in their content. We propose a method of aligning documents considering not only content information but also structural information in documents. Our method consists of three steps; baseline alignment considering document order, merging, and swapping. We used papers which have been presented at a domestic conference and an international conference, then obtained their alignments by using several methods in our evaluation experiments. The results revealed the effectiveness of the use of document structures.

Keywords: document alignment, structured document, cross-lingual alignment.

1 Introduction

We can obtain the correspondence between parts of given documents which are in different forms for the same topic or in different versions. For example, a paragraph from one document corresponds to a paragraph or paragraphs in another document. Such documents include pairs of a conference paper presented at an international conference and a journal paper, which was an improved version of the conference paper, or two distinct versions of Wikipedia articles.

The information on corresponding relationships is very useful to understand documents. For example, if one feels that part of a document is hard to understand, the corresponding parts in another document can help one to better understand the given part. In addition, if one wants to find differences between a new document and a document which one has read in the past, corresponding information can provide them. Furthermore, they can be used to complement parts which have poor content by using corresponding parts which have more content. Other important applications include detection of plagiarism.

However, it is difficult to associate parts which have been heavily modified only using information from their content. Therefore, we considered using not only information from content but also the structural information in documents

L. Chen et al. (Eds.): APWeb 2014, LNCS 8709, pp. 201–211, 2014.

such as sections or paragraphs. We can align and associate parts appropriately by using structural information.

Much important content on the Web can be modeled as structured documents. Our motivation is to associate corresponding parts in structured documents, and we propose a method of using the content and structural information of documents for fine-grained document alignments.

Using document structures would be especially effective for cross-lingual cases. It is a way to use machine translation such as Google Translate[1] in advance in order to take alignments of cross-lingual documents. However, machine translation does not have sufficiently good quality to obtain appropriate alignments by only using information from content. In contrast, as structural information is not changed by machine translation, it would be effective for cross-lingual alignments.

We carried out experiments to confirm the effectiveness of using document structures for alignments, where we used pairs of papers such as a conference paper and its modified version which had been published as a journal paper. The results revealed that we could obtain more appropriate alignments by using document structures and there were especially effective for cross-lingual cases.

This paper is organized as follows. Section 2 discusses related work and its differences from our work. Section 3 explains the method of alignment. Section 4 presents results obtained from experiments and discusses the results. Conclusions and future work are presented in Section 5.

2   Related Work

2.1   Document Alignment

Document alignment has been widely studied. Daumé III and Marcu [1] considered alignments at the phrase level between one document and its abstract, and proposed a method using a hidden Markov model (HMM). Jeong and Titov [2] used a Bayesian model for alignments.

Our motivation was to associate corresponding parts of documents, i.e., to obtain alignments, which was similar to the previous work. However, they considered alignments based on information from the content of documents. In contrast, we introduced structural information into alignments.

Romary et al. [3] proposed a multilevel alignment method for structured documents. However, their target structure is balanced tree and they do not consider swapping.

2.2   Similarity of Documents

The idea of using document structures has been presented in studies on calculating similarities in documents. Zhang and Chow [4] regarded a document as having a two-level tree structure which had a root node representing the entire

---

[1] http://translate.google.com/

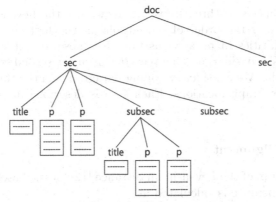

Fig. 1. Example of document tree

document and child nodes representing paragraphs, and they calculated similarities by using the Earth Mover's Distance (EMD). They also applied their method to detect plagiarism [5]. Wan [6] regarded a document as a sequence of its subtopics and he calculated similarities with EMD. Tekli and Chbeir [7] used the Tree Edit Distance to calculate similarities in XML documents.

They considered document structures in their work, but their motivation was to calculate similarities of documents, which was different from our motivation to find alignments.

2.3   Cross-Lingual Alignment

Yahyaei et al. [8] proposed a method using Divergence from Randomness. Yeung et al. [9] regarded document alignment to be a matter where Wikipedia pages had various quantities of descriptions for various languages. They used alignment technique to complete their content by using the same pages written in different languages. Smith et al. [10] used alignment to gather parallel sentences for training of statistical machine translation (SMT). Vu et al. [11] proposed a method to obtain similar news texts written in different languages.

Our method can be applied to cross-lingual alignments by using machine translation. Their work focused on content information of documents. On the other hand, our work introduce the structural information into alignments.

3   Alignment Method

We regard structured documents as tree structures and call them document trees (Figure 1). The input for our method is two document trees and the output is the result from alignment. The granularity of alignment is paragraphs.

If corresponding parts are heavily modified, it is hard to associate them by only using similarities in their content. Therefore, our method takes into considerations the order of paragraphs and the structures of documents.

Our method consists of three steps, where we use the Levenshtein distance algorithm to consider the order of paragraphs in the first step. We not only consider the similarities in paragraphs but also those in sections to associate two paragraphs. We consider merging paragraphs in the second step to associate multiple paragraphs. We consider swapping paragraphs in the third step to deal with changing paragraph locations. Each step is described in subsections 3.1, 3.2, and 3.3.

3.1 Baseline Alignment

We use the algorithm of the Levenshtein distance [12] for the baseline alignment. The Levenshtein distance is calculated as

$$d(s_i, t_j) = \min \begin{pmatrix} d(s_{i-1}, t_j) + cost_{del}(s[i]), \\ d(s_i, t_{j-1}) + cost_{ins}(t[j]), \\ d(s_{i-1}, t_{j-1}) + cost_{ren}(s[i], t[j]) \end{pmatrix} \tag{1}$$

s_i is the substring of string s which has i characters from the begining of s, and $s[i]$ is the i th character of s. The same thing can be said for t_j, $t[j]$, and t.

We regard documents as paragraph sequences and obtain alignment by applying this algorithm to them. When the bottom expression in Eq. (1) is minimum, i.e., when a rename operation is applied, we associate $s[i]$ and $t[j]$. Thus, we can obtain alignment which takes into account the order of paragraphs.

We set the rename cost of similar paragraphs to a lower value to associate similar paragraphs. The cost functions are defined as

$$cost_{del}(p) = cost_{ins}(p) = \alpha \quad (0 \le \alpha \le 1) \tag{2}$$

$$cost_{ren}(p, q) = 1 - similarity(p, q) \tag{3}$$

where p and q are paragraphs. As delete and insert operations are symmetric, we set their costs to be equal. The *similarity* calculates the similarities between p and q in 0 to 1.

In order to associate two paragraphs which are hard to associate only using their similarity, we use sim_{global} which is the similarity between the sections which contain the paragraphs to be associated and sim_{local} which is the similarity between the paragraphs. sim_{global} and sim_{local} are calculated as the cosine similarity between the term vectors by tf-idf. The *similarity* is defined as follows, where C is a parameter which is in 0 to 1.

$$similarity(p, q) = C sim_{global}(p, q) + (1 - C) sim_{local}(p, q) \tag{4}$$

Thus, the similarity between sections will help in associating paragraphs.

This is the association using the Levenshtein distance algorithm. Figure 2 outlines an example of alignment in step 1, where associated paragraphs are

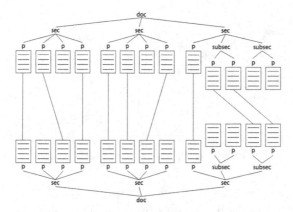

Fig. 2. Example of alignment in step 1

linked in the lines. Paragraphs which are not associated are regarded as deleted or inserted in this step. The alignment process is finished when all paragraphs or no paragraphs are associated in this step.

3.2 Merging

Paragraphs can be split into multiple parts, but the alignments in the previous step are in 1-to-1. We then need to consider alignments in m to n. we can do this by merging paragraphs.

The merging targets are paragraphs which have not been associated yet in the previous step (Section 3.1). We try to merge each paragraph into adjoining paragraphs which have been already associated. That means, we assume that parts of paragraphs which are split are associated in the previous step.

We determine whether paragraphs should be merged by checking for the similarities, i.e., if similarities increased by merging, the paragraphs are merged. If similarity decreased, the paragraphs remain not associated.

We considered using document structures for merging. The merge process was used to deal with split paragraphs, and paragraphs would not split into different sections. Therefore, as we assumed that merging between paragraphs which were in different sections will not occur, we prevented such merging by decreasing similarities. We introduced a parameter, *penalty*, in our method, which was multiplied to the similarity of merged paragraphs of different sections. We can determine whether the merging is done over different sections by checking whether the parents of the paragraphs to be merged are the same. We could reduce false merging by doing this.

We applied the merging process described in this step to the results of the previous step. Figure 3 has an example of alignments in this step, where paragraphs which are associated with the same paragraph have been merged.

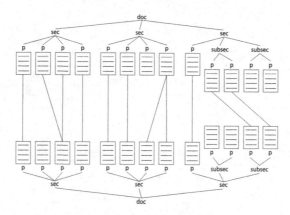

Fig. 3. Example of alignment in step 2

There are also paragraphs which have not been associated yet in this step. They were not merged since similarities decreased if they merged. If all paragraphs are associated in this step, the alignment process is finished.

3.3 Swapping

Alignments which took into consideration associations in multiple paragraphs were achieved in the previous steps. However, there are cases where the locations of paragraphs have changed where we need to consider cross associations. We took cross associations into account in this step, i.e., where paragraphs were swapped.

Like the merging process, the targets for the swapping process are paragraphs which have not been associated yet in the merging step (Section 3.2). Swapped paragraphs can remain not being associated in the previous steps. The targets in the swapping process are paragraphs in a document which are not associated and we try to find corresponding paragraphs in another document which are also not associated.

We need to check for similarities to find swapped corresponding paragraphs. For example, if similarities are greater than a threshold, then paragraphs become associated. However, it is hard to find corresponding paragraphs which are heavily modified only using the information from content as in the previous steps. Furthermore, as the swapping process does not take into consideration the order of paragraphs unlike in the previous steps, false associations can be increased. We need to set the threshold for associations in the swapping process to a greater value. Therefore, there need to be greater similarity of swapped paragraphs to be associated appropriately.

We then introduce the use of document structures into the swapping process. Before finding corresponding paragraphs, we enumerate subtrees which are composed only of the paragraphs that are not associated. We then try to swap the subtrees. Figure 4 shows an example of targets of swapping, where the subtrees enclosed by the dotted lines are the targets. We check for similarities for each

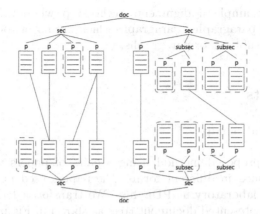

Fig. 4. Example of targets of swapping

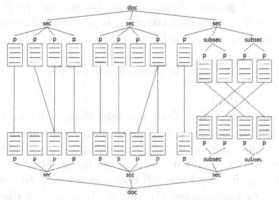

Fig. 5. Example of alignment in step 3

subtree in one document with subtrees in another document and if the similarities are greater than the threshold, then we regard the subtree as corresponding. Thus, we can find corresponding paragraphs by using the structural information in subtrees even when it is hard to swap paragraphs by content information only.

We use the Tree Edit Distance (TED) [13] to calculate the similarities between subtrees. We can find appropriate corresponding subtrees by using the structural information in subtrees even if there are few similarities by using the content of paragraphs. We choose a subtree which has the largest similarity value greater than the threshold as the corresponding subtree.

We focus on the two subtrees and apply our method from step 1 again if a corresponding subtree is found. The alignment process is recursively performed and stops when any of the following three states is achieved

1. All paragraphs are associated, or no paragraphs are associated in step 1.
2. All paragraphs are associated in step 2.
3. No paragraphs are associated in step 3.

Figure 5 shows an example of alignments in this step, where the crossed associations are swapped paragraphs. Paragraphs which are not associated could not find corresponding subtrees or paragraphs.

4   Experiments

4.1   Experimental Setup

We evaluated the proposed method using 8 pairs of papers which had been presented or published in different forms. The papers used in the experiment were stored in our laboratory as PDF files. We transformed the PDF files to XML files, which represented document trees as shown in Figure 1. Among the 8 pairs, 5 pairs are cross-lingual (papers in Japanese and English) and Japanese papers were translated into English by Google Translate as the preprocessing.

We manually judged proper alignments as the ground truth and calculated the precision and recall of the associations. We preliminarily examined optimal values for the parameters and set α in Eq. (2) to 0.425, C in Eq. (4) to 0.2, and *penalty* to 0.8.

We used two other approaches to evaluate our method.

- simple matching method
  It associates paragraphs and does not take their order into consideration. Our method consists of 3 steps, i.e., step 1: alignments using the Levenshtein distance, step 2: merging, and step 3: swapping. However, the merging and swapping steps are required since alignments using the Levenshtein distance are (1) associations in 1 to 1 and (2) these are not able to deal with changes in the locations of paragraphs. We use the Levenshtein distance in step 1 since we take into consideration the order of paragraphs and assume the alignments to be more appropriate.

  The simple matching method works as follows to confirm the effectiveness of considering the order of paragraphs. Each paragraph in one document is associated with a paragraph in another document which is the most similar to and its similarity is greater than threshold $1 - 2\alpha$. Thus, it identifies alignments and does not take into account the order of paragraphs.

- non-structural method
  The main idea of this research was that alignments would be improved by using document structures. We arranged this method, which is based on the proposed approach, and modified it in three ways to confirm this.

  1. It does not use sim_{global} in step 1 (alignments using the Levenshtein distance), i.e., C in Eq. (4) is set to 0.
  2. It does not impose a penalty on merging between different sections in step 2 (merge), i.e., the *penalty* is set to 1.
  3. It swaps using paragraphs in step 3 (swap), not subtrees.

  Thus, it makes alignments using only the content and the order information.

Table 1. Precision and recall for each method

Pair ID	proposed method		non-structural method		simple matching method	
	precision	recall	precision	recall	precision	recall
p1	0.95 (36/38)	0.95 (36/38)	0.91 (32/35)	0.84 (32/38)	0.62 (31/50)	0.82 (31/38)
p2	0.94 (34/36)	0.89 (34/38)	0.91 (30/34)	0.79 (30/38)	0.65 (24/37)	0.63 (24/38)
p3	0.85 (34/40)	0.76 (34/45)	0.80 (33/41)	0.73 (33/45)	0.68 (34/50)	0.76 (34/45)
p4	0.86 (44/51)	0.92 (44/48)	0.81 (38/47)	0.79 (38/48)	0.44 (35/80)	0.73 (35/48)
p5	0.95 (37/39)	0.90 (37/41)	0.93 (37/40)	0.91 (37/41)	0.69 (31/45)	0.76 (31/41)
p6	0.98 (51/52)	0.98 (51/52)	0.98 (51/52)	0.98 (51/52)	0.98 (51/52)	0.98 (51/52)
p7	1.0 (51/51)	0.93 (51/55)	0.98 (51/52)	0.93 (51/55)	0.88 (45/51)	0.82 (45/55)
p8	0.97 (37/38)	1.0 (37/37)	0.95 (37/39)	1.0 (37/37)	0.97 (31/32)	0.84 (31/37)

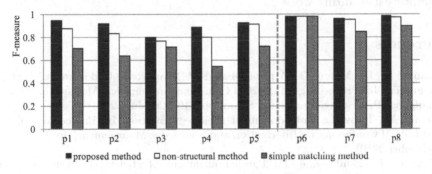

Fig. 6. F-measures for each method

4.2   Results

Table 1 lists the results of alignments for the methods. Precision and recall are calculated as follows.

- Number of correct associations in result / Number of associations in result
- Number of correct associations in result / Number of correct associations

Figure 6 shows the F-measures for the methods. The proposed method performed the best for each pair according to Figure 6.

There were many false alignments in the results for the simple matching method, which ignored the order of paragraphs. In contrast, the proposed method and non-structural method, which took into consideration the order of paragraphs, obtained natural alignments. These results confirm that taking into consideration the order of paragraphs is effective for alignments.

In contrast to the results of the non-structural method, the effectiveness of using document structures can be seen in the results of the proposed method. The proposed approach associated paragraphs which had not been associated by the non-structural method by using structural information. These results confirmed that taking document structures into consideration is effective for alignments.

Furthermore, the proposed method outperformed the other methods especially in the cross-lingual cases (p1, p2, p3, p4, and p5) on the left part of Figure 6. They were translated by machine translation in preprocessing. This means that using structures is especially effective for finding cross-lingual alignments.

5   Conclusion

We proposed a method of document alignment, in which we applied the algorithm of the Levenshtein distance and took into consideration document structures. The method also took into account the merging and swapping of paragraphs. We confirmed its effectiveness of using the structures of documents for alignments in our experiments. We will apply our method to more documents and improve it in future work.

References

1. Daumé III, H., Marcu, D.: A phrase-based HMM approach to document/abstract alignment. In: Proceedings of the 2004 Conference on Empirical Methods in Natural Language Processing, Barcelona, Spain, pp. 119–126 (July 2004)
2. Jeong, M., Titov, I.: Multi-document topic segmentation. In: Proceedings of the 19th ACM Conference on Information and Knowledge Management, pp. 1119–1128 (October 2010)
3. Romary, L., Bonhomme, P.: Parallel alignment of structured documents. In: Véronis, J. (ed.) Parallel Text Processing, pp. 233–253. Kluwer Academic Publishers (2000)
4. Zhang, H., Chow, T.W.S.: A multi-level matching method with hybrid similarity for document retrieval. Expert Systems with Applications 39(3), 2710–2719 (2012)
5. Zhang, H., Chow, T.W.S.: A coarse-to-fine framework to efficiently thwart plagiarism. Pattern Recognition 44(2), 471–487 (2011)
6. Wan, X.: A novel document similarity measure based on earth mover's distance. Information Sciences 177(18), 3718–3730 (2007)
7. Tekli, J., Chbeir, R.: A novel XML document structure comparison framework based-on sub-tree commonalities and label semantics. Journal of Web Semantics 11, 14–40 (2012)
8. Yahyaei, S., Bonzanini, M., Roelleke, T.: Cross-lingual text fragment alignment using divergence from randomness. In: Grossi, R., Sebastiani, F., Silvestri, F. (eds.) SPIRE 2011. LNCS, vol. 7024, pp. 14–25. Springer, Heidelberg (2011)
9. Au Yeung, C., Duh, K., Nagata, M.: Providing cross-lingual editing assistance to wikipedia editors. In: Gelbukh, A. (ed.) CICLing 2011, Part II. LNCS, vol. 6609, pp. 377–389. Springer, Heidelberg (2011)
10. Smith, J.R., Quirk, C., Toutanova, K.: Extracting parallel sentences from comparable corpora using document level alignment. In: Human Language Technologies: Conference of the North American Chapter of the Association of Computational Linguistics, Los Angeles, USA, pp. 403–411 (June 2010)

11. Vu, T., Aw, A., Zhang, M.: Feature-based method for document alignment in comparable news corpora. In: Proceedings of the 12th Conference of the European Chapter of the Association for Computational Linguistics, Athens, Greece, pp. 843–851 (2009)
12. Levenshtein, V.I.: Binary codes capable of correcting deletions, insertions and reversals. Soviet Physics Doklady 10(8), 707–710 (1966)
13. Zhang, K., Shasha, D.: Simple fast algorithms for the editing distance between trees and related problems. SIAM Journal on Computing 18(6), 1245–1262 (1989)

Acquiring Stored or Real Time Satellite Data via Natural Language Query

Xu Chen[1,2], Jin Liu[1,*], Xinyan Zhu[3], and Ming Li[3]

[1] State Key Laboratory of Software Engineering, Wuhan University, Wuhan, China
[2] Language Technologies Institute, School of Computer Science, Carnegie Mellon University, Pittsburgh, USA
[3] State Key Laboratory of Information Engineering in Surveying Mapping and Remote Sensing, Wuhan University, Wuhan, China
{xuchen,jinliu}@whu.edu.cn

Abstract. With the advent of Sensor Web, the satellite data acquired by sensor systems could be shared among users immediately. Our research has led to an implementation of natural language queries such that users without particular knowledge of satellite imagery can describe easily for what they need. We use a rules-based method to retrieve named entities, with the help of a knowledge base and uses existing Sensor Web services for acquiring stored or real time satellite data. We use rule-based methods to align time, location and domain task entities in natural language queries with Sensor Web services with standard times, geographical coordinates, and satellite attributes. To evaluate our system, we wrote a series of natural language queries in the domains of surveying and mapping, forestry, agriculture, and disaster response. Our queries and satellite data retrieved by the queries were corrected by a group of experts to create a gold standard. Using their remarks as correct, we scored our system results using precision and recall metrics standard for information retrieval. The results of our experiment demonstrate that the proposed method is promising for assisting in Earth observation applications.

Keywords: Observation Task, Satellite Data, Sensor Web, Ontology.

1 Introduction

The core of our research concerns how to bridge the technical parameters of satellite data with natural language queries from users who might be unfamiliar with satellite parameters. More people would like to examine real-time satellite data, or integrate these data into their own services. Archives of satellite data are available through keyword search of geo-portals such as the Google MAP[1], the National Aeronautics and Space Administration (NASA) Earth Observing System Data and the Information System EoDIS[2].

---

* Corresponding author.
[1] https://www.google.com/maps/preview
[2] http://reverb.echo.nasa.gov/reverb/#utf8=%E2%9C%93&spatial_map=satellite&spatial_type=rectangle

L. Chen et al. (Eds.): APWeb 2014, LNCS 8709, pp. 212–223, 2014.

The Sensor Web [2] allows satellite data to be obtained in real time. But how to find it? Sensor Web services integrate easily with other Web services. However, most people find the interfaces of service (such as Sensor Observation Service [12] or Sensor Planning Service [14]) opaque due to their technical parameters and specifications.

In this study, we propose a novel method that allows natural language query to search and retrieve archived or real-time satellite data. We use a rules-based method to find named entities, with the help of a knowledge base. We use rule-based methods to link time, location and domain tasks entered by users with the technical specifications of the existing infrastructure for the Sensor Web.

The remainder of this paper is organized as follows: Section 2 outlines an architecture of our system. A structured natural language template and knowledge base are described in Section 3. Section 4 explains how keywords and named entities are identified. A system implementation and the experimental study are discussed in Section 5. Section 6 describes related work, and Section 7 summarizes the conclusions and gives potential directions for future research.

2   Architecture

Many Sensor Web services have been implemented and can be accessed by Internet, eg., the company 52°North, with its Sensor Web community[3], which can be used as a data layer for acquiring satellite data. We require an intelligent analysis layer as a sort of middleware between client and existing Sensor Web services. Therefore, the framework could be divided into three layers: user interface layer, intelligent analysis layer, and data layer, as shown in Fig. 1.

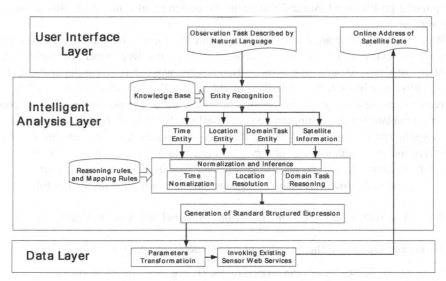

Fig. 1. Acquiring stored or real time satellite data via natural language query

---

[3] http://52north.org/communities/sensorweb/

User Interface Layer: is a simple and user-friendly Web browser client. Anyone can use it to input some keywords or a natural language sentence for describing an observation task. Multi-condition combination query and a bulk feed are also supported. Results are also shown in this layer.

Intelligent analysis layer: is the core layer that achieves task recognition and reasoning. It includes a rules-based classifier for named entities which draws upon the knowledge base. In section 3.2, we describe how the knowledge base includes a time ontology, location ontology, satellite ontology, domain task ontology. The output of this layer are normalized values based on the format which we defined.

Data Layer: This provides satellite data based on the services layer. A parameter transformation function is provided in this layer which transform the result of Intelligent Analysis Layer to values of interface parameters of the standard Sensor Web services, then we can invoke existing Sensor Web services such as the Sensor Observation Service, or the Sensor Planning Service.

3   A Structured Natural Language Template and Knowledge Base

3.1   Template for Input

In generally, users prefer to describe the observation task by natural language rather than formalized language. However, keyword search of data collections often lack precision, and automated parsing of unrestricted natural language may be inaccurate [16]. In this study, we propose a structured natural language template, to reduce the parsing problems of Natural Language Processing and remove the limitations of keyword search.

We investigate four areas where such satellite data might be useful, including Bureau of Surveying and Mapping, Department of Forestry, Department of Agriculture, Ministry of Civil Affairs. We asked officials who worked in these departments for parameters for what satellite data they might need. We collected more than 200 requirement descriptions were collected. Then we used a ground-up approach to construct a template for future unseen queries based on their requirements. It is based on this experiment that we found that time, location, domain task and satellite requirement are the basic elements of observation task, which we included in our template. These basic elements can be used to construct a data query or a satellite plan. Therefore, we present a structured natural language template, which is defined as follows:

- *ObservationTask* = { *Time, Location, DomainTask, SatelliteRequirement* }

Time expresses when the task should be executed, eg., About 2003.8.21.

Location expresses where the task covers with, e.g., southwest Montana.

DomainTask describes a specific domain task, e.g., monitoring of wildfires.

SatelliteRequirement expresses the detailed description of image parameters and sensor parameters, e.g., MODIS.

User could easily describe an observation tasks based on this template:

" About 2003.8.21, monitoring of wildfires in southwest Montana, the sensor should be MODIS. "

3.2   Knowledge Base

Ontologies are used to model the domain knowledge, and organize the concepts and properties of time, spatial information, domain task and satellite. In order to recognize the entities in a user query, we collected vocabulary specific to four domains: forestry, agriculture, surveying and mapping, and disaster response. We collect terms, relationships from Wikipedia[4], WenkuBaidu[5], terminological dictionaries and standards of each domain (such as ISO Standards for Geographic Information[8]), website of organizations and institutions (such as ISO/TC211[6]). Then we built a knowledge base with a time ontology, a location ontology, ontologies for our given task domains, a satellite ontology, task reasoning rules and spatiotemporal calculation rules.

Ontologies in the Knowledge Base. Time information describes the time or duration of a user observation task (such as assess the wildfire's area). Location describes the observation location of the task. Domain tasks indicate a specific task in a specific domain, satellite information is about satellite data to achieve observation task. Therefore, we built four types of ontologies to model the requirement of observation task.

Time Ontology: OWL-time is a temporal ontology that provides a vocabulary for expressing data on the topological relations between instants and intervals, together with the duration and date–time information [6].We adopt the OWL-time as a basis for the time ontology. Time ontology includes temporal terms (e.g., festival, season), temporal units (e.g., year, month, week, day), temporal qualifier (e.g., before, after). The Chinese temporal ontology is built in the study additionally, most of concepts refer to Time ontology in English. However, Mandarin has some special temporal concept, the concepts of the Chinese lunar calendar and the traditional solar term are added into the Chinese time ontology, which provide better support for the observation task described in Chinese.

Location Ontology: We reference GeoNames Ontology[7] and build the Location ontology. Location ontology is used to organize concepts of toponym, spatial relationships, feature types, spatial range and so on, which consists of the geo-feature entity, geo-feature-type, and spatial relationship ontologies. The geo-feature entity ontology

---

includes the place name, geocoding, feature type, and footprint. The geo-feature-type ontology is a classification ontology of the feature type. The spatial relationship ontology is built to describe the spatial relationship which defined in the DE-9IM model [3]. Toponyms in gazetteer are regarded as instances of Location Ontology.

Domain Task Ontology: The vocabulary came from speaking with experts and noting keywords about tasks that might use the satellite data, terminological dictionaries and standards of domain. The inter-relations were made by hand with the help of domain experts. In this study, "task" refers to the observation task, especially for Earth observation task. Domain means application domain of Earth observation technology, different domain has different tasks, vocabularies, and concepts, building domain task ontology is a heavy work. The domain task ontology consists of observation object, observation action, object attribute, and their relations.

Satellite Ontology: The vocabulary came from Wikipedia and some satellite websites. The inter-relations were also made by hand with the help of domain experts. Properties of Satellite Ontology include id, mission type, operator, reference system, regime, semi-major axis, eccentricity, period, epoch and so on. Satellite Ontology refer to Sensor Ontology and Satellite Data Ontology. Sensor Ontology describes specific properties of sensor, e.g. orbit, scan rate, swath. Satellite Data Ontology describes specific properties of data, e.g. spatial resolution, fabric width, band, and signal noise ratio.

Reasoning Rules in the Knowledge Base. In addition to these ontologies, we use rules to find enough information in order to determine which satellite to call upon.

Task Reasoning Rules: Many observation tasks described by natural language are incomplete. If the query lacks satellite-related information, for example, it is hard to find satellite data. Therefore, we defined a variety of task requirements based on template in several specific domains (disaster response, agriculture, surveying and mapping, forestry) and encode the reasoning in Semantic Web Rule Language.[8] For example, "monitoring of forest fire" is a typical observation task, which demands satellite data with a spatial resolution of less than 1000 meters and a near-infrared wave band. The rules can be expressed as follows:

Monitoring of Forest fire (?task) $\rightarrow$ satelliteData(?x) $\wedge$ hasSpatialResolution(?x,?y) $\wedge$ swrlb:lessThan(?y,1000) $\wedge$hasBand(?x,?z) $\wedge$ bandName(?z,?bName)$\wedge$ swrlb:stringEqualIgnoreCase(?bName,"Near Infrared")

Spatiotemporal Calculation Rules: We also use rules to find a specific time and location. For example, we use spatial analysis calculation, spatial relationship calculation, coordinate transformation (WGS 84 is the first choice), time transformation, normalization of relative temporal expressions (e.g. today) and implicit temporal expressions (e.g. spring season) and so on.

---

[8] http://www.w3.org/Submission/SWRL/

We have found experimentally that our ontologies, reasoning rules, and gazetteer provide a sufficient resources to support Named Entities Recognition, normalization and inference of user queries in natural language.

4   How Our Recognition Algorithm Works in Details

The observation task described by natural language is processed by a rule-based algorithm that recognizes keywords and named entities with the help of the knowledge base described in section 3.2. The way it works is that time entities, location entities, domain task entities, and satellite requirements are recognized. Then normalization and inference is used to gain deeper understanding of the user query.

Algorithm. A Rule-based Recognition

Input : User query Q_i
Output: $R\{T_i|P_i, L_i|A_i, S_i\}$
1 **for** each Q_i
2   Named Entities Recognition(Q_i) ;
3   **if** (time entities exist and NumofTime == 2) **then**
4   TemporalCalculation(T_1,T_2);
5   Period of Pi, add Pi to R;
6   **else if** (time entities exist and NumofTime == 1) **then**
7   time normalization T_i;
8   add T_i to R;
9   **if** (location entities exist and 6>NumofLocation>1) **then**
10   SpatialCalculation ($L_1,L_2...L_{Num}$);
11   MBR of A_i;
12   add A_i to R;
13   **else if** (location entities exist and NumofLocation==1) **then**
14   resolution Location L_i;
15   add L_i to R;
16   **if** domain task entities exist **then**
17   task reasoning S'_i;
18   **if** satellite requirement exist **then**
19   resolution satellite information S''_i;
20   S_i= intersection(S'_i,S''_i) ;
21   add S_i to R;
22   **return** R;

The above is pseudocode for our algorithm. The input to the algorithm is a user query or set of queries, Q_i. The output is set R, which includes normalization time T_i or a period of time P_i, geographical coordinates of L_i or a minimum enclosing rectangle of observation area A_i, satellite information S_i which is a interaction result of task reasoning S'_i and   satellite requirement S''_i.

4.1   Expression Rules

We inferred these rules based on collecting actual data from professionals in our domain fields. We discovered four types of expression rules: for time, location, task and satellite parameters, then we defined these rules based on Backus–Naur Form. Each rule is explained below.

Time. Time data divides into instants and intervals. The terms contain "Day," "Month," "Year," "Christmas," "August," and so on. An example of an instant is 2003-08-21 21:00, and an example of an interval is a month. The qualifier for the time contains "before," "after," "between," and so on. These vocabularies are used to describe time in the observation, e.g., "before August 21, 2003," The expression rules of the temporal information are described as follows:

Time Information::={Qualifier} + <Value> + [Month] + <Value> + [Day] +<Value>+ [Year].

Location. "In the boundary between Montana and Idaho" and "in southwest Montana," are examples of the location information in the observation task, which include toponym or spatial range, terms of spatial relationship and spatial direction. The expression rule of the spatial information resemble in the following, the Qualifier indicates words that describe the position and direction, e.g., "in," "at," "between". The Relationship indicates the spatial relationship terms, e.g., "across," "intersect". Toponym indicates terms such as "administrative division," "river," "mountain", spatial range is another choice to describe a observation range.

Location Information::= [Qualifier] + [Relationship] + {<Toponym> / <Spatial Range> + [Qualifier]}.

Task. Domain task information is the core of the observation task. This is subdivided into task actions (found in natural language in terms such as "monitoring" or "updating"), task aspect (found in natural language queries in terms such as "area," or "desertification"), and task object (found in natural language in terms such as "wildfires," or "digital terrain map").

Domain Task::=<Action> + {[Aspect]} + <Object>.

Satellite Parameters. In the description of the observation task, users impose some restrictions on the satellite parameters (such as "the spatial resolution should be better than 10 m."). Qualifier indicates the words that express comparison, such as "better than" or "equal." Value indicates a quantifier to express the parameters, e.g., "5" or "five." Unit is the unit of the parameters, e.g., "m" or "km."

Satellite Requirement::=[Satellite parameters] + {Qualifier} + <Value> + <Unit>.

4.2   Normalization and Inference

After we get the named entities of user query, in some cases we still cannot find suitable satellite data because we lack specific time, latitude and longitude, and/or satellite information. Therefore, we execute normalization and inference based on the result of Named Entities Recognition.

For example, the user input this query:

"About 2003.8.21, monitoring of wildfires in southwest Montana, the sensor should be MODIS."

After the Named Entities Recognition, the time entities, location entities, and domain task entities and satellite requirement are extracted based on expression rules and knowledge base. The intermediate result resembles the following:

Time Entity: About 2003.8.21

Location Entity: southwest Montana

Domain Task Entity: monitoring of wildfires

Satellite Requirement: MODIS

Then in another step, which also called normalization and inference. It is used to transform the named entity to standard time information, spatial information, and satellite information, the result as following:

Time information, which is described in a standard time representation:

Start time: 2003-08-21T00:00:00, End time: 2003-08-21T24:00:00.

Spatial information, southwest Montana is transformed to longitude and latitude by spatial calculation:

Latitude: N45°01′57.39″ ~ N46°40′56.90″, Longitude: W107°12′01.38″~W111°45′38.87″.

Satellite information, which is the intersection of task reasoning results and original satellite requirement, e.g., "monitoring of forest fire" is a typical observation task, which requires sensor with a spatial resolution of less than 1,000 m and a near-infrared wave band, and in this task, the MODIS sensor requirement is expressed definitely, which also satisfies the requirement of monitoring of forest fire. Therefore, the intersection result is:

Satellite information: MODIS.

5   Prototype System and Experiment

5.1   Prototype System

We developed a prototype system to test and verify this method of retrieving satellite data archived or in real time. The Web client of the prototype system is shown in Fig.2. A input field is on the top panel, we can input an observation task described by natural language into the field. After we run the processing function, the time, location, task entities and satellite requirement are extracted by Named Entities Recognition (NER), the result is shown in left panel. Then, we can get result of the normalization and inference, the normalization of temporal information, spatial coordinates, the detailed satellite information are shown on the right panel. Then, we can invoke existing Sensor Web services based on the results to acquire satellite data.

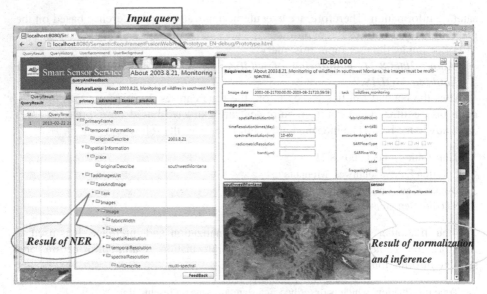

Fig. 2. The web client of prototype system

5.2   Evaluation

We tested the ability of our system to retrieve satellite data based on natural language query. We used observation task queries in the domains of surveying, forestry, agriculture, disaster reduction. We collected 212 observation task keywords in Mandarin described by experts. Then the authors of this paper ourselves wrote 623 more sets of tasks with related, but not duplicate keywords. We had experts re-read the queries that the authors had written to verify their plausibility, and to modify the queries if necessary. The break-down of queries by domain in the sample data set appears in Table1.

We show four examples translated to English as follows:

Sample query_1, from surveying and mapping domain: *2012,   producing Digital Line Graphic of Beijing Changping district, the scale of the product   is 1: 460000.*

Sample query_2, from forestry domain: *In the autumn of 2011, wooded area investigation of Heilongjiang Province, resolution is not less than 10m.*

Sample query_3, from agriculture: *2011.06.21-2011.07.10,   yield monitoring of spring wheat in the north.*

Sample query_4, from disaster response: *On 2003/8/21, assess the wildfire's area in northeast Idaho, the spatial resolution should be better than 10m.*

To evaluate, we randomly selected six groups queries (each group has 100 queries) from these domain samples. Then we gave both query and results to a group of experts in each domain to make a gold standard. Then we scored the recall and precision, with the results shown in Table 2.

Table 1. Test samples statistics

Domain	Surveying and Mapping	Forestry	Agriculture	Disaster Reduction
#Sample queries	199	210	209	217

We score results in terms of precision and recall:

$$Precision\ of\ NER = \frac{numbers\ of\ correct\ recognized\ query}{numbers\ of\ recognized\ query} \tag{1}$$

$$Recall\ of\ NER = \frac{numbers\ of\ correct\ recognized\ query}{numbers\ of\ query} \tag{2}$$

If one of the named entities in a query is not extracted, we judge the query is not recognized. For example, in Sample query_2, If *"In the autumn of 2011"* is not recognized, despite *"wooded area investigation, Heilongjiang Province, resolution is not less than 10m"* are recognized correctly, this query is not recognized correct. This represents the first pass of the query through the system. However, this is sometimes insufficient because we lack specific time, latitude and longitude, and/or satellite information. Therefore, we score results of normalization and inference:

$$Precision\ of\ normalization\ and\ inference = \frac{numbers\ of\ correct\ normalization\ and\ inference\ query}{numbers\ of\ normalization\ and\ inference\ query} \tag{3}$$

$$Recall\ of\ normalization\ and\ inference = \frac{numbers\ of\ correct\ normalization\ and\ inference\ query}{numbers\ of\ correct\ recognized\ query} \tag{4}$$

The precision and recall of normalization and inference is based on the results of NER, if one of the named entities is not normalized or reasoning correctly, we judge the query is not understood. For example, if we can't calculate the spatial range of *Heilongjiang Province* correctly, this query is not inference correctly, although we get the standard time and satellite specific information.

Table 2. Precision and recall statistics

	1	2	3	4	5	6	Average
Precision of NER	98.3	98.7	96.5	98.9	93.4	96.4	97.03
Recall of NER	96.4	96.3	97.2	95.1	95.6	96.1	96.11
Precision of normalization and inference	96.1	95.6	94.3	96.9	91.1	94.9	94.81
Recall of normalization and inference	95.4	97.8	96.5	97.2	93.7	95.3	95.98

The average precision and recall of NER is above 96%, because we utilize the a large knowledge base and variety expression rules, but a good result relies on the completeness of knowledge base and rules, we provide a function to add new knowledge and rules, to enhance the extendibility of our system. The average precision and recall ration of normalization and inference is also above 94%, assuming that results from NER are correct. Therefore, our prototype system is promising for assisting in Earth observation applications.

6   Related Work

Our system is able to return satellite data to users based on their task domains, while comparable systems by the NASA and the ESRI Company return data only in direct response to user keywords.   Recall that the core of our research concerns how to bridge the technical parameters of satellite data with natural language queries from users who might be unfamiliar with satellite parameters. We break this into sub-parameters in order to review the literature.

Location. Recognizing geospatial information in document files (for example, from txt, html, xml and doc) is an active research direction in the geo-spatial domain. Most studies focus on place name, also called toponym recognition. The recognition of toponyms based on Gazetteer [7] is a fundamental method.   Many NER approaches are used for toponym recognition, the approach that employs dictionaries and hand-made rules is very popular [9]. The approach based on Machine Learning is another popular method for toponym recognition, including Maximum Entropy[1], Conditional Random Field sequence models [4] and so on. A combination of rule-based method and Machine Learning is a new trend for toponym recognition [10, 5].

Location and Time. Some algorithms combine temporal and geographic information. Strötgen et al. use temporal and geographic information extracted from documents and recorded in temporal and geographic document profiles[15].

Location, Time and Task. Events happen at a given place and time[11]. Most of the research focuses on identifying events from temporally-ordered streams of documents and organizes these documents according to the events they describe[17]. Our observation task is a special type of event, which is more closely linked to temporal and spatial information than other events.

Research indicates that even state-of-the-art entity recognition systems are brittle, meaning that they are developed for one domain but do not typically perform well on other domains [13]. Therefore, research on entity recognition to acquire satellite data is significant.

7   Conclusion

In this study, we describe a novel method to acquire stored or real time satellite data via a natural language query based on existing SWE services. Based on users input, our algorithm uses Named Entities Recognition, normalization and inference to find relevant items in the satellite data. Our evaluation is based on our in-house prototype system which showed precision and recall. Open questions for future research include how to expand the reasoning rules that match between users input and ontologies of data automatically by machine learning.

Acknowledgment. This work was supported by the grants of the National Basic Research Program of China (2011CB707101), the National Natural Science Foundation of China (41201405, 61070013), China Scholarship Council No. 201308420300.

References

1. Bender, O., Och, F., Ney, H.: Maximum Entropy Models for Named Entity Recognition. In: Proceedings of the 7th Conference on Natural Language Learning (CoNLL 2003), Edmonton, Canada, pp. 148–151 (2003)
2. Delin, K.A., Jackson, S.P.: The Sensor Web: A New Instrument Concept. In: Proceedings of the SPIE's Symposium on Integrated Optics, San Jose, CA, vol. 4284, pp. 1–9 (2001)
3. Egenhofer, M.J., Franzosa, R.D.: Point-set topological spatial relations. International Journal of Geographical Information Systems 5(2), 161–176 (1991)
4. Finkel, J.R., Grenager, T., Manning, C.: Incorporating non-local information into information extraction systems by gibbs sampling. In: Proceedings of the 43rd Annual Meeting of the Association for Computational Linguistics, Ann Arbor, MI, pp. 363–370 (2005)
5. Gelernter, J., Zhang, W.: Cross-lingual geo-parsing for non-structured data. In: 7th Workshop on Geographic Information Retrieval (GIR) Orlando, Florida, USA, pp. 64–71 (2013)
6. Hobbs, J.R., Pan, F.: An Ontology of Time for the Semantic Web. ACM Transactions on Asian Language Processing: Special issue on Temporal Information Processing 3(1), 66–85 (2004)
7. Hill, L.: Georeferencing – The Geographic Associations of Information, pp. 92–154. MIT Press, Cambridge (2006)
8. Kresse, W., Fadaie, K.I.: Standards for Geographic Information. Springer (2004)
9. Leidner, J.L., Lieberman, M.D.: Detecting Geographical References in the Form of Place Names and Associated Spatial Natural Language. The SIGSPATIAL Special 3(2), 5–11 (2011)
10. Lieberman, M.D., Same, H.: Multifaceted Toponym Recognition for Streaming News. In: Proceedings of the 34th International ACM SIGIR Conference on Research and Development in Information Retrieval, Beijing, China, pp. 843–852 (2011)
11. Miller, G.A., Beckwith, R., Fellbaum, C., Gross, D., Miller, K.J.: Introduction to wordnet: an on-line lexical database. International Journal of Lexicography 3, 235–244 (1990)
12. Na, A., Priest, M.: OGC Implementation Specification 06-009r6: OpenGIS Sensor Observation Service. OpenGIS Sensor Observation Service. Open Geospatial Consortium Inc., Wayland (2007)
13. Poibeau, T., Kosseim, L.: Proper Name Extraction from Non-Journalistic Texts. In: Computational Linguistics in the Netherlands Meeting, Amsterdam, New York, pp. 144–157 (2001)
14. Simonis, I., Echterhoff, J.: OGC Implementation Specification 09-000: OpenGIS Sensor Planning Service. Open Geospatial Consortium Inc., Wayland (2011)
15. Strötgen, J., Gertz, M., Popov, P.: Extraction and Exploration of Spatio-temporal Information in Documents. In: Proceedings of the 6th Workshop on Geographic Information Retrieval (GIR 2010), Zurich, Switzerland, pp. 1–8 (2010)
16. Tamand, A.M., Leung, C.H.C.: Structured Natural-Language Descriptions for Semantic Content Retrieval of Visual Materials. Journal of the American Society for Information Science and Technology 52(11), 930–937 (2007)
17. Vavliakis, K.N., Symeonidis, A.L., Mitkas, P.A.: Event identification in web social media through named entity recognition and topic modeling. Data and Knowledge Engineering 88, 1–24 (2013)

EISA: An Efficient Information Theoretical Approach to Value Segmentation in Large Databases

Weiqing Wang, Shazia Sadiq, and Xiaofang Zhou

School of Information Technology and Electrical Engineering
University of Queensland, Brisbane, Australia
weiqingwang@uq.edu.au, {shazia,zxf}@itee.uq.edu.au

Abstract. Value disparity is a widely known problem, that contributes to poor data quality results and raises many issues in data integration tasks. Value disparity, also known as column heterogeneity, occurs when the same entity is represented by disparate values, often within the same column in a database table. A first step in overcoming value disparity is to identify the distinct segments. This is a highly challenging task due to high number of features that define a particular segment as well as the need to undertake value comparisons which can be exponential in large databases. In this paper, we propose an efficient information theoretical approach to value segmentation, namely EISA. EISA not only reduces the number of the relevant features but also compresses the size of the values to be segmented. We have applied our method on three datasets with varying sizes. Our experimental evaluation of the method demonstrates a high level of accuracy with reasonable efficiency.

Keywords: segmentation, attribute, data quality, data profiling, information theory, large database.

1 Introduction

As the need to integrate data from multiple sources continues to grow, the disparity of values, often within the same column in a table, is also on the increase. Value disparity or column heterogeneity [8] is widely known problem that contributes to several data quality and data integration issues.

Segmentation of the values is one way to overcome the value disparity problem. This can be done by tagging the values with keywords, descriptions, or assigning them to several categories. Each segment has its specific patten and these patterns assist in understanding the data. Segmentation is also helpful in finding outliers or noise in the data. Clustering similar values is a classical way to segment the data. There are also many other approaches such as CFD(conditional functional dependency) [3] inferring, partitioning of a database horizontally [1] and others, which have been used in value segmentation.

Dai et al. proposed the "column heterogeneity" problem in [8]. This problem often arises when merging data from different sources. The example given in [8]

L. Chen et al. (Eds.): APWeb 2014, LNCS 8709, pp. 224–235, 2014.

is that one application might use email addresses as the customer identifier while another might use phone numbers for the same purpose. Given a heterogeneous attribute, partitioning the values into several more homogeneous segments is a natural solution to this problem.

Intuitively, there are two types of segment methods for the values in one attribute: value-based and format-based segment. Table 1(a) is a concrete example of attributes suitable for value-based segment. For this instance, a good segmentation can be achieved by grouping the strings with common q-grams [20] together. The attribute in table 1(b) is an instance suitable for format-based segmentation. This table contains distinct transport stops of buses, trains and boats. Stops coming from different companies are encoded in distinct formats. In this case, clustering l_1 and l_2 (same format: "BT"+ number) into the same segment is more reasonable than clustering l_1 and l_3 (common gram: "1213") together. This means that value-based segmentation does not suit to this case. In this paper, our focus is limited to cases where value-based segmentation is more suited.

Table 1. Examples for value-based and format-based segmentations

(a) E-mails

	emails
l_1	david@gmail.com
l_2	mike@gmail.com
l_3	anny@hotmail.com
l_4	theresa@hotmail.com

(b) Stops

	stops
l_1	BT011213
l_2	BT051708
l_3	1213
l_4	1708
l_5	C12
l_6	C17

In [12], Tishby et al. stipulate that good clustering should be informative about the values they contain. This method is called information bottleneck. With values being distributions over selected features, this approach recasts clustering as the compression of the values into a compact representation which preserves as much information as possible about the features. The mutual information between the clusters and features is a good indicator of information preserved.

Based on information bottleneck, the problem setting in this paper is as follows: Given a set of values X whose size $|X|$ is large and the number of segments $|T| \ll |X|$(which is often the case in practical situations in large database). The problem is to find a set of distinguishable features Y and identify a natural partition T of X efficiently, meanwhile maintaining the mutual information between T and Y (represented as $I(T;Y)$) as large as possible.

Producing distinguishable Y is significant for reliable segmentation. For value-based segmentation, intuitively, introducing more q-grams into features gives more distinct information. For example, 1-gram is not enough to distinguish "C12" and "C21". But if we introduce 2-grams, they can be separated effectively. However, when used for segmentation in large database, this extending has potential risks, such as the explosion of $|Y|$ and the existence of noisy features. As a matter of fact, there exists redundancy between features. Consider table 1(a) as an example, every value has the same distribution on any gram extracted from "mail.com". Thus, we can keep one gram from "mail.com" instead of all the grams. Due to the limited vocabulary, this kind of redundancy is common. As a result, we apply a dimensionality reduction process on Y to produce a more compact feature set.

The approach presented in this paper (namely EISA: An Efficient Information Theoretical Approach to Value Segmentation in Large Database) is based on the above principles. Once the compact features are produced, "Agglomerative Information Bottleneck" algorithm [12] is applied on X to get a greedy agglomerative clustering result. EISA records the related statistics for the clusters and identifies a natural segmentation though the analysis of these statistics. In this way, without being given the number of segments in advance, EISA identifies a natural segmentation. The computation cost of agglomerative algorithm is high which is quadratic in $|X|$. In our experiments, we find that, even after the reduction, $|Y|$ is still on the scale of thousands for large databases. The cost of inferring the distance between two clusters is still rather high. This makes the computation cost of agglomerative method even higher. Due to this, EISA uses scalable information bottleneck [10] to compress X. Then agglomerative method is applied on the compressed set of values.

The main contributions of EISA are as follows:

1. EISA produces a highly distinguishable set of features.
2. EISA effectively reduces the number of the features.
3. EISA compresses the size of the values to be segmented significantly.
4. EISA identifies a natural segmentation for the values.
5. EISA facilitates data quality through improved value consistency.

The organization of this paper is as follows. Section 2 is a discussion about the related work. The section 3 gives a detailed description of EISA. The subsequent section evaluates the approach on several data sets. Lastly, summary and outlook of the paper is presented.

2   Related Work

Many existing works focus on data analysis to facilitate data quality management. Among all these works, clustering [8], inferring conditional functional dependency (CFD) [3], information-theory-based tools [1] and labelling data patterns [18] are the major existing approaches related to value segmentation.

A value-based clustering method(RICH) is applied in [8] during inferring the heterogeneity of one column. It samples a small amount of data and divides them into soft-clusters. Then the soft-cluster entropy is inferred as the heterogeneity of this column. RICH represents sampled values in the attribute with weighted distributions on the 1- and 2-grams of all the strings. Then, it loads all the distributions into memory and clusters them based on an iterative optimization information bottleneck algorithm. RICH performs well in rapid identification of column heterogeneity. However, if used for segmentation in large database, it needs to introduce q-grams of larger length to facilitate the separation of the values with similar components(i.e. ID and phone) and also give a good consideration about the high computation cost. EISA uses similar model (q-grams) to transform the values into distributions. Representing attributes as q-grams has been shown useful in [8], [16], [18]. The q-gram distribution is proven to contain information about the underlying topic and the semantic type of the data in [13]. However, EISA produces more distinguishable feature set and applies more efficient clustering method. On the other hand, EISA offers a natural solution to the heterogeneity problem by segmenting the column into several homogeneous partitions.

Conditional functional dependency [6], [7], [5], [3] binds semantically related values by incorporating a pattern with these values. Fan et al. show how to capture data inconsistencies based on CFD analysis [6], [3]. Discovering CFD is an approach for segmentation. However, not all values are involved in CFD in an attribute [6].

Information-theory-based tools quantifying information content has been quite successful as a way of extracting structure from data [1], [15], [17]. Andritsos et al. concentrate on discovering the database structure from large data sets[1]. They also use scalable information bottleneck to make the algorithm scalable. But they model the data in a different way and have different application from EISA.

There are many work on finding out patterns from data and labelling it[18,19,4]. Ahmadi et al. categorize the relational attributes based on their data type. They identify the signatures indicating the semantic type of the data and the signatures can subsequently be used for other applications, like clustering. The signatures can be used in EISA as the label of the segmentations and also EISA is helpful in identifying these signatures. They complement each other.

3   Our Approach

3.1   Naive Solution

For value-based segmentation, intuitively, we use all the q-grams as the feature Y. Then, we need to find out a proper information bottleneck algorithm. A detailed introduction to the information bottleneck algorithms is beyond the scope of this paper. What we merely point out is that its essential idea is to minimize the function 1 given in [12].

$$F = I(T; X) - \beta * I(T; Y) \tag{1}$$

$I(T; X)$ quantifies the compression and $I(T; Y)$ is a measure of the quality of the clustering. They are both maximized when $T = X$. β is the trade-off between compression and quality. When $\beta = 0$, quality does not matter. On the other hand, when $\beta \longrightarrow \infty$, compression does not matter. The constraint $|T| \ll |X|$

in the setting of this paper implies a significant compression. In this case, we are interested in maximizing the quality [12]. A direct way to achieve this is to take $\beta \longrightarrow \infty$. Thus, agglomerative and sequential optimization algorithms [11] are natural choices.

Sequential optimization algorithm requests a cardinality value k as an input. In real world applications, the cardinality of an attribute is generally unknown. However, in [1], by applying agglomerative method, a value of k corresponding to a natural partition can be identified. So agglomerative method is the proper clustering algorithm.

The computation cost of this naive solution is $O(|Y||X|^2)$. When applied on large database, it is highly expensive. Thus, EISA is proposed.

3.2   EISA

The work flow of EISA is illustrated as Figure 1.

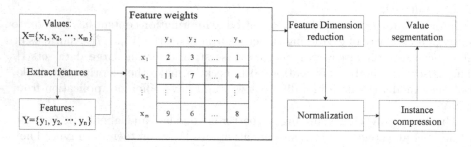

Fig. 1. EISA work flow

EISA uses PCA [21] to reduce $|Y|$. To conquer the computation bottleneck in agglomerative method, X is compressed. A scalable algorithm [10] is applied to achieve such a compression. It reads the values one by one to construct a BTree-similar tree, and during the process, it merges the values which are sufficiently closed to each other. At the end, the leaves of the tree are the initial clusters. The size of the leaves is much smaller than $|X|$. Then, agglomerative algorithm is applied on these leaves to get smaller number of clusters. These clusters perform as the seed cluster centroids and EISA reads all the values to assign them to one of the seed cluster centroids.

3.3   Features Extraction

Features in this paper are extracted as the following steps:

1. Construct the set of all-length q-grams for all strings in X, denoted as Y.
2. Construct a matrix F whose rows are X and columns are Y, and the entry $m_{xy} = f(x, y)$, where $f(x, y)$ is the number of occurrences of y in x.
3. Conduct PCA on F, resulting in a matrix S.

4. Normalize the matrix S so that the sum of all the entries is 1, and the result matrix is denoted as M. Every entry in M denotes $p(x, y)$.
5. With matrix M, $p(x)$ and $p(y|x)$ are inferred as equation 2 and 3.

$$p(x) = \sum_y p(x, y) \tag{2}$$

$$p(y|x) = \frac{p(x, y)}{p(x)} \tag{3}$$

3.4   Instances Compression

Infer DCFs. Scalable information bottleneck method [10] is applied in EISA to implement this compression. The spirit of this method is just maintain sufficient statistics instead of the whole clusters in the memory. These statistics are called "distributional cluster features(DCF)". In EISA, the DCF of a value x is defined as equation 4. The DCF of the new merged cluster $\bar{t}$ is denoted as equation 6. $p(\bar{t})$ is computed with equation 5. $p(Y|\bar{t})$ is inferred with equation 7.

$$DCF(x) - (p(x), p(Y|x)) \tag{4}$$

$$p(\bar{t}) = p(t_i) + p(t_j) \tag{5}$$

$$DCF(\bar{t}) = (p(\bar{t}), p(Y|\bar{t})) \tag{6}$$

$$p(Y|\bar{t}) = \frac{p(t_i)}{p(\bar{t})} p(Y|t_i) + \frac{p(t_j)}{p(\bar{t})} p(Y|t_j) \tag{7}$$

The distance between two clusters is measured by the information loss caused by merging these two clusters. For instance, at step s_n, two clusters t_i and t_j are merged into $\bar{t}$. The information loss caused by this merge is $\Delta I(t_i, t_j) = I(T_n; Y) - I(T_{n-1}; Y)$. Tishby et al. has shown that $\Delta I(t_i, t_j)$ has nothing to do with other clusters other than t_i and t_j in [12]. It is inferred with the equation 8. $\bar{d}(t_i, t_j)$ is inferred using equation 9.

$$\Delta I(t_i, t_j) = p(\bar{t}) * \bar{d}(t_i, t_j) \tag{8}$$

$$\bar{d}(t_i, t_j) = JS_\Pi[p(Y|t_i), p(Y|t_j)] \tag{9}$$

Construct Summary Tree. The values are read one by one to construct a BTree-similar tree. Each read value x is converted into $DCF(x)$. Then EISA finds out the node A containing the closest DCF entry $DCF(t)$ to $DCF(x)$. If $\Delta I(x, t) \leq \Phi \frac{I(X; Y)}{|X|}$, x is merged into t. Otherwise, x is inserted into the node A as a new cluster. Φ is a indicator of the compression of the summary tree.

3.5   Values Segmentation

After the construction of the DCF tree, the leaf nodes hold the DCFs of an initial clustering of X, denoted as T_i. $|T_i|$ is much smaller than $|X|$. Then the agglomerative method[12] is applied on T_i. It proceeds iteratively, reducing the number of clusters by one in each step. At each iteration, two chosen clusters are merged into one so that the information loss caused by this merge is minimum.

EISA picks a value k_{max} that is sufficiently large(for example, 200 clusters) and applies agglomerative method on T_i to obtain k_{max} clusters denoted as $T_{k_{max}}$, which is stored on the disk. During the agglomerative process, to avoid the repeat computing, EISA computes the distances between every two clusters only once. In the subsequent merge, EISA only updates the distances between the new produced cluster and every other cluster.

With the cluster number k range from k_{max} to 1, EISA uses the statistics proposed in [1] to identify k corresponding to natural segmentations. These statistics include$\Delta I(T; Y)$ and $\Delta H(T|Y)$. $\Delta I(T; Y)$ is an indicator of the rate of change in the clustering quality and $\Delta H(T|Y)$ captures the rate of change in dissimilarity across clusters. EISA infers $\Delta H(T|Y)$ with Equation 10. $H(T)$ is inferred by assigning a probability $p(t_i)$ to each cluster which is equal to the fraction of the values it contains [14]. These two statistics are good signs to have a overview about the information change in the clusterings.

$$H(T \mid Y) = H(T) - I(T; Y)$$
$$p(\bar{t}) = p(t_i) + p(t_j)$$
$$\Downarrow$$
$$\Delta H(T \mid Y) = \Delta H(T) - \Delta I(T; Y)$$
$$= p(\bar{t}) \log p(\bar{t}) - p(t_i) \log p(_i)$$
$$- p(t_j) \log p(_j) - \Delta I(T; Y)$$

(10)

At the end of agglomeration on $T_{k_{max}}$, the clusters T is produced. The next thing to do is to scan the X again to assign every $x \epsilon X$ to its closest cluster $t \epsilon T$.

3.6   Performance Analysis

The most related work for EISA is RICH in [8]. EISA prepares data in similar way with RICH. Like the analysis in [8], the time spent on preparing the data is negligible. The main time bottleneck of RICH is the iteration and its time cost is $O(N(2|X||T||Y|))$. N is the times of iterations. Without any knowledge about the number of clusters, RICH sets $|T| = |X|/2$, which means that the complexity of RICH is $O(N|Y||X|^2)$.

In EISA, the main time cost is the feature reduction, sample compression and agglomeration. PCA, as we know, is a mature algorithm and there are many optimized and parallel computation implementations available. Agglomeration is quadratic in $|X|$. If EISA compresses the $|X|$ by n times, then the time cost of agglomeration reduces to $t_{original}/n^2$. Thus, we mainly focus on the performance analysis of sample compression. As shown in [10], the cost of creating the DCF tree is $O(|X|hB + UB^2)$. B is a constant and it is the branching factor of the tree. h is the height of the DCF tree and U is the number of non-leaf nodes. It has been proved that scalable information bottleneck produces compact trees of small height which means that both h and U are bounded.

4   Evaluation

4.1   Experiment Settings

We run the evaluation in the environment with Intel Xeon E5-2690 × 2 CPU , 192GB memory, Windows Server 2008 R2 x64 platform.

4.2   Small Scale Experiments

We firstly run some experiments on two small scale datasets to evaluate the effectiveness of EISA and its facilitation on data quality management.

Parameters. For PCA, we need to choose the proportion p of the sum of the chosen latent value to the sum of all latent values. As the scale of the datasets is small, we set p=1 which indicates no loss of the features. For the same reason, Φ is set to 0 to achieve a non-compression on the instances. On the other hand, from the analysis in [10], we know that B(the branching factor) just affects the execution time in this construction and it does not significantly affect the quality of the clustering. We set $B = 8$ in this experiment.

Datasets and Results. The following datasets are used in our evaluation:
● *Integrated Dataset*: To evaluate the ability of EISA in solving the *"column het-erogeneity"* problem, we integrate four different types of data into one column. The characteristic of these four types of data is similar to the dataset used in [8]. ID contains 609 numeric values, PHONE is a collection of 453 telephone numbers which contain the period as well. EMAIL is a set of 259 email addresses and CIRCUIT contains 500 alphanumeric values. As we already know there are 4 natural segmentations in this data set, we set k=4 in the experiment. In fact, from the figure 2(a) and figure 2(b) , we find that when k is little smaller than 5 ($k \approx 4$), the change

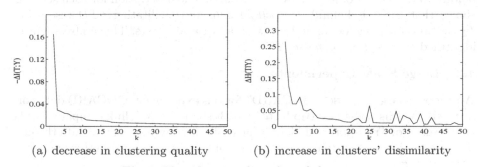

(a) decrease in clustering quality   (b) increase in clusters' dissimilarity

Fig. 2. Identification of number of clusters

of both statistics is steady. This means that the quality is not decreasing rapidly and the dissimilarity between clusters is not increasing sharply which indicates that k=4 is a proper selection. This provides proof of the reasonableness of choosing k in EISA. EISA works well on this dataset since only two values mistaken-segmented.

Table 2. Segment result of e-mails

Segment ID & Description		Examples
T_1	The e-mails from the state of North Carolina	dhsr.webmaster@ncmail.net Debbie.Brantley@ncmail.net
T_2	The only one with people's name in capital letters	THOMASCOLLINS@DHHMAIL .DHH.STATE.LA.US.gov
T_3	The e-mails from the state of Colorado	dora_ins_seniorhealthstaff@state.co.us cdphe.information@state.co.us
T_4	The e-mail addresses contain 'state' and 'us' but no 'co'	Delores.Pinkerton@medicaid.state.ar.us comsumer.protection@tdi.state.tx.us
T_5	The e-mail addresses contain "health"	info@stratishealth.org medicalfacilities@health.ok.gov
T_6	The e-mails from the state of Florida	infoctr@fdhc.state.fl.us administration@doh.state.fl.us
T_7	The e-mails from the ESRD State Survey Agency	kmayo@nw7.esrd.net info@nw6.esrd.net
T_8	The e-mail addresses end with '.com'	mygeorgiacares@yahoo.com kansashospices@gmail.com
T_9	The e-mails from the governments	insurance.shiip@arkansas.gov eoa@doh.hawaii.gov
T_{10}	The e-mails from the organizations	helpline@akfinc.org arpro.sjohnson@sdps.org

• *Email in Medicare*: This is a real-life data set abstracted from "medicareContact" [22]. As a result, we get 259 email addresses. Different from the "integrated dataset", nothing about segmentations on this set is known in advance. However, EISA finds that the email addresses can be segmented into 10 meaningful segmentation as shown in table 2. The email addresses in one segment have common q-grams and these grams are the characteristics for each segmentation. According to the common q-grams, we give the description for each segmentation in table 2. Some email addresses belong to the same state while some others belong to the same domain(".gov" or ".com"). The description for each segment shows that EISA is helpful in *labelling data* and facilitating *CFD* resolution. T_2 contains only one email address with all capital letters. This address can be identified as *exception or noise* [2].

4.3   Large Scale Experiments

We choose a larger dataset "GOCARD" for this experiment. GOCARD data contains six months passenger trip history in Brisbane TRANSlink company [1]. The Department of Transport and Main Roads collects a large amount of data through the go card ticketing system. There are about 69 million records in this dataset.

---

[1] http://translink.com.au/

In this experiment, we choose the column of "Boarding Stop" as the object to be segmented. There are 17773 distinct stops. After abstracting the q-grams of these stops, we get 53666 distinct q-grams.

Parameters. For p during PCA, The relationship between p and $|Y|$ is given in figure 3(a). This figure shows that when $|Y|$ approaches to 10000, p is almost 100%. This indicates that EISA produces a significant compression on Y. We choose $p = 90\%$ resulting in $|Y|$ reduced to 1731. In [10], when the compact rate Φ is set to 1, the number of leaf entries becomes sufficiently small while obtaining clusterings of exactly the same quality as for $\Phi = 0$. Thus, we set $\Phi = 1$.

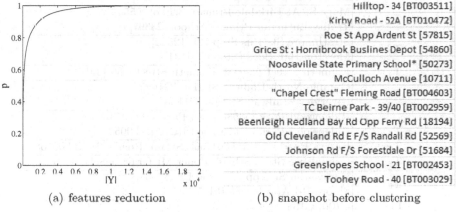

| (a) features reduction | (b) snapshot before clustering |

Fig. 3. Feature reduction and Snapshot

Performance Analysis. As EISA and RICH prepare data in a similar way and the time spent in preparing data is negligible. We only concentrate on the time cost of the remaining steps. From the analysis in [8], we know that if $|X| = 200$ and $|Y| = 1100$, the time cost of RICH per-iteration is about 5s. The main time cost of RICH is $O(N|Y||X|^2)$. Based on this , we can infer that RICH, used for segmentation on this dataset, takes at least several days. Meanwhile, EISA only takes less than 3 hours on the same dataset.The time consumed by EISA in each step on different scales of datasets is given in Table 3.

Table 3. Time cost

Original size		Compressed size		Time cost			
$|X|$	$|Y|$	$|X|$	$|Y|$	FR	IC	VS	overall
17773	53666	2290	1731	7315 s	178 s	1789 s	9282 s
13000	48855	1620	1678	3964 s	135 s	870 s	4969 s
8000	41811	1107	1414	1654 s	67 s	343 s	2064 s
3000	28446	516	866	287 s	15 s	48 s	350 s

FR for feature reduction, **IC** for instance compress, **VS** for value segment

Effectiveness. A snapshot of these stops before segmenting is given in figure 3(b). Even though we do not make $p = 100\%$ and $\Phi = 0$, we can still get a reasonable segmentation result on this data set as shown in Table 4. EISA finds many meaningful segments, such as: the district stops, the stops at primary school, the railway stations, stops at park, stops at school(other than primary school), the stops at the cross between two streets("Moore Rd App Roche Rd") and so on.

Table 4. Result of segmentation on stops

Segment ID	Samples
T_1	Saturn Crescent - District Stop [BT010471]
	District stop Ashridge Road [BT005394]
T_2	Mary St At Birkdale Primary School [55536]
	Trinity Lutheran Primary School [23391]
T_3	Strathmore St (Bus Stop 92) [12562]
	Moreton Bay Boys (Stop 63) [1313]
T_4	Kenneth Street [29983], Kenneth Street - 36 [3010]
T_5	Gympie North Railway Station [C169]
	Riverview Railway Station [C115]
T_6	Ridgewood Park [5858], Cash Park - 32 [2732]
	Ridgewood Park" Ridgewood Road [BT005858]
T_7	Harrys Road - 18 [BT001766], Swann Road - 28 [BT001684]
T_8	Caboolture State School, Upper Mt Gravatt School - 43
T_9	Karawatha St App Alfriston Dr [57004]
	Moore Rd App Roche Rd [55924]
T_{10}	C100, C154
T_{11}	Southport Golf Club [23860]
	Cannon Hill Shopping Centre - Zone F [BT005930]

5   Summary and Outlook

In this paper, we argue that segmenting one attribute in large databases is essential for better understanding of data and data quality. To achieve this, we design an effective and efficient approach EISA that allows an informative theoretical approach to value segmentation. We demonstrate that EISA can produce an accurate value-based segment with reasonable efficiency. In the future, we plan to introduce the format information and combine it with value information to achieve a more comprehensive means of segmentation.

Acknowledgement. The work described in this paper is partially supported by ARC Discovery Project (DP140103171): Declaration, Exploration, Enhancement and Provenance: The DEEP Approach to Data Quality Management Systems (20132016).

References

1. Andritsos, P., Miller, R.J., Tsaparas, P.: Information-theoretic tools for mining database structure from large data sets. In: SIGMOD, pp. 731–742 (2004)
2. Dang, X.H., Assent, I., Ng, R.T., Zimek, A., Schubert, E.: Discriminative Features for Identifying and Interpreting Outliers. In: ICDE (2014)
3. Li, J., Liu, J., Toivonen, H., Yong, J.: Effective Pruning for the Discovery of Conditional Functional Dependencies. The Computer Journal (2012)
4. Zhang, M., Hadjieleftheriou, M., Ooi, B.C., Procopiuc, C.M., Srivastava, D.: Automatic Discovery of Attributes in Relational Databases. In: SIGMOD (2011)
5. Golab, L., Karloff, H., Korn, F., Srivastava, D., Yu, B.: On generating Near-Optimal Tableaux for Conditional Functional Dependencies, In: PVLDB (2008)
6. Fan, W., Geerts, F., Li, J., Xiong, M.: Discovering Conditional Functional Dependencies. In: TKDE (2011)
7. Yeh, P.Z., Puri, C.A.: Discovering Conditional Functional Dependencies to Detect Data Inconsistencies. In: VLDB (2010)
8. Dai, B.T., Srivastava, D., Koudas, N., Venkatasubramanian, S., Ooi, B.C.: Rapid Identification of Column Heterogeneity. In: ICDM, pp. 159–170 (2006)
9. Dasu, T., Johnson, T., Muthukrishnan, S., Shkapeny, V.: Mining Database Structure; Or, How to Build a Data Quality Browse. In: SIGMOD (2002)
10. Andritsos, P., Tsaparas, P., Miller, R.J., Sevcik, K.C.: LIMBO: Scalable clustering of categorical data. In: Bertino, E., Christodoulakis, S., Plexousakis, D., Christophides, V., Koubarakis, M., Böhm, K. (eds.) EDBT 2004. LNCS, vol. 2992, pp. 123–146. Springer, Heidelberg (2004)
11. Slonim, N., Tishby, N.: Agglomerative information bottleneck, pp. 617–623. MIT Press (1999)
12. Tishby, N., Pereira, O.C., Bialek, W.: The information bottleneck method, pp. 368–377. University of Illinois (1999)
13. Keselj, V., Peng, F., Cercone, N., Thomas, C.: N-gram-based author profiles for authorship attribution. In: Pacific Association for Computational Linguistics (2003)
14. Cover, T.M., Joy, A.T.: Elements of information theory. Wiley Interscience, New York (1991)
15. Arenas, M., Libkin, L.: An information-theoretic approach to normal forms for relational and XML data. JACM 52(2), 246–283 (2005)
16. Dai, B.T., Koudas, N., Srivastavat, D., Tung, A.K.H., Venkatasubramaniant, S.: Validating Multi-column Schema Matchings by Type. IEEE (2008)
17. Srivastava, D., Venkatasubramanian, S.: Information Theory For Data Management. In: SIGMOD (2010)
18. Ahmadi, B., Hadjieleftheriou, M., Seidl, T., Srivastava, D., Suresh: Type-Based Categorization of Relational Attributes, In: EDBT (2009)
19. Wang, J., Lochovsky, F.H.: Data Extraction and Label Assignment for Web Databases. In: WWW (2003)
20. N-gram, http://en.wikipedia.org/wiki/N-gram
21. Principle components analysis, http://en.wikipedia.org/wiki/Principle_components_analysis
22. Medical care data of the government, https://data.medicare.gov/

Learning to Compute Semantic Relatedness Using Knowledge from Wikipedia

Chen Zheng, Zhichun Wang*, Rongfang Bie, and Mingquan Zhou

College of Information Science and Technology, Beijing Normal University,
Beijing 100875, China
zc_cheney@mail.bnu.edu.cn, {zcwang,rfbie,mqzhou}@bnu.edu.cn

Abstract. Recently, Wikipedia has become a very important resource for computing semantic relatedness (SR) between entities. Several approaches have already been proposed to compute SR based on Wikipedia. Most of the existing approaches use certain kinds of information in Wikipedia (e.g. links, categories, and texts) and compute the SR by empirically designed measures. We have observed that these approaches produce very different results for the same entity pair in some cases. Therefore, how to select appropriate features and measures to best approximate the human judgment on SR becomes a challenging problem. In this paper, we propose a supervised learning approach for computing SR between entities based on Wikipedia. Given two entities, our approach first maps entities to articles in Wikipedia; then different kinds of features of the mapped articles are extracted from Wikipedia, which are then combined with different relatedness measures to produce nine raw SR values of the entity pair. A supervised learning algorithm is proposed to learn the optimal weights of different raw SR values. The final SR is computed as the weighted average of raw SRs. Experiments on benchmark datasets show that our approach outperforms baseline methods.

Keywords: Semantic relatedness, Wikipedia, Supervised Learning.

1 Introduction

Computing semantic relatedness (SR) between terms is an important task for many natural language processing applications, such as information retrieval [4], word sense disambiguation [11] and entity linking [10,18] . Many approaches for computing SR have been proposed in these years. Some approaches use statistical analysis of large corpora to get SR between words; other approaches make use of hand-crafted lexical resources for computing SR. However, both of these two groups of approaches have their limitations. Corpora-based methods only use collections of texts, which do not make any use of available structured knowledge, and their results might be influenced by noise in the texts. The other group of approaches utilize lexical resources such as WordNet [8], Roget's Thesaurus [13];

---

* Corresponding author.

L. Chen et al. (Eds.): APWeb 2014, LNCS 8709, pp. 236–246, 2014.

but these resources are usually created by human experts and therefore usually cover a small part of language lexicon.

Recently, lots of work has shown that Wikipedia can be used as the resource for computing SR between words or text fragments. Wikipedia is one of the largest online encyclopedias on the web, which contains more than 20 million articles written in 285 languages by March 2013. Wikipedia contains large number of hypertext pages that are interconnected by links. A page that has encyclopedic information in it is called a Wikipedia article, or entry. Articles are the most important elements of Wikipedia, each of them identifies a notable encyclopedic topic and summarizes that topic comprehensively. Except article pages, there are other meta pages which are used for administrative tasks, including Category page, Statistic page and Help page, etc. Fig. 1 is an example of a Wikipedia article page.

Fig. 1. The structure of a Wikipedia article

Different kinds of information in Wikipedia has been used for computing SR. The category system of Wikipedia is used in [16,12], links among Wikipedia articles are used in [17], links between articles and categories are used in [1]. Information of the same kind can also be used in different ways to compute the SR. For example, inlinks of two articles are compared as two sets in [17], but they are compared as two vectors in [5]. We have observed that different combination of Wikipedia information and SR measures usually result in different SR results. Table 1 shows the top 10 entities that have the highest relatedness with the entities *Mathmatics* for three different SR measures based on articles' inlinks, including Inlink-DC (Dice Coefficient of inlinks), Inlink-GD (Google Distance of inlinks), and Inlink-VB (Vector based distance of inlinks). Entities listed in each column in Table 1 are ranked in descending order of SR. It shows that most the 10 entities have different ranks in three columns. Table 2 shows the top 10 most related articles *Mathematics* based on the the same SR measure Dice Coefficient, but with three different kinds of Wikipedia information, including the inlinks, outlinks and categories. It shows that using the same SR measure but with different kinds of information will also generate different results. Therefore, how to use different kinds of information in Wikipedia to accurately compute SR between entities becomes a challenging problem.

Table 1. Top 10 most related articles with *Mathematics* based on inlinks

Inlink-DC	Inlink-GD	Inlink-VB
Physics	Physics	Physics
Mathematician	Mathematician	Mathematician
Chemistry	Chemistry	Topological space
Science	Science	Group (mathematics)
Biology	Function (mathematics)	Real number
Computer science	Group (mathematics)	Function (mathematics)
Philosophy	Real number	Vector space
Real number	Topological space	Chemistry
Astronomy	Field (mathematics)	Field (mathematics)
Function (mathematics)	Complex number	Science

Table 2. Top 10 most related articles with *Mathematics* based on dice coefficient

Inlink-DC	Outlink-DC	Category-DC
Physics	Glossary of areas of mathematics	Lemma (mathematics)
Mathematician	Areas of mathematics	Emphasis
Chemistry	Outline of mathematics	Micro-X-ray fluorescence
Science	Philosophy of mathematics	Philomath
Biology	History of mathematics	Skolem arithmetic
Computer science	Pure mathematics	Noology
Philosophy	Mathematician	Analytic
Real number	Geometry	Zone
Astronomy	Axiom	Logic
Function (mathematics)	Number	Formal science

In this paper, we propose a supervised learning approach for computing SR between entities based on Wikipedia. Our approach uses articles' inlinks, outlinks, and categories in Wikipedia, and employs three different SR measures to compute raw SRs between entities. A supervised learning algorithm is proposed to learn the weights of different raw SRs to get the final SR. We evaluate our approach on three standard datasets, the results show that our approach can get better results than the comparison approaches.

The rest of this paper is organized as follows, Section 2 discusses some related work; Section 3 describes the proposed approach; Section 4 presents the evaluation results and Section 5 concludes this work.

2   Related Work

There have been several approaches that compute SR based on Wikipedia.

Strube and Ponzetto [16,12] firstly proposed to compute SR based on Wikipedia. Their approach WikiRelate first maps the given words to Wikipedia pages, and then hooks these pages to the category tree by extracting the categories the pages belong to. The SR between the given words is computed by path-based measures based on the category taxonomy.

Gabrilovich and Markovitch [5] proposed Explicit Semantic Analysis (ESA) for computing SR. ESA first represents each Wikipedia concept as an attribute vector of words that occur in the corresponding article, and assigns weights to the words in vectors by using TF-IDF method [15]. For any given words or long texts, ESA then represents them as weighted vectors of concepts based on the words-concept associations in the former step. And ESA finally computes SR of texts or words as the cosine distances between their vectors.

Milne and Witten [17] proposed a approach, Wikipedia Link-based Measure (WLM), which computes SR using the hyperlink structure of Wikipedia instead of its category hierarchy or textual content. Given two terms, WLM fist identifies the corresponding Wikipedia articles of them. Then it uses two measures to compute the SR: the first measure represents each article as the vector of weighted inlinks and then computes the cosine similarity between the vectors of two articles; the second measure represents each article as a set of inlinks, and then computes the Normalized Google Distance [3] between the feature sets of two articles.

Hassan and Mihalcea [7] proposed to measure the SR of words by using their concept-based profiles. A profile is constructed using the co-occurring salient concepts found within a given window size in a very large corpus. A word is defined by a set of concepts which share its context and are weighted by their point-wise mutual information. To compute the SR, a modified cosine similarity is computed between words' profile vectors.

Yeh et al. [19] proposed to compute SR by using personalized PageRank on a graph derived from Wikipedia. Their approach first converts Wikipedia into a graph, and then maps the input texts into the graph. Random walks on the graph based on Personalized PageRank are performed to obtain stationary distributions that characterize each text. And the SR between two texts is computed by comparing their distributions.

Hassan and Mihalcea [6] also extended the ESA approach and proposed a method for computing cross-lingual SR between words. By using the cross-lingual links in Wikipedia, their method can compute the cosine similarity between ESA concept vectors in different languages. Several modifications of ESA are also done to improve the performance of their method.

Chan et al. [2] solve a problem that words with comparatively low frequency cannot always be well estimated based on ESA. They proposed a method for using not only word frequency but also layout information in Wikipedia articles by regression to better estimate the relevance of a word and a concept. Empirical evaluation shows that on the low frequency words, this method achieves better estimate of SR over ESA.

Table 3 summarizes the key features of the above approaches. Being different from these approaches, our approach uses several different components of Wikipedia article and several measures together; instead of empirical designed measures, our approach use supervised learning algorithm to predict the SR.

Table 3. Semantic relatedness computing based on Wikipedia

Algorithm	Measures	Component	Task
ESA [5]	TF-IDF + Cosine similarity	Textual content	Word and Document relatedness
WikiRelate [16]	Path length, information content, text overlap	Category taxonomy	Word relatedness
Milne et al. [10]	Similarity of hyperlinks	Inlinks and Outlinks	Word relatedness
Crosslingual ESA [6]	TF-IDF + Cosine similarity	Cross-lingual links	Cross-lingual word relatedness
Chan et al. [2]	Regression	Textual content and layout information	Document relatedness
Yeh et al. [19]	PageRank	Links structure	Word and Document relatedness

3   The Proposed Approach

In this section, we introduce our proposed approach. Given two entities, our approach first maps them to the articles in Wikipedia; then it computes several different raw SRs between the corresponding articles, and uses a supervised learning algorithm to get the final SR.

3.1   Raw Semantic Relatednesses

Our approach utilizes 3 features of Wikipedia articles, which are then combined with 3 different relatednesses measures to form 9 raw SRs.

Article Features. Here we first define three features of Wikipedia articles.

Definition 1. *Outlinks.* *For a Wikipedia article a, the outlinks of a is the set of articles O_a that a links to by hyperlinks.*

$$O_a = \{a_1, a_2, a_3, \ldots, a_m\} \tag{1}$$

Definition 2. *Inlinks*. *For a Wikipedia article a, the inlinks of a is the set of articles I_a that link to a by hyperlinks.*

$$I_a = \{a'_1, a'_2, a'_3, \ldots, a'_m\} \tag{2}$$

Definition 3. *Categories*. *For a Wikipedia article a, the categories of a is the set of categories C_a that that a belongs to.*

$$C_a = \{c_1, c_2, c_3, \ldots, c_m\} \tag{3}$$

Relatedness Measures. Our approach uses 3 measures for computing SR.

Definition 4. *Dice Coefficient*. *Given two feature sets A and B of two Wikipedia article a and b, Dice Coefficient computes the relatedness of a and b as*

$$S_{DC}(a,b) = \frac{2|A \cap B|}{|A| + |B|} \tag{4}$$

Definition 5. *Google Distance*. *Given two feature sets A and B of two Wikipedia article a and b, Google Distance computes the SR of a and b as*

$$S_{GD}(a,b) = 1 - \frac{log(max(|A|,|B|)) - log(|A \cap B|)}{log(|W|) - log(min(|A|,|B|))} \tag{5}$$

where W is the set of all articles in Wikipedia.

Definition 6. *Vector-based Similarity*. *The vector-based similarity is calculated between the feature vectors of articles' features. Before the similarity computation, a virtual document is generated for the feature of each article. Then the virtual document of each article is represented as a vector, where the elements in the vector are weights assigned to the words in the virtual document using TF-IDF method [15]. For a word i in an article's virtual document j, the weight of the word is computed as*

$$\omega_{ij} = tf_{ij} \cdot \lg \frac{N}{df_i} \tag{6}$$

where tf_{ij} is the number of occurrences of i in j, df_i is the number of virtual documents that contain i, and N is the total number of virtual documents. The vector-based similarity between two article is computed as the cosine value between their virtual documents:

$$S_{VB}(d,k) = \frac{\sum_{i=1}^{M} \omega_{id} \cdot \omega_{ik}}{\sqrt{\sum_{i=1}^{M} \omega_{id}^2} \cdot \sqrt{\sum_{k=1}^{M} \omega_{ik}^2}} \tag{7}$$

where M is the total number of distinct words in all of the virtual documents.

Raw Semantic Relatedness. Based on the above features and relatedness measures, 9 different raw SRs are computed for each pair of entities. These raw SRs are outlined in Table 4.

Table 4. Raw semantic relatednesses

Raw SR	Feature	Measure
SR_1	Inlinks	Dice Coefficient
SR_2	Outlinks	Dice Coefficient
SR_3	Categories	Dice Coefficient
SR_4	Inlinks	Google Distance
SR_5	Outlinks	Google Distance
SR_6	Categories	Google Distance
SR_7	Inlinks	Vector-based Similarity
SR_8	Outlinks	Vector-based Similarity
SR_9	Categories	Vector-based Similarity

3.2 Learning to Compute Relatednesses

To get the final SR, our approach computes the weighted sum of 9 raw SRs between two articles by the following function:

$$R(a,b) = \frac{\sum_{i=1}^{9} \omega_i \cdot SR_i(a,b)}{\sum_{i=1}^{9} \omega_i} \tag{8}$$

One challenge problem here is how to determine the proper weights $\omega_i, (i = 0, ..., 9)$ for each raw SR. We propose a supervised learning algorithm to learn the optimum weights. The goal of learning algorithm is to make the predicted SR to be close to human judgement as much as possible.

In order to learn the weights of different raw SRs, training data need to be built by human experts. Instead of asking people to decide the SR values of given entity pairs, we ask human experts to tell whether a given entity e_1 is more related to a referent entity e_2 than another reference entity e_3. Because we think it is natural and easy for people to answer such kind of questions. After collecting a number of the answers, we are able to build a training dataset D that consists of triples in the form of $t_j = \langle e_{j1}, e_{j2}, e_{j3} \rangle, (j = 1, ..., m)$; here t_j indicates $SR(e_{j1}, e_{j2}) > SR(e_{j1}, e_{j3})$.

Given training dataset $D = \{\langle e_{j1}, e_{j2}, e_{j3} \rangle\}_{j=1}^{m}$, our algorithm learns the weights to ensure

$$\boldsymbol{\omega} \cdot (\boldsymbol{SR}(e_{j1}, e_{j2}) - \boldsymbol{SR}(e_{j1}, e_{j3})) > 0, \tag{9}$$

where $\boldsymbol{\omega} = \langle \omega_1, ..., \omega_9 \rangle$ and $\boldsymbol{SR}(\cdot) = \langle SR_1(\cdot), ..., SR_9(\cdot) \rangle$. If we define the probability of $R(e_{j1}, e_{j2}) > R(e_{j1}, e_{j3})$ as

$$P(R(e_{j1}, e_{j2}) > R(e_{j1}, e_{j3})) = \frac{1}{1 + e^{-\boldsymbol{\omega} \cdot (\boldsymbol{SR}(e_{j1}, e_{j2}) - \boldsymbol{SR}(e_{j1}, e_{j3}))}}, \tag{10}$$

then for each triple $t_j = \langle e_{j1}, e_{j2}, e_{j3} \rangle$ in D, we have $P(R(e_{j1}, e_{j2}) > R(e_{j1}, e_{j3})) > 0.5$ and $P(R(e_{j1}, e_{j3}) > R(e_{j1}, e_{j2})) < 0.5$.

In this case, the weights $\boldsymbol{\omega}$ can be determined by the MLE (maximum likelihood estimation) technique for logistic regression. We generate a new dataset

$D' = \{(\boldsymbol{x}_j, y_j)\}_{j=1}^m$ based on D to train a logistic regression model; $\boldsymbol{x}_j$ is the input vector and y_j represents the class label (positive or negative). For each triple $t_j = \langle e_{j1}, e_{j2}, e_{j3} \rangle$, a positive example $(\boldsymbol{SR}(e_{j1}, e_{j2}) - \boldsymbol{SR}(e_{j1}, e_{j3}), positive)$ and a negative example $(\boldsymbol{SR}(e_{j1}, e_{j3}) - \boldsymbol{SR}(e_{j1}, e_{j2}), negative)$ is generated. After a logistic regression model is trained on D', the learned weights ω^* is used to compute the SR by formula (8).

4   Experiments

We implemented our proposed approach based on the English Wikipedia data that is archived in August 2012. After parsing the Wikipedia XML dump and removing redirect pages, we obtained 7.5 GB of text in 4 million concept pages and 889,527 category pages. Each article linked to 19.262 articles and be linked from 16.914 articles on average.

4.1   Datasets

We evaluated our proposed approach on three datasets of entity pairs and manually defined SR, Table 5 shows the detail information of these datasets.

Table 5. Evaluation datasets

Dataset	Year	Pairs	Scores	Subjects
M&C30	1991	30	[0,4]	38
R&G65	1965	65	[0,4]	51
Fin353	2002	353	[0,10]	13/16

M&C30. Miller and Charles [9] replicated the experiment with 38 test subjects judging on a subset of 30 pairs called M&C30 taken from the original 65 pairs (i.e. R&G65). We argue that evaluations restricted to those datasets were limited with respect to the number of word pairs involved, the parts of speech of word pairs, approaches to select word pairs (manual vs. automatic, analytic vs. corpus based), and the kinds of semantic relations that hold between word pairs. However, an evaluation involving the aspects described above is crucial to understand the properties of a specific measure. A significant evaluation of SR measures requires a higher number of word pairs such as the next datasets.

R&G65. Rubenstein and Goodenough [14] obtained similarity judgments from 51 test subjects on 65 noun pairs written on paper cards. These noun pairs range from the high synonyms to the irrelevant words on semantics. Test subjects were instructed to order the cards according to the similarity of meaning and then assign a continuous similarity value [0,4] to each card, where 0 represents the fact that two words art not related, and 4 indicates that both are synonymous. The final dataset called R&G65 contains 65 English noun pairs, which is commonly used for semantic computation.

Fin353. Finkelstein et al. [4] created a larger dataset for English called Fin353, which is a significant famous manual dataset of SR containing 353 word pairs including also the 30 word pairs from M&C30. To assess word relatedness, we use the Fin353 benchmark dataset, available online, which contains 353 word pairs. Each pair was judged, on average, by 13-16 human annotators. This dataset, to the best of our knowledge, is the largest publicly available collection of this kind, which is used by the most works (detailed in related works paragraph) in their evaluation.

4.2   Evaluation Metric

We evaluated performance by taking the Pearson product-moment correlation coefficient between the relatedness measure scores and the corresponding human judgments. It is computed as:

$$\rho_r(X,Y) = \frac{n\sum x_i y_i - \sum x_i \sum y_i}{\sqrt{n\sum x_i{}^2 - (\sum x_i)^2} \cdot \sqrt{n\sum y_i{}^2 - (\sum y_i)^2}} \tag{11}$$

where $X = \{x_i\}_{i=1}^N$ and $Y = \{y_i\}_{i=1}^N$. Here we consider the computed SRs as one variable X and the relatedness in the evaluation dataset as another variable Y, and then compute their correlation. High correlation indicates that the computed SRs are closed to the relatedness defined by humans.

4.3   Results Comparison

Table 6 shows the experimental results of our approach and five comparison approaches. The results of comparison approaches were reported in already published papers, we compare the results of our approach with these ones. It shows that our approach achieves the best results on all the three datasets. Our approach outperforms the second best approaches on three datasets by 0.18, 0.13 and 0.03 respectively. It is obvious that combining different features and relatedness measures by supervised learning algorithm can improve the accuracy of computed SRs.

Table 6. Comparison of experimental results (Pearson correlation)

Approach	Data set		
	M&C30	R&G65	Fin353
WikiRelate (Path) [16]	0.40	0.49	0.47
WikiRelate (Content) [16]	0.23	0.31	0.37
WikiRelate (Overlap) [16]	0.46	0.46	0.20
Milne et al. [10]	0.70	0.64	0.69
Yeh et al. [19]	0.56	/	0.49
Proposed approach	**0.88**	**0.77**	**0.72**

5   Conclusion and Future Work

In this paper, we propose a supervised learning approach for computing SR between entities based on Wikipedia. Our approach first maps entities to articles in Wikipedia, and then computes 9 different raw SRs between them. A learning model based on logistic regression is used to obtain the optimal weights for each raw SR, and the final SR is computed as the weighted average of 9 original ones. The experimental results show that our approach can accurately predict the SR, and it performs better than the comparison approaches.

Currently, computing SR between entities in one language is widely studied, but the problem of computing cross-lingual SR has not been well solved. Therefore, we want to extend our approach to the cross-lingual domain to compute cross-lingual SR based on Wikipedia in the future work.

Acknowledgement. The work is supported by NSFC (No. 61202246, 61003225, 61170203, 61171014, 61272475, 61371185), NSFC-ANR(No. 61261130588), and the Fundamental Research Funds for the Central Universities (2013NT56, 2013NT57), and by SRF for ROCS, SEM.

References

1. Bu, F., Hao, Y., Zhu, X.: Semantic relationship discovery with wikipedia structure. In: Proceedings of the Twenty-Second International Joint Conference on Artificial Intelligence, IJCAI 2011, vol. 3, pp. 1770–1775. AAAI Press (2011)
2. Chan, P., Hijikata, Y., Nishida, S.: Computing semantic relatedness using word frequency and layout information of wikipedia. In: Proceedings of the 28th Annual ACM Symposium on Applied Computing, SAC 2013, pp. 282–287. ACM (2013)
3. Cilibrasi, R., Vitanyi, P.: The google similarity distance. IEEE Transactions on Knowledge and Data Engineering 19(3), 370–383 (2007)
4. Finkelstein, L., Gabrilovich, E., Matias, Y., Rivlin, E., Solan, Z., Wolfman, G., Ruppin, E.: Placing search in context: The concept revisited. In: Proceedings of the 10th International Conference on World Wide Web, pp. 406–414. ACM (2001)
5. Gabrilovich, E., Markovitch, S.: Computing semantic relatedness using wikipedia-based explicit semantic analysis. In: Proceedings of the 20th International Joint Conference on Artifical Intelligence, IJCAI 2007, pp. 1606–1611. Morgan Kaufmann Publishers Inc., San Francisco (2007)
6. Hassan, S., Mihalcea, R.: Cross-lingual semantic relatedness using encyclopedic knowledge. In: Proceedings of the 2009 Conference on Empirical Methods in Natural Language Processing, EMNLP 2009, vol. 3, pp. 1192–1201. Association for Computational Linguistics, Stroudsburg (2009)
7. Hassan, S., Mihalcea, R.: Semantic relatedness using salient semantic analysis. In: Proceedings of AAAI Conference on Artificial Intelligence (2011)
8. Miller, G.A.: Wordnet: a lexical database for english. Commun. ACM 38(11), 39–41 (1995)
9. Miller, G.A., Charles, W.G.: Contextual correlates of semantic similarity. Language and Cognitive Processes 6(1), 1–28 (1991)

10. Milne, D., Witten, I.H.: Learning to link with wikipedia. In: Proceedings of the 17th ACM Conference on Information and Knowledge Management, CIKM 2008, pp. 509–518. ACM, New York (2008)
11. Patwardhan, S., Banerjee, S., Pedersen, T.: Senserelate: Targetword: a generalized framework for word sense disambiguation. In: Proceedings of the ACL 2005 on Interactive Poster and demonstration Sessions, pp. 73–76. Association for Computational Linguistics (2005)
12. Ponzetto, S.P., Strube, M.: Knowledge derived from wikipedia for computing semantic relatedness. J. Artif. Intell. Res(JAIR) 30, 181–212 (2007)
13. Roget, P.M.: Roget's Thesaurus of English Words and Phrases. TY Crowell Company (1911)
14. Rubenstein, H., Goodenough, J.B.: Contextual correlates of synonymy. Commun. ACM 8(10), 627–633 (1965)
15. Salton, G., Yang, C.-S.: On the specification of term values in automatic indexing. Journal of Documentation 29, 351–372 (1973)
16. Strube, M., Ponzetto, S.P.: Wikirelate! computing semantic relatedness using wikipedia. In: Proceedings of the 21st National Conference on Artificial Intelligence, AAAI 2006, vol. 2, pp. 1419–1424. AAAI Press (2006)
17. Witten, I., Milne, D.: An effective, low-cost measure of semantic relatedness obtained from wikipedia links. In: Proceeding of AAAI Workshop on Wikipedia and Artificial Intelligence: an Evolving Synergy, pp. 25–30. AAAI Press, Chicago (2008)
18. Xu, M., Wang, Z., Bie, R., Li, J., Zheng, C., Ke, W., Zhou, M.: Discovering missing semantic relations between entities in wikipedia. In: Alani, H., Kagal, L., Fokoue, A., Groth, P., Biemann, C., Parreira, J.X., Aroyo, L., Noy, N., Welty, C., Janowicz, K. (eds.) ISWC 2013, Part I. LNCS, vol. 8218, pp. 673–686. Springer, Heidelberg (2013)
19. Yeh, E., Ramage, D., Manning, C.D., Agirre, E., Soroa, A.: Wikiwalk: Random walks on wikipedia for semantic relatedness. In: Proceedings of the 2009 Workshop on Graph-based Methods for Natural Language Processing, TextGraphs-4, pp. 41–49. Association for Computational Linguistics, Stroudsburg (2009)

Discovering Condition-Combined Functional Dependency Rules

Yuefeng Du, Derong Shen, Tiezheng Nie, Yue Kou, and Ge Yu

College of Information Science and Engineering, Northeastern University, China
duyuefeng@research.neu.edu.cn,
{shenderong,nietiezheng,kouyue,yuge}@ise.neu.edu.cn

Abstract. Conditional functional dependency (CFD) on a relation schema is an important technique of data consistency analysis. However, huge number of CFD rules will lead to lower the efficiency of data cleaning. Thus, we hope to reduce the number of rules by raising support degree of CFD. As a result, some crucial rules may be discarded and the accuracy of data cleaning will be decreasesd. Hence, in this paper, we present a new type of rules which combines the condition values. Using the rules, we can reduce the number of CFD rules and maintain the accuracy of data cleaning. We also propose 1) a 2-process search strategy to discover the combined condition rules, 2) the method of combining the CFD rules by combining the inconflict values and 3) pruning method to improve efficiency of the search. Finally, Our experiments show the efficiency and effectiveness of our solution.

Keywords: conditional functional dependency, discovering rules, search strategy.

1 Introduction

Data consistency analysis is one of the central issues in connection with data quality [1]. Functional dependency (FD) [2] and conditional functional dependency (CFD) [3] are the suitable techniques for data consistency analysis. FD rules can be used to detect data inconsistency rapidly. But the FDs are inadequate and the result of data cleaning doesn't meet our demands. Owing to this, we use CFDs to promote the result. By restricting the values of conditional attributes, CFDs make better results than FDs. However, the huge number of CFDs also reduce the efficiency of data cleaning. Normally, similar to approximate FD, we set the threshold for CFD rules and reduce the number of CFDs by raising the threshold. Consequently, some crucial rules are also discarded just because they are below the threshold. Aiming to use the fewest rules and maintain the crucial rules, we combine condition values to replace several rules by one.

Example 1. Table 1 shows a relation schema R_0 with records from the 1994 US Adult Census database [4] that contains education level(Edu), education number(EN), marital status(MS), family relationship(Rel), race(Race), gender(Gen) and native country(NC). And Fig.1 shows some business rules over R_0.

L. Chen et al. (Eds.): APWeb 2014, LNCS 8709, pp. 247–257, 2014.

Table 1. Records from 1994 US Adult Census Database

	Edu	EN	MS	Rel	Race	Gen	NC
t_1	Doctorate	16	Married-civ-spouse	Husband	Asian-Pac-Island	Male	China
t_2	Masters	14	Married-civ-spouse	Husband	Asian-Pac-Island	Male	China
t_3	Masters	14	Separated	Not-in-family	Asian-Pac-Island	Male	China
t_4	HS-grad	9	Married-civ-spouse	Wife	Asian-Pac-Island	Female	China
t_5	HS-grad	9	Divorced	Unmarried	Black	Female	US
t_6	Masters	14	Married-civ-spouse	Husband	White	Male	US
t_7	Some-college	10	Married-civ-spouse	Husband	Black	Male	Jamai-
t_8	Some-college	10	Married-AF-	Husband	Black	Male	Jamai-
t_9	Masters	14	Never-married	Own-child	Black	Female	Jamai-

$$\phi_1 : [\text{ Edu }] \rightarrow [\text{ EN }]$$
$$\varphi_2 : [\text{ MS } = \text{"Married-civ-spouse" Gen } = \text{"\_"}] \rightarrow [\text{ Rel } = \text{"\_"}]$$
$$\varphi_3 : [\text{ MS } = \text{"Married-AF-spouse" Gen } = \text{"\_"}] \rightarrow [\text{ Rel } = \text{"\_"}]$$

Fig. 1. Business Rules over R_0

Here, ϕ_1 shows that if any two people have the same education level, their education number must be the same. ϕ_1 is a FD. φ_2 shows that a person's married status is Married-civ-spouse (married in law and live together), on condition that, his gender can determine his family relationship. If his gender is male, then he must be husband. Otherwise, her gender is female, then she must be wife. φ_3 is similar to φ_2. Specially, a person's married status is either Married-civ-spouse or Married-AF-spouse, as long as he is married, his gender can determine his family relationship. Therefore, we can combine the two conditional values into a rule as

$$\psi_4 : [\text{ MS } = \text{"Married-civ-spouse, Married-AF-spouse" Gen } = \text{"\_"}] \rightarrow [\text{ Rel } = \text{"\_"}]$$

In the comparison of the number of tuples affected by the rules, ϕ_1 affects all tuples over R_0. φ_2 affects five tuples t_1, t_2, t_4, t_6, t_7. φ_3 only affects one tuple t_8. ψ_4 affects six tuples $t_1, t_2, t_4, t_6, t_7, t_8$. The number of tuples affected by combined rules is more than that affected by CFD rules.

When we detect the consistency of tuples on MS, Gen and Rel, we use φ_2 and φ_3. We need two rules. But if we use the combined values rule ψ_4, we just only need one rule. And the results of detection are the same.

When the threshold of the number of tuples is 5, φ_2 and φ_3 will be rejected and the accuracy of detection will be reduced. Nevertheless, the relationship between MS, Gen and Rel is valid in real life and shouldn't be discarded. Otherwise, ψ_4 can be remained and accuracy of detection will also be maintianed.

We aim to discover rules such as ψ_4 which replaces several rules by one. However, not all the rules can be combined. Given a rule as

$$\varphi_5 : [\text{ MS } = \text{"Divorced" Gen } = \text{"\_"}] \rightarrow [\text{ Rel } = \text{"\_"}]$$

We can't add "Disvorced" to ψ_4. For MS = "Married-civ-spouse, Married-AF-spouse, Divorced", if one's Gen is Female, her Rel may be either wife or unmarried. It causes inconsistency.

Especially, in this paper, we focus on the following three challenges. 1) What structures will be proposed to express combined value rules. 2) Which of the condition values can be combined and how to combine. 3) The search space for CFD is $2^{2^{|N|}}$, where $|N|$ is the number of attributes. Hence, an efficient algorithm is necessary to decrease the time cost of discovering rules.

In this paper, we make contributions as follow. 1) We present the definition of CCFD which combines some condition values and give the definition of discovering CCFD. 2) We propose a method of discovering CCFD rules. Firstly, we propose a 2-process search strategy. Then we discover condition values as the candidates. Secondly, we propose an approach to combine the candidates to build CCFD rules. Lastly, we prune the search space via the valid rules that can reduce the computation cost. 3) Our experiment shows the efficiency and effectiveness of our solution.

This paper is organized as follow. We introduce the related work in Section 2. Then we present the definition of CCFD and problem statement in Section 3. Next we give out the method of discovering CCFD rules in Section 4. Algorithm for the method will be proposed in Section 5. The experiments are showed in Section 6. And we draw a conclusion in Section 7.

2   Related Works

Our work finds similarities to three main lines of work: functional dependency discovery, conditional functional dependencies, and association rule mining.

Functional dependency (FD) discovery involves mining for all dependencies that hold over a relation, including discovery of functional [2, 5, 6], multi-valued [6] and approximate [2] functional dependencies. Conditional functional dependencies, are a form of constrained functional dependencies (introduced by Maher [3]), extending Armstrong's axioms to present a (minimal) set of inference rules for CFDs [3, 8]. CFD rules can be discovered by using lattice rapidly [9, 10]. Association rule mining (ARM) focuses on identifying relationships among a set of items in a database. Large item sets that satisfy minimum support and confidence thresholds are most interesting [11]. And FD is considered as special CFD because it contains all condition values.

Our work is to discover the rules between FDs and CFDs. By combining the condition values, the rules not only reflect on the association of attributes in certain condition like CFDs, but also contain several condition values.

3   Quality Rules

In this section, we review FD and CFD, present 1) the definition of the condition - combined functional dependencies, and 2) problem statement.

3.1   Preliminaries

Given a relation schema R, all of the attributes set over R is $attr(R)$ and domain of attribute A is $dom(A)$.

FD. A FD ϕ over R can be expressed $X \rightarrow A$, where $X \subseteq attr(R)$, $A \in attr(R)$. ϕ is valid over R if for all pairs of tuples $t,u \in R$. We have: if $t[B]=u[B]$ for all $B \in X$, then $t[A]=u[A]$.

CFD. A CFD φ over R is a pair $(X \rightarrow A, tp)$, where 1) $X \subseteq attr(R)$, $A \in attr(R)$. 2) $X \rightarrow A$ is a standard FD, referred to as the FD embedded in φ, and 3) tp is a pattern tuple with attributes in X and A, where for each B in $X \cup A$, $tp[B]$ is either a constant "a" in $dom(B)$, or an unnamed variable "_" that draws values from $dom(B)$. We denote X as $LHS(\varphi)$ and A as $RHS(\varphi)$.

3.2   Condition-Combined Functional Dependencies

CCFD. A CCFD ψ over R is defined by $\psi:(C|Y \rightarrow A, Sc)$, where 1) C is the conditional attribute sets, Y is the variable attribute sets, C and Y are separated by "|", $C, Y \subset attr(R)$ and $C \cap Y = \emptyset$. $C \cup Y$ is denoted as the $LHS(\psi)$, single attribute A is denoted as the $RHS(\psi)$. 2) $Y \rightarrow A$ is a standard FD. 3) We denote a condition value of C by Ci, a combined conditional value set by Sci and $Ci \in Sci$. Sc is the set of Sci.

Example 2. For CCFD ψ_4 in example 1 can be expressed as $\psi_4:(MS|Gen \rightarrow Rel, Sc = \{"Married-civ-spouse, Married-AF-spouse"\})$. $Sc_1 = "Married-civ-spouse, Married-AF-spouse"$. Here, Sc contains only one element Sc_1.

$LHS(\varphi)$ of CFD can be seemed to consist of conditional attribute sets C and variable attribute sets Y.

A CCFD $\psi:(C|Y \rightarrow A, Sc)$ is valid if and only if for and all pairs of tuples $t,u \in R$, if $t[C], u[C] \in Sci$ in Sc, $t[Y]=u[Y]$, then $t[A]=u[A]$. An instance I of R satisfying the CCFD ψ is denoted as $I \models \psi$, otherwise as $I \not\models \psi$. Σ is CCFDs set. I satisfying Σ is denote as $I \models \Sigma$. Any two Ci and Cj ($i \neq j$), under condition of $Ci \cup Cj$, if $Y \rightarrow A$ is valid, we say that Ci and Cj are **inconflict**, otherwise Ci and Cj are **conflict**.

Specially, if $|Sci|=|\pi_C|$, then CCFD is a FD, where $|Sci|$ is the number of different condition values in Sci, $|\pi_C|$ is the number of different values in attribute C.

3.3   Problem Statement

We define support degree of Sci of CCFD ψ as $sup(\psi_{Sci})$. The rules discovering of CCFD is expressed as, given a relation schema R and a threshold θ, we need to find minimal CCFD set Σ over R and for each CCFD ψ in Σ, each $sup(\psi_{Sci}) > \theta$.

For a certain CCFD ψ, attributes sets C, Y, A and condition values Ci are specified. To find minimal Σ is to find minimal ψ. The problem is how can we combine Ci into Sci, making sure we can use the fewest Sci which contains the most Ci. As the same time, we also ensure each $sup(\psi_{Sci}) > \theta$ and ψ can not be derived by other rules. To find Sci is *maximum clique problem* which is proven as NP-complete.

For instance I, a CCFD ψ: $(C|Y\rightarrow A,Sc)$ is minimal that is 1) $I \not\models \psi$:$(C|Y'\rightarrow A,Sc)$ where $C' \cup Y' = C \cup Y$, $C' \subset C$. 2) $I \not\models \psi'$: $(C \mid Y' \rightarrow A,Sc)$ where $Y' \subset Y$. 3) $I \not\models \psi'$:$(C|Y\rightarrow A,Sc')$ where $Sc \subseteq Sc'$. 4) $I \not\models \psi'$:$(C|Y\rightarrow A,Sc')$ where $|Sc| \geq |Sc'|$ and $|U_{Ci\ in\ Sc}\ Ci| \leq |U_{Ci\ in\ Sc'}\ Ci|$ where $|Sc|$ is the number of Sci in Sc and $|U_{Ci\ in\ Sc}\ Ci|$ is the number of different Ci in Sc, there dose not exist ψ' having fewer $|Sc|$ than ψ.

Through the experiment, we can get a suitable threshold θ for a certain dataset.

4   Search Strategy

The discovering of CCFDs is based on CFDs. We find CFDs and classify CFDs as candidates by condition values in 2-process search space. Then we combine the inconflict values to build a CCFD and prune the space.

4.1   2-process Search Space

In order to find the minimal nontrivial CCFDs, we propose a 2-process method denoted by **CCFDfinder**. The 1st process is denoted by FD classification. In FD classification, according to the number of attributes, we divide FD ϕ whose $LHS(\phi)$ has the same number of attributes into the same level. If the number of $LHS(\phi)$ is i, then ϕ is in the level i. The 2nd process is denoted by condition classification. Condition classification is similar to FD classification. According to the number of conditional attributes, we divide CFDs φ into layers.

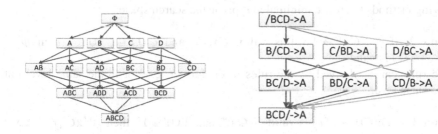

Fig. 2. FD Classification   **Fig. 3.** Condition Classification

FD classification is the same as TANE[2] as Fig.2. We execute FD classification via lattice. Each edge is a process of search, the former vertex is $LHS(\phi)$ and the latter vertex is $RHS(\phi)$. For example, edge(ABC, $ABCD$) represents FD ϕ: $ABC\rightarrow D$.

If FD ϕ is not valid, we will execute condition classification as Fig.3. We classify ϕ into different layers via lattice. For example, if $BCD\rightarrow A$ is not valid. We will search in $B|CD\rightarrow A$, $C|BD\rightarrow A$, $D|BC\rightarrow A$ till $BCD|\rightarrow A$.

4.2   Condition Values Combination

To find the minimal CCFDs is NP-complete, we present a heuristic method. We consider the valid CFDs condition values as candidates. We define the ratio by $p(\varphi_i) = C(\varphi_i)/|\pi_Y(\varphi_i)|$, where $C(\varphi_i)$ is the number of tuples affected by CFD φ_i, $|\pi_Y(\varphi_i)|$ is the number of different values in Y. We compute all $p(\varphi_i)$ and greedily combine Ci with the largest $p(\varphi_i)$ into Sci if Ci is inconflict with any Cj in Sci. Then we delete Ci from candidates. If none else can be combined into Sci and $sup(\psi_{Sci}) > \theta$, a Sci is obtained. If $sup(\psi_{Sci}) < \theta$, we combine the Ci in the former Sci till $sup(\psi_{Sci}) > \theta$. We implement the process till no one can be combined.

Example 3. We use the relation schema R_0 and rules in example 1. We add new rules:

$$\varphi_6: [\text{MS} = \text{"Separated"} \ \text{Gen} = \text{"\_"}] \to [\text{Rel} = \text{"\_"}]$$
$$\varphi_7: [\text{MS} = \text{"Never} - \text{married"} \ \text{Gen} = \text{"\_"}] \to [\text{Rel} = \text{"\_"}]$$

For ψ_4 :(MS|Gen $\to$ Rel, Sc), Ci in $\varphi_2, \varphi_3, \varphi_5, \varphi_6$ and φ_7 are candidates. $p(\varphi_2) =$ 2.5 , $p(\varphi_3) = p(\varphi_5) = p(\varphi_6) = p(\varphi_7) = 1$, $Sc=\{$"Married-civ-spouse, Married-AF-spouse", "Divorced, Separated", "Never-married"$\}$.

Specially, if $|C| = |LHS(\varphi)|$, then all Ci in C are inconflict.

4.3   Pruning Method

CCFDfinder works in the lattice until the minimal CCFDs are found. A CCFD ψ is minimal is that ψ can not be derived by any other of the valid CCFDs. We use the following methods to ensure minimal and prune the search space.

Lemma 2. If ψ: $(C \,|\, Y \to A, Sc)$ is valid, $C \subseteq C'$ and $C \cup Y \subseteq C' \cup Y'$, then ψ': $(C' \,|\, Y' \to A, Sc)$ is valid.

The rules can be derived by the rules in the former level or in the same level but not the same layer.

Lemma 3. If ψ:$(C|Y \to A, Sc)$ is valid, $C \subseteq C'$, and $A \cup Y \subseteq Y'$, then ψ':$(C'|Y' \to X, Sc)$ is not minimal.

If a valid CCFD exists in $C' \,|Y'$ of ψ', whether ψ' is valid that can be derived by rules in former level. Specially, if only such CCFD ψ exists, no matter what attribute in the $RHS(\psi')$, ψ' is not minimal. For example, whether ψ':(MS,Race| Gen,Rel,NC $\to$ X, Sc) is valid that is equal to whether ψ'': (MS,Race|Gen,NC $\to$ X,Sc) is valid. So ψ' is not minimal.

Lemma 4. If ψ:($C|Y \to A, Sc$) and ψ':$(C'|A \to B, Sc')$ are valid, $C \subseteq C'$, $Sc \subseteq Sc'$, then ψ'':($C|Y \to B, Sc$) is valid.

We only consider the nontrivial CCFDs which have single attribute in $RHS(\psi)$. Hence, the quantity of Y in ψ' is 1. According to Armstrong theorem, rules can be derived by delivering of other rules.

The lemmas above are helping finding minimal CCFDs. We only need to test ψ with $Ci \notin Sc$.

Especially, if CFD $\varphi':(C|Y \to A,tp)$ is valid, $\varphi':(C|Y' \to A,tp')$ is valid and $tp \cup tp'$ $=dom(C)$. No Ci exists when we test $C|Y \cup Y' \to A$. We define **pruning rules (PRs)** by $\eta:(C/Y \to A)$. PRs can be only used to prune the search space but not detect data consistency like FDs. When we use PRs to prune the search space in the former lemmas, what only we need to know is attributes of ψ, we do not need to know the condition values at all.

Example 4. We use CFDs $\varphi_2, \varphi_3, \varphi_5, \varphi_6$ and φ_7 in example 2. $\cup tp(\varphi_i)=dom(\mathrm{MS})$. Then we have PRs $\eta:(\mathrm{MS}|\mathrm{Gen}) \to \mathrm{Rel}$. In fact, FD ϕ: MS,Gen$\to$Rel is not valid.

5   Algorithm for the Rules Discovering

In this section, we will show the algorithm 2-processs search strategy. Algorithm combineCCFD describes how to combine the condition values.

5.1   2-process Search Strategy

Our algorithm uses 2-process search strategy to discover the candidates. 1st-process is used to divide FDs into levels, 2nd-process is used to divide CFDs into layers. The process of 1st-process is shown in algorithm CCFDfinder.

Algorithm 1. CCFDfinder
Input: relation schema R and threshold θ
Output: minimal non-trivial CCFDs that hold over R
1   FDr, CFDr=null, *prune*(FDr)=null
2   **for** i=0 to $|$attr(R)$|$-1 **do**
3   **for** each A in attr(R) **do**
4   **for** each X in *subset*(R/(A $\cup$ *prune*(FDr)), i) **do**
5   **If**($|$X$|$=$|$XUA$|$) **then** FDr=FDr $\cup$ {$X \to A$}, *prune*(FDr)
6   **Else** CFDfinder(X, A, FDr, θ)
7   **return** CCFDr

Step2-4 shows that the FDs are divided into different levels according to *LHS* (ϕ) and *RHS*(ϕ). In the dividing process, we also prune the search space. Step5 shows that if FD $X \to A$ is valid, then *prune*(FDr) computes the space need to prune. Otherwise, we start 2nd-process by using CFDfinder to layer the FD.

Algorithm 2. CFDfinder(X, A, FDr, θ)
1   CCFDr=null
2   **for** j=i-1 to 0 **do**
3   **for** each Y in *subset*(X/*cprune*(**FDr, CFDr**), j) **do**
4   C=X/Y $\cup$ *clprune*(CFDr), $C_{Set} = \pi_C/cprune$(**FDr, CFDr**), CFDset=null
5   **for** each C_k in C_{Set} **do**
6   **If**($|$Y$|$=$|$YUA$|$) **then** CFDr=CFDr $\cup$ { C_k/Y$\to$A}, CFDset=CFDset $\cup$ {C_k/Y$\to$A}, *cprune*(FDr,CFDr)
7   *clprune*(**CFDr**)
8   **return** CCFDr=CCFDr $\cup$ Combine CCFD(CFDset, C, Y, A, θ)

Step2-4 shows that we will separate C and Y and divide FD into different layers. We also do pruning in the layering process. In step 3, we use lemma 4. In step 4, we use lemma 2 and 3. Then we get the condition values need to test. Step5-6 shows that if CFD φ is valid when $C = Ci$, then Ci becomes a candidate and $cprune$(FDr,CFDr) computes the space need to prune and $clprune$(CFDr) will compute the PRs. When we get all candidates, we use CombineCCFD to combine the condition values.

5.2   Heuristic Algorithm of Combining Condition Values

We present a heuristic algorithm CombineCCFD to combine the candidates. The process of combining is shown in algorithm CombineCCFD.

Algorithm 3. CombineCCFD(CFDset, C, Y, A, θ)
1   **for** each Cm in CFDset **do**
2   Compute the ratio of Cm, sort Cm by the ratio into CS
3   **for** each cs in CS and not in Sc **do**
4   If($inconflict(cs, Sci)$) **then** Sci=Sci ∪ cs
5   **If**($sup(\psi_{Sci})> \theta$) **then** Sc=Sc ∪ Sci
6   **Else if**($inconflict(cs'$ in $Sc, Sci)$) **then** Sci=Sci ∪ cs' till $sup(\psi_{Sci})> \theta$, Sc=Sc ∪ Sci, i=i+1
7   **If**($sup(\psi_{Sci})< \theta$ && $conflict(cs'$ in $Sc, Sci)$) **then** Sci=Sci ∪ cs' till $sup(\psi_{Sci})> \theta$, Sc=Sc ∪ Sci, i=i+1
8   **return** CCFD with Sc

Step1-2 shows that we sort the valid condition values. Step4-6 shows that a few condition values can be combined into Sci. If $sup(\psi_{Sci}) < \theta$, then we select the condition value which has been combined to combine till $sup(\psi_{Sci}) > \theta$. Step 7 shows that if a condition value can not be combined int Sci and $sup(\psi_{Sci}) < \theta$, then we consider the conditional values which have been combined. $Inconflict(cs,Sci)$ is used to test whether cs is conflict with the values in Sci.

Furthermore, the complexity of CombineCCFD is $O(n^2)$, where n is number of valid values in CFDset. If the $sup(\psi_{Sci})$ of CFD ψ with one values-pair is above θ, then we use ψ alone to clean the data.

6   Experiment Study

We next present an experimental study of discovering CCFD rules. Using real-life data, we evaluated 1) the effectiveness of CCFDs discovering algorithm, 2) the scalability of our algorithms, 3) the efficiency of data cleaning using CCFDs, 4) the result of data cleaning affected by threshold.

6.1   Experimental Setting

We used 2 real-life data sets. (1) Adults data was from the UCI Machine Learning Repository[3] and contained 32561 records of US citizens with 15 attributes, which described attributes related to their salary. (2) The Census-Income dataset[3] contains 300K tuples with 347 domain values.

Dirty datasets were produced by introducing noise to data from Adults. Noise ratio **noi%** is the ratio of number of noise tuples and the total number of tuples. We randomly changed the value of one tuple's number to make this tuple a noise tuple.

6.2   Quality Measuring

We adopted support rate, F-measure and C-precision to evaluate our algorithms. For one rule, the support rate is the ratio of the number of tuples satisfying the rule to the total number of tuples. Average support rate is the average of all of the support rates. F-measure=2*(precision*recall)/(precision ı recall) where the precision is the ratio of true tuples correctly found in the tuples satisfying the condition values and recall is the ratio of true tuples correctly found in the tuples in all condition values. C-precision=$|N_e|/|N_E|$ where $|N_e|$ is the number of found mistakes and $|N_E|$ is the number of actually existing mistakes.

Our experiments were run using Intel Core i7-2600(3.4GHz) with 8 GB of memory. We used Java to implement our algorithms.

6.3   Experimental Results

Exp-1: Discovering CCFD Rules. We used the Adults dataset with 10 attributes and varied the threshold θ to test the effect of our algorithms. The overall performance is reported in Fig.4.(a-c) when varying threshold θ. With the increasing of the threshold, more tuples can not satisfy the threshold and to be pruned, we used the pruning method deduce the search space so that the running time diminished. So was the quantity of rules. (a) shows that the combining time is 1.3 minutes and is 6% of CCFD-running time. (b) shows that CCFD gets much fewer rules than CFD at low threshold. Specially, when threshold is 0.5, none of CFDs can be find, but 5 CCFDs remained. (c) shows that CCFDs have greater support ratio than CFDs.

Exp-2. Scalability in Attributes. We used the Census-Income dataset and varied the number of attributes and number of tuples to test its effect on the running time. Fig.4.(d) shows the running time with varied number of attributes fixing 2000 tuples and threshold θ=0.5. When the number of attributes is above 10, we observe that the running time increases more rapidly. Fig.4.(e) shows the running time with varied number of tuples fixing 8 attributes and threshold θ=0.5. We observe that the running time increases smoothly.

Exp-3. Performance of Data Cleaning w.r.t. noi%. We tested the performance of data cleaning by varying the noise rate from 2% to10% on Adults dataset with the rules fixing threshold θ=0.01. The result is reported in Fig.4.(f) and (g). (f) shows F-measure decreases when the noi% increases. Compare to CFD, one CCFD can be used to clean more tuples. (g) shows running time increases when the noi% increases. By using only one rule to cleaning, cleaning with CCFD takes more time. But due to fewer CCFD rules than CFD, the sum of running time using CCFDs is much less.

Exp-4. Performance of Data Cleaning w.r.t. Threshold θ. With the same experiment set but setting noi%=10, we test the performance of data cleaning by varying the threshold θ. The result is reported in Fig.4 (h) and (i). (h) shows that CCFDs have better C-precision than CFD. (i) shows that the time of cleaning gets linear decrease and CCFD is stable. When the value of θ is between 0.01 to 0.1, it is more suitable for Adults dataset.

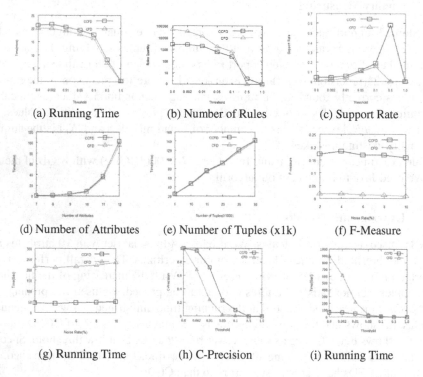

(a) Running Time   (b) Number of Rules   (c) Support Rate

(d) Number of Attributes   (e) Number of Tuples (x1k)   (f) F-Measure

(g) Running Time   (h) C-Precision   (i) Running Time

Fig. 4. CCFDFinder Performance(a-c), CCFDFinder Scalability(d-e), Data Cleaning Performance w.r.t. noi%(f-g) Data Cleaning Performance w.r.t. θ(h-i)

Our experiments results show that our method can combine the condition values effectively and clean the data efficiently.

7   Conclusion

Basing on the CFD rules, we combine condition values of several rules and present a consistency rule known as a CCFD. We have proposed an approach to discover CCFD rules. We have developed a 2-process search strategy for CCFD discovery, described the method to merge those true CFD condition values and the method for pruning. Our experiments demonstrate the effectiveness and the efficiency of our solution.

We are investigating the relationship across levels and layers of condition set, and condition set search strategy and the pruning approach, for purpose of improving the coverage and the accuracy of the rules.

Acknowledgement. This research was supported by the National Basic Research 973 Program of China under Grant No. 2012CB316201, the National Natural Science Foundation of China under Grant No. 61033007.

References

1. Fan, W., Geerts, F.: Foundations of data quality management. Synthesis Lectures on Data Management 4(5), 1–217 (2012)
2. Huhtala, Y., Karkkainen, J.: Porkka.: Efficient discovery of functional and approximate dependencies using partitions. In: Proceedings of Data Engineering, pp. 392–401. IEEE (1998)
3. Asuncion, A., Newman, D.J.: Uci machine learning repository (2007)
4. Lopes, S., Petit, J.-M., Lakhal, L.: Efficient discovery of functional dependencies and armstrong relations. In: Zaniolo, C., Grust, T., Scholl, M.H., Lockemann, P.C. (eds.) EDBT 2000. LNCS, vol. 1777, pp. 350–364. Springer, Heidelberg (2000)
5. Wyss, C., Giannella, C., Robertson, E.: FastFDs: A heuristic-driven, depth-first algorithm for mining functional dependencies from relation instances - extended abstract. In: Kambayashi, Y., Winiwarter, W., Arikawa, M. (eds.) DaWaK 2001. LNCS, vol. 2114, pp. 101–110. Springer, Heidelberg (2001)
6. Savnik, I., Flach, P.A.: Discovery of multivalued dependencies from relations. Intelligent Data Analysis 4(3), 195–211 (2000)
7. Kivinen, J., Mannila, H.: Approximate inference of functional dependencies from relations. Theoretical Computer Science 149(1), 129–149 (1995)
8. Bohannon, P., Fan, W., Geerts, F., Jia, X., Kementsietsidis, A.: Conditional functional dependencies for data cleaning. In: Data Engineering, ICDE 2007, pp. 746–755. IEEE (2007)
9. Fan, W., Geerts, F., Li, J., Xiong, M.: Discovering conditional functional dependencies. TKDE 23(5), 683–698 (2011)
10. Chiang, F., Miller, R.: Discovering data quality rules. In: VLDB (2008)
11. Agrawal, R., Imieli'nski, T., Swami, A.: Mining association rules between sets of items in large databases. ACM SIGMOD Record 22, 207–216 (1993)

Summarizing Relational Database Schema Based on Label Propagation

Xiaojie Yuan[1], Xinkun Li[1], Man Yu[1], Xiangrui Cai[1],
Ying Zhang[2,*], and Yanlong Wen[1]

[1] College of Computer and Control Engineering, Nankai University
[2] College of Software, Nankai University,
No. 94 Weijin Road, Tianjin, P.R.China 300071
{yuanxj,lixk,yuman,caixr,zhangying,wenyl}@dbis.nankai.edu.cn

Abstract. Real enterprise databases are usually composed of hundreds of tables, which make querying a complex database a really hard task for unprofessional users, especially when lack of documentation. Schema summarization helps to improve the usability of databases and provides a succinct overview of the entire schema. In this paper, we introduce a novel three-step schema summarization method based on label propagation. First, we exploit varied similarity properties in database schema and propose a measure of table similarity based on Radial Basis Function Kernel, which measures similarity properties comprehensively. Second, we find representative tables as labeled data and annotate the labeled schema graph. Finally, we use label propagation algorithm on the labeled schema graph to classify database schema and create a schema summary. Extensive evaluations demonstrate the effectiveness of our approach.

Keywords: Relational database, schema graph, schema summarization, label propagation.

1 Introduction

Enterprise database always has hundreds of inner-linked tables. Users who are unfamiliar with the dataset must comprehend the database schema before their query or development. Consider the example schema based on the TPCE [1] benchmark in Fig. 1, which is small, compared to most enterprise databases. Even so, it is challenging to understand such a complex schema, which leads to a growing interest in automatic methods for summarizing the database schema called schema summarization, an effective method of reducing the database schema complexity.

An expected schema summarization provides a succinct overview of the entire schema in the form of clustered categories, each of which is represented by a topical table, making it possible to explore relevant schema components. Recently there have been much related research work on how to generate schema summarization automatically. Existing research on schema summarization is conducted

---

* Corresponding author.

L. Chen et al. (Eds.): APWeb 2014, LNCS 8709, pp. 258–269, 2014.

mainly on three types [2]. The first one focused on ER model abstraction [3]. It aims to cluster ER entities into abstract entities and rely heavily on the semantic relationships. The second one focused on semi-structured database, such as XML database [4]. It generates schema summarization of hierarchical data models. The third one summarizes schema on relational database schema [5]. This paper focuses on the last type of schema summarization.

Considering the existing relational database schema summarization researches, most of them use unsupervised clustering algorithm to summarize schemas. For example, the method in [6] is developed for schema summarization with the Weighted k-Center Algorithm and the method in [7] uses hierarchical clustering algorithm to build hierarchy clusters. We defer a detailed discussion of these algorithm to Section 4.4. Our experiments show that they are not effective enough for large scale database.

In this paper, we describe SSLP: a Schema Summarization Approach based on Label Propagation. It generates the schema summarization of a relational database automatically based on semi-supervised label propagation algorithm [8,9], which can predict the information of unlabeled nodes by a few of labeled nodes. It finds that unlabeled data, when used in conjunction with a small amount of labeled data, can produce considerable improvement in learning accuracy. Labels propagate to all nodes according to their similarity. We define a table similarity kernel function to compute the table similarity, based on Radial Basis Function kernel(RBF kernel) [10], mathematically analyze some of its properties comprehensively. The design of a good kernel function underlies the success of schema summarization. Proper similarity measure can improve the accuracy of label propagation. All the tables in the schema graph will have their own label at the end of the propagation. Intuitively, tables having the same label belong to the same category. SSLP can generate a schema summarization in the form of a set of categories, and each category is represented by a topical table. Further discussion of SSLP approach appears in Section 3.

In summary, this paper makes the following contributions:

- We propose a new approach to quantifying table similarity using a novel table similarity kernel function.
- We propose the SSLP approach to create the schema summarization, which is proved more effective than the existing approaches.
- We have extensively evaluated SSLP over TPCE. The results demonstrate that our approach can outperform the existing approaches significantly.

2   Preliminaries

A schema graph G is defined as (V, E), where each node $v \in V$ in the graph denotes as a table and each edge $e \in E$ denotes as a foreign key constraint. A table may have multiple foreign keys. If there are multiple foreign key constraints between the same pair of tables, we collect and represent them with one edge. A labeled schema graph G_L is appending the function L to the schema graph G and extending G to a fully connected graph, as definition 1 interprets.

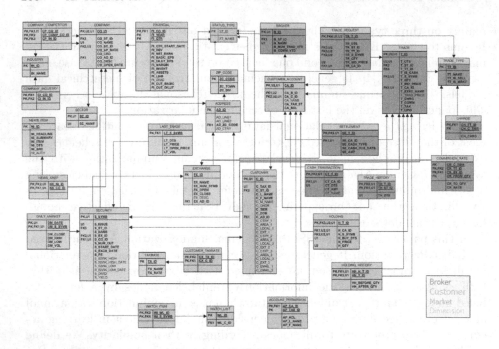

Fig. 1. TPCE schema graph

Definition 1. Labeled Schema Graph. A labeled schema graph G_L is a complete graph, denoted as a triple (V, E, L), where V is a set of tables in schema graph G and $E = V \times V$ is a set of edges. L is a labeling function that assigns a label to each table. $L(v) = l$ denotes that the label of table v is l. The weight on each edge, denoted as $weight(v_i, v_j)$, is a function of the similarity between nodes v_i and v_j.

The labeled schema graph can be regarded as a sparse labeled data region $V_L = \{v_1, v_2, \cdots, v_k\} (V_L \subseteq V)$, where $L(v_1) = l_1, \cdots, L(v_k) = l_k$ and $k \ll n$ (n is the number of graph nodes and k is the initial number of the labeled nodes), combining with a dense unlabeled data region $V_U = \{v_{k+1}, v_{k+2}, ..., v_n\} (V_U \subseteq V)$, where $\forall v \in V_U$, $L(v) = null$.

Our approach aims to estimate the label of V_U from V_L automatically and group tables into categories based on their labels. Based on the above notions, we define our problem as follows.

Definition 2. Schema Summarization. Given a labeled schema graph $G_L = (V, E, L)$ for a relational database, a summary of G_L with size k is a k-partition $C = \{C_1, C_2, \cdots, C_k\}$ over the tables in V. Each category $c \in C$ has a labeled topical table in V_L, defined as $t(c)$. For each category c, all the tables included have the same label with $t(c)$: $\forall c \in C, \forall v \in c, L(v) = L(t(c))$. The summarized summary of the labeled schema graph is represented as the k-partition $C = \{C_1, C_2, \cdots, C_k\}$.

3   The SSLP Approach

This section describes our approach of relational database schema summarization. SSLP takes a relational database schema graph as the input and returns the partition of tables as the output. It is made up of three major modules: table similarity computing, table importance tagging and label propagation.

3.1   Table Similarity Computing

Intuitively, a cogent summary should be one such that tables within the same category are similar while tables from different categories are diverse. A problem with previous similarity measures is that each of them is tied to a particular dataset or assumes a particular domain model. For example, name-based similarity model[11] assume that table names conform to the nomenclature. If database tables are named non-compliantly, name-based measures will not work.

This paper presents a definition of similarity that satisfies our intuitions about similarity. These intuitions are listed here. Each followed by a detailed review explanation of its underlying rationale.

Intuition 1. Name Similarity. If two tables are similar, their table names and attribute names may "look" like similar.

We extend *Vector Space Model* to calculate the similarity between the instance names. Each table, denoted as a vector W, is represented as a text document, which contains keywords from the name of the table and the names of its attributes. W is obtained by *TF*IDF* function [12]. Given table v_i and table v_j. Let $Sim_n(v_i, v_j)$ be the name similarity of v_i and v_j, corresponds to the similarity between two vectors W_i and W_j, which may be evaluated via the *Cosine* function as follows.

$$Sim_n(v_i, v_j) = \frac{W_i \cdot W_j}{\|W_i\| \times \|W_j\|} \tag{1}$$

Intuition 2. Value Similarity. If two tables are similar, they may have several attributes containing similar values [13].

We employ the *Jaccard* similarity coefficient function to calculate the value similarity. For every two attributes A and B, the similarity between them is defined as follows.

$$J(A, B) = \frac{|A \cap B|}{|A \cup B|} \tag{2}$$

The value similarity of a table pair can be computed as the average attribute similarity. Given table v_i and table v_j. Let $Sim_v(v_i, v_j)$ be the value similarity of v_i and v_j, which is defined as follows.

$$Sim_v(v_i, v_j) = \frac{\sum_{(A,B) \in Z} \{J(A, B)\}}{\max(|v_i|, |v_j|)} \tag{3}$$

where $|v|$ is the number of attributes in v and Z is an attribute collection of all the matching attribute pairs based on a greedy-matching strategy.

Intuition 3. Cardinality Similarity. The cardinality defines the relationship between the entities in terms of numbers. The three main cardinality relationships are: one-to-one, expressed as $1 : 1$; one-to-many, expressed as $1 : M$; and many-to-many, expressed as $M : N$. Based on intuition, the table similarity in $1 : 1$ relationship is much greater than in $1 : M$ and $M : N$ relationship.

Given table v_i and table v_j, let $Sim_c(v_i, v_j)$ be the cardinality similarity of v_i and v_j, which is defined as follows.

$$Sim_c(v_i, v_j) = \frac{q_i}{\sum fan(\tau_i)} \times \frac{q_j}{\sum fan(\tau_j)} \tag{4}$$

where τ are the tuple of table v, $fan(\tau)$ is the number of edges incident to tuple τ, q counts the number of tuples satisfying $fan(\tau) \ll 0$.

In machine learning, the (Gaussian) radial basis function kernel, or RBF kernel, is a popular kernel function. We define a table similarity kernel function based on RBF kernel to get the accurate table similarity.

Definition 3. Table Similarity Kernel Function. The table similarity kernel function on table v_i and table v_j is defined as

$$K(v_i, v_j) = \langle \Phi(v_i), \Phi(v_j) \rangle = \exp(-\frac{dist(v_i, v_j)^2}{2\sigma^2}) \tag{5}$$

where $K(v_i, v_j)$ is the measure of the table similarity. Φ is a feature map which maps the space of inputs into some dot product space. This kernel function is controlled by a parameter σ, which is studied by average label entropy method in Section 4.2. $dist(v_i, v_j)$ measures the distance between two tables, which is defined with all the similarity properties mentioned above. The distance function is defined as

$$dist(v_i, v_j) = b - \beta \cdot Sim(v_i, v_j) \tag{6}$$

where Sim represents the p-dimensional similarity feature vector and p is the number of similarity properties. Note that each property is normalized to adjust similarities measured on different scales to a notionally common scale. β is denoted as a p-dimensional parameter vector which is applied to quantify the strength of the relationship between $dist$ and Sim. b is defined to capture all other factors which influence the $dist$ function other than the known similarity feature.

The table similarity kernel function has high scalability. If other novel similarity features are proposed in future work, the similarity function still works.

A weight to each edge of the labeled schema graph is positively correlated with the table similarity, see below.

$$weight(v_i, v_j) = K(v_i, v_j) \in [0, 1] \tag{7}$$

3.2   Table Importance Tagging

Intuitively, a cogent summary should be informative. We select important tables as the labeled data in labeled schema graph. The definition of the table importance introduced in [6] is equivalent to the stationary distribution of a random walk process. Each table is first given an initial importance as

$$IC(v) = \log |v| + \sum_{v.A \, inv} H(v.A) \tag{8}$$

where $IC(v)$ represents the initial information content of the table v, $|v|$ is the number of tuples in v, $v.A$ is an attribute of v and $H(v.A)$ presents the entropy of the attribute A, which is defined as

$$H(v.A) = \sum_{i=1}^{k} p_i \log(1/p_i) \tag{9}$$

where k is the number of different values of attribute $v.A$. Let $v.A = \{a_1, \ldots, a_k\}$ and p_i is the fraction of tuples in v that have value a_i on attribute A.

An $n \times n$ probability matrix Π reflects the information transfer between tables. Let v_i, v_j present two tables, q_A denote the total number of join edges involving attribute $v_i.A$.

$$\Pi[v_i, v_j] = \sum_{v_i.A - v_j.B} \frac{H(v_i.A)}{\log |v_i| + \sum_{v_i.A'} q_{A'} \cdot H(v_i.A')} \tag{10}$$

The importance vector I denotes the stationary distribution of the random walk defined by the probability matrix Π. It can be computed by the iterative approach until the stationary distribution is reached.

We tag the k most important tables as the labeled data in labeled schema graph G_L. In our approach, we regard the k labeled tables as the $t(c)(c \in C)$ for k categories $C = \{C_1, C_2, \cdots, C_k\}$, which means the clustered category will center on the most important tables and the summarized summary will present important schema elements.

3.3 Label Propagation

Label propagation algorithm starts with a labeled schema graph G_L, which aims to estimate the label of unlabeled data in G_L. Each node can be reconstructed from its neighborhood. This process will iterate until convergence is reached, and all the tables are labeled. The label of a table propagates to other tables through the edges for each iteration. The larger edge weights, the easier label propagates. Meanwhile, we fix the labels on the labeled data to make labeled tables act like sources that push out labels through unlabeled tables.

We define a $n \times n$ probabilistic transition matrix T (by probability matrix we mean a matrix of non-negative numbers so that each row sums up to 1) as follows.

$$T(v_i, v_j) = P(j \to i) = \frac{weight(v_i, v_j)}{\sum_{m=1}^{n} weight(v_m, v_j)} \tag{11}$$

where $T(v_i, v_j)$ is the probability of label propagation from table v_j to v_i. We also define a $n \times k$ label matrix Y, whose i-th row representing the label probabilities of table v_i. The final label distribution in Y does not depend on the initial values, which means the initialization of them is not important. The initialization independence was proved in [14].

The label propagation algorithm is as follows.

Algorithm 1. Label Propagation

Input: (1) labeled schema graph G_L, (2) label matrix Y, (3) probabilistic transition matrix T
Output: the convergent label matrix Y
1: row normalize T as $\overline{T}$
2: **while** Y is not convergence **do**
3:     $Y \leftarrow \overline{T}Y$
4:     row normalize Y to maintain the category probability interpretation
5:     clamp the labeled data
6: **end while**
7: **return** Y

Step 5 is critical, we clamp the category distributions of labeled tables to avoid the labeled source fade away, so the probability mass is concentrated on the given category. The intuition is that, any possible classification of unlabeled data should not influence the data that we have known their labels exactly. Step 2-6 are the iteration process to propagate labels until Y is convergent. Here, "convergence" means that the predicted labels of the data will not change in several successive iterations.

As shown in Algorithm 2, SSLP proceeds as follows. First, get the weight on each edge by the function of the table similarity. Next, choose the top-k ones as the labeled tables ranking by the table importance. Finally, use the label propagation algorithm to extend the labeled set consisting of tables for summarization based on the labeled schema graph. Tables are then grouped into categories according to their labels and displayed in the form of a partition.

Algorithm 2. Schema Summarization

Input: (1) schema graph G, (2) summary size k
Output: a partition of schema graph C
1: compute the similarity of any two tables in G via table similarity kernel function
2: obtain top-k important tables in G
3: annotate the labeled schema graph G_L
4: label propagation through G_L
5: get the label vector I with maximum probability
6: assign all tables into $C = \{C_1, C_2, \cdots, C_k\}$ according to I
7: **return** C

---

4   Experimental Evaluation

In this section, we firstly introduce our experimental settings, including the datasets and accuracy evaluation. Then we conducted a set of extensive experimental study to compare our SSLP approach against recent proposals on schema summarization with the same accuracy evaluation.

4.1   Experimental Setups

Datasets: We evaluate our schema summarization methods over TPCE benchmark dataset. TPCE is a benchmark database portraying a brokerage firm with customers who generate transactions related to trades, account inquiries, and market research. The brokerage firm in turns interacts with financial markets to execute orders on behalf of the customers and updates relevant account information. The table classification is provided as part of the benchmark. That is the reason why we use this dataset. It makes convenient to compare the generated summaries with the pre-defined table classification.

TPCE has 33 tables. However, since no active transactions are considered, table $TRADE\_REQUEST$ is empty. Therefore, our experiment is performed only on the remaining 32 tables. The TPCE database tables are pre-grouped into four categories: *Customer, Broker, Market, Dimension*. Thus, we are interested in discovering the four categories.

Evaluation Metric: We use the accuracy model mentioned in [6] to compare the performance of the SSLP approach and other approaches. It assumes that a proper clustering model should be one such that tables within the same category are more similar to each other than tables in different categories. It measures how many tables are categorized correctly as follows.

For each category C_i, $t(C_i)$ determines the topical table. Let $m(C_i)$ denote the number of tables in the category C_i that belongs to the same category as $t(C_i)$, in the pre-defined labeling. Then the accuracy of a summary $C = \{C_1, C_2, \cdots, C_k\}$ is

$$acc(C) = \frac{\sum_{i=1}^{k} m(C_i)}{n} \qquad (12)$$

where n is the total number of database tables.

4.2   Parameter Learning

There is a kernel parameter σ in the table similarity kernel function. The optimization parameter will make the function have the best performance. When $\sigma \to 0$, the weight on every edge is close to 0, which means each point belongs to a separate category. When $\sigma \to \infty$, the weight on every edge is close to 1, which means the whole dataset shrinks to a single point. Both of the limiting cases totally overlook the real similarity relationship because of the unbefitting parameter.

The usual parameter learning criterion is to maximize the probability of the labeled data. However, in our approach the labeled data are fixed, so data label probability does not make sense as a criterion in our setting, especially with very few labeled data. Intuitively the quality of the solution depends on how unlabeled data assigned labels, we use average label entropy as the heuristic criterion for parameter learning. The average label entropy H is defined as

$$H = -\sum_{ij} Y_{ij} \log Y_{ij} \tag{13}$$

where H is the sum of the entropy on unlabeled data.

Fig. 2 shows that H has a minimum 0 at $\sigma \to 0$, but it is not always desirable. This can be fixed by smoothing T. We smooth T with a uniform transition matrix U, where $U_{ij} = 1/n$.

$$\widetilde{T} = \varepsilon U + (1 - \varepsilon)T \tag{14}$$

$\widetilde{T}$ is then used in place of T in the SSLP approach. Fig. 2 shows H vs. σ before and after smoothing with different ε values. With the smoothing, the nuisance minimum at 0 gradually disappears as the smoothing factor ε grows as shown in Fig. 2. When we set $\varepsilon = 0.05$, the minimum entropy is 33.417 at $\sigma = 0.3$. In the following, we use the value $\varepsilon = 0.05$ and $\sigma = 0.3$. Although we have to add one more parameter ε to learn σ, the advantage will be apparent if we introduce multiple parameter in the future work. In the table similarity kernel function, distance between tables is computed with β parameter vector. We propose three features to measure the table similarity, *Name Similarity*, *Value Similarity* and *Cardinality Similarity*. The distance between table v_i and table v_j can be rewritten as follows.

$$dist(v_i, v_j) = b - \beta_1 * Sim_n - \beta_2 * Sim_v - \beta_3 * Sim_c \tag{15}$$

We estimate the unknown parameters by multivariable linear regression model. The experiment result shows that $\beta_1 = 6.3877$, $\beta_2 = 4.8351$, $\beta_3 = 2.0534$ and $b = 0.7918$. In the following experiments, we use them in the table similarity kernel function.

4.3   Table Similarity Kernel Function

In this section, we evaluate the table similarity model compared with the name similarity [11], value similarity [11] and cardinality similarity [6]. To simplify the problem, we first tie the other two dimensions, table importance and label propagation algorithm.

Fig. 3 plots the accuracy for the four similarity functions mentioned above. In each case, the SSLP similarity model has the highest accuracy. For $k = 4$, the accuracy of SSLP similarity model reaches 82.14%, which is nearly 50% higher than other models. Clearly, SSLP similarity model performs better. Thus, the table similarity kernel function emphasizes to measure various similarity properties comprehensively and guarantee to cluster the most similar tables correctly. Notice that the accuracy remains the same when $k = 3$ and $k = 4$, which is related

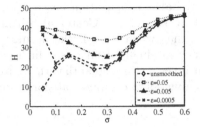

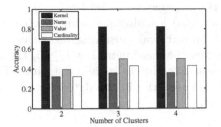

Fig. 2. Smoothing Average Label Entropy

Fig. 3. Comparison among similarity models

with the fixed dimension, label propagation algorithm. The detailed analysis is shown in Section 4.4.

4.4 Label Propagation Algorithm

In this section, we compare Weighted k-Center(WKC), Hierarchical Clustering Algorithm(HCA), and Label Propagation Algorithm(LPA), by fixing table importance dimension and table similarity dimension.

Weighted k-Center: It is an approximation algorithm for the NP-hard K-means problem. It starts by creating one cluster and assigning all tables to it. It then iteratively chooses the table whose weighted distance from its cluster center is largest and creates a new cluster with that table as its center. However, if a newly chosen cluster center is isolated in the graph, clusters are unbalanced. For TPCE, when $k = 2$, the first cluster has 27 tables, whose center is $TRADE$ (has the highest table importance), and the second cluster contains only 5 tables, whose center is $CUSTOMER$ (has the minimum similarity with $TRADE$ and the maximum table importance among the left tables). When $k = 3$, the new cluster whose center is $FINANCIAL$ includes only two tables. For $k = 4$ or more, it follows a similar trend. Although the accuracy is increasing which is shown in Fig. 4, the unbalanced clustering result shows that Weighted k-Center does not work very well over TPCE.

Hierarchical Clustering Algorithm: It builds a hierarchy from the individual elements by progressively merging clusters, mentioned in [7]. Each observation starts in its own cluster, and only merges two elements as one moves up the hierarchy, which makes it too slow for large data sets. Moreover, hierarchical clustering algorithm does not have a redistributive capacity, which will affect the accuracy of the clustering result. For TPCE, table $SECURITY$ and table $WATCH\_ITEM$ are merged into a cluster at some move, however, they actually belong to different categories. This merge leads a set of tables that are similar with $WATCH\_ITEM$ clustered into $SECURITY$ group, which affects the accuracy greatly. Fig. 4 plots the accuracy for the methods above, as well as the alternative Label Propagation. Clearly, Label Propagation based semi-supervised learning performs much better than Weighted k-Center algorithm and hierarchical clustering algorithm. Notice that when $k = 4$, the accuracy reaches the maximum. For $k \geq 5$, the accuracy gradually decreases, which we do not show due to space constraints. Thus, it gives a clear signal that there are only 4 categories in this dataset, and it is meaningless to compute categories for $k > 4$.

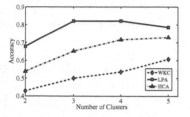 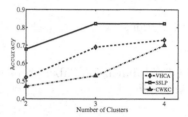

Fig. 4. Comparison of Label Propagation and Weighted k-Center

Fig. 5. Comparison of summarization solution accuracy

4.5   The SSLP Approach

In this section, we evaluate the effectiveness of schema summarization approach. In our experiment, we also study two alternative schema summarization solution. The CWKC approach defined in [6] requires Cardinality Similarity Model to compute the table similarity and Weighted k-Center Algorithm to summarize the schema summary, as proposed in previous work. The VHCA approach defined in [7] requires the value similarity measure to compute the affinity along tables, and use Hierarchical Clustering Algorithm as the schema clustering algorithm.

In Fig. 5, we plot the accuracy value for these approaches. As mentioned in Section 4.4, it is meaningless to compute $k > 4$ clusters. The graph clearly shows that the most accurate summaries are obtained for the SSLP approach. It is expected because the SSLP approach outperforms others on whatever dimension. It further indicates the effectiveness of SSLP.

5   Conclusion

We introduced the problem of retrieving information from complex schema of modern database. In this paper, we propose a new approach for generating schema summarization automatically. The SSLP approach is unique in that we use a new kernel function to measure the table similarity by considering several relevant features comprehensively. Based on the table similarity, we proposed to exploit label propagation algorithm to compute high quality schema summaries automatically. An experimental assessment of our summaries shows that our approach can find good summaries for a given database and outperform the existing approaches significantly. We believe a set of categories summarized is a really valuable means to help users understand complex databases.

Acknowledgments. This work is supported by National Natural Science Foundation of China under Grant No. 61170184, and Tianjin Municipal Science and Technology Commission under Grant No. 13ZCZDGX02200, 13ZCZDGX01098 and 14JCQNJC00200.

References

1. TPCE, http://www.tpc.org/tpce/tpc-e.asp
2. Jagadish, H.V., Chapman, A., Elkiss, A., et al.: Making database systems usable. In: Proceedings of the 2007 ACM SIGMOD International Conference on Management of Data, pp. 13–24. ACM (2007)
3. Akoka, J., Comyn-Wattiau, I.: Entity-relationship and object-oriented model automatic clustering. Data & Knowledge Engineering 20(2), 87–117 (1996)
4. Yu, C., Jagadish, H.V.: Schema summarization. Proceedings of the VLDB Endowment, 319–330 (2006)
5. Sampaio, M., Quesado, J., Barros, S.: Relational Schema Summarization:A Context-Oriented Approach. In: Morzy, T., Härder, T., Wrembel, R. (eds.) Advances in Databases and Information Systems. AISC, vol. 186, pp. 217–228. Springer, Heidelberg (2013)
6. Yang, X., Procopiuc, C.M., Srivastava, D.: Summarizing relational databases. Proceedings of the VLDB Endowment 2(1), 634–645 (2009)
7. Wang, X., Zhou, X., Wang, S.: Summarizing Large-Scale Database Schema Using Community Detection. Journal of Computer Science and Technology 27(3), 515–526 (2012)
8. Zhu, X., Ghahramani, Z., Lafferty, J.: Semi-supervised learning using gaussian fields and harmonic functions. In: ICML, vol. 3, pp. 912–919 (2003)
9. Wang, F., Zhang, C.: Label propagation through linear neighborhoods. IEEE Transactions on Knowledge and Data Engineering 20(1), 55–67 (2008)
10. Vert, J.P., Tsuda, K., Schölkopf, B.: A primer on kernel methods. Kernel Methods in Computational Biology, 35–70 (2004)
11. Wu, W., Reinwald, B., Sismanis, Y., Manjrekar, R.: Discovering topical structures of databases. In: Proceedings of the 2008 ACM SIGMOD International Conference on Management of Data, pp. 1019–1030. ACM (2008)
12. Salton, G., McGill, M.J.: Introduction to modern information retrieval (1983)
13. Rahm, E., Bernstein, P.A.: A survey of approaches to automatic schema matching. The VLDB Journal 10(4), 334–350 (2001)
14. Zhu, X., Ghahramani, Z.: Learning from labeled and unlabeled data with label propagation. Technical Report CMU-CALD-02-107, Carnegie Mellon University (2002)

Delta-K^2-tree for Compact Representation of Web Graphs

Yu Zhang[1,2], Gang Xiong[1,*], Yanbing Liu[1], Mengya Liu[1,2],
Ping Liu[1], and Li Guo[1]

[1] Institute of Information Engineering, Chinese Academy of Sciences,
Beijing, 100093, China
[2] University of Chinese Academy of Sciences, Beijing, 100049, China
{zhangyu,xionggang,liuyanbing,liumengya,liuping,guoli}@iie.ac.cn

Abstract. The World Wide Web structure can be represented by a directed graph named as the web graph. The web graphs have been used in a wide range of applications. However, the increasingly large-scale web graphs pose great challenges to the traditional memory-resident graph algorithms. In the literature, K^2-tree can efficiently compress the web graphs while supporting fast querying in the compressed data. Inspired by K^2-tree, we propose the Delta-K^2-tree compression approach, which exploits the characteristics of similarity between neighbor nodes in the web graphs. In addition, we design a node reordering algorithm to further improve the compression ratio. We compare our approach with the state-of-the-art algorithms, including K^2-tree, WebGraph, and AD. Experimental results of web graph compression on four datasets show that our Delta-K^2-tree approach outperforms the other three in compression ratio (1.66-2.55 bits per link), and meanwhile supports fast forward and reverse querying in graphs.

Keywords: Web graphs, Compact data structures, Graph compression, Adjacency matrix.

1 Introduction

In the applications of web management and mining, the World Wide Web structure can be represented by a directed graph, where each web page corresponds to a graph node and each hyperlink corresponds to a graph edge. Such a directed graph is known as web graph. Lots of basic algorithms and operations are based on the web graphs to analysis and mine the inner structure of the web. For example, some famous webpage ranking algorithms, such as Pagerank [1] and HITS [2] used in the primary search engines, are based on the web graph structure. Their key techniques are computing the out-degree and in-degree of each node and analysis the connected relations between different nodes. With the explosive development of the Internet, the scale of web graphs is growing at an amazing speed. To meet the need of large-scale graph data management, there is a trend

---

* Corresponding author.

L. Chen et al. (Eds.): APWeb 2014, LNCS 8709, pp. 270–281, 2014.

towards studying efficient compression techniques and fast querying algorithms in recent years.

Traditional methods for storing and manipulating the web graphs mostly store a graph in an adjacency matrix or list. In order to guarantee efficient querying, it requires the entire adjacency matrix or list to be loaded into the memory. However, it's not practical for the increasingly large scale of graph data with millions of nodes and edges to be memory-resident. According to the official report by CNNIC (China Internet Network Information Center) [3], the numbers of web pages and hyperlinks were about 86.6 billion and 1 trillion respectively by the end of 2012 in China. This web graph has to be stored using adjacent list over 16TB. The huge memory space poses great challenge to the traditional storing methods.

There exist three aspects of researches to solve excessive storage problem: (1) Storing the graph in external memory since the external memory is much cheaper and larger compared with main memory [4, 5]. (2) Using distributed system to partition the graph into small subgraphs and manipulating subgraphs in distributed computers [6–8]. (3) Converting the graph to compact form which requires less space while supporting fast querying [9–12].

In our research, we focus on the third aspect and aim to represent web graphs in highly compact form, thus manipulating huge graphs in main memory. In practice, such compression algorithm is beneficial for the former two aspects of research. For the external memory scheme, the locality of access will be promoted since much more compressed graph data is available in the main memory at one time. For the distributed system scheme, highly compact structure will allow fewer computers to do the same work and reduce the network traffic.

Among all the algorithms for compressing graphs, K^2-tree [11] is a representative algorithm with high compression ratio and fast querying performance. This algorithm uses an adjacency matrix to represent a graph and exploits its sparsity for effective compression. However, K^2-tree ignores an important characteristic of the similarity between adjacent rows or columns in the adjacency matrix, which can be exploited for improving the compression ratio.

In this paper, we proposed a new tree-form structure named as Delta-K^2-tree. A series of experiments indicate that our approach outperforms K^2-tree in compression ratio while still supporting fast querying. Furthermore, a node reordering algorithm is proposed to make better use of the similarity between nonadjacent rows or columns, which can further improve the compression ratio of Delta-K^2-tree.

2   Related Works

Researchers in the field of web graph compression are mostly interested in forming a compact representation which supports efficient querying operations, such as checking the connected relation between two page nodes, extracting the successors of any page node, etc. The most influential representative in this trend is WebGraph [9] framework. When we use WebGraph for compressing the web graphs made up by URLs (Uniform Resource Locator), the URLs have been previously sorted in lexicographical order aiming to make similar URLs appear in adjacent locations. According to the similarity between the adjacent URLs, the method achieves a good trade-off between compression ratio and querying speed. Variants of the WebGraph [13–16] keep optimizing the storage space by more effective encoding and reordering techniques.

With the same reordering process as WebGraph in the previous stage, [12] further exploits the structural characteristics of the web graph adjacency matrix. In the research, six kinds of regular sub-graphs are extracted and compressed to achieve high compression ratio. Whereas the querying speed of finding all neighbors of the given page is particularly slow since the query requires numerous accesses to all the sub-graphs.

Instead of using the lexicographical order, AD algorithm proposed in [10] reorders the web graph nodes based on the Bradth First Search (BFS) scheme. Taking the advantage of similarity between adjacent nodes in the adjacency list after node reordering, AD is competitive with WebGraph in compression efficiency and querying speed.

All approaches mentioned above just provide forward querying operation and that they can be simply converted into one that supports bidirectional querying operations. In [16], a web graph is divided into two sub-graphs, where one contains all bidirectional edges and the other contains all unidirectional edges. The method compresses both of the above two sub-graphs and a transposed graph of the unidirectional sub-graph. However, such extended methods require extra space to store the transposed graph.

In [11], Brisaboa et. al. present a K^2-tree structure that offers forward and reverse query without constructing the transposed graph. It highly considers the properties of large empty areas of the graph adjacency matrix and gives very good compression ratio. In this paper, we improve the performance of K^2-tree via exploiting the similarity between adjacent nodes in the graph adjacency matrix and reordering nonadjacent nodes to further improve the compression ratio. We compared our method with the best alternatives in the literature, offering a series of space/time analysis according to the underlying experimental results.

3   Preliminary

3.1   Notation

As used herein, a directed graph $G = (V, E)$ indicates a web graph, where V represents the set of nodes and E represents the set of edges in the graph. Each node corresponds to a page and each edge corresponds to a link. Using $n(n = |V|)$ indicates the number of nodes and $m = |E|$ indicates the number of edges. A square matrix $\{a_{i,j}\}$ only containing 0s and 1s indicates the adjacency matrix. $a_{i,j}$ is 1 if there is an edge from v_i to v_j and 0 otherwise.

3.2 K^2-tree

In [11], an unbalanced tree structure named K^2-tree represents an adjacency matrix. In the K^2-tree, each node stores 1 bit information, 0 or 1. Every node in the last level of the K^2-tree represents an element in the matrix and every other node represents a sub-matrix in the matrix. Except in the last level of the K^2-tree, the node stored 1 corresponds to the sub-matrix containing at least one 1 and the node stored 0 corresponds to the sub-matrix containing all 0s.

In the phase of K^2-tree construction, the $n \times n$ adjacency matrix is divided into K^2 equal parts and each part is a $\frac{n}{K} \times \frac{n}{K}$ sub-matrix. Each of the sub-matrixes corresponds to a child of the root of K^2-tree. If and only if a sub-matrix contains at least one 1, the child is 1, otherwise the child is 0. For those children who are 1, go on dividing them into K^2 equal parts recursively until the sub-matrix contains all 0s or only one element.

In real web graphs, m is far less than n^2 so that the adjacency matrix is extremely sparse. Due to the characteristic of sparsity, K^2-tree achieves high compression ratio of the web graphs by using one node to represent a sub-matrix containing all 0s. [11] proves that, in the worst case, the total space of K^2-tree is $K^2 m(\log_{K^2} \frac{n^2}{m} + O(1))$ bits which is asymptotically twice the information-theoretic lower bound necessary to represent all the matrices of $n \times n$ with m 1s.

In the phase of query, for two given nodes v_i and v_j, we can use K^2-tree to determine if $a_{i,j}$ is 0 or 1. Using the root as the current node, find a child which represents the sub-matrix containing $a_{i,j}$. $a_{i,j}$ is 0 if the child stores 0. Otherwise, using the child as the current node, go on finding a child of the current node until the child stores 0 or the current node has no child. $a_{i,j}$ is 0 if the last node we find store 0 and $a_{i,j}$ is 1 otherwise.

In practice, if n is not a power of K, the matrix could be extended to $K^{\lceil \log_K n \rceil} \times K^{\lceil \log_K n \rceil}$ by adding 0s at the right and the bottom. The K^2-tree is stored in two bit arrays, T and L. T stores nodes except those in the last level via traversing the K^2-tree level by level from left to right. L stores nodes in the last level from left to right. Fig. 1 shows an adjacency matrix and K^2-tree according to the matrix when $K = 2$, and 0s in the grey area are added to solve the problem that n is not a power of K.

In order to find a child of the given node of K^2-tree efficiently by using T and L, T needs to permit Rank query. Rank$(T, i)(0 \leqslant i < |T|)$ counts the number of 1s from position 0 up to position i in T. The first position in T is 0. For example, a given node of K^2-tree represented by $T[i]$ has children if $T[i] = 1$, then the s-th child of the node is at position Rank$(T, s) \cdot K^2 + s$ of $T : L$. $T : L$ represent the connection of T and L. [17] proves that Rank can be calculated in constant time using sub-linear space.

3.3   Rank

The implementation of Rank in [17] achieves very good results theoretically, however the realization is complicated. [18] proposes a simple implementation and shows that in many practical cases the simpler solutions are better in terms

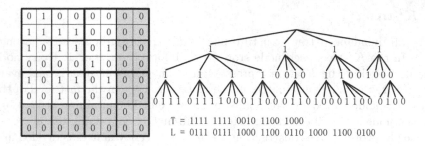

Fig. 1. The adjacency matrix and the corresponding K^2-tree

of time and extra space. For a bit array T, the method uses an array R to store every B position of Rank, $R[\lfloor \frac{i}{B} \rfloor] = \mathsf{Rank}(T, \lfloor \frac{i}{B} \rfloor \cdot B)$, and uses an array popc to store number of 1s in all the different b-bit array. Then $\mathsf{Rank}(T, i) =$ $R[\lfloor \frac{i}{B} \rfloor \cdot B] + \sum_{k=0}^{\lfloor \frac{i}{b} \rfloor - 1} \mathsf{popc}[T[\lfloor \frac{i}{B} \rfloor \cdot B + k \cdot B, \lfloor \frac{i}{B} \rfloor \cdot B + (k+1) \cdot B - 1] + \mathsf{popc}[T[\lfloor \frac{i}{b} \rfloor \cdot b, \lfloor \frac{i}{b} \rfloor \cdot b + b - 1] \& \underbrace{1...1}_{i \bmod b} \underbrace{0...0}_{b - (i \bmod b)}]$, where $T[i, j]$ indicates T from i-th position to j-th position and B is a multiple of b. When the length of T is t, the length of R is $\lfloor \frac{t}{B} \rfloor$ and the length popc is 2^b.

Due to that we can use _mm_popcnt_u64 in SSE (Streaming SIMD Extensions) to calculate the number of 1s in 64-bit integer, we set b to 64 and use T, an array of 64-bit integers, to store every 64 bits of the bit array in practical applications in Fig. 2. B is set to $2^w \cdot b$ for the convenience of the programming. As w increases, the computation increases and the space decreases simultaneously.

```
procedure Rank(T, i)
    result := R[i>>(6+w)] // 2^6 is 64
    for(k := (i>>(6+w))<<w, k < (i>>6)), k ++)
        result += _mm_popcnt_u64(T[k])
    result += _mm_popcnt_u64(T[k]>>(0x3F-i&0x3F)) // 0x3F is 64
    return result
```

Fig. 2. The Rank algorithm

4   Delta-K^2-tree

4.1   Motivation

By taking advantage of adjacency matrix's sparsity, K^2-tree compresses the web graph efficiently and its space is $k^2 m (\log_{K^2} \frac{n^2}{m}) + O(1))$ bits in the worst case. We prove Theorem 1 that as m decrease the total space of K^2-tree, in the worst case, decreases when K and n are not changed. According to the theoretical analysis, if we can reduced the number of 1s and unchanged the size of the matrix simultaneously, it can reduce the space of K^2-tree.

Theorem 1. *The space of K^2-tree of the sparse matrix, in the worst case, decreases with number of 1s decreases in the case of unchanging n and K.*

Proof. For $y = K^2 m (\log_{K^2} \frac{n^2}{m} + O(1))$, let $a = K^2$, $b = n^2$, $c = O(1)$, and $x = \frac{n^2}{m}$, then $y = a\frac{b}{x}(\log_a x + c)$. The derivative of y is y'. $y' = \frac{ab}{x^2 \ln a} \cdot (\ln \frac{e}{a^c} - \ln x)$. when $x > \frac{e}{a^c}$, $y' < 0$ and y decreases with x increases. According to sparsity of the matrix, x is greater than $\frac{e}{a^c}$ obviously.

4.2 Construction and Query

The characteristic of similarity between neighbors of different pages has been found and is used widely in compression algorithms such as WebGraph and AD. We also use the characteristic to reduce the number of 1s. We use a matrix named Delta-matrix to store the difference between adjacent rows or columns in the adjacency matrix. We take rows for example. The Delta-matrix can be constructed with the method in Fig. 3, where Count1s($matrix[i]$) and Count-Dif($matrix[i]$, $matrix[j]$) represent the number of 1s in i-th row in the matrix and the number of differences between same positions in i-th row and j-th row in the matrix. D in Fig. 3 is a n-bit array to record which rows in the Delta-matrix represent the differences. According to the construction, the number of 1s in the Delta-matrix is not greater than that in the adjacency matrix.

```
procedure Delta-matrix_Construction(matrix[n][n])
    D[0] := 0
    Delta-matrix[0] := matrix[0].
    for(i := 1, i < n, i++)
        if(Count1s(matrix[i]) < CountDif(matrix[i], matrix[i-1]))
            D[i] := 0
            Delta-matrix[i] := matrix[i]
        else
            D[i] := 1
            create a n-bit array R
            for(k:=0, k<n, k++)
                if(matrix[i][k] == matrix[i-1][k]) R[k] := 0
                else R[k] := 1
            Delta-matrix[i] := R
    return Delta-matrix, D
```

Fig. 3. The construction for Delta-matrix

The Delta-matrix and the n-bit array D instead of the adjacency matrix can be used to represent web graphs. We use $\{a_{i,j}\}$ to represent the adjacency matrix and $\{a'_{i,j}\}$ to represent the Delta-matrix. Elements in the adjacency matrix can be obtained from the Delta-matrix and D by formulate (1) where $\oplus$ means exclusive-OR and s is the number of consecutive 1s in D from i-th position forward.

$$a_{i,j} = \begin{cases} a'_{i,j}, & \text{if } D[i] = 0 \\ a'_{i,j} \oplus a'_{i-1,j} \oplus \ldots \oplus a'_{i-s,j}, & \text{if } D[i] = 1 \end{cases} \tag{1}$$

We use K^2-tree to compress the Delta-matrix instead of the adjacency matrix to reduce the space. However, we need to access the K^2-tree of the Delta-matrix several times to obtain an element in the adjacency matrix. So if the number of consecutive 1s in D is very large, query will become very time-consuming. To resolve this problem, we propose two methods: (1) We replace nodes in the last level of K^2-tree of the Delta-matrix with elements of the same positions in the adjacency matrix. We call the modified K^2-tree Delta-K^2-tree. For example in Fig. 4, the dotted line indicates nodes replaced. (2) When using Delta-K^2-tree, if we access a node stored 0 which is not in the last level, then it means all elements in the sub-matrix represented by the node are all 0s. So one access can obtain several elements. In practical applications using the above two methods, one query to obtain an element in the adjacency matrix merely needs about 2 accesses to Delta-K^2-tree on average. In addition, Delta-K^2-tree can use similarity between adjacent columns as same as adjacent rows, which can be selected according to the actual situation.

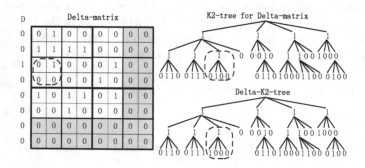

Fig. 4. The K^2-tree for the Delta-Matrix and the corresponding Delta-K^2-tree

4.3   Nodes Reordering

Delta-K^2-tree uses the characteristic of similarity between adjacent nodes in web graphs. Actually, the similar nodes may not be adjacent. We can use nodes reordering method to change the order of nodes in the web graph to make better use of the characteristic. That is to find an order of nodes in order to obtain the Delta-matrix with the minimal 1s.

We use a directed graph $G = (V, E)$ to represent the similarity of nodes in the matrix. In this subsection, G does not represent the web graph. v_i in V represents i-th node and the weights of $e(v_i, v_j)$ for every two different vertexes is the the minimum of the number of i-th node's neighbors and the number of difference between i-th node's neighbors and j-th node's neighbors. For an n nodes web graph, there is a graph G containing n vertexes and $n(n-1)$ edges. Every Hamiltonian path in G corresponds to an order of nodes in the web graphs and the weights of the path is the number of 1s in the Delta-matrix. So, the problem is transferred into the shortest Hamiltonian path problem.

The shortest Hamiltonian path is a NP-complete problem, so we propose a heuristic algorithm to solve it. The algorithm randomly selects a starting vertex and traverses all vertexes once by edge of the current vertex with minimal value. The order of vertexes in the shortest Hamiltonian path is the order of nodes in the web graph.

5 Experiments

5.1 Experimental Environment and Test Data

Our test dataset are real web graphs obtained from the Laboratory for Web Algrithmics [9]. Table 1 describes the numbers of nodes and edges and the the filenames on their website [19].Our experiments are based on the operation system Red Hat Enterprise Linux 6.0 Server (64 bits) with Intel(R) Core(TM) i7-3820CPU@3.60GHz and 32GB RAM. All tests use only one CPU core. The compilers used are gcc version 4.4.7 and java version 1.7.0_09.

Table 1. Description of testing practical Web graphs

Web graphs	Nodes	Edges	Filename
uk	100,000	3,050,615	uk-2007-05@100000
cnr	325,557	3,216,152	cnr-2000
eu	862,664	19,235,140	eu-2005
in	1,382,908	16,917,053	in-2004

We compare Delta-K^2-tree with the state-of-the-art algorithms, including K^2-tree, WebGraph, and AD, in memory space and querying speed over the test data. We implement K^2-tree and Delta-K^2-tree in C++. The version of WebGraph we use is 3.2.1 which is publicly available at [19]. The version of AD we use is 0.3.2 which is publicly available at [20]. WebGraph and AD both are implemented in Java.

5.2 Memory Space Comparison with Different Options

Table 2 shows the comparison in memory space between K^2-tree and Delta-K^2-tree with different options. Space is measured in bpe (bits per edge), by dividing the total space of the compressed data by the number of edges in the web graphs.

We configure K^2-tree and Delta-K^2-tree with parameter $K = 2, 4$. $Rank$ is configured with parameter $B = 512$. For Delta-K^2-tree, we test four different options. Delta-K^2-tree use similarity between adjacent rows or columns in the adjacency matrix are labeled with row and column. Nodes reordering before compression is labeled with reorder.

Results show that our proposal leads to about 40% reduction in space with K^2-tree. In different options, compression efficiency by using similarity of columns is better than rows. Compression efficiency can be improved significantly by our nodes reordering method.

Table 2. Memory space comparison (in bpe) between K^2-tree and Delta-K^2-tree with different options

	uk		cnr		eu		in	
	K=2	K=4	K=2	K=4	K=2	K=4	K=2	K=4
K^2-tree	2.97	3.70	3.58	4.81	4.19	5.91	2.99	3.77
Delta-K^2-tree(row)	2.31	3.18	3.02	4.23	3.42	4.92	2.34	3.12
Delta-K^2-tree(column)	2.12	3.01	2.94	4.17	3.15	4.79	2.17	2.89
Delta-K^2-tree(row+reorder)	1.78	2.47	2.51	2.91	2.64	4.10	1.90	2.62
Delta-K^2-tree(column+reorder)	**1.66**	**2.31**	**2.36**	**2.77**	**2.55**	**3.98**	**1.76**	**2.46**
Reduction in space	44%	38%	34%	42%	39%	33%	41%	35%

5.3   Memory Space Comparison with Other Approaches

Table 3 shows the comparison in memory space among K^2-tree, WebGraph, AD and Delta-K^2-tree. Space is measured in bpe.

We configure WebGraph with parameters $w = 70$ and $m = 300$, configure AD with parameters $l = 100$ and configure K^2-tree and Delta-K^2-tree with parameter $K = 2$ and $B = 512$ to favor compression over speed. As WebGraph and AD are based on adjacency list, they only support forward querying. We use the technique proposed in [16] to solve the problem by using some extra space, which has been introduced in related work.

Results show that the space of our proposal is minimal among all algorithms while supporting both forward and reverse querying.

Table 3. Memory space comparison (in bpe) with other approaches

Web graphs	K^2-tree	WebGraph	AD	Delta-K^2-tree
uk	2.97	2.99	3.07	**1.66**
cnr	3.58	5.06	3.80	**2.36**
eu	4.19	5.59	5.47	**2.55**
in	2.99	3.72	2.86	**1.76**

5.4   Space/Speed Trade-Off Comparison with Other Approaches

We do this experiment while WebGraph and AD only supporting forward query-ing without any extra space. We test querying speed in tow aspects, query for link and query for neighbors. Query for link represents checking the connecting relation between two given nodes. Query for neighbors is to obtain all neigh-bors of the given node. Space is measured in bpe. Speed is measured in nspe (nanoseconds per edge). Speed of query for link is the time of one query. Speed of query for neighbors is calculated by dividing the time of one query by the number of the neighbors.

Fig. 5 shows the space/speed trade-off comparison of query for link, and Fig. 6 shows the space/speed trade-off comparison of query for neighbors.We config-ure WebGraph with parameters $(w, m) = (1, 1), (3, 3), (70, 300)$, configure AD with parameters $l = 4, 8, 16, 100$ and configure K^2-tree and Delta-K^2-tree with parameter $K = 2$ and $B = 64, 128, 256, 512$.

On querying speed, our proposal does not have advantages. When querying for link, K^2-tree is the fastest. When querying for neighbors, WebGraph is the fastest. However, our proposal shows better space/speed trade-off performance especially in querying for link. When querying for link, if we need high compres-sion and fast speed at the same time, Delta-K^2-tree is the best choice.

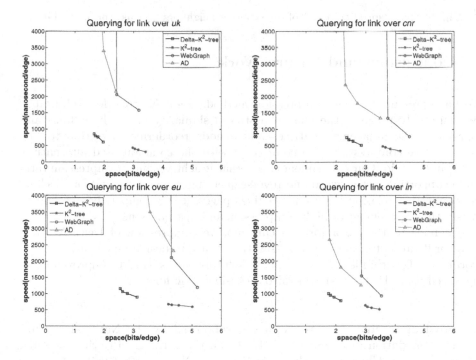

Fig. 5. Space/speed trade-off of querying for link over uk, cnr, eu and in

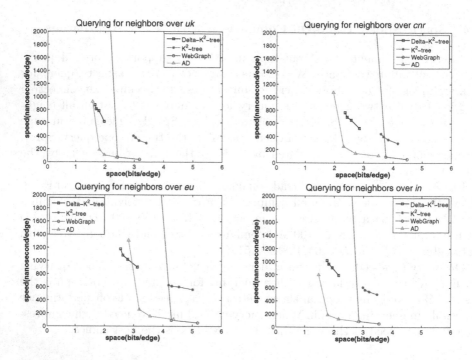

Fig. 6. Space/speed trade-off of querying for neighbors over uk, cnr, eu and in

6   Conclusions and Future Work

We have presented a new compression method, Delta-K^2-tree, for web graphs by taking advantage of the characteristics of similarity of the hyperlinks and sparsity of the adjacency matrices and a node reordering algorithm to further improve compression. We compare it with the common used alternatives [9–11] in the field. Our experiments show that it achieves high compression ratio while supporting fast forward and reverse querying. When querying for checking the connecting relation between two given pages, it is a competitive method to satisfy the requirement of high compression and fast querying.

The node reordering algorithm can improve compression of Delta-K^2-tree, however it can not get the optimal solution. Thus, to design new heuristic node reordering algorithm is one of our possible future works. How to improve querying speed using Delta-K^2-tree is also a consideration for us.

Acknowledgement. This research was supported by the National Natural Science Foundation of China (No. 61202477); the Strategic Priority Research Program of the Chinese Academy of Sciences (No. XDA06030602); the National High Technology Research and Development of China (863 Program) (No. 2011AA010705, 2012AA012502).

References

1. Brin, S., Page, L.: The anatomy of a large-scale hypertextual Web search engine. Computer Networks and ISDN Systems 30(1), 107–117 (1998)
2. Kleinberg, J.M.: Authoritative sources in a hyperlinked environment. Journal of the ACM (JACM) 46(5), 604–632 (1999)
3. China Internet Network Information Center, http://www.cnnic.net.cn/research/bgxz/tjbg/201201/t20120116_23668.html
4. Vitter, J.S.: External memory algorithms and data structures: Dealing with massive data. ACM Computing Surveys (CsUR) 33(2), 209–271 (2001)
5. Vitter, J.S.: Algorithms and data structures for external memory. Foundations and Trends in Theoretical Computer Science 2(4), 305–474 (2008)
6. Badue, C., Baeza-Yates, R., Ribeiro-Neto, B., Ziviani, N.: Distributed query processing using partitioned inverted files. In: Proceedings of Eighth International Symposium on SPIRE 2001, pp. 10–20. IEEE (2001)
7. Tomasic, A., Garcia-Molina, H.: Performance of inverted indices in shared-nothing distributed text document information retrieval systems. In: Proceedings of the Second International Conference on Parallel and Distributed Information Systems, pp. 8–17. IEEE (1993)
8. Yu, G., Gu, Y., Bao, Y.B., Wang, Z.G.: Large scale graph data processing on cloud computing environments. Chinese Journal of Computers 34(10), 1753–1767 (2011)
9. Boldi, P., Vigna, S.: The Webgraph Framework I: Compression techniques. In: The 13th International Conference on World Wide Web, pp. 539–602. ACM (2004)
10. Apostolico, A., Drovandi, G.: Graph compression by BFS. Algorithms 2(3), 1031–1044 (2009)
11. Brisaboa, N.R., Ladra, S., Navarro, G.: k^2-trees for compact web graph representation. In: Karlgren, J., Tarhio, J., Hyyrö, H. (eds.) SPIRE 2009. LNCS, vol. 5721, pp. 18–30. Springer, Heidelberg (2009)
12. Asano, Y., Miyawaki, Y., Nishizeki, T.: Efficient compression of web graphs. In: Hu, X., Wang, J. (eds.) COCOON 2008. LNCS, vol. 5092, pp. 1–11. Springer, Heidelberg (2008)
13. Boldi, P., Vigna, S.: The WebGraph Framework II: Codes For The World-Wide Web. In: The Conference on Data Compression, p. 528. IEEE Computer Society (2004)
14. Boldi, P., Santini, M., Vigna, S.: A large time-aware web graph. ACM SIGIR Forum 42(2), 33–38 (2008)
15. Boldi, P., Santini, M., Vigna, S.: Permuting web graphs. In: Avrachenkov, K., Donato, D., Litvak, N. (eds.) WAW 2009. LNCS, vol. 5427, pp. 116–126. Springer, Heidelberg (2009)
16. Boldi, P., Rosa, M., Santini, M., Vigna, S.: Layered label propagation: A multiresolution coordinate-free ordering for compressing social networks. In: The 20th International Conference on World Wide Web, pp. 587–596. ACM (2011)
17. Jacobson, G.: Space-efficient static trees and graphs. In: 30th Annual Symposium on Foundations of Computer Science, pp. 549–554. IEEE (1989)
18. Gonzalez, R., Grabowski, S., Makinen, V., Navarro, G.: Practical implementation of rank and select queries. Poster Proceedings Volume of 4th Workshop on Efficient and Experimental Algorithms (WEA 2005), pp: 27–38 (2005)
19. WebGraph Homepage, http://webgraph.dsi.unimi.it
20. Drovandi, G.: PhD Web Site, http://www.dia.uniroma3.it/~drovandi/software.php

An EMD-Based Similarity Measure
for Multi-type Entities Using Type Hierarchy

Liang Zheng and Yuzhong Qu

State Key Laboratory for Novel Software Technology, Nanjing University,
Nanjing 210023, PR China
zhengliang@smail.nju.edu.cn, yzqu@nju.edu.cn

Abstract. Recommending entities with similar types is an important
part of entity recommendation, particularly for multi-type entities. So
there is a necessity to measure similarity between multi-type entities.
However, most existing similarity measures are simply based on either
type collection intersection or type vector similarity, and pay little attention to the weighting of types. In this paper, we propose an EMD-based
similarity measure for multi-type entities, which not only takes into account pairwise type similarity, but also the weighting of types. We also
present a novel PageRank-based weighting scheme by using type hierarchy. The experimental results show that our weighting scheme outperforms base-line weighting schemes and that our EMD-based similarity
measure outperforms traditional similarity measures.

Keywords: entity recommendation, similarity measure, Earth Mover's
Distance (EMD), entity type weighting.

1 Introduction

Today most users' activities are pivoted around entities in Web browsing and
search [3]. To help users explore further, more and more online systems, such as
Google and Baidu, provide entity recommendation services based on background
knowledge base, including public knowledge bases (e.g., DBpedia [2], YAGO [10],
etc.) in the Linking Open Data (LOD) cloud. As we know, the user's intuitive
understanding of entity is linked to the types of the entity. For example, when
we talk about Albert Einstein, he is usually considered as an instance of the
type "JewishScientists". Entity type is used to describe and distinguish the
entities. Therefore recommending entities with similar types is an important part
of entity recommendation.

In general, an entity is associated to a set of types in a knowledge base. For
example, the entity Albert Einstein in DBpedia has 55 types, such as Person,
JewishScientists and NobelLaureatesInPhysics, just to name a few. All
those types are correct but some may be too general to be important (e.g.,
Person), while some others may be particular and meaningful to the user (e.g.,
JewishScientists, NobelLaureatesInPhysics). Moreover, there is a hierarchy
of types like "JewishScientists is a subtype of Person".

L. Chen et al. (Eds.): APWeb 2014, LNCS 8709, pp. 282–293, 2014.

In previous research, the traditional similarity measures between two multi-type entities are determined by collection intersection, such as the overlap measure and the Jaccard measure [1]. Since the intersection-based similarity measure only takes into account the common types, it is unable to identify types that have a similar meaning but do not match exactly. In order to solve this problem, pairwise type similarity measures have been proposed by exploiting hierarchical structure in some domain (e.g., WordNet [7]), such as the Lowest Common Ancestor (LCA) [5]. Subsequently, several pairwise multi-type entity similarity measures have been presented based on type vector similarity, such as the cosine similarity measure [5,9], and a type collection is represented by a type vector. However, the weighting of type is paid little attention in similarity computation.

The weighting of each type within a type collection, represents the contribution to the similarity between the two entities. For example, some types (e.g., JewishScientists, NobelLaureatesInPhysics) are crucial when we talk about Albert Einstein. On the contrary, other types describe non-salient facts (e.g., Person). Thus, the Person is the least important one and has little or no contribution to similarity computing. There has been a lot of work related to "term weighting" in information retrieval (IR), such as TF-IDF. However, it does not take into account the relationships between types within type hierarchy.

In this study, we measure multi-type entity similarity based on the earth mover's distance (EMD) [8], which not only takes into account pairwise type similarity, but also the weighting of entity type. The EMD is based on a solution to the transportation problem. It computes the minimal "work" that must be paid to transport goods from several suppliers to several consumers. The weighting of types is the key factor in the EMD. In this paper, we also present a PageRank-based weighting scheme by using type hierarchy.

The rest of the paper is structured as follows. Section 2 introduces the multi-type entity similarity measure based on EMD. Section 3 introduces two baseline weighting schemes and presents our PageRank-based weighting scheme. Our evaluation is reported in Section 4. Section 5 describes related work and Section 6 concludes this paper.

2   Similarity Measure Based on EMD

The Earth Mover's Distance (EMD) is one of the most popular distance functions, which is used in various fields, such as searching similar multimedia contents [8] and measuring document similarity [13].

The EMD is modeled as a solution to the transportation problem. Suppose that several suppliers, each with a given amount of goods, are required to supply several consumers, each with a given limited capacity. For each supplier-consumer pair, the cost of transporting a single unit of goods is given. The transportation problem is then to find a least-expensive flow of goods from the suppliers to the consumers that satisfies the consumers' demand.

Measuring multi-type entities similarity can be naturally cast as a transportation problem. We define one entity as the supplier and the other as the consumer, and set the cost for a supplier-consumer pair to equal the ground distance between a type in the first entity and a type in the second. Intuitively, the solution is then the minimum amount of "work" required to transport types from one entity to the other. The problem is formalized as follows:

Given two multi-type entities a and b,

- Let $\mathbf{A} = \{(t_{a1}, w_{a1}), (t_{a2}, w_{a2}), \dots, (t_{am}, w_{am})\}$ be the entity a with m types, where t_{ai} represents a type of entity a and w_{ai} is the weight of t_{ai}.
- Let $\mathbf{B} = \{(t_{b1}, w_{b1}), (t_{b2}, w_{b2}), \dots, (t_{bn}, w_{bn})\}$ be the entity b with n types, where t_{bj} represents a type of entity b and w_{bj} is the weight of t_{bj}.
- Let $\mathbf{D} = [d_{ij}]$ the ground distance matrix where d_{ij} is the ground distance between entity types t_{ai} and t_{bj}. In our case, semantic similarity can be converted to distance as $d_{ij} = 1 - sim_{LCA}(t_{ai}, t_{bj})$, where $sim_{LCA}(t_{ai}, t_{bj})$ is the LCA [5] similarity between t_{ai} and t_{bj}.

We want to find a flow $\mathbf{F} = \{f_{ij}\}$, with f_{ij} the flow between t_{ai} and t_{bj}, that minimizes the overall cost

$$WORK(A, B, F) = \sum_{i=1}^{m} \sum_{j=1}^{n} f_{ij} d_{ij}, \tag{1}$$

subject to the following constraints:

$$f_{ij} \geq 0, \ 1 \leq i \leq m, \ 1 \leq j \leq n \tag{2}$$

$$\sum_{j=1}^{n} f_{ij} \leq w_{ai}, \ 1 \leq i \leq m \tag{3}$$

$$\sum_{i=1}^{m} f_{ij} \leq w_{bj}, \ 1 \leq j \leq n \tag{4}$$

$$\sum_{i=1}^{m} \sum_{j=1}^{n} f_{ij} = min(\sum_{i=1}^{m} w_{ai}, \sum_{j=1}^{n} w_{bj}) \tag{5}$$

Constraint (2) allows moving types from $\mathbf{A}$ to $\mathbf{B}$ and not vice versa. Constraint (3) limits the amount of supplies that can be sent by the types in $\mathbf{A}$ to their weights. Constraint (4) limits the types in $\mathbf{B}$ to receive no more supplies than their weights; and constraint (5) forces to move the maximum amount of supplies possible. Once the transportation problem is solved, the EMD is defined as the work normalized by the total flow:

$$EMD(A, B) = \frac{\sum_{i=1}^{m} \sum_{j=1}^{n} f_{ij} d_{ij}}{\sum_{i=1}^{m} \sum_{j=1}^{n} f_{ij}} \tag{6}$$

Finally, the similarity between entities a and b is defined as follows:

$$sim_{EMD}(a, b) = 1 - EMD(A, B) \tag{7}$$

$sim_{EMD}(a, b)$ is in the range of $[0, 1]$. The higher the value of $sim_{EMD}(a, b)$ is, the more similar entities a and b are.

Efficient algorithms for solving the EMD problem are available. However, the computational complexity is a major hurdle to the EMD computing, which is between $\mathcal{O}(N^3)$ and $\mathcal{O}(N^4)$ in general (N represents the total number of the types in entity a and b). In our context, the performance is not the key consideration since the size of the collection of entity types is not very large. We used the transportation-simplex method [8] to compute the EMD, which is a streamlined simplex algorithm.

3   Entity Type Weighting

Given an entity a and its type collection $\mathbf{T_a} = \{t_{a1}, t_{a2}, \ldots, t_{am}\}$ in a given knowledge base, we define a type weighting function $w : \mathbf{T_a} \to [0, 1]$, and let $\sum_{i=1}^{m} w(t_{ai}) = 1$. $w(t_{ai}) > w(t_{aj})$ represents that the type t_{ai} is more important than t_{aj} among the type collection $\mathbf{T_a}$. In RDFS/OWL, the $\mathbf{T_a}$ can be derived from triples in the form $(uri, rdf : type, t)$, where uri identifies the entity a.

In this section, we introduce two base-line weighting schemes, including statistics-based and depth-based schemes. Finally, we propose a novel PageRank-based weighting scheme by using type hierarchy.

3.1   Base-Line Schemes

Statistics-Based Scheme. The *tf-idf* [9], short for term frequency-inverse document frequency, is a numerical statistic that is intended to reflect how important a word is to a document in a collection or corpus. It is often used as a weighting factor in IR and text mining.

We adopt the *tf-idf* for weighting an entity type. In our context, an entity is regarded as a document, an entity type is regarded as a word. First, we compute the *tf* and *idf* values of an entity type.

$$tf(t_{ai}) = \frac{n_{tai,a}}{\sum_{j=1}^{m} n_{taj,a}}, \quad idf(t_{ai}) = \log \frac{N}{df(t_{ai})} \tag{8}$$

where $n_{tai,a}$ is the number of times that the type t_{ai} occurs in the type collection of the entity a, in this case the $n_{tai,a}$ equals 1 or 0. N is the total number of entities in the dataset and $df(t_{ai})$ is the number of entities having the type t_{ai}.

Finally, the *tfidf*-based weighting scheme for entity type is derived as follows:

$$tfidf(t_{ai}) = tf(t_{ai}) \times idf(t_{ai}), \quad w(t_{ai}) = \frac{tfidf(t_{ai})}{\sum_{j=1}^{m} tfidf(t_{aj})} \tag{9}$$

Depth-Based Scheme. The large-scale knowledge bases (e.g., DBpedia, YAGO, etc.) provide very rich ontologies, which consist of a set of concepts and relations among them.

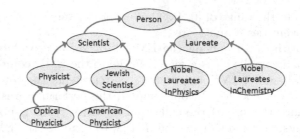

Fig. 1. An example of type hierarchy

In our context, we focus on the hierarchy of classes. In RDFS/OWL, the class hierarchy is specified in triples in the form $(c1, rdfs : subClassOf, c2)$. A simple example of the type hierarchy is shown in Figure 1.

Knowing the relations among types and their depth in the hierarchy is often helpful when automatically weighting entity types. Tonon et al. [12] introduced an approach ($ancDepth$) for ranking entity types. Note that the type hierarchy of an entity is usually not a tree, but forms a directed acyclic graph (DAG). To obtain a single type tree from DAG, they eliminated the cycles manually, and added some relationships by domain experts. We use the $ancDepth$ for weighting an entity type. Given an entity type hierarchy, the $ancDepth$ is defined as follows:

$$ancDepth(t_{ai}) = \sum_{t_{aj} \in Ancestor(t_{ai}) \land t_{aj} \in \mathbf{T_a}} depth(t_{aj}) \tag{10}$$

where $Ancestor(t_{ai})$ is the ancestors of t_{ai} in the type hierarchy, the $depth(t_{aj})$ is the depth of t_{aj} in the type hierarchy. Finally, the $ancDepth$-based weighting for entity type is defined as follows:

$$w(t_{ai}) = \frac{ancDepth(t_{ai})}{\sum_{j=1}^{m} ancDepth(t_{aj})} \tag{11}$$

3.2   PageRank-Based Scheme

The process of understanding entity type is regarded as a random surfing on entity type graph. In general, there are two common ways of thinking (*vertical thinking* and *horizontal thinking*). The former is sequential pathway thinking and can deepen the understanding of things. The latter is to investigate the thinking wider not deeper.

In our context, the two kinds of thinking are reflected in process of understanding entity type. Given an entity type hierarchy, we define two kinds of edge: *vertical edge* and *horizontal edge*.

- **Vertical Edge:** There is a vertical edge starting at one type t_u and ending at one type t_v if t_v is a subclass of t_u.
- **Horizontal Edge:** There is a horizontal edge starting at one type t_u and ending at one type t_v if t_u and t_v share the a direct parent type.

Furthermore, the user may have a preference on which kind of edge to follow, when a user is navigating inside the entity type graph. We characterize the preference by a parameter p, which is a value between 0 and 1 representing the probability of following vertical edges, and thus $1-p$ of following horizontal edges.

To characterize the user's preference edges, we derive a weighted type graph as follows: First, the type hierarchy is usually a directed acyclic graph (DAG) in the knowledge base. We extracted an entity type hierarchy from DAG, which is Hasse diagram and denoted by TT.

Then a graph $G = (V, E, W)$ is a weighted and directed graph, where each vertex represents an entity type. Given $i, j \in V$ and $i \neq j, (i, j) \in E$ iff there exists at least one vertical edge or horizontal edge from i to j, where V and E stand for the set of vertices and edges. W is weighting function, which is defined in (12).

$$w(i, j) = \begin{cases} p, & \text{if } v_j \text{ is a child of } v_i \text{ in } TT \\ 1 - p, & \text{if } v_i \text{ and } v_j \text{ share a parent in } TT \\ 0, & \text{otherwise} \end{cases} \tag{12}$$

where p is the navigational preference of a surfer. The weighted type graph of Albert Einstein in DBpedia is shown in Figure 2.

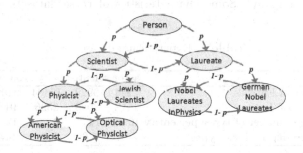

Fig. 2. An example of weighted type graph

Next, we devise the focused PageRank (PR) [4], to measure importance of entity type based on weighted type graph. The PR value of entity type can be computed as following:

$$PR(i) = \frac{1 - d}{N} + d * \sum_{(j,i) \in E} \frac{w(j, i) * PR(j)}{\sum_{(j,k) \in E} w(j, k)} \tag{13}$$

where d is the damping factor and N is the total number of vertices.

The *PageRank*-based weighting for entity type is defined as follows:

$$w(t_{ai}) = \frac{PR(t_{ai})}{\sum_{j=1}^{m} PR(t_{aj})} \tag{14}$$

4 Evaluation

In this section, we evaluate the performance of the *PageRank(PR)*-based type weighting scheme and the EMD-based similarity measure on real-world datasets (i.e., DBpedia, Last.fm).

We use DBpedia as the knowledge base, and select four entities from different popular types as our test case. Using crowdsourced judgments on the test case, we create a "golden standard" including two parts, one is about type ranking for each of the four entities, the other is about similar entities for each of the four entities. We compare the effectiveness of our *PR*-based scheme with the *tfidf*-based and the *ancDepth*-based weighting schemes. We also evaluate the performance of our EMD-based similarity measure and traditional similarity measures (i.e., *Jaccard*, $Cosin_{tfidf}$).

Next, we create a ground truth of artist recommendation from Last.fm. For the recommendation accuracy, we compare our EMD-based similarity measure with two traditional recommendation methods (i.e., Simple Tag-Cloud Comparison [11], Tag Vector Similarity [11]).

4.1 Experiment on DBpedia

Dataset. We used the DBpedia dataset and selected 4 common types (i.e., actor, scientist, city, company). Some characteristics of these datasets are shown in Table 1.

Table 1. Experimental datasets

	actor	scientist	city	company
Number of Entities	2244	9920	13494	31096
Number of Types	1513	7980	2596	9137
Average number of types per entity	16.07	14.33	13.8	12.96
Average depth of the types	5.22	5.68	7.63	6.71

Crowdsourced Judgement. We invited 24 participants (comprising graduate and undergraduate students majoring in computer science) to take part in the evaluation.

For each dataset, we constructed a ranked entity list according to the number of related entities [3] of each entity in DBpedia. Then we selected one entity from top 500 entities of each list at random. Altogether there are four entities, `Jackie Chan` (383 related entities, 21 types), `Albert Einstein` (129 related entities, 55 types), `Sydney` (2948 related entities, 24 types) and `IBM` (508 related entities, 22 types) separately, to be regarded as "selections" for the testing tasks. We prepared the tasks as follows:

- *Extract the important entity type.* For each "selection", the user is asked to pick the important types, and report (a) "important", (b) "somewhat related", or (c) "unimportant", corresponding to ratings 3, 2 and 1, respectively.

- *Extract the similar entity.* Meanwhile, for each "selection", the user is asked to assess the similarity of entity type between the recommended entity and the "selection", and report (a) "similar", (b) "somewhat similar", or (c) "not similar", corresponding to ratings 3, 2 and 1, respectively.

Note that, for each "selection", we can hardly ask users to give a ranking of all the other entities by the similarity in dataset, but rather, we apply the depth-10 pooling technique, which is widely adopted for evaluating IR systems. To be specific, we apply three similarity measures (i.e., *Jaccard*, $Cosin_{tfidf}$, *EMD*) to score all the other entities in dataset respectively. Then, for each result, we retain those having positive relatedness values, and collect the top-10 ones. Finally, we obtain the recommended entities by combining the three top-10 ones together.

Evaluation Metric. We used the Normalized Discounted Cumulative Gain (NDCG) [6], which is a widely used metric for IR evaluation. NDCG@k, inside the interval [0,1], measures the quality of the top-k ranked element list against the golden standard list. The NDCG is defined for a cut-off level k as:

$$NDCG@k = \frac{DCG@k}{DCG_{ideal}@k} \ , \ DCG@k = \sum_{i=0}^{k} \frac{2^{g(e_i)}-1}{\log_2(i+1)} \quad (15)$$

and $DCG_{ideal}@k$ is the maximum attainable DCG value, $g(e_i)$ is the gain assigned to element e_i. In our experiment, $k = 3, 5, 8, 10$.

Experimental Results for Type Weighting Schemes. We present the performance comparison between PR-based weighting scheme and the two base-line weighting schemes (i.e., *tfidf, ancDepth*).

For the fitness of the PR-based scheme, we set navigation preference p with the different values (i.e., p=0.0, 0.2, 0.5, 0.8, 1.0). An interesting observation in Figure 3 is that: when p increases, the NDCG scores keep ascend or stable. It shows that the specific type is more important, as it is closer to human intuition. However when p= 1, the approach has a poor effectiveness. It can be interpreted

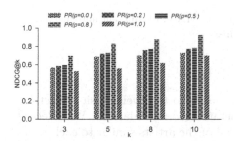

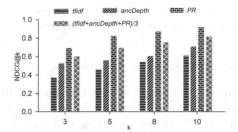

Fig. 3. NDCG of the PageRank-based weighting scheme with different p

Fig. 4. NDCG of different type weighting schemes

as following: $p = 1$ means the horizontal edges are ignored. The weighted type graph becomes simplified, only considering the vertical edges in the weighted type graph. By observing the result, we set $p= 0.8$ in latter evaluation.

Next, we compare the PR-based scheme with other two schemes (i.e. *tfidf*, *ancDepth*). In addition, we combine the above three kinds of scheme by using simple linear combination to see whether better results can be achieved. The result is shown in Figure 4. In all cases, the *PR*-based scheme performs better than the *tfidf*-based and the *ancDepth*-based schemes. We also observe that the combined weighting scheme has the worse performances compared with the *PR*-based scheme.

Experimental Results for Different Similarity Measures. The performance comparison among EMD-based measures with different weighting schemes is depicted in Figure 6.

For the fitness of the EMD-based measure, we chose a commonly used method (i.e. *LCA* [5]) as the pairwise type similarity measure, and used four kinds of type weighting scheme (i.e. *1/m*, *tfidf*, *ancDepth*, *PR*). Notice that "1/m" represented that "$w_{ai} = 1/m$ *and* $w_{bj} = 1/n$". We observe that EMD_{PR} performs better than $EMD_{1/m}$, EMD_{tfidf} and $EMD_{ancDepth}$, as seen in Figure 5.

Next, we consider the NDCG scores for different similarity measures as shown in Figure 6. It illustrates that the EMD-based similarity measure outperforms the *Jaccard* and the $Cosin_{tfidf}$ measures.

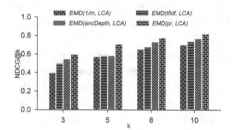 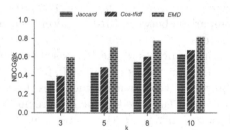

Fig. 5. NDCG of EMD-based measure with different type weighting schemes

Fig. 6. NDCG of different similarity measures

4.2   Experiment on Last.fm

Dataset. Last.fm is a music website, allows users to tag their music collection, and uses the wisdom of the crowd to generate recommendations. We selected the top-1000 popular artists, and collected all of the artists similar to each artist through the API of Last.fm[1]. For each artist, we extracted the top-50 similar artists from returned data, and created the ground truth recommendation as baseline. We get 16,285 music artists from recommendation of Last.fm in total.

---

[1] http://www.last.fm/api

Next, we use DBpedia as the knowledge base, and select all instances of db-pedia:MusicalArtist from DBpedia as our test case, including 10288 entities. Through the "string match" of the artist's name, we finally identify only 4076 common artists between Last.fm and DBpedia.

Evaluation Metric. We use precision and recall, which are standard metrics in Top-N recommendation (N ranging over 3 to 50 in our experiment).

For an entity e, $R(e)$ denotes the similar entities recommended from our method. $U(e)$ denotes the baseline from Last.fm. The precision and recall for an entity e are calculated as follows:

$$\text{Precision} = \frac{R(e) \bigcap U(e)}{R(e)}, \quad \text{Recall} = \frac{R(e) \bigcap U(e)}{U(e)} \tag{16}$$

Experimental Results for Entity Recommendation. Our EMD-based similarity measure can be applied to the tag-based Top-N recommendation.

We present the performance comparison on recommendation accuracies between our EMD-based measure with two traditional recommendation methods. One is called Simple Tag-Cloud Comparison (STCC) method [11], which is similar to the *Jaccard* measure. The other, Tag Vector Similarity (TVS) [11], which is similar to the $Cosin_{tfidf}$ measure. For the fitness of the EMD-based measure, we chose the LCA as the ground distance, and used two kinds of type weighting scheme (i.e. $1/m$, PR).

The result is shown in Figure 7. In all cases, the EMD-based measures outperform STCC and TVS, and the EMD_{PR} measure has the best performance. As indicated in Figure 7, all methods have low precision and recall scores, it can be explained by the fact that our "ground truth" recommendation from Last.fm includes many new artists, which do not appear in DBpedia.

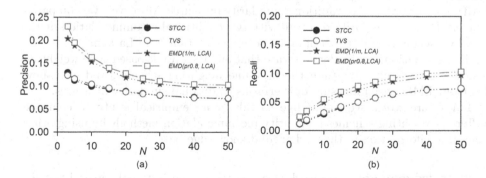

Fig. 7. Comparison of different recommendation methods in terms of (a) precision and (b) recall

5   Related Work

The traditional similarity measures between two collections of types have been proposed by using the set-intersection, such as the Jaccard measure and the overlap measure [1]. Since the intersection-based similarity measure only uses the common types, it does not take into account pairwise similarity between two types. To solve this problem, similarity measures between two types have been proposed by exploiting type hierarchical structure, such as using the depth of the lowest common ancestor (LCA) [5] between two concepts. Subsequently, several pairwise multi-type entity similarity measures have been presented based on type vector similarity. Salton and Buckley [9] used the cosine-similarity measure based on tf-idf for evaluating document similarity, and the document is modeled as bag of words. Ganesan et al. [5] introduced the cosine-similarity measure based on LCA for computing object similarity.

The Earth Mover's Distance (EMD) is proposed by Rubner et al. [8] to measure dissimilarity between two multi-dimensional distributions in a feature space, which is widely applied in various fields, such as searching similar multimedia contents [8], measuring document similarity [13] and so on. Moreover, entity type weighting has played an important role in various fields, such as entity summary, ranking search results [12] and so on. Existing weighting approaches are mainly based on statistics analysis (e.g., TF-IDF) [9] and the type hierarchy (e.g., the depth of ancestors of entity type) [12].

6   Conclusion

For recommending entities with similar types, we investigated the similarity measure between type collections. In this paper, we proposed an EMD-based similarity measure for multi-type entity recommendation, and also devised a PageRank-based weighting scheme by using type hierarchy. By using a hand-crafted golden standard on real dataset, we compared our type weighting scheme with the base-line weighting schemes, and also compared our EMD-based similarity measure with the traditional similarity measures. Moreover, we compared our EMD-based similarity measure with two traditional recommendation methods by using a ground truth of artist recommendation from Last.fm.

The evaluation results demonstrate that our PageRank-based type weighting scheme is more effective than the base-line weighting schemes, and also show that our EMD-based measure outperforms traditional similarity measures.

For future work, we would like to take more empirical study to compare different weighting schemes and entity recommendation methods by using other semantic information in the background knowledge base.

Acknowledgements. This work is supported by the National Natural Science Foundation of China (NSFC) under Grants 61170068 and 61100040, and it is also supported by National Social Science Foundation of China under Grant 11AZD121. We would like to thank Dr. Gong Cheng for his valuable suggestion on this work. We are also grateful to the 24 students who participated in the construction of the "golden standard" of recommendation lists for the selected four entities.

References

1. Baeza-Yates, R., Ribeiro-Neto, B.: Modern information retrieval. ACM Press, New York (1999)
2. Bizer, C., Lehmann, J., Kobilarov, G., Auer, S., Becker, C., Cyganiak, R., Hellmann, S.: DBpedia-A crystallization point for the Web of Data. J. Web Sem. 7(3), 154–165 (2009)
3. Blanco, R., Cambazoglu, B.B., Mika, P., Torzec, N.: Entity Recommendations in Web Search. In: Alani, H., Kagal, L., Fokoue, A., Groth, P., Biemann, C., Parreira, J.X., Aroyo, L., Noy, N., Welty, C., Janowicz, K. (eds.) ISWC 2013, Part II. LNCS, vol. 8219, pp. 33–48. Springer, Heidelberg (2013)
4. Diligenti, M., Gori, M., Maggini, M.: A unified probabilistic framework for web page scoring systems. IEEE Transactions on Knowledge and Data Engineering 16(1), 4–16 (2004)
5. Ganesan, P., Garcia-Molina, H., Widom, J.: Exploiting hierarchical domain structure to compute similarity. ACM Trans. Inf. Syst. 21(1), 64–93 (2003)
6. Järvelin, K., Kekäläinen, J.: IR evaluation methods for retrieving highly relevant documents. In: 23rd Annual International ACM SIGIR Conference on Research and Development in Information Retrieval, pp. 41–48. ACM, New York (2000)
7. Miller, G.A., Beckwith, R., Fellbaum, C., Gross, D., Miller, K.J.: Introduction to wordnet: An on-line lexical database. Int. J. Lexicography 3(4), 235–244 (1990)
8. Rubner, Y., Tomasi, C., Guibas, L.: The earth mover's distance as a metric for image retrieval. Int. J. Comput. Vision 40(2), 99–121 (2000)
9. Salton, G., Buckley, C.: Term-weighting approaches in automatic text retrieval. Inf. Process. Manage. 24(5), 513–523 (1988)
10. Suchanek, F.M., Kasneci, G., Weikum, G.: YAGO: A Large Ontology from Wikipedia and WordNet. J. Web Sem. 6(3), 203–217 (2008)
11. Szomszor, M., Cattuto, C., Alani, H., O'Hara, K., Baldassarri, A., Loreto, V., Servedio, V.D.: Folksonomies, the semantic web, and movie recommendation. In: Proceedings of the Workshop on Bridging the Gap between Semantic Web and Web 2.0 at the 4th European Semantic Web Conference, pp. 71–84. Springer, Heidelberg (2007)
12. Tonon, A., Catasta, M., Demartini, G., Cudré-Mauroux, P., Aberer, K.: TRank: Ranking Entity Types Using the Web of Data. In: Alani, H., et al. (eds.) ISWC 2013, Part I. LNCS, vol. 8218, pp. 640–656. Springer, Heidelberg (2013)
13. Wan, X.: A novel document similarity measure based on earth mover's distance. J. Inf. Sci. 177(18), 3718–3730 (2007)

Optimizing Alignment Selection
in Ontology Matching
via Homomorphism Constraint

Xiangqian Li, Jiwei Ding, and Yuzhong Qu

State Key Laboratory for Novel Software Technology,
Nanjing University, Nanjing 210093, China
skyline0623@gmail.com, jiweiding@outlook.com, yzqu@nju.edu.cn

Abstract. Ontology matching is an important issue for integrating information from distributed ontologies on the Web. While lots of research is related to similarity measures, little attention has been paid to the methods for selecting alignments from a similarity matrix. In this paper, we propose two alignment selection methods based on homomorphism constraint and weak constraint on homomorphism respectively. Experiments on various OAEI tests show that the two methods have an advantage when the matching ontologies have sufficient subsumption relations while performing competitively in other cases. Finally, we design a strategy to dynamically choose a suitable method according to the characteristics of the compared ontologies. Experimental results demonstrate that this strategy leads to a stable advantage in both precision and F1-measure in average.

Keywords: ontology matching, homomorphism constraint, alignment selection.

1 Introduction

An ontology typically provides a vocabulary that describes a domain of interest and a specification of the meaning of terms in the vocabulary. Due to the decentralized nature of the Web, there usually exist multiple ontologies from overlapped application domains or even within the same domain [1]. The semantic heterogeneity problem existing in the ontologies from various sources is a big issue. Ontology matching is an effective way of handling the semantic heterogeneity problem between ontologies. It finds correspondences between semantically related terms from two different ontologies and is useful to Semantic Web applications, such as information integration and distributed query processing [1].

In Semantic Web research field, several ontology matching tools have been developed, such as Falcon-AO [1], RiMOM [2] and AgreementMaker [3]. They usually have a similar process of matching ontologies. The typical process of them usually has two steps listed as follows:

L. Chen et al. (Eds.): APWeb 2014, LNCS 8709, pp. 294–305, 2014.
© Springer International Publishing Switzerland 2014

1. Similarity calculation based on terminological, structural or background information.
2. Alignment selection based on the similarity matrix got in the first step.

While lots of research is related to the issue of computing and refining similarity measures, only little attention has been paid to alignment selection [4]. Alignment selection is to select a set of reliable alignments from a matrix of similarity values of any pair of entities from two ontologies, which is given by the ontology matching tool in the first step. For the requirements of different ontology matching tasks, the selected alignment can be one to one, one to many, or many to many alignments.

It is well-known that alignment selection can be seen as an optimization problem. Currently there are mainly three kinds of optimization methods: greedy optimization by local decisions [4], global optimization based on Hungarian algorithm [4] and optimization based on structure information [7–9]. However, as far as we know, there isn't a systematic study on alignment selection that takes homomorphism constraint into consideration. In this work, we transform alignment selection into a 0-1 integer programming problem, in which the objective function is the total similarity in some sense, and the constraint is essentially the homomorphism constraint or the variant. Specially we propose two methods, called Seal-H and Seal-WH, to optimize alignment selection, which can increase the precision of results while keeping a similar recall. Moreover, we provide a combined method Seal-HWG to dynamically select a suitable selection method based on the characteristics of matching ontologies. Experimental results show that the combined method Seal-HWG has an increase in both precision and F1-measure in average.

The rest of this paper is organized as follows. In Section 2 we review related work and illustrate the necessity of our work. In Section 3, we give the definition of homomorphism constraint and propose a method to select alignments via homomorphism constraint. In Section 4, we propose a method to select alignments via weak constraint on homomorphism. In Section 5, a strategy for choosing and combining different methods is designed for different ontology matching tasks. In Section 6, we evaluate the three proposed methods by comparing them with three baseline methods in three Ontology Alignment Evaluation Initiative[1](known as OAEI for short) test series. Finally, Section 7 concludes the paper.

2   Related Work

In the literature [5], Euzenat and Shvaiko have discussed using thresholds to cut off low similarity alignments to get n-m alignments. To select 1-1 alignments, Meilicke et.al. [4] have surveyed two alignment selection methods that make local decisions to find high similarity alignments in a greedy style. Naive descending selection method is widely used by many ontology matching tools, such as Falcon-AO [1] and RiMOM [2]. It iteratively selects the alignment with the maximum

---

[1] http://oaei.ontologymatching.org/

similarity larger than a threshold and remove it and all the alignments that have the same source or target concept with it until no alignment could be selected. We call it G-Des method in the rest of this paper. Naive ascending selection method iterates over all the alignments in an ascending order of the similarity score and selects one alignment if there is no alignments that have the same source or target concept with it having a higher similarity score. We call it G-Asc method. G-Asc method is more restrictive than the G-Des method.

The two greedy-style methods don't consider the whole selection task as a priority. A selection method that seeks a set of alignments with the maximum sum of similarity using the Hungarian algorithm is discussed by Meilicke et.al. [4]. It treats concepts in two ontology as nodes in a bipartite graph and the input candidate alignments as the edges between the nodes on two sides with the similarity value as the weight. It uses the Hungarian algorithm to find a bipartite matching that maximise the total weight.

However, the methods above rely on the similarities of alignments and don't utilize the structure information. In [7], Meilicke et.al. use logical reasonings to identify inconsistencies and automatically remove erroneous alignments from the previously selected alignments. It only identifies those alignments that are provably inconsistent according to a description logics formulation. Meilicke.et.al further extends this to define the mapping stability as a criterion of alignments which is much more restrictive than mapping consistency. ASMOV [9] extends the process of Meilicke's work and introduces additional rules that seek to find positive verification by which computed alignments could comply with desired characteristics.

Meilicke.et.al's two works [7, 8] and ASMOV [9] try to repair or fill up alignments based on logical constraint or reasonings after getting a set of 1-1 alignments got by other selection methods. Our proposed selection methods seek a global optimization and utilize homomorphism constraint and weak constraint on homomorphism, which is able to combine the "repairing or filling up" process into the process of alignment selection.

3   Selecting Alignment via Homomorphism Constraint

In this section we will give a formal definition of homomorphism constraint, and then propose a selection method based on homomorphism constraint, which is called Seal-H.

3.1   Homomorphism Constraint

In graph theory, a graph G_1 is said to be homomorphic to a graph G_2 if there is a mapping, called a homomorphism, from $V(G_1)$ to $V(G_2)$ such that if two vertices are adjacent in G_1 then their corresponding vertices are adjacent in G_2. The definition of homomorphic mapping for class inheritance hierarchy is quite similar. Intuitively, if a homomorphic mapping preserves hyponymy among entities, for example, the alignment set A=$\{a_1, a_2, a_3\}$, as shown in Fig. 1, is a homomorphic mapping. We first give a definition of ontology alignment, which is borrowed from [1].

Definition 1. *Ontology Alignment.* *Given two ontologies O_1 and O_2, an alignment is a 5-tuple: $\langle id, e_1, e_2, u, v \rangle$ where id is a unique identifier; e_1 is an entity in O_1, and e_2 is an entity in O_2; u is an equivalence ($=$), subsumption ($\sqsubseteq$ or $\sqsupseteq$) or disjointness ($\perp$) relationship holding between e_1 and e_2; and v is a similarity between e_1 and e_2 in the [0,1] range.*

In this paper, we mainly focus on equivalence relation. We will use a 3-tuple $\langle id, e_1, e_2 \rangle$ to refer to an alignment if not particularly stated. A homomorphism mapping and the homomorphism constraint is defined formally as follows:

Definition 2. *Homomorphic mapping and homomorphism constraint.* *For a set of alignments $A = \{a_1, a_2, ..., a_n\}$, we say A is a homomorphic mapping if it conforms to the homomorphism constraint as follows:*

$$\forall \ \langle i, e_{1i}, e_{2i} \rangle, \langle j, e_{1j}, e_{2j} \rangle \in A \ \ e_{1i} \prec e_{1j} \ iff \ e_{2i} \prec e_{2j}. \qquad (H)$$

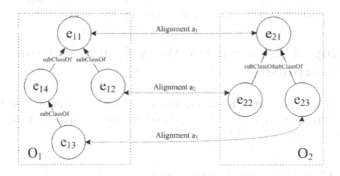

Fig. 1. An example of homomorphic mapping

3.2   A Selection Method Based on Homomorphism Constraint

In order to select 1-1 alignments that conform to the definition of a homomorphic mapping in Definition 2 from a given similarity matrix, we introduce a method, called Seal-H, which transforms the problem into a 0-1 integer programming problem, in which the objective function is the total similarity in some sense, and the constraint is essentially the homomorphism constraint. If two alignments a_1 and a_2 violate homomorphism constraint, at most one of them could take place in the result. Formally, the target and constraint can be defined as follows:

$$Target :Maximize \sum_{\substack{0 \leqslant i < n \\ 0 \leqslant j < m}} f(S(i,j)) * X(i,j)$$

$$Constraints :0 \leqslant i < n, \sum_{0 \leqslant j < m} X(i,j) \leqslant 1$$

$$0 \leqslant j < m, \sum_{0 \leqslant i < n} X(i,j) \leqslant 1$$

$$For\ 0 \leqslant i, r < n, 0 \leqslant j, s < m,\ X(i,j) + X(r,s) \leqslant 1,$$
$$if\ e_i \prec e_r\ and\ e_j \not\prec e_s$$
$$For\ 0 \leqslant i, r < n, 0 \leqslant j, s < m,\ X(i,j) + X(r,s) \leqslant 1,$$
$$if\ e_j \prec e_s\ and\ e_i \not\prec e_r$$

Where S is the similarity matrix, $X(i,j)$ is a binary value which determine whether this alignment belongs to the result set, $f(x)$ is an alignment weight function which is an increasing function on $[0,1]$, such as x^n, $n = 1, 2, 3....$ By experiments, we have found that the performance of selection is best when $n = 2$.

It will be shown in Section 6.2 that the Seal-H method can improve the performance of alignment selecting in the cases that have rich subsumption relations and have fewer diversities in taxonomies between two ontologies.

4   Selecting Alignment via Weak Constraint on Homomorphism

In this section we will give a formal definition of weak constraint on homomorphism, and then propose a selection method via weak constraint on homomorphism, which is called Seal-WH.

4.1   Weak Constraint on Homomorphism

According to reference alignments of OAEI benchmark series, about 8.75% of alignments pairs $\langle i, e_{1i}, e_{2i}\rangle, \langle j, e_{1j}, e_{2j}\rangle \in A$ satisfies the condition that $e_{1i} \prec e_{1j}$ while $e_{2i} \not\prec e_{2j}$, which means some reference mappings are not homomorphic mappings. So the homomorphism constraint may be too strong for some of the ontology matching tasks, and a weaker constraint on homomorphism should be introduced. Before we give the definion of weak constraint on homomorphism, we first define the alignment conflict relation as follows:

Definition 3. Alignment conflict. *Alignment conflict is a relation between two alignments, $a_i = \langle i, e_{1i}, e_{2i}\rangle$ and $a_j = \langle j, e_{1j}, e_{2j}\rangle$, we say a_i conflicts with a_j iff $e_{1i} \prec e_{1j}$ and $e_{2j} \prec e_{2i}$, or $e_{1j} \prec e_{1i}$ and $e_{2i} \prec e_{2j}$. We denote this relation by $Conf(a_i, a_j)$.*

The definition of the weak constraint on homomorphism is as follows:

Definition 4. *Weak constraint on homomorphism.* *For a set of alignments $A=\{a_1, a_2, ..., a_n\}$, we say A conforms to weak constraint on homomorphism if the following condition is satisfied:*

$$\forall\ a_i, a_j \in A \text{ we have NOT } Conf(a_i, a_j). \qquad (WH)$$

As shown in Figure 2, there is an alignment conflict relation between alignment a_1 and a_2. Alignment conflict relation is an irreflexive and symmetric relation. The existence of this relation in the result alignment set would badly hurt the quality of hyponymy-preserving. Actually, there is only one pair of alignments in conflict existing in the reference alignments of OAEI benchmark series. So the weak constraint on homomorphism defined in Definition 4 we can remove some alignments in conflict with others to reduce the scale of the alignment without hurting the recall of the results.

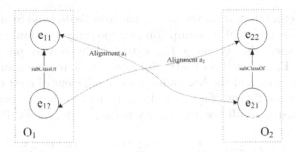

Fig. 2. Alignment conflict

4.2 A Selection Method Based on Weak Constraint on Homomorphism

Just like Seal-H, we introduced a method, called Seal-WII, which transforms the problem into a 0-1 integer programming problem, in which the objective function is the total similarity in some sense, and the constraint is essentially the weak constraint on homomorphism. If there exists conflict between alignments a1 and a2, at most one of them could take place in the result. Formally, the target and constraint can be defined as follows:

$$Target: Maximize \sum_{\substack{0 \leqslant i < n \\ 0 \leqslant j < m}} f(S(i,j)) * X(i,j)$$

$$Constraints: For\ 0 \leqslant i < n, \sum_{0 \leqslant j < m} X(i,j) \leqslant 1$$

$$For\ 0 \leqslant j < m, \sum_{0 \leqslant i < n} X(i,j) \leqslant 1$$

$$For\ 0 \leqslant i, r < n, 0 \leqslant j, s < m, X(i,j) + X(r,s) \leqslant 1, if\ Conf(a_{ij}, a_{rs})$$

Where S, $X(i,j)$ and $f(x)$ take the same definition in Section 3.2.

It will be shown in Section 6.2 that Seal-WH performs better than the G-Des method and the Seal-H method in average, but in the cases that the structure of two matching ontologies are quite similar, it performs not as good as Seal-H.

5   Combining Strategy

Experiments show that both the Seal-H and Seal-WH method can improve the precision and F1-measure significantly in many cases but not all cases. In this section, we first define two measures to estimate the characteristics of the two matching ontologies and then introduce a combined method to dynamically choose a suitable method according to the designated measures.

5.1   Measures

There are two factors that affect the performance of Seal-H and Seal-WH method: the first one is the extent of subsumption or hyponymy relations existing in two matching ontologies; the second is the extent of hyponymy preserving in the target mapping. Based on this observation, we will define the comparability coefficient of a hierarchy and the homomorphism coefficient of a set of alignments.

Comparability coefficient of a hierarchy is defined as the percent of subsumption relations existed in all possible entity pairs in a hierarchy. It is defined as follows:

$$CCoef(O) = \frac{|(e_1, e_2)|e_1 \preceq e_2 \ or \ e_2 \preceq e_1, \ e_1, e_2 \in O|}{|O| * |O|} \tag{1}$$

Homomorphism coefficient of a alignment set A is defined to evaluate how well A keeps the subsumption relations in both ontologies, i.e. how well the alignments confirm to the homomorphism constraints. It is defined as follows:

$$HCoef(A) = \frac{|\{ \begin{array}{c} (\langle i, e_{1i}, e_{2i}\rangle, \langle j, e_{1j}, e_{2j}\rangle)| \\ (e_{1i} \preceq e_{1j} \ and \ e_{2i} \preceq e_{2j}) \ or \ (e_{1j} \preceq e_{1i} \ and \ e_{2j} \preceq e_{2i}) \end{array} \}|}{|\{ \begin{array}{c} (\langle i, e_{1i}, e_{2i}\rangle, \langle j, e_{1j}, e_{2j}\rangle)| \\ e_{1i} \preceq e_{1j} \ or \ e_{2i} \preceq e_{2j} \ or \ e_{1j} \preceq e_{1i} \ or \ e_{2j} \preceq e_{2i} \end{array} \}|} \tag{2}$$

It is observed from our experiments on various ontology matching tasks that the above two measures are relevant to the performance of the Seal-H and Seal-WH method. The extent of subsumption relations in a hierarchy of matching ontologies greatly affect the power of the constraint on homomorphism including the weak constraint. When the comparability coefficient is higher than a threshold, Seal-H and Seal-WH performs better than traditional methods. Specifically, Seal-H performs best when the homomorphism coefficient is higher than a threshold. When the comparability coefficient is low, the traditional method G-Des perform best among all methods used in our experiments. Based on these observations, we think these measures are useful to help us dynamically choose a suitable selection method.

5.2   A Combined Method

We have defined comparability coefficient for a hierarchy and homomorphism coefficient for a set of alignments in the last section. However, there often does not exist a reference mapping for an upcoming ontology matching task. To estimate the homomorphism coefficient of the target mapping, we need to use a reliable method to select some alignments with high confidence as a "reference" alignment set.

Based on our empirical study, we propose a combined method, called Seal-HWG, to take advantage of three methods, say Seal-H, Seal-WH and G-Des. The flow chart of the combined method is given in Fig. 3.

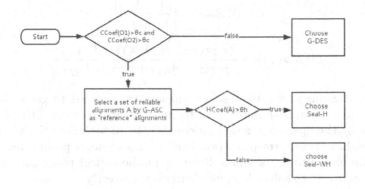

Fig. 3. The flow chart of the method Seal-HWG

We first compute the comparability coefficient of both hierarchies in matching ontologies. When its value is lower than a predefined threshold θ_c (we set it to 0.01), we choose the traditional method G-Des, because it performs best among traditional methods in terms of average F-measure. Otherwise, we use G-Asc method to get a set of "reference" alignments with a similarity higher than a predefined threshold (we set it to 0.4). The reason we choose G-Asc method is that it costs less time and it can get a reliable mapping by our empirical study. Based on the "reference" alignments, we compute the homomorphism coefficient and if it is higher than a predefined threshold θ_h (we set it to 0.95), we choose Seal-H method; otherwise, Seal-WH is our choice.

6   Evaluation

In this section, we first introduce the used test series followed by the measures used in our experiments. Then, we report our experimental results to demonstrate the validness of our proposed methods.

6.1   Experiment Settings

We have chosen the latest test series in OAEI with a reference mapping. We use the benchmark series[2] of test in OAEI2012 (including 48 matching tasks), the conference series[3] in OAEI2010 (including 21 matching tasks) and directory series[4] in OAEI2005 (including 2,265 matching tasks) as the three test series.

If the output set of alignments is A, and the set of corresponding reference alignments is A_{ref}, the precision, recall and F1-measure of output alignments are defined as:

$$prec(A, A_{ref}) = \frac{|A \cap A_{ref}|}{|A|} \tag{3}$$

$$rec(A, A_{ref}) = \frac{|A \cap A_{ref}|}{|A_{ref}|} \tag{4}$$

$$f1(A, A_{ref}) = \frac{2 * prec(A, A_{ref}) * rec(A, A_{ref})}{prec(A, A_{ref}) + rec(A, A_{ref})} \tag{5}$$

Before using our methods to select alignments, we need to get a similarity matrix of concepts in both ontologies. In our experiments, we use the similarity matrix got by the open source tool Falcon-AO [1]. In both Seal-H and Seal-WH method, we have transformed the problem into a 0-1 integer programming problem and we have utilized a state-of-the-art mathematical programming solver Gurobi Optimizer[5] to solve them efficiently and correctly.

To evaluate the three selection methods proposed in this paper, we compare them with three baseline selection methods including the G-Des, the G-Asc and the Hungarian method. We compute the average values of F1-measure, precision and recall of the selection results in each test series for each of the all six methods respectively. It is noted that for the best performance in comparing with other alignment weight functions, we choose $f(x) = x^2$ as the alignment weight function in the Hungarian, Seal-H and Seal-WH methods.

Because properties often have fewer subsumption relations and instances don't have any, our selection methods are mainly adopted to select alignments of corresponding classes rather than properties or instances. We use the widely used G-Des method to select alignments in properties and instances.

6.2   Experimental Results

The performance of the six methods on OAEI benchmark series is depicted in Fig. 4. The Seal-HWG method performs best among all methods in terms of F1-measure. The G-Asc method has a good performance in precision but hurts the

---

[2] http://oaei.ontologymatching.org/2012/benchmarks/index.html

[3] http://oaei.ontologymatching.org/2010/conference/index.html

[4] http://oaei.ontologymatching.org/2005/directory/

[5] http://www.gurobi.com/

score of recall. In average, the G-Des method performs best in the three baseline methods and the Seal-H and Seal-WH methods have a competitive performance.

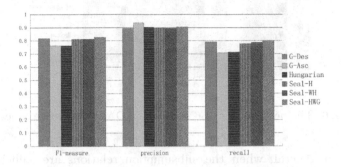

Fig. 4. The performance of 6 methods on OAEI benchmark series

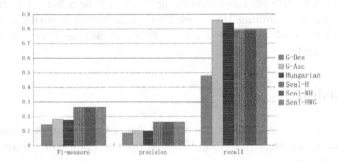

Fig. 5. The performance of 6 methods on OAEI directory series

The performance of the six methods on OAEI directory series is depicted in Fig. 5. In directory series, our proposed methods all have a dominant advantage over the three baseline methods. After investigating the matching ontologies in directory series, we have found that the matching ontologies usually have a similar structure which could make our homomorphism constraint powerful in the alignment selection process.

Fig. 6 shows the performance of these methods on the conference series. Both the G-Des and G-Asc method have a competitive performance in average. The Seal-WH method has a better performance than the Seal-H and three baseline methods in average but not in every single task. However, the combined method Seal-HWG performs best among the six methods which is a demonstration of the effectiveness of dynamical method selection performed in the process of the Seal-HWG method.

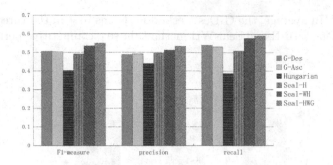

Fig. 6. The performance of 6 methods on OAEI conference series

Speaking in general, when the subsumption relations are sufficient, both Seal-H and Seal-WH method could have a stable performance in our tests. Otherwise, they could also perform competitively comparing to the baseline methods. Among the baseline methods, the G-Des method has a good performance in terms of F1-measure on most matching tasks. We also find that the G-Asc method performs best among the three baseline methods in terms of precision. Our combined method Seal-HWG has a stable advantage over the other five methods in our tests.

7   Conclusion

In this paper, we have systematically studied the optimization problem of alignment selection in ontology matching. To sum up, the main contributions of this paper are as follows:

Firstly, we modeled the optimization problem of alignment selection in ontology matching as an 0-1 integer programming problem, in which the objective function is the total similarity in some sense, and some constraint on homomorphism should be taken into consideration. Specifically, we designed two methods for selecting alignments, called Seal-H and Seal-WH, which are based on homomorphism constraint and weak constraint on homomorphism, respectively.

Secondly, to take advantage of three selection methods, say Seal-H, Seal-WH and G-Des method, we designed a combined method to integrate these three methods. The combined one is called Seal-HWG, and it can dynamically choose a suitable selection method according to some designated estimation.

Finally, to evaluate the effectiveness of our presented methods, we conducted extensive tests of six related methods on three OAEI test series. The results demonstrate that both the Seal-H and Seal-WH have an advantage when the subsumption relations are sufficient in the matching ontologies and perform competitively in other cases. Especially, the combined method Seal-HWG has a stable advantage among the six methods in terms of the F1-measure.

In future work, we are interested in designing an effective divide-and-conquer strategy to make our selection methods more scalable and efficient. Besides, it is also an interesting research work to make sense of classes by mapping class hierarchy to WordNet via homomorphism constraint.

Acknowledgement. This work is supported by the National Natural Science Foundation of China (NSFC) under Grants 61223003, 61170068 and 61370019. We would like to thank Dr. Wei Hu and Dr. Gong Cheng for their valuable suggestion on this work.

References

1. Hu, W., Qu, Y., Cheng, G.: Matching large ontologies: A divide-and-conquer approach. Data & Knowledge Engineering 67(1), 140–160 (2008)
2. Li, J., Tang, J., Li, Y., Luo, Q.: Rimom: A dynamic multistrategy ontology alignment framework. IEEE Transactions on Knowledge and Data Engineering 21(8), 1218–1232 (2009)
3. Cruz, I.F., Antonelli, F.P., Stroe, C.: AgreementMaker: efficient matching for large real-world schemas and ontologies. Proceedings of the VLDB Endowment 2(2), 1586–1589 (2009)
4. Meilicke, C., Stuckenschmidt, H.: Analyzing Mapping Extraction Approaches. OM (2007)
5. Euzenat, J., Shvaiko, P.: Ontology matching. Springer, Heidelberg (2007)
6. Kuhn, H.W.: The Hungarian method for the assignment problem. Naval Research Logistics Quarterly 2(1-2), 83–97 (1955)
7. Meilicke, C., Stuckenschmidt, H.: Applying logical constraints to ontology matching. In: Hertzberg, J., Beetz, M., Englert, R. (eds.) KI 2007. LNCS (LNAI), vol. 4667, pp. 99–113. Springer, Heidelberg (2007)
8. Meilicke, C., Stuckenschmidt, H., Tamilin, A.: Repairing ontology mappings. AAAI 3(2.1), 6 (2007)
9. Jean-Mary, Y.R., Patrick Shironoshita, E., Kabuka, M.R.: Ontology matching with semantic verification. Web Semantics: Science, Services and Agents on the World Wide Web 7(3), 235–251 (2009)

Matrix Factorization Meets Cosine Similarity: Addressing Sparsity Problem in Collaborative Filtering Recommender System

Hailong Wen[2], Guiguang Ding[1], Cong Liu[2], and Jianmin Wang[1]

[1] School of Software, Tsinghua University, Beijing, China
[2] Department of Computer Science and Technology,
Tsinghua University, Beijing, China
{wenhl11,cong-liu11}@mails.tsinghua.edu.cn,
{dinggg,jimwang}@tsinghua.edu.cn

Abstract. Matrix factorization (MF) technique has been widely used in collaborative filtering recommendation systems. However, MF still suffers from data sparsity problem. Although previous studies bring in auxiliary data to solve this problem, auxiliary data is not always available. In this paper, we propose a novel method, Cosine Matrix Factorization (CosMF), to address the sparsity problem without auxiliary data. We observe that when data is sparse, the magnitude of user/item vector could not be properly learned due to lack of information. Based on that observation, we propose to use cosine to replace inner product for sparse users/items, thus eliminating the negative effects of poorly trained magnitudes. Experiments on various real life datasets demonstrate that CosMF yields significantly better results without help of auxiliary dataset.

Keywords: Matrix Factorization, Cosine Similarity, Collaborative Filtering, Sparsity Problem.

1 Introduction

Recommender systems are widely used on the Internet nowadays. Web sites such as Amazon, EBay, Hulu and Netflix rely on recommender systems to promote sales and improve user experience. These systems analyze users' purchasing records, predict users' preference (ratings) to different items, and recommend those with the highest ratings, i.e., the highest potential to attract users. Due to the great commercial value, recommender system has attracted much attention in different fields of research during the last decade, such as information retrieval [1–3], data mining [4–7] and machine learning [8].

Matrix factorization [9] is one of the most commonly used approaches in recommender systems. Despite of its efficiency, MF still suffers from sparsity problem, i.e., users who rate only a small portion of items could not get proper recommendation, and items with few ratings may not be recommended well.

Researchers have tried to utilize auxiliary datasets to alleviate sparsity problem, such as social recommendation and transfer learning [10–12, 1, 13–15, 2, 16,

L. Chen et al. (Eds.): APWeb 2014, LNCS 8709, pp. 306–317, 2014.

6, 5, 17, 7, 18, 19]. From the auxiliary datasets, recommender system could get additional profile of sparse users/items, thus making a more accurate recommendation. Although these methods are very useful to cope with sparse datasets, they have 4 major drawbacks: 1) Auxiliary datasets are not always available. The transfer learning method requires that the auxiliary data have at least one common set (user set or item set). The social recommendation needs user-user interaction data. 2) Auxiliary datasets may not be of good quality even if they are available. Data under different assumption or data with noise would be of limited help, or even harmful. [20] reports a negative case in which social data contributes nothing to the final result, probably due to the poor quality of data. 3) The balance between target and auxiliary datasets needs fine-tuning. [17] and [7] both mentioned that relying too much on either side would not generate good performance. 4) These models usually have high complexity and could not be easily implemented and scaled. Most of the above models involve graph computation, which would be a challenge when the amount of users/items goes up.

Instead of taking in auxiliary datasets, we focus more on further utilizing the existing dataset to get better performance. In this paper, we combine the commonly used cosine similarity with the matrix factorization model to form a novel approach, called Cosine Matrix Factorization (CosMF). There are two main contributions in CosMF:

- We explain matrix factorization in an information retrieval scenario. We demonstrate that there are actually two stages in model training, the *direction identification* and the *magnitude adjustment*. Then we analyze how vector norm and cosine similarity trained by these two stages finally affect the performance when data is extremely sparse. This analysis further motivates us to apply cosine similarity in the low-rank approximation.
- We developed a novel approach, the CosMF. CosMF requires no auxiliary datasets, yet still works well. To our best knowledge, this is the first attempt to incorporate cosine similarity for improving the recommendation quality of MF.

The rest of the paper is organized as follows. Chapter 2 gives an overview of the related work, especially how MF model works. In Chapter 3, we analyze why MF does not work so well in sparse dataset. Chapter 4 introduces the CosMF method. Chapter 5 demonstrates the experiments and results. Chapter 6 draws a conclusion and discusses the future work.

2   Related Work

2.1   Overview

The Matrix Factorization (MF) technique aims to train a lower-rank model to approximate the rating matrix R by user latent vector U and item feature vector V. The underlying assumption of MF is that user preference is influenced by a small number of latent factors, and the rating of an item is determined by how each of its feature factor applies to the user preference [21–23, 8, 24, 25, 9]. MF works efficiently and effectively and becomes one of the most widely used methods in collaborative filtering.

Lots of research had been done to improve the performance of basic Matrix Factorization. In [21] Lee et al. proposed Non-negative Matrix Factorization (NMF) to enforce non-negativity in U and V, which was proved to be useful in computer vision fields. In [23], Zhang et al. proposed Weighted Non-negative Matrix Factorization (WNMF) to improve NMF by using weights as indicator matrix to denote the observability of entries in R. In [8], Salakhutdinov et al. gave Probabilistic Matrix Factorization (PMF), which used Gaussian distribution to initialize U and V, and applied logistic function to limit the range of predicted to [0,1]. Koren et al. summarized these work in [9] and gave an generic framework for Matrix Factorization.

Researchers also managed to incorporate information from other data sources. Zhang et al. used review sentiment analysis to construct virtual ratings for users who have not explicitly expressed their opinions on the item [10]. Gu et al. proposed the Graph Weighted Nonnegative Matrix Factorization (GWNMF) [19] to use user/item neighborhood graph to preserve neighbourhood information in user/item latent vectors. [5, 1, 17] utilized social network information under the assumption that friends share similar tastes and interests.

2.2   Matrix Factorization

Suppose we have n users, m items and a rating matrix $R = [R_{i,j}]_{m \times n}$ with each element $R_{i,j}$ representing the rating of user i to item j. To make a recommendation for user i, the recommender system needs to predict missing value of i-th row of R, and picks items with high predicted ratings. In Matrix Factorization, the rating of user i to item j is predicted as

$$R_{i,j} = U_i V_j^T \tag{1}$$

where U_i denotes the latent preference row vector of user i and V_j denotes latent feature row vector of item j, and both of them have k dimensions (latent factors). To train the model, we need to minimize the squared error between predicted and observed ratings while keeping the model as simple as possible. This leads to the following objective function of Matrix Factorization(MF),

$$\mathcal{L} = \min_{U,V} \sum_{i=1}^{n} \sum_{j=1}^{m} I_{i,j}(R_{i,j} - U_i V_j^T)^2 + \frac{\lambda_u}{2} \sum_{i=1}^{n} \|U_i\|_{Frob}^2 + \frac{\lambda_v}{2} \sum_{j=1}^{m} \|V_j\|_{Frob}^2 \tag{2}$$

where $(R_{i,j} - U_i V_j^T)^2$ is the loss function. $I_{n \times m}$ is an indicator matrix with observed ratings set to 1 and unobserved ones 0. The $\|\cdot\|_{Frob}$ denotes the Frobenius norm, which acts as a regularizer and constrains the model's complexity. $\lambda_u, \lambda_v \geq 0$ are penalty parameters of the above constraints.

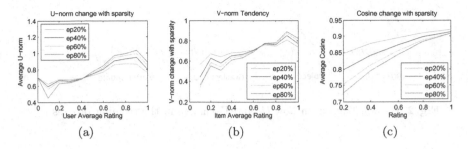

Fig. 1. Average U-norm, V-norm and Cosine on Epinions with different sampling ratio

3   Insights on Matrix Factorization

In this chapter, we give an alternative interpretation of Matrix Factorization
in the perspective of information retrieval. We treat recommending items as retrieving items with the highest similarity. Thus $R_{i,j}$ represents the inner product
similarity between U_i and V_j, which is determined by the angle between these
two vectors and their magnitudes:

$$R_{i,j} = U_i V_j^T = \|U_i\| \, \|V_j\| \cos(U_i, V_j) \tag{3}$$

The $\|\cdot\|$ denotes the L2-norm of a vector, and $\cos(\cdot, \cdot)$ denotes the cosine sim-
ilarity of two vectors. The *norm* and *cosine* play different roles in the preference
approximation. $\|U_i\|$ and $\|V_j\|$ respectively carry the macroscopic(global) infor-
mation of the strength of user i's preference vector and item j's feature vector. A
small $\|U_i\|$ means that user i generally has low preference on most of the items,
and a small $\|V_j\|$ means that item j generally has low attraction to most of the
users. While cosine similarity $\cos(U_i, V_j)$ carries the microscopic(local) information of the pairwise inter-action between U_i and V_j. A small $\cos(U_i, V_j)$ means
that the feature of item j does not appeal to user i's preference.

To better understand how cosine and norm work in the similarity approximation, we conduct the following experiment. We use the famous Epinions dataset
and sample it with different ratios 20%, 40%, 60% and 80% to construct training
set with different sparsity. For each training set, matrix factorization model is
trained. We calculate user average ratings and the U-norm $\|U_i\|$ for user i. For
each user average rating, we further compute the average of U-norm, thus forming the "User Average Rating"-"Average U-norm" graph in Figure 1(a). For example, a data point $(0.8, 0.9)$ means that for all users whose average ratings is 0.8,
their average U-norm is 0.9. The same goes for "Item Average Rating"-"Average
V-norm" graph in Figure 1(b). Then, for each training instance $\langle i, j, rating \rangle$, we
calculate the average cosine similarity $\cos(U_i, V_j)$ for each rating and draw the
"Rating"-"Average Cosine" graph in Figure 1(c). From Figure 1 we observe that
both vector norm and cosine similarity have a positive correlations with the ratings. A higher rating usually indicates a higher cosine similarity. Users and items
with higher average ratings tend to have higher vector norms. Also, we notice

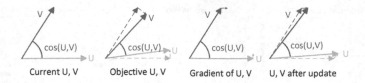

Fig. 2. Demonstration on how U_i and V_j change in the training process

that as data sparsity decreases, the cosine curve gets lower, while the U-norm and V-norm curves become steeper. We can draw 2 insights from the above observation:

1. *The focus of low-rank approximation shifts from cosine similarity to vector norm when more information comes.*
2. *In MF model, cosine and norm get trained in parallel, since the cosine similarity and vector norm change with the sparsity at the same time.*

Insight 1 is in consistent with how people make recommendation in their daily life. For example, if we know that Bob has watched Star Wars and rated it 5-star, we may guess Bob is a Science-Fiction movie lover. This only one message gives us the basic direction of Bob's user latent vector. We name this process *direction identification*. Without further information, we still could not know how much he likes Sci-Fi. But if we get more Bob's rating history, we could depict Bob's the length of latent factor vector more precisely. We name this process *magnitude adjustment*. MF works in a similar way. For example, suppose MF has already learned that Bob likes watching Star Wars. If it is told that Bob often watches Sci-Fi movie and gives them high ratings, the angle of U_{Bob} stays the same, while the norm inclines to fit the high ratings. If it further knows that he watches thrill movie too, the direction of U_{Bob} deviates from V_{Sci_Fi}, and their cosine similarity declines. To make up for the loss of cosine, the norm of U_{Bob} increases. The only problem of MF resides at the very beginning, where MF starts to do *direction identification*. According to insight 2, MF trains cosine and norm in parallel, which means that it processes *direction identification* and *magnitude adjustment* simultaneously. During the *direction identification* (cosine training), the magnitudes of U_i and V_j both get adjusted to make up the approximation error. Figure 2 demonstrates the above situation. If data is sparse, e.g., only one training instance is related to U_i or V_j, the cosine similarity could not get enough training (under-fitted) while norm gets too much training (over-fitted).

4 Cosine Matrix Factorization

4.1 Motivation

As we mention in chapter 3, norm represents the macroscopic strength of user/item vectors. Such corpus-wide information cannot be estimated accurately if data is sparse. While cosine similarity indicates the microscopic inter-action of user i to item j. Even only one rating given by user i to item j can also give the preference direction of him/her (but not the strengths). This motivates us to focus on cosine similarity approximation at the first stage and norm approximation at the second stage.

4.2 Direction Identification: Factorization with Cosine Similarity

We focus on *direction identification* by eliminating norm of U and V from (1):

$$R_{i,j} = \frac{U_i V_j^T}{\|U_i\| \|V_j\|} = \cos(U_i, V_j) \tag{4}$$

which means that the task of the low-rank factorization from answering "what rating user i will give item j" to an easier question "how likely user i interacts with item j". The objective function of (4) is:

$$\mathcal{L} = \min_{U,V} \sum_{i=1}^{n} \sum_{j=1}^{m} I_{i,j}(R_{i,j} - \frac{U_i V_j^T}{\|U_i\| \|V_j\|})^2 + \frac{\lambda_u}{2} \sum_{i=1}^{n} \|U_i\|_{Frob}^2 + \frac{\lambda_v}{2} \sum_{j=1}^{m} \|V_j\|_{Frob}^2 \tag{5}$$

This objective function has no global optimal solution, yet a local minimal could be acquired by performing stochastic gradient descent. The derivation of U_i and V_j are given by the following two equations:

$$\frac{\partial \mathcal{L}}{\partial U_i} = \sum_{j=1}^{m} I_{i,j}(R_{i,j} - \frac{U_i V_j^T}{\|U_i\| \|V_j\|})(\frac{V_j - \frac{U_i V_j^T}{U_i U_i^T} U_i}{\|U_i\| \|V_j\|}) + \lambda_u U_i \tag{6}$$

$$\frac{\partial \mathcal{L}}{\partial V_j} = -\sum_{i=1}^{n} I_{i,j}(R_{i,j} - \frac{U_i V_j^T}{\|U_i\| \|V_j\|})(\frac{U_i - \frac{U_i V_j^T}{V_j V_j^T} V_j}{\|U_i\| \|V_j\|}) + \lambda_v V_j \tag{7}$$

The purpose of this step is to train U_i and V_j to capture the detail of $U - V$ interactions microscopically, thus avoiding the under-fitting of cosine similarity in the ordinary MF methods.

4.3 Magnitude Adjustment: Compensating with Traditional MF

The above cosine based model discards the magnitude information of U_i and V_j, which means that it loses the ability to describe U_i and V_j with detailed preference/attraction strengths. Thus, for most non-sparse users/items, the performance of the above model should not be better than the traditional MF. To compensate the limitations of them, we separately train these two models, and ensemble their respective results through linear combination. That is to say, there are two user preference vectors, U_i for MF, U_i' for cosine-based model, and two item feature vectors, V_j for MF, V_j' for cosine-based model. U_i and V_j are trained by stochastic gradient descent using the following equations:

$$\frac{\partial \mathcal{L}}{\partial U_i} = -\sum_{j=1}^{m} I_{i,j}(R_{i,j} - U_i V_j^T) V_j + \lambda_u U_i \tag{8}$$

$$\frac{\partial \mathcal{L}}{\partial V_j} = -\sum_{i=1}^{n} I_{i,j}(R_{i,j} - U_i V_j{}^T)U_i + \lambda_v V_j \tag{9}$$

The final predicted rating $\hat{R}_{i,j}$ is given by:

$$\hat{R}_{i,j} = \alpha U_i V_j{}^T + (1-\alpha)\cos(U_i', V_j') \tag{10}$$

where α is the weight balance parameter between MF and the cosine-based model. When $\alpha = 1$, the model degenerates into the traditional MF. When $\alpha = 0$, the model discards all magnitudes method. Notice that α does not take part in the training process, and could be adjusted and fixed by cross-validation afterwards.

5   Experiments

5.1   Datasets

CosMF requires the original rating dataset only. Hence, this model could be used in most of the recommendation system. We use 4 datasets to testify the effectiveness of our model.

Epinions[1] Epinions.com is a well-known web site where customers could read and post reviews on a variety of items. Each review relates to a rating ranging from 1 to 5. This dataset is issued in [6]. It consists of 40,163 users, 139,738 items and totally 664,824 ratings.

Douban[2] Douban.com is a Chinese web site where users could share their interests on films, books, music and events by scoring the items (ranging from 1 to 5). This dataset is crawled and shared by Ma et al. [17]. It consists of 129,490 users, 58541 items and 16,830,839 ratings.

Flixster[3] Flixster.com is a web site where users can rate movies. The ratings are in the range of [0.5, 5] with step size 0.5. After eliminating invalid users and items, the dataset contains 787,214 users, 48,795 items and 8,196,077 ratings.

MovieLens10M[4] MovieLens10M consists of 10,000,054 ratings and 95,580 tags of 71,567 users for 10,681 movies. The preference of the user for a movie is rated from 1 to 5 and 0 indicates that the movie is not rated by any user.

The Douban, Flixster and MovieLens10M are all dense datasets. We lower the sample ratio of training set, manually creating more sparse users/items. This would provide us more test cases for each sparse user/item. For Douban, Flixster and MovieLens10M, 20% and 40% sampling are applied. Epinions is sparse enough, so we only sample 80% as training set.

We use $\mathcal{U}_t$ to denote the set of users who have rated no more than t items, $\mathcal{I}_t$ to denote the set of items which have been rated by no more than t users.

---

[1] http://www.trustlet.org/wiki/Epinions_datasets
[2] https://www.cse.cuhk.edu.hk/irwin.king/pub/data/douban
[3] http://www.sfu.ca/sja25/datasets/
[4] http://files.grouplens.org/datasets/movielens/ml-10m.zip

Table 1. Description of the datasets

Statistics	Epinions 80% sampling	Douban 20% sampling	40% sampling	Flixster 20% sampling	40% sampling	MovieLens10M 20% sampling	40% sampling
Train set sparsity	9.47e-5	4.44e-4	8.88e-4	4.27e-5	8.53e-5	2.92e-4	5.85e-4
$|\mathcal{U}_{t=1}|$	18665	15237	8577	729120	709037	2137	1693
$|\mathcal{U}_{t=1}|/|U|$	37.87%	11.77%	6.624%	92.62%	90.07%	2.986%	2.366%
$|\mathcal{I}_{t=1}|$	87596	30472	23877	28057	21407	55386	54907
$|\mathcal{I}_{t=1}|/|I|$	62.69%	52.05%	40.79%	57.50%	43.87%	85.04%	84.30%
$|\mathcal{R}_{t=1}^{train}|$	78225	18142	16806	42218	46664	883	283
$|\mathcal{R}_{t=1}^{train}|/|R^{train}|$	14.71%	0.539%	0.249 %	2.575%	1.423 %	0.044%	0.007%
$|\mathcal{R}_{t=1}^{test}|$	30716	158111	50459	304895	134052	15698	1329
$|\mathcal{R}_{t=1}^{test}|/|R^{test}|$	23.10%	0.0117%	0.005 %	0.047%	0.027 %	0.002%	2e-4%

$\mathcal{R}_t = \{R_{i,j} | i \in \mathcal{U}_t \vee j \in \mathcal{I}_t\}$ is called the sparse set. $\mathcal{R}_1$ is used in the following test to evaluate the performance of MF and CosMF on sparse users/items.

Finally we constructed 7 datasets in total, and each dataset has its sparse set. These datasets are in various sparsity, and should be sufficient to give us an overview of the performance. Basic descriptions of all datasets could be found in Table 1. From Table 1 we can see that all these datasets are extremely sparse (sparsity below 0.1%). Epinions and Flixster are extremely sparse both in user and item. In Epinions, sparse instances can even takes up to 15% of the whole training set. Douban and MovieLens10M are dense in user while sparse in item.

5.2 Metrics

We adopt two widely used evaluation metrics for our experiment, the Mean Absolute Error (MAE) and the Root Mean Square Error (RMSE):

$$MAE = \frac{\sum_{i,j} \left| R_{ij} - \tilde{R}_{ij} \right|}{|T_E|} \qquad RMSE = \sqrt{\frac{\sum_{i,j} \left(R_{ij} - \tilde{R}_{ij} \right)^2}{|T_E|}}$$

where $R_{i,j}$ denotes the rating user i gives to item j, $\tilde{R}_{i,j}$ denotes the predict rating for user i with item j, $|T_E|$ is the amount of ratings in test dataset. By definition, smaller MAE and RMSE are better.

5.3 Baseline and Parameters

To the best of our knowledge, we are the first one to attempt to improve Matrix Factorization from information retrieval perspective in extremely sparse datasets without auxiliary data. Other methods either use auxiliary data, or do not address the sparsity problem (especially for users and items with only one training data). So we only use method proposed by Koren et al. in [9] as the evaluation baseline.

Table 2. Performances on different datasets with $\alpha = 0.5$

Dataset	Cold Set				Whole			
	MF		CosMF		MF		CosMF	
	MAE	RMSE	MAE	RMSE	MAE	RMSE	MAE	RMSE
Epinions 80%			**0.9125**	**1.1175**			**0.8445**	**1.078**
	1.098	1.3115	*16.89%*	*14.79%*	0.894	1.143	*5.54%*	*5.69%*
Douban 20%			**0.742**	**0.9165**			**0.591**	**0.7455**
	0.99	1.2065	*25.05%*	*24.04%*	0.594	0.752	*0.51%*	*0.86%*
Douban 40%			**0.751**	**0.928**			**0.573**	**0.723**
	1.031	1.2475	*27.16%*	*25.61%*	0.5775	0.7315	*0.78%*	*1.16%*
Flixster 20%			**0.869**	**1.0965**			**0.6855**	**0.906**
	1.0015	1.2305	*13.23%*	*10.89%*	0.702	0.932	*2.35%*	*2.79%*
Flixster 40%			**0.8815**	**1.1105**			**0.6505**	**0.8665**
	1.0045	1.2355	*12.24%*	*10.12%*	0.66	0.884	*1.44%*	*1.98%*
MovieLens 20%			**0.81**	**1.0365**			**0.6755**	**0.874**
	0.855	1.085	*5.26%*	*4.47%*	0.685	0.8895	*1.39%*	*1.74%*
MovieLens 40%			**0.7375**	**0.9395**			**0.638**	**0.8285**
	0.894	1.112	*17.51%*	*15.51%*	0.6465	0.8415	*1.31%*	*1.54%*

For each of the training set, we compare MF with CosMF on sparse set as well as the whole set. Different numbers of latent factors k settings $\{5, 10, 15, 20\}$, and different balance parameter α $\{0.0\text{-}1.0, 0.01$ each step$\}$ are tried. The learning rate of the stochastic gradient descent is set to 0.03, and the regularization parameter λ_u, λ_v are set to 0.001 empirically. Each method is repeated 3 times, and the average MAE and RMSE are reported. Each experiment iterates until its objective function converges.

5.4 Performance

The experiment results using $\alpha = 0.5$ are shown in Table 2. The standard deviations of the results are all around 0.002. Best result are highlighted in bold style. From the results, we observe that the proposed CosMF consistently outperform the original MF in both cold set and the whole set. Percentages in italic are the improvement of CosMF over the original MF. Due to the higher sparse test set ratio, the improvement on whole set of Epinions is much higher than others.

5.5 Parameter Sensitivity

We investigate the parameter sensitivity of dimension k and weight balance factor α by varying their values and demonstrate the results in Figure 3 and Figure 4.

As Figure 3 shows, on Epinions 80%, performance of MF and CosMF both improve as k goes bigger. While on Douban 40%, Flixster 40% and MovieLens10M 40%, MF starts to perform bad when k get even bigger, while CosMF almost stays the same. The reason for this is that as k goes up, the norms of U_i and V_j also tend to become bigger, and impact of magnitude grows stronger, making the model more vulnerable to over-fitting. CosMF relies less on the magnitude and does not get over-fitted easily. Douban 20%, Flixster 20% and MovieLens10M are too sparse that models trained on them over-fit at the very beginning. Increasing k only makes things worse.

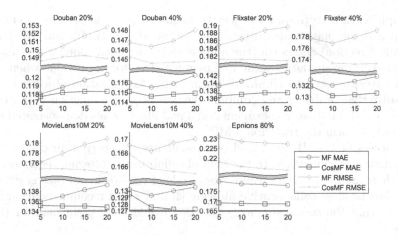

Fig. 3. Impact of dimension of latent factors on different datasets

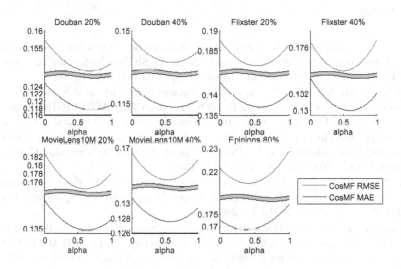

Fig. 4. Impact $of \alpha$ on different datasets

Figure 4 shows the impact of α. When $\alpha = 0$, we discard all magnitude information, resulting in performance worse than the original MF. When $\alpha = 1$, it becomes the traditional MF. α around 0.5 always give the best result, which means that we should neither rely too much on the magnitude(norm) information, nor directly ignore and discard it.

6   Conclusion and Future Work

In this paper, we focused on the sparsity problem in collaborative filtering recommender system without the help of auxiliary data. Based on the observation that people learn features of an object through two process, the direction identification and the magnitude adjustment, we found that traditional MF trains cosine (the direction) and norm (the magnitude) in parallel, which would lead to under-fitted cosine similarity value and over-fitted vector norm value when data is sparse. We proposed to eliminate norm in the factorization objective function to solve that problem, and combine the new objective function with MF to form the CosMF method. Experiments on 4 real life datasets demonstrated that CosMF out-perform the traditional MF.

The success of CosMF increased our confidence to incorporate cosine similarity in matrix factorization. In the field of collaborative filtering recommender system, there are many scenes where magnitude of vectors do not matter greatly, such as the one-class collaborative filtering [4] and social recommendation [17]. We believe that the cosine similarity function would be of great help for those problems.

References

1. Ma, H., King, I., Lyu, M.R.: Learning to recommend with social trust ensemble. In: Proceedings of the 32nd International ACM SIGIR Conference on Research and Development in Information Retrieval, pp. 203–210. ACM (2009)
2. Konstas, I., Stathopoulos, V., Jose, J.M.: On social networks and collaborative recommendation. In: Proceedings of the 32nd International ACM SIGIR Conference on Research and Development in Information Retrieval, pp. 195–202. ACM (2009)
3. Sarwar, B., Karypis, G., Konstan, J., Riedl, J.: Item-based collaborative filtering recommendation algorithms. In: Proceedings of the 10th International Conference on World Wide Web, pp. 285–295. ACM (2001)
4. Pan, R., Zhou, Y., Cao, B., Liu, N.N., Lukose, R., Scholz, M., Yang, Q.: One-class collaborative filtering. In: Eighth IEEE International Conference on Data Mining, ICDM 2008, pp. 502–511. IEEE (2008)
5. Jamali, M., Ester, M.: Trustwalker: a random walk model for combining trust-based and item-based recommendation. In: Proceedings of the 15th ACM SIGKDD International Conference on Knowledge Discovery and Data Mining, pp. 397–406. ACM (2009)
6. Massa, P., Avesani, P.: Trust-aware bootstrapping of recommender systems. In: ECAI Workshop on Recommender Systems, pp. 29–33. Citeseer (2006)
7. Shi, J., Long, M., Liu, Q., Ding, G., Wang, J.: Twin bridge transfer learning for sparse collaborative filtering. In: Pei, J., Tseng, V.S., Cao, L., Motoda, H., Xu, G. (eds.) PAKDD 2013, Part I. LNCS, vol. 7818, pp. 496–507. Springer, Heidelberg (2013)
8. Salakhutdinov, R., Mnih, A.: Probabilistic matrix factorization. NIPS 1, 2–1 (2007)
9. Koren, Y., Bell, R., Volinsky, C.: Matrix factorization techniques for recommender systems. Computer 42(8), 30–37 (2009)
10. Zhang, W., Ding, G., Chen, L., Li, C.: Augmenting chinese online video recommendations by using virtual ratings predicted by review sentiment classification. In: 2010 IEEE International Conference on Data Mining Workshops (ICDMW), pp. 1143–1150. IEEE (2010)

11. Jamali, M., Ester, M.: A transitivity aware matrix factorization model for recommendation in social networks. In: Proceedings of the Twenty-Second International Joint Conference on Artificial Intelligence, vol. 3, pp. 2644–2649. AAAI Press (2011)
12. Pan, W., Liu, N.N., Xiang, E.W., Yang, Q.: Transfer learning to predict missing ratings via heterogeneous user feedbacks. In: Proceedings of the Twenty-Second International Joint Conference on Artificial Intelligence, vol. 3, pp. 2318–2323. AAAI Press (2011)
13. Ma, H., King, I., Lyu, M.R.: Learning to recommend with explicit and implicit social relations. ACM Transactions on Intelligent Systems and Technology (TIST) 2(3), 29 (2011)
14. Ma, H., Yang, H., Lyu, M.R., King, I.: Sorec: social recommendation using probabilistic matrix factorization. In: Proceedings of the 17th ACM Conference on Information and Knowledge Management, pp. 931–940. ACM (2008)
15. Ma, H., Lyu, M.R., King, I.: Learning to recommend with trust and distrust relationships. In: Proceedings of the Third ACM Conference on Recommender Systems, pp. 189–196. ACM (2009)
16. Shen, Y., Jin, R.: Learning personal+ social latent factor model for social recommendation. In: Proceedings of the 18th ACM SIGKDD International Conference on Knowledge Discovery and Data Mining, pp. 1303–1311. ACM (2012)
17. Ma, H., Zhou, D., Liu, C., Lyu, M.R., King, I.: Recommender systems with social regularization. In: Proceedings of the Fourth ACM International Conference on Web Search and Data Mining, pp. 287–296. ACM (2011)
18. Gu, Q., Zhou, J.: Neighborhood preserving nonnegative matrix factorization. In: BMVC, pp. 1–10 (2009)
19. Gu, Q., Zhou, J., Ding, C.H.: Collaborative filtering: Weighted nonnegative matrix factorization incorporating user and item graphs. In: SDM, pp. 199–210. SIAM (2010)
20. Liu, N.N., Cao, B., Zhao, M., Yang, Q.: Adapting neighborhood and matrix factorization models for context aware recommendation. In: Proceedings of the Workshop on Context-Aware Movie Recommendation, pp. 7–13. ACM (2010)
21. Lee, D.D., Seung, H.S.: Algorithms for non-negative matrix factorization. In: Advances in Neural Information Processing Systems, pp. 556–562 (2000)
22. Srebro, N., Jaakkola, T., et al.: Weighted low-rank approximations. In: ICML, vol. 3, pp. 720–727 (2003)
23. Zhang, S., Wang, W., Ford, J., Makedon, F.: Learning from incomplete ratings using non-negative matrix factorization. In: SDM. SIAM (2006)
24. Takács, G., Pilászy, I., Németh, B., Tikk, D.: Investigation of various matrix factorization methods for large recommender systems. In: IEEE International Conference on Data Mining Workshops, ICDMW 2008, pp. 553–562. IEEE (2008)
25. Takács, G., Pilászy, I., Németh, B., Tikk, D.: Matrix factorization and neighbor based algorithms for the netflix prize problem. In: Proceedings of the 2008 ACM Conference on Recommender Systems, pp. 267–274. ACM (2008)

Recommendation Based on Frequent N-adic Concepts

Di Wang and Jun Ma

School of Computer Science and Technology, Shandong University, 250101 Jinan, China
wangdi2044@sina.com, majun@sdu.edu.cn

Abstract. In social networks, many users tend to share items such as movies, books, songs and images by rating them with a series of discrete numbers or annotating them with a set of tags. Clearly, there are some semantic relationships among the users, items, ratings, tags and other information. Most of the past works only focused on some ternary relationships such as users-items-ratings or users-items-tags to make recommendations. But the ternary relationships which do not make good use of the given information are insufficient to provide accurate recommendations. In this paper, we propose a novel recommendation method based on frequent n-adic concepts which can mine the hidden conceptualization in the relationships. If there are tags, we model the relationships into the quadruples <users, items, ratings, tags> and if there are no tags, we also have some other information and model the relationships into the quintuples <users, items, ratings, contexts, features>. Experimental results on MovieLens dataset demonstrate that our method has shown a significant improvement over the state-of-the-art recommendation approaches in terms of precision.

Keywords: Recommendation, Frequent N-adic Concepts, Tags, Contexts.

1 Introduction

With the explosion growth of information available on the World Wide Web, we are flooded with a lot of information. Therefore, the information filtering techniques such as recommender systems have become more and more popular. Recommender systems attempt to provide the best options matching the users' interests and have been used in various applications, such as Amazon and Last.fm.

In the times of Web 2.0, people have two ways to express their opinions on items. One is that the users are allowed to rate items with numbers within a certain range. This forms a structure that consists of three sets U, I, R as well as a ternary relation among them, where U, I and R are the sets of users, items and ratings respectively. The user's preferences for an item can be reflected by the ratings. Another is that the users can label diverse items with freely chosen tags. The resulting structure is folksonomy [3, 16] which consists of three sets U, I, T and a ternary relation among them, where T is the set of tags. Some tags such as "aliens" or "shark attacks" can represent the items' contents and some tags such as "excellent" or "overrated" may implicitly reflect the user's preferences. Many existing recommender systems including rating-based

L. Chen et al. (Eds.): APWeb 2014, LNCS 8709, pp. 318–330, 2014.

and tag-based methods use only ternary relationships to derive their recommendations. The main difference is that the rating-based methods [2, 6, 13] usually utilize
the users-items-ratings relationships while the tag-based methods [7, 20, 21] make use
of the users-items-tags relationships to generate recommendations.

However, the recommendations based on ternary relationships may be inaccurate
because they only use a portion of the given information. Users may annotate the
same tags for an item but give different ratings on it. Items may have multiple tags
indicating their different facets and users could give different ratings on the same item
based on different facets that they care. Table 1 shows an example of ternary relationships. Both u_1 and u_2 have labeled i_1 with the same tag "comedy". However, u_2 likes i_1
but u_1 does not. User u_1 has rated i_2 with high score while u_2 has given low rating.
Maybe i_2 is a good thriller movie for u_1 and not a good love movie for u_2. Hence using
rating or tag information alone is insufficient.

Table 1. An example of ternary and quaternary relationships

users-items-tags			users-items-ratings			users-items-tags-ratings			
U	I	T	U	I	R	U	I	T	R
u_1	i_1	comedy	u_1	i_1	1	u_1	i_1	comedy	1
u_1	i_2	thriller	u_1	i_2	5	u_1	i_2	thriller	5
u_2	i_1	comedy	u_2	i_1	5	u_2	i_1	comedy	5
u_2	i_2	love	u_2	i_2	1	u_2	i_2	love	1

Actually, we can merge the original ternary relationships and form a new quaternary relationship. The quaternary relationships <users, items, ratings, tags> can reveal
more information that cannot be obtained in ternary relationships. Although the method in [5] groups the quaternary relationships among users, items, ratings and tags as
a 4-order tensor, it costs too much time and memory to learn the model.

Except for the quaternary relationships, other information such as contexts and user's features can also be used. The information of contexts which is associated with
the user-item interaction [1] has been recognized as an important factor in recommender systems. The contexts could be the location or the time of the interaction happens. Obviously, we can significantly improve the recommendation accuracy compared to the methods solely based on user-item interactions [1, 13, 17]. In addition,
the information of user's features such as gender, age and profession is also important. Users play an important role in the social networks and the process of item sharing is accomplished by the users. Therefore, we can get high quality recommendations when adding user's features [4, 11].

In this paper, we propose a novel recommendation method based on frequent n-
adic concepts. The frequent n-adic concepts can reveal the shared conceptualization
hidden in the non-formalized data [9]. We design two different methods that consist
of the quadruples <users, items, ratings, tags> and the quintuples <users, items, ratings, contexts, features> corresponding to the models with tags and without tags respectively. We group the quadruples into structures called 4-adic concepts and simi-

larly the quintuples into 5-adic concepts. A possible 4-adic concept can be: "some users give the same ratings and tags to some movies" and the hidden conceptualization is that the users with similar interests tend to have same preference for similar items. We also devise two different item recommendation algorithms when we get the concepts. The experimental results on a large MovieLens dataset show that our method outperforms the state-of-the-art algorithms in terms of accuracy.

2   Related Work

In this section, we review several major approaches for recommender systems, especially for rating-based and tag-based methods.

Collaborative Filtering (CF) is one of the most widely used rating-based methods. CF algorithms mainly focus on the user-item rating matrix and can be divided into two types, i.e. memory-based approaches [2, 6, 12, 15] and model-based approaches [8, 18, 19, 25].

Except for rating-based methods, some works also focus on the recommendations based on tags. In [7], Diederich et al. proposed to create user profiles using the tags associated with some specified objects. These tag based profiles are used to find the neighbors with similar interests based on some similarity measure. In [22], the authors presented a generic method that incorporates tags to CF algorithms. They first reduce the ternary relationships users-items-tags to three binary relationships including users-items, users-tags and items-tags. Then, they design a fusion mechanism to capture the ternary relationships. The work in [20] predicted user's preferences for items based on their inferred preferences for tags. Symeonidis et al. in [21] developed a framework to model the ternary relationships users-items-tags into a 3-order tensor and perform a dimensionality reduction for recommendation.

Recently, some works based on quaternary relationships have emerged. In [5], the authors proposed a unified framework based on quaternary semantic analysis. They model the quaternary relationships among users, items, ratings and tags as a 4-order tensor and cast the problem as a multi-way latent semantic analysis problem. A Higher-Order Singular Value Decomposition (HOSVD) is applied in the 4-order tensor to reveal the latent semantics among the four entities. The time complexity is quartic in the size of the latent dimensions and the space complexity is $O(|U| \times |I| \times |R| \times |T|)$. Although they model the quaternary relationships as a 4-order tensor, it needs more running time and memory to learn the model. The authors in [11] gave a personalized recommendation method based on user's profiles in folksonomies. They suggest a quaternary relationship <users, items, tags, profiles> which considers the user's profiles as a new dimension of a folksonomy and make recommendations matching user's profiles rather than popular ones. But they ignore the information of ratings which represent most of a user's tastes.

3   Frequent N-adic Concepts

In order to discover the shared conceptualizations hidden in the relationships, we introduce the notion of n-adic concepts [23]. We first present the notion of n-adic context[1].

A formal context consists of a set of objects, a set of attributes and a binary relation between the two sets. This framework means that the objects have the attributes. Many models are proposed which are inspired by the use of this framework for data analysis. This setting has been extended in [24] to a triadic context that consists of three sets and a ternary relation among them. These three sets are objects, attributes and conditions and the ternary relation means that the objects have the attributes under the conditions. Based on the notions mentioned above, we now generalize to an n-adic context.

Definition 1. (n-adic context) [23] An n-adic context is an (n+1)-tuple $K = (\mathcal{K}_1, \mathcal{K}_2, \ldots, \mathcal{K}_n, Y)$, where $\mathcal{K}_1, \mathcal{K}_2, \ldots, \mathcal{K}_n$ are finite entity sets and Y is an n-ary relation among $\mathcal{K}_1, \mathcal{K}_2, \ldots, \mathcal{K}_n$, i.e., $Y \subseteq \mathcal{K}_1 \times \mathcal{K}_2 \times \ldots \times \mathcal{K}_n$.

Table 2 shows an example of an n-adic context when n=3, which are also known as folksonomy. According to the table we can see that the 3-adic context $K = (\mathcal{U}, I, \mathcal{T}, Y)$ includes three sets $\mathcal{U} = \{u_1, u_2, u_3, u_4\}$, $I = \{i_1, i_2, i_3, i_4\}$ and $\mathcal{T} = \{t_1, t_2, t_3\}$. $Y \subseteq \mathcal{U} \times I \times \mathcal{T}$ and each $y \in Y$ can be represented by a triple: $y = \{(u, i, t) \mid u \in \mathcal{U}, i \in I, t \in \mathcal{T}\}$. Each triple indicates an item sharing process that a user u from $\mathcal{U}$ labels an item i from I with a tag t from $\mathcal{T}$. For example, the user u_1 has tagged the item i_1 with tags t_1, t_2 and t_3, and the items i_2, i_3 and i_4 with tags t_2 and t_3. We can also see that both u_1 and u_2 have tagged the items i_3 and i_4 with tags t_2 and t_3.

Table 2. An example of an n-adic context

I	i_1			i_2			i_3			i_4		
$\mathcal{U}/\mathcal{T}$	t_1	t_2	t_3	t_1	t_2	t_3	t_1	t_2	t_3	t_1	t_2	t_3
u_1	1	1	1		1	1		1	1		1	1
u_2	1		1	1	1		1	1	1	1	1	1
u_3		1		1	1	1	1	1		1		1
u_4	1		1	1	1		1	1		1	1	1

We now define an n-adic concept.

Definition 2. (n-adic concept) [23] An n-adic concept of an n-adic context $K = (\mathcal{K}_1, \mathcal{K}_2, \ldots, \mathcal{K}_n, Y)$ is an n-tuple $(A_1, A_2, \ldots, A_n)$ with $A_i \subseteq \mathcal{K}_i$, $i = 1, 2, \ldots, n$, and $A_1 \times A_2 \times \ldots \times A_n \subseteq Y$ such that the n-tuple $(A_1, A_2, \ldots, A_n)$ is maximal, i.e. none of these sets can be extended without shrinking one of the other dimensions.

---

[1]   This context is a framework for data analysis and is different from the context which is associated with the user-item interaction in context-aware recommendation.

Table 3. An example of an n-adic concept

U	I	T
u_1	i_1	t_1, t_2, t_3
u_1	i_1, i_2, i_3, i_4	t_2, t_3
u_2	i_1, i_3, i_4	t_1, t_3
u_1, u_2	i_3, i_4	t_2, t_3
u_1, u_2, u_3	i_1, i_2, i_3	t_2
...	...	...

Table 3 shows an example of a portion of the n-adic concept of the n-adic context in Table 2. If there are no restrictions, we will have a lot of n-adic concepts from the given n-adic context. These n-adic concepts are highly redundant and it is hard to find the most important information. In order to obtain a condensed representation and keep the most significant ones, we impose some restrictions on each dimension of the context with minimum thresholds.

Problem 1. (Mining all frequent n-adic concepts) Let $K = (\mathcal{K}_1, \mathcal{K}_2,..., \mathcal{K}_n, Y)$ be an n-adic context and $minsupp_1$, $minsupp_2$, ..., $minsupp_n$ be the user-defined minimum thresholds. The task of mining all frequent n-adic concepts consists in determining all n-adic concepts $(A_1, A_2,..., A_n)$ of K with $|A_i| \geqslant minsupp_i$, $i = 1,2,...,n$.

After setting the thresholds, the n-adic concepts we get are called frequent. For example, in Table 2, if we set $minsupp_u = 2$, $minsupp_i = 2$ and $minsupp_t = 2$. Then, we can extract three frequent 3-adic concepts such as $\{(u_1, u_2), (i_3, i_4), (t_2, t_3)\}$, $\{(u_2, u_3, u_4), (i_2, i_3), (t_1, t_2)\}$, $\{(u_2, u_4), (i_1, i_4), (t_1, t_3)\}$. It is important to note that the extracted representation of n-adic concepts is very dense and it can represent the most of the original information [10]. We can easily find the latent conceptualizations from the frequent n-adic concepts.

4   Recommendation Models

After the introduction to the background of the n-adic concepts, in this section, we present our recommendation methods.

We design two different methods including the models with tags and without tags. Actually, most of the social networks aim at a specific application and some allow the users to give ratings on items while others let the users label the items with tags. Therefore, the forms of information in different networks are different. In most social networks, the process of item rating is very easy for the users while item tagging is a little complicated. This is why the information of ratings is a little more than the tags in most of the networks. We provide a framework that consists of two different models so that the recommendations will be more accurate.

4.1   Models with Tags

Existing recommender systems only use the ternary relationships such as users-items-ratings or users-items-tags. However, both ratings and tags are necessary and we will miss important information if lacking any one of them. We now present the models with tags and introduce the quadruples <users, items, ratings, tags>.

We have introduced the notion of n-adic context and the 4-adic context is a special case when n=4. The 4-adic context is a quintuple $K = (\mathcal{U}, \mathcal{I}, \mathcal{R}, \mathcal{T}, Y)$, where $\mathcal{U}, \mathcal{I}, \mathcal{R}$ and $\mathcal{T}$ are finite sets that represent users, items, ratings and tags respectively. $Y \subseteq \mathcal{U} \times \mathcal{I} \times \mathcal{R} \times \mathcal{T}$ and each $y \in Y$ can be represented by a quadruple: $y = \{(u, i, r, t) \mid u \in \mathcal{U}, i \in \mathcal{I}, r \in \mathcal{R}, t \in \mathcal{T}\}$ which denotes that a user u gives the rating r and provides the tag t to an item i if s/he has watched i before.

Similarly, the 4-adic concept is also a special case of n-adic concept when n=4. The 4-adic concept of a 4-adic context $K = (\mathcal{U}, \mathcal{I}, \mathcal{R}, \mathcal{T}, Y)$ is a quadruple (U, I, R, T) with $U \subseteq \mathcal{U}, I \subseteq \mathcal{I}, R \subseteq \mathcal{R}, T \subseteq \mathcal{T}$ and $U \times I \times R \times T \subseteq Y$ such that the quadruple (U, I, R, T) is maximal. Then, we set the thresholds and get frequent 4-adic concepts. We refer to the obtained frequent 4-adic concepts as F4C.

4.2   Models without Tags

Tags are not always available in different social networks even if the information of tags is very useful. Therefore, we consider the models without tags.

Although there is no tag information, we have access to some additional information, such as contexts and user's features. Contextual information has proved to be valuable for providing more accurate predictions in various application domains [17] including recommender systems [1, 13]. The contextual information is associated with the user-item interaction and could be the location or the time of the interaction. The user's features such as gender, age and profession greatly increase the accuracy of personalized recommendation.

After adding the information of contexts and user's features, we introduce the quintuples <users, items, ratings, contexts, features>. Similarly, when n=5, we can get 5-adic context $K = (\mathcal{U}, \mathcal{I}, \mathcal{R}, \mathcal{C}, \mathcal{F}, Y)$, where $\mathcal{U}, \mathcal{I}, \mathcal{R}, \mathcal{C}$ and $\mathcal{F}$ are finite sets representing users, items, ratings, contexts and user's features respectively and $Y \subseteq \mathcal{U} \times \mathcal{I} \times \mathcal{R} \times \mathcal{C} \times \mathcal{F}$. The 5-adic concept of a 5-adic context $K = (\mathcal{U}, \mathcal{I}, \mathcal{R}, \mathcal{C}, \mathcal{F}, Y)$ is a quintuple (U, I, R, C, F) with $U \subseteq \mathcal{U}, I \subseteq \mathcal{I}, R \subseteq \mathcal{R}, C \subseteq \mathcal{C}, F \subseteq \mathcal{F}$ and $U \times I \times R \times C \times F \subseteq Y$ such that the quintuple (U, I, R, C, F) is maximal. We refer to the obtained frequent 5-adic concepts as F5C.

In order to mine all frequent 4-adic or 5-adic concepts from the given 4-adic or 5-adic context, we apply the QUADRICONS [10] which is one of the existing algorithms in the literature. We take the 4-adic or 5-adic context as well as minimum thresholds as input and output the set of F4C or F5C fulfilling these thresholds.

4.3   Recommendation Algorithms Based on Frequent N-adic Concepts

After obtaining the frequent 4-adic or 5-adic concepts, we design two recommendation algorithms corresponding to the models with tags or without tags respectively.

Algorithm 1. Recommendation based on F4C

Input:

1. F4C: the set of frequent 4-adic concepts
2. a user u and the set of tags T that u has used to label items which s/he likes
3. N: the number of recommended items

Output:

RI: the set of top-N recommended items

1: **For each** 4-adic concept $f4c \in$ F4C
2:      **For each** $tag \in f4c.t$
3:        **If** $tag \in T$
4:          RI = RI $\cup$ $f4c.i$;
5:          Count the occurrences of $f4c.i$;
6:        **End**
7:      **End**
8: **End**
9: Keep the most frequent N items in RI;
10: **Return** RI;

The pseudo code of the algorithm with tags is sketched by Algorithm 1. It takes a set of frequent 4-adic concepts F4C, a user u, a set of tags T, a number N as input and outputs a set of top-N recommended items. We assume that a user likes a movie if s/he has given a top rating to the item. T is the set of tags that u has used to label items which s/he likes. The algorithm runs the set of frequent 4-adic concepts to find those where the tags in F4C belongs to T. Then, we count the occurrences of the items in each 4-adic concept that we have found and return the most frequent N items.

Algorithm 2 shows the pseudo code of the algorithm without tags. It takes F5C, a user u with features f, a number N as input and outputs a set of top-N recommended items. The set of recommended items has two parts and one is determined by the user's features and the other by the relevant user's tastes. First, we find the items from F5C corresponding to u's features. Then, we run the set of frequent 5-adic concepts to find those where u belongs to and put the items which are liked by the users we have found in each 5-adic concept into the recommended set. Finally, we combine the two parts and return the most frequent N items.

Both Algorithm 1 and Algorithm 2 rely on frequent n-adic concepts. The process of the extraction of frequent n-adic concepts is an off-line phase and is only performed once. The time and space complexity of QUADRICONS are $O(N^2)$ and $O(N)$ respectively, where N is the number of item sharing interactions such as (u, i, r, t) or (u, i, r, c, f). Our algorithms do not cost a lot of time and can present recommendations timely.

Algorithm 2. Recommendation based on F5C

Input:
1. F5C: the set of frequent 5-adic concepts
2. a user u with features f
3. N: the number of recommended items

Output:
RI: the set of top-N recommended items
1: **For each** 5-adic concept $f5c \in$ F5C
2:      If $f \in f5c.f$
3:          RI = RI $\cup f5c.i$;
4:          Count the occurrences of $f5c.i$;
5:      **End**
6:      If $u \in f5c.u$
7:          **For each** user $u' \in f5c.u/u$ /* except u */
8:              RI = RI $\cup u'.likeditems$;
9:              Count the occurrences of $u'.likeditems$;
10:         **End**
11:     **End**
12: **End**
13: Keep the most frequent N items in RI;
14: **Return** RI;

5   Experiment

In this section, we conduct several experiments to compare our models with existing methods. We first give a detail description of the datasets and protocol that are used in the experiments. Then, we evaluate the recommendation performance of our two models and give a detail analysis of the impact of minimum thresholds.

5.1   Experimental Setup

For this research, we use the MovieLens[2] dataset which is publicly available[3]. MovieLens is a recommender system and virtual community website where users can share movies with ratings and tags. The users can receive recommended movies that matching their own interests. This dataset consists of two parts. The first part contains the users' ratings with a scale of 0.5 to 5 on different movies and the second part contains the users' tags on different movies. This dataset contains 2113 users who have rated or labeled 10197 different items. There are 855598 ratings and 47957 tag assignments using 13222 tags. According to the models we have proposed, after conducting a combination and an extraction, we obtain 36885 quadruples <users, items, ratings, tags> and 855598 quintuples <users, items, ratings, contexts, features>. We use 90% of the data as the training set and the remaining 10% as the test set for each part.

---

[2] http://movielens.umn.edu/
[3] http://grouplens.org/

The evaluation metrics we use is the Hit Ratio [14, 5]. For each user u, we only consider the items s/he likes. So, we randomly choose one item i that has a rating of 5 and keep the tuples involving u and i. If the item i is among the top-N recommended items, we say that a hit has occurred. The hit ratio is defined as:

$$HitRatio = \frac{Number of hits}{|U|}.$$

5.2   Experiments on Recommendation with Tags

We first evaluate the precision of the proposed recommendation models with tags (F4C). We compare our method with the following approaches:

1. UCF: The user based collaborative filtering is a memory-based approach. It uses PCC to cluster similar users and recommends items based on these similar users.
2. PMF [19]: This method is a state-of-the-art model based collaborative filtering algorithms. It just considers the user-item rating matrix using probabilistic matrix factorization for recommendations.
3. F3CR: This method focuses on ternary relationships users-items-ratings and uses frequent 3-adic concepts to make recommendations.
4. F3CT: Like F3CR, F3CT only utilizes the relationships of users-items-tags.
5. QSA [5]: The method of quadratic semantic analysis applies the HOSVD in the 4-order tensor to reveal the latent semantics among users, items, ratings and tags.

Fig. 1 shows the results of all comparison partners as we vary N. From the result, we can see that our model F4C significantly outperforms the other methods in terms of Hit Ratio and its advantage is more obvious when $N \geqslant 4$. This is because F4C can discover the shared conceptualizations hidden in the structure of the quadruples <users, items, ratings, tags>. Both F3CR and F3CT get worse results compared to F4C, which demonstrates that using tag or rating information alone is insufficient. We also notice that UCF and PMF obtain relatively worse results and we think this phenomenon is caused by two factors. One is that UCF and PMF only use user-item ratings and do not take the tags into consideration for collaborative filtering recommendations. The other is that both UCF and PMF aim at more accurate rating prediction, which does not necessarily lead to better top-N recommendation.

5.3   Experiments on Recommendation without Tags

In order to evaluate the performance of the models without tags (F5C), we first determine the additional information about contexts and user's features. Based on the information available in the datasets, we extract three types of contextual information: (1) period-of-day, i.e. which time period a rating is given, morning, afternoon or evening; (2) period-of-week, i.e. which day a rating is given, weekday or weekend; (3) category of the target item. We get two types of user's features: (1) level-of-activity, i.e. how many ratings s/he has rated; (2) habit-of-ratings, i.e. in which level her/his average ratings are, high, normal or low.

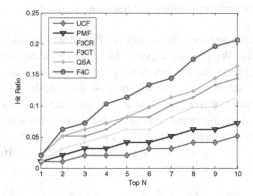

Fig. 1. Performance Comparison on Top-N Item Recommendations with Tags

Besides UCF, PMF and F3CR, we compare F5C with TF [13] which is a context-aware recommendation method based on tensor factorization.

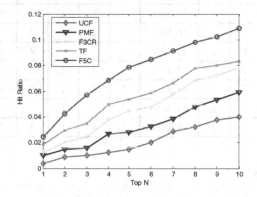

Fig. 2. Performance Comparison on Top-N Item Recommendation without Tags

Fig. 2 shows the performance of all comparison partners on Top-N item recommendations without tags. It is clear that F5C achieves a higher Hit Ratio compared to other methods. UCF and PMF which only consider user-item ratings still don't achieve good results. When we apply frequent n-adic concepts, F3CR get a better result than UCF and PMF. Although TF considers the contextual information, it doesn't discover the associations between them. Our models F5C can reveal latent associations using frequent 5-daic concepts with additional information including contexts and user's features.

5.4   Impact of Minimum Thresholds

In the process of the extraction of frequent n-adic concepts, the minimum thresholds determine the representation of the shared conceptualizations and further affect the recommendation results. Table 4 shows the impact of minimum thresholds on Top-10

Hit Ratio of the models with tags. Since the users can rate a particular item only once, the $minsupp_r$ can just be 1.

From the table we can see that the minimum thresholds impact the recommendation results significantly. We can get a good Hit Ratio when the minimum thresholds are 1-1-1-1. This is because the dataset is very sparse and we can obtain many concepts if the thresholds are 1-1-1-1. As we increase the thresholds, we get lower Hit Ratios because the number of frequent n-adic concepts decreases and the concepts are not very condensed. When the thresholds are 2-2-1-2, we obtain the best results. We not only get adequate n-adic concepts but also a condensed representation. The results become worse when the thresholds are larger because of the significant reduction of the number of frequent n-adic concepts.

Table 4. Impact of minimum thresholds

Minimum Thresholds				*HitRatio*	Minimum Thresholds				*HitRatio*
u	*i*	*r*	*t*		*u*	*i*	*r*	*t*	
1	1	1	1	18.56%	2	2	1	3	10.31%
1	1	1	2	16.50%	2	3	1	2	8.25%
1	2	1	1	16.50%	3	2	1	2	11.34%
2	1	1	1	17.53%	3	3	1	3	6.19%
1	2	1	2	15.46%	3	3	1	4	3.09%
2	1	1	2	11.34%	3	4	1	3	4.12%
2	2	1	1	11.34%	4	3	1	3	5.15%
2	**2**	**1**	**2**	**19.59%**	4	4	1	4	2.06%

6   Conclusions

In this paper, we propose a novel recommendation method based on frequent n-adic concepts and have shown that it can get higher accuracy in top-N item recommendations. When there is tag information, we model the item sharing process into a quadruple <users, items, ratings, tags> and reveal the latent associations between them. When there are no tags, we introduce the additional information including contexts and user's features and model the relations into the quintuples <users, items, ratings, contexts, features>. Experiments conducted on a real dataset show that F4C or F5C evidently outperform the state-of-the-art models in terms of precision and can reveal more information from the quadruples or quintuples which are not captured by other methods.

Acknowledgement. This work is supported by the Natural Science Foundation of China (61272240, 60970047, 61103151, 71301086), the Doctoral Fund of Ministry of Education of China (20110131110028), the Natural Science foundation of Shandong province (ZR2012FM037) and the Excellent Middle-Aged and Youth Scientists of Shandong Province (BS2012DX017).

References

1. Adomavicius, G., Sankaranarayanan, R., Sen, S., Tuzhilin, A.: Incorporating contextual information in recommender systems using a multidimensional approach. ACM Trans. Inf. Syst. 23, 103–145 (2005)
2. Breese, J.S., Heckerman, D., Kadie, C.: Empirical analysis of predictive algorithms for collaborative filtering. In: UAI 1998: Proceedings of Uncertainty in Artificial Intelligence (1998)
3. Cattuto, C., Schmitz, C., Baldassarri, A., Servedio, A., Loreto, V., Hotho, A., Grahl, M., Stumme, G.: Network properties of folksonomies. In: Proc. of AICSI on NANSE, Amsterdam, The Netherlands, pp. 245–262 (2007)
4. Chen, K., Chen, T., Zheng, G., Jin, O., Yao, E., Yu, Y.: Collaborative Personalized Tweet Recommendation. In: Proc. of SIGIR 2012, pp. 661–670 (2012)
5. Chen, W., Hsu, W., Lee, M.: A Unified Framework for Recommendations Based on Quaternary Semantic Analysis. In: Proc. of SIGIR 2011, pp. 1023–1032 (2011)
6. Deshpande, M., Karypis, G.: Item-based top-n recommendation. ACM Transactions on Information Systems 22(1), 143–177 (2004)
7. Diederich, J., Iofciu, T.: Finding communities of practice from user profiles based on folksonomies. In: Proceedings of the 1st International Workshop on TEL-CoPs, Crete, Greece, pp. 288–297 (2006)
8. Hofmann, T.: Latent semantic models for collaborative filtering. ACM Trans. Inf. Syst. 22(1), 89–115 (2004)
9. Jaschke, R., Hotho, A., Schmitz, C., Ganter, B., Stumme, G.: Discovering shared conceptualizations in folksonomies. Web Semantics 6(1), 38–53 (2008)
10. Jelassi, M.N., Yahia, S.B., Nguifo, E.M.: A scalable mining of frequent quadratic concepts in d-folksonomies. ArXiv e-prints (December 2012)
11. Jelassi, M.N., Yahia, S.B., Nguifo, E.M.: A Personalized Recommender System Based on Users' Information In Folksonomies. In: WWW 2013, pp. 1215–1223 (May 2013)
12. Jin, R., Chai, J.Y., Si, L.: An automatic weighting scheme for collaborative filtering. In: SIGIR 2004: Proceedings of the 27th Annual International ACM SIGIR Conference on Research and Development in Information Retrieval, pp. 337–344. ACM, New York (2004)
13. Karatzoglou, A., Amatriain, X., Baltrunas, L., Oliver, N.: Multiverse recommendation: n-dimensional tensor factorization for context-aware collaborative filtering. In: RecSys 2010, pp. 79–86. ACM, NY (2010)
14. Karypis, G.: Evaluation of item-based top-n recommendation algorithms. In: CIKM, pp. 247–254 (2001)
15. Linden, G., Smith, B., York, J.: Amazon.com recommendations: Item-to-item collaborative filtering. IEEE Internet Computing, 76–80 (January/February 2003)
16. Mika, P.: Ontologies are us: A unified model of social networks and semantics. Web Semantics 5(1), 5–15 (2007)
17. Palmisano, C., Tuzhilin, A., Gorgoglione, M.: Using context to improve predictive modeling of customers in personalization applications. IEEE Trans. on Knowl. and Data Eng. 20(11), 1535–1549 (2008)
18. Pennock, D.M., Horvitz, E., Lawrence, S., Giles, C.L.: Collaborative filtering by personality diagnosis: A hybrid memory and model-based approach. In: Proc. of UAI, pp. 473–480 (2000)
19. Salakhutdinov, R., Mnih, A.: Probabilistic matrix factorization. In: Advances in Neural Information Processing Systems, vol. 20 (2008)

20. Sen, S., Vig, J., Riedl, J.: Tagommenders: connecting users to items through tags. In: WWW, pp. 671–680 (May 2009)
21. Symeonidis, P., Nanopoulos, A., Manolopoulos, Y.: A unified framework for providing recommendations in social tagging systems based on ternary semantic analysis. IEEE TKDE 22, 179–192 (2010)
22. Tso-Sutter, K.H.L., Marinho, L.B., Schmidt-Thieme, L.: Tag-aware recommender systems by fusion of collaborative filtering algorithms. In: SAC, pp. 1995–1999 (2008)
23. Voutsadakis, G.: Polyadic concept analysis. Order 19(3), 295–304 (2002)
24. Wille, R.: The basic theorem of triadic concept analysis. Order 12, 149–158 (1995)
25. Xue, G.R., Lin, C., Yang, Q., Xi, W., Zeng, H.J., Yu, Y., Chen, Z.: Scalable collaborative filtering using cluster-based smoothing. In: Proc. of SIGIR 2005, pp. 114–121 (2005)

Refreshment Strategies for the Shortest Path Caching Problem with Changing Edge Weight

Xiaohua Li, Tao Qiu, Xiaochun Yang, Bin Wang, and Ge Yu

College of Information Science and Engineering,
Northeastern University, Liaoning 110819, China
lixiaohua@ise.neu.edu.cn

Abstract. The problem of caching shortest paths which aims at reducing the computational time of servers has been widely studied. All the existing methods addressing this problem assume that the graph status does not change with time. Based on this assumption, they analyze shortest paths query logs and prefer to load paths with the most query frequency into the cache. However, the graph status is actually affected by many factors and undoubtedly changes with time in the real work. As the existing approaches ignore the change of graph status, they cannot guarantee the efficient use of caches. In this paper, we first exploit properties related with changing graphs. Then we develop an algorithm to detect shortest paths affected by weight change of edges. After detection affected paths in a cache, several heuristic based refreshment strategies are proposed to update the cache. In the experimental section, performances of proposed refreshment strategies are compared.

Keywords: shortest path caching, cache refreshment, weight change, affected shortest paths, refreshment strategy.

1 Introduction

The shortest path query in location based service is now widely used in daily life [1–6]. When a user has a shortest path query, a cache in a local server is accessed, and the result, if any, will be directly returned to the user. If there is no off-the-shelf result for the query in the cache, the system has to access a global server for the result, which costs communication and computational time [7–11]. The caching content is therefore, very critical for the efficiency of the whole query system.

In the shortest paths caching problem, given a road network and a cache, existing works either select paths with high query frequency in the query log, or those paths that contain the most number of nodes [12, 13]. None of them have talked about the scenario of changing road network. The assumption of an unchanged network, is obviously too strong. In practice, road network actually changes with time. For example, rush hours or traffic congestion change the weight of some edges on the road network, making certain paths in a cache become invalid or the utilization of the cache decreases. When confronting a changing road network, a straightforward way to refresh a cache is to evaluate the attractiveness of all the present shortest paths in the road network, and reload the cache. Such a method is far more from inefficient, because evaluating all

L. Chen et al. (Eds.): APWeb 2014, LNCS 8709, pp. 331–342, 2014.

the shortest paths is time-consuming and unnecessary. In this paper, we discuss how
to refresh a cache when the weight of a certain edge changes. This scenario depicts
situations in practice where a main road has traffic congestion (increased weight), or
traffic congestion on a main road is reduced (decreased weight). Assuming the weight
change of only one edge is reasonable, as in the real road network, traffic congestion
often happens in only a few roads and these roads are not interrelated. All the congested
roads can be seen as independent roads and dealt with separately.

1.1 Challenges

The refreshment of shortest path caches is challenging in two folds. The first challenge
is: when an edge changes its weight, how to detect which paths are affected in a short
time. Though some extant works have already proposed methods to monitor affected
paths caused by edge weight changes, they have to store extra information. Whereas,
in local servers, storage spaces are used to cache shortest paths as many as possible,
leaving no spare space to store extra information. Another challenge is how to devise
an efficient refreshment strategy, so as to ensure a high utilization of caches.

1.2 Contributions

To the best of our knowledge, our work is the first one to discuss the shortest path
caching problem with a changing graph. This problem is undoubtedly more close to the
real application. To address this problem, we develop an algorithm to detect the shortest
paths which are affected by edge changes. In addition, we propose four cache refreshment strategies and analyze the performance of proposed strategies by conducting a
series of experiments.

2 Related Work

The published work related with our problem has two streams. One stream is concerned
with the monitoring of shortest paths; while the other stream addresses the problem of
caching shortest paths.

With respect to the monitoring of shortest paths, there exists a wide spectrum of
works. Lee et al. [14] propose an ellipse bound method (EBM), where each shortest path
corresponds to an elliptic geographical area and all the updated edges are considered to
affect their corresponding paths. The shortcoming of such a method is that they cover a
large number of unrelated edges and a lot of computational time is wasted to recompute
unchanged paths. Tian et al. [15] develop the notion of query scope to identify affected
paths and devise a partial path computation algorithm (PPCA) to quickly recompute
the updated paths. Although Lee et al. [14] and Tian et al. [15] effectively monitor
affected min-cost paths, their methods work only if auxiliary data structures (elliptic
geographical areas and query scope indexes) are available.

Cache is widely used to improve the performance of many support systems. Communication cost and query response time are two important indicators in a client-server
system, and a cache is therefore employed in the client-side to reduce communication

and improve query response time. However, a cache, if located at a client, can only serve queries from the client itself, not other clients. As a consequence, only query-intensive users can be benefited from such a cache. Two caching approaches (dynamic caching and static caching) are proposed by Markatos et al. [11]. The dynamic caching aims to adjust the caching content based on recently received queries, while the static caching exploits the way to effectively initialize system caches. Thomsen et al. [12] and Li et al. [13] carry out static caching techniques for caching shortest paths. They utilize statistics from query logs to estimate the benefit of caching a specific shortest path and employ greedy algorithms to load beneficial paths in a cache. However, none of the above works considers the shortest path caching problem with a changing graph.

The rest of the paper is organized as follows.In Section 2, we study work related to the shortest path caching problem. In Section 3, we introduce all the concepts and formally define the problem. Then we explore the properties of a changing graph and present our algorithm for detecting affected shortest paths accordingly in Section 4. It is followed by four cache refreshment strategies in Sections 5. In Section 6, we conduct experimental comparison among the proposed methods on real data sets. Finally, we give some closing remarks in Section 7.

3 Preliminaries

Definition 1. *Graph model. Any transportation network can be modeled as an undirected graph $G = (V, E)$ where $V = \{v_1, v_2,..., v_n\}$ is the set of nodes and E is the set of edges. Each edge in this graph is represented by a pair of nodes $e(v_i, v_j)$. Moreover, the weight of each edge $e(v_i, v_j)$ is denoted as $w(v_i, v_j)$.*

Definition 2. *Shortest Paths. For any given graph $G = (V, E)$, the shortest path from node v_a to node v_b is denoted as $P_{a,b} = \langle v_{x_0}, v_{x_1}, ..., v_{x_n} \rangle$ here $v_{x_0} = v_a$, $v_{x_n} = v_b$ and the distance is $D_{a,b} = \sum_{i=0}^{n-1} w(v_{x_i}, v_{x_{i+1}})$.*

Definition 3. *Cache. A cache is denoted by Ω and its capacity is $|\Omega|$. Ψ refers to the caching content. The size of a cache and caching content are measured in terms of the number of nodes. It is clearly that the size of Ψ is always no larger than the cache capacity, i.e., $|\Psi| \leq |\Omega|$ all the time.*

Definition 4. *Subpaths set $S(P_{a,b})$. All the subpaths of $P_{a,b}$ compose set $S(P_{a,b})$.*

$$S(P_{a,b}) = \{P_{v_i,v_j} | v_i \in P_{a,b} \text{ and } v_j \in P_{a,b}, \text{ for any } i < j\}. \tag{1}$$

For example, for the shortest path $P_{1,8}$ in Fig. 1, its subpaths set $S(P_{1,8})$ contains paths $P_{1,3}$, $P_{1,6}$, $P_{1,8}$, $P_{3,6}$, $P_{3,8}$ and $P_{6,8}$.

Definition 5. *Affected paths. Suppose the shortest path between v_a and v_b is originally $P_{a,b} = \langle v_a, v_i, ..., v_j, v_b \rangle$. Due to the change of edge weights, if the shortest path between v_a and v_b becomes $P'_{a,b} = \langle v_a, v_m, ..., v_n, v_b \rangle$ ($P'_{a,b} \neq P_{a,b}$), then $P_{a,b}$ is called an affected path.*

Lemma 1. *Optimal subpath property [16]. A subpath of any shortest path is a shortest path of the ends of that subpath. That is, for a given shortest path* $P_{a,b} = \langle v_a, v_i, ..., v_j, ..., v_k, ..., v_b \rangle$ *and any pair of nodes* (v_i, v_j) *on it, the subpath* $\langle v_i, ..., v_j \rangle$ *is the shortest path of* $P_{i,j}$.

Lemma 1 tells us that if we store a certain shortest path in a cache, we can answer all of the shortest path queries whose end nodes are on that path.

Problem Description. Given a user query log L, a cache Ω, and a computational system which can compute the shortest paths on a graph $G = (V, E)$, we assume that cache Ω has been fully loaded and the weight of one edge e is changed from w to w'. The objective of our problem is to refresh the content of cache Ω.

4   Affected Paths Dectection

In this Section, we first summarize the properties owned by affected paths and then develop an algorithm to compute affected paths. Given the weight of e can increase as well as decrease, we discuss the two situations respectively.

(1) The weight of edge e increases.

Theorem 1. *For graph G, suppose the ends of e is v_a and v_b and $P_{a,b} = e$. When w_e increases, if $P'_{a,b} \neq e$, then each path p containing e must be an affected path. In other situations, no shortest paths are affected.*

Proof. When w_e increases, it has three cases:
   1). If $P_{a,b} = e$ originally but it becomes $P'_{a,b} \neq e$, then $P_{a,b}$ is an affected path, and any path containing $P_{a,b}$ is also an affected path.
   2). If $P_{a,b} = e$ originally and it remains $P_{a,b} = e$ even if w_e increases, then no path is affected.
   3). If $P_{a,b} \neq e$ originally, then the increase of w_e does not affect any shortest paths at all.

(2) The weight of edge e decreases.

Theorem 2. *For graph G, when the weight of e decreases, if $P_{a,b}$ is an affected path, then $P'_{a,b}$ must contain edge e.*

Proof. Assume a shortest path $P_{a,b}$ is an affected path, and $P'_{a,b}$ does not contain edge e, then it has $P_{a.b} = P'_{a,b}$, indicating that $P_{a,b}$ is not an affected path. There is a conflict with the assumption. Therefore, $P'_{a,b}$ must contain edge e.

When w_e decreases, we deploy Algorithm 1 to find all the affected paths. Assume the ends of e is v_a and v_b. Its basic idea is to determine start node v_s and end node v_e and for each pair of start and end node, check whether $P_{s,e}$ is an affected path. As there are many nodes can be start nodes and end node, we use C_s and C_e to denote the set of candidate start and end nodes, respectively. The determination of C_s and C_e

is performed by a nested loop. First, C_s is initialized with v_a, the only start node. In the outer loop, pop one candidate start node from C_s as current start node v_s and all the adjacent nodes with current start node v_s become candidate start nodes when the shortest path $P'_{s,b}$ contains e, thus, they are added into C_s (lines 5–7). If a node has been used as a start node before, then do not add it into C_s. In the inner loop, the start node v_s can be seen as given, and then vary the end node v_e. The variation of end nodes is similarly with that of outer variation. v_e is obtained by popping a node from C_e and the adjacent nodes of current end node v_e are added into C_e except for those which have entered into C_e before (lines 9–18). Given v_s and v_e, Algorithm 1 decides whether $P_{s,e}$ is affected and if yes, put it into the set of affected paths S_{aff}. The pseudo code is shown in Algorithm 1.

Algorithm 1: CALAFFECTEDPATHS

> **Input**: A graph $G(V, E)$, the edge e changed its weight, its node v_a and v_b, the original
> weight w of e, the new weight w' of e;
>
> **Output**: The set of affected paths S_{aff};
>
> 1 $C_s \leftarrow v_a$;
> 2 **while** $C_s \neq \Phi$ **do**
> 3 $\quad$ $v_s \leftarrow$ pop the first element from C_s;
> $\quad$ // $P'_{s,b}$ is the new shortest path between v_s and v_b
> 4 $\quad$ **if** $P'_{s,b}$ contains e **then**
> 5 $\quad\quad$ **for** each adjacent vertex v_{adj} of v_s **do**
> 6 $\quad\quad\quad$ **if** v_{adj} have not entered C_s **then**
> 7 $\quad\quad\quad\quad$ $C_s \leftarrow v_{adj}$;
> 8 $\quad$ $C_e \leftarrow v_b$;
> 9 $\quad$ **while** $C_e \neq \Phi$ **do**
> 10 $\quad\quad$ $v_e \leftarrow$ pop the first element from C_e;
> 11 $\quad\quad$ Calculate the short path $P'_{s,e}$ with $weight(e) = w'$;
> 12 $\quad\quad$ **if** $P'_{s,e}$ contains e **then**
> 13 $\quad\quad\quad$ **for** each adjacent vertex v_{adj} of v_e **do**
> 14 $\quad\quad\quad\quad$ **if** v_{adj} have not entered C_e **then**
> 15 $\quad\quad\quad\quad\quad$ $C_e \leftarrow v_{adj}$;
> 16 $\quad\quad$ Calculate the short path $P_{s,e}$ with $weight(e) = w$;
> 17 $\quad\quad$ **if** $P_{s,e} \neq P'_{s,e}$ **then**
> 18 $\quad\quad\quad$ $S_{aff} \leftarrow P_{s,e}$;
>
> 19 **return** S_{aff};

Theorem 3. *Our affected shortest paths computing method satisfies both soundness and completeness.*

Proof. We first prove that the algorithm CALAFFECTEDPATHS is sound, i.e. any path in S_{aff} is an affected path. According to the algorithm , if a path $P_{s,e}$ exists in S_{aff}, then there must exist that the path $P_{s,e} \neq P'_{s,e}$, in which $P'_{s,e}$ is the new shortest path between v_s and v_e with $weight(e) = w'$, so $P_{s,e}$ is an affected path.

Now we prove that the algorithm CALAFFECTEDPATHS is complete. Assume that there exist an affected path $P_{s,e}$, and $\langle v_s, v_e \rangle$ is not in S_{aff}. Based on Theorem 2, we know the new shortest path $P'_{s,e}$ connecting v_s and v_e must contain the changed edge e, then according to the algorithm, v_s and v_e must be added into C_s and C_e, respectively. So the path $P_{s,e}$ must be considered, and compared with $P'_{s,e}$. Therefore, the algorithm can get the affected path $P_{s,e}$, the assumption does not hold and the algorithm is complete.

Fig. 1 shows an example of computing affected paths when the weight of $e(v_3, v_6)$ decrease from 5 to 3. $e(v_3, v_6)$ are first considered, obtaining affected path v_3-v_4-v_6. Afterwards the algorithm computes remaining paths containing $e(v_3, v_6)$, such as v_2-v_3-v_6, v_1-v_3-v_6, v_4-v_3-v_6 and so on. When computing v_3-v_6-v_5 and v_3-v_6-v_8, affected paths v_3-v_4-v_6-v_5 and v_3-v_4-v_6-v_8 are obtained, respectively .

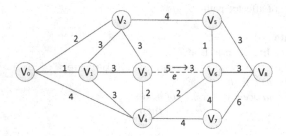

Fig. 1. An example of the weight of e decreased

In reality, a cache normally stores a large number of paths, making it time-consuming to directly recompute all the new shortest paths in the cache. Nevertheless, affected paths caused by w_e are fewer, because the change of a single edge only affects its surrounding paths. It is efficient to firstly compute the set of affected shortest paths caused by w_e, and then check whether the cache contains any affected paths. Though we discuss the problem assuming that only one edge changes its weight, we can still detect affected paths if multiple edges change weights concurrently by deploying Algorithm 1 multiple times.

5   Refreshment Strategies

In this section, we introduce four heuristic rule-based path refreshment strategies.

5.1   Through Reload

The first refreshment strategy is to empty the entire cache and reload it. This is the most straightforward idea to refresh the cache. In Li et al. [13], they propose a benefit oriented model to load shortest paths. To make this paper self-contained, we briefly introduce how the benefit oriented model works.

All of us know that the cache utilization, or the cost reduction by using cache, is affected by the query frequency and the computational time of shortest paths. When calculating the cost saved by loading a path $P_{a,b}$ into a cache, we consider: 1) which queries can be answered by the path $P_{a,b}$; and 2) the saved computational cost if answering a query $Q_{a,b}$ by a cache directly.

For the first consideration, according to Lemma 1, we know that a path can answer all the queries on its subpath set. For the second consideration, it depends on how frequently a query arrives and the computational cost of that query. More specifically, it is the multiplier of the query frequency and the computational cost.

From the above analysis, we have the utilization of storing $P_{a,b}$ in caches as the following form.

$$B(P_{a,b}) = \frac{\sum_{P_{s,t} \in S(P_{a,b})} F_{s,t} \cdot C_{s,t}}{|P_{a,b}|}. \tag{2}$$

Here, the numerator is the total cost reduction saved by caching path $P_{a,b}$. After normalized by the size of path $P_{a,b}$, $B(P_{a,b})$ is the unit-size benefit brought by path $P_{a,b}$ if it is loaded into a cache. Due to the limited cache capacity, the unitization can better reflect the value of loading a path after normalization. Readers can understand this as the value of per unit weight in a knapsack problem. Paths with larger $B(P_{a,b})$ have higher priority to be loaded into a cache.

The method wastes a lot of time. Since only an edge changes its weight, its impact on the whole network is limited. The majority of shortest paths do not change at all. As a result, through reload is redundant.

5.2   Affected Paths Update

The second strategy is to detect all the affected paths in a cache, and then update these paths in the new network. The advantage of this method is that the computational time is the least; it does not involve comparison of path benefits. The shortcoming of this method is that the ends of affected paths may not be of high benefits after the network changes. It may be better to replace affected paths with other paths.

5.3   Highest Frequency First

To overcome the shortcoming of the second method, in the third method, we delete the affected paths in a cache first and then try to fill the cache until it cannot contain paths any more. Each time, one path is selected. In order to increase the speed of refreshment, we greedily select the path with the highest query frequency. It avoids to compute the benefits of each path which are dynamic values based on the current content of the cache. Query frequency, instead, can be easily obtained from the query log and never changes even though the network changes.

5.4 Roulette Wheel Selection

At last, the forth strategy is to delete all the affected paths in the cache and load new paths to the cache by the method of *roulette wheel*. As the historical queries are not the true queries in the future, on one hand, we consider it as a reference for the future queries; on the other hand, we avoid over fitting the cache content to it.

We use a roulette wheel to determine which paths should be loaded into the cache. One feature of the roulette wheel selection is that alternatives with low attractiveness can also be selected, although with a relatively low possibility. We adopt the idea of roulette wheel as the following: for a path p in the query log, its probability of being selected $\Pr(p)$ is proportional to its query frequency f_p, as shown in Equation 3.

$$\Pr(p) = \frac{f_p}{\sum_i f_i}. \tag{3}$$

The summation of the probabilities of all the paths are just 1. The probability of selecting each path corresponds to the probability of a variable X with a standard uniform distribution falling into an interval as shown in Equation 4.

$$\Pr(p) = \Pr(X \in [\frac{\sum_{i=1}^{p-1} f_i}{\sum_i f_i}, \frac{\sum_{i=1}^{p} f_i}{\sum_i f_i}]). \tag{4}$$

In another word, to realize the probabilities for all the paths is equivalent to generate a random number failing at interval [0,1].

Take Table 1 for an example, it records the path-interval correspondence. When we need to select a path into the cache, we generate a random number according to the standard uniform distribution. Suppose the randomly generated number is 0.6, then $P_{2,11}$ will be selected because 0.6 belongs to $[0.5, 0.75]$.

Table 1. A example of roulette wheel selection

Path	Frequency	Probability	Interval
$P_{1,12}$	6	0.3	$[0, 0.3]$
$P_{1,10}$	3	0.15	$[0.3, 0.45]$
$P_{6,9}$	1	0.05	$[0.45, 0.5]$
$P_{2,11}$	5	0.25	$[0.5, 0.75]$
$P_{1,8}$	2	0.1	$[0.75, 0.85]$
$P_{7,12}$	3	0.15	$[0.85, 1.0]$

In terms of the computational time, the roulette wheel selection is slower than the affected paths update and the highest frequency first, faster than the through reload. As for the performance, it is better than the former two and worse than the through reload. Choosing which refreshment strategy is based on the scenario requirement. When time is not a concern, then the through reload or the roulette wheel selection may be used; When real time response is a big issue, the affected paths update or the highest frequency first may be utilized. There is no absolutely good or absolutely bad.

6 Experiments

The benchmark data sets used are the commonly known data sets: the road network of Aalborg and Beijing. Both data sets consist of a large number of nodes, edges, and associated weights. Table 2 summarizes the information on the data sets.

Table 2. Data set information

Data set	Number of nodes	Number of edges	Description
Aalborg	4.6Million	3.9Million	Road network
Beijing	2.7Million	2.4Million	Road network

We divide each data set into two parts: one part for training and the other part for testing. Training sets act as historical logs while test sets act as future queries. The frequency statistics is extracted from the training set, and the cache is fulfilled based on frequency information. For Aalborg, the training set is 176.2KB and the test set is 177.3KB; for Beijing, the training set is 483.4KB and the test set is 481.7KB.

To simulate the weight change of an edge, we generate 50 instances based on each data set. Out of the 50 instances, 20 times are of weight increase and 30 times are of weight decrease. In each instance, randomly select one edge and change its weight. The increase of a weight ranges from 1% to 100%. To simulate the weight decrease, we first increase the edge weight and load the cache, then recover the weight to its original value after loading the cache. The experimental results in Section 6.1 and Section 6.2 are the average of 50 instances. As for the result in Section 6.3 (the hit-ratios of different refreshment strategies), we sum up results of 50 instances for ease of read, since the hit-ratio differences among different strategies are tiny.

We assume that the query trend on training sets and test sets are similar, and the statistic information from training sets can predict future queries to some extent. All the code were implemented in GNU C++. The experiments were run on a PC with an Intel i7 Quad Core CPU clocked at 3.10 GHz.

6.1 Efficiency of Detecting Affected Paths in the Cache

Detecting affected paths in a cache is an important step before refreshing a cache. To demonstrate the performance of our algorithm (Algorithm 1), a basic method named BASICPATHS is used as a benchmark method. BASICPATHS recomputes the new shortest paths for all the ends pairs in the cache and compare them with the original ones in the cache. If the two paths for a ends pair are different, then an affected path is detected. We test algorithms CALAFFECTEDPATHS and BASICPATHS on Aalborg and Beijing data set and the running time of the two detection methods is regarded as the performance indicator.

As seen from Fig. 2, algorithm CALAFFECTEDPATHS has a better performance than algorithm BASICPATHS. For example, in the Aalborg data set, when the cache size is 9MB, the running time of CALAFFECTEDPATHS is only 267ms; while the running time of BASICPATHS reaches 28.67seconds. In addition, we can see that CALAFFECTEDPATHS algorithm uses less time on Aalborg data set than it does on Beijing data set. The reason is that the graph of Beijing data set is more compact. Hence, CALAFFECTEDPATHS need check more paths in the graph to yield all the affected paths.

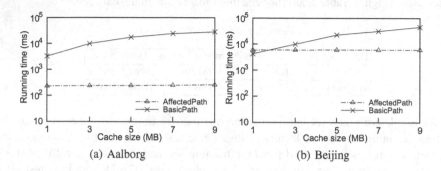

(a) Aalborg   (b) Beijing

Fig. 2. Performance comparison on affected paths detection methods

6.2 Overhead of Different Refreshment Strategies

In Section 5, we propose four cache refreshment strategies, which are based on different heuristic rules. For ease of illustration, TR is short for the through reload method, APU is short for the affect paths update method, HFF is short for the highest frequency first method and RWS is short for the roulette wheel selection method. We test the running time of these four replacement strategies v.s. various cache sizes as shown in Fig. 3. It reveals that TR spends the most running time and the other three spend similar running time. It is because the overhead reported by the computer is not that accurate under 1000ms. Meanwhile, It is surprisingly to find that HFF and RWS do not spend much time, just almost at the same scale with APU. It indirectly indicates that the scale of affected paths is rather small compared with the content of the cache.

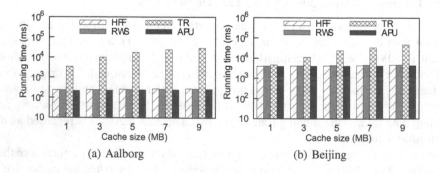

(a) Aalborg   (b) Beijing

Fig. 3. Overhead comparison of different refreshment strategies

6.3 Hit Ratio of Different Refreshment Strategies

Fig. 4 shows the hit-ratios of four refreshment strategies under different scales of caches. We can observe that the through reload (TR) achieves the highest hit ratio. And the hit ratios of HFF and RWS are similar. At last, APU is the worst. Such a result is consistent with the discussion in Section 5.

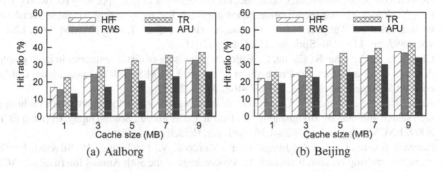

(a) Aalborg   (b) Beijing

Fig. 4. Hit ratio comparison of different refreshment strategies

7 Conclusion

We address the problem of refreshing cache content in a changing network. To the best of our knowledge, our work is the first one to discuss the cache refreshment problem when the road network changes with time. Road network changes are commonly seen in the real world, for example traffic congestion or road construction. Shortest path caches are necessary to be refreshed periodically, so that the information in them is accurate, valid and the utilization of the cache is maximized. In this paper, we first introduce the concept of affected paths, and then exploit the properties associated with affected paths. In the following, we develop an algorithm to detect affected shortest paths in the cache caused by road network changes. Sequentially, four cache refreshment strategies are illustrated. We give a full explanation of these strategies, and conduct a series of experiments to compare their performance, i.e., the computational time and the hit ratio on bench mark data sets.

Acknowledgments. The work is partially supported by the National Natural Science Foundation of China (Nos. 61322208, 61272178), the Joint Research Fund for Overseas Natural Science of China (No. 61129002), the Doctoral Fund of Ministry of Education of China (No. 20110042110028), and the Fundamental Research Funds for the Central Universities (No. N120504001, N110804002).

References

1. Wu, L., Xiao, X., Deng, D., Cong, G., Zhu, A.D., Zhou, S.: Shortest path and distance queries on road networks: An experimental evaluation. Proceedings of the VLDB Endowment 5(5), 406–417 (2012)

2. Long, X., Suel, T.: Three-level caching for efficient query processing in large web search engines. In: World Wide Web Conference, WWW, pp. 257–266 (2005)

3. Potamias, M., Bonchi, F., Castillo, C., Gionis, A.: Fast shortest path distance estimation in large networks. In: Proceedings of the 18th ACM Conference on Information and Knowledge Management, CIKM, pp. 867–876 (2009)

4. Wei, F.: Tedi: Efficient shortest path query answering on graphs. In: Proceedings of the 2010 ACM SIGMOD International Conference on Management of Data, pp. 99–110. ACM (2010)

5. Liu, X., Yang, X.: A generalization based approach for anonymizing weighted social network graphs. In: Wang, H., Li, S., Oyama, S., Hu, X., Qian, T. (eds.) WAIM 2011. LNCS, vol. 6897, pp. 118–130. Springer, Heidelberg (2011)

6. Cheng, J., Ke, Y., Chu, S., Cheng, C.: Efficient processing of distance queries in large graphs: A vertex cover approach. In: Proceedings of the 2012 ACM SIGMOD International Conference on Management of Data, pp. 457–468. ACM (2012)

7. Altingovde, I.S., Ozcan, R., Ulusoy, Ö.: A cost-aware strategy for query result caching in web search engines. In: Boughanem, M., Berrut, C., Mothe, J., Soule-Dupuy, C. (eds.) ECIR 2009. LNCS, vol. 5478, pp. 628–636. Springer, Heidelberg (2009)

8. Baeza-Yates, R., Gionis, A., Junqueira, F., Murdock, V., Plachouras, V., Silvestri, F.: The impact of caching on search engines. In: Proceedings of the 30th Annual International ACM SIGIR Conference on Research and Development in Information Retrieval, pp. 183–190. ACM (2007)

9. Kriegel, H.-P., Kroger, P., Renz, M., Schmidt, T.: Hierarchical graph embedding for efficient query processing in very large traffic networks. In: Scientific and Statistical Database Management Conference, SSDBM, pp. 150–167 (2008)

10. Gan, Q., Suel, T.: Improved techniques for result caching in web search engines. In: Proceedings of the 18th International Conference on World Wide Web, pp. 431–440. ACM (2009)

11. Markatos, E.P.: On caching search engine query results. Computer Communications 24(2), 137–143 (2001)

12. Thomsen, J.R., Yiu, M.L., Jensen, C.S.: Effective caching of shortest paths for location-based services. In: Proceedings of the 2012 ACM SIGMOD International Conference on Management of Data, pp. 313–324. ACM (2012)

13. Li, X., Wang, S., Yang, X., Wang, B., Ge, Y.: An improved algorithm to enhance the utilization of shortest path caches. In: Web Information System and Application, pp. 419–424. IEEE (2013)

14. Lee, C.-C., Wu, Y.-H., Chen, A.L.P.: Continuous evaluation of fastest path queries on road networks. In: Papadias, D., Zhang, D., Kollios, G. (eds.) SSTD 2007. LNCS, vol. 4605, pp. 20–37. Springer, Heidelberg (2007)

15. Tian, Y., Lee, K.C.K, Lee, W.-C.: Monitoring minimum cost paths on road networks. In: Proceedings of the 17th ACM SIGSPATIAL International Conference on Advances in Geographic Information Systems, pp. 217–226. ACM (2009)

16. Cormen, T.H., Leiserson, C.E., Rivest, R.L., Stein, C., et al.: Introduction to Algorithms, vol. 2. MIT Press, Cambridge (2001)

Based on Citation Diversity to Explore Influential Papers for Interdisciplinarity

Keqiang Wang[1], Chaofeng Sha[2], Xiaoling Wang[1], and Aoying Zhou[1]

[1] Shanghai Key Laboratory of Trustworthy Computing,
Institute for Data Science and Engineering,
East China Normal University, Shanghai 200062, China
[2] School of Computer Science,
Shanghai Key Laboratory of Intelligent Information Processing,
Fudan University, Shanghai 200433, China
sei.wkq2008@gmail.com, xlwang@sei.ecnu.edu.cn

Abstract. Interdisciplinary scientific research (IDR) has been obtained more and more attention in recent years. This paper studies the problem of which papers are important for IDR. According to the citation relationships among papers, we focus on the influential papers where novel methods or idea are proposed and these new methods are used in different research areas. A two-stage approach is given to find influential papers for interdisciplinarity based on citation diversity. Firstly, the topic distribution of each paper is estimated by training Latent Dirichlet Allocation (LDA) topic model on the papers repository. Then the diversity of cited papers and citing papers are designed to measure the paper's influence. The effectiveness of the proposed approach is demonstrated through the extensive experiments on a real dataset and a synthetic dataset.

Keywords: Topic model, Diversity, Interdisciplinarity.

1 Introduction

Interdisciplinary scientific research (IDR)[2] is important to create new research areas, such as quantum information processing and bioinformatics, by utilize several subjects theories or methods. It is important to find promising methods that can be used in multiple areas. Christos[16] said that "*The criterion is that if I see a method being applied two or three times, or being reinvented two or three times, then it is probably a method that could have application also in databases.*" If one method can be applied in several scientific fields, the diversity of its citing papers is often high while the diversity of its cited papers and the paper itself is often low. This paper is aiming to identify those influential papers for IDR by proposing a ranking measure that takes the diversity of the citations into consideration. We also combine the Latent Dirichlet Allocation topic model with diversity measure to find the influential paper for interdisciplinarity.

The main contributions can be summarized as follows.

L. Chen et al. (Eds.): APWeb 2014, LNCS 8709, pp. 343–354, 2014.

1. We study the problem of finding influential papers from the literature of academic world. According to the citation relationships, all of papers are classified into three categories.
2. A citation diversity-based approach is proposed to measure the importance of the influential papers.
3. We conduct extensive experiments both on real and synthetic datasets to demonstrate the effectiveness of our proposed methods.

The rest of the paper is organized as follows. In Section 2, the related work is discussed based on diversity. Section 3 describes the taxonomy of papers considering the citing relationship and propose the methods to explore the influential papers. Experimental evaluation using real and generated data are shown in Section 4. Conclusion and future work are discussed in section 5.

2   Related Work

There are many metrics to measure the influence or importance of one paper, such as the citation number (in-degree), H-index, and PageRank value. Recently, [15] proposes a graph ranking method by utilizing citations, authors, journals/conferences, and the publication time information. However, the impact on interdisciplinary is overtaken by these measures.

In recent years, various diversity measures have been employed to measure the impact of paper for interdisciplinary research [3,10,11,13]. [13] proposes three different attributes of diversity: variety, balance and disparity. "Variety" is the number of topics, "balance" is the topics distribution and "disparity" is the distance between each pair topics. The classic diversity measure, such as Shannon entropy, combines the variety and balance while ignores disparity. Stirling[13] proposes a general diversity heuristic function as follows:

$$div_d = \sum_{i \in T} \sum_{j \in T} (1 - sim(i,j))^\alpha (P(i|d)P(j|d))^\beta \tag{1}$$

where d is a document, $P(i|d)$ and $P(j|d)$ are the proportions of category i and j, $sim(i,j)$ is the similarity between category i and j, and α, β are the tuning parameters. When $\alpha = \beta = 1$, the expression (1) is collapsed to a variant of Rao's diversity [12]. [10] uses the number of disciplines, their distribution and distance between knowledge sources to measure the diversity by (1). Their experiments conducted on publications from six research domains between 1997 and 2005 to demonstrate the rising interdisciplinarity. Rafols[11] treats the diversity and network coherence as indicators of interdisciplinarity and carries out case studies on bionanoscience publications. The intuition behind these two indicators are verified from the experiments: diversity reflects the breadth of a paper's knowledge, and coherence represents the novelty. Text-based measures are employed in [3] and the LDA topic model is adopted to measure the variety, balance and disparity.

Similar to former work, this paper follows [3] to calculate the paper/publication's diversity. However, instead of detecting the interdisciplinarity or diversity of each paper itself, we focus on detecting the influential papers with diverse citation from different areas. Those influential papers, where some promising methods or theories are proposed, are very important for IDR. Besides the variety, balance and disparity of each paper, we also take into account the citations, which are an important factor to measure the diverse influence of a paper/publication.

3   Finding Influential Papers

This section presents our method to find influential papers for interdisciplinarity. Firstly, we discuss the characteristics of papers and classify them into three categories according to the citation relationships.

3.1   Categories of Papers

Given a paper d, cited papers are the references of d, denoted as $R(d)$, while citing papers are these papers which cite d, denoted as $C(d)$. As Figure 1, we observe that most of the papers can be classified into three categories: interdisciplinary, influential and single-domain. Here, the recently published papers are ignored, because there is no citation information for them. In the following section, we propose a method to find these influential papers.

- **Interdisciplinary Paper:** These papers in this category not only cite papers from multiple areas but also are cited by many papers of different fields. For example, **D1** in Figure 1 are interdisciplinary papers. Former work [8,9,6,7,11] is to find this kind of papers. Interdisciplinary papers provide the novel methods or theories in other research fields.
- **Influential Paper:** The paper like **D2** in Figure 1 belongs to this category. These paper is cited by many different areas, however only contains cited papers from single research field. We argue that these papers with fundamental theories and methods are in low diversity of topics. These papers are the original ones and play an important role on interdisciplinary scientific research.
- **Single-Domain Paper:** The last category of papers is single-domain paper which has cited papers and citing papers of one specific field, such as **D3** in Figure 1.

This paper is focusing on identifying the influential papers belong to the second category.

3.2   Our Measure

Intuitively, if one method can be applied in several scientific fields, the diversity of its citing papers is often high while the diversity of its cited papers and the paper itself is often low. For example, the paper which proposes Latent Dirichlet Allocation(LDA) topic model has been cited by many papers in theoretical computer

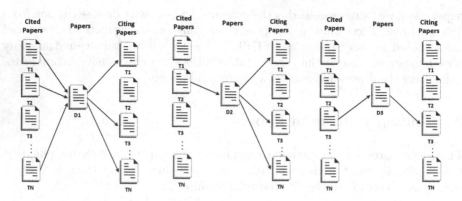

(a) Interdisciplinary papers   (b) Influential papers   (c) Single-domain papers

Fig. 1. Two Subfigures

science, natural language processing, computer vision and recommender systems. Combining both diversity of a paper d, paper's cited papers and its citing papers, we propose the following score to measure its influence for interdisciplinarity.

$$\varphi(d) = \lambda div_{c\_all}^{(d)} - (1 - \lambda)div_{r\_all}^{(d)} \tag{2}$$

where $div_{c\_all}^{(d)}$ is the diversity of $C(d)$, $div_{r\_all}^{(d)}$ is the diversity of $R(d)$ and d, and λ is a tradeoff parameter in the range $[0, 1]$.

The Rao's diversity [12] is adopted as in [3].

$$div_d = \sum_{i \in T} \sum_{j \in T} P(i|d)P(j|d)\delta(i,j) \tag{3}$$

where $P(i|d)$ is the probability of topic i in a paper d (i.e., $P(i|d) = \frac{n_{di}}{n_d}$, where n_{di} is the number of words in d belonging to topic i, n_d is the number of words in d), $\delta(i,j)$ is the distance between two topics i and j and T is the topics set.

The topic distribution $P(i|d)$ can be estimated through training Latent Dirichlet Allocation (LDA) topic model [4] on publication repository.

To calculate both the diversity of $R(d)$ and $C(d)$, $div_{r\_all}^{(d)}$ and $div_{c\_all}^{(d)}$, the topic distribution of citing papers (denoted as $P^c(\cdot|d)$) and cited papers (denoted as $P^r(\cdot|d)$) should be estimated from the paper repository. Besides those distributions, the distance between them should also be calculated. The next two sections will discuss the detail.

3.3 Topic Co-occurrence Similarity Analysis

The topic distance $\delta(i,j)$ is opposite to the topic co-occurrence similarity. We use $\delta(i,j) = 1/sim(i,j)$ as the distance between topic i and topic j. Several similarity measures can be used. The formula of the cosine similarity is as follows:

$$sim(i,j) = \frac{\sum_d n_{di}n_{dj}}{\sqrt{\sum_d n_{di}^2}\sqrt{\sum_d n_{dj}^2}} \tag{4}$$

The joint probability of two topics appearing in one paper is defined as:

$$sim(i,j) = P(i,j) = \sum_d P(i|d)P(j|d)P(d) \tag{5}$$

where $P(d)$ is estimated by $\frac{n_d}{N}$ and N is the number of words of all papers.

The above similarity measure assumed that each word contributes equally. Alternatively, we can treat each document equally. The similarity can be computed as the function of topic distributions:

$$sim(i,j) = \frac{\sum_d P(i|d)P(j|d)}{\sqrt{\sum_d P(i|d)^2}\sqrt{\sum_d P(j|d)^2}} \tag{6}$$

or,

$$sim(i,j) = P(i,j) = \frac{1}{|D|}\sum_d P(i|d)P(j|d) \tag{7}$$

where D is the paper set and $|D|$ is the number of papers.

Note that there are a large number of topic pairs i,j, the similarity $sim(i,j)$ between them may be very small or even equal to zero which leads $\delta(i,j)$ to be very large or singular. When using the Rao's diversity, it has little impact on measuring the diversity of paper itself. Because $sim(i,j)$ is near to zero, $P(i|d)P(j|d)$ is also very small or near to zero. The diversity of the paper is not affected by them. Then it is reasonable to define $P(i|d)P(j|d)\delta(i,j) = 0$ if $sim(i,j) = 0$. The similarity between topics does not need to be smoothed.

However, when computing the diversity of a paper's cited or citing papers, it is sensitive to the disparity attribute. For some topic pair i,j, it happens that $P(i|d)P(j|d)$ is not negligible while $\delta(i,j)$ is very large, which leads to the over-amplification of the diversity score. In order to mitigate this problem, the Dirichlet prior smoothing [17] is employed:

$$sim(i,j) = \frac{\sum_d (n_{di} + \mu_d P(i|D))(n_{dj} + \mu_d P(j|D))}{\sqrt{\sum_d (n_{di} + \mu_d P(i|D))^2}\sqrt{\sum_d (n_{dj} + \mu_d P(j|D))^2}} \tag{8}$$

$$P(i,j) = \sum_d \frac{n_d(P(i|d) + \mu_d P(i|D)}{n_d + \mu_d}\frac{n_d(P(j|d) + \mu_d P(j|D)}{n_d + \mu_d}\frac{n_d + \mu_d}{N + \sum_d \mu_d} \tag{9}$$

where μ_d is a constant or a variable value based on the word count of paper d (e.g., $\mu_d = 0.1|d|$)

3.4   Topic Distribution Analysis of Cited Papers and Citing Papers

Now the remaining problem is estimating the topic distributions of $R(d)$ and $C(d)$. Intuitively, we can treat $R(d)$ or $C(d)$ as one document respectively. Then their topic distributions can be estimated as follows:

$$P^r(i|d) = \frac{\sum_{r \in R(d)} n_{ri}}{\sum_{r \in R(d)} n_r}, \quad P^c(i|d) = \frac{\sum_{c \in C(d)} n_{ci}}{\sum_{c \in C(d)} n_c} \tag{10}$$

Note that when defining the formula (10), it is assumed that each word contributes equally. When the length of papers varies largely in the dataset, the influence of longer papers may be overestimated by this method. To overcome this deficiency, we treat all the cited or citing papers equally. We sum the $P(i|d)$s of $R(d)$ and $C(d)$ respectively as normalization factors. This normalization is defined as follows:

$$N^r(i|d) = \sum_{k \in R(d)} P^r(i,k|d), \quad N^c(i|d) = \sum_{k \in C(d)} P^c(i,k|d) \tag{11}$$

$$P^r(i|d) = \frac{N^r(i|d)}{\sum_{j \in T} N^r(j|d)}, \quad P^c(i|d) = \frac{N^c(i|d)}{\sum_{j \in T} N^c(j|d)} \tag{12}$$

where $P^r(i,k|d)$ or $P^c(i,k|d)$ is the probability of topic i in the document k which is a cited or citing paper of d.

However, for papers with many citations, some topics' proportion may be very large. When $P^c(i|d)$ for some topic i is high, the overall diversity score may be dominated by this topic distribution unevenly.

Example 1. *Consider the case shown in Table 1. The paper d_1 has 900 citations on topic A and 100 citations on topic B respectively. Another paper d_2 has 70 citations on topic A and 30 citations on topic B respectively. The proportion of each topic $P^c(i|d)$ calculated using formula (12) are listed in the right two columns. We assume that $\delta(A, B) = 1$ and $\delta(A, A) = \delta(B, B) = 0$. So $div_{c\_all}^{d_1} = 0.9 \times 0.1 \times 1 = 0.09$ and $div_{c\_all}^{d_2} = 0.7 \times 0.3 \times 1 = 0.21$. As can be seen that $div_{c\_all}^{(d_2)}$ is more than two times $div_{c\_all}^{(d_1)}$. Although the topic distribution of d_1 are more imbalanced than d_2, the influence for interdisciplinarity of d_1 is more than d_2.*

Table 1. *Illustration for Example 1*

Document	Citations		Distribution	
	Topic A	Topic B	Topic A	Topic B
d_1	900	100	0.9	0.1
d_2	70	30	0.7	0.3

From the above example, we know that for papers with more citations, the balance attribute affects the diversity score too much. To tackle this problem, we should reduce the weight of balance. Therefore we propose the following adjusted formulation by adding a discounting weight α_i for each topic i:

$$N^c(i|d) = \sum_{k=1}^{|C|} \alpha_i^{\sum_{j=1}^{k-1} P^c(i,j|d)} P^c(i,k|d) \tag{13}$$

To calculate this measure, we need to rank cited papers and citing papers firstly. One straightforward and efficient way is ordering papers by years of publication. For each topic i, the total distance from other topics, $\sum_{j \in T} \delta(i,j)$, represents the similarity with other topics. Therefore, we take $\sum_{j \in T} \delta(i,j)$ into account the following definition of α_i: $\alpha_i = \frac{\sum_{j \in T} \delta(i,j)}{max_{k \in T} \sum_{j \in T} \delta(k,j)} - \epsilon$, where ϵ is a small constant (e.g. ϵ is set to 0.05 or 0.01) to avoid $\alpha_i = 1$.

4 Experiments

We evaluated the method proposed in this paper using both synthetic and real datasets. In this section, we first elaborate on datasets and experimental setting. We then compared the three methods on those datasets under specific parameter setting.

4.1 Settings

Firstly, the stemming technique is used to process all documents in the paper collection. Then we use MALLET [1] to train LDA topic model, where standard stop-word removal, lowercase transformation and word segmentation were conducted. When training LDA topic model, the parameters setting follows [3]. We learn LDA topic models with 10, 30, and 100 topics.

As there is no ground truth dataset, we generate artificial citation relationship between papers. We use five journals from PubMed Central Open Access dataset (PubMed) to set up the pseudo-relationships. These five journals are shown in Table 2 and they are all unrelated. Here we create two kinds of artificial citation relationships. In the first setting, we assign each paper with 10 cited papers and 1 to 80 citing papers. Both cited papers and citing papers are selected randomly from one or two journals. So there are three kinds of artificial documents representing **D1,D2** and **D3**. For each case, we create 200 papers and 600 papers respectively. By this setting, we aim to examine the effectiveness of our method on distinguishing the influential papers from other papers. The second one is set to measure the effectiveness of three methods with different variety or citations. We use the same number of citing papers (e.g., five papers) of each journal and different number of journals to simulate different variety. In another way, the same number of journals and different number of citing papers (e.g., one kind has 5 citing papers of each journal and another has 10 citing papers with the same number of journals.) are created to simulate different citations.

We also carry out case studies on a real dataset, the ArnetMiner dataset [14]. We train the LDA on the paper's abstract repository. However, the abstract of many papers is missed. We crawl them from the Microsoft Academic Search [1].

---
[1] http://academic.research.microsoft.com/

Table 2. Five Journals from PubMed Central Open Access Dataset

Journal	Description	Published number
Arthritis_Res_Ther	A journal about arthritis	2374
Breast_Cancer_Res	A journal about breast cancer	1797
Malar_J	A journal about malaria	2584
Diabetes_Care	A journal about diabetes	2284
Nanoscale_Res_Lett	A journal about nanotechnology	2226

We choose the papers whose number of cited papers are greater than 5 and have more than 10 citations. There are about 20k documents and 290k referring or citing relationships.

4.2 Experimental Results on Pseudo-Document Dataset

In this section, we discuss the experimental results on pesudo-document dataset. Since the results are similar with cosine similarity and joint probability, we just report the results with the cosine similarity. We compare the performances of three methods on the synthetic dataset:

- All cited or citing papers as One document(AO): treats all cited or citing papers as one document, as described by formula (10).
- Normalized Cumulative Topic Distributions(NCTD): uses the cumulative topic distributions followed by normalization process, as described by formula (11),(12).
- Normalized Discounted Cumulative Topic Distributions(NDCTD): uses the discounted cumulative topic distributions followed by normalization process, as described by formula (13),(12).

According to [3], the area under the receiver operating characteristic (ROC) curve, known as the AUC[5], is used to evaluate the effectiveness of our approaches. The ROC plots on the X-axis and TP(14) on the Y-axis.

$$FP = \frac{negatives\ incorrectly\ classified}{total\ negatives}, TP = \frac{positives\ correctly\ classified}{total\ positive}$$

$$(14)$$

The AUC represents the probability that a randomly chosen negative example will have a smaller estimated probability of belonging to the positive class than a randomly chosen positive example.

Firstly, we examine the ability of three approaches on distinguishing influential papers from others. In this set of experiments, the parameter λ is set to 0.4. The results are shown in Table 3. It can be seen that all three methods can be used to distinguish the influential papers from others well. The approach NDCTD outperforms other two methods, while AO and NCTD have similar performance.

Moreover, the best results are achieved for the three methods with 30 topics. When the number of topics is set to more than 30, the effectiveness of the three methods degrades. The reason is that the diversity is sensitive to high topic distance $\delta(i,j)$ even using Dirichlet prior smoothing. We also conduct another experiment where we take papers from 4 or 5 journals into cited or citing papers (high diversity). On the other hand, the low diversity papers are with cited or cited papers from 1 or 2 journals. We find that the results are more better and all are higher than 0.97. These results indicate that these methods can distinguish the influential papers from other two kinds effectively.

Table 3. AUC scores of different methods with different topic numbers

	10 topics	30 topics	100 topics
AO	0.940	0.947	0.924
NCTD	0.941	0.948	0.922
NDCTD	**0.961**	**0.962**	**0.940**

To test the sensitiveness of method on the parameter λ, we set the value of λ from 0.2 to 0.6 with 10, 30 and 100 topics. From the results shown in the Figure 2, we can find that it is reasonable to set λ to be less than 0.5. In the most cases, the best results of three methods are achieved when $\lambda \approx 0.3$ or 0.4. It means that the cited papers' influence is a little more than the citing papers.

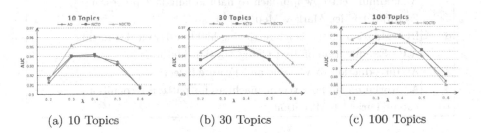

(a) 10 Topics   (b) 30 Topics   (c) 100 Topics

Fig. 2. AUC scores for different λ

Next we examine the effectiveness of three methods with different variety or citations. Table 4 shows the results with different variety. "1vs2" means that the data set has two kinds of artificial citing relationships to compare: "1" means that there is only one kind/category of journals in the citing papers and "2" means two kinds/categories. "2vs3", "3vs4" and "4vs5" denotes the similar meaning. The results show that when the number of journals grows, it is harder to distinguish. Especially, while the number of journals is not less than 2, it is not easy to distinguish them.

For the influential papers, the citations are also an important factor besides variety, balance and disparity. The importance of papers is reflected by the number of citations. So we conduct another experiment. We fix the journals and vary the number of citations from five to ten. The result is shown in Table 5. As expected, the method NDCTD is the best. However, all three methods have no good performance. This problem is left to explore and improve in the future.

Table 4. AUC scores for three methods with different variety

	1vs2	2vs3	3vs4	4vs5
AO	0.947	0.626	0.599	0.594
NCTD	0.948	0.648	0.594	0.569
NDCTD	**0.962**	**0.676**	**0.642**	**0.623**

Table 5. AUC scores for three methods with different citations

Journal number	2	3	4	5
AO	0.581	0.539	0.581	0.469
NCTD	0.561	0.521	0.591	0.439
NDCTD	**0.675**	**0.686**	**0.698**	**0.727**

Table 6. Top 10 Papers Title in real dataset with 30 topics, $\lambda = 0.4$

	Title
1	Fast string kernels using inexact matching for protein sequences
2	Random Forests
3	Comparison of multiobjective evolutionary algorithms: Empirical results
4	A maximum entropy approach to natural language processing
5	Factorial Hidden Markov Models
6	IR evaluation methods for retrieving highly relevant documents
7	A Re-Examination of Text Categorization Methods
8	An Introduction to Variable and Feature Selection
9	A tutorial on support vector machines for pattern recognition
10	Latent Dirichlet Allocation

4.3 Case Studies on Real Dataset

We also conduct experiments on the real dataset. We show the top 10 papers' title ranked by our method with 30 topics in Table 6. Note that LDA topic model used in this paper ranks 10th which we examined the topics distribution of cited papers and citing papers. We find that the cited papers of LDA have the low diversity. The probability of their top 5 topics is about 0.89 as shown in Table 7. On the other hand, the probability of top 5 topics in citations only about 1/3 as shown in Table 8. As we know that LDA topic model is proposed to process text (topic modeling), while it can applied in many other areas, such as computer vision, recommender systems and location based service, etc. Besides LDA, we can see that most of top 10 papers are the classic influential papers.

Table 7. Top 5 topics in cited papers of LDA

$P(i|d)$	top 5 words in each topic
0.21	model estim measur method distribut
0.21	text word languag extract base
0.21	data cluster learn algorithm method
0.16	data queri web databas inform
0.10	learn comput student research technolog

Table 8. Top 5 topics in citing papers of LDA

$P(i|d)$	top 5 words in each topic
0.095	text word languag extract base
0.067	data queri web databas inform
0.060	data cluster learn algorithm method
0.056	imag method base propos object
0.055	learn comput student research technolog

5 Conclusion

This paper is to explore the influential paper for interdisciplinarity. To the best of our knowledge, this is the first work to find such kind of important literature among many research areas. LDA and diversity techniques are used to quantify the influence of a paper for interdisciplinarity. And this score can be also as an indicator of the importance of a paper. Experiments have shown the effectiveness of the proposed approach. In the future, we want to consider the link analysis, such as PageRank, to improve the effectiveness; and the efficiency is also our consideration.

Acknowledgments. This work was supported by the 973 project (No. 2010CB328106), NSFC grant (No. 61170085 and 61033007), Program for New Century Excellent Talents in China (No.NCET-10-0388) and Shanghai Knowledge Service Platform Project (No. ZF1213).

References

1. Mccallum, A.K.: Mallet: A machine learning for language toolkit, http://www.cs.umass.edu/~ccallum/mallet
2. Interdisciplinarity, http://en.wikipedia.org/wiki/Interdisciplinary
3. Bache, K., Newman, D., Smyth, P.: Text-based measures of document diversity. In: Proceedings of the 19th ACM SIGKDD International Conference on Knowledge Discovery and Data Mining, pp. 23–31. ACM (2013)
4. Griffiths, T.L., Steyvers, M.: Finding scientific topics. PNAS 101, 5228–5235 (2004)

5. Huang, J., Ling, C.X.: Using auc and accuracy in evaluating learning algorithms. IEEE Transactions on Knowledge and Data Engineering 17(3), 299–310 (2005)
6. Kajikawa, Y., Mori, J.: Interdisciplinary research detection by citation indicators. In: IEEM 2009, pp. 84–87. IEEE (2009)
7. Larivière, V., Gingras, Y.: On the relationship between interdisciplinarity and scientific impact. Journal of the American Society for Information Science and Technology 61(1), 126–131 (2010)
8. Porter, A.L., Chubin, D.E.: An indicator of cross-disciplinary research. Scientometrics 8(3), 161–176 (1985)
9. Porter, A.L., Cohen, A.S., Roessner, J.D., Perreault, M.: Measuring researcher interdisciplinarity. Scientometrics 72(1), 117–147 (2007)
10. Porter, A.L., Rafols, I.: Is science becoming more interdisciplinary? measuring and mapping six research fields over time. Scientometrics 81(3), 719–745 (2009)
11. Rafols, I., Meyer, M.: Diversity and network coherence as indicators of interdisciplinarity: case studies in bionanoscience. Scientometrics 82(2), 263–287 (2010)
12. Rao, C.R.: Diversity and dissimilarity coefficients: a unified approach. Theoretical Population Biology 21(1), 24–43 (1982)
13. Stirling, A.: A general framework for analysing diversity in science, technology and society. Journal of the Royal Society Interface 4(15), 707–719 (2007)
14. Tang, J., Zhang, J., Yao, L., Li, J., Zhang, L., Su, Z.: Arnetminer: Extraction and mining of academic social networks. In: KDD 2008, pp. 990–998 (2008)
15. Wang, Y., Tong, Y., Zeng, M.: Ranking scientific articles by exploiting citations, authors, journals, and time information. In: AAAI (2013)
16. Winslett, M.: Christos faloutsos speaks out: on power laws, fractals, the future of data mining, sabbaticals, and more. ACM SIGMOD Record 34(4), 85–89 (2005)
17. Zhai, C.: Statistical language models for information retrieval. Synthesis Lectures on Human Language Technologies 1(1), 1–141 (2008)

Multi-constrained Optimal Path Search Algorithms

Jinling Bao[1,2], Bin Wang[1], Shuchao Yan[1], and Xiaochun Yang[1]

[1] College of Information Science and Engineering, Northeastern University, China
[2] Department of Computer Science,Baicheng Normal College, China
baojinling@research.neu.edu.cn, {binwang,yangxc}@mail.neu.edu.cn,
yanshuchaoneu@gmail.com

Abstract. The problem of trip planning has received wide concerns in recent years. More and more people require the service of automatically confirming the optimal tour path. When users assign the source, the destination and the permitted time of the tour, how do we help them find the optimal path with the maximum popularity score? The multi-constrained optimal path search solutions have been used to solve the trip planning problem widely. However, when the permitted time is not enough to visit all attractions in any path, existing methods can not find the path satisfying the constraints. The time and the popularity score are different when we select the different attractions to visit in the same path. So we propose a new search rule to answer above issue, making a choice on any node (visit or pass by) according to the tradeoff between permitted time and popularity score of attractions. As our search rule need to make a choice on any attraction (visit or pass by), the search cost will be larger. This problem is NP hard. In this paper, we propose an exact algorithm to find the optimal path in relatively small data sets, and we also present a heuristic algorithm which is efficient and scalable to large data sets. The experimental results on real data sets reveal that our algorithms are able to find the optimal path efficiently.

Keywords: trip planning, multi-constrained, optimal path search.

1 Introduction

More and more people upload their travel information to Flickr, Baidu Lvyou and other social networking sites for sharing their travel experiences. By analyzing such data, researchers can mine a popular tourist attractions and tourism paths to recommend. Existing researches include: recommending the path according to users' demand [3, 4, 6, 7, 9] and recommending attractions based on the popularity of the path [2, 10, 11].

Considering the real-life demand of a new path search: a tourist, traveling in an unfamiliar city, requires help for planning the trip: "In order to obtain the most popular tourist paths, how to select the attractions if I departure from the hotel at 8:00 and need to catch the train at 18:00?" When users assign the source

L. Chen et al. (Eds.): APWeb 2014, LNCS 8709, pp. 355–366, 2014.

(hotel), the destination (railway station), and the permitted time (10 hours) of the tour, how to find the optimal tour path?

The problem above is multi-constraint optimal path search (MCOPS) problem. The solution of this MCOPS problem is NP hard. Existing methods can not find the optimal path under the constraints while the permitted time is not enough to visit all attractions in any path, because their search rule is visiting either all attractions or no attraction in a path. The time and the popularity score are different when we select the different attractions to visit in the same path. For example, a path contains five attractions and the tourist does not have enough time to visit all. In order to answer the problem, we propose a new search rule to find the optimal path, making a choice on any attraction (visit or pass by) in any path, according to the tradeoff between permitted time and popularity score of attractions. As our search rule need to make a choice on any attraction (visit or pass by), the search cost will be larger.

How to reduce the search cost of finding the optimal path is a challenge for us. We devise an exact algorithm based on breadth-first search to find the optimal path efficiently when the data sets are relatively small. And we propose a heuristic algorithm based on the shortest path, which searches the optimal path nearby the shortest path. It is scalable to relatively large data sets. In the paper, we mainly make the following contributions:

(1) We propose a new search rule to find the optimal path with multi-constraint making a choice on any node (visit or pass by) of all valid path according to the tradeoff between permitted time and popularity score of attractions.

(2) We present an exact algorithm based on breadth-first search. when the attractions is relatively few, to find the optimal path more efficiently, we prune invalid path according to the lower bound of time and the upper bound of popularity score.

(3) We propose a heuristic algorithm based on the shortest path, which finds the optimal path nearby the shortest path. In this algorithm, We also prune invalid path according to the lower bound of time and the upper bound of popularity score on path. It is efficient and scalable to relatively large data sets.

(4) The experimental results on real data sets reveal that our algorithms are efficient and scalable.

The rest of the paper is organized as follows. We briefly review the related work in Section 2. Section 3 gives the definition of MCOPS problem and prove its NP-hardness. In Sections 4 and 5 we propose an exact algorithm and a heuristic algorithm, respectively. Section 6 gives the empirical study. Finally, Section 7 concludes the paper.

2   Related Work

In recent years, a large number of relevant studies on tourist paths recommendations and searches, usually contain two cases as following: recommending the path according to users' demand and based on the GPS trajectories.

The work [6] proposes an exact algorithm, namely Trip-Mine, which can find the optimal trip having the highest total popularity score from the source node s and finally back to s. It takes the attraction map as a complete graph and use the permutation of all attractions to solve the problem. Lu X. et al. [7] collect geo-tagged photos from Flickr and built travel paths based on these photos. They define popularity scores on each attraction and each path, and recommend a path having the highest popularity score within a travel duration in the whole map. The exact recommendation algorithm rans in an extreme long time based on dynamic programming. The work [1] proposes a greedy algorithm to solve MCOPS problem as ours, but its accuracy is not well. The problems in the work [6, 7] are similar to ours, but Trip-Mine approach and dynamic programming algorithm can not efficient to solve our problem.

The work [9] proposes a KOR problem. It aims to find an optimal path, in which a set of user-specified keywords is covered, a specified budget constraint is satisfied, and an objective score of the path is optimal. In this work, two approximation algorithms are proposed.

With the development of GPS mobile positioning system, using GPS trajectory data to mine the best path receives wide concerns. The work [3] finds popular paths from users historical trajectories. The popularity score is defined as the probability from the source location to the target location estimated using the Absorbing Markov Chain based on the trajectories. Chen et al. [2] propose k-BCT and IKNN query algorithm to get k routes which can go through the user-specified location track well. Cong et al. [4] propose a BCK-tree indexing technology to quickly search the shortest path covering all keywords.

The problems in the work [2–4, 9] concern the popularity of path between attractions. But in this paper, we pay attention to the popularity of attractions in itself, it is more suitable the demand of users who want to experience the value of attractions.

3   Problem Statement

This section describes the related definitions of multi-constraint optimal path search problem and complexity analysis.

3.1   Optimal Path Search

We use a graph G to express a road network graph, or a graph extracted from users' historical trajectories. For example, if G is a traffic network, the attributes can be travel duration, travel distance, popularity, travel cost and so on. For simplicity, we consider undirected graphs in this paper. However, our discussion can be extended to directed graphs straightforwardly.

Given a graph $G = (V, E)$, it consists of a set of nodes V and a set of edges $E \subseteq V \times V$. Each node $v \in V$ represents a location; each edge in E represents a directed path between two locations in V, and the edge from v_i to v_j is represented by $e(v_i, v_j)$.

Let P be a path from v_0 to v_n, $P = \langle v_0, \ldots, (v_i), \ldots, v_n \rangle$, where v_i with a bracket denotes an unvisited node, while the others denote visited nodes. For example, $P = \langle v_0, (v_1), v_2 \rangle$ represents a path from v_0 to v_2, and the node v_1 is unvisited (simply passed by), while the nodes v_0 and v_2 are visited.

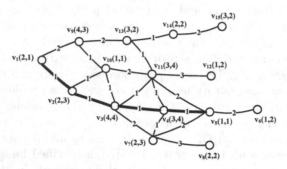

Fig. 1. An example graph G, where the pair (w_p, w_c) of each node represents the popularity w_p and cost w_c of the node, and the label in each edge represents the cost of the edge

Definition 1. Popularity Score and Cost Score. *Given a graph $G = (V, E)$. For each node $v \in V$, we use a pair (w_p, w_c) to express its popularity w_p and cost w_c, and for each edge $e = (v_i, v_j)$ we use a weight w to express its cost.*

For any path $P = \langle v_0, v_1, \ldots, v_n \rangle$, the popularity score of P is denoted as $PS(P)$, and the cost score of P is denoted as $C(P)$. Let V_P be the set of the nodes in the path P and V_A be the set of visited nodes, $V_A \subseteq V_P$. The cost score for path P is defined as the summation of the cost values of all visited nodes and all the edges in P:

$$C(P) = \sum_{\forall v_i \in V_A} w_c(v_i) + \sum_{\forall e = (v_i, v_j) \in P} w(e), \tag{1}$$

and the popularity score of the path P is the summation of the popularity score of all visited nodes:

$$PS(P) = \sum_{\forall v_i \in V_A} w_p(v_i). \tag{2}$$

For example, Fig. 1 shows an example of a graph G, in which each node v has a pair of scores (w_p, w_c), and each edge $e = (v_i, v_j)$ also has a cost score w. Consider the path $P = \langle v_1, (v_2), v_3, (v_4), v_5 \rangle$ in Fig. 1. The popularity score of P is $PS(P) = w_p(v_1) + w_p(v_3) + w_p(v_5) = 7$, and the cost score of P is $C(P) = w_c(v_1) + w(v_1, v_2) + w(v_2, v_3) + w_c(v_3) + w(v_3, v_4) + w(v_4, v_5) + w_c(v_5) = 10$.

Problem Formulation. Given a query $q = (v_s, v_d, \mathcal{C})$, where v_s is the source node, v_d is the destination node, and $\mathcal{C}$ is the permitted cost by users.

Find the optimal path P from v_s to v_d such that it satisfies the following two conditions:

[C_1]: $arg \max PS(P)$, and
[C_2]: $C(P) \leq C$.

Example 1. Consider the graph shown in Fig. 1. Let query $q = (v_1, v_5, 10)$. Find an optimal path with the maximum popularity score.

As shown from the Fig. 1, the optimal path is $P = \langle v_1, (v_2), v_3, (v_4), v_5 \rangle$, $PS(P) = 7$, $C(P) = 10$. In this case, there are not all nodes can be visited in any path due to permitted cost C, so existing methods can not find the optimal path. When we traverse any node based on breadth-first search, we must consider two states of this node (visited or pass by). In the path, the nodes v_2 is the node only passed by but unvisited. If there are m nodes on one path, we can get the 2^m combinations. After we get all combinations of all paths satisfying multi-constraint, we select the maximum popularity score as the optimal path.

3.2 Complexity of the Problem

Theorem 1. *The problem of solving MCOPS problem is NP-hard.*

Proof Sketch: If a node has the cost score and popularity score, the node can be expressed as the node has an edge with cost score and popularity score to itself. Then this problem can be reduced from the NP-hard shortest weight-constrained path problem (SWCPP) [8]. Given a graph in which each edge has a length and a weight, SWCPP finds a path that has the shortest length with the total weight not exceeding a specified value. The problem of answering MCOPS queries is a generalization of SWCPP. The problem of solving MCOPS becomes equivalent to the SWCPP.

4 Pruning Strategies for Exact Search

When the graph is relatively small, we do exact search to get the optimal path answering our MCOPS problem. A naive approach is to traverse all paths based on the breadth-first search. When we get all combinations of all paths satisfying multi-constraint, we select the path with maximum popularity score as the optimal finally. The main problem of the naive approach is that too many partial paths need to be stored on each node. In order to make it efficient, we propose two pruning strategies according to the lower bound of cost and the upper bound of popularity score in this section respectively.

To simplify the expression, we introduce the following notations in Table 1.

By observing real-life attractions information, we find that the attraction with more popularity always cost more. So we assume that all attractions have the same popularity score per unit cost in this paper and we set $\rho_i = \rho$. And $\kappa_{i,j}$ is the key node in the shortest path. We can find all nodes of the shortest path based on the key node efficiently.

Table 1. Related Notations

Notation	Description
$c_{i,j}$	The minimum cost between any two nodes v_i and v_j.
$\kappa_{i,j}$	The next to last node in the current shortest path from v_i to v_j.
ρ_i	The popularity score per unit cost, $\rho_i = \frac{w_p(v_i)}{w_c(v_i)}$.

Theorem 2. *Given a graph G and a query $q = (v_s, v_d, \mathcal{C})$, v_i is the current node to extend and c' is the cost of current path, if $(c' + c_{i,d}) > \mathcal{C}$, then the path is an invalid path.*

Proof Sketch: $c_{i,d}$ is the lower bond of cost spending from the current node v_i to the destination v_d, and $(c' + c_{i,d})$ is the lower bond of the cost from the current path to v_d through v_i. $(c' + c_{i,d}) > \mathcal{C}$ means that the path extending from the node v_i does not satisfy the permitted cost, so it is an invalid path, and all paths extending from the current path through v_i are all invalid ones.

Theorem 3. *Given a graph G and a query $q = (v_s, v_d, \mathcal{C})$, ps_{max} is the maximum popularity score of all path found. Let v_i is the current node to extend, c' is the cost of current path, and ps' is the popularity score of current path. The current path is an invalid path if $ps' + \rho(\mathcal{C} - c' - c_{i,d}) < ps_{max}$.*

Proof Sketch: According to the lower bound of the cost spending in the path, we can compute the upper-bound of remaining cost, which is equal to $(\mathcal{C} - c' - c_{i,d})$, i.e., the maximum cost to spend in the attractions. ρ is the popularity score per unit cost, so the upper bound of the popularity we get in the remaining cost is no more than $\rho(\mathcal{C} - c' - c_{i,d})$. If $ps' + \rho(\mathcal{C} - c' - c_{i,d}) < ps_{max}$, it means that the popularity score of any path from the current path to the destination v_d is less than ps_{max}. So the current path extending from v_i is not a valid path.

In order to improve the searching efficiency and reduce the memory storage requirement, we proposed the pruning algorithm according to the Theorem 2 and Theorem 3, i.e., we prune the invalid path according to the lower bound of cost and the upper bound of popularity score. The pseudo code is presented in Algorithm 1.

We use a queue Q to organize the partial path. We initialize the queue Q and p as NULL (p is used to store the partial path), and use variable ps_{max} to store the maximum popularity score we have got currently. p_i^k represents the k-th partial path from the source node v_s to the current node v_i. If the cost from the source node v_s to the destination node v_d is less than the permitted cost $\mathcal{C}$, We create a path p_s^0 at the starting node v_s and enqueue it into Q (lines 1-3). Then we calculate the popularity score per unit cost and use variable ρ to store it (line 4). We keep dequeuing path from Q. If the popularity score of current path is more than the maximum popularity score, we replace the ps_{max} with it (line 7). We terminate the algorithm when Q is empty (line 5).

For each outgoing neighbor v_j of the current node v_i, we extend the current path. If the lower bound of the cost in this path is more than the permitted cost $\mathcal{C}$, or the upper bound of the popularity score in this path is less than the maximum popularity score ps_{max} we have got, we stop extending for the path is invalid. Otherwise, we create the partial path (p_j^k) passing by the node v_j: add the cost $w(v_i, v_j)$ to (p_i^k) and set the state of v_j as FALSE. If v_j is not the destination, enqueue (p_j^k) into Q (lines 8-12). Compute the new lower bound of cost and upper bound of popularity score visiting the node v_j. If the lower bound is less than the permitted cost C, and the upper bound is more than the maximum popularity score, we create the partial path (p_j^{k+1}): add the cost $w_c(v_j)$ to $C(p_j^k)$, add $w_p(v_j)$ to $PS(p_j^k)$ and set the state of v_j as TRUE. If v_j is not the destination, enqueue (p_j^k) into Q (lines 13-19). Finally, the path p with the maximum popularity score is the optimal path (line 20).

Algorithm 1. Exact Search Algorithm

Input: graph G and $q = (v_s, v_d, C)$;
Output: The optimal path with largest popularity score: p;
1 Initialization queue Q; $p \leftarrow$ NULL; $ps_{max} \leftarrow 0$;
2 **if** $c_{s,d} \leq C$ **then**
3 $\quad$ create the path p_s^0 at v_s:$PS(p_s^0) \leftarrow ps(v_s)$; $C(p_s^0) \leftarrow c(v_s)$; $Q.\text{push}(p_s^0)$;
4 $\quad$ set $\rho \leftarrow \frac{w_p(v_s)}{w_c(v_s)}$;
5 $\quad$ **while** Q *is not empty* **do**
6 $\quad\quad$ $p_i^k \leftarrow Q.\text{pop}()$;
7 $\quad\quad$ **if** $PS(p_i^k) \geq ps_{max}$ **then** $ps_{max} \leftarrow PS(p_i^k)$;
8 $\quad\quad$ **for** *each edge* $e = (v_i, v_j)$ **do**
9 $\quad\quad\quad$ $cost_{lower} \leftarrow C(p_i^k) + w(e) + c_{j,d}$;
10 $\quad\quad\quad$ $ps_{upper} \leftarrow PS(p_i^k) + \rho(C - cost_{lower})$;
11 $\quad\quad\quad$ **if** $cost_{lower} \leq C$ *and* $ps_{upper} \geq ps_{max}$ **then**
12 $\quad\quad\quad\quad$ Create the path p_j^k: $C(p_j^k) \leftarrow C(p_i^k) + w(e)$;
13 $\quad\quad\quad\quad$ set $v_j.visit \leftarrow$ FALSE;
14 $\quad\quad\quad\quad$ **if** $v_j \neq v_d$ **then** $Q.push(p_j^k)$;
15 $\quad\quad\quad\quad$ $cost_{lower} \leftarrow cost_{lower} + w_c(v_j)$;
16 $\quad\quad\quad\quad$ $ps_{upper} \leftarrow ps_{upper} + w_p(v_j)$;
17 $\quad\quad\quad\quad$ **if** $cost_{lower} \leq C$ *and* $ps_{upper} \geq ps_{max}$ **then**
18 $\quad\quad\quad\quad\quad$ Create the path p_j^k: $C(p_j^{k+1}) \leftarrow C(p_j^k) + w_c(v_j)$;
$\quad\quad\quad\quad\quad\quad$ $PS(p_j^{k+1}) \leftarrow PS(p_j^k) + w_p(v_j)$; Set $v_j.visit \leftarrow$ TRUE;
19 $\quad\quad\quad\quad\quad$ **if** $v_j \neq v_d$ **then** $Q.push(p_j^k)$;

20 $\quad$ $p \leftarrow$ the path with the maximum popularity score;
21 return p;

---

5 Heuristic Search

The exact search algorithm is used to the case with relatively few nodes. In order to answer the MCOPS problem in a relatively large graph, we propose a heuristic search algorithm based on the shortest path.

By observing, we draw a conclusion that we can get more popularity score path when spending less cost on the path. Because we spend the less cost in the edge, we get more remaining cost to visit the nodes. Thus we can get more popularity score because the popularity score per unit cost of all nodes is equal. Then we can obtain the maximum popularity score extending the path nearby the shortest path from the source to the destination.

Theorem 4. *If the permitted cost C is just equal to the cost of visiting all nodes in the shortest path, the shortest path is the optimal path.*

Proof Sketch: If the query $q = (v_s, v_d, C)$, the popularity score per unit cost is ρ, and p is the shortest path from the source node v_s to the destination node v_d, the cost spending in the path only is $c_{s,d}$. And if the path p' is any path from the source node v_s to the destination node v_d, the remaining cost to spend in attractions is $C - C(p)$ along the path p', while the remaining cost to spend in attractions along the shortest path p is $C - c_{s,d}$. Therefore, $C - c_{s,d} \geq C - C(p)$, then $\rho(C - c_{s,d}) \geq \rho(C - C(p))$, i.e., the popularity score of the path p is equal or larger than that of the path p'. We can conclude that the shortest path p is the optimal path.

Based on the Theorem 4, we get the Lemma 1.

Lemma 1. *If the permitted cost C is just equal to the cost of visiting partial nodes in the shortest path, the path composed of the partial nodes along the shortest path is the optimal path.*

The basic idea of heuristic search algorithm based on shortest path is: we get the shortest path from the source to the destination firstly, then we extend the path to one-hop nodes nearby the shortest path.

The path we find based on the cases setting in Theorem 4 and Theorem 5, is just the optimal path. However, the optimal path is probably not in the shortest path, but it should be nearby the shortest path. We get the optimal path along the shortest path using exact search firstly, then we extend the current optimal path to one-hop node between any pair nodes in the shortest path. We iterate the above process till the cost is not enough to visit any other node. Finally, we get a approximate optimal path. When we search in the shortest path exactly and extend the path nearby the shortest path, we prune the invalid path according to the Theorem 2 and Theorem 3. The pseudo code is presented in Algorithm 2.

We initialize the optimal path: p as NULL and a query $q = (v_s, v_t, C)$ (line 1). we get the shortest path p from the source node to the destination node, and compute the related cost and the popularity of path p (lines 2-4). we compare $cost_{min}$ with C. If $C > cost_{min}$, and $C < cost_{max}$, we exact search in the shortest path and get the current optimal path (lines 5-7). Otherwise, if $C > cost_{max}$, we take the shortest path as current optimal path (lines 8-10). If the remaining cost is more than 0, we extend the path to one-hop node between any two visited nodes in p till the remaining cost is not enough to visit any other node (lines 11-12). Finally, the path p is the optimal path we find (line 13).

For example, given a query $q(s, d, C) = (v_1, v_5, 12)$, in order to find the optimal path p, we first get the shortest path from node v_0 to node v_5: $p = \langle v_1, v_2, v_3, v_4, v_5 \rangle$.

Algorithm 2. Heuristic Search Algorithm

Input: A graph G and a query $q = (v_s, v_d, \mathcal{C})$;
Output: The optimal path p with largest popularity score;

1 Initialization optimal path $p \leftarrow$ NULL;
2 $p \leftarrow$ the shortest path from v_s to v_d in G;
3 $cost_{min} \leftarrow 0$; $cost_{max} \leftarrow 0$; $ps_{max} \leftarrow w_p(v_s)$; $v_i \leftarrow v_s$;
4 **foreach** $edge\ e = (v_i, v_j)\ in\ p$ **do**
5 $\quad$ $cost_{min} \leftarrow cost_{min} + w(e)$; $ps_{max} \leftarrow ps_{max} + w_p(v_j)$;
$\quad$ $cost_{max} \leftarrow cost_{max} + w_c(v_j) + w(e)$; $v_i \leftarrow v_j$;;

6 **if** $cost_{min} < \mathcal{C}$ **then**
7 $\quad$ **if** $\mathcal{C} < cost_{max}$ **then**
8 $\quad\quad$ $p \leftarrow$ optimal path exact searching on the shortest path;
9 $\quad\quad$ the remaining cost $cost_{remain} \leftarrow \mathcal{C} - C(p)$;

10 $\quad$ **if** $\mathcal{C} \geq cost_{max}$ **then** the remaining cost $cost_{remain} \leftarrow \mathcal{C} - C(p)$;
11 $\quad$ **while** $cost_{remain} > 0$ **do**
12 $\quad\quad$ $p \leftarrow$ optimal path extending nearby the shortest path;

13 return p;

Then we find the optimal combination using the exact search: $p = \langle v_1, (v_2), v_3, (v_4), v_5 \rangle$ as the current optimal path, $C(p) = 10 < \mathcal{C}$, $PS(p) = 7$ and the remaining cost is 2. We extend the path to one-hop node nearby the shortest path: v_7, v_{10}, and v_{11}, respectively. The path $p = \langle v_1, (v_2), v_{10}, v_3, (v_4), v_5 \rangle$ has the maximum popularity score. So The path p is the optimal path and $C(p) = 12$ and $ps(p) = 8$.

We utilize the pre-processing results in order to accelerate the algorithms. We use the Floyd-Warshall algorithm [5], which is a well-known algorithm for finding all pairs shortest path. We store the minimum cost between any two nodes $c_{i,j}$, and the next to last node in the current shortest path $\kappa_{i,j}$.

6   Experiments

This section mainly studies the efficiency of all algorithms.

6.1   Experimental Settings

We use nine data sets in our experimental study. Five are generated from real attractions data. By extracting the subgraph of Beijing from Baidu Lvyou, we obtain five data sets containing 100, 150, 200, 250 and 300 nodes, respectively. To create the graph, we use the travel distance as the cost on each edge, the star level remarking by users as the popularity score in the range (1,5), and the average visiting time of an attractions as the cost on each node.

The other four are generated from real map data. By extracting the subgraph of Beijing road network, we obtain 4 data sets containing 800, 1000, 2000 and 3000 nodes, respectively. The travel distance is used as the cost on each edge, and we randomly generate the popularity score and the cost in the range (1,5) on each node to create the graph.

We generate a query set with any pairs of all nodes from data sets, and select 50 queries from all pairs randomly. Finally, we computed the average running time for each query set.

All algorithms were implemented in VC++ and ran on an Intel(R) Xeon(TM)2 CPU E7300@2.93GHz with 8GB RAM.

6.2   Experimental Results

The objective of this set of experiments is to study the efficiency of DAP [7], Trip-Mine [6] and the algorithms that we proposed with variation on the data set size and permitted time $\mathcal{C}$.

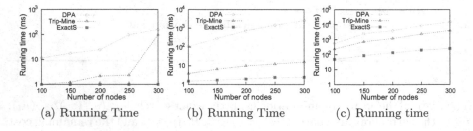

(a) Running Time   (b) Running Time   (c) Running time

Fig. 2. Running Time Vary the Number of Nodes

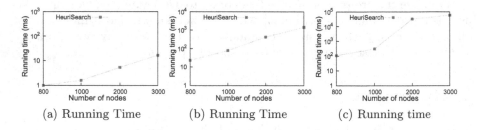

(a) Running Time   (b) Running Time   (c) Running time

Fig. 3. Running Time Vary the Number of Nodes

(1) Varying the Size of Data Set

Fig. 2 (a), (b) and (c) shows that the running time of three exact algorithms: DAP, Trip-Mine and Exact-Searh we proposed, processing the query set varying the number of the nodes respectively, when the permitted time $\mathcal{C}$ is 4 hours, 8 houres and 16 hours limit. Exact-Searh algorithm always outperforms DAP and Trip-Mine in terms of runtime. The reason is that the pruning strategies we proposed are relatively efficient. As expected, all algorithms run slower as we increase the permitted time.

Fig. 3 (a), (b) and (c) shows that the running time of Heuristic Search algorithms: processing the query set varying the number of the nodes respectively, when the permitted time $\mathcal{C}$ is 8 hours, 12 hours and 16 hours limit, respectively. The running time of this algorithm is affected by the data set size. It runs slower with increasing the data set size. However, when the permitted time is no more than 16 hours and the number of nodes is 3000, it is efficient.

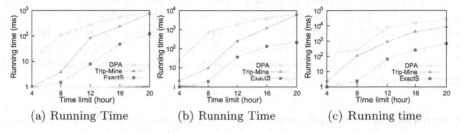

(a) Running Time   (b) Running Time   (c) Running time

Fig. 4. Running Time Vary the time limit $\mathcal{C}$

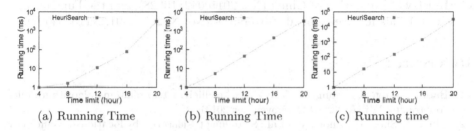

(a) Running Time   (b) Running Time   (c) Running time

Fig. 5. Running Time Vary the time limit $\mathcal{C}$

(2) Varying the Time Limit $\mathcal{C}$

Fig. 4 (a), (b) and (c) shows the running time of three exact algorithm processing querys varying the permitted time $\mathcal{C}$ when the number of nodes is 100, 200 and 300, respectively. Exact-Searh algorithm always outperforms DAP and Trip-Mine in terms of runtime. The reason is that the pruning strategies we proposed are relatively efficient. As expected, all algorithms run slower as we increase the permitted time.

Fig. 5 (a), (b) and (c) shows that the running time of Heuristic Search algorithms: processing the query set varying permitted time $\mathcal{C}$ when the number of nodes is 800, 1000, 2000 and 3000, respectively. The running time of this algorithm is affected by the permitted time $\mathcal{C}$. It run more slower with the increasing of permitted time. However, when the permitted time is no more than 16 hours and the number of nodes is 3000, it is efficient.

7   Conclusions

This MCOPS problem is NP hard. In order to answer the problem, we propose a new search rule. How to reduce the search cost for finding the optimal path efficiently is a challenge for us. We devise an exact algorithm based on breadth-first search to find the optimal path for relatively small data sets. In this algorithm, we prune invalid path according to the lower-bound of time and the upper-bound of popularity score on path. And we propose a heuristic algorithm based on the shortest path, which finds the optimal path nearby the shortest path. It is scalable to relatively large data sets. The experimental results on the real data sets reveal that our algorithm is able to find the optimal path in high efficiency. In the future work, we would like to improve the efficiency of the algorithms and current pre-processing approach.

Acknowledgments. The work is partialcly supported by the National Natural Science Foundation of China (Nos. 61322208, 61272178), the Joint Research Fund for Overseas Natural Science of China (No. 61129002), the Doctoral Fund of Ministry of Education of China (No. 20110042110028), and the Fundamental Research Funds for the Central Universities (No. N120504001, N110804002).

References

1. Bao, J., Yang, X., Wang, B., Wang, J.: An efficient trip planning algorithm under constraints. WISA, 429–434 (November 2013)
2. Chen, Z., Shen, H., Zhou, X., et al.: Searching trajectories by locations-an efficiency study. In: SIGMOD, pp. 255–266 (2010)
3. Chen, Z., Shen, H.T., Zhou, X.: Discovering popular routes from trajectories. In: ICDE, pp. 900–911 (2011)
4. Cong, G., Lu, H., Ooi, B.-C., et al.: Efficient spatial keyword search in trajectory databases. Arxiv Preprint, pp. 1–12 (2012)
5. Li, F., Cheng, D., Hadjieleftheriou, M., Kollios, G., Teng, S.: On trip planning queries in spatial databases. ASTD, 273–290 (2005)
6. Lu, E., Lin, C.Y., Tseng, V.S.: Trip-mine:an efficient trip planning approach with travel time constraints. MDM, 152–161 (November 2011)
7. Lu, X., Wang, C., Yang, J., Pang, Y., Zhang, L.: Photo2trip: generating travel routes from geotagged photos for trip planning. MM, 143–152 (2010)
8. Garey, M.R., Johnson, D.S.: Computers and Intractability: A Guide to the Theory of NP-Completeness. Freeman and Company, San Francisco (1979)
9. Cao, X., Chen, L., Cong, G., Xiao, X.: Keyword aware optimal route search. VLDB 5(11), 1136–1147 (2012)
10. Huang, Y., Bian, L.: A bayesian network and analyti hierarchy process based personalized recommendations for tourist attractionsover the internet. Expert Systems with Applications 36(1), 933–943 (2009)
11. Zheng, Y., Zhang, L., Xie, X., Ma., W.: Mining interesting locations and travel sequences from gps trajectories. In: WWW, pp. 791–800 (2009)

SPKV: A Multi-dimensional Index System for Large Scale Key-Value Stores

Qi Wang, Hailong Sun, Yu Tang, and Xudong Liu

School of Computer Science and Engineering, Beihang University,
Beijing, China 100191
{wangqi,sunhl,tangyu,liuxd}@act.buaa.edu.cn

Abstract. A number of key-value databases have emerged with the development of cloud computing, which provide the ability of large scale data storage, but they do not efficiently support the multi-dimensional range queries and kNN queries which are important in online applications. Thus, we introduce the Sliced Pyramid Index for Key-Value Stores (SPKV), an index system that bridges the gap between data scale and querying functionality for highly available and scalable distributed key-value databases. SPKV implements a distributed index system with an improved pyramid index scheme called SP-Index, which allows efficient multi-dimensional query processing. In our experiments, SPKV achieves dozens of times faster than other index systems for key-value databases.

1 Introduction

In recent years, the Internet data has been growing rapidly with the development of large scale Internet applications, such as social networking, e-commerce and so on. As a result of the requirements of big data and cloud computing, the data storage system is expected to achieve a series of new requirements which the traditional relational database cannot satisfy. Thus, a plenty of distributed NoSQL databases are developed. Key-value database is the most important category of NoSQL. They efficiently support simple queries based on the primary key, but most of the key-value databases do not efficiently support range queries, kNN queries and other complicated queries based on non-primary keys because of lacking of efficient indexes. For these queries, the whole dataset has to be scanned, which leads to excessive costs. This defect makes their application scenario mainly limited to simple applications or some offline data analysis applications with the help of MapReduce[2]. And it is not suitable for complex query requirements of online applications.

Although key-value stores follow a schema-free design, in practice developers prefer to store schema specific application data for convenient data processing with them. Therefore, in recent years, there have been many research on the indexing technology of key-value database for schema data, such as CCIndex[4] and BIDS[7]. However, existing indexing technologies are basically designed for specific architecture of key-value databases and are highly coupled with the underlying database storage engine, which limits the application scope of existing

L. Chen et al. (Eds.): APWeb 2014, LNCS 8709, pp. 367–378, 2014.

index technologies. Therefore, the index technology for key-value databases still needs to be further studied to be adapted to more general application scopes.

In this paper, we propose the design of SPKV, an index system which provides efficient multi-dimensional query processing for different key-value databases. The key of SPKV is an efficient multi-dimensional index scheme called SP-Index, which is designed on the basis of the pyramid technique[1]. Since the pyramid technique mainly uses only one dimension to calculate the index value, which causes that multiple data points are mapped to a single pyramid value on large-scale datasets with less distinct values. In order to understand the impact of pyramid value, we perform an experiment to evaluate how the pyramid technique performs with changing number of distinct values and size of the dataset. Fig 1 shows that the number of candidate points to be scanned in a point query can be up to 400,000 for the dataset containing 20 million points with 50 distinct values in each dimension. The linear scan for so many points on the disk severely degrades the query performance. In order to decrease the number of points to be scanned, we specify the dimensions with less distinct values and divide the pyramid space much finer based on the information of all dimensions. Theoretical analysis shows that our division strategy leads to exponential improvement about the dimensionality on query performance compared to the original pyramid technique.

Then we apply SP-Index to Cassandra, a popular open-source key-value database, to implement a prototype system of SPKV. Experiments on synthetically generated dataset and the dataset of TPC-H benchmark[11] show SPKV can efficiently process complex multi-dimensional range queries and kNN queries. And it greatly outperforms some other index methods on key-value databases with tens of times faster.

The rest of the paper is organized as follows. In next section, we conduct a literature review of related works. In Section 3, we describe the design of SP-Index and its query processing. The implementation details of SPKV are presented in Section 4. In Section 5, we evaluate the performance of SPKV and conclude this paper in Section 6.

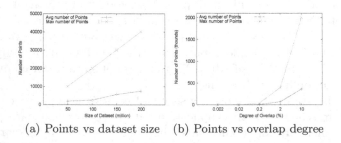

(a) Points vs dataset size   (b) Points vs overlap degree

Fig. 1. The *overlap degree* means the percentage of the points with the same pyramid value in total points, which is negatively correlated to the number of distinct values. The number of distinct values in (a) is 50 and the dataset size of (b) is 20 million.

2   Related Work

Nowadays, there are various key-value databases. Dynamo[3], Hbase[5] and Cassandra[6] are representative key-value stores. They cannot efficiently deal with complex queries based on non-primary key because of lack of efficient secondary index. In production environment, the solution is using MapReduce technology to scan the whole database in parallel to establish special data tables as indexes. This scheme can satisfy the requirements of the query, but the index can only be established in batch and cannot be updated in real time. Besides, it is not a general method which can bring excess work to database users.

Complemental Cluster Indexing technology (CCIndex)[13,4] is proposed based on Hbase and Cassandra. However, CCIndex need to store a replica for every dimensions in a row which results in large amounts of disk space consumption in high-dimensional cases, and it does not support for kNN query. BIDS[7] achieves very low space cost and provides efficient multi-dimensional range queries and join queries with highly compressed bitmap index. But it is more suitable for offline data analysis applications with rare updates rather than online applications because of the defect of the bitmap index in updating.

Pyramid technique[1] is proved to be an efficient multi-dimensional index structure. The pyramid technique adopts the strategy of the non-uniform space division and filter to distribute the data points into space pyramids. It calculates the pyramid index value (Pv) according to the multi-dimensional values. Then it builds one dimensional index in B^+-tree according to the Pv. The final query results are obtained through filtering the candidate points which are searched from the B^+-tree with the Pv of the query. The performance of pyramid technology far exceeds the tree-like indexing methods[1]. But the pyramid index calculates the Pv only considering the value of the dimension which is the furthest from the space center and ignoring the information of other dimensions, incurring that two points whose values which largely differ from each other in some dimensions have the same Pv. Other index technology derived from the pyramid technique, such as P^+-Tree[12], has no obvious performance improvement under the uniform datasets because they mainly focus on the query for the skewed distributed or clustered datasets[12]. So far there is no fundamental solution to the high cost in filtering the candidate points corresponding to the query.

3   The SP-Index

In order to cope with the query requirements of huge volumes of data in various types, we propose SP-Index on the basis of the pyramid technique. So we take a look at pyramid technique before introducing the SP-Index.

The pyramid technique divides the d-dimensional data space into $2d$ pyramids that share the center point of the space as their top (Fig 2(a)), and the $(d-1)$-dimensional surfaces of the space are their bases. Each pyramid has a pyramid id p according to some rule. The distance between a point X and the center in dimension p (or $p-d$ if $p \geq d$) is defined as the height of the point, h_X. Then, the pyramid value of X is $Pv_X = (p + h_X)$.

Two problems of the pyramid technique make it fail to preserve its excellent performance when facing a huge amount of multi-dimensional data. First, the number of points corresponding to each Pv increases with the increasing amounts of data. Second, the number of Pv becomes less when there are less distinct values in each dimensions. These problems make the data points corresponding to a Pv will out of range of a leaf node in B^+-tree. Large numbers of candidate points increase the times of disk I/O because one query operation has to search data across multiple disk pages, which results in longer response time and degrades the performance of the index.

Therefore, the main objective of SP-Index is to reduce the number of data points with the same pyramid value (Pv) in the case of large-scale datasets or datasets with less distinct values, which can improve query processing efficiency with the decreasing of the needed disk scanning.

3.1   Space Division of SP-Index

With this consideration, the basic idea of SP-Index is to enlarge the pyramid value scope of each pyramid and to provide finer division on the pyramid space so as to make each Pv corresponds to as less data points as possible. First, the d-dimensional data space is divided into $2d$ pyramids as original pyramid method does. Second, we specify the columns with less distinct values and perform the slice division to insurance the index items with the same Pv can be stored in a disk page. Then each corresponding pyramid will be further split into 2^{d-1} slices. Since we set the interval size of each slice to 1, the Pv of some points in a pyramid may greater than the upper bound of this pyramid which leads to collisions with the points in next pyramid. So we need to extend the interval of each pyramid to avoid the collisions. And in each slice, a data point is identified by the height of the point, which is similar to original pyramid method. Above all, in SP-Index, a data point will be addressed through a triple $< pyramidid, sliceid, height >$ (Fig 2(b)). The detailed method is described as following steps:

S1. We assume the dimension of data is d, a row of data is presented by a point $X = (x_0, x_1, ..., x_{d-1})$ in d-dimensional space. Normalize X according to the range of the value of each dimension and put it into d-dimensional [0,1] space. Then we get point $X' = (x'_0, x'_1, ...x'_{d-1})$.

S2. Get the id p of the pyramid which X' is belonging to as below.

$$p = \begin{cases} j_{max} & x'_{j_{max}} < 0.5) \\ j_{max} + d & x'_{j_{max}} \geq 0.5) \end{cases} \tag{1}$$

j_{max} is the number of the dimension which has the biggest value of $|x'_j - 0.5|$.

S3. In this step, we determine pyramids need to be divided into slices. Considering the general case, the number of points in each node and in each dimension is similar with other nodes and dimensions. We set N to be the estimated number of rows in the dataset, n is the number of nodes in the cluster and V is the

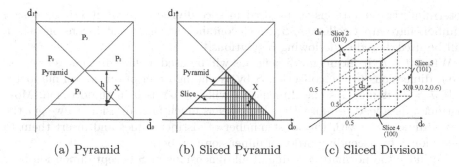

(a) Pyramid   (b) Sliced Pyramid   (c) Sliced Division

Fig. 2. Space division of Pyramid and SP-Index

number of distinct values. So the average number of points corresponding to a pyramid value is $\frac{N}{ndV}$. In order to optimize the query performance, the number is expected to be less than the max number of index items in a disk page. Let K to be the disk page size and S is the size of an index item. Generally, K is 4KB and S is about 64B. Then we can get the following formula.

$$\frac{N}{ndV} \geq \frac{K}{S} \rightarrow V \leq \frac{NS}{ndK} \tag{2}$$

In Formula (2), V is the max distinct values number of the columns which need to be further divided. Specifically, given a 200 million 6-dimensional dataset and a cluster with 10 nodes, V is about 50,000, which means the pyramids corresponding to the columns with less than 50,000 distinct values are required finer division.

S4. We divide each pyramid into multiple slices in the process of calculating the height of point X. As mentioned above, we need to extend the interval of each pyramid to avoid the collision of Pv with the points in next pyramids. We set the size of the interval of each *sliced pyramid* to 2^s and uniformly divide the interval $[0, 2^s]$ into 2^s slices, the interval of each slice is 1. And the *sliced pyramid* id sp is denoted by the low bound of its interval, which is defined as $sp = p \cdot 2^s$.

So the interval of *sliced pyramid* p is $[p \cdot 2^s, (p+1) \cdot 2^s]$. s indicates the times that we divide the pyramid and it is defined as $s = Min(d-1, T)$.

However, a larger s would produce too many slices since the volume of slices grows exponentially with dimensions. Since large numbers of slices will increase the times of scans and reduce the performance in range queries, we set T to 8 based on experiment results, which is not presented in this paper because of the length limitation of the article, to limit the size of s.

S5. For the pyramids corresponding to the dimensions needn't to be slice divided, we calculate the height as $h = |0.5 - x'_{p\%d}|$ directly. And the pyramid value of the points in this dimensions is defined as $Pv_X = sp + h$, which is similar with original pyramid technique.

On the other hand, for the pyramids corresponding to the dimensions with less distinct values, we will get the slice id $q_{X'}$ of point X'. At first, we need to determine the dimensions to be used in slice division. So we insert dimension numbers into empty collection S, which contains the number of dimensions which will be used, based on following regulations.

When $d \leq T$, it means all dimensions will be used in slice division, so we add the d dimensions to the collection S by ascending order of dimension number;

If $d > T$, it means some dimensions will not be used in the division. More distinct values lead to more Pv which means much finer division, so we get the first s dimensions with the most number of distinct values and insert them to collection S by ascending order of dimension number.

We judge the normalized value of all dimensions in S except dimension $p\%d$ and set the corresponding bit of q to 1 if the value $x' \leq 0.5$, otherwise we set the bit to 0. For example, there is a 4-dimensional point $X' = (0.9, 0.2, 0.6, 0.95)$, we can get $p = 7$ and $s = 3$ according to S2 and S4. Then we put X' into a 3-dimensional space showed in Fig 2(c). The 4th dimension is excluded because it has been used to determine the pyramid id. Since $x'_0 > 0.5$, we set the 1st bit of q to 1. And so on, we set the 2nd and 3rd bit of q to 0 and 1 because $x'_1 < 0.5$ and $x'_2 > 0.5$. In this way, we know that X' is located in $Slice$ 5 because $q_{X'} = 5$.

S6. In last step, we not only divide 4-dimensional space into $2d = 8$ pyramids but also divided each pyramid into $2^s = 8$ slices. Inside the slice, the distance from a data point to the inner edge of each slice is defined as height $h = |0.5 - x'_{p\%d}|$. Finally, the pyramid value of SP-Index is defined as $Pv_X = sp + q + h$.

In order to dynamically insert a point X, we first determine the pyramid value Pv_X of the point through the steps above and then insert the point into B$^+$-tree or other data structures which efficiently support point and range queries to construct the SP-Index using Pv_X as the key.

3.2   Query Processing

The process of queries for the pyramids corresponding to the dimensions without slice division is similar with origin pyramid technique. So we mainly discuss on the queries in sliced pyramids in this section.

Point Query. The process of point query based on column values is simple, we compute the Pv_Q of query point $Q = (x_0, x_1, ..., x_{d-1})$ using the methods in section 3.1 and querying the B$^+$-tree with Pv_Q, then we will obtain a set of candidate points sharing the Pv_Q. We can scan the set and determine whether the point is satisfied with conditions of each dimension of Q to obtain the final result.

Range Query. Given a range query $Q = ((x_{0_{min}}, x_{0_{max}}), ..., (x_{d-1_{min}}, x_{d-1_{max}}))$, it will be processed as following steps.

S1. At first, we normalize Q to d-dimensional $[0, 1]$ space. Get the pyramids intersected with the query range. A pyramid p is intersected with the query Q if and only if it satisfies the following formula. And we set the *sliced pyramid* id to $sp = p \cdot 2^s$.

$$x_{i_{min}} \le x_{j_{max}}, x_{i_{min}} \le 1 - x_{j_{min}} \qquad j = 0, 1, ..., d - 1, p < d, i = p$$
$$1 - x_{i_{max}} \le x_{j_{max}}, 1 - x_{i_{max}} \le 1 - x_{j_{min}} \quad j = 0, 1, ..., d - 1, d \le p < 2d, i = p\%d$$

S2. In this step, we determined the slices need to be queried by the following algorithm in each *sliced pyramid*. Let x be the id of the slice need to be queried. We determine the upper bound and lower bound of query range in each dimension and set the corresponding bit of x to 0 if the upper bound is less than 0.5 or set the bit to 1 if the lower bound is greater than 0.5. If the point 0.5 is included in the range, we need to search two slices and the corresponding bit of the id of the first slice is set to 0 and the other slice is set to 1. For example, the query range is $((0.3, 0.4), (0.4, 0.7), (0.5, 0.6), (0.0, 0.1))$. The pyramid id $p = 3$, and we can get two slice number $x_1 = 1(001)$ and $x_2 = 3(011)$ because the query range of 2nd dimension includes the point 0.5. We will get the slices to be queried after all dimensions except the dimension $p\%d$ are judged.

S3. In the last step, we need to determine the query ranges $r = (r_{low}, r_{high})$ within each slice to be queried according to Formula (3).

$$f = 0.5 - q_{x\%d_{min}} * 0.5 - q_{x\%d_{max}}$$

$$r_{low} = \begin{cases} sp + q + Min(|0.5 - x_{p\%d_{min}}|, |0.5 - x_{p\%d_{max}}|) & f \ge 0 \\ sp + q & f < 0 \end{cases}$$

$$r_{high} = \begin{cases} sp + q + Max(|0.5 - x_{p\%d_{min}}|, |0.5 - x_{p\%d_{max}}|) & f \ge 0 \\ sp + q + |0.5 - x_{p\%d_{min}}| & f < 0, p < d \\ sp + q + |0.5 - x_{p\%d_{max}}| & f < 0, p \ge d \end{cases}$$

$$(3)$$

Through the steps above, we finally obtain a set of one dimensional ranges for each slice q of each intersect pyramid p. The points outside the ranges can be ensured exclusion from the query rectangular, and every point within the range is the candidate points to be processed. Thus, we can scan the set obtained from several range queries on B$^+$-tree and determine whether the point is satisfied with the query range of Q to obtain the final result.

kNN Query. To find the kNN of a query point $X = (x_0, x_1, ..., x_{d-1})$, we adopt a kNN search algorithm with modified decreasing radius strategy[10]. We use a priority queue A to contain k candidate nearest neighbors sorted by the distance from X in decreasing order. Let $D(v, X)$ be the Euclidean distance between a candidate point v and point X, and D_{max} be the maximum distance between the points in A and point X. Besides, let $C(X, r)$ be a circle centered at X with a radius r. We will get the result in queue A after following steps.

S1. A is initialized to be empty, and we calculate the $Pv_X = p_i + q_j + h$ using the method in section 3.1. We search the B$^+$-tree to locate the leaf node which has the key equal to Pv_X, or the largest key less than Pv_X. After locating the leaf node, we check the data points in the node towards both to the left and right, meanwhile, we calculate the $D(v, X)$ to determine if the point v is one of the k nearest neighbors, and update A accordingly. The search process stops when the key of the leaf node is less than $\lfloor Pv_X \rfloor$ or greater than $\lfloor Pv_X \rfloor + 0.5$, or there are k data points in A and the difference between the current key value in the node and the pyramid value of X is greater than D_{max}.

S2. If the size of queue A is less than k after we finish searching the interval $[\lfloor Pv_X \rfloor, \lfloor Pv_X \rfloor + 0.5]$ then we need to repeat S1 in the slice which is the nearest from the point X. We find dimension l which has the smallest $|0.5 - x_l|$ from the collection S which is mentioned in section 3.1. Then we invert the l-th bit of the slice number q_j to get q_j' and repeat S1 with $Pv_{X'} = p_i + q_j' + h$.

S3. We get a big enough query range (radius) through the first 2 steps and the query range will gradually decrease after the range queries in each pyramid. We generate a query square W enclosing $C(X, r)$ to perform an range search, which guarantees the correctness of the query results. We assume there are k data points in A after the first two steps. We examine the rest of the pyramids one by one. If the pyramid intersects W, we perform a range search to check if the points in this pyramid are among the k nearest neighbors by compared to the D_{max}. The side length of W and D_{max} is updated after each pyramid is examined. If the pyramid does not intersect W, we can prune the search in this pyramid. We will get the finally results when all the pyramids are checked.

4 Implementation of SPKV

We implement SPKV with SP-Index and deploy SPKV on the nodes of the key-value database to support the complex queries on huge amounts of multi-dimensional data. In this paper, we use Cassandra as the data layer of SPKV. Cassandra is a popular open-source key-value database, in addition, it provides the SQL-like CQL language which introduces a schema-like data model and friendly query interfaces. It is valuable and necessary to apply SPKV to Cassandra to improve its query performance limited by its original inefficient secondary index. Moreover, it is convenient to apply SPKV to other key-value databases.

In the design of SPKV, we can adopt the same partition strategy and replication strategy with database layer basing on the current node states and the partition information of the cluster. The index layer in each node only indexes the local data partition by consistent hashing of Cassandra or other partition methods of underlying databases. Besides, SPKV ensures the availability of index layer when some nodes are subject to failures by the replication of SP-Index.

The persistent storage of index tables is implemented with MapDB[8], which is a B-tree-like storage engine. When inserting new data, we first compute the Pv value by the method described in section 3.1. Then we insert it to MapDB using "$Pv : RowKey$" as the key. We implement replication and partition functions for index tables based on the strategy of underlying key-value database to guarantee the high availability and scalability of the index system. Considering the inefficient insert performance of B-tree-like data structure, we provides memtable and commitlog for SP-Index to improve the insert performance. Besides, we divide the non-index columns into two parts. The columns which are mainly queried by multi-dimensional conditions, in terms of *Index Content*, are stored in the index table. And the other columns which mainly queried by the rowkey are stored only in the underlying database in order to control the space cost of SPKV. Although we store the columns into different tables, we can get all columns of the row through an additional low-cost key-value query in database layer or point query in SP-Index.

5   Evaluation

In this section, we present a set of evaluation results to show the performance of SPKV. Specifically, we evaluate SPKV through the comparison with MySQL Cluster 7.3.2[9], CCIndex for Cassandra[4] and SPKV implemented with original pyramid technique in terms of multi-dimensional point query, range query and kNN query. Our experimental cluster has 10 nodes. Each node has 2.0 GHz quad-cores CPU, 16 GB memory and more than 200 GB HDD. All nodes are connected by 1Gbps Ethernet. SPKV is implemented on Cassandra 1.2.8.

We both use the synthetically generated random datasets (The number of distinct values in each column ranges from 100 to 100,000) and the dataset of TPC-H in our evaluation. The total size of a row in generated dataset ranges from 128 to 164 Bytes according to the dimensions. We use the dataset of TPC-H, an acknowledged database benchmark which can simulate real business applications, to test the performance of SPKV in real world datasets. In order to test the performance of index, all experiments do not return the non-*IndexedContent* so as to avoid the influence of massive key-value query in Cassandra.

5.1   Effects of Data Size

In this section, we measure the performance with varying number of rows compared to other system. We perform point queries, range queries with 50,000 rows of selectivity and kNN queries with k=50 in a 6-dimensional dataset. Figure 3 displays the result of the experiments. The kNN query of original pyramid is implemented based on [10]. However, CCIndex and MySQL Cluster don't supported kNN queries so we skip the comparison with them. As is shown in Figure 3, all techniques perform well in the point query. Thanks to the finer division, SPKV outperformed other systems with speed factor 4∼8 in range query and speed factor 10∼20 in kNN query with every data sizes and performed well in large volume of data.

5.2   Effects of Selectivity

In this section we see how the selectivity and the number of K effect the performance of SPKV. In these experiments, we use 6-dimensional dataset and let the data size to be 100 million. Figure 4(a)(b) shows the results. SPKV always performs best and achieves the largest speedup factor in low selectivity or low K value. The reason is that the smaller query ranges lead to less slices need to

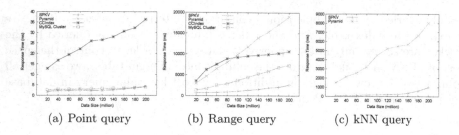

Fig. 3. Effect of Data Set Size

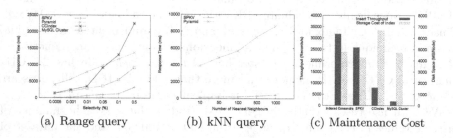

Fig. 4. Effect of Selectivity and Throughput

be query which decrease both the query times and the size of rows to be scan. When selectivity becomes larger the performance decreases, nevertheless, SPKV still outperforms other technique with 7~20 times faster and can be competent to various of selectivity and K value.

5.3   Insert Throughput and Storage Cost

In the evaluation of insert throughput, we use 10 concurrent clients to insert rows to the system which has already stored 100 million rows of 6-dimensional data and the experiment result is showed in Figure 4(c). The insert throughput of SPKV is lower than Indexed Cassandra because of the additional write operations and network communication cost brought by the index table. However, SPKV performs far better than CCIndex which need to write 6 index tables and MySQL Cluster whose insert throughput is limited by the relational and transactional storage engine.

Figure 4(c) also indicates that each node of SPKV costs about 4GB disk space for a 6-dimension dataset of 100 million rows, which is less than the cost of 6GB disk space with CCIndex. Besides, it is similar to that of the secondary index in Cassandra and the b-tree index of MySQL cluster. According to the above analysis and experimental results, the costs are acceptable while great query performance improvement is achieved.

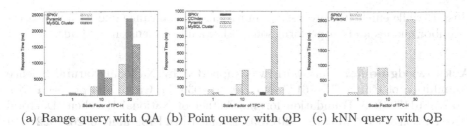

(a) Range query with QA   (b) Point query with QB   (c) kNN query with QB

Fig. 5. Performance with TPC-H Dataset

5.4   TPC-H Benchmark

In this section, we use $Q6$ in TPC-H as QA to illustrate the practical effect on range queries of SPKV. We also define a simple query QB to evaluate the performance of point queries and kNN queries. For the queries we build a 5-dimensional index on the *Lineitem* table in TPC-H.(We change some columns of the table in order to adapt to Cassandra's data model.)

QA is defined as:

`SELECT sum(extendedprice*discount) as revenue FROM Lineitem`
`WHERE shipdate≥x AND shipdate<x+1 year AND`
`discount≥y AND discount<y-0.02 AND quantity<z`

We also define QB as below:

`SELECT extendedprice FROM Lineitem WHERE shipdate=sd AND commitdate`
`=sd+1 month AND discount=d AND tax=t AND quantity=q`

The result is showed in Figure 5. SPKV still performs well but a bit lower than the experiments on generated dataset since the number of distinct values of index columns in *Lineitem* table are much smaller. In addition, the QA only specify the query range for 3 dimensions, that is, the other 2 dimensions of the queries are full domains. Even so, SPKV still achieves remarkable performance and outperforms other system because of the slice division on the dimensions whose query ranges are specific. The performance of CCIndex and pyramid technique rapidly deteriorates when the distinct values are less. They respectively fail to respond in 30 seconds during the range and kNN query, so we skip them in Figure 5(a)(c). All of above show that SPKV can well perform on columns with both less and more distinct values.

6   Conclusions

In this paper, we introduce an efficient multi-dimensional index technique named SP-Index. Through the much finer division on the pyramid space, we significantly improve the query performance on huge amounts of data. We present the design of SPKV that builds SP-Index over the partitioned key-value store, which allows efficient multi-dimensional query processing. In our experiments, the results demonstrate that SPKV can handle high scale of data using a modest 10 node cluster, while efficiently processing multi-dimensional range queries and nearest neighbor queries and outperform some other multi-dimension methods.

Acknowledgments. This work was supported by National Natural Science Foundation of China (No. 61370057, No. 61103031), China 863 program (No. 2012AA011203), A Foundation for the Author of National Excellent Doctoral Dissertation of PR China (No. 201159), Beijing Nova Program(No. 2011022) and Specialized Research Fund for the Doctoral Program of Higher Education (No. 20111102120016).

References

1. Berchtold, S., Böhm, C., Kriegal, H.P.: The pyramid-technique: towards breaking the curse of dimensionality. ACM SIGMOD Record 27, 142–153 (1998)
2. Dean, J., Ghemawat, S.: Mapreduce: simplified data processing on large clusters. Communications of the ACM 51(1), 107–113 (2008)
3. DeCandia, G., Hastorun, D., Jampani, M., Kakulapati, G., Lakshman, A., Pilchin, A., Sivasubramanian, S., Vosshall, P., Vogels, W.: Dynamo: amazon's highly available key-value store. In: SOSP, vol. 7, pp. 205–220 (2007)
4. Feng, C., Zou, Y., Xu, Z.: Ccindex for cassandra: A novel scheme for multi-dimensional range queries in cassandra. In: 2011 Seventh International Conference on Semantics Knowledge and Grid (SKG), pp. 130–136. IEEE (2011)
5. Hbase, A.: http://hbase.apache.org/
6. Lakshman, A., Malik, P.: Cassandra: a decentralized structured storage system. ACM SIGOPS Operating Systems Review 44(2), 35–40 (2010)
7. Lu, P., Wu, S., Shou, L., Tan, K.-L.: An efficient and compact indexing scheme for large-scale data store. In: 2013 IEEE 29th International Conference on Data Engineering (ICDE), pp. 326–337. IEEE (2013)
8. MapDB, http://www.mapdb.org/
9. MySQLCluster, http://dev.mysql.com/downloads/cluster/
10. Shi, Q., Nickerson, B.: Decreasing radius k-nearest neighbor search using mapping-based indexing schemes. Tech. rep., University of New Brunswick (2006)
11. TPC-H, http://www.tpc.org/tpch/
12. Zhang, R., Ooi, B.C., Tan, K.-L.: Making the pyramid technique robust to query types and workloads. In: Proceedings of 20th International Conference on Data Engineering, pp. 313–324. IEEE (2004)
13. Zou, Y., Liu, J., Wang, S., Zha, L., Xu, Z.: CCIndex: A complemental clustering index on distributed ordered tables for multi-dimensional range queries. In: Ding, C., Shao, Z., Zheng, R. (eds.) NPC 2010. LNCS, vol. 6289, pp. 247–261. Springer, Heidelberg (2010)

Popularity Prediction in Microblogging Network

Shuai Gao, Jun Ma, and Zhumin Chen

School of Computer Science and Technology, Shandong University, Jinan, China
gao_shuai@mail.sdu.edu.cn, {majun,chenzhumin}@sdu.edu.cn

Abstract. Popularity prediction in microblogging network aims to predict the future popularity of a tweet based on the observation in the early stages. Existing studies have investigated many features for prediction. However, features from the users who have potential to retweet a tweet have not been fully explored for this problem. Also, the impact of tweet's post time on its early-stage popularity has been neglected. To address these issues, we study two prediction tasks in this paper, i.e. predicting the popularity of a tweet based on the observation in 1 Hour after being posted (PP1H) or the observation of its first k retweets (PPkR), and investigate a wide spectrum of features to identify effective features for each prediction task. We extract structural features including *retweet network features* and *border network features* from the underlying user network, and *temporal features* from the observed retweets. To mitigate the impact of tweet's post time on its early-stage popularity, we introduce the notation of *tweet time* and use it to measure the temporal features. We treat both prediction tasks as classification problems and apply five standard classifiers (i.e. naive bayes, k-nearest-neighbor, support vector machine, logistic regression and bagging decision trees) for prediction. Experiments on Sina Weibo show that for PP1H task, bagging decision trees with all feature yield the best performance and border network features outperform other groups of features. For PPkR task, we find that satisfied prediction performance can be obtained based on only the temporal features of first 10 retweets. Furhter, by introducing tweet time, we can significantly improve the prediction performance of temporal features.

Keywords: Popularity Prediction, Social Media, Classification, Information diffusion.

1 Introduction

Online social networks have become increasingly important for information sharing and interpersonal communication. Recently, the study of predicting the popularity of online content in social networks has drawn much attention because of its remarkable practical value in a variety of business and administrative applications, including media advertising [1, 2], trend forecasting [3, 4] and understanding the collective behaviors of users [5–7] etc. Future popularity of online content indicates the intensity with which people would react and hence has the potential to influence polity decisions.

L. Chen et al. (Eds.): APWeb 2014, LNCS 8709, pp. 379–390, 2014.

Popularity prediction in microblogging network aims to predict the future popularity of a tweet based on the observation in the early stages. It is challenging since there are numerous factors to be considered. Recently, several pioneering work have been made and many features have been investigated [8–10]. However, previous studies have not considered the impact of the time of day when a tweet is posted on its popularity in the early stages. Since the user activity varies over time, the post time of a tweet can affect its popularity in the early stages. For example, considering the number of retweets that a tweet receives in the first hour after being posted, a tweet posted at 11 am is expected to receive more retweets on average than a tweet posted in midnight, since users are more active in daytime. If we do not eliminate the effect of user activity, we may misinterpret the relative interestingness of a tweet only based on the observation in the early stages. Also, users who have not retweeted the tweet but followed those who have already retweeted the tweet could be potentially useful for prediction. For tweet popularity prediction problem, features from these users have not been fully explored.

In this paper, we study the popularity prediction problem on Sina Weibo, a Twitter-like microblogging network in China. Different from previous studies, we consider two prediction tasks, which are predicting the popularity of a tweet based on the observation in 1 Hour after being posted (PP1H) or the observation of its first k retweets (PPkR). We investigate a wide spectrum of features including structural features and temporal features to identify effective features for each prediction task. By utilizing the historical mention relationships, we construct the underlying user network and then extract two groups of structural features, i.e. *retweet network features* from the network formed by users who have retweeted the tweet and *border network features* from the network formed by users who have been exposed to the tweet but not retweeted the tweet. Further, to mitigate the impact of tweet's post time on its early-stage popularity, we introduce the notation of *tweet time* and use it to measure the *temporal features* derived from the observed retweets. The PP1H task is treated as a multi-class classification problem which predicts the popularity range of a tweet, while the PPkR task is considered as a binary classification problem which predicts whether the tweet will be popular in the future. We apply five widely used classifiers for prediction, including Naive Bayes, K-Nearest-Neighbors, Support Vector Machine, Logistic Regression and Bagging Decision Trees. Experimental results show that for PP1H task, bagging decision trees with all features can achieve the best performance and the border network features are more effective than the other two groups of features. For PPkR task, we find that temporal features are more effective than structural features and the prediction performance of temporal features can be highly improved when measured by tweet time. Note that temporal features can be effortlessly extracted only based on the first few retweets, without need of the knowledge of user network. This provides new insights for administrative applications such as media control. Quick decisions can be made effortlessly based on only the observation of the early stages of diffusion process. Our main contributions are as follows:

- We study two popularity prediction tasks on microblogging networks, i.e. predicting the future popularity of a tweet based on the observation in one hour after being posted or the observation of first k retweets.
- We investigate a wide spectrum of features including structural and temporal features and identify effective features for each prediction task.
- We introduce the notation of tweet time and use it to measure the temporal features. Through this, we can mitigate the impact of tweet's post time on its early-stage popularity and further improve the prediction performance of temporal features.

The rest of paper is organized as follows. We review related work in Section 2. In Section 3, we define the research problems studied in this paper and present the methods. We give a detailed description of features in Section 4. The results and discussions are presented in Section 5. We conclude our paper in Section 6.

2   Related Work

Online content exists in various forms such as news articles, videos, hashtags and tweets etc. There have been many studies on predicting the popularity of online content in social networks. In [11], Tsagkias et al. explored five feature sets to predict the comment volume of news articles prior to publication. Lerman et al. [12] modeled users' vote process on Digg by considering both the interestingness and visibility of online content and then use the model for popularity prediction. By investigating Digg and Youtube, Szabo et al. [13] found that the final popularity is highly correlated to the popularity in the early period and then employed a direct extrapolation method to predict the long-term popularity. Recent studies on microblogging networks mainly include hashtag (or trend) popularity prediction and tweet popularity prediction. Focusing on hashtag popularity prediction, Tsur et al. [3] examined features from the hashtag itself and employed a regression model to predict hashtag popularity on a weekly basis. Further, Ma et al. [4] considered both content and context features and proposed to predict hashtag popularity on a daily basis. They found that the context features are more effective than content features. For tweet popularity prediction, Hong et al. [8] formulated the popularity prediction problem as a classification task and investigate the important features which influence information propagation in Twitter. Bao et al.[9] incorporated the structural characteristics of early adopters of a tweet into models developed in [13] and showed that the prediction accuracy can be significantly improved. Previous studies have not considered the impact of tweet post time on its early-stage popularity. Also, features from users who are exposed to a tweet have not been fully explored in tweet popularity prediction problem. In our study, both of these issues are addressed.

3   Problem Setting

In this paper, we focus on predicting the future popularity of a tweet based on the observation in the early stages. Since for most tweets in our dataset, they seldom receive retweets after being posted for 48 hours, hence we use the number of retweets that a tweet receives in 48 hours since been posted to represent its future popularity. In our problem setting, we consider two different definitions of "early stages": 1) one hour after the tweet has been posted, 2) when the tweet receives k retweets. Then, we define two prediction tasks:

1. **PP1H:** **P**redicting the **P**opularity of a tweet based on the observation in **1 H**our after being posted.
2. **PPkR:** **P**redicting the **P**opularity of a tweet based on the observation of its first k **R**etweets.

For a given tweet s, we denote its future popularity as Φ^s. Note that predicting the exact value of Φ^s is extremely hard and often not necessary. Hence, we relax the problem and predict the range of popularity. We define a popularity threshold ϕ and then define five ranges of popularity: $[0, \phi/2), [\phi/2, \phi), [\phi, 2\phi), [2\phi, 4\phi), [4\phi, +\infty)$, which represent *not popular, marginally popular, popular, very popular*, and *extremely popular*, respectively. The PP1H task is treated as a multi-class classification problem which predicts the range of tweet's future popularity. Since we use relatively small k in PPkR task, we further relax the problem to be predicting whether the popularity of a tweet will exceed ϕ, which is a binary classification problem.

Methods. Since the key focus of this research is to identify and evaluate the effectiveness of features for prediction, we apply five widely used classifiers [14] in our experiments: NB (Naive Bayes), KNN (K-Nearest Neighbor), SVM (Support Vector Machine), LR (Logistic Regression) and BDT (Bagging Decision Trees). Besides the five standard classifiers, we further apply two baseline methods: *Random baseline* chooses tweet's popularity range randomly with no bias and *Distribution bias baseline* chooses tweet's popularity range following a prior probability distribution on all ranges.

4   Features for Popularity Prediction

In this section, we first detail features used for popularity prediction, including two groups of structural features and a group of temporal features. Then we give a brief analysis of efforts needed to access these features. The features are listed in Table 1.

4.1   Structural Features

User Network Construction. To extract structural features, we first construct a global user network $G = (U, E)$ by utilizing the historical mention relationships in the data collection, similar to that in [15]. In G, a user $u \in U$ is a node and a directed edge $e(u_p, u_q) \in E$ from u_p to u_q is established when u_p directed at least m @-messages to u_q. This definition is one way of defining a proxy for the attention that user u_p pays to other user u_q. Here, we empirically set m to 3.

Table 1. Features for popularity prediction

Feature	ID	Abbr.	Description
	F_{r1}	$rUserCount$	Number of users $|rU_s|$
	F_{r2}	$rDensity$	Density of rG_s
	F_{r3}	$DiffusionDepth$	Longest length of path from u_0^s to any user in rU_s
	F_{r4}	$rReciprocity$	Portion of co-links in rE_s
Retweet	F_{r5}	$rClusterCoeff$	Clustering Coefficient of rG_s
Network	F_{r6}	$rSourceAuthority$	Authority score of u_0^s
Features	F_{r7}	$rMaxAuthority$	Maximum authority score of users in rU_s
	F_{r8}	$rAvgAuthority$	Average authority score of users in rU_s
	F_{r9}	$NumConCom$	Number of Connected Components in rG'_s
	F_{r10}	$NumConCom2$	Number of Connected Components in rG'_s (size ≥ 2)
	F_{r11}	$MaxConComSize$	Maximum size of Connected Components in rG'_s
	F_{b1}	$bUserCount$	Number of border users $|bU_s|$
Border	F_{b2}	$bDensity$	Density of bG_s
Network	F_{b3}	$bReciprocity$	Portion of co-links in bE_s
Features	F_{b4}	$bMaxAuthority$	Maximum authority score of users in bU_s
	F_{b5}	$bAvgAuthority$	Average authority score of users in bU_s
	F_{b6}	$ExposureDistrib$	15-Dimension exposure distribution vector
Temporal	F_{t1}	$ArriveTime$	k-Dimension vector of the time taken for the first k retweets to arrive
Features	F_{t2}	$MaxTimeInterval$	Maximum time interval between two adjacent retweets
	F_{t3}	$AvgTimeInterval$	Average time interval between two adjacent retweets

Retweet Network Features. We illustrate an example diffusion network for a tweet in Fig. 1(a). For a given tweet s, we sort all its observed retweets in ascending time order, forming a chain of retweets C_s. We use u_i^s (for $i = 1, 2, \cdots$) to denote the author of the ith retweet. Specially, we denote the author of s as u_0^s. Considering all the observed retweets in C_s, we denote the union of tweet author and retweets authors as rU_s, i.e. $rU_s = \cup_{i=0}^{|C_s|}\{u_i^s\}$ (union of red and blue nodes in Fig. 1(a)). We consider that users in rU_s form a virtual community and the popularity of tweet s can be highly affected by the social relationships among these users, as well as their followers. By extracting relationships from G, we form a retweet network $rG_s = (rU_s, rE_s)$. From rG_s, we extract 8 retweet network features. F_{r1} is the number of users who have already retweeted s, i.e. $|rU_s|$. Density of rG_s (F_{r2}), is defined as

$$density(rG_s) = |rE_s|/(|rU_s| \times (|rU_s| - 1)) \tag{1}$$

which is the number of edges divided by the number of possible edges in the retweet network. It is a common feature in graph mining to measure the sparsity of the graph. Diffusion depth (F_{r3}) is the longest length of the path from the tweet author u_0^s to users in rU_s. Existing study [9] has shown that there exists a strong positive near-linear correlation between the final popularity and the diffusion depth. Reciprocity of rG_s (F_{r4}) is another quantity to specifically characterize directed networks. Link reciprocity measures the tendency of vertex pairs to form mutual connections between each other [16]. It is defined as

$$reciprocity(rG_s) = |\text{co-link}(rE_s)|/|rE_s| \tag{2}$$

which is the ratio of the number of co-links (links pointing in both directions) to the total number of links. Clustering coefficient of rG_s (F_{r5}) is defined as the average of the local clustering coefficients of all nodes in rU_s [17].

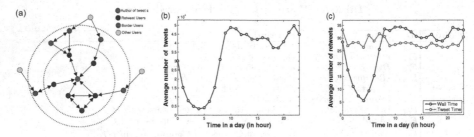

Fig. 1. (a) Example diffusion network for a tweet. (b) The average number of tweets posted per hour. (c) The average number of retweets that a tweet receives after being posted for one hour (blue curve) and one tweet hour (red curve). The horizontal axis represents the time when a tweet is posted.

Larger clustering coefficient indicates stronger ties among users. The authority score is adopted to measure the influence level of users. Intuitively, if a user is followed or mentioned by many users, he or she is likely to be influential. We calculate the authority scores for all users by performing PageRank algorithm [18] on G. F_{r6} is the authority score of tweet author u_0^s. F_{r7} and F_{r8} are the maximum and average authority score of users in rU_s respectively.

Further, by considering only the retweet authors, $rU_s' = \cup_{i=1}^k \{u_i^s\}$ (blue nodes in Fig. 1(a)), we construct a strict retweet graph $rG_s' = (rU_s', rE_s')$. From rG_s', we extract 3 retweet network features, which are the number of connected components (F_{r9}), the number of connected components which size is larger or equal to 2 (F_{r10}) and the maximum size of the connected components (F_{r11}).

Border Network Features. Besides the users who have already retweeted tweet s, users who have not retweeted s but been "exposed" to s could be potentially very useful for our popularity predicting problem. We denote these users as *border users* (black nodes in Fig. 1(a)). More formally, based on the global network G, the border users bU_s are followers of rU_s who still have not retweeted tweet s, i.e. $bU_s = \{u_q | \exists e(u_p, u_q) \in E, u_p \in rU_s, u_q \notin rU_s\}$. By extracting relationships between rU_s and bU_s, we construct a border network $bG_s = (rU_s, bU_s, bE_s)$, which is a bipartite network. From bG_s, we extract 6 border network features.

We extract the number of border users (F_{b1}), density of bG_s (F_{b2}), reciprocity of bG_s (F_{b3}), maximum and average authority score of border users (F_{b4} and F_{b5}), in the same way as in rG_s. Further, analogous to [15], we define that a border user is *x-exposed* to tweet s if he/she has not retweeted s, but has edges to x other users in rU_s. Border users with more exposures to tweet s are expected to be more likely to retweet s. We denote $A_s(x)$ as the set of border users who are x-exposed to s. Then we get the exposure distribution vector F_{b6}, in which the xth dimension $P(x) = |A_s(x)|/|bU_s|$ is the ratio of the number of border users who are x-exposed to s to the total number of border users. Specially, we limit the maximum value of x to be 15 since there are only a few border users whose exposed times are greater than 15. When calculating $P(15)$, we consider border users who have at least 15 edges to users in rU_s.

4.2   Temporal Features

Before extracting temporal features, we first examine the hourly variations of user activity in our data collection by investigating the number of tweets posted during a given hour of a day. We show the average number of tweets posted per hour in Fig. 1(b). Clearly, we can see that user activity varies over time, namely that users are highly active during daytime and inactive in midnight. Hence, for a given tweet, the number of its retweets in the first few hours will differ greatly depending on the time of day when it is posted. Specifically, we show the average number of retweets that a tweet receives in the first hour after being posted in Fig. 1(c) (blue curve). As can be expected, tweets posted at higher active periods of a day will on average receive more retweets in the first hour than tweets posted at less active periods. The Pearson correlation coefficients between the blue curve in Fig. 1(b) and the blue curve in Fig. 1(c) is 0.946, which indicates that the number of retweets that a tweet receives in the first hour is highly correlated with the user activity. Therefore, if we do not eliminate the effect of user activity, we may misinterpret the relative interestingness of a tweet only based on the observation made in a few hours after it has been posted.

Inspired by [13], we introduce the notion of *tweet time* to eliminate the effect of user activity, where we measure time not by wall time (seconds), but by the number of posted tweets. We define the tweet time t_t as

$$t_t = N(t)/\delta \tag{3}$$

where t is the time of a day, $N(t)$ is the average number of tweets posted from the beginning of the day to t and δ is the average number of tweets posted per time scale. In our data collection, the average number of tweets posted per second is 9, hence when we refer to t_t in tweet second, δ is set to be 9. Similarly, we can measure t_t in tweet minute and tweet hour by setting δ to be 540 and 32400 respectively. By defining tweet time, we can mitigate the impact of tweet's post time on its early-stage popularity. As can be seen from Fig. 1(b), the number of tweets posted during 10am-11am is nearly ten times larger than that during 4am-5am, thus the duration of one tweet second during 4am-5am is ten times longer than that during 10am-11am. Further, we show the average number of retweets that a tweet receives in the first tweet hour after being posted in Fig. 1(c) (red curve). We can see that the number of retweets slightly changes over the post time, indicating that the effect of user activity has been largely eliminated.

From the retweet chain C_s, we extract 3 temporal features and use the defined tweet time to measure them. F_{t1} is k-dimensional vector where the kth dimension is the time taken for the kth retweet to arrive. We measure the time intervals between every two adjacent retweets in the retweet chain C_s and extract the maximum time interval feature F_{t2} and average time interval feature F_{t3}.

4.3   Efforts Needed to Access Features

In order to extract structural features, we first need to construct the underlying user network. Here, the user network is constructed based on massive historical mention relationships in the data collection. However, since the network evolves with time, the constructed network can be either incomplete or inaccurate. Hence, sometime it is hard to access the structural features. On the contrary, temporal features can be effortlessly extracted only based on the first few retweets, without need of the knowledge of user network.

5   Experiments

5.1   Experimental Setting

Dataset. We used Sina Weibo dataset published by WISE 2012 Challenge[1]. First, we constructed the global user network based on mention relationships from Jan to Aug 2011. The user network consists of 10.8 million users and 87.1 million edges. Then we selected a subset of tweets that were posted in July 2011 and receive at least 10 retweets in the first hour after being posted. This gave us a dataset of 51,835 original tweets and 4,645,067 retweets from 1,031,899 users. We reserved 50% of the tweets for evaluation, using the other 50% for training.

Evaluation Metrics. For multi-class classification problem PP1H, we use *Accuracy* to measure the performance of each method. For binary classification problem PPkR, we use Macro-*Pr* (macro-precision), Macro-*Re* (macro-recall), Macro-*F1* (macro-F1 score), Accuracy and AUC (area under ROC curve) to evaluate the prediction performance. We give their definitions as follows. $\mathcal{T}$ is the set of testing samples and $n = |\mathcal{T}|$ is the number of testing samples. The set of class labels is denoted as L. Let $\hat{y} = (\hat{y_1}, \hat{y_2}, \cdots, \hat{y_n})$ be the classification result vector and $y = (y_1, y_2, \cdots, y_n)$ be the ground truth vector. Then

$$\text{Macro-}Pr = \frac{1}{|L|} \sum_{l \in L} p(l) \qquad \text{Macro-}Re = \frac{1}{|L|} \sum_{l \in L} r(l)$$

$$\text{Macro-}F_1 = \frac{1}{|L|} \sum_{l \in L} \frac{2 \times p(l) \times r(l)}{p(l) + r(l)} \qquad Accuracy = \frac{\sum_{i \in \mathcal{T}} \text{I}\{y_i = \hat{y_i}\}}{n} \qquad (4)$$

where

$$p(l) = \frac{\sum_{i \in \mathcal{T}} \text{I}\{y_i = \hat{y_i} = l\}}{\sum_{i \in \mathcal{T}} \text{I}\{\hat{y_i} = l\}} \qquad r(l) = \frac{\sum_{i \in \mathcal{T}} \text{I}\{y_i = \hat{y_i} = l\}}{\sum_{i \in \mathcal{T}} \text{I}\{y_i = l\}} \qquad (5)$$

$p(l)$ and $r(l)$ are precision and recall for class l respectively. $\text{I}(X)$ is an indicator function which returns 1 if the statement X is true and 0 otherwise.

Implementation Details. We empirically set the popularity threshold $\phi = 50$ and set k in PPkR to be 10. For KNN, we use Euclidian distance and set $K = 15$. We use the C-Support Vector Classification in LIBSVM [19] with linear kernel to implement a multi-class SVM classifier and empirically set $C = 20$. The number of decision trees in BDT is 60.

---

[1] http://www.wise2012.cs.ucy.ac.cy/challenge.html

5.2   Results

PP1H Task. We show the classification accuracies for all methods in Table 2. For each classifier, we conducted experiments with retweet network features (RN), border network features (BN), temporal features (T) and all features (ALL) to check the effectiveness of each feature group. We can see that baseline methods which do not use any feature perform the worst. The best performance is achieved by BDT with all features. Generally, for each classifier, the best performance is achieved by combining all features. Moreover, we can see that among all feature groups, BN features performs the best and can achieve comparable good performance as all features. The only exception is NB, where the prediction accuracy for NB with BN features is quite low, even worse than baseline methods and combing all features yields a worse performance than only using RN features. One possible reason is that the exposure distribution vector (F_{b6}) contains too many zeros which makes the NB classification model imprecise. When removing F_{b6}, we observe that the accuracy for NB with BN features has been improved to 0.5444 which further confirms the effectiveness of BN features.

Table 2. The classification accuracy for PP1H task

Methods	RN	BN	T	ALL
Random			0.2000	
DistBias			0.2529	
NB	0.5326	0.1425	0.4011	0.2652
KNN	0.5085	0.5201	0.4827	0.5326
SVM	0.4115	0.4684	0.3759	0.4770
LR	0.5422	0.5540	0.5157	0.5640
BDT	0.5446	0.5769	0.5106	0.5817

PPkR Task. Since bagging decision trees classifier has shown its effectiveness in PP1H task, we also apply it in PPkR task. We compared the performance of BDT with all features with two baselines and present the results in the upper part of Table 3. Obviously, combining all features yields the best performance.

In order to investigate the contribution of each feature to the prediction performance, we performed a *stepwise forward feature selection* algorithm to identify effective features. The algorithm starts with an empty feature set F_0 and runs iteratively. In the jth iteration of this algorithm, we created feature set F_j by adding the best single feature which maximizes the objective function (AUC) to the set F_{j-1}. Since it only selects one feature at a time, this algorithm prevents us from adding more than a single copy of highly correlated features. We show the top-5 features selected by this algorithm in Table 4. We can see that a rela-

Table 3. The classification results for PPkR task

Methods	Macro-Pr	Macro-Re	Macro-$F1$	ACC	AUC
Random	0.5000	0.5000	0.4994	0.5000	0.5000
DistBias	0.5000	0.5000	0.5000	0.5023	0.5000
All features	0.7418	0.7354	0.7364	0.7403	0.7354
- RN features	0.7385	0.7321	0.7231	0.7370	0.7321
- BN features	0.7330	0.7259	0.7267	0.7311	0.7259
- T features	0.6312	0.6285	0.6285	0.6333	0.6285

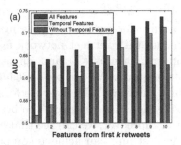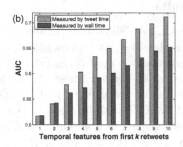

Fig. 2. Performance for PPkR task when predicting using only the features derived from the first k retweets

tive small set of features can achieve comparable performance as all features. It is reasonable that the best single feature is the maximum authority score of users in rU_s since if the tweet is posted or retweeted by a user with higher authority, it will have more chance to be seen and retweeted. Note that, two of the top-5 features are from the temporal feature group and there is a significant performance gain after adding these features. The other two features are from border network feature group which can be interpreted as the number of exposed users and the tie strength between retweet users and border users.

Table 4. Results of stepwise forward feature selection. Each row represents the performance for all features listed in that row and above.

Feature added	AUC
F_{r7}: $rMaxAuthority$	0.6212
+ F_{t1}: $ArriveTime[10]$	0.6721
+ F_{b1}: $bUserCount$	0.7065
+ F_{t1}: $ArriveTime[7]$	0.7204
+ F_{b3}: $bReciprocity$	0.7268

Seeing that the top features are from different feature groups, we further checked the effectiveness of each feature group by removing each feature group and examining how the prediction performance is affected. The results are presented in lower part of Table 3. We can see that the performance drops significantly when temporal features are removed. On the contrary, when retweet network features or border network features are removed, the performance slightly changes. That indicates the temporal features contribute greatly to the overall performance and the combination of other features is unable to make up the loss. We highlight this by comparing the prediction performance when using "all features" "temporal features" and "without temporal features" of the first k retweets and show the results in Fig. 2(a). Obviously, the best performance is always achieved by combining all the features. Also, we can see that when the temporal features are removed, the performance of the other features slightly changes when k varies. On explanation is that, since we have observed that the best single feature for PPkR task is maximum authority score of users in

rG_s, for a large portion of tweets which gain at least 10 retweets, maximum authority score of users in rU_s is equal to the authority score of u_0^s, which is unchanged when k varies. It is worth noting that the performance gap between all features and temporal features gradually narrows with the increasing of k. When $k = 10$, the performance gap has been reduced to 0.0235. Note that, as mentioned before, sometimes it is hard to extract structural features due to the limited knowledge of underlying user network. However, the temporal features can be effortlessly extracted only based on the first few retweets. The results indicate that we can get a satisfied prediction performance for predicting whether a tweet will be popular in the future, by only using the temporal features of the first 10 retweets.

Effectiveness of Tweet Time. To investigate the effectiveness of tweet time, focusing on PPkR task, we compared the prediction performance of BDT with temporal features extracted from first k retweets which are measured by wall time and tweet time respectively. The results are presented in Fig. 2(b). Clearly we can see that temporal features measured by tweet time show better performance for most k, indicating that by introducing the notation of tweet time, the prediction performance of temporal features can be significantly improved.

6   Conclusion

In this paper, focusing on popularity prediction on microblogging networks, we studied two prediction problems, i.e. predicting the popularity of a tweet based on the observation in 1 hour after the tweet being posted (PP1H) and the observation of the first k tweets (PPkR). To identify effective features for prediction, we extracted structural features including *retweet network features* and *border network features* from the underlying user network, and *temporal features* from the observed retweets. Further, to mitigate the impact of tweet's post time on its early-stage popularity, we introduced the notation of *tweet time* and used it to measure the temporal features. We treated both prediction tasks as classification problems and applied five widely used classifiers, i.e. naive bayes, k-nearest-neighbor, support vector machine, logistic regression and bagging decision trees. Experiments on Sina Weibo show that, when predicting the exact range of tweet's popularity (PP1H task), border network features extracted from the users who are exposed to the tweet show the best performance. When predicting whether a tweet will be popular in the future (PPkR task), only using the temporal features of the first 10 retweet can achieve a satisfied prediction performance. Further we show that by introducing tweet time, we can significantly improve the prediction performance of temporal features.

In the future, we will focus on exploring other potential features and developing more effective models for prediction problem.

Acknowledgments. This work is supported by the Natural Science Foundation of China (61272240, 61103151), the Doctoral Fund of Ministry of Education of

China (20110131110028), the Natural Science foundation of Shandong province (ZR2012FM037) and the Excellent Middle-Aged and Youth Scientists of Shandong Province(BS2012DX017).

References

1. Figueiredo, F., Benevenuto, F., Almeida, J.M.: The tube over time: characterizing popularity growth of youtube videos. In: WSDM, pp. 745–754. ACM (2011)
2. Lakkaraju, H., Ajmera, J.: Attention prediction on social media brand pages. In: CIKM, pp. 2157–2160. ACM (2011)
3. Tsur, O., Rappoport, A.: What's in a hashtag?: content based prediction of the spread of ideas in microblogging communities. In: WSDM, pp. 643–652. ACM (2012)
4. Ma, Z., Sun, A., Cong, G.: Will this# hashtag be popular tomorrow? In: SIGIR, pp. 1173–1174. ACM (2012)
5. Crane, R., Sornette, D.: Robust dynamic classes revealed by measuring the response function of a social system. PNAS 105(41), 15649–15653 (2008)
6. Bakshy, E., Hofman, J.M., Mason, W.A., Watts, D.J.: Everyone's an influencer: quantifying influence on twitter. In: WSDM, pp. 65–74. ACM (2011)
7. Asur, S., Huberman, B.A.: Predicting the future with social media. In: WI-IAT, vol. 1, pp. 492–499. IEEE (2010)
8. Hong, L., Dan, O., Davison, B.D.: Predicting popular messages in twitter. In: WWW Companion, pp. 57–58 (2011)
9. Bao, P., Shen, H.-W., Huang, J., Cheng, X.-Q.: Popularity prediction in microblogging network: a case study on sina weibo. In: WWW Companion, pp. 177–178 (2013)
10. Can, E.F., Oktay, H., Manmatha, R.: Predicting retweet count using visual cues. In: CIKM, pp. 1481–1484. ACM (2013)
11. Tsagkias, M., Weerkamp, W., De Rijke, M.: Predicting the volume of comments on online news stories. In: CIKM, pp. 1765–1768. ACM (2009)
12. Lerman, K., Hogg, T.: Using a model of social dynamics to predict popularity of news. In: WWW, pp. 621–630. ACM (2010)
13. Szabo, G., Huberman, B.A.: Predicting the popularity of online content. Commun. ACM 53(8), 80–88 (2010)
14. Bishop, C.M., Nasrabadi, N.M.: Pattern recognition and machine learning, vol. 1. Springer, New York (2006)
15. Romero, D.M., Meeder, B., Kleinberg, J.: Differences in the mechanics of information diffusion across topics: idioms, political hashtags, and complex contagion on twitter. In: WWW, pp. 695–704 (2011)
16. Garlaschelli, D., Loffredo, M.I.: Patterns of link reciprocity in directed networks. Physical Review Letters 93(26), 268701 (2004)
17. Watts, D.J., Strogatz, S.H.: Collective dynamics of 'small-world' networks. Nature 393(6684), 440–442 (1998)
18. Page, L., Brin, S., Motwani, R., Winograd, T.: The pagerank citation ranking: bringing order to the web (1999)
19. Chang, C.-C., Lin, C.-J.: Libsvm: a library for support vector machines. ACM TIST 2(3), 27 (2011)

DivRec: A Framework for Top-N Recommendation with Diversification in E-commerce

Kejun He, Junyu Niu, and Chaofeng Sha

Software School, Fudan University, No.220, Handan Road, Shanghai, 200433, P.R. China
{hekejun,jyniu,cfsha}@fudan.edu.cn

Abstract. In order to increase sales for e-commerce websites and meet customer expectations, recommender systems need to recommend more niche products consumers might like. However, traditional product recommender systems usually aim to improve the recommendation accuracy while overlook the diversity within the recommendation lists. In this paper, firstly we examine the importance of diversity within recommended lists through a psychological survey. Motivated by our observations, we develop a general framework, called DivRec, to improve recommendation diversity without lowering accuracy. Experimental results on an e-commerce dataset demonstrate that our approach outperforms state-of-the-art techniques in terms of both accuracy and diversity.

Keywords: Recommender Systems, Collaborative Filtering, Diversification.

1 Introduction

The information overload problem has made the task of decision making a real challenge for Internet users especially for online shoppers. Recommender System (RS) is a promising solution for this problem and has shown great potential to help users find interesting items from a huge information source. Most previous work has focused on improving the accuracy of RS. These studies inclined to use the accuracy metrics such as RMSE, MAE to measure the performance of recommendation algorithm.

In addition to recommendation accuracy, more factors should be considered to satisfy users' need, such as diversity. For e-commerce websites, to recommend users with a broader range of products is beneficial. A RS with more diversity can easily help user to find products which may surprise them so it is possible that niche products grow to be popular. Chris Anderson coined the evolutions from niche products to popular ones on Internet market as "The Long Tail". Most of successful Internet companies, including Amazon, Yahoo, and Apple etc., have used long-tail as part of their business strategy to improve their online services.

A good top-N recommendation list with diversity in e-commerce is a list of items that are relevant to the target user's interests, as well as dissimilar with each other (e.g. they do not belong to the same product category). In this paper, we address the importance of the diversity from a psychological perspective which has been overlooked by previous studies. The second contribution of this paper is that a general RS framework (DivRec) is proposed to improve diversity without lowering accuracy. The effectiveness of the framework is demonstrated through experiments on a real dataset.

L. Chen et al. (Eds.): APWeb 2014, LNCS 8709, pp. 391–400, 2014.

The rest of the paper is organized as follows: we overview the related work in Section 2. We motivate the diversity into recommendation with a psychological experiment Section 3. We present our approach in Section 4 and evaluate it in Section 5. Section 6 concludes the paper.

2 Related Work

The Collaborative Filtering (CF) which establishes the connection between users and items is commonly used in recommendation systems. Two popular approaches are the neighborhood models (user or item based) [1] and the latent factor models, e.g. Regression-Based Latent Factor Model [2], Probabilistic Matrix Factorization [3], and Singular Value Decomposition [4].

In recent year, there has been some work on diversifying the recommendation lists to increase users' satisfactions. These works can be classified to two categories based on the way how diversity is measured: (1) Content-based diversity, which is known as an instance of p-dispersion problem [5]. Most of the content-based recommendation diversification methods so far are attributes based. In [6], the diversity of recommendation lists is increased through maximizing the topic attribute difference between items. In [7], item explanation is employed to measure the distance between items to achieve diversification instead of item attributes. (2) Temporal diversity. There are works to use temporal information for recommendation diversification, e.g. [8] examines the temporal characteristics of item rating patterns to increase recommendation diversity, and [9] increases temporal diversity with product purchase intervals.

There are few previous work discuss why diversity is important especially for e-commerce websites, although they proposed the approaches how to improve the diversity of recommendation lists. Another problem is how to diversify the item lists efficiently. Taking attribute-based method as an example, the search step for analyzing intrinsic properties of items is time consuming when the product database is large, especially when the attributes are not leveraged by recommendation strategies (some related work has been discussed in [5]). We focus on how to tackle these problems in this paper. We start our work with a psychological study in the next section.

3 Why to Offer Diverse Recommendations

Associative Interference has been widely studied in psychology and advertising fields [10] [11]. The core of this theory is that the amount of the retroaction will increase in accordance with the degree of similarity between the original material and the new material in learning and memory. Associative Interference studies the negative effect of similar materials in a learning process [12]. Inspired by Associative Interference theory, we hypothesize that potential negative effects remaining in the interactions between RS and users when recommendations provided are similar to each other.

We simulate the interactions between RS and online shoppers through a psychological survey. The participants are 50 undergraduates who had online shopping experience. They had been asked to provide their demographic data. In our survey, each recommendation was tagged with two attributes, product relevance and product category.

Participants were randomly divided into two groups, Similar Group (SG) and Diverse Group (DG). Participants in SG were offered with relevant recommendations which concentrate on same few categories. Unlike SG, recommendations in DG are both relevant and diverse in product categories. We did not select personalized CF algorithms for these recommendations to avoid the impact of the quality of the algorithm itself.

The survey was conducted as follows. In each time all participants were offered a questionnaire with 8 recommendations followed a simple product introduction. The participants were asked to rate these recommendations on a 1-5 score scale. All participants were required to finish 5 questionnaires once in a day. After finishing all rating tasks, participates were asked to evaluate the whole recommendations.

In our survey, we recommended 453 products to DG users and 221 products to SG users. 53 items are recommended to both groups. The ratings of these 53 products from two groups are examined to verify the hypothesis. In Fig. 1, the average rating of DG on these 53 products is 3.77, and 3.05 of SG. The rating difference is larger than 0.7. This means that the users in DG are much more satisfied with the recommendations. There is negative effect within the more similar recommendation lists.

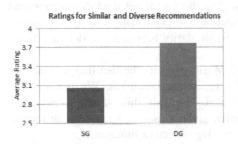
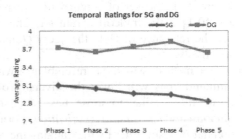

Fig. 1. Survey results for the same recommendations in SG and DG

Fig. 2. Survey results for recommendations in SG and DG in continuous stages

Let us examine the average rating values in each round. As shown in Fig. 2, all values in DG are larger than the value of SG. The ratings in SG decrease with time. But the ones in DG remain around 3.7. We can see that the negative effect is more significant within similar item set and lowers the recommendation quality.

We also test the statistical significance of the survey results. The analysis of variance is as follows: the null hypothesis of our survey is that a product receives same ratings in any case. We reject the null hypothesis with 99% confidence with the p-value 7.65e-04 which is less than 0.01.

As the final part of our survey, the participants are asked about how to measure the recommendation performance. In summary, 94% said RS should offer the user relevant product and 6% chose neutral option.82% said RS should provide more different recommendations and 14% were neutral about the choice. 76% of participants in SG responded that the diversity of recommendations is more important. It is apparent that a good recommendation list should contain products less similar to each other.

4   DivRec Framework

The observations in Section 3 motivate us to design a new framework to ensure both recommendation accuracy and diversity in recommendation lists. Moreover, we should diversify the recommendation lists efficiently. We will show how to achieve our goals in this section.

4.1   Diversification Framework

To the best of our knowledge, the first work combing result diversity and relevance is Maximal Marginal Relevance (MMR) [13] from information retrieval. It aimed to reduce the redundancy within search results. In MMR, each remaining document is checked which combines the relevance to query and the similarity with resulted list. It is defined as:

$$MMR \overset{\text{def}}{=} arg\ max_{D_i \in R \setminus S}[ë(sim_1(D_i, Q) - (1 - \lambda)\ max_{D_j \in S}\ sim_2(D_i, D_j))] \quad (1)$$

where R is the set of original documents, S is the set of resulted documents and $\lambda \in [0,1]$ is the tradeoff parameter. The function sim_1 and sim_2 are used to measure the relevance of D_i to the query Q and the similarity between two documents respectively.

Our method, which has resemblance with MMR, exploits the fact that similar recommendations will lower the diversity of a recommendation list. We penalize the items that similar to those has been selected. We call this variation as *relevance-aware max-sum diversification*. Formally, given a user u, we return the recommendation result set S by maximizing the following objective function:

$$F(u, S) = \sum_{i \in S} rel(u, i) \left(1 - \lambda \sum_{j \in S, j \neq i,} sim(i, j)\right) \quad (2)$$

where $rel(u,i)$ is the relevance between item i and user u, $sim(i,j)$ is the similarity between items i and j, and $\lambda \in [0,1]$ is the tradeoff parameter to balance the relevance and diversity. The reasons for this combination are from two-fold: (1) We do realize that MMR performs well in result diversification task but it needs amendments for top-N recommendations; (2) Some methods such as SVD can be used to extract item attributes efficiently for following diversification step.

To instantiation the relevance function $rel(u,i)$ and similarity measure $sim(i,j)$ in the above framework, we resort to the matrix factorization method, Singular Value Decomposition (SVD) [14], which maps both users and items to a joint latent factor space of dimensionality f so the user-item interactions are modeled as inner products in that space. Each item i is associated with a vector $q_i \in R^f$ and each user u is associated with a vector $p_u \in R^f$. The rating of user u on item i, $\hat{r}_{ui}$ is estimated as follows:

$$\hat{r}_{ui} = \mu + b_u + b_i + q_i^T p_u \quad (3)$$

where μ, b_u and b_i denote the overall average ratings, bias of user u and bias of item i respectively. The parameters are learned through minimizing the regularized squared error function:

$$\min_{b*,q*,p*} \sum_{(u,i)\in\Re} (r_{ui} - \mu - b_u - b_i - q_i^T p_u)^2 + \lambda_1(b_i^2 + b_u^2 + \|q_i\|^2 + \|p_u\|^2) \quad (4)$$

where the regularization parameter $ë_1$ is determined by cross validation.

After training, we can define the relevance between item i and user u as follows:

$$rel(u,i) = b_i + q_i^T p_u \quad (5)$$

For an item i, the elements in vector q_i measure the extent for each corresponding factor. Intuitively, the vectors corresponding to two similar items are more closed to each other which has been verified in [15]. Thus, $sim(i,j)$ can be cosine similarity:

$$sim(i,j) = cos(i,j) = \frac{q_i^T q_j}{\|q_i\|\|q_j\|} \quad (6)$$

4.2   Improvement on Recommendation Accuracy

In the above framework *relevance-aware max-sum diversification*, we seek to tradeoff between recommendation accuracy and diversity. In other words, diversity is achieved at the cost of recommendation accuracy loss. However, even if a RS is good at providing more niche items while ignoring users' preference, it might have poor performance. Therefore, more improvement should be proposed to enhance the recommendation accuracy of our framework.

Recommendation accuracy can be improved by taking implicit correlations between items into consideration, which provides a useful indication of user preferences. We can introduce co-occurrence between two items as item correlation into our framework. Formally, the correlation R between item i and j is defined as follows:

$$R(i,j) = \frac{|U_i \cap U_j|}{|U_i \cup U_i|} \quad (7)$$

where U_i denotes the set of users who already rated or bought item i. This correlation measure can be combined linearly into Equation (2).

Another improvement we used is *case amplification*. Case amplification refers to a transformation of item weights. It is a kind of "Richer get rich" strategy which ignores the tiny items and highlights the distinct ones. By using case amplification, the similarity measure $sim(i,j)$ is modified as follows:

$$sim(i,j)' = sim(i,j) \cdot |sim(i,j)|^{\rho-1} , \rho \geq 1 \quad (8)$$

where ρ is used to control the effect of case amplification. The same transformation can be also applied to the item correlation R:

$$R(i,j)' = R(i,j) \cdot |R(i,j)|^{\rho-1}, \rho \geq 1 \quad (9)$$

By employing these improved methods, we change Equation (2) into the following formulation:

$$F(u,S) = \sum_{i \in S} rel(u,i)(1 - \lambda \sum_{j \in S} sim(i,j)' + \theta \sum_{i \neq j, j \in I(u)} R(i,j)') \qquad (10)$$

where $I(u)$ denotes the set of items already rated by user u and the parameters λ and θ are used to control the extent of diversity and item relevancy respectively.

4.3   DivRec

The framework described in Equation (10) is called DivRec. The corresponding diversification algorithm (pseudo-code) outlined in Algorithm 1 is a greedy heuristic.

Algorithm 1. The Top-N recommendation Algorithm for DivRec
Input: item set **I**. Parameters: $min\_rel, \lambda, \theta, \rho$
Output: top-N item list L_u
Initialization: $B = \{i \in I : rel(u,i) > min\_rel\}$, $L_u = \emptyset$
Steps:
1: $i = argmax_{i \in B} rel(u,i)$.
2: $L_u = L_u \cup \{i\}$.
3: for $n \leftarrow 2$ to N
4:    $i = argmax_{i \in B \setminus L_u} F(u,B)$.
5:    $L_u = L_u \cup \{i\}$.
6: end for

Algorithm 1 takes these three steps: (1) the relevant item ($rel(u,i) > min\_rel$) set B to user u is selected; (2) the recommendation list to user u L_u is initialized with the most relevant item; (3) other items are moved one-by-one from B to L_u until N (the result list size) of them have been selected. Note that the item moved each time has the maximum ranking score calculated by DivRec. Parameter min_rel denotes the minimum relevance threshold for user u and parameters λ, θ, ρ are defined in DivRec.

5   Evaluations

We conducted our experiments on a dataset gathered from *Jingdong* which is one of the biggest B2C e-commerce websites in China. The data we collected consist of 310,000 users, 18,000 products 1,650,000 ratings between 1st December 2003 and 15th January 2010. We preprocessed the dataset and removed users whose rates are less than 20. The final dataset has 15,680 users, 15,171 products and 553,875 ratings and its density is 0.233%. We randomly selected 80% of the users' rating as the training set R_{train} and the other 20% are treated as the test set R_{test}.

Our baseline models include three algorithms: (1) *TopPop*. It is a simple non-personalized algorithm which recommends top-N most popular products to users; (2) *SVD*. The SVD algorithm proposed in [14]; (3) *MMR*. MMR is a base diversification framework and we use the implementation presented in [13]. Although these models are not explicitly support recommendation accuracy and diversity, they are considered as reasonable baselines to evaluate the performance of our approach.

We studied the effectiveness of all methods on predicting top-N recommendation lists for each user. Experiments were started with 4 different top-N result list size: N= 5, 10, 15, and 20. For all methods in our experiments, the cross validation is conducted to tuning the parameters achieving he best Recall value.

5.1   Evaluation Metrics

We used two different metrics to measure a recommendation list: (1) CIS, which is used to measure the diversity within a recommendation list; (2) the Precision and Recall of the recommendation list.

Following [6], we adopted the *on-Category Intra-list Similarity* (CIS) to measure the similarity in a recommendation list with a size N:

$$CIS(S) = \frac{\sum_{i \in S} \sum_{j \in S, i \neq j} cat(i,j)}{N(N-1)} (n > 1) .$$

Here we used a product category in commercial systems to determine two items whether they are similar, e.g. the *APPLE iPhone 5S* is similar to *SAMSUNG Galaxy S5* because they belong to a product category named *Cellphone*. If two items i and j belong to the same product category, $cat(i,j) = 1$. Otherwise, $cat(i,j) = 0$. The higher CIS value of a recommendation list, the less diverse be within it.

We adapted a variant of Recall and Precision, which was proposed in [16], to evaluate the accuracy quality. Denote M as the amount of items in R_{test} and N as the top-N list size:

$$Recall = \frac{hits}{M},$$

$$Precision = \frac{hits}{N \cdot M}.$$

where $hits$ is the amount of successful test cases. For a test case, we randomly select 500 additional items unrated by user u and mixed them with a user-rated item i ($r_{ui} = 5$). We define a successful test case as a *hit* when item i is correctly recommended to user u in the top-N recommendation list.

5.2   Results

Fig.3 shows the average CIS values of recommendation lists generated by prediction algorithms. Among the baselines, MMR is the best one in terms of diversity because it is designed for result diversification. The results achieved by DivRec are much closer to MMR and show the advantages to other baselines. This maybe thank to the fact that our DivRec framework has resemblance to MMR.

Next, we analyzed the effectiveness measured by the Recall and Precision of the different approaches. In Fig.4 (a), we can see that as the list size increases, the Recall value increases. It matches our intuition that an item is most likely to be recommended if the top-N list size is large enough. MMR performs worse than SVD because it achieves diversity in recommendation lists while lowers the accuracy. Our algorithm, DivRec, outperforms both MMR and SVD in terms of recall. (70%+ to MMR, and 25%+ to SVD). We can see that DivRec does improve the accuracy of top-N recommendation list. We can draw the same conclusion from Fig.4 (b), which shows that DivRec has a significant improvement on precision compared to baseline models.

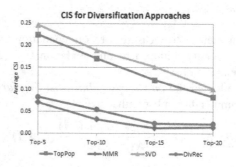

Fig. 3. Average CIS of the top-N lists for test models

5.3   Long-Tail Product Recommendation

We find that the top-100 most popular products in our dataset used receive more than 20% of total ratings. Fig.5 shows the rating count of the products in our dataset. Most of the products were rated by only a few times (≤ 5). The distribution of product popularity follows power law (long-tail). To provide an overall evaluation, we will examine the performance of DivRec on long-tail recommendation.

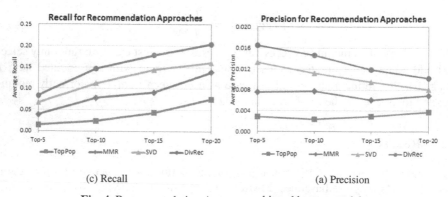

(c) Recall   (a) Precision

Fig. 4. Recommendation Accuracy achieved by test models

We define popular products and long-tail products by the 80:20 rule in a long tail distribution. 0.62% of all products which take up 20% of all ratings are the popular products and the rest are long -tail products. Then we change the experimental setting: the test set R_{test} only contains all 5-score long-tail products and repeat the experiments. Fig.6 shows the performances of prediction algorithms on the long-tail product recommendation tasks. We omit TopPop because it only concerns the popularity and is invalid to recommend long-tail products. We can see that DivRec outperform others with all settings of size N on the long-tail product recommendation task. One possible explanation is that though DivRec is not targeted for recommending long-tail products, DivRec tends to add more different items into a recommendation list as well as ensure the recommendation accuracy. The DivRec algorithm is able to capture users' preferences feedbacks for the long-tail products and is demonstrated to be efficient.

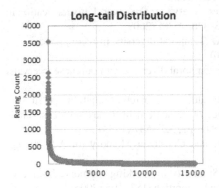

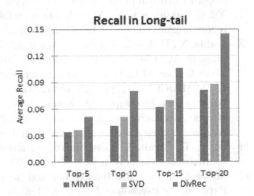

Fig. 5. Rating counts for all products in our dataset

Fig. 6. Recommendation Accuracy achieved by test models in long-tail task

6 Conclusions

In this paper, we studied the problem of top-N recommendation with diversification. We showed that diversity is an important feature for recommended lists through a psychological survey. Then we proposed a general recommendation framework, DivRec, to improve the diversity without lowering the accuracy. Finally, we investigated the effect of our framework on a real dataset from *Jingdong*. The experimental results demonstrate that our approach outperforms other baseline models. With DivRec, even niche items which do not have an extensive rating history are easier to be recommended.

Acknowledgement. The work is partially supported by National High Technology Research and Development Program 863 of China (Grant No. 2009AA01Z4).

References

1. Su, X., Khoshgoftaar, T.M.: A Survey of Collaborative Filtering Techniques. Advances in Artificial Intelligence 2009, Article ID431425S (2009)
2. Agarwal, D., Chen, B.: Regression-based latent factor models. In: ACM SIGKDD 2009, pp. 19–28 (2009)
3. Salakhutdinov, R., Mnih, A.: Probabilistic matrix factorization. Advances in Neural Information Processing Systems 20, 1257–1264 (2008)
4. Koren, Y., Bell, R.: Advances in collaborative filtering. In: Recommender Systems Handbook, pp. 145–186 (2011)
5. Drosou, M., Pitoura, E.: Search result diversification. ACM SIGMOD Record 39(1), 41–47 (2010)
6. Ziegler, C., McNee, S., Konstan, J., Lausen, G.: Improving Recommendation Lists Through Topic Diversification. In: WWW 2005, pp. 22–32 (2005)
7. Yu, C., Lakshmanan, L., Amer-Yahia, S.: It takes variety to make a world: diversification in recommender systems. In: EDBT 2009, pp. 368–378. ACM (2009)
8. Lathia, N., Hailes, S., Capra, L., Amatriain, X.: Temporal diversity in recommender systems. In: ACM SIGIR 2010, pp. 210–217 (2010)
9. Zhao, G., Lee, M.L., Hsu, W., et al.: Increasing temporal diversity with purchase intervals. In: ACM SIGIR 2012, pp. 165–174 (2012)
10. Baumgardner, M., Leippe, M., Ronis, D., Greenwald, A. In: search of reliability persuasion effects: Associative interference and persistence of persuasion in a message-dense environment. Journal of Personality and Social Psychology, 524–537 (1983)
11. Burke, R., Skrull, T.: Competitive Interference and Consumer Memory for Advertising. Journal of Consumer Research, 55–68 (1988)
12. Michael, B.: Proactive Interference and Item Similarity in Working Memory. Journal of Experimental Psychology:Learning, Memory, and Cognition, 183–196 (2006)
13. Carbonell, J., Goldstein, J.: The use of MMR, diversity-based reranking for reordering documents and producing summaries. In: SIG 1998, pp. 335–336. ACM (1998)
14. Koren, Y., Bell, R., Volinsky, C.: Matrix factorization techniques for recommender systems, pp. 30–37. IEEE Computer Society (2009)
15. Kurucz, M., Benczúr, A.A., Csalogány, K.: Methods for large scale SVD with missing values. In: Proceedings of KDD Cup and Workshop, vol. 12, pp. 31–38 (2007)
16. Cremonesi, P., Koren, Y., Turrin, R.: Performance of recommender algorithms on top-n recommendation tasks. In: RecSys2010, pp. 39–46. ACM (2010)

An Efficient Graph Processing System

Xianke Zhou, Pengfei Chang, and Gang Chen

College of Computer Science and Technology
Zhejiang University, Hangzhou, China
{xiankz,changpeng3336,cg}@zju.edu.cn

Abstract. Conventional graph processing algorithms are not designed for those unprecedented large graphs and result in suboptimal performance. To address the problem, Google proposed its Pregel system, which adopts a vertex-centric processing framework for simplifying the development of parallel graph algorithms. In Pregel, the graph computation proceeds iteratively and each iteration is called a superstep. Pregel's processing engine adopts the Bulk Synchronous Parallel (BSP) model, which simplifies the synchronization mechanism and ensures that the system reaches a global synchronization at the end of each superstep. This strategy however significantly increases the system overhead for algorithms that entail many iterations. In this paper, we propose a new graph processing framework based on Pregel. It extends Pregel by introducing a new data structure, *super-vertex*, and a new API, *internalCompute*. Our system is fully compatible with Pregel in that the codes of Pregel can run on it without modification. Moreover, we allow the programmers to optimize their codes with the unique two-phase processing strategy. We evaluated the advantages of our approach by two popular graph algorithms, Shortest Path and PageRank, with real dataset from twitter.

1 Introduction

MapReduce [2] has been widely adopted in various big data applications. Its simple but flexible interface allows the programmers to develop high-performance parallel algorithms without delving into the scheduling, synchronization and other non-trivial implementation issues. However, as argued in [8][9], MapReduce is inefficient in processing graph data. Consequently, Google introduces an alternative system called Pregel [9], which is specifically designed for large-scale graph processing.

Pregel is based on the vertex-centric computation model. The vertices communicate with each other via messages. It defines the *Compute* function to process the incoming messages, and adopts Bulk Synchronous Parallel (BSP) model [14] as a means to synchronize the processing where the computation is split into multiple iterations (aka superstep). In each superstep, the vertex retrieves its incoming messages and processes them sequentially. Pregel monitors the status of the vertices. If all vertices consume their messages of a given step and finish the processing, it can progress to a new superstep. In this way, a global synchronization is achieved at the end of each iteration.

In Pregel, except the CPU cost for processing the *Compute* function, the main cost consists of the message forwarding cost and synchronization cost. We use Figure 1 to demonstrate the cost estimation. Suppose we have two workers (the compute nodes),

L. Chen et al. (Eds.): APWeb 2014, LNCS 8709, pp. 401–412, 2014.

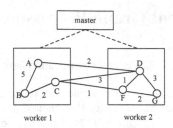

Fig. 1. Example of Graph Processing

and the graph vertices are randomly distributed to the workers. To compute the shortest path from B to the other vertices, B forwards the initial message to A and C in the first superstep. In the second superstep, A and C become active and update their paths to B accordingly. To broadcast the message, C forwards its shortest path to D and F, while A notifies D about its new path. Vertex D and F are hosted by the other worker. Therefore, the communication incurs network overhead. At the end of superstep 2, A and C turn inactive and vote to stop. The process has three drawbacks for the first two supersteps.

1. Vertex C sends the same message to D and F. As both D and F are located in worker 2, C generates redundant messages between worker 1 and worker 2.
2. Both vertex A and C forward their shortest paths to D. However, as C's path is better than A's, it is not necessary for A to notify D.
3. The first two supersteps only involve vertices in worker 1. In fact, we can combine them into one superstep to reduce the synchronization cost.

Moreover, at the end of each superstep, the workers communicate with the master to reach a synchronized status (whether to start the next superstep or stop). Such synchronization is costly, as straggling workers may cause the delay of the whole system in reaching a global synchronization point. Some complex algorithms may require a few hundreds of supersteps, and the synchronization cost is likely to dominate the total processing cost. If we can reduce the number of required supersteps, we can significantly boost the performance of such algorithms.

In this paper, we propose P++, an improved graph processing framework based on the Pregel. P++ defines a new data structure, *super-vertex*, and a new processing interface, *internalCompute*. The super-vertex represents a set of connected vertices. It maintains a subgraph for those vertices. A super-vertex can dynamically shrink or expand by removing or adding new vertices, and multiple super-vertices that are connected can be merged together. By introducing the concept of super-vertex, the computation is split into two phases in each superstep. In phase one, we apply the *internalCompute* function to process the data inside each super-vertex. In phase two, the original *Compute* function of Pregel is invoked to continue the computation for the whole super-vertex.

The remainder of the paper is organized as follows. In Section 2, we propose our new framework P++ and compare it with Pregel via Shortest Path graph algorithm. We evaluate the new framework in Section 3 and review the related work in Section 4. The paper is concluded in Section 5.

2 Computation Model of P++

Pregel adopts a vertex-centric computation model, where all interfaces are defined for the vertices. Table 1 lists the main interfaces provided by Pregel. The user-defined processing logic is typically implemented in the *Compute* function. For the space limitation, the detail description of Pregel is referred to [9][14][4].

Table 1. Pregel Interfaces

Function	Description
Compute(msgList)	process the messages
SendMessageTo(destV, &msg)	send message to neighbor vertex
VoteToHalt()	vote to be inactive
superstep()	get current superstep number
GetValue()	get the vertex value
GetOutEdgeIterator()	get the out edges

To reduce the message cost and synchronization cost, we design our new framework P++ by extending the open-source implementation of Pregel, GPS[10]. P++ is compatible with the Pregel's interface and the users' programs can therefore run in the new framework without modifications. In P++, we introduce a two-phase processing model and a new interface *internalCompute*. *internalCompute* is designed for the new compute unit, *super-vertex*, which represents a set of connected vertices.

2.1 Interface of P++

In parallel graph processing, the large graph is typically partitioned into subgraphs [11][17]. Each subgraph is assigned to a compute node and all compute nodes start their processing in parallel. Based on the same philosophy, we define a new concept, super-vertex, for the P++ processing framework.

Definition 1. Connected Subgraph
For the graph $G = (V,E)$, its subgraph $G' = (V',E')$ is a connected subgraph, if

1. *$V' \subset V$ and $E' \subset E$*
2. *$\forall v_i \in V', \forall v_j \in V'$, there is a path $v_i \rightsquigarrow v_0 \rightsquigarrow ... \rightsquigarrow v_n \rightsquigarrow v_j$ and $v_x \in V'$ for $0 \le x \le n$.*

Definition 2. Super-Vertex
For a connected subgraph $G' = (V',E')$, we define a super-vertex S, which represents all vertices in V'. S maintains two types of edges, internal edge E_{in} and external edge E_{ex}. $E_{in} = E'$, while E_{ex} is defined as:

- *If there is an edge $e = (v_i, v_j)$ and $v_i \in V' \wedge v_j \notin V'$, then we use a new edge $e' = (S,S')$ to replace e, where S' is the super-vertex for v_j. $e' \in E_{ex}$.*

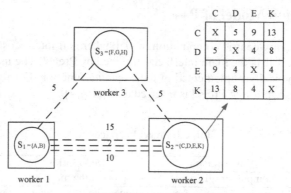

Fig. 2. Super-Vertices

For the example of Shortest Path algorithm, we transform the subgraph of each worker to a super-vertex and the result is shown in Figure 2. The external edges of super-vertices are the edges of the new graph. Note that there are three edges between super-vertices S_1 and S_2, as they are linked by three external edges representing $A \rightsquigarrow D$, $B \rightsquigarrow C$ and $B \rightsquigarrow D$, respectively. Inside each super-vertex, we keep the structure of the corresponding subgraph, namely the vertices and internal edges of the subgraph. The transformation allows us to use the super-vertex as the processing unit in Pregel. Note that in real scenario, each worker can have multiple connected subgraphs and hence multiple super-vertices are created.

The super-vertex can expand or shrink adaptively via the *merge* and *split* operations.

Definition 3. Super-Vertex Merge
Two super-vertices S_i and S_j can be merged, if there exist edges between them. Let G_i and G_j denote the subgraphs of S_i and S_j, respectively. The merged super-vertex S is generated for the new subgraph $G = (G_i.V \cup G_j.V, G_i.E \cup G_j.E \cup E_{ij})$, where E_{ij} represents the edges between G_i and G_j.

split is a reverse operation of *merge*, which partitions the subgraphs into two disjoint connected subgraphs. The sizes of the subgraphs are configurable. By applying the *merge* and *split* operations, we can adaptively tune the size of the super-vertex. To communicate between super-vertices, we define the super-message as:

Definition 4. Super-Message
Super-message follows the format of

$$(\{(m, \{v_0, ..., v_n\}), (m', \{v'_0, ..., v'_n\}), ..., \}, S)$$

where m is the message value, v_i denotes the ID of a vertex and S is the receiver's super-vertex ID.

In one super-message, the super-vertex can send different messages to multiple vertices from the same super-vertex. Moreover, the message value can be shared among the vertices. For example, the message from S_1 to S_2 in Figure 2 is represented as:

$$(\{(20, \{C\}), (12, \{D\}), (15, \{D\})\}, S_2)$$

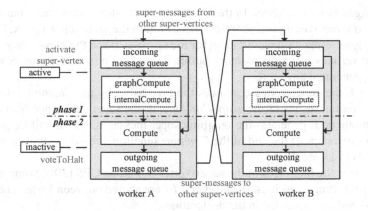

Fig. 3. Two-Phase Model

2.2   Two-Phase Processing Model

If we adopt the super-vertex as the processing unit, the computation within each superstep will be performed in two phases. As shown in Figure 3, the incoming super-messages from the other super-vertices are buffered in the queue and if the super-vertex is inactive, it will be woken up.

Algorithm 1. graphCompute(Iterable<M> supermsgs)

1: int microstep = 1
2: **while** !isStop() **do**
3:      **for** every vertex v in this.*subGraph* **do**
4:          **if** microstep==1 **then**
5:              internalCompute(v, getMessage(supermsgs,v), 1)
6:          **else**
7:              internalCompute(v,getMessageFromBuffer(v), microstep)
8:      microstep++

In phase 1, the messages are passed to the *graphCompute* function, which invokes the new *internalCompute* interface to process the subgraph of the corresponding super-vertex. The algorithms can update the internal vertices and their values, but cannot interact or access the data in other super-vertices. *internalCompute* follows the same definition as Pregel's *Compute* interface. In most cases, users can directly copy their codes from the *Compute* function to the *internalCompute* function. The only difference between the two interfaces is that they perform computation for the vertex and super-vertex, respectively. *graphCompute* specifies how the subgraph is processed. Although users can define their own *graphCompute* function, we recommend them to use the default implementation, which is shown as Algorithm 1.

graphCompute splits the processing into micro-steps. In the first micro-step, each vertex processes messages received from other super-vertices in the last super-step and send messages to its neighbors. In the following micro-steps, the vertex continues the processing if it receives messages from vertices within the same super-vertex. Note that there is no synchronization requirement for the micro-step and the messages are passed to different vertices using the memory buffer. The whole process terminates when no message is generated any more.

In phase 2, the super-vertex continues the processing by the *Compute* interface. It exploits the partial results of the *graphCompute*. If one super-vertex needs to communicate with others, it generates the outgoing super-messages, which will be processed in the next superstep. At the end of the *Compute* function, the super-vertex can vote to stop, if all its tasks are done.

Figure 4 lists the interfaces of the super-vertex (based on GPS [10]). Some inherited interfaces from Pregel, such as *SendMessageTo*, are shared between *Vertex* and *Super-Vertex* class and are discarded in the declarations.

```
public abstract class  SuperVertex<V extends MinaWritable,
E extends MinaWritable, M extends MinaWritable> extends Vertex{

    private Graph subGraph;

    public Graph getSubGraph(){return subGraph;}
    protected abstract void graphCompute(Iterable<M> messageValues);
    public abstract void merge(SuperVertex neighbor);
    public abstract SuperVertex split();
    //for subgraph processing
    public abstract void internalCompute(Vertex v, Iterable<M> messageValues,
                        int microstepNo);
    @Override
    public abstract void compute(Iterable<M> messageValues,
                        int superstepNo);
}
```

Fig. 4. Interface of Super-Vertex

2.3   Shortest Path Processing

In the shortest path algorithm, we use Figure 2 to illustrate how P++ processes the graph data. The *internalCompute* function (Algorithm 2) defines how the normal vertex in a super-vertex performs its computation. In fact, we follow the same processing logic as the shortest path algorithm in Pregel. Specifically, the programmers can copy their codes for previous *Compute* function to the *internalCompute* function with a little change for using the new argument v. In the initial micro-step, the vertex broadcasts a new path to its neighbors (line 1-4). In the following micro-steps, the vertex updates its shortest path to the other vertices inside the same super-vertex progressively (line 6-13). The *SendMessageTo* (line 4 and 13) buffers the messages in memory, instead of forwarding them via the network connection.

Note that between two consecutive micro-steps, no synchronization is needed. *graph-Compute* function (Algorithm 1) defines how the computation is scheduled. *graphCompute* checks the message buffer before starting a new micro-step. If there are messages inside the buffer, a new micro-step will start and *internalCompute* will be invoked immediately. Otherwise, *graphCompute* will terminate its processing. As a result, we can obtain the shortest distance between every pair of graph vertices in a super-vertex. Figure 2 shows the result of super-vertex S_2, when *graphCompute* terminates.

Algorithm 2. internalCompute(Vertex v, Iterable<M> msgs, int mno)

1: **if** *mno* == 1 **then**
2:      **for** every neighbor vertex v_i of v **do**
3:          Path P = new Path(v, v_i, getWeight(v, v_i))
4:          SendMessageTo(v_i, P)
5: **else**
6:      **for** M *msg* : *msgs* **do**
7:          Path P = (Path)*msg*
8:          Path P' = getShortestPath(P.root)
9:          **if** P'.weight> P.weight **then**
10:             $\bar{v}$.setShortestPath(P.root, P)
11:             **for** every neighbor vertex v_i of v **do**
12:                 Path *nextP* = new Path(P'.root, v_i, getWeight(v, v_i))
13:                 SendMessageTo(v_i, *nextP*)

In the processing, each super-vertex may receive multiple shortest paths from the last superstep. It will iteratively generate all new paths and only the shortest one is selected. More formally, if super-vertex S_i receives a path set P from the last superstep, it can compute its shortest paths as follows. Let $g(p)$ return the last vertex in a path p. We retrieve a corresponding subset of vertices $\theta(g(p))$ from S_i. Vertices in $\theta(g(p))$ are directly connected to $g(p)$ with an edge. We use $f(v_k, v_j)$ to denote the shortest path from v_k to v_j, which is computed in *graphCompute*. The shortest paths of S_i can be computed as:

$$\{min(p \circ f(v_k, v_j)) | \forall p \in P, \forall v_k \in \theta(g(p)), \forall v_j \in S_i\}$$

where *min* returns the path with the shortest distance and $\circ$ denotes the concatenation of two paths.

By adopting the two-phase processing strategy, we reduce the number of supersteps to three and the inter-vertex messages to four, which is a significant improvement over the original algorithm. The key difference is that by iteratively evoking *internalCompute* function, we obtain the shortest distance paths for every pair of inside vertices, instead of waiting for the next superstep to generate the results. Compared to the original Pregel, the number of supersteps is reduced from $O(N)$ to $O(N')$ in P++, where N and N' are the number of graph vertices and super-vertices, respectively.

3   Performance Evaluation

To show the superior performance of P++, we implement the Shortest Path algorithm discussed in Section 3 and PageRank algorithm from [15], with the real dataset from Twitter. Twitter dataset has about 40 million vertices and more than 1 billion edges [5]. The user profiles were crawled from July 6th to July 31st, 2009. For the dataset,

Table 2. Experiment Settings

Parameter	Range and Default Value
Cluster Size	50
Memory Buffer per Super-Vertex	10M
Twitter Graph Size	4M-32M (32M)
HDFS Chunk Size	64M

we generate some synthetic datasets by only using the first K vertices and their edges. The synthetic dataset was used to evaluate the scalability of P++. The experiments were conducted on our in-house cluster. Each cluster node (machine) is powered with an intel Xeon 2.4GHZ CPU, 8GB memory and 512GB disk. All cluster nodes are connected via a high-speed 1GB Cisco switch. To reduce resource contention, each cluster node only hosts one P++ worker. The metrics used in the experiments are processing time and number of supersteps. Table 2 lists the configurations of the cluster and the experiments.

3.1 Shortest Path

In the shortest path algorithm, we randomly select a vertex as the root and compute the shortest pathes from the other vertices to the root. In above experiments, we show the average performance. In fact, the selection of root significantly affects the performance. Some root has many out-edges and thus triggers a large number of messages. Some root has few neighbors and the pathes are easy to compute.

Figure 5 and 6 show the effect of data size. P++ is more scalable and provide a stable performance. The processing time of both approaches does not increase linearly with the data size. Because increasing data size in Twitter does not necessarily lead to a higher processing cost for those users, as their reachable users are limited.

In Figure 7 and Figure 8, the performance of GPS is affected by the root selection. Twitter has a skewed user-base. Some popular users will incur very high computation cost, while some inactive users only require a few super-steps. By employing P++, we can effectively reduce the performance variance. The popular users and their friends are grouped into one super-vertex, where the computation is performed by *internal-Compute*. The data skewness is neutralized by the adoption of super-vertex structure.

3.2 PageRank

P++ is fully compatible with the Pregel (GPS) interface. If the users does not define the *internalCompute*, P++ will adopt the original processing logic defined in the *Compute* function. But P++ still provides a better performance because P++ groups vertices into super-vertices and no message exchange is required inside a super-vertex. To illustrate the benefit of P++, we use *GPS-P++* to denote the performance of original GPS codes running on P++. We remove the diagram of GPS, as it always performs worse than GPS-P++. In the PageRank computation, we set a stop threshold ε. When the changes of rank values of all vertices are bounded by ε in a consecutive super-step, we assume that the algorithm converges and terminate the computation. On the other hand, we set a maximal super-step number S. If the PageRank algorithm does not converge after N super-steps, we will stop it forcedly. The initial rank value of a vertex is set to $\frac{1}{N}$, where

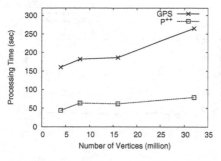

Fig. 5. Shortest Distance for Varied Data Size (Processing Time)

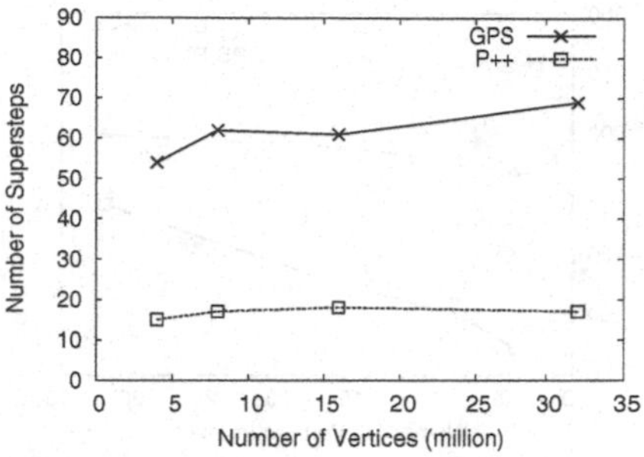

Fig. 6. Shortest Distance for Varied Data Size (# of Super-Steps)

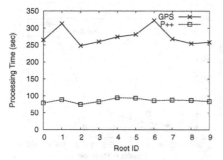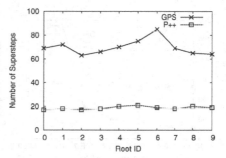

Fig. 7. Shortest Distance for Varied Roots (Processing Time)

Fig. 8. Shortest Distance for Varied Roots (# of Super-Steps)

N is the total number of vertices in the dataset. In the experiments, the default values of ε and S are $10E - 8$ and 50, respectively.

Figure 9 and Figure 10 show the effect of data size. It costs more time for P++ to process a large graph, because its *internalCompute* needs to handle more local PageRank computation. However, the performance of GPS-P++ seems to be less affected by the data size. In fact, that is because GPS-P++ cannot converge before 50 iterations. We stop it before it can provide the satisfied PageRank results.

In Figure 11 and Figure 12, we vary the threshold from $10E - 3$ to $10E - 9$. Performance of P++ is only slightly affected by the threshold, as the local PageRank values are computed in the *internalCompute*. GPS-P++ can terminate faster for a loose threshold, as it triggers few super-steps before completion. However, when the threshold becomes tighter, the performance of GPS-P++ drops dramatically. Clearly, for a tight stop threshold, P++ shows superior performance than GPS-P++.

3.3 Comparison with GraphLab

Due to the recent interest generated by asynchronized processing model, we also compare the performance of P++ with GraphLab. In this experiment, we only run the PageRank algorithm to measure the loading cost and query processing cost. Figure 13 shows the results. P++ incurs less loading cost, as its partitioning technique is well

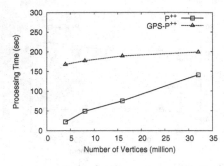

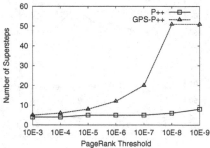

Fig. 9. PageRank for Varied Data Size (Processing Time)

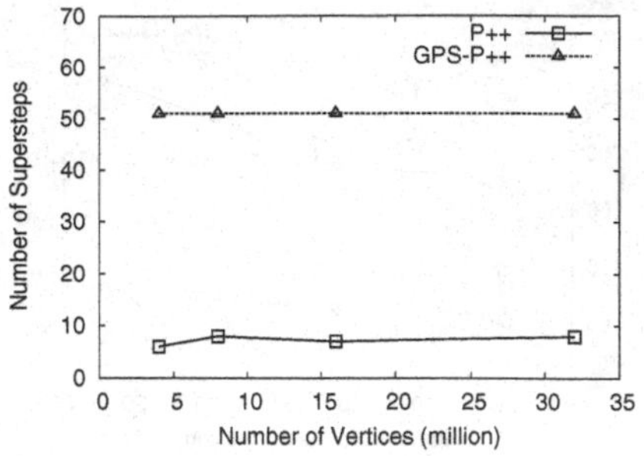

Fig. 10. PageRank for Varied Data Size (# of Super-Steps)

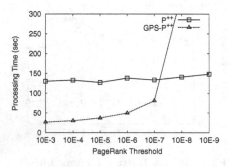

Fig. 11. PageRank for Varied Threshold (Processing Time)

Fig. 12. PageRank for Varied Threshold (# of Super-Steps)

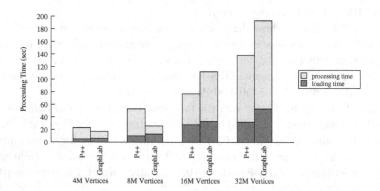

Fig. 13. P++ VS GraphLab of PageRank

integrated with Pregel, whereas GraphLab uses a sophisticated vertex-cut partitioning approach [3]. For the PageRank algorithm, P++ outperforms GraphLab for large datasets. Its two-phase strategy speeds up the convergence of the PageRank algorithm and no synchronization cost is incurred for computing the local PageRank values of each subgraph. In our ongoing work, we are extending and incorporating the P++'s two-phase model into GraphLab.

4 Related Work

To process large-scale graphs, previous work transformed the graph algorithms into a set of MapReduce jobs[1] which are executed sequentially. However, MapReduce is not designed for such iterative processing. For this purpose, Google introduced its Pregel [9] for large-scale graphs processing. In Pregel, the programmers write codes for each vertex. Many graph algorithms, such as PageRank and KMeans, can be implemented in a few lines in Pregel. Pregel has become another popular tool after MapReduce.

Similar to Pregel, GraphLab [7][8], PowerGraph [3] and Graph-Chi [6], provide alternative graph processing model. The main difference between Pregel and others is the synchronization model. For example, Pregel splits the processing into multiple supersteps and requires a global synchronization at the end of each superstep, while GraphLab does not have such requirement and it is completely asynchronous. GraphLab provides three different consistent models: full, edge, and vertex consistency.

Recently, some memory-based distributed processing platforms, such as Spark [18] and Trinity [12], are proposed as high-performance data analytical systems. They share some similar design philosophy with the Pregel-like systems. We can simulate Pregel on top of Spark or Trinity. However, to improve the efficiency, those systems maintain the graph structures or intermediate results in memory to reduce the I/O cost. Our technique can benefit those systems by avoiding the unnecessary iterations as in the Pregel system. Some recent works[16][13] also proposed the idea similar with super-vertex, but they differ from our vertex construction and computing processing model.

5 Conclusion

Pregel was recently proposed as a processing engine for large graphs. In Pregel, the algorithm is invoked iteratively and each iteration is called a superstep. All vertices need to reach the same status at the end of each superstep, which incurs high synchronization cost. To address this problem, we have extended Pregel to our new framework P++. P++ introduces a new data structure, the *super-vertex*, and a new processing interface, *internalCompute*. The super-vertex represents a set of graph vertices and is hosted by a single cluster node. All computations within the super-vertex can be processed locally within each superstep. and hence, the algorithm requires fewer supersteps to complete. Consequently, the synchronization cost is greatly reduced. P++ is completely compatible with the Pregel in that all Pregel codes can run in the P++ without modification in order to gain performance improvement. We used shortest path algorithm to illustrate the benefit of P++. P++ is evaluated using real datasets and the results demonstrate its superior performance.

Acknowledgement. This research has been supported by The National Key Technology R&D Program of the Ministry of Science and Technology of China (Grant No. 2013BAG06B01) and the National Science Foundation of China (NSFC Grant 61202047).

References

1. Bahmani, B., Chakrabarti, K., Xin, D.: Fast personalized pagerank on mapreduce. In: SIGMOD (2011)
2. Dean, J., Ghemawat, S.: Mapreduce: Simplified data processing on large clusters. In: OSDI (2004)
3. Gonzalez, J.E., Low, Y., Gu, H., Bickson, D., Guestrin, C.: Powergraph: Distributed graph-parallel computation on natural graphs. In: OSDI (2012)
4. Hewitt, C., Bishop, P., Steiger, R.: A universal modular actor formalism for artificial intelligence. In: IJCAI (1973)
5. Kwak, H., Lee, C., Park, H., Moon, S.: What is Twitter, a social network or a news media? In: WWW (2010)
6. Kyrola, A., Blelloch, G., Guestrin, C.: Graphchi: Large-scale graph computation on just a pc. In: OSDI (2012)
7. Low, Y., Gonzalez, J., Kyrola, A., Bickson, D., Guestrin, C., Hellerstein, J.M.: Graphlab: A new framework for parallel machine learning. In: UAI (2010)
8. Low, Y., Gonzalez, J., Kyrola, A., Bickson, D., Guestrin, C., Hellerstein, J.M.: Distributed graphlab: A framework for machine learning in the cloud. PVLDB 5(8) (2012)
9. Malewicz, G., Austern, M.H., Bik, A.J.C., Dehnert, J.C., Horn, I., Leiser, N., Czajkowski, G.: Pregel: a system for large-scale graph processing. In: SIGMOD (2010)
10. Salihoglu, S., Widom, J.: Gps: A graph processing system. In: Technical Report, Stanford (2012)
11. Schloegel, K., Karypis, G., Kumar, V.: Parallel multilevel algorithms for multi-constraint graph partitioning. In: Bode, A., Ludwig, T., Karl, W.C., Wismüller, R. (eds.) Euro-Par 2000. LNCS, vol. 1900, p. 296. Springer, Heidelberg (2000)
12. Shao, B., Wang, H., Li, Y.: Trinity: A distributed graph engine on a memory cloud. In: SIGMOD (2013)
13. Tian, Y., Balmin, A., Corsten, S.A., Tatikonda, S., McPherson, J.: From "think like a vertex" to "think like a graph". PVLDB 7(3), 193–204 (2013)
14. Valiant, L.G.: A bridging model for parallel computation. Communications of the ACM 33(8) (1990)
15. Wang, Y., DeWitt, D.J.: Computing pagerank in a distributed internet search engine system. In: VLDB (2004)
16. Xie, W., Wang, G., Bindel, D., Demers, A.J., Gehrke, J.: Fast iterative graph computation with block updates. PVLDB 6(14), 2014–2025 (2013)
17. Yang, S., Yan, X., Zong, B., Khan, A.: Towards effective partition management for large graphs. In: SIGMOD (2012)
18. Zaharia, M., Chowdhury, M., Franklin, M.J., Shenker, S., Stoica, I.: Spark: Cluster computing with working sets. In: HotCloud (2010)

An Approximate Duplicate-Elimination in RFID Data Streams Based on d-Left Time Bloom Filter[*]

Xiujun Wang[1,3], Yusheng Ji[2], and Baohua Zhao[1]

[1] University of Science and Technology of China, Hefei, China
wxj@mail.ustc.edu.cn
[2] National Institute of Informatics, Hefei, China
kei@nii.ac.jp
[3] Anhui University of Technology, Hefei, China

Abstract. There are a larger number of duplicates in RFID data streams, due to the multiple readings of an RFID tag by one RFID reader or by some RFID readers deployed to the same region in an RFID based system. Existing duplicate-elimination methods based on Time Bloom filter (TBF) require multiple counters to store the detected time of an element in RFID data streams, thus waste valuable memory resources. In this paper, we devise d-left Time Bloom filter (DLTBF) as an extension of d-left Counting Bloom filter. With the d-left hashing, a balanced allocation mechanism, DLTBF can store the detected time of an element into one counter. Then we propose an one-pass approximate method to remove duplicates in RFID data streams based on DLTBF. In an RFID data stream, suppose that the detected time of an element is T-bit, i.e., T bits are required to store the detected time of an element in RFID data streams, the number of non-duplicate elements within a time length of τ is W and the probability that a non-duplicate element is taken to be a duplicate by our method is ε (the false positive probability), then the number of bits used by our method is $O(W \log_2(1/\varepsilon) + WT)$. Experimental results on the synthetic data verify the effectiveness of our method.

1 Introduction

RFID (Radio Frequency Identification) based system usually contains many tags and readers. A tag is attached to a physical object with the aim to track the movement of this object. An reader, which has a limited detection region, is deployed to detect the tags that occurs in the region without contact; then it sends a sequence of RFID data to a server for real-time analysis. Given that the RFID data is generated and sent to the server continuously by many RFID readers in an RFID based system, the RFID data comes to the server in the form of an input RFID data stream [10, 13]. The server conducts some kinds

---

[*] This work is supported in part by Natural Science Foundation of Anhui Province (1408085QF128) and NII International Internship Program.

L. Chen et al. (Eds.): APWeb 2014, LNCS 8709, pp. 413–424, 2014.

of real-time analysis based on the input RFID data stream. It is defined in [13] that each element in RFID data streams includes: a tag identifier, the location of the reader that detects the tag, and the detected time of the tag (similar to [13], we also call it the detected time of an element in RFID data streams).

Due to the low price of tags and the non-intrusive way that the reader detects tags, RFID based systems have been applied in many fields [1, 10, 11, 12, 14], such as postal package tracking and customer behavior analysis. In real RFID based systems, multiple RFID readers are deployed in the same area to prevent missing readings of RFID tags. Because, if RFID tags move quickly and a large number of tags pass simultaneously through the detection region of an RFID reader, the reader can't ensure to detect all of them [13]. On the other hand, if an RFID tag moves slowly or stands still in the detection region of an reader, many unnecessary RFID data of this tag (called duplicate elements in RFID data streams) is generated [13]. Thus, usually, there are a larger number of duplicates in RFID data streams. These duplicates will degenerate the accuracy of real-time analysis in an RFID based system if they are not eliminated.

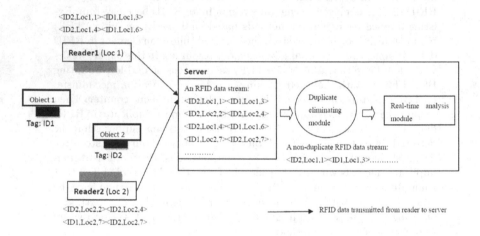

Fig. 1. An example for duplicate-elimination in an RFID based system

For example, an RFID based system can be used to tracking the user behavior in a large department store, where each customer is attached with a unique tag and each area of the department is deployed with some readers. Readers send the RFID data of tags (elements in RFID data streams) to a server for the real-time analysis of customers behavior, such as the real-time number of customers in every store. In this application, when a customer stays at the same region for a long time, a larger number of unnecessary RFID data will be generated [13]. Obviously these duplicates must be dropped.

As raw RFID data obtained from RFID readers contains false and uncertain readings, there has been some research on RFID data cleaning [2, 3, 6, 9, 10]. However these researches don't consider approximate duplicate-elimination in RFID data streams.

It has been pointed out in [13] that eliminating the duplicates in an RFID data stream exactly requires a large number of memory bits to store all elements in RFID data streams within a time length of τ, thus is an inefficient approach. There are also many methods for approximate duplicate detection in data streams, e.g. [7, 8]. However these approaches can't store the detected time of an element in RFID data streams. To eliminate duplicates in an RFID data stream approximately, some methods have been proposed. The authors in [13] propose Time Bloom filters (TBF), which uses a time counter to substitute the bit used in a Bloom filter. They store the detected time of an element in RFID data streams into the k time counters hashed by this element, and eliminate duplicates based on the values of time counters in TBF. They also propose Time Interval Bloom filters (TIBF) to reduce the false positive rate of TBF. However, these methods are not memory efficient, since multiple time counters are required to store the detected time of an element in RFID data streams in TBF or TIBF. In [11], the authors deploy a TBF in each RFID reader, with the aim to reduce the bandwidth requirement to transfer those duplicates to the server.

Our work is mainly motivated by [4] and [13]. We devise a d-left Time Bloom filter (DLTBF), which is an extension of d-left Counting Bloom filter in [4]. Based on DLTBF, we propose an one-pass approximate method to remove duplicates in RFID data streams. In an RFID data stream, suppose that the detected time of an element is T-bit, the number of non-duplicate elements within a time length of τ is W and false positive probability is ε, the number of bits used by DLTBF in our method is $O(W \log(1/\varepsilon) + WT)$, while the existing methods based on TBF in [13] need $O(W \log_2(1/\varepsilon)T)$ bits.

The rest of this paper is organized as follows. In Section 2, we give some background on the definitions of duplicate element and the duplicate-elimination problem in RFID data streams. We describe d-left Time Bloom filter (DLTBF) and an one-pass duplicate-elimination method based on DLTBF in Section 3. In Section 4, experimental results on synthetic data set demonstrate the effectiveness of our method. Section 5 concludes this paper.

2   Problem Definition

An RFID based system is depicted in Fig. 1. Each reader generates RFID data continuously and an RFID data stream comes into the server. There is a module for duplicate elimination in the server, which sends a non-duplicate RFID data stream to the real-time analysis module. To be more specific, the duplicates are effectively dropped out from the raw RFID data stream by the duplicate-elimination module. Thus the real-time analyis module can give more accurate result based on a non-duplicate RFID data stream.

In [13], an RFID data stream $RFIDStream$ is defined as a sequence of elements: $RFIDStream = s_1, ..., s_n, ...$, where each element s_i is a triple $s_i =< TagID, Loc, Time >$. $TagID$ is an unique electronic product code (EPC) of a tag [10]. Loc is the location of the reader that detects the tag with $TagID$. $Time$ is the detected time of a tag (we also call it the detected time of s_i an element in *RFIDStream*). Considering the example in Fig. 1, there are two readers (*Reader*1,*Reader*2), and two tags with the identifier (EPC) $ID1$ and $ID2$ (the two tags are attached to two objects respectively). Two Readers generate the detection information such as $< TagID, Location, Time >$. For example, *Reader*1 may detect the tag with $ID1$ and generate an element: $s_n =< ID1, Loc1, 3 >$ in an RFID data stream. $ID1$ is the EPC of a tag, $Loc1$ is the location of *Reader*1, and 3 represents the detected time of s_n.

It is also defined in [13] that an element s_i in *RFIDStream* is considered as a duplicate if there exists an element $s_j \in RFIDStream, j \neq i$, such that $s_i.TagID = s_j.TagID$ and $s_i.Time - s_j.Time \leq \tau$, where τ is a positive value depends on an application. This definition is intuitive because that elements in *RFIDStream* with the same $TagID$ that are generated repeatedly at time intervals that are less than or equal to τ are usually useless [13]. Considering the RFID data stream in the server in Fig. 1 and assuming $\tau = 2.5$, based on the definition of duplicate in *RFIDStream*, we know the third element $< ID2, Loc2, 2 >$ is a duplicate because of the first element $< ID2, Loc1, 1 >$; the fourth element $< ID2, Loc2, 4 >$ is a duplicate because of the third element $< ID2, Loc2, 2 >$. The non-duplicate elements sent to the real-time analysis module is $< ID2, Loc1, 1 >, < ID1, Loc1, 3 >, < ID1, Loc1, 6 >, < ID2, Loc2, 7 >$. The non-duplicate RFID data stream for *RFIDStream* is an RFID data stream after eliminating all duplicates in *RFIDStream*, see Fig. 1.

3   d-Left Time Bloom Filter

In this section, we describe the d-left Time Bloom filter (DLTBF) , which is an extension of d-left Counting Bloom filter in [4], for approximate duplicate-elimination in RFID data streams. The main working principle of DLTBF is to store the fingerprints (produced based on the $TagID$) and the detected time of elements in an RFID data stream evenly into four hash tables, based on the d-left hashing (a variation of the balanced allocations mechanism [15]). Based on the stored fingerprints and detected times of elements, we can approximately remove duplicates in an RFID data stream.

3.1   d-Left Time Bloom Filter Design

We assume that the maximum number of non-duplicate elements in an RFID data stream is W within a time length of τ. The d-left Time Bloom filter (DLTBF) is depicted in Fig. 2. (For convenience $W/24$ is assumed to be an integer.) The DLTBF uses 4 independent hash functions (h_1, h_2, h_3, h_4) with range $\{1, 2, ..., W/24\}$, and one hash function f with range $\{0, 1, ..., 2^R - 1\}$ (f produces the fingerprint of an element in RFID data streams).

The explicit data structure of DLTBF is as follows. There are 4 hash tables in DLTBF. Each hash table contains $W/24$ buckets: $B[1], ..., B[W/24]$ and each bucket contains 8 slots. Each slot in one bucket $B[i]$ includes a R-bit (the R-bit is used for storing the fingerprint $f(x.TagID)$ of an element x in RFID data

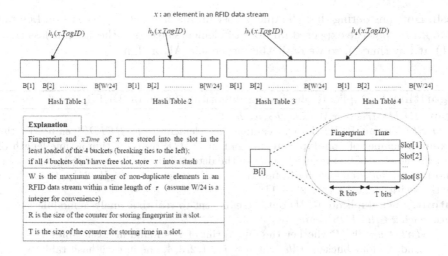

Fig. 2. The structure of DLTBF

streams) and a T-bit counter (the T-bit is used for storing the detected time $x.Time$ of x). The reason that we adopts 4 hash tables, each with $W/24$ buckets (8 slots in a bucket) in DLTBF, is that this setting is good enough to prevent bucket overflow (more than 8 elements are put into the same bucket) in DLTBF with very high probability (we give the proof in Lemma 1).

The steps for storing an element x in RFID data streams into DLTBF are as follows. we first find 4 possible buckets $B[h_i(x.TagID)], i = 1, 2, 3, 4$ in Hash Table $1 - 4$. $B[h_1(x.TagID)]$ is the $h_1(x.TagID)$-th bucket in Hash Table 1, $B[h_2(x.TagID)]$ the $h_2(x.TagID)$-th bucket in Hash Table 2 and so on. Then we place the fingerprint $f(x.TagID)$ and time $x.Time$ into the least loaded bucket (the bucket contains the largest number of free slot); in case of a tie, $f(x.TagID)$ and $x.Time$ are stored into the bucket of the leftmost Hash Table. When the 4 buckets all don't have free slot, we store $f(x.TagID)$ and $x.Time$ of x into a stash, which contains a number of counters. In the following, we will prove that the expected number of elements stored in the stash is less than $O(1)$ at any time t.

In order to check whether an incoming element x from an RFID data stream is a duplicate or not, we check the 4 buckets $B[h_i(x.TagID)], i = 1, 2, 3, 4$, one in each hash table. If there exists a slot $Slot[j]$ in one bucket such that $Slot[j].Fingerprint = f(x.TagID)$ and $x.Time - Slot[j].Time \leq \tau$, x is taken to be a duplicate (there may be some false positive errors in this case due to hash collisions). Otherwise, we are sure that x is not a duplicate. Because if x is a duplicate of y (this means $y.TagID = x.TagID$ and $x.Time - y.Time \leq \tau$), then y must have occupied one slot in the 4 buckets with the fingerprint $f(y.TagID) = f(x.TagID)$ ($y.TagID = x.TagID$) and the time $y.Time$ ($x.Time - y.Time \leq \tau$). It should be noted that when we can't find a slot $Slot[j]$ in the four buckets such that $Slot[j].Fingerprint = f(x.TagID)$, in order to prevent false negative error, we still have to check the fingerprints and detected times stored in the stash. But considering that the query cost in this case is $O(1)$ (Based on Lemma 1, we know that the expected number of elements stored in the stash is less than $O(1)$ at any time t), so we omit this process in Algorithm 1.

Algorithm 1. Duplicate-elimination algorithm based on DLTBF

Input: $RFIDStream, x, W, T, h_1, h_2, h_3, h_4, f$

$RFIDStream$: an RFID data stream; x: an element from $RFIDStream$; W: the maximum number of non-duplicate element in $RFIDStream$ within a time length of τ; T: the number of bits required to store the detected time $x.Time$ of x; h_1, h_2, h_3, h_4: uniform and independent hash functions with range $\{1, 2, ..., W/24\}$; f: an hash function with range $\{0, 1, ..., 2^R - 1\}$;

Output: a non-duplicate RFID data stream sent to real-time analysis module;

1　**For** each $x \in RFIDStream$;
2　　　$InTable = 0$; //*whether the fingerprint of x is found in hash tables*//
3　　　find the four buckets $B[h_i(x.Tag)], i = 1, 2, 3, 4$, one in each hash table;
4　　　**For** each slot of the four buckets
5　　　　**If** (exists a slot $Slot[j]$ such that $Slot[j].Fingerprint = f(x.TagID)$)
6　　　　　**If** ($x.Time - Slot[j].Time \leq \tau$)
7　　　　　　drop x from $RFIDStream$; //*x is taken to be duplicate*//**End If**
8　　　　　$Slot[j].Time = x.Time; InTable = 1$; //*update*//**End If End For**
9　　　**If** ($InTable == 0$)//* the fingerprint of x is not in the four buckets $B[h_i(x.Tag)], i = 1, 2, 3, 4$*//
10　　　**For** each slot $Slot[j]$ in the four buckets
11　　　　**If** ($x.Time - Slot[j].Time > \tau$)
12　　　　　$Slot[j].Time = -1, Slot[j].Fingerprint = -1$; **End If**
　　　　　//*clear the outdated information in $Slot[j]$*//**End For**
13　　　Find the bucket B that contains the largest number of free slot, and break ties to the left, in $B[h_i(x.Tag)], i = 1, 2, 3, 4$;
14　　　**If** (B has a free slot $Slot[j]$) //*store x into DLTBF*//
15　　　　Set $Slot[j].Time = x.Time$ and $Slot[j].Fingerprint = f(x.Tag)$;
16　　　**Else** store $x.Time$ and $f(x.Tag)$ into stash; **End If End If End For**

How to eliminate duplicates in an RFID data stream $RFIDStream$ based on DLTBF is depicted in in Algorithm 1. The algorithm can efficiently remove all duplicates in one-pass scan of $RFIDStream$. The two counters in each slot $Slot[i]$ are initially set as: $Slot[i].Time = -1$ and $Slot[i].Fingerprint = -1$ (-1 represents that $Slot[i]$ is free). When an element x of $RFIDStream$ arrives at the server, it will pass through the DLTBF in the duplicate-elimination module (x will be dropped or sent to the real-time analysis module). To be more specific, when x passes through the DLTBF, firstly we check the condition: if there exists a slot $Slot[j]$ such that $Slot[j].Fingerpint = f(x.TagID)$ and $x.Time - Slot[j].Time \leq \tau$ in the 4 buckets $B[h_i(x.Tag)], i = 1, ..4$ (Line 5-6 in Algorithm 1). If so, x is taken to be a duplicate and dropped from the RFID data stream (Line 7). It should be noted that, in this case, x may be a non-duplicate element, since $Slot[j]$ may be set by another non-duplicate element y due to hash collisions ($y.TagID \neq x.TagID$, there exists a $i \in$ $\{1, 2, 3, 4\}$ such that y is stored in the $B[h_i(y.TagID)]$-th bucket in the i-th hash table, and $B[h_i(y.TagID)] = B[h_i(x.TagID)]$, $f(y.TagID) = f(x.TagID)$, $x.Time - y.Time \leq \tau$). Otherwise x is surely a non-duplicate element and sent to the real-time analysis module. Finally, we store $x.Time$ and $f(x.TagID)$ into a slot or a position in the stash whenever x is duplicate or not (Line 8 and 13-16).

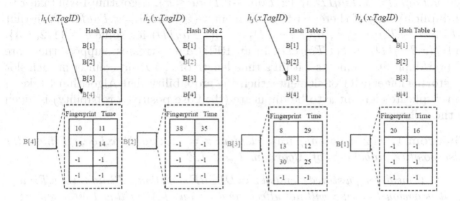

Fig. 3. The state of DLTBF before a newly coming element x

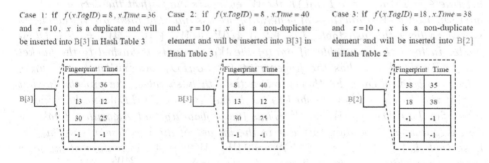

Fig. 4. Three cases for the insertion of x into DLTBF

Fig. 3 shows the state of DLTBF before the arrival of an element $x \in RFIDStream$. For ease of illustration, in Fig. 3, we assume $W/24 = 4$ and each bucket contains 4 slots (Actually, each bucket in DLTBF contains 8 slots). In Fig. 3, x is hashed to the four buckets (one in each hash table) by h_1, h_2, h_3, h_4. In Fig. 4, three cases for the insertion of x into DLTBF are showed. In case 3, x is surely a non-duplicate element, so it will be stored into the least loaded bucket. In case 2, x is also surely a non-duplicate element, but given that there a slot contains the same fingerprint as $f(x.TagID)$, so we just update this slot. For case 1, x is assumed to be a duplicate element and the update is same as that in case 2.

3.2   Theoretical Performance Analysis of DLTBF

In this section, we shall analyze the false positive probability of Algorithm 1 and compare its performance with that of the approximate duplicate-elimination method based on Time Bloom filter (TBF) in [13]. We assume that the readers detect various tags independently from one another in the following analysis.

If a newly incoming element x is non-duplicate (there is not an element y such that $y.TagID = x.TagID$ and $x.Time - y.Time \leq \tau$), Algorithm 1 will take x to be duplicate only if there exists an element z ($z.TagID \neq x.TagID$) such that $x.Time - z.Time \leq \tau$, $h_i(x.TagID) = h_i(z.TagID)$ for some $i \in \{1,2,3,4\}$, and $f(x.TagID) = f(z.TagID)$. In an RFID data streams, suppose there are W non-duplicate elements within a time length of τ, a R-bit counter in each slot for storing fingerprint of elements, then the probability that Algorithm 1 takes a non-duplicate element x to be duplicate (the false positive probability) is given in the following.

Theorem 1. *For a non-duplicate element $x = (x.TagID, x.Loc, x.Time)$, the false positive probability of Algorithm 1 is $24/2^R$.*

Proof. Considering a stored element z in DLTBF such that $z.Time \in (0, x.Time - \tau)$, it is obviously that z will not affect the decision of Algorithm 1 on x, since z is an expired element in time $x.Time$.

Given that the number of the non-duplicate elements stored in DLTBF within a time length of τ is W (denote y one of the W elements, then y satisfies $y.Time \in [x.Time - \tau, x.Time)$), the W elements may affect the decision of Algorithm 1 on x. Without loss of generality, we assume that there are W_i elements stored in the i-th hash table, $i = 1,2,3,4$ ($W_1 + W_2 + W_3 + W_4 = W$). Obviously, in the i-th hash table, if one of the W_i elements is hashed to the bucket $B[h_i(x.TagID)]$ and has the fingerprint $f(x.TagID)$, Algorithm 1 will surely take x to be duplicate. Furthermore, in the i-th hash table, the probability that one of the W_i elements is hashed to the bucket $B[h_i(x.TagID)]$ and has fingerprint $f(x.TagID)$ is $24W^{-1}2^{-R}$. Thus the probability that Algorithm 1 takes a non-duplicate x to be duplicate due to the impact of the W_i elements in the i-th hash table is $1 - (1 - 24W^{-1}2^{-R})^{W_i} \approx 24W_i/(W2^R)$. A summation of the false positive probabilities over the four hash tables is $\sum_{i=1,2,3,4} \frac{24W_i}{W2^R} = 24/2^R$.

Obviously, Algorithm 1 uses the randomized multiple-choice allocation scheme same as the Always-Go-left algorithm in [15]. In the following, we will use the Theorem 1 (generalized version) in [15] to show that the expected number of elements that are stored in the stash used in Algorithm 1 is O(1) at any time t. In this paper, we say an event A to occur with high probability if $P(A) \geq 1 - W^{-\alpha}$ for an arbitrarily constant $\alpha \geq 1$. We use "w.h.p." as an abbreviation of "with high probability".

Lemma 1. *Suppose there are at most W non-duplicate elements $x_1, .., x_W$ ($t - x_i.Time \leq \tau, i = 1, .., W$) stored in DLTBF of Algorithm 1 at any point of time t. Then the maximum loaded bucket in DLTBF contains $\frac{\ln\ln(W/6)}{4\ln 1.927} + 6$ elements, w.h.p., at any time t.*

Proof. Plugging $d = 4, \phi_4 = 1.927$ (see in [5]) and $h = 6$ (there are altogether $W/6$ buckets in DLTBF) into the Theorem 1 (generalized version) in [15], we get the conclusion.

Given that W is usually smaller than 6×10^{20} in an RFID based system, then at any point of time t, the maximum loaded buckets in Algorithm 1 is less than $\frac{\ln \ln (10^{20})}{4 \ln 1.927} + 6 = 7.4596 < 8$, w.h.p. (with probability at least $1 - W^{-\alpha}, \alpha \geq 1$). Then we can see that the probability that one of the W non-duplicate elements within the time interval $(t - \tau, t)$ is stored in the stash is less $W^{-\alpha}$, thus the expected number of the elements stored in the stash is less than $W^{-\alpha}W = O(1)$ (noting that an element will be stored in stash only if there is an bucket contains 8 elements). Actually, the expected number of the elements stored in the stash is much less than 1, since in the above analysis, we don't consider the probability that the maximum loaded buckets are selected by one of the W elements.

Since there is not a closed form formula of false positive rate for the approximate duplicate-elimination algorithm based on Time Interval Bloom filter (TIBF) in [13], so we compare Algorithm 1 with the method based TIBF experimentally in Section 4.

We compare the approximate duplicate-elimination algorithm based on TBF in [13] with Algorithm 1 in Theorem 2. In an RFID data stream, suppose that the detected time of an element is T-bit, the number of non-duplicate elements within a time length of τ is W and false positive probability is ε, then we have the following.

Theorem 2. *Given the same false positive rate ε, the number of bits used by the approximate duplicate-elimination algorithm based on TBF in [13] is $(\log_2 e)\log_2(1/\varepsilon)WT$, while Algorithm 1 uses $[\log_2(1/\varepsilon) + T + \log_2 24]4W/3$ bits.*

Proof. According to Theorem 1 in [13], given m counters (each is a T-bit counter) and W non-duplicate elements within a time length of τ, the false positive probability of the approximate duplicate-elimination algorithm based on TBF is $(1/2)^{(m \ln 2)/W}$, and the number of bits used by this algorithm is mT. Let $\varepsilon = (1/2)^{(m \ln 2)/W}$, we have $m = (\log_2 e)\log_2(1/\varepsilon)W$, Thus we get the number of bits used by the algorithm based on TBF is $(\log_2 e)\log_2(1/\varepsilon)WT$.

In Algorithm 1, DLTBF uses $[T + R]W4/3$ bits. This is because that there are $W/6$ buckets in DLTBF, and the number of bits used by a bucket is $8[T + R]$ (a bucket contains 8 slots and each slot contains a T-bit and a R-bit counters). By Theorem 1, we know the false positive rate of Algorithm 1 is $24/2^R$. Let $\varepsilon = 24/2^R$, we can get the number of bits used by Algorithm 1 is $[\log_2(1/\varepsilon) + T + \log_2 24]4W/3$ (Since the stash contains $O(1)$ elements, we neglect the constant bits used in the stash).

Considering that there are W non-duplicate elements within a time length of τ, thus to obtain a false positive rate ε, Algorithm 1 uses $m_1 = 1.33(\log_2(1/\varepsilon) + T + 4.5)$ bits per element, while the algorithm based on TBF needs $m_2 = 1.44\log_2(1/\varepsilon)T$ bits. It is easy to see that when $\varepsilon \leq 0.125$ and $T > 3.5$, m_1 is less than m_2, and $m_2 - m_1$ increases with the increase of T and $1/\varepsilon$.

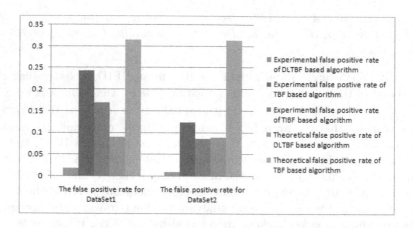

Fig. 5. The false positive rates over DataSet1 and DataSet2

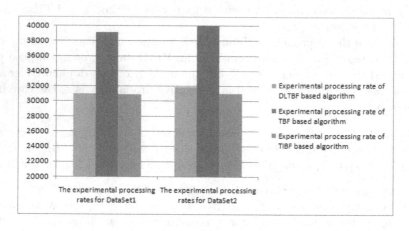

Fig. 6. The processing rates over DataSet1 and DataSet2

4   Experiments

In this section, we use the detection model in [10, 13] to generate synthetic RFID data streams. In this model, tags move in a straight line with different velocities that are assigned randomly when the tags are generated. There are many detection locations in this line and multiple readers may be used to monitor each location in order to increase detection ratio. Similar to [13], we deploy one reader in each detection location and generate an RFID data stream of 10^7 elements (denoted by DataSet1); and we deploy three readers in each detection location and generate an RFID data stream of 10^7 elements (denoted by DataSet2). Obviously, DataSet2 (83% elements in DataSet2 are duplicate) contains more duplicates than DataSet1 (39% elements in DataSet1 are duplicate). The maximum numbers of non-duplicate elements within a time length of τ in Dataset1 and Dataset2 are 1265 and 1333 respectively ($\tau = 100$). The experiments are conducted on 2GHz PC with 4GB main memory using Matlab.

We evaluate Algorithm 1 (the algorithm based on DLTBF), the algorithms based on Time Bloom filter and Time Interval Bloom filter with respect to a false positive rate and a processing rate. In the experiments, the three algorithms use the same number of memory bits.

Fig. 5 shows the false positive rates of the three algorithms in DataSet1 and DataSet2. The false positive rate is sum of false positive errors divided by the 10^7 (the number of elements in DataSet1 or DataSet2 that will be processed by the three algorithms). In Fig. 5, we can see that given the same number of memory bits, DLTBF based algorithm produces a least false positive rate among the three algorithms. It should be noted that the theoretical false positive rate of DLTBF based algorithm is obtained when an element is actually non-duplicate, while there are a large number of duplicates in Dataset1 and Dataset2. Thus the theoretical false positive rate of DLTBF based algorithm is larger than the experimental false positive rate of this algorithm. The reason why the theoretical false positive rate of TBF based algorithm is larger than its experimental false positive rate is the same.

Fig. 6 shows the processing rates of the three algorithms. A processing rate of an approximate duplicate-elimination algorithm is the number of elements that the algorithm can process in one second. In Fig. 6, we can see that given the same number of memory bits, The processing rate of TBF based algorithm is about 1.4 times as that of the other two algorithms over DataSet1 and DataSet2. However from Fig. 5, we can see that the false positive rate of TBF based algorithm is about 10 times as that of DLTBF based algorithm. DLTBF based algorithm has a processing rate similar to that of TIBF based algorithm in Fig. 5, but we note that the false positive rate of TIBF based algorithm is about 8 times as that of DLTBF based algorithm.

5   Conclusion

Usually, there are a larger number of duplicates in RFID data streams, and these duplicates must be eliminated efficiently before an accurate analysis can be conducted on RFID data streams. Existing duplicate-elimination methods based on Time Bloom filter require multiple counters to store the detected time of an element in RFID data streams, thus waste valuable memory resources. In this paper, we devise d-left Time Bloom filter (DLTBF) as an extension of d-left Counting Bloom filter. With the d-left hashing, a balanced allocation mechanism, DLTBF can store the detected time of an element into one counter. Then we propose an one-pass approximate method to remove duplicates in RFID data streams based on DLTBF. Experimental results on the synthetic data verify the effectiveness of our method.

References

[1] Aggarwal, C.C., Han, J.: A survey of rfid data processing. In: Managing and Mining Sensor Data, pp. 349–382. Springer (2013)

[2] Bai, Y., Wang, F., Liu, P.: Efficiently filtering rfid data streams. In: CleanDB Workshop, pp. 50–57 (2006)

[3] Bleco, D., Kotidis, Y.: RFID data aggregation. In: Trigoni, N., Markham, A., Nawaz, S. (eds.) GSN 2009. LNCS, vol. 5659, pp. 87–101. Springer, Heidelberg (2009)

[4] Bonomi, F., Mitzenmacher, M., Panigrahy, R., Singh, S., Varghese, G.: An improved construction for counting bloom filters. In: Azar, Y., Erlebach, T. (eds.) ESA 2006. LNCS, vol. 4168, pp. 684–695. Springer, Heidelberg (2006)

[5] Broder, A., Mitzenmacher, M.: Using multiple hash functions to improve ip lookups. In: Proceedings of Twentieth Annual Joint Conference of the IEEE Computer and Communications Societies, INFOCOM 2001, vol. 3, pp. 1454–1463. IEEE (2001)

[6] Chen, H., Ku, W.S., Wang, H., Sun, M.T.: Leveraging spatio-temporal redundancy for rfid data cleansing. In: Proceedings of the 2010 ACM SIGMOD International Conference on Management of Data, pp. 51–62. ACM (2010)

[7] Dautrich Jr., J.L., Ravishankar, C.V.: Inferential time-decaying bloom filters. In: Proceedings of the 16th International Conference on Extending Database Technology, pp. 239–250. ACM (2013)

[8] Dutta, S., Narang, A., Bera, S.K.: Streaming quotient filter: a near optimal approximate duplicate detection approach for data streams. Proceedings of the VLDB Endowment 6(8), 589–600 (2013)

[9] Fazzinga, B., Flesca, S., Furfaro, F., Parisi, F.: Cleaning trajectory data of rfid-monitored objects through conditioning under integrity constraints. In: EDBT, pp. 379–390 (2014)

[10] Jeffery, S.R., Garofalakis, M., Franklin, M.J.: Adaptive cleaning for rfid data streams. In: Proceedings of the 32nd International Conference on Very Large Data Bases, VLDB Endowment, pp. 163–174 (2006)

[11] Jiang, W., Wang, Y., Zhang, G.: A two-layer duplicate filtering approach for RFID data streams. In: Wang, Y., Zhang, X. (eds.) IOT 2012. CCIS, vol. 312, pp. 226–233. Springer, Heidelberg (2012)

[12] Ku, W.S., Chen, H., Wang, H., Sun, M.T.: A bayesian inference-based framework for rfid data cleansing. IEEE Transactions on Knowledge and Data Engineering 25(10), 2177–2191 (2013)

[13] Lee, C.H., Chung, C.W.: An approximate duplicate elimination in rfid data streams. Data & Knowledge Engineering 70(12), 1070–1087 (2011)

[14] Martínez-Sala, A.S., Egea-López, E., García-Sánchez, F., García-Haro, J.: Tracking of returnable packaging and transport units with active rfid in the grocery supply chain. Computers in Industry 60(3), 161–171 (2009)

[15] Vöcking, B.: How asymmetry helps load balancing. Journal of the ACM (JACM) 50(4), 568–589 (2003)

MOARLE: Matrix Operation Accelerator Based on Run-Length Encoding

Masafumi Oyamada, Jianquan Liu, Kazuyo Narita, and Takuya Araki

Green Platform Research Labs., NEC Corp.
1753 Shimonumabe, Nakahara-ku, Kawasaki, Kanagawa, 211-8666 Japan
{j-liu,k-narita}@ct.jp.nec.com, t-araki@dc.jp.nec.com,
m-oyamada@cq.jp.nec.com

Abstract. Matrix computation is a key technology in various data processing tasks including data mining, machine learning, and information retrieval. Size of matrices has been increasing with the development of computational resources and dissemination of big data. Huge matrices are memory- and computational-time-consuming. Therefore, reducing the size and computational time of huge matrices is a key challenge in the data processing area. We develop **MOARLE**, a novel matrix computation framework that saves memory space and computational time. In contrast to conventional matrix computational methods that target to sparse matrices, **MOARLE** can efficiently handle both sparse matrices and dense matrices. Our experimental results show that **MOARLE** can reduce the memory usage to 2% of the original usage and improve the computational performance by a factor of 124x.

Keywords: Matrix, Compression, Run-length encoding, Similarity search, Euclidean distance.

1 Introduction

Matrix is a fundamental structure to represent structured data, including feature-vector sets in information retrieval, relational tables in databases, graphs in social network analysis, and user-item associations in recommender systems [5]. Nowadays, abundant data yield huge matrices, which consume a large amount of storage space and take a long time to be computed. This situation motivates a classical problem: how to reduce the data size and computational time of huge matrices?

There is a lot of work that tackled the above-mentioned problem [8, 11, 13], and most of the work are based on the technique called *sparse matrix representation* [8]. Sparse matrix representation concisely represents a sparse matrix that is mostly filled with a *default value*. When the default value is zero, we can omit computations on matrix by utilizing algebraic laws such as multiplying any values to zero yields zero.

However, actual matrices are not only sparse but also dense. Unfortunately, methods that depend on sparse matrix representation cannot represent and compute dense matrices concisely and efficiently. Thus, in this paper, we tackle a challenging problem: reducing the data size and computational time for both sparse matrices and dense matrices.

L. Chen et al. (Eds.): APWeb 2014, LNCS 8709, pp. 425–436, 2014.

To this end, we propose **MOARLE** *(Matrix Operation Accelerator based on Run-Length Encoding)*, a novel matrix computation framework. **MOARLE** compresses an input matrix with *run-length encoding* and conducts computations on the compressed matrix directly without decompression, thus reducing computational time and memory usage. Furthermore, **MOARLE** can improve the compression rate of the input matrix without changing computational results. When **MOARLE** finds that the result of a computation to a matrix is not affected by row- or column-reordering, it reorders the rows or columns of the matrix in order to improve the compression rate, in a grace way.

We summarize our contributions:

1. We propose **MOARLE**, a matrix computation framework that compresses an input matrix and conducts computations on the compressed matrix directly without decompression, thus reducing computational time and memory usage.
2. For several representative computations, we propose techniques to conduct the computations on compressed matrices without decompression (Section 2).
3. We propose a way to improve the compression rate without changing computational results. We define the problem of maximizing the compression rate formally, and propose approximate solutions that run in polynomial time (Section 3).
4. We implement **MOARLE** and present an experimental analysis demonstrating the effectiveness of our proposed techniques (Section 4).

The rest of this paper is organized as follows. Section 2 describes how **MOARLE** compresses and computes input matrices. Section 3 describes how **MOARLE** improves the compression rate of input matrices. Section 4 evaluates **MOARLE** by experiments with various datasets. Section 5 describes related work. Section 6 concludes the paper.

2   Computation of Compressed Matrix

In this section, we present the mechanism of **MOARLE**'s computational part, which compresses a matrix with run-length encoding and conducts computations without decompression to reduce computational time.

2.1   Run-Length Encoding of Matrix

We employ *run-length encoding(RLE)*, a basic data compression technique, in compression part of **MOARLE**. RLE represents a sequence of consecutive same data elements with a pair *(length, element)*, where *length* is the number of the data elements, and *element* is the data element. For example, RLE encodes a data sequence 1, 1, 1, 1, 1, 2, 2, 2, 2, 2, 2, 2, 2, 1, 1, 1 to a sequence of pairs (5, 1), (9, 2), (3, 1), reducing the number of elements to represent the data from 17 to 6. One downside of RLE is that it cannot efficiently encode a sequence of data in which the number of consecutive same data elements is small. To alleviate this problem, **MOARLE** can optionally employ *Pack-Bits* [1], an improved version of RLE. PackBits handles two types of length: *positive length* and *negative length*. When PackBits finds a sequence of consecutive same data elements, it replaces the sequence by a pair with positive length, as in RLE. Otherwise, PackBits meets a sequence of consecutive *different data elements* and inserts the length of the sequence before the sequence in negative format. For example, PackBits encodes a data sequence 1, 2, 3, 4, 1, 1, 1, 1 to (-4, 1, 2, 3, 4), (4, 1) successfully reducing the data size, whereas RLE encodes the sequence to (1, 1), (1, 2), (1, 3), (1, 4), (4, 1) increasing the data size. We will compare the performance of RLE and PackBits in Section 4.

MOARLE encodes a matrix with RLE in two ways: either encoding row-vectors (row-compression) or column-vectors (column-compression). For example, a matrix

$$\begin{pmatrix} 1\,1\,2\,2\,2 \\ 2\,2\,1\,2\,2 \\ 2\,3\,3\,3\,3 \\ 2\,3\,3\,2\,2 \\ 2\,3\,1\,2\,2 \end{pmatrix} \tag{1}$$

is encoded to

(2, 1) (3, 2)

(2, 2) (1, 1) (2, 2)

(1, 2) (4, 3)

(1, 2) (2, 3) (2, 2)

(1, 2) (1, 3) (1, 1) (2, 2)

in row-compression, or

$$\begin{array}{c|c|c|c|c} (1,1) & (1,1) & (1,2) & (2,2) & (2,2) \\ (4,2) & (1,2) & (1,1) & (1,3) & (1,3) \\ & (3,3) & (1,3) & (2,2) & (2,2) \\ & (1,1) & & & \end{array}$$

in column-compression.

2.2 Computation over RLE Vectors without Decompression

MOARLE conducts several computations on RLE vectors directly without decoding the vectors. This technique reduces the computational time and the memory usage, achieving our original goal. The key insight in the technique is that an RLE-encoded data sequence contains preliminary knowledge that an element x appears n times. In the rest part of this section, we demonstrate how **MOARLE** uses this knowledge to perform computations without decoding.

Square Sum of RLE Vector. First, we demonstrate how **MOARLE** computes square sum of a compressed vector. Square sum of a vector is a basic but essential computation because it appears in many complex computations including Euclidean distance, cosine similarity, coordinate descent [7], and so forth.

Let us consider square sum computation of the first row of the matrix in Eq.1. A naïve approach is to compute the square sum as

$$1^2 + 2^2 + 2^2 + 2^2 + 2^2 \tag{2}$$

where it needs to conduct five product and four addition operations.

In **MOARLE**, we can process RLE vectors directly without decoding. Given the RLE vector of the first row of the matrix in Eq.1, $(1, 1), (4, 2)$, **MOARLE** computes the square sum of the vector as

$$1^2 + 4 \cdot 2^2 \tag{3}$$

where it needs to conduct three product and one addition operations, of which the computation cost is less than the naïve one.

Dot Product of RLE Vectors. Next, we will demonstrate how **MOARLE** computes dot product of a compressed vector. Dot product of a vector is also an important computation, which appears in a lot of more complicated operations.

Let us consider dot product computations of the first row-vector and the second row-vector of the matrix in Eq.1. A naïve approach is to compute the dot product as

$$1 \cdot 2 + 1 \cdot 2 + 2 \cdot 1 + 2 \cdot 2 + 2 \cdot 2 \tag{4}$$

where it needs to conduct five product operations and four addition operations.

Given RLE-encoded vectors for the first row and second row of the matrix in Eq.1, **MOARLE** computes the dot product of the vectors as

$$1 \cdot (2 \cdot 2) + 2 \cdot (1 \cdot 1 + 2 \cdot 2) \tag{5}$$

where it needs to conduct two product operations and four addition operations, of which the computation cost is less than the naïve one.

2.3   Euclidean Distance of RLE Vectors

So far, we have described two basic computations of RLE vectors: square sum and dot product. Here, we show that some complex operations of RLE vectors can be done by composing basic computations.

Let us consider the Euclidean distance of two RLE vectors. The Euclidean distance of vector $\mathbf{a} = (a_1, ..., a_n)$ and vector $\mathbf{b} = (b_1, ..., b_n)$ is defined as

$$\sqrt{\sum_i^n (a_i - b_i)^2}. \tag{6}$$

Since Eq.6 can be expanded to

$$\sqrt{\sum_i^n a_i^2 + \sum_i^n b_i^2 - 2 \sum_i^n a_i b_i}, \tag{7}$$

and it consists only of aforementioned square sum and dot product, **MOARLE** can compute the Euclidean distance without decoding. This kind of approach can also be applied to other computations like cosine similarity, but we do not show concrete examples here owing to space limitations.

3 Improving Compression Rate by Reordering Rows or Columns

In the previous section, we have described how **MOARLE** compresses a matrix with RLE and conducts computations directly without decoding. In this section, we show that the RLE compression rate of a matrix can be improved by reordering the row- or column-vectors, and such reordering does not affect results of the computations we have seen.

3.1 Reordering and Computation

By reordering rows or columns of a matrix properly, we can improve the RLE's compression rate of the matrix, reducing the memory usage and the computational time. Consider the matrix $X \in \mathbb{R}^{6 \times 3}$ in Fig.1. By applying column compression to the matrix X, we get the collection of RLE column-vectors in Fig.2, which consists of 15 pairs. If we reorder the rows of the matrix X, we can further reduce the number of pairs to represent X, thus improving the compression rate. Let us consider the matrix X^* in Fig.3, which is derived from X by reordering rows. If we apply column-compression to X^*, we get the collection of the RLE column-vectors in Fig.4, which consists of 11 pairs, smaller than the 15 pairs needed by the original matrix X.

$$\begin{pmatrix} 2 & 1 & 2 \\ 1 & 0 & 1 \\ 5 & 1 & 1 \\ 4 & 0 & 2 \\ 3 & 2 & 1 \\ 1 & 2 & 1 \end{pmatrix}$$

Fig. 1. Original matrix X

(1, 2)	(1, 1)	(1, 2)
(1, 1)	(1, 0)	(2, 1)
(1, 5)	(1, 1)	(1, 2)
(1, 4)	(1, 0)	(2, 1)
(1, 3)	(2, 2)	
(1, 1)		

Fig. 2. Compressed original matrix

$$X^* = \begin{pmatrix} 2 & 1 & 2 \\ 5 & 1 & 1 \\ 3 & 2 & 1 \\ 1 & 2 & 1 \\ 1 & 0 & 1 \\ 4 & 0 & 2 \end{pmatrix}$$

Fig. 3. Reordered matrix X^*

(1, 2)	(2, 1)	(1, 2)
(1, 5)	(2, 2)	(4, 1)
(1, 3)	(2, 0)	(1, 2)
(2, 1)		
(1, 4)		

Fig. 4. Compressed reordered matrix

MOARLE reorders a matrix to improve its compression rate, based on an insight that the results of certain computations are not affected by row- or column-reordering. We call such a computation an *order-insensitive computation*. For example, square sum and dot product computations illustrated in Section 2.2 are order-insensitive computations. Relational operations in relational algebra also are order-insensitive computations when we consider a matrix as a relational table. Furthermore, even more complex computations such as convex-optimization algorithms including coordinate descent [7] and stochastic gradient descent [6] also are order-insensitive computations.

3.2 Problem Definition

Since reordering a matrix can improve the RLE compression rate and the reordering does not change the results of order-insensitive operations, **MOARLE** reorders the matrix if computations are known to be order-insensitive. However, the number of possible reordering patterns for a matrix is huge, and thus finding the best pattern from possible patterns is not a trivial task. In the rest of this section, we limit the discussion to row-reordering for ease of exposition, and tackle the following problem:

Problem 1 (Row-reordering). *Given a matrix $X \in \mathbb{R}^{m \times n}$, find a matrix X' that satisfies the following condition*

$$minimize: Size(X')$$
$$subject\ to:\ X' \in \mathbb{X},\ Size(X') \leq Size(X)$$

where Size : $\mathbb{R}^{m \times n} \to \mathbb{N}$ is a function that counts the number of pairs to represent a given matrix with column-order RLE and $\mathbb{X}$ is a set of all matrices derived from X by reordering rows.

3.3 Exhaustive Search

The most naïve solution for the Problem 1 is exhaustive search method. Exhaustive search method checks all reordering matrix patterns $\mathbb{X}$, and picks up the matrix with minimum *Size*. Since the number of patterns $|\mathbb{X}|$ is $m!$ and each *Size* process traverses all elements in X, which checks $m \cdot n$ elements, the computational complexity of exhaustive search method is $O(m \cdot m!\ n)$. Although exhaustive method can find the best matrix, it is not feasible for real-world problems because the computational complexity is non-polynomial.

In the rest of this section, we introduce two reordering methods: greedy method and scored-lex-sort method, which run in polynomial time.

3.4 Greedy Method

First, we introduce *greedy method*, a greedy approach to find a feasible solution for the Problem 1. Greedy method selects a row as the beginning row, and then repeatedly selects the row that has minimum hamming distance with the previously selected row. Finally the matrix is reordered in the selection order. Algorithm 1 shows the complete algorithm of greedy method. In Algorithm 1, we use $a_{i*} \leftarrow b_{j*}$ to denote replacing i-th row of the matrix A with j-th row of the matrix B, and $O_{m,n}$ to denote a zero matrix whose size is $m \times n$.

Greedy method runs in polynomial time. In greedy method, we can choose a beginning row from m rows, and for each beginning row, there are $(m-1) + (m-2) + \dots + 1 =$

Algorithm 1. Greedy method

Input: $X \in \mathbb{R}^{m \times n}$, Input matrix
Output: Reordered matrix
Data: P, Row pool; $\mathbb{X}_{cand}$, Candidates set; X', Reordered matrix
1 **foreach** $i \in \{1, ..., m\}$ **do**
2      $X' \leftarrow O_{m,n}$
        /* Select i-th row in matrix X as the beginning row, and add
        other rows to the pool P.   */
3      $P \leftarrow \{1, ..., m\} \setminus \{i\}$
4      $x'_{1*} \leftarrow x_{i*}$
5   **for** $k \leftarrow 2$ **to** m **do**
           /* Pick up j-th row that has minimum hamming distance with the
           beginning row from pool P, and add it to reordered matrix
           X'.   */
6         $j \leftarrow \underset{j \in P}{\arg \min} \, \mathrm{HammingDistance}(X, k-1, j)$
7         $P \leftarrow P \setminus \{j\}$
8         $x'_{k*} \leftarrow x_{j*}$
9      $\mathbb{X}_{cand} \leftarrow \mathbb{X}_{cand} \cup \{X'\}$
10 **return** $\underset{X' \in \mathbb{X}_{cand}}{\arg \min} \, Size(X')$

$m(m-1)/2$ patterns of selecting remaining rows in the greedy way based on hamming distance. Each hamming distance computation needs n element comparison. Thus, the computational complexity of greedy method is $O(m^3 n)$. Although $O(m^3 n)$ is a polynomial time, it contains m^3 and thus is not appropriate for processing large matrices.

3.5 Scored-Lex-Sort Method

Second, we introduce *scored-lex-sort method*, an efficient approach to find a feasible solution for the Problem 1 based on lexicographical sort. scored-lex-sort method runs in $O(n m \log m)$, which is better than greedy method's $O(m^3 n)$. To introduce scored-lex-sort method, we first describe lexicographical sorting of a matrix. Lexicographical sorting of a matrix is to reorder rows of a matrix where the order of two rows is defined as lexicographical order. For example, if we sort the matrix X in Fig.1 lexicographically, then the sorted matrix X_{lex} is as follows:

$$X_{lex} = \begin{pmatrix} 1 & 0 & 1 \\ 1 & 2 & 1 \\ 2 & 1 & 2 \\ 3 & 2 & 1 \\ 4 & 0 & 2 \\ 5 & 1 & 1 \end{pmatrix}. \tag{8}$$

Since lexicographical sorting of a matrix preferentially sorts left-side columns, it sometimes does not much improve the compression rate of the matrix. For instance,

---

Algorithm 2. Row-compare function in scored-lex-sort method

Input: $X \in \mathbb{R}^{m \times n}$, Input matrix; $p \in \{1, ..., m\}$, Row number of the first input row;
$\quad\quad\quad q \in \{1, ..., m\}$, Row number of the second input row;
Output: A numerical number indicating whether p-th row is bigger/smaller than or equal
$\quad\quad\quad$ to q-th row
Data: Q, Priority queue

1 **foreach** $k \in \{1, ..., n\}$ **do**
2 $\quad$ Get the score of k-th column, and add the column number k to the priority queue Q
$\quad\quad$ using the score as the priority.

3 **while** Q *is not empty* **do**
4 $\quad$ $k \leftarrow$ Dequeue(Q)
5 $\quad$ **if** $x_{pk} > x_{qk}$ **then**
6 $\quad\quad$ **return** *1, which indicates p-th row > q-th row.*

7 $\quad$ **else if** $x_{pk} < x_{qk}$ **then**
8 $\quad\quad$ **return** *-1, which indicates p-th row < q-th row.*

9 **return** *0, which indicates p-th row = q-th row.*

X_{lex}'s compression rate is worse than the original matrix X's one. To alleviate this problem, we introduce *scored-lex-sort method*. scored-lex-sort method first computes scores of all columns of the matrix, and then preferentially sorts columns that have high score. Effectiveness of scored-lex-sort method highly depends on the definition of the score. We use $1/\text{Cardinality}(\mathbf{x})$ as the score of a column $\mathbf{x}$, where the function Cardinality($\mathbf{x}$) counts the number of distinct elements in column $\mathbf{x}$. This score definition is based on the insight that a column with low-cardinality contains a lot of same elements, and preferentially sorting such columns improves the compression effect of RLE.

Algorithm 2 shows the algorithm of row comparison function in scored-lex-sort method. In the algorithm, x_{ij} indicates the (i, j) element in the matrix X. For the sorting part, we can use arbitrary sorting algorithms. This allows us to reorder a huge matrix by using external sorting algorithms like merge-sort.

Scored-lex-sort method runs in polynomial time, and its computational complexity is smaller than of the greedy method. As mentioned before, scored-lex-sort method can use arbitrary general sorting algorithms. General sorting algorithms are known to sort m records in $O(m \log m)$ [4]. In a comparison operation of two rows, scored-lex-sort method needs to compare n elements as described in Algorithm 2. Thus, the computational complexity of scored-lex-sort method is $O(n\, m \log m)$, which is sufficiently applicable to large matrices.

4 Experiments

4.1 Experimental Setup

System. All of our experiments were run on a machine that has 16GB RAM and dual-core 3.6GHz CPU running Linux 3.8.0. Our proposed system, **MOARLE**, is implemented in C++ and compiled by GNU g++ 4.7.3.

Datasets. We used both sparse matrices and dense matrices for experiments. Table 1 shows the information of the datasets we have used. The sparse matrices are bag-of-words model matrices [2]. For the details of the dense matrices, see [10].

Table 1. Datasets used in experiments

	Sparse [2]			Dense [10]		
	nips	kos	enron	madelon	arcene	gisette
Rows	12,419	6,906	28,102	500	10,000	5,000
Columns	1,500	3,430	39,861	2,000	100	6,000
Non-zero elements ratio	0.040	0.014	0.003	0.999	0.540	0.129

4.2 Compression Rate

First, we evaluate **MOARLE**'s compression part, checking how RLE is effective for real-world matrices and how our scored-lex-sort method improves the compression rate. In this experiment, we applied row-order RLE described in Section 2.1 to the matrices shown in Table 2, and examined the compression rate that is defined as $\frac{compressed\ size}{original\ size}$. In the experiment, we used two compression methods: normal RLE and PackBits described in Section 2.1. We measured the compression rate of these methods for both an input matrix and reordered by scored-lex-sort method described in Section 3.5.

Table 2. Compression rate of sparse/dense matrices (MB)

	Sparse			Dense		
	nips	kos	enron	madelon	arcene	gisette
Original	71.0	90.3	4273.1	3.8	3.8	114.4
RLE	10.5 (14.8%)	5.1 (5.7%)	54.9 (1.2%)	7.5 (197.4%)	5.9 (156.4%)	55.1 (48.2%)
Sort+RLE	9.9 (14.0%)	4.8 (5.4%)	53.4 (1.2%)	7.4 (195.6%)	5.1 (134.4%)	46.8 (40.9%)
PackBits	10.0 (14.0%)	5.0 (5.6%)	53.6 (1.2%)	3.8 (101.4%)	3.8 (100.9%)	49.9 (43.6%)
Sort+PackBits	9.1 (12.8%)	4.7 (5.2%)	51.7 (1.2%)	3.8 (101.7%)	3.2 (83.9%)	39.0 (34.1%)

Table 2 shows the compression rates of different compression methods. In the table, "RLE" or "PackBits" means the compression method, and "Sort" indicates whether we applied scored-lex-sort method or not. Here, we summarize the insights from Table 2 as follows:

– **RLE/PackBits are especially effective for sparse matrices:** PackBits yielded the highest compression rate 1.21% when it compressed the sparse matrix *enron*.
– **PackBits is effective for dense matrices:** Compared to RLE, PackBits succeeded to reduce the compressed data size of the dense matrices *madelon*, *arcene*, and *gisette* by 96%, 55%, and 4.58%, respectively.
– **Scored-lex-sort is especially effective for dense matrices:** Scored-lex-sort succeeded to reduce the compressed data size of the dense matrix *gisette* by 9.5%.

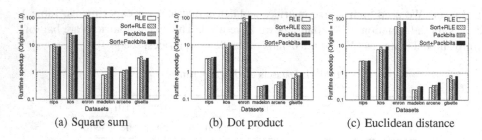

(a) Square sum   (b) Dot product   (c) Euclidean distance

Fig. 5. Runtime speedups (log-scaled)

4.3   Runtime Speedup

Second, we evaluate **MOARLE**'s computation part, checking how the computations on compressed matrices outperform the computations on original matrices. In this experiment, we measured the performance of the computations described in Section 2.2 for both compressed matrices and original matrices. Specifically, we computed square sums of each row-vectors, and dot products and Euclidean distances between the first row vector and each of the rest row-vectors. Fig.5 shows runtime speedup factors of the computations on compressed matrices compared to the computations on original matrices.

In the results of square sum for sparse matrices (left part of Fig.5(a)), we confirmed the notable speedup by a factor of 10x to 120x, and further speedups by scored-lex-sort method (e.g., factor increased from 115x to 120x in *enron*). Although PackBits yielded more compact data compared to RLE, speedup factors of PackBits are lower than those of RLE. We conducted a profiling and found that this phenomena is caused by branch-prediction misses: PackBits switches processes based on whether a run's length is positive or negative, causing frequent branch-prediction misses. To reduce branch-prediction misses is one of our future work. For dense matrices (right part of Fig.5(a)), we also confirmed the speedup by a factor of 1.5x to 3.7x and the effect of scored-lex-sort method (e.g., factor increased from 3.2x to 3.7x in *gisette*).

In the results of dot product for sparse matrices (left part of Fig.5(b)), we confirm the notable speedup by a factor of 3.5x to 124x, and further speedups by scored-lex-sort method (e.g., factor increased from 76x to 124x in *enron*). In contrast to square sum, PackBits outperformed RLE in both the compression rate and the runtime speedup. This is because RLE and PackBits versions of dot product implementations are a bit complicated, and both implementations incur branch-prediction misses. Overheads of current complicated implementations can also be seen in the results for dense matrices (right part of Fig.5(b)). We plan to optimize the implementations in the future.

Fig.5(c) shows the results of Euclidean distance. We omit the discussion for the results here because Euclidean distance is composition of square sum and dot product we have discussed.

4.4   Correlation between Compression Rate and Runtime Speedup

Finally, we discuss the correlation of compression rates and runtime speedups. Fig.6 shows the correlations between the compression rates and the runtime speedups measured in experiments in Section 4.2 and 4.3. In the figure, each sample corresponds to a dataset. Since correlation charts in Fig.6 are both log-scaled and show linear correlations, we can say that compression rates and runtime speedups follow power-law. By using this knowledge, we can estimate the corresponding runtime speedup from a compression rate, allowing us to choose whether to conduct a computation on a compressed matrix or an original matrix; if the estimated speedup by the compression is below 1.0, we can choose the naïve computation.

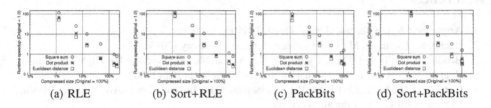

(a) RLE   (b) Sort+RLE   (c) PackBits   (d) Sort+PackBits

Fig. 6. Correlation charts of compression rates and runtime speedups (both log-scaled)

5   Related Work

MOARLE relates to computation frameworks that utilize sparse matrix and sparse vector representations. For example, Eigen [9], a vector computation library, can represent sparse matrices and sparse vectors by concise data structures, and efficiently conduct computations on them. In contrast to Eigen, which aims to process sparse data efficiently, **MOARLE** tries to compress and process dense matrices efficiently as well. We plan to compare **MOARLE** with Eigen through experiments in the future.

Rendle proposed a way to accelerate machine-learning algorithms by utilizing block structures in a matrix [12]. His method assumes certain structures in input matrices, the block structures generated by relational joins, whereas **MOARLE** does not have any assumptions for the input matrices.

Brodie *et al.* tackled the row-reordering problem we have defined in Section 3.2, and proposed a method that is similar to our greedy method, whose computational complexity is $O(m^3 n)$ [3]. In their situation, greedy method was enough, because their aim was to compress the state-transition tables of regular expression, and commonly such tables are not so large. However, we also targets huge matrices that cannot be processed by greedy method in realistic time. In this case, our scored-lex-sort method, whose computational complexity is $O(n m \log m)$, is better.

6   Conclusion

In this paper, we proposed **MOARLE**, a matrix computation framework. **MOARLE** compresses an input matrix with RLE/PackBits, and conducts computations on the compressed matrix directly without decoding, thus reducing the computational time and the memory usage. We first proposed techniques that directly conduct several representative computations over compressed matrices. Second, we proposed a way to improve the compression rate without changing computational results. The insight is that results of certain computations over a matrix are not affected by row- or column-reordering, allowing us to reorder the rows/columns of matrix in order to improve the compression rate. We defined the reordering problem formally, and proposed a solution named *scored-lex-sort*, which runs in $O(n\,m\log m)$. Our experimental results confirmed the effectiveness of **MOARLE**, showing the computational time improvement from naïve one by a factor of 10x to 120x and the memory usage reduction up to 98%.

References

1. Apple Inc.: Apple Technical Note TN1023 (1996)
2. Bache, K., Lichman, M.: UCI machine learning repository (2013)
3. Brodie, B.C., Taylor, D.E., Cytron, R.K.: A Scalable Architecture for High-Throughput Regular-Expression Pattern Matching. In: ISCA, pp. 191–202 (2006)
4. Cormen, T.H., Stein, C., Rivest, R.L., Leiserson, C.E.: Introduction to Algorithms, 2nd edn. McGraw-Hill Higher Education (2001)
5. Deshpande, M., Karypis, G.: Item-based top-N Recommendation Algorithms. ACM Trans. Inf. Syst. 22(1), 143–177 (2004)
6. Feng, X., Kumar, A., Recht, B., Ré, C.: Towards a unified architecture for in-RDBMS analytics. In: SIGMOD, pp. 325–336. ACM (2012)
7. Fu, W.J.: Penalized Regressions: The Bridge versus the Lasso. Journal of Computational and Graphical Statistics 7(3), 397–416 (1998)
8. Golub, G.H., Van Loan, C.F.: Matrix Computations, 3rd edn. Johns Hopkins University Press, Baltimore (1996)
9. Guennebaud, G., Jacob, B., et al.: Eigen v3 (2010), http://eigen.tuxfamily.org
10. Guyon, I., Gunn, S.R., Ben-Hur, A., Dror, G.: Result analysis of the nips 2003 feature selection challenge. In: NIPS (2004)
11. Pinar, A., Heath, M.T.: Improving Performance of Sparse Matrix-vector Multiplication. In: SC. ACM, New York (1999)
12. Rendle, S.: Scaling Factorization Machines to Relational Data. PVLDB 6(5), 337–348 (2013)
13. Willcock, J., Lumsdaine, A.: Accelerating Sparse Matrix Computations via Data Compression. In: ICS, pp. 307–316. ACM, New York (2006)

Measuring User Similarity with Trajectory Patterns: Principles and New Metrics

Xihui Chen[1], Ruipeng Lu[2], Xiaoxing Ma[3], and Jun Pang[1,2]

[1] Interdisciplinary Centre for Security, Reliability and Trust, University of Luxembourg
[2] Faculty of Science, Technology and Communication, University of Luxembourg
[3] State Key Laboratory for Novel Software Technology,
Department of Computer Science and Technology, Nanjing University

Abstract. The accumulation of users' whereabouts in location-based applications has made it possible to construct user mobility profiles. Trajectory patterns, i.e., traces of places of interest that a user frequently visits, are among the most popular models of mobility profiles. In this paper, we revisit measuring user similarity using trajectory patterns, which is an important supplement for friend recommendation in on-line social networks. Specifically, we identify and formalise a number of basic principles that should hold when quantifying user similarity with trajectory patterns. These principles allow us to evaluate existing metrics in the literature and demonstrate their insufficiencies. Then we propose for the first time a new metric that respects all the identified principles. The metric is extended to deal with location semantics. Through experiments on a real-life trajectory dataset, we show the effectiveness of our new metrics.

1 Introduction

Nowadays, most people are equipped with mobile devices that are able to acquire their real-time positions. This technical progress leads to the emergence and popularity of *geo-social networks* (GSN) such as Bikely and Foursquare. What is attractive in GSNs is that people can share their locations with their friends. For example, photos and videos can be tagged by their shooting places. Even the traditional on-line social networks, e.g., Google+ and Facebook, have also upgraded to support location sharing. With GSNs becoming popular, an enormous number of locations have been posted and accumulated into large datasets of users' movements. This access to users' mobility history offers an opportunity to improve the friend recommendation service of GSNs because a user's historical movements significantly reveal his personal interests [1, 2]. Thus, recommending friends with similar interests can be supplemented by finding people with similar movements.

One method to identify users with similar movements is to construct and compare their *mobility profiles* which are composed of their *trajectory patterns* [3]. Intuitively, a trajectory pattern is a sequence of places of interest which a user frequently visits. The frequency by which the pattern is followed is called its *support value*. For instance, every morning Pierre, a student in Oxford travels by train from his home to Oxford from which he walks to Trinity College. This daily routine can be described as a trajectory pattern: *Home → Oxford station → Trinity College*. Typical transition time between two successive visits can also be extracted and annotated on trajectory patterns.

L. Chen et al. (Eds.): APWeb 2014, LNCS 8709, pp. 437–448, 2014.

Profiling user mobility has attracted a lot of research in recent years, and different models have been proposed, e.g., Lévy-walk [4–6] and Markov chains [7]. Compared with these mobility profile models, trajectory patterns provide a more concise representation of users' *typical* movements as only the places which are *meaningful* to users are taken into account. This subsequently results in a more efficient comparison due to the elimination of the positions during transition between places, especially compared to those methods based on users' raw trajectories [8, 2]. Thus, in this paper, we concentrate on measuring user similarity using trajectory patterns.

Related Work. Measuring user similarity with trajectory patterns has been studied in a few papers. Ying et al. [9] propose a metric based on *maximal trajectory pattern* (MTP) similarity. A maximal trajectory pattern is a pattern that is not contained in any other patterns. For any two trajectory patterns from two users respectively, a similarity value is calculated by referring to the length of their longest common sequences. Two users' similarity is then calculated as the weighted average of the similarity values of all pattern pairs. The weight assigned to two patterns is the average support values. Later, Chen et al. [10] identify and fix a weakness in the metric of Ying et al. [9] that the maximum similarity value (1.0) cannot be achieved even for two identical users.

Our Motivations. In the literature, the effectiveness of a metric is assessed by the difference between the calculated similarity values and the ground-truth similarity obtained in other ways, e.g., by questionnaires. However, there are no formal principles to capture the basic properties that a valid user similarity metric on trajectory patterns should respect. Take the relation *equality* as an example. Intuitively, two users are equal or their similarity is maximum if and only if their mobility profiles are exactly the same. However, even the metric proposed by Chen et al. [10] fails to satisfy this property as it ignores the differences between support values. In other words, two users are considered identical when they have the same trajectory patterns even if they visit these patterns with significantly distinctive frequencies. Without identifying design principles first, we cannot propose a meaningful user similarity metric to capture the real similarity between users based on their trajectory patterns.

Our Contributions. In this paper, we identify and define the basic principles that hold when measuring user similarity based on trajectory patterns. These principles enable us to re-evaluate existing metrics and discuss their insufficiency in capturing user similarity. Instead of fixing them, we propose for the first time a new metric which respects all the basic principles. Due to the importance of location semantics in identifying users' hobbies, we extend our new metric to measure user similarity to take into account the semantics of visited locations. Last but not least, we perform extensive experiments on real-life trajectory datasets and demonstrate the effectiveness of our metrics.

2   Preliminaries

In this section, we briefly introduce the basic concepts related to profiling user mobility and describe existing user similarity metrics based on trajectory patterns.

Basic Concepts. A trajectory is the path followed by a user through space in a certain time period. It can be considered as a trace of chronologically ordered spatio-temporal points which record the user's geographical positions at different time points. Let $\mathcal{L}$ be the set of possible positions and $\mathcal{T}$ the totally ordered set of time points. A trajectory can be denoted as the sequence $(\langle \ell_1, t_1 \rangle, \ldots, \langle \ell_n, t_n \rangle)$ where $\ell_i \in \mathcal{L}$ and $t_i \in \mathcal{T}$ $(1 \leq i \leq n)$.

We use *regions of interest* (RoI) to represent the places which are meaningful to users, e.g., Trinity College in the example of Section 1. In fact, an RoI R can be seen as a set of adjacent geographic positions. Thus we have $R \subset \mathcal{L}$. As we previously mentioned, a trajectory pattern indicates one of a user's regular traces of RoIs [3]. Thus we represent a trajectory pattern P as a sequence of RoIs, i.e., $P = (R_1, \ldots, R_n)$ $(n \geq 1)$. It is also denoted as $R_1 \to \ldots \to R_n$ in this paper. We use $len(P)$ to denote its length, i.e., $len(P) = n$. If a user sequentially travels all the RoIs of a trajectory pattern in a trajectory, then we say that the trajectory *spatially contains* the trajectory pattern or the trajectory pattern has an *occurrence* in the trajectory.

Definition 1 (Spatial Containment). *For a trajectory T and a trajectory pattern $P = R_1 \to \ldots \to R_n$, we say that P is spatially contained in T if and only if there exists a subsequence of T, i.e., $T' = (\langle \ell'_1, t'_1 \rangle, \ldots, \langle \ell'_n, t'_n \rangle)$ such that $\forall 1 \leq i \leq n, \ell'_i \in R_i$.*

The movements of a user u in a time period can be stored as a dataset of trajectories and one trajectory pattern may have multiple occurrences in this dataset. We use *support value* (denoted as $sup_u(P)$) to quantify the frequency of its occurrence. Its value is calculated as the percentage of the trajectories containing pattern P among all his trajectories. A trajectory pattern is *frequent* if its support value is larger than a threshold σ. Let $\mathcal{P}_u^\sigma$ be user u's set of frequent trajectory patterns. Then $\mathcal{P}_u^\sigma = \{P \mid sup_u(P) \geq \sigma\}$.

As we discussed above, trajectory patterns captures users' regular movements and their support values quantify their visiting frequencies. These two aspects actually cover the regularity of user mobility. Thus we model user u's mobility profile $\mathcal{M}_u$ as the pair $\langle \mathcal{P}_u^\sigma, sup_u \rangle$. In the sequel, we use $\mathcal{P}_u$ for short by assuming that σ is given implicitly.

In some works (e.g., see [10]), transition time between successive RoIs is also considered when comparing two users. It is usually used as a discounter to the calculated user similarity. In this paper we only focus on the key step of user similarity calculation and users' regularity on transition time can be added similarly as in [10, 11].

MTP-Based Metrics. We briefly describe the metric proposed by Ying et al. [9] and its revision by Chen et al. [10]. Both methods use the set of *maximum trajectory patterns* (MTP) to represent a user mobility profile so as to avoid duplicate comparison between trajectory patterns. Given two patterns $P = (R_1, \ldots, R_n)$ and $Q = (R'_1, \ldots, R'_m)$, we say that Q is a subsequence of P (denoted by $Q \sqsubseteq P$) if there exists $j_1, \ldots, j_m$, such that $R_{j_i} = R'_i$ $(1 \leq i \leq m)$. Given user u's trajectory pattern set $\mathcal{P}_u$, the maximal trajectory pattern set is defined as $M(\mathcal{P}_u) = \{P \in \mathcal{P}_u \mid \nexists P' \in \mathcal{P}_u \ s.t. \ P \sqsubseteq P'\}$.

The main idea of the two MTP-based metrics is to compute the similarity between maximal trajectory patterns and then combine the similarity values. The two metrics calculate the similarity between maximal patterns in the same way, which is based on the length of their *longest common sequences*. For two patterns P and Q, the set of their longest common sequences is $\{S \mid S \sqsubseteq P \wedge S \sqsubseteq Q \wedge (\forall S' \sqsubseteq P \wedge S' \sqsubseteq Q, len(S) \geq len(S'))\}$. Let $lenLCS(P, Q)$ be the length of their longest common sequences. Then the similarity between P and Q is $sim(P,Q) = \frac{2 \cdot lenLCS(P,Q)}{len(P)+len(Q)}$. Furthermore, a weight is calculated for the pair of maximal patterns, i.e., $w(P,Q) = \frac{1}{2}(sup_u(P)+sup_{u'}(Q))$.

The difference between the two MTP-based metrics is the way to combine the similarity values between maximal trajectory patterns. Ying et al. [9] calculate the average weighted similarity as the final user similarity:

$$sim(u,u') = \frac{\displaystyle\sum_{P_i \in M(\mathcal{P}_u)} \sum_{Q_j \in M(\mathcal{P}_{u'})} w(P_i,Q_j) \cdot sim(P_i,Q_j)}{\displaystyle\sum_{P_i \in M(\mathcal{P}_u)} \sum_{Q_j \in M(\mathcal{P}_{u'})} w(P_i,Q_j)}.$$

Chen et al. [10] find that the average similarity cannot guarantee the maximum similarity value (1.0) for identical mobility profiles. For example, suppose mobility profile $\mathcal{M}_u$ with pattern set $\{P_1, \ldots, P_n\}$ where any two patterns have the same support value but share no common parts, i.e., $lenLCS(P_i, P_j) = 0$ and $sup_u(P_i) = sup_u(P_j)$ for any $1 \leq i \neq j \leq n$, Thus, for $1 \leq j \leq n$ we have $sim(P_i, P_i) = 1$ and $sim(P_i, P_j) = 0$ if $i \neq j$. The similarity of $\mathcal{M}_u$ to itself, i.e., $sim(u,u)$, will be calculated as $\frac{1}{n}$, instead of the intuitive value 1.0. Thus, Chen et al. [10] propose a different combination method. First, for each maximal pattern P_i of user u, the method finds the most similar maximal pattern of u', denoted as $\psi_{u,u'}(P_i)$. Then they compute his *relative similarity* to u' as

$$sim(u \mid u') = \frac{\sum_{P_i \in M(\mathcal{P}_u)} sim(P_i, \psi_{u,u'}(P_i)) \cdot w(P_i, \psi_{u,u'}(P_i))}{\sum_{P_i \in M(\mathcal{P}_u)} w(P_i, \psi_{u,u'}(P_i))}.$$

In the end, the user similarity between u and u' is defined as the average of the two relative similarities: $sim(u,u') = \frac{1}{2}(sim(u \mid u') + sim(u' \mid u))$. In the above example, the two relative similarities are both 1.0, hence $sim(u,u) = 1.0$.

In the rest of paper, we use MSTP to refer to the measurement of Ying et al. [9] as it is originally designed to measure user similarity with location semantics and MTP for the metric of Chen et al. [10].

3   Principles

In this section, we present the basic principles that should hold when comparing users based on their trajectory patterns. Then we demonstrate by examples the insufficiencies of existing metrics with respect to the principles.

As we reduce the calculation of user similarity to the comparison of their mobility profiles, we investigate the basic principles that a valid similarity metric for two mobility profiles should satisfy. To begin with, we introduce two concepts about users' mobility profiles. First, given two users u_1 and u_2, we say that u_1's mobility profile is *contained* in u_2's mobility profile, denoted by $\mathcal{M}_{u_1} \prec \mathcal{M}_{u_2}$, if $\mathcal{P}_{u_1} \subseteq \mathcal{P}_{u_2}$ and $\forall P \in \mathcal{P}_{u_1}, sup_{u_1}(P) \leq sup_{u_2}(P)$ and $\mathcal{M}_{u_1} \neq \mathcal{M}_{u_2}$. Intuitively, this means that user u_1's regular movements are only part of those of u_2. Second, we use $\mathcal{M}_{u_1 \triangleleft u_2}$ to represent the mobility profile whose pattern set consists of all the common patterns shared by u_1 and u_2, i.e., $\mathcal{P}_{u_1 \lhd u_2} = \mathcal{P}_{u_1} \cap \mathcal{P}_{u_2}$ and for any $P \in \mathcal{P}_{u_1 \lhd u_2}$, its support value equals to that of user u_1, i.e., $sup_{u_1 \lhd u_2}(P) = sup_{u_1}(P)$. It is obvious that the mobility profile $\mathcal{M}_{u_1 \lhd u_2}$ is contained in the mobility profile of u_1, i.e., $\mathcal{M}_{u_1 \lhd u_2} \prec \mathcal{M}_{u_1}$.

Example 1. Suppose four users whose pattern sets are

$$\mathcal{M}_{u_1} = \{A(0.1), C(0.2)\}; \qquad \mathcal{M}_{u_2} = \{A(0.1), C(0.3)\};$$
$$\mathcal{M}_{u_3} = \{A(0.1), B(0.2), C(0.4)\}; \quad \mathcal{M}_{u_4} = \{A(0.3), B(0.1), D(0.2)\}.$$

For the sake of simplicity, we put the support value in the parentheses for each pattern. Then $\mathcal{M}_{u_1} \prec \mathcal{M}_{u_2} \prec \mathcal{M}_{u_3}$. Furthermore, $\mathcal{M}_{u_3 \lhd u_4} = \{A(0.1), B(0.2)\}$ and $\mathcal{M}_{u_4 \lhd u_3} = \{A(0.3), B(0.1)\}$

Definition 2 (Principles). *A valid similarity metric based on user mobility profiles should satisfy all the principles described below:*

1. $sim(\mathcal{M}_{u_1}, \mathcal{M}_{u_2}) \geq 0$;
2. $sim(\mathcal{M}_{u_1}, \mathcal{M}_{u_2}) \leq 1$;
3. $sim(\mathcal{M}_{u_1}, \mathcal{M}_{u_2}) = sim(\mathcal{M}_{u_2}, \mathcal{M}_{u_1})$;
4. $sim(\mathcal{M}_{u_1}, \mathcal{M}_{u_2}) = 0$ *if and only if* $\mathcal{P}_{u_1 \lhd u_2} = \emptyset$;
5. $sim(\mathcal{M}_u, \mathcal{M}_u) = 1$;
6. $sim(\mathcal{M}_{u_1}, \mathcal{M}_{u_2}) > sim(\mathcal{M}_{u_1}, \mathcal{M}_{u_3})$ *if* $\mathcal{M}_{u_3} \prec \mathcal{M}_{u_2} \prec \mathcal{M}_{u_1}$;
7. $sim(\mathcal{M}_{u_1}, \mathcal{M}_{u_2}) > sim(\mathcal{M}_{u_1}, \mathcal{M}_{u_3})$ *if* $sim(\mathcal{M}_{u_1}, \mathcal{M}_{u_2 \lhd u_1})) > sim(\mathcal{M}_{u_1}, \mathcal{M}_{u_3 \lhd u_1}))$
   and $sim(\mathcal{M}_{u_2}, \mathcal{M}_{u_2 \lhd u_1})) > sim(\mathcal{M}_{u_3}, \mathcal{M}_{u_3 \lhd u_1})$.

The first two principles regulate the range of the similarity value between two users. Principle 3 says that user similarity is *symmetric* and principle 4 states that two users have the minimum similarity value, i.e., 0 if and only if they have no common regular movements. Principle 5 indicates that user similarity should be maximum, i.e., 1.0, when a user is compared to himself. The last two principles are about comparing the similarity of a user to different users. The intuition of principle 6 is that users sharing more regular movements with a user should be more similar to him than users sharing less common behaviours. For instance, in Example 1 user u_2 is more similar to u_3 than u_1 as u_2 travels pattern C more regularly than u_1. Principle 7 says that a user is more similar to users who share more movements and have less different movements than those sharing less but having more different movements. The similarity values calculated with a valid metric should be consistent with this reasoning.

With these principles, we re-evaluate the existing metrics MSTP and MTP and find that they cannot satisfy all the principles. We use the following example to demonstrate their weaknesses.

Example 2. Suppose the following five users:

$$\mathcal{M}_{u_1} = \{A\,(0.4), B\,(0.4), C\,(0.4), A \to B\,(0.1)\};$$
$$\mathcal{M}_{u_2} = \{A\,(0.4), B\,(0.4), C\,(0.4), A \to B\,(0.2)\};$$
$$\mathcal{M}_{u_3} = \{A\,(0.4), B\,(0.4), C\,(0.4), A \to B\,(0.3)\};$$
$$\mathcal{M}_{u_4} = \{A\,(0.4), B\,(0.4), C\,(0.4), B \to A\,(0.3)\};$$
$$\mathcal{M}_{u_5} = \{A\,(0.4), C\,(0.4), D\,(0.4), A \to D\,(0.3)\}.$$

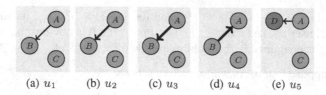

(a) u_1 (b) u_2 (c) u_3 (d) u_4 (e) u_5

Fig. 1. Mobility profiles in Example 2

Table 1. Pairwise user similarity

		MSTP					MTP			
	u_1	u_2	u_3	u_4	u_5	u_1	u_2	u_3	u_4	u_5
u_1	0.5	0.5	0.5	0.42	0.42	1.0	1.0	1.0	0.83	0.83
u_2	0.5	0.5	0.5	0.42	0.42	1.0	1.0	1.0	0.58	0.58
u_3	0.5	0.5	0.5	0.39	0.39	1.0	1.0	1.0	0.79	0.79
u_4	0.42	0.42	0.39	0.5	0.39	0.83	0.58	0.79	1.0	0.79
u_5	0.42	0.42	0.39	0.39	0.5	0.83	0.58	0.79	0.79	1.0

Table 2. User similarity by our method

	u_1	u_2	u_3	u_4	u_5
u_1	1.0	0.96	0.93	0.76	0.50
u_2	0.96	1.0	0.97	0.71	0.47
u_3	0.93	0.97	1.0	0.67	0.44
u_4	0.76	0.71	0.67	1.0	0.44
u_5	0.50	0.47	0.44	0.44	1.0

Figure 1 depicts the mobility profiles in a rectangle region. We use grey circles to indicate RoIs and arrows between RoIs to represent the transition direction whose thickness implies support values. Table 1 shows the results given by the two metrics.

From Table 1, it is clear that both metrics satisfy principles 1, 2, 3 and 4. Principle 5 is violated by metric MSTP as the similarity of any user to himself is not 1.0, which has been pointed out by Chen et al. [10]. Principle 6 is violated by both of them. Since $\mathcal{M}_{u_1} \prec \mathcal{M}_{u_2} \prec \mathcal{M}_{u_3}$, according to principle 6, we have $sim(\mathcal{M}_{u_3}, \mathcal{M}_{u_1}) < sim(\mathcal{M}_{u_3}, \mathcal{M}_{u_2})$. However, both metrics compute the same similarity values for them, i.e., 0.5 and 0.1, respectively. Principle 7 does not hold for both of the metrics either. Take the MTP metric as an example. According to its definition,

$$sim(\mathcal{M}_{u_2}, \mathcal{M}_{u_4 \triangleleft u_2}) = 0.82; \quad sim(\mathcal{M}_{u_2}, \mathcal{M}_{u_5 \triangleleft u_2}) = 0.86$$
$$sim(\mathcal{M}_{u_4}, \mathcal{M}_{u_4 \triangleleft u_2}) = 0.82; \quad sim(\mathcal{M}_{u_5}, \mathcal{M}_{u_5 \triangleleft u_2}) = 0.86.$$

As $sim(\mathcal{M}_{u_2}, \mathcal{M}_{u_5 \triangleleft u_2}) > sim(\mathcal{M}_{u_2}, \mathcal{M}_{u_4 \triangleleft u_2})$ and furthermore $sim(\mathcal{M}_{u_5}, \mathcal{M}_{u_5 \triangleleft u_2}) > sim(\mathcal{M}_{u_4}, \mathcal{M}_{u_4 \triangleleft u_2})$, if principle 7 holds we will have the relation $sim(\mathcal{M}_{u_2}, \mathcal{M}_{u_5}) > sim(\mathcal{M}_{u_2}, \mathcal{M}_{u_4})$. However, the metric cannot distinguish u_2's similarity to u_4 and u_5 and outputs the same similarity value (0.58) in both cases.

Neither of the metrics can give a precise evaluation of similarity for all users. From Figure 1, it is clear that the similarity values should decrease when comparing u_1 with the other users (from u_2 to u_5) – u_2 should be the most similar one to u_1 as they share a same set of trajectory patterns while u_5 is the least.

4 New Metrics

In this section, we propose for the first time user similarity metrics that satisfy all the basic principles discussed above. We first present a metric to measure user similarity based on their movement called *mobility similarity* and then extend the metric to handle location semantics, called *location-semantic similarity*.

4.1 Mobility Similarity

The MTP-based metrics [9, 10] are problematic in comparing user similarity due to the inappropriate comparison between maximal trajectory patterns. In this section, we propose a new metric which does not compare maximal patterns but directly compare users' original mobility profiles. Moreover, instead of longest common patterns, we consider all common patterns of two users. Our main idea is to (1) compare two users based on the *relative importance* of their common patterns to each user's mobility profile and (2) take into account the difference of two users' frequencies by which they follow the common regular movements. Intuitively, if a user shares more common patterns with another user and their support values are also closer, then he is more similar to this user. This idea is consistent with the principles identified in Section 3.

We start with the calculation of the relative importance of the common patterns to a user mobility profile. A trajectory pattern can be interpreted as a description of users' movement *regularity*. The more RoIs it contains and the more frequent it occurs, the more regularity of the user it can represent. With the regularity of trajectory patterns, we can then quantify the regularity of a users' mobility profile. Given a user u, the regularity that his mobility profile represents can be calculated as follows:

$$\Gamma_u = \sum_{P \in \mathcal{P}_u} lcn(P) \cdot sup_u(P).$$

Given two users u and u', the relative importance of their common patterns with respect to u's mobility profile can be assessed by the ratio between the regularity of the common patterns and the whole pattern set of u. Recall that $\mathcal{M}_{u \lhd u'}$ is the mobility profile whose pattern set is composed of u' and u's common patterns and the support value of any trajectory pattern is equal to that of user u. Thus, $\Gamma_{u \lhd u'}$ is the movement regularity of user u expressed by the common patterns. Let $\Phi_{u,u'|u}$ be the relative importance of the common movements of u and u' to u's mobility profile, then it can be calculated as $\Phi_{u,u'|u} = \frac{\Gamma_{u \lhd u'}}{\Gamma_u}$.

We proceed to quantify the difference between the support values of two users' common trajectory patterns. The *Bray-Curtis similarity* [12] delivers reliable similarity measurements, especially in ecology. It can also be adopted as a metric of the similarity between two vectors. Given a user u, his support values of the trajectory patterns shared with u' can be modelled as a vector of real numbers each of which corresponds to the support value of a common pattern. Due to its popularity and simplicity, we make use of Bray-Curtis similarity to assess the closeness of two users' support values of their common patterns as the following:

$$\Psi_{u,u'} = 1 - \frac{\sum_{P \in \mathcal{P}_u \cap \mathcal{P}_{u'}} |sup_u(P) - sup_{u'}(P)|}{\sum_{P \in \mathcal{P}_u \cap \mathcal{P}_{u'}} (sup_u(P) + sup_{u'}(P))}.$$

Finally, the similarity between users u and u' can be calculated as

$$sim(u, u') = \sqrt{\Phi_{u,u'|u} \cdot \Phi_{u,u'|u'}} \cdot \Psi_{u,u'}.$$

It is easy to verify that our metric satisfies all the principles discussed in Section 3. We apply our metric to Example 2, and the results are shown in Table 2. We can see that our metric can give more precise similarity values which reflect the different similarities among users. Especially, the similarities of u_1 to the other users decrease from u_1 to u_5. We use CPS to refer to our metric, as it mainly utilises common pattern sets of users.

4.2   Location-Semantic Similarity

It has been addressed that the consideration of the functionalities of places can reveal more about users' similar hobbies. For instance, two users who live in different cities both like reading. According to their mobility, we cannot find their similarity because they go to different book stores. However, when considering the functionalities of places, e.g., 'book store', we will be able to discover their common interest. We call the functionalities of places *location semantics*. People always stay at a place for the service provided by the place. Given a trajectory, we can learn the trace of places where the user stayed for a certain amount of time [10, 11]. By labelling each of such places with its functionality, we can obtain a trace of location semantics, called a *semantic trajectory*. Similar to mining trajectory patterns from geographic trajectories, we can also mine *semantic trajectory patterns* from a user's semantic trajectories.

Let $\mathcal{LS}$ be the set of location semantics. Then a semantic trajectory pattern can be defined as a sequence of location semantic, i.e., $(\mu_1, \ldots, \mu_n)$ where for each $1 \leq i \leq n$, $\mu_i \in \mathcal{LS}$. It can also be represented as $\mu_1 \rightarrow \ldots \rightarrow \mu_n$. However, in practice a place usually corresponds to multiple location semantics. For instance, some shopping malls contain both shops and restaurants. For a visit to a place, its functionality that a user really uses is thus not certain. This uncertainty can be modelled as a probability distribution over all possible location semantics of the place, indicating the likelihood of how users use a functionality during their visits. A location semantic trajectory can thus be in the form of a sequence of sets of location semantics each of which corresponds to a probability distribution. Mining semantic trajectory patterns from such probabilistic semantic trajectories has been studied and termed as *probabilistic pattern mining* [13]. However, due to its underlying complexity, we propose in this paper a different method to obtain the set of semantic trajectory patterns by exploring user mobility profiles.

Although the metric such as the MSTP metric [9] can calculate user similarity with location semantics, it ignores the uncertainty of the real purposes of users' visits. Each location is assigned with a set of semantic tags, instead of a probability distribution on the tags. Furthermore, due to its dependence on maximal patterns, the MSTP metric with location semantics suffers the same problems as discussed in Section 3. In this paper, the calculation of user similarity with location semantics consists of two steps:

1. Transform trajectory patterns into semantic trajectory patterns and calculate their corresponding support values;
2. Calculate user similarity based on the obtained semantic trajectory patterns.

Once semantic trajectory patterns and their support values are available, the metric given in the previous section can be used. Thus we focus on the first step. Associating a location with its location semantics a user uses have been recognised as the problem of labelling locations with *semantic tags* [14]. A semantic tag corresponds to a type of location semantics. Given an RoI R and $\mu \in \mathcal{LS}$, we use $Pr(tag(R) = \mu)$ to denote the probability that a user stays at R for its functionality μ. For a trajectory pattern $P = (R_1, \ldots, R_n)$, we represent its induced semantic pattern as $lsp(P)$. We assume the tag labelling of RoIs in a trajectory is independent from each other. The likelihood that $lsp(P)$ is $Q = (\mu_1, \ldots, \mu_n)$, i.e., $Pr(lsp(P) = Q)$, can be calculated as follows:

$$Pr(lsp(P) = Q) = \prod_{1 \leq i \leq n} Pr(tag(R_i) = \mu_i).$$

For a semantic trajectory Q of a fixed length, any trajectory patterns of the same length in a user's profile may have a (positive) probability to induce Q. Thus, the support value of Q can be calculated as:

$$sup_u^{LS}(Q) = \sum_{P \in \mathcal{P}_u} Pr(lsp(P) = Q) \cdot sup_u(P).$$

Similar to trajectory patterns, we should choose the representative location-semantic patterns to compare users' similarity. A proper threshold of support values is thus required. From the calculation of the support values of semantic patterns, we can see that they depend on their length and the number of trajectory patterns of the same length. Therefore, the threshold for semantic patterns cannot be uniform, which is different from frequent trajectory patterns. Let $minPro$ be the minimum probability that a semantic tag is non-negligible to be the real semantic tag of an RoI. Then the threshold for a semantic pattern of length n can be calculated as the following:

$$\sigma_{LS}(n, \mathcal{P}_u) = minPro^n \cdot \sigma \cdot |\{P \in \mathcal{P} \mid len(P) = n\}|.$$

Intuitively, it equals to the support value of a semantic pattern, each of whose semantic tags has a larger probability than $minPro$ in all the trajectory patterns of the same length. In the end, the semantic trajectory pattern set of user u is obtained as

$$\mathcal{P}_u^{LS} = \{Q \mid (\exists P \in \mathcal{P}_u, len(P) = len(Q)) \wedge sup_u^{LS}(Q) \geq \sigma_{LS}(len(Q), \mathcal{P}_u)\}.$$

Example 3. Consider $\mathcal{M}_{u_3}$ from Example 2 and suppose that $\mathcal{LS}$ consists of only two location semantic tags, e.g., $\mu_1 =$ hotel and $\mu_2 =$ restaurant. For the sake of simplicity, we denote the distribution of an RoI R as a pair $d_R = \langle p_1, p_2 \rangle$ with $p_1 = Pr(tag(R) = \mu_1)$ and $p_2 = Pr(tag(R) = \mu_2)$. Suppose $d_A = \langle 0.4, 0.6 \rangle$, $d_B = \langle 0.2, 0.8 \rangle$ and $d_C = \langle 0.5, 0.5 \rangle$. For the semantic trajectory pattern μ_1, as patterns A, B and C can all induce it, its support value is calculated as: $sup_{u_3}^{LS}(\mu_1) = 0.4 \times 0.4 + 0.2 \times 0.4 + 0.5 \times 0.4 = 0.44$. If $\sigma = 0.2$ and $minPro = 0.2$, since we have 3 trajectory patterns with length 1 in $\mathcal{M}_{u_3}$, the support value threshold for semantic pattern μ_1, i.e., $\sigma_{LS}(1, \mathcal{P}_{u_3})$ is $0.2 \times 0.2 \times 3 = 0.12$. As the semantic pattern μ_2 has the same length as μ_1, its support value threshold is also $\sigma_{LS}(1, \mathcal{P}_{u_3})$. The calculation for other patterns is similar. Finally, we compute the set $\mathcal{P}_{u_3}^{LS}$ as follows

$$\{\mu_1(0.44), \mu_2(0.76), \mu_1 \rightarrow \mu_2(0.096), \mu_1 \rightarrow \mu_1(0.024), \mu_2 \rightarrow \mu_1(0.036), \mu_2 \rightarrow \mu_2(0.144)\}.$$

If the distribution for RoI D is also $\langle 0.2, 0.8 \rangle$ which is the same for RoI C, then u_3 and u_5 will have identical semantic pattern sets, i.e., $\mathcal{P}_{u_3}^{LS} = \mathcal{P}_{u_5}^{LS}$. Thus, u_3 and u_5 become much more similar when considering location semantics.

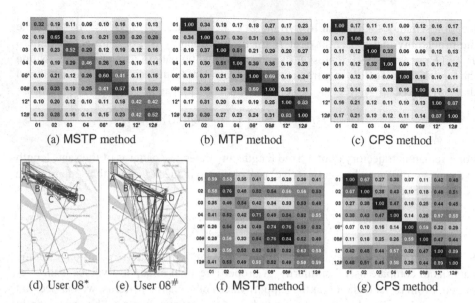

Fig. 2. User mobility similarity by three metrics (a, b, c) & the mobility profiles of users 08* and 08# (d, e) & user location-semantic similarity (f, g)

5   Evaluation

Our aim of the evaluation is to check whether our metric can accurately capture the real similarity between users in practice as well as its consistency with the basic principles.

The Dataset. We explore a real-life dataset of GPS trajectories collected by Yonsei University in Korea to evaluate the effectiveness of our metrics. It consists of 1,865 daily trajectories from 12 users, which cover a total length of 32,626 km. Although users moved in different cities or even countries, we focus on their local movements in Seoul. We select six users in terms of the number of their trajectories. We construct another two additional users based on the dataset so as to help compare the performance of different metrics. One is based on the user with the identity 08 in the dataset by dividing the user into two (08* and 08#) since the user has different movement patterns in two different periods. The other two users (12* and 12#) are derived from user 12 by evenly dividing his trajectories into two parts.

When constructing users' mobility profiles, we adopt the approach of Chen et al. [10]. In their approach, stay points are first detected from trajectories, which represent the places a user are likely to have stayed in the trajectories. Then all stay points are clustered into RoIs by a hierarchical clustering algorithm. Trajectories of stay points are then transformed into traces of RoIs from which user's mobility profiles are constructed using a trajectory pattern mining tool [3]. The minimum support value is set to 0.1 in the experiments. Due to the page limit, we omit the values of other related parameters.

In Figure 2, we show the mobility similarities and location-semantic similarities between all pairs of selected users by the three metrics – MSTP, MTP, and CPS. We use different grey levels to distinguish the similarity values between users. A darker cell indicates that the corresponding pair of users are more similar.

User Mobility Similarity. We have mentioned that the MTP-based metrics have been validated in the literature as effective ways to quantify users' similarity using ground-truth data. Thus, by comparing the similarity values of our metric to the values of these two metrics, we can verify whether our metric correctly assesses user similarity.

In general, we have two main observations. First, if users are ordered according to their similarity values to a same user, our metric will output a similar order to the other two metrics. We take the similarity value of a user to another user computed with a given metric as a variable. Then we can calculate the covariance of two variables of a user with regard to different metrics. A positive covariance will indicate the user's similarity values calculated by the two metrics are consistent. In other words, the similarity of a user to a given user has a similar ranking when calculated with the metrics. On average, the covariances of our metric with respect to MSTP and MTP are 0.09 and 0.04, respectively, which validates our observation that CPS is also consistent with the ground-truth. Second, when comparing Figure 2(b) and Figure 2(c), we observe that for some pairs of users, the similarity values calculated with our new metric have significant differences from the other two metrics. However, after projecting users' original GPS trajectories on the map, we see that the similarity calculated with our metric is more precise. For example, the similarity values between users 08* and 08# have a rather large difference among the three metrics MSTP and MTP output 0.41 and 0.69 respectively, while CPS only gives 0.16. We plot their trajectories on the map and present them in Figure 2(d) and Figure 2(e). RoIs are labelled by red rectangles and users' stay points are tagged by yellow dots. Blue lines represent the transition between stay points in a trajectory. We also name the RoIs and put their identities beside them. User 08# has two more RoIs (E, F) than 08*. Furthermore, more than 57% of user 08#'s trajectories go through these two RoIs and only about 15% of his trajectories contain RoIs A, B and C. However, about 78% of 08*'s trajectories contain A, B and C. Therefore, the reasonable similarity value between 08# and 08* should be around 0.20 after considering the small proportion of common patterns and the large difference between their support values. By this example, we show that our metric indeed gives rise to a more precise similarity measurement.

User Location-Semantic Similarity. We proceed to illustrate the effectiveness of our metric when adding location semantics in user similarity calculation. Our major purpose is to check whether our metric can capture users' similarity when location semantics are added, but not to learn the real similarity between the users. Thus, in our experiments we select five location semantic tags, and for each RoI we assign to it a probability distribution over the tags. Since only the metric proposed by Ying et al. [9] can handle location semantics, we show and compare the similarity values calculated by their method and our new CPS-based metric in Figure 2(f) and 2(g). Since the MSTP metric only considers the location semantic tags that an RoI may associate with non-negligible likelihoods, in the implementation of the metric, we set the minimum probability as 0.2 and for each RoI we only consider the subset of location semantic tags with probabilities larger than 0.2. From Figure 2(f) and 2(g), we can see that our metric calculates similar similarity values to MSTP. This means our metric keeps the right ranking between the similarity values of different pair of users as the effectiveness of the MSTP metric has been evaluated in [9]. Compared to the mobility similarity, an interesting observation is that the similarity between users 08* and 08# increases to 0.59 from 0.16. This is mainly because the RoIs E and F have similar distributions to B and C. From the above discussion, we can conclude that our metric not only satisfies all the basic principles but also outputs more precise measurements for users' similarity based on trajectory patterns and location semantics.

6 Conclusion

We have identified a number of principles and proposed new metrics (with/without location semantics), when quantifying users' similarity based on their trajectory patterns. The effectiveness of our metics is illustrated through extensive experiments. In the future, we want to evaluate our metrics on more real-life datasets, especially when considering location semantics. This might lead to more efficient and effective ways to treat semantics in mobility data.

References

1. Crandall, D.J., Backstrom, L., Cosley, D., Suri, S., Huttenlocher, D., Kleinberg, J.: Inferring social ties from geographic coincidences. PNAS 107(52), 22436–22441 (2010)
2. Zheng, Y., Zhang, L., Ma, Z., Xie, X., Ma, W.Y.: Recommending friends and locations based on individual location history. ACM Transactions on the Web 5(1), 1–44 (2011)
3. Giannotti, F., Nanni, M., Pedreschi, D., Pinelli, F., Axiak, M.: Trajectory pattern mining. In: Proc. KDD, pp. 330–339. ACM Press (2007)
4. Rhee, I., Shin, M., Hong, S., Lee, K., Kim, S.J., Chong, S.: On the levy-walk nature of human mobility. IEEE/ACM Transaction on Networking 19(3), 630–643 (2011)
5. Song, C., Koren, T., Wang, P., Barabási, A.-L.: Modelling the scaling properties of human mobility. Nature Physics 6, 818–823 (2010)
6. Brockman, D., Hufnagel, L., Geisel, T.: The scaling laws of human travel. Nature 439(26), 462–465 (2006)
7. Shokri, R., Theodorakopoulos, G., Troncoso, C., Hubaux, J.P., Boudec, J.Y.L.: Protecting location privacy: optimal strategy against localization attacks. In: Proc. CCS, pp. 617–627. ACM Press (2012)
8. Xiao, X., Zheng, Y., Luo, Q., Xie, X.: Finding similar users using category-based location history. In: Proc. GIS, pp. 442–445. ACM Press (2010)
9. Ying, J.C., Lu, H.C., Lee, W.C., Weng, T.C., Tseng, S.: Mining user similarity from semantic trajectories. In: Proc. SIGSPATIAL, pp. 19–26. ACM Press (2010)
10. Chen, X., Pang, J., Xue, R.: Constructing and comparing user mobility profiles for location-based services. In: Proc. SAC, pp. 261–266. ACM Press (2013)
11. Chen, X., Pang, J., Xue, R.: Constructing and comparing user mobility profiles. TWEB (accepted, 2014)
12. Bray, J.R., Curtis, J.T.: An ordination of upland forest communities of southern Wisconsin. Ecological Monographs 27, 325–349 (1957)
13. Zhao, Z., Yan, D., Ng, W.: Mining probabilistically frequent sequential patterns in large uncertain databases. IEEE Transaction on Knowledge and Data Engineering (2013) (preprint)
14. Ye, M., Shou, D., Lee, W.C., Yin, P., Janowicz, K.: On the semantic annotation of places in location-based social networks. In: Proc. KDD, pp. 520–528. ACM Press (2011)

Graph-Based Summarization
without Redundancy

Hai-Tao Zheng and Shao-Zhou Bai

Tsinghua-Southampton Web Science Laboratory,
Graduate School at Shenzhen, Tsinghua University, Shenzhen, China
zheng.haitao@sz.tsinghua.edu.cn,
baishaozhou@gmail.com

Abstract. In this paper we present a new text summarization method based on graph to generate concise summaries for highly redundant documents. By mapping the source documents into a textual graph, we turn the summarization into a new problem of finding the key paths composed by essential information. Unlike the extraction of original sentences, our method regenerates sentences by word nodes in the textual graph. In order to avoid the selection of unreasonable paths with grammatical or semantical problems, some syntax rules are defined to guide the path selecting process, and we merge the common paths shared by different sentences to reduce content redundancy. Evaluation results show that our method can get concise summaries with a higher content accuracy.

Keywords: summarization, sentence regeneration, textual graph.

1 Introduction

Text summarization is the reductive transformation of source text to summaries through content condensation by selection or generalisation on what is important in the source [1]. With the exponential growth of textual information online, resulting in useless information blast, manually accessing to useful information becomes a highly difficult task, so summarization becomes a critically important technique to help users quickly gain the important knowledge by generating the essential information in a concise way. Concerning on the approaches used in text summarization, there are two types of summaries [2]: extractive summaries that composed by a set of original sentences selected from the source documents, and abstractive summaries that composed by materials which may not appear in the source documents.

Extractive summarization is based on the extraction of important sentences from the source documents. The importance of a sentence is usually measured by some kind of scoring models such as term frequency, and sentences are ranked by their scores, then the sentences with the highest scores are selected in turn to constitute the summary with the required length. On the contrary, abstractive summarization attempts to understand the concepts in source documents and reorganize language to cover the essential information in a concise way. It usually

L. Chen et al. (Eds.): APWeb 2014, LNCS 8709, pp. 449–460, 2014.

involves prior knowledge [3] or deeper natural language generation technology [4], which either relies heavily on manual efforts or is domain specified.

Associating to the complexity of the limited abstractive methods, most summarizations today are based on the extractive methods [2]. However, the extraction of original sentences from the source documents is flawed [5], which usually selecting verbose sentences that lead to incomplete information such as information loss or information redundancy in the summaries. Firstly, the extracted sentence is usually longer which contain much unnecessary terms and consuming the limited word space. Secondly, selecting sentences based on importance leads to redundancy which reduces the coverage of different information in the summaries. Lastly, extracted sentences often lead to semantical coherence problem because some sentences may lose their referents when extracted out of the text.

In this paper, we propose a graph-based summarization method to reduce content redundancy in the previous extractive methods. In contrast with the previous works, our method uses the word as basic unit rather than sentence, which represents the text by a textual graph and turns summarization into a new problem of finding key paths that contain the essential information. Some syntax rules are defined to avoid the selection of unreasonable paths, and common paths are recomposed to generate sentences with little redundancy.

2   Related Work

Earlier works on summarization explored the superficial approaches [6]. Term frequency is the simplest method to score the importance of a sentence as in [7], and tf*idf combines it with the document frequency [8]. The underlying assumption is that the frequency of a word is proportional to its relevant to the main information of the document, but the weight of a word decreases with the increasing documents that contain this word. The part of speech (POS) also influences the word weight [9], the nouns usually contain more semantic information than others like conjunction and get a higher score. The position of sentences is also relevant to the importance [10], the leading sentences usually contain the main information and selecting sentences from the beginning of the text could be a reasonable selection. What's more, the titles usually summarize the essential information of source documents, so the sentences contain title words should be more important than others [11].

Knowledge-based approaches either extend superficial approaches by the incorporation of lexical resources or discourse organization theories. Lexical thesaurus such as WordNet is used to identify related words (e.g., Synonyms) and connect the cohesive links between sentences, the summary sentences are selected based on the resulting linked structure [12]. The discourse organization theories consider the text as a linguistic unit, and the important sentences can be selected by the specific organization of clue information such as "conclusions", "purpose", "results" [13]. Machine learning methods such as Bayesian classifier, Hidden Markov Models, Support Vector Machine etc., are also used to combine the superficial methods in text summarization [14].

Graph-based ranking algorithms have also been shown to be effective in text summarization [15],[16]. The basic idea is that the nodes of the graph represent text elements such as words or sentences, and edges represent the relations between these text elements such as the similarity between sentences, then some graph-based random walk algorithms such as PageRank [17] can be used to compute the importance of sentences. TextRank [15] is a typical graph-based summarization method, which uses the PageRank algorithm to score these sentences in a graph structure.

As mentioned above, most extractive summarization methods treat sentences independently and select sentences based on the weight scores, which means that sentences in summary may repeat content and lead to content redundancy [6]. This is usually dealt by filtering sentences too similar to the selected ones, and Maximal Marginal Relevance [18] is commonly used to make a tradeoff between the similarity and difference between sentences. Although this kind of methods can reduce redundancy in some degree, they still confront the poor accuracy because of verbose sentences. Instead of selecting original sentences, our method regenerates sentences by the words to reduce redundancy and covers more different essential information so as to improve the content accuracy.

3   Proposed Method

The basic idea of our proposed method GSWR (Graph-based Summarization without Redundancy) is that, we firstly construct a textual graph by the words from the given source documents through the preprocess procedure, and then we select and label the key paths in the graph, finally we regenerate sentences to compose the summary by the labeled nodes under the restraining of syntax rules. The main steps are shown as Fig. 1.

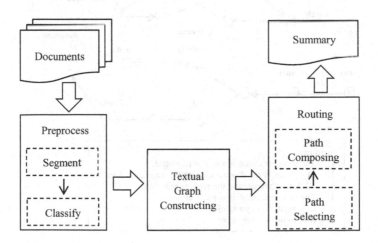

Fig. 1. The main steps of GSWR

Given the source documents, the first step of preprocess is to segment the text into sentences and words with the properties such as term frequency, part of speech, position etc, which are the materials for textual graph constructing. The second step of preprocess is to classify the sentences into different categories based on the key words which are the nouns that contain the main information. The role of this step is to simplify the structure of textual graph by clustering the relevant sentences to form an independent subgraph, which can reduce the time consuming of path traversals.

3.1 Textual Graph

Textual graph is also commonly used in other extractive summarization methods such as TextRank [15] and LexRank [16]. The difference is that the previous methods use the sentences as nodes and similarity between sentences as edges, and important sentences are selected by the graph rank algorithms such as PageRank [17]. While our graph uses the words as nodes and adjacent relations between words as edges, which is closer to Opinosis [19] where the graph is

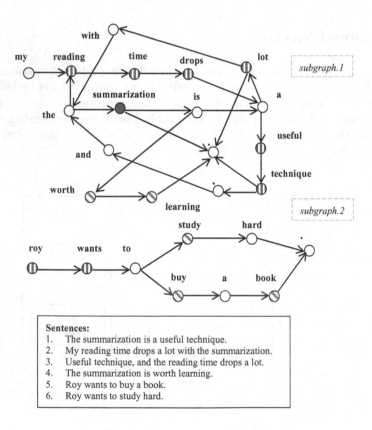

Fig. 2. A sample textual graph

used to enumerate all the possible sentences, but our method GSWR regenerates
sentences by key paths selecting and composing in the textual graph.

Figure. 2 is a sample textual graph of the given 6 sentences. Each node represents a unique word, and the directed edges are the adjacent relations between
the words. Different circles indicate different word frequencies and the hollow
circles are stopwords (words without semantic meanings, such as "a", "of"). By
classifying sentences based on the nouns, we get two sets of sentences, sentences
1-4 and 5-6, which are corresponding to subgraphs 1 and 2, each of which is
highly redundant. The same non-stopwords in different sentences are mapped
into one node in the textual graph, then the phrases appeared more than once
are represented by the common paths of same nodes and edges. The common
paths indicate the redundant content of source text, and the summary will be
more concise if we merge the common paths.

3.2 Syntax Rules

Without the restraining of any rules, the path routing algorithm will enumerate all the possible paths in the graph and regenerate many grammatically or
semantically incorrect sentences. In order to guarantee the reasonability of the
path routing, we use the sample path $P = \{v_1, \ldots, v_m, \ldots, v_n\}$ to define the
syntax rules. v_1 is start node and v_n is the end node, v_m is a node in path P.

BeginWord. BeginWord is the word that can start a new sentence. v_m is a
BeginWord only if it satisfies the conditions:

1. $IsStopWord(v_m) = false$;
2. $POS(v_m) = NN$;
3. $m \leq \min\{\delta_{start}, n - \delta_{end}\}, \quad \delta_{start} = 4, \ \delta_{end} = 2$;
4. $POS(v_i) \notin \{NN, VB, RB\}, \quad m \geq 2, \forall v_i \in \{v_1, \ldots, v_{m-1}\}$.

Firstly v_m mustn't be a stopword, and the POS (part of speech) is noun. The
position of v_m in the sentence path should not larger than the threshold δ_{start},
at the same time keeps a distance larger than δ_{end} from the last word v_n. And
the words before v_m should not contains any nouns, verbs or adverbs.

BranchPre. Path P is the previous branch of a selected path, only if it satisfy
the conditions:

1. $W_{unlabel} = \sum_{i=1}^{n} W(v_i), \quad Labeled(v_i) = false$;
2. $W_P = \sum_{i=1}^{n} W(v_i)$;
3. $\frac{W_{unlabel}}{W_P} \leq \delta_{ul}, \quad \delta_{ul} = 0.5$.

$W_{unlabel}$ is the summation weights of the unlabeled nodes in path P, and W_P
is the summation weights of all the nodes in P. The ratio between $W_{unlabel}$ and
W_P indicates the novelty of path P, which is compared with the threshold δ_{ul}.
The ratio less than δ_{ul} means most of the words in P have been visited and P
is a BranchPre. The definition of BranchPre is to avoid selecting the paths that
have been selected before.

BranchNext. A partial path $P_1 = \{v_m, \ldots, v_n\}$ is the next branch of a selected
path $P_2 = \{v_x, \ldots, v_y\}$only if it satisfies the conditions

1. $POS(v_i) = VB, \quad \exists v_i \in P_1$;
2. $v_i \in P_2, \quad if\ v_i \neq v_m$;
3. $IsBeginWord(v_j) = true, \quad \exists v_j \in P_1 \cap P_2, j > 1$;
4. $Labeled(v_k) = true, \quad \forall v_k \in \{v_i, \ldots, v_j\}$.

Firstly we trace back along path P_1 from node v_m, and find a verb v_i, if v_i is not equal to v_m then v_i must be a common word in path P_2. Once we find the verb v_i, we trace back along common path of P_1 and P_2 from v_i and find a BeginWord v_j. The words between v_i and v_j must all be labeled. If P_1 is a BranchNext then it can be jointed to the already selected path P_2 and regenerate a new sentence by the two paths.

AccessNext. In the process of path composing, v_m in $P_1 = v_1, \ldots, v_n$ is the next accessible node of the current path $P_2 = \{v_x, \ldots, v_y\}$, only if it satisfies the conditions

1. $Labeled(v_m) = ture$
2. $IsBeginWord(v_i) = ture, \quad \exists v_i \in P_2 \cap \{v_1, \ldots, v_m\}$.

The next accessible node of the current path P_2 must be labeled, and we must find a $BeginWord$ in the common path between P_2 and P_1.

3.3   Path Score

We use the common textual features to compute the word weight, including term frequency, part of speech, whether is a stopword/title word or not. Given that $P = \{v_1, v_2, \ldots, v_n\}$ is a path of n nodes in the textual graph, v_1 is the start point and v_n is the end point, the path length $L = n - 1$, then the path score of $W(P)$ is defined as follows:

$$W(P) = \frac{1}{1 + \log L} \sum_{i=1}^{n} W(v_i) \tag{1}$$

In (1), $W(v_i)$ is the word weight of v_i. The path score $W(P)$ is the summation of the words' weight along the path, and divided by the length function $1 + \log L$. The definition of word weight $W(v_i)$ is:

$$W(v_i) = TFIDF(v_i) \cdot IsStopWord(v_i) \cdot POS(v_i) \cdot IsTitleWord(v_i) \tag{2}$$

TFIDF is commonly used to score sentences and defines as follows:

$$TFIDF(v_i) = N_{v_i} \cdot (1 + \log \frac{|D|}{|D_{v_i}|}) \tag{3}$$

N_{v_i} is the frequency of v_i, $|D|$ is the total number of the source documents, $|D_{v_i}|$ is the number of documents that contains word v_i. $IsStopWord(v_i)$ weights the impact of stopwords, which is 0 for stopwords and 1 otherwise, since the stopwords contain not any useful semantic meanings. $POS(v_i)$ measures the impact of part of speech, which is 2 for nouns and verbs that usually contain more important information, and 1 for others. $IsTitleWord(v_i)$ measures the impact of words that appear in the title, which is 3 for title words and 1 for others, because the title words usually contain the essential information of the source documents. Both coefficients for $POS(v_i)$ and $IsTitleWord(v_i)$ are determined by the experiment results after testing a range of values.

3.4 Path Selecting

The Path Selecting algorithm is used to select the word nodes that composes the summaries. The basic idea is as follows: Select the key paths in the textual graph iteratively until get a summary with the limited size, and the nodes in the

---

Algorithm 1. PathSelect

Input: Textual graph $G = (V, E)$, Summary length L
Output: List of BeginWords $BV = \{V_1, \ldots, V_n\}$
 1: **repeat**
 2:     $P_{max} \leftarrow \phi$
 3:     **for** $V_i \in IsNotLabeled(V) \parallel IsBeginWord(V_i)$ **do**
 4:         **if** $IsPunctuation(V_i)$ **then**
 5:             **continue**
 6:         **end if**
 7:         $PS \leftarrow GetPath(V_i)$
 8:         **for** $P \in PS$ **do**
 9:             **if** $IsBranchPre(P)$ **then**
10:                 **continue**
11:             **end if**
12:             **if** $!(IsBeginWord(V_i) \parallel IsBranchNext(P))$ **then**
13:                 **continue**
14:             **end if**
15:             **if** $W(P) > W(P_{max})$ & $Len_P \leq L$ **then**
16:                 $P_{max} \leftarrow P$
17:             **end if**
18:         **end for**
19:     **end for**
20:     **if** $P_{max} \neq \phi$ **then**
21:         $L \leftarrow L - Len(P_{max})$
22:         $SetNodesLabeled(P_{max})$
23:         $V_{first} \leftarrow P_{max}.getFirstNode()$
24:         **if** $IsBeginWord(V_{first})$ **then**
25:             $BV \leftarrow BV \cup V_f$
26:         **end if**
27:     **else**
28:         **return** BV
29:     **end if**
30: **until** $L \leq 0$
31: **return** BV

---

selected paths are labeled. At each iteration, the path started with an unlabeled node with the maximal path score is selected, at the same time the path must satisfy the syntax rules.

Algorithm 1 describes the process of path selecting in detail. The input parameters are the textual graph $G(V, E)$ and the summary length L, the output parameter is a list of the begin words BV which will be used as the input parameters of the path composing algorithm. The path selecting algorithm is an iteration process until we get a summary of length L or there is nothing to be selected any more. At each iteration, we select a key path P_{max} with the maximal path score, which starts with an unlabeled node or a BeginWord and satisfies the following conditions: P_{max} is not a BranchPre of the labeled paths which will create content redundancy; P_{max} is a BranchNext or BeginWord; The length of P_{max} is less than the remain summary size L. If we can find such a key path, namely $P_{max} \neq \phi$, then update the remain length of summary L by subtracting the length $Len(P_{max})$, and label all the nodes on path P_{max}, at the same time, if the first node of P_{max} is a BeginWord then we add it into the list BV. Otherwise if we can't find a valid key path, namely $P_{max} = \phi$, it means all the key paths have been labeled and we return list BV to quit this procedure.

3.5   Path Composing

After path selecting, we labeled the word nodes that will compose the summary and get a BeginWord list BV. The path composing is to use these labeled Begin-Words to start the depth-first traversal to regenerate sentences, and the common paths representing the redundant content are merged during this process. Finally we get the summary by these regenerated sentences from each BeginWord.

Algorithm 2 describes the path composing process of a single BeginWord V, and the regenerated sentence S is returned. Firstly we initialize the sentence S to be empty and get the collection of next accessible nodes V_{next} by the syntax rule $AccessNext$. If V_{next} is empty, then there are two cases: V is a punctuation or not. In the first case we return this punctuation, which means we find a valid sentence ending with V. In the second case V is not a punctuation, there is not any accessible next node for V, which means the current node path from V is invalid and we return an empty $S = \phi$. Otherwise when V_{next} isn't empty, namely there are several accessible next nodes, we recursively generate the subsentence for each next node V_i and compose these subsentences with the common path before node V, which helps to reduce the content redundancy. In Fig. 2, if we start with the BeginWord "summarization", we will get two accessible next nodes "a" and "worth" in the branch node "is", and the subsentences "a useful technique" and "worth learning" respectively, then we regenerate a new sentence "summarization is a useful technique and worth learning".

4   Experiment and Results

In order to compare GSWR with the extractive summarization methods, we select two typical methods: MMR and TextRank. The former uses the MMR

Algorithm 2. PathCompose

Input: BeginWord V
Output: Regenerated sentence S
1: $S \leftarrow \phi$
2: $V_{next} \leftarrow GetAccessNextNodes(V)$
3: **if** $V_{next} = \phi$ **then**
4:      **if** $IsPunctuation(V)$ **then**
5:          $S \leftarrow V.word$
6:      **end if**
7:      **return** S
8: **else**
9:      **for each** $V_i \in V_{next}$ **do**
10:          $S_i \leftarrow PathCompse(V_i)$
11:          **if** $S_i \neq \phi$ **then**
12:              $S \leftarrow S \cup S_i$
13:          **end if**
14:      **end for**
15: **end if**
16: **if** $S \neq \phi$ **then**
17:      $S \leftarrow V.word \cup S$
18: **end if**
19: **return** S

---

and superficial methods to tackle with the content redundancy problem, the latter uses random walk algorithms in graph structure to weight sentences, both of which make the corresponding comparison with GSWR in different aspects. In this experiment we use the dataset[1] of DUC 2007, which is composed of 45 different news topics, and there are 25 news reports under each topic. we use the ROUGE [20] toolkit[2] for evaluation, which is an automatic summarization evaluation widely adopted by DUC.

Table 1 is the comparison of different summarization methods, it is obvious to find that GSWR gets a better experimental results compared to the baselines MMR and TextRank, which means GSWR makes an improvement of the content accuracy compared with the typical extractive summarization methods.

As a typical extractive summarization method, TextRank usually generates summaries contain much verbose sentences and redundant content, which wastes the limited number of words in summaries and leads to the incomprehensive coverage of main information, thus reducing the accuracy of summaries. MMR is also an extractive summarization method, but it considers both relevance and novelty when selecting a sentence, which reduces the content redundancy by making a tradeoff between similarity and difference. The results of MMR is better than TextRank for the processing of content redundancy, however, as an extractive summarization method, MMR also influenced by the drawbacks of verbose sentences, which weakens its advantage to TextRank. By using the idea of sentence

---

[1] http://www-nlpir.nist.gov/projects/duc/data/2007data.html
[2] http://www.berouge.com/Pages/default.aspx

Table 1. ROUGE values of different methods

	50	100	150	200	250
ROUGE-1					
GSWR	**0.24531**	**0.29238**	**0.32544**	**0.35266**	**0.36792**
MMR	0.23593	0.28003	0.29577	0.32282	0.33926
TextRank	0.22055	0.26742	0.28951	0.30964	0.3329
ROUGE-2					
GSWR	**0.04379**	**0.05416**	**0.05475**	**0.06054**	**0.06498**
MMR	0.04050	0.04262	0.04770	0.05462	0.06023
TextRank	0.03775	0.04171	0.04459	0.05151	0.05839
ROUGE-SU4					
GSWR	**0.07396**	**0.08971**	**0.10143**	**0.11258**	**0.12005**
MMR	0.07384	0.08411	0.09266	0.10274	0.11173
TextRank	0.06533	0.0804	0.09011	0.10033	0.11145

regenerating, GSWR has the best results compared to TextRank and MMR, for it can cover more different main information by selecting non-overlapping node paths and reduce content redundancy by merging the common paths in the textual graph, which two factors together determine the good performance of GSWR on the content accuracy of summaries.

On the other hand, the summary length varies with the application environment, so it's important to keep the robustness of summarization algorithms under different summary lengths. The summary length ranges from 50 to 250, because the summary with too little words is not enough to contain any main information, so we set the minimal length to 50 empirically, and we set the maximal length 250 because the reference summaries are about 250 words. In the following, we will investigate the influence of different summary lengths to the ROUGE metrics by Fig. 3(a), Fig. 3(b), Fig. 3(c).

It is obviously to be found that all the ROUGE scores decrease with the decreasing of summary length. The reason is that the reference summaries written by human is more subjective when the summary length is little, and it will be more difficult for the automatic summarization methods to identify these subjective content. With the increasing of summary length, the summaries will contain more information which makes the content to be more objective, and then improve the probability that the summarization methods identifies the important information which agrees to the human.

On the other hand, in Fig. 3(a) and Fig. 3(c), we can find that the performance of GSWR is closer to MMR when the summary length approaches to 50, because the summary can contain little content when the length is little and GSWR covers less different information in this condition, which weakens GSWR's advantage to MMR., but they are all better than TextRank because of the influence of redundancy reduction.

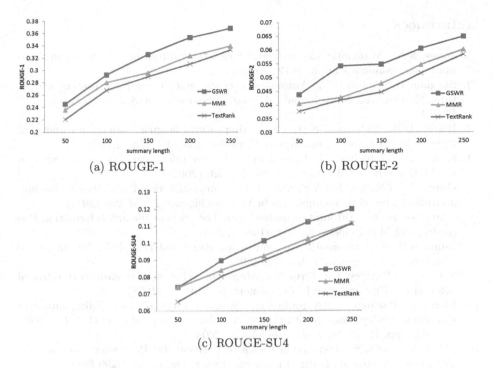

(a) ROUGE-1   (b) ROUGE-2

(c) ROUGE-SU4

Fig. 3. ROUGE values vary with the summary length

5   Conclusion

In this paper we present a graph-based summarization method without redundancy GSWR. Unlike the commonly used extractive summarization methods that select the original sentences to constitute summaries, GSWR constructs a textual graph based on words to regenerate sentences which can make a comprehensive coverage of different essential information and reduce content redundancy, so as to improve the accuracy of summaries. However, there are still much things we can do to improve our algorithm. Instead using the basic superficial features to score sentences, we can introduce the lexical resources such as WordNet to optimize the score model. And we need more different kinds of data corpus to validate and optimize our syntax rules in the process of path selecting. Finally, we will concentrate more on the readability of the summaries content in the future work, which is another big challenge for text summarization.

Acknowledgment. This research is supported by the 863 project of China (2013AA013300), National Natural Science Foundation of China (Grant No. 61375054) and Tsinghua University Initiative Scientific Research Program (20131089256).

References

1. Jones, K.S.: Automatic summarizing: factors and directions. Advances in Automatic Text Summarization, 1–12 (1999)
2. Saggion, H., Poibeau, T.: Automatic text summarization: Past, present and future. Multi-source, Multilingual Information Extraction and Summarization, 3–21 (2013)
3. Radev, D.R., McKeown, K.R.: Generating natural language summaries from multiple on-line sources. Computational Linguistics 24, 470–500 (1998)
4. Saggion, H., Lapalme, G.: Generating indicative-informative summaries with sumUM. Computational Linguistics 28, 497–526 (2002)
5. Gupta, V., Lehal, G.S.: A Survey of Text Summarization Extractive Techniques. Journal of Emerging Technologies in Web Intelligence 2, 258–268 (2010)
6. Sparck Jones, K.: Automatic summarising: The state of the art. Information Processing and Management 43, 1449–1481 (2007)
7. Luhn, H.P.: The automatic creation of literature abstracts. IBM Journal of Research and Development 2, 159–165 (1958)
8. Salton, G., Buckley, C.: Term-weighting approaches in automatic text retrieval. Information Processing and Management 24, 513–523 (1988)
9. Lloret, E., Palomar, M.: A gradual combination of features for building automatic summarisation systems. In: Matoušek, V., Mautner, P. (eds.) TSD 2009. LNCS, vol. 5729, pp. 16–23. Springer, Heidelberg (2009)
10. Lin, C.Y., Hovy, E.: Identifying topics by position. In: Proceedings of the Fifth Conference on Applied Natural Language Processing, pp. 283–290 (1997)
11. Edmundson, H.P.: New methods in automatic extracting. Journal of the ACM 16, 264–285 (1969)
12. Barzilay, R., Elhadad, M.: Using lexical chains for text summarization. In: Proceedings of the ACL Workshop on Intelligent Scalable Text Summarization, pp. 10–17 (1997)
13. Teufel, S., Moens, M.: Argumentative classification of extracted sentences as a first step towards flexible abstracting. Advances in Automatic Text Summarization (1999)
14. Lloret, E., Palomar, M.: Text summarisation in progress: a literature review. Artificial Intelligence Review 37, 1–41 (2012)
15. Mihalcea, R., Tarau, P.: TextRank: Bringing order into texts. In: Proceedings of the Conference on Empirical Methods in Natural Language Processing, pp. 404–411 (2004)
16. Erkan, G., Radev, D.R.: LexRank: Graph-based lexical centrality as salience in text summarization. Journal of Artificial Intelligence Research 22, 457–479 (2004)
17. Page, L., Brin, S.: The PageRank citation ranking: Bringing order to the web. Stanford InfoLab (1999), http://ilpubs.stanford.edu:8090/422/
18. Carbonell, J., Goldstein, J.: The use of MMR, diversity-based reranking for reordering documents and producing summaries. In: Proceedings of ACM SIGIR, pp. 335–336 (1998)
19. Ganesan, K., Zhai, C.X., Han, J.: Opinosis: a graph-based approach to abstractive summariza-tion of highly redundant opinions. In: Proceedings of the 23rd International Conference on Computational Linguistics, pp. 340–348 (2010)
20. Lin, C.Y.: Rouge: A package for automatic evaluation of summaries. In: Proceedings of the ACL Text Summarization Workshop, pp. 74–81 (2004)

Structural-Based Relevance Feedback in XML Retrieval

Kamoun Fourati Inès, Tmar Mohamed, and Ben Hamadou Abdelmajid

Multimedia Information systems and Advanced Computing Laboratory,
Higher Institute of Computer Science and Multimedia, University of Sfax,Tunisia
http://www.miracl.rnu.tn/

Abstract. Contrarily to classical information retrieval systems, the systems that treat structured documents include the structural dimension through the document and query comparison. Thus, relevant results are all the document fragments that match the user need rather than the whole document. In such case, the document and query structure should be taken into account in the retrieval process as well as during the reformulation. Query reformulation should also include the structural dimension. In this paper we propose an approach of query reformulation based on structural relevance feedback. We start from the original query on one hand and the fragments judged as relevant by the user on the other. Structure hints analysis allows us to identify nodes that match the user query and to rebuild it during the relevance feedback step. The main goal of this paper is to show the impact of structural hints in XML query optimization. Some experiments have been undertaken into a dataset provided by INEX[1] to show the effectiveness of our proposals.

Keywords: relevance feedback, XML, INEX, line of descent matrix.

1   Introduction

The goal of information retrieval systems (IRS) is to satisfy the information needs of a user. This need is expressed by a query to be matched to all the documents in the corpus to select those that could answer to the user need. Because of the ambiguity, and the incompleteness of his query, the user is, in most cases, not satisfied with the returned results. To overcome this problem, there can be alternatives to the initial query so as to improve the results. Among the most popular patterns in information retrieval (IR), we cite the relevance feedback (RF) which is based on the judgments of relevance of the documents found by the IRS and is intended to re-express the information need from the initial query in an effort to find more relevant documents. But with the standardization of the Web to XML schemas[2] presents new problems and hence new needs for

---

[1] INitiative for the Evaluation of XML retrieval, an evaluation forum that aims at promoting retrieval capabilities on XML documents

[2] A structured document (as XML document) is characterized by a content and a structure. This structure possibly completes semantics expressed by the content and becomes a constraint with which IRS must comply in order to satisfy the user information needs.

L. Chen et al. (Eds.): APWeb 2014, LNCS 8709, pp. 461–468, 2014.

customized information access. However, the traditional IRS do not exploit this structure of documents, including the RF function. Indeed, the user can express his need by a set of keywords, as in the traditional IRS, and can add structural constraints to better target the sought semantics. Thus, taking into account the structure of the documents and that of the query by the information retrieval systems handling structured documents is necessary in the feedback process. Many initiatives of relevance feedback have been proposed to rewrite the user query. The majority of these approaches are content-based, which means that only the query terms are updated, and relatively reweighted to improve the result. Only a few approaches modifies the query structure. In this paper, we propose an approach of structure-based relevance feedback. We assume that the query structure could be reformulated based on the structure of the document elements judged as relevant. This paper is organized as follows: in the second section, we give a survey on the related works to XML relevance feedback. We present in the third section our approach of query reformulation, based on the structure relevance feedback. In the fourth section, we present the experiments and the obtained results. The fifth section concludes.

2 Related Work

Many initiatives of XML query reformulation has been proposed. In the most cases, RF approaches has been adapted in order to take into account the structural dimension. Villatoro-Tello et al. describes in [12] a system developed by the Language and Reasoning Group of UAM for the Relevance Feedback track of INEX 2012. The system focuses on the problem of ranking documents in accordance to their relevance. It is mainly based on different hypotheses such as that current IR machines are able to retrieve relevant documents for most of general queries, but they cannot generate a pertinent ranking and focused relevance feedback could provide more and better elements for the ranking process than isolated query terms. The authors aim to demonstrate that using some query-related relevance feedback it is possible to improve the final ranking of the retrieved documents. Balog et al. propose a general probabilistic framework for entity search to evaluate and provide insight in the many ways of using these types of input for query modelling [1]. They focus on the use of category information and demonstrates the effectiveness of category-based expansion using example entities. Schenkel and Theobald [11] describe two approaches which focus on the incorporation of structural aspects in the feedback process. Their first approach re-ranks results returned by an initial keyword-based query using structural features derived from results with known relevance. Their second approach involves expanding traditional keyword queries into content-and-structure queries. Official results, evaluated using the INEX 2005 [5] assessment method based on rank-freezing, show that reranking outperforms the query expansion method on this data.

Among these approaches, only a few consider that RF in the query structure is necessary. It is common to rewrite the query based on its structure, and the content of the relevant elements as in [3], [9] and [15] , but modification of the query structure itself is not addressed. In our approach, we consider that the structural RF is necessary, particularly if the XML retrieval system takes into account the structural dimension in the matching process. Since we use an XML retrieval system that matches the structure in addition to the content [2], we assume that the structure reformulation could improve the retrieval performance.

3 Structural-Based Relevance Feedback: Our Approach

In our approach we focus essentially on the structure of the original query and that of document fragments deemed to be relevant to the user structure hints. Indeed, this study allows us to reinforce the importance of these structures in the reformulated query to better identify the most relevant fragments to the user's needs. The analysis of structures allows us to identify the most relevant nodes and the involved relationships. The content of these fragments and those of the initial query are also taken into account. Their analysis allows us to select the most relevant terms that will be injected in new query. Our approach is based on two major phases. The first aims at representing the query and the judged relevant fragments in a single representative structure. The second is focused on query rewriting.

3.1 Query and Relevant Fragments Representation

According to most approaches of relevance feedback, the query construction is done by building a representative pattern for relevant objects and another pattern for irrelevant ones, and then build a representation close to the first and far from the second.

For example, the Rocchio's method [4] considers a representative pattern of a document set by their centrod. A linear combination of the original query and the centrods of the relevant documents and irrelevant ones can be assumed as a potentially suitable user need.

Although simplistic, the Rocchio's method is the most widespread. This simplicity is due to the nature of the manipulated objects. Indeed, Rocchio's method is adapted to the case where documents are full text, in such case, each document is expressed by a vector (generally a vector of weighted terms). Where the documents embody structural relations, the vector representation becomes simplistic, this results in a significant loss of structural contrast and therefore the reconstruction of a unified structure becomes impossible. As for us, we believe that the structure is an additional dimension.

A unique dimension is not enough to encode the structural information (one dimension vector), thus we need to encode all documents into two dimensions, by using matrices rather than vectors.

That reasoning has led us to traduce the documents and the query in a matrix format instead of a weighted term vector. Those matrices are enriched by values calculated from transitive relationship function. Then, the representative structure of query and judged relevant fragments (that we call S) is constructed under a matrix form.

Line of Descent Matrix. We build for each document a matrix called *line of descent matrix* (LDM), which must show all existing ties of relation between different nodes. This representation should also reflect the positions of the various nodes in the fragments as they are also important in the structural relevance feedback. For an XML tree (or sub-tree) A, we associate the matrix defined by M_A:

$$M_A[n, n'] = \begin{cases} P & \text{if } n \to n' \in A \ (n \text{ is the parent of } n') \\ 0 & \text{otherwise} \end{cases}$$

Where P is a constant value which represents the weight of the descent relationship, n and n' are two nodes of the tree A.

As for us, we represent each of the relevant fragments and the initial query in the LDM form[3]. The value of the constant P for the query LDM construction is greater than that used for the construction of other LDMs (which represent the relevant fragments) to strengthen the weight of the initial query edges following the principle used in the Rocchio's method which uses reformulation parameters having different effects (1 for the initial query, α for the relevant documents centrod and β for the non relevant documents centrod where $0 \leq \alpha \leq 1$ and $-1 \leq \beta \leq 0$).

Content Integration in LDM. The content of each element represented in LDM must be taken into account. In RF in XML retrieval we aim to rewrite query's structure and the set of terms of this query. So, we propose to integrate terms of each element in LDM.

Each element node n in LDM is characterized by a tag name and a set of weighted terms: $n_i = (tag_i, \{(t_1, w(t_1, n, i)), (t_2, w(t_2, n, i)) \ldots (t_m, w(t_m, n, i))\})$ where: tag_i: tag name of element n_i, t_k: k^{th} term in n_i, $w(t_k, n, i)$: weight of term t_k in element n_i based on the its frequency in n_i and the total number of elements that contain it [2], m: number of elements.

Let us consider that the element node A appears in three positions in a XML tree as follows:

$A[1] = (A, \{(t_1, 0.5), (t_2, 0.8), (t_3, 0.3), (t_4, 0.0), (t_5, 0.0), (t_6, 0.0)\})$
$A[2] = (A, \{(t_1, 0.5), (t_2, 0.7), (t_3, 0.0), (t_4, 0.2), (t_5, 0.0), (t_6, 0.0)\})$
$A[3] = (A, \{(t_1, 0.0), (t_2, 0.0), (t_3, 0.0), (t_4, 0.2), (t_5, 0.8), (t_6, 0.3)\})$

$A[1]$ and $A[2]$ have relatively the same content which is different from $A[3]$. In the LDM matrix, A will appear twice, with two different contents (t_1, t_2, t_3, t_4)

---

[3] Note that no complexity analysis is here needed because of the low number of relevant judged documents comparing to the corpus size. In our experiments, we undertake the relevance feedback in a pseudo-feedback way on the top 20 ranked fragments resulting from the first round retrieval. In the other hand, the total number of tags is over 160 in all the collection (INEX'05 collection) and about 5 in a single fragment, so the matrix size can not exceed 25.

and (t_4, t_5, t_6). The content similarity is done by the inner product like in vector model [8], we assure that $A[1]$ and $A[2]$ are similar since they have the same tag name (A) and $A[1] \times A[2] = 0.926 \geq Th$ which is not the case for $A[1] \times A[3] = 0.051 < Th$ or $A[2] \times A[3] = 0.0$ (Th is an experimental threshold. In this example, we take $Th = 0.5$). $A[1]$ and $A[2]$ will be aggregated and represented in LDM as follow by a single A and the centrod of $A[1]$ and $A[2]$ as follows: $A = (A, \{(t_1, 0.5), (t_2, 0.75), (t_3, 0.3), (t_4, 0.2)\})$

Setting Relationships between a Node and Its Descendants. XML retrieval is usually done in a vague way [14]. The XML retrieval system has to query with tolerated differences (a few missing elements or more additional ones) between the query structure and the document. Consequently, we believe that the most effective way to bring this tolerance is to assure that one element is not only connected to its childs nodes, but to all its descendants. A relationship between nodes in the same line of descent is weighted by their distance in the XML tree. So, we use the Transitive Relationship function TR which is defined as follows:

$$\forall (n, n', n'') \in N^3, M_A[n, n''] \leftarrow M_A[n, n''] + TR(M_A[n, n'], M_A[n', n''])$$

where N is the set of all different nodes in the tree A and M_A is its LDM, and $TR(x, y) = \frac{x \times y}{\sqrt{x^2 + y^2}}$

Matrix S Construction. The new query structure is built starting from the obtained LDMs. Let us consider $F = \{F_1, F_2 \ldots F_n\}$ with F_i are the relevant judged fragments and Q_{old} the initial query, the query structure is built starting from the cumulated LDM S:

$$\forall (n, n')^2 \in N^2, S[n, n'] = M_{Q_{old}}[n, n'] + \frac{1}{|F|} \sum_{f \in F} M_f[n, n']$$

and for each n: $w(t, n, S) = \alpha w(t, n, Q_{old}) + \frac{\beta}{|F|} \sum_{f \in F} w(t, n, f)$

The constants α and β are the same used in line of descent matrix construction to strengthen the weight of old query's terms. If a column in S contains several low values, then the node will tend to appear as a leaf node in the reformulated query. If on the contrary one row contains several low values, then the node will tend to be seen as a root node in the reformulated query if, in addition, the corresponding column contains several high values, otherwise, the node will tend to appear as an internal node. Thus, in order to build the new query structure, we can determine the new root.

3.2 Query Rewriting

Root Identification. The structure query construction starts by identifying its root. The root is characterized by a high number of child nodes and a weak number of parents. For example, to find the root we simply return the element

R, which has the greatest weight in the rows of the matrix S and the lowest weight in its columns. The root R is then such that:

$$R = \arg\max_{n \in N} \sum_{n' \in N} S[n, n'] . \log \left(\frac{\sum_{n' \in N} S[n', n]}{\sum_{(n', n'') \in N^2} S[n', n'']} + 1 \right)$$

The argument to maximize reflects that the candidate nodes to represent the root should have as maximal low values as possible in the relative row ($\sum_{n' \in N} S[n, n']$) and as minimal low values as possible in the column ($\sum_{n' \in N} S[n', n]$) relatively to the total sum of the matrix values ($\sum_{(n', n'') \in N^2} S[n', n'']$). We are inspired from the $tf \times idf$ factor (*term frequency, inverse of document frequency*) commonly used in traditional information retrieval [7] which affects importance to a term t for a document proportionally to its frequency in the document d (term frequency) and inversely proportionally to the number of documents in the collection where it appears at least once.

Building the New Query Structure. Once the root has been established from the matrix S, we proceed to the recursive development phase of the tree representing the structure of the new query. The development of the tree starts by the root R, and then by determining all the child nodes of R, the same operation is performed recursively for the child nodes of R until reaching the leaf nodes. Each element n is developed by attributing to it its potentially child nodes n' ($n' \neq n$) whose $S[n, n'] > Threshold_n$, calculated from the mean average μ_n and the standard deviation σ_n of its relative child nodes. Indeed, the mean average and the standard deviation will illustrate the probability that a node is an actual child-node of the current node n. This threshold is defined as: $Threshold_n = \mu_n + \gamma * \sigma_n$ with $\mu_n = \frac{1}{|N|} \sum_{n' \in N} S[n, n']$ and $\sigma_n = \frac{1}{|N|} \sqrt{\sum_{n' \in N} (S[n, n'] - \mu_n)^2}$.

If the value of γ is relatively high, the tree outcome will tend to be shallow and ramified and vice versa. The value of γ allows the estimation for each element of the number of child nodes. The objective of this interval is to reconstruct a tree as wide and deep as the XML fragments from which the query should be inferred. This value is then defined experimentally.

4   Experiments and Results

To carry out our experiments we use INEX'05 dataset and we only considered the VVCAS [5] (topics whose relevance vaguely depends on the structural constraints) queries type. Indeed the need for reformulation of the query structure is appropriate to the task. We use also the metrics proposed by INEX which are based on on the extended cumulated gain (XCG) [6].For a given rank i, the value of $nxCG[i]$ reflects the relative gain the user accumulated up to that rank. We only present the results of the generalized quantization function which is most suitable for VVCAS queries (10 queries proposed by INEX).

The table 1 shows the results obtained from XIVIR a research system based on tree matching [2]. This table presents a comparison between the values obtained before (BRF) and after RF (ARF). AA is the absolute improvement of the relevance feedback run over the original base run proposed by INEX.

Table 1. Comparative results before (BRF) and after (ARF) structural RF

Run	$nxCG[10]$	$nxCG[25]$	$nxCG[50]$	MAep
BRF	0.1225	0.1104	0.083	0.0509
ARF	0.2643	0.2348	0.2093	0.0784
AA	+115.75 %	+112.681%	+152.16%	+54.027%

In our experiments we assume that the top k fragments are relevant, the table 2 shows the results obtained from different numbers of relevent fragments.

Table 2. Results from different number of relevant fragments

Run	$nxCG[10]$	$nxCG[25]$	$nxCG[50]$	MAep
$k=5$	+47.08%	+57.38%	+56.76%	-1.63%
$k=10$	+49.15	+59.78%	+58.92%	+1.52%
$k=20$	+47.47%	+57.38%	+60.57%	+23.87%
$k=30$	+47.02	+57.05%	+57.82%	+22.31%
$k=50$	+46.97	+56.71%	+56.74%	+22.29%

We can see through our experiments that our RF approach significantly improves the results. We note that during these experiments we reformulate only the queries structures without changing their original content, and therefore we believe that this reformulation has brought an evolution that could be accentuated by the reformulation of the content.

5   Conclusions and Future Work

We have proposed in this paper an approach to structural relevance feedback in XML retrieval. We proposed a representation of the original query and relevant fragments under a matrix form. After some processing and calculations on the obtained matrix and after some analysis we have been able to identify the most relevant nodes and their relationships that connect them.

The obtained results show that structural relevance feedback contributes to the improvement of XML retrieval. The strategy of the reformulation is based on a matrix representation of the XML trees deemed to be relevant to the fragments and the original query. This representation preserves the original links of descent and the transformations achieved are suitable for the retrieval flexibility.

References

1. Balog, K., Bron, M., de Rijke, M.: Category-based Query Modeling for Entity Search. In: Gurrin, C., He, Y., Kazai, G., Kruschwitz, U., Little, S., Roelleke, T., Rüger, S., van Rijsbergen, K. (eds.) ECIR 2010. LNCS, vol. 5993, pp. 319–331. Springer, Heidelberg (2010)
2. Mohamed, B.A., Mohamed, T., Mohand, B.: Flexible document-query matching based on a probabilistic content and structure score combination. In: ACM Symposium on Applied Computing (SAC), Sierre, Switzerland (2010)
3. Crouch, C.J., Mahajan, A., Bellamkonda, A.: Flexible Retrieval Based on the Vector Space Model. In: Fuhr, N., Lalmas, M., Malik, S., Szlávik, Z. (eds.) INEX 2004. LNCS, vol. 3493, pp. 292–302. Springer, Heidelberg (2005)
4. Rocchio, J.: Relevance feedback in information retrieval. Prentice Hall Inc., Englewood Cliffs (1971)
5. Fuhr, N., Lalmas, M., Malik, S., Kazai, G. (eds.): INEX 2005. LNCS, vol. 3977. Springer, Heidelberg (2006)
6. Kazai, G., Lalmas, M.: INEX 2005 evaluation measures. In: Fuhr, N., Lalmas, M., Malik, S., Kazai, G. (eds.) INEX 2005. LNCS, vol. 3977, pp. 16–29. Springer, Heidelberg (2006)
7. Salton, G.: A comparison between manual and automatic indexing methods. Journal of American Documentation 20(1) (1971)
8. Salton, G.: The SMART Retrieval System - Experiments in automatic Document Processing. Prentice Hall Inc., Englewood Cliffs (1963)
9. Pan, H.: Relevance feedback in XML retrieval. In: Lindner, W., Fischer, F., Türker, C., Tzitzikas, Y., Vakali, A.I. (eds.) EDBT 2004. LNCS, vol. 3268, pp. 187–196. Springer, Heidelberg (2004)
10. Ralf, S., Anja, T., Gerhard, W.: XXL @ INEX 2003. In: Proceedings of the Second INEX Workshop, Dagstuhl, Germany, pp. 59–66 (2004)
11. Schenkel, R., Theobald, M.: Relevance Feedback for Structural Query Expansion. In: Fuhr, N., Lalmas, M., Malik, S., Kazai, G. (eds.) INEX 2005. LNCS, vol. 3977, pp. 344–357. Springer, Heidelberg (2006)
12. Villatoro-Tello, E., Sánchez-Sánchez, C., Jiménez-Salazar, H., Luna-Ramírez, W.A., Rodríguez-Lucatero, C.: UAM at INEX 2012 Relevance Feedback Track: Using a Probabilistic Method for Ranking Refinement. In: CLEF 2012 (2012)
13. Mihajlović, V., Ramírez, G., Westerveld, T., Hiemstra, D., Blok, H.E., de Vries, A.P.: TIJAH Scratches INEX 2005: Vague Element Selection, Image Search, Overlap, and Relevance Feedback. In: Fuhr, N., Lalmas, M., Malik, S., Kazai, G. (eds.) INEX 2005. LNCS, vol. 3977, pp. 72–87. Springer, Heidelberg (2006)
14. Mihajlovic, V., Hiemstra, D., Blok, H.E.: Vague Element Selection and Query Rewriting for XML Retrieval. In: Proceedings of the Sixth Dutch-Belgian Information Retrieval Workshop, pp. 11–18 (2006)
15. Mass, Y., Mandelbrod, M.: Relevance Feedback for XML Retrieval. In: Fuhr, N., Lalmas, M., Malik, S., Szlávik, Z. (eds.) INEX 2004. LNCS, vol. 3493, pp. 303–310. Springer, Heidelberg (2005)

Query Authentication over Cloud Data
from Multiple Contributors[*]

Ge Xie, Zhiyong Peng, and Wei Song[**]

Computer School, Wuhan University, Wuhan, China
{xiege,peng,songwei}@whu.edu.cn

Abstract. As data stored in the cloud may encounter the malicious attack from the cloud service provider (CSP), to ensure data authenticity and integrity, it is necessary to authenticate the query results from CSP. However, most existing authentication methods focus on query over data from a single contributor in the outsourced database. This paper puts forward authentication method for query over data from multiple contributors in the cloud environment. The method can validate data from multiple contributors on only one authentication data structure (ADS) based on Merkle Hash Tree (MHT), which achieves low storage costs and high computational efficiency. Experimental results show that our mechanism can efficiently enable query authentication over cloud data from multiple contributors.

Keywords: cloud storage, multiple contributors, query authentication, data security, Merkle Hash Tree.

1   Introduction

With the rising popularity of cloud storage [1] and the gradual establishment of various authorization relationships between cloud storage users, there exists a special data authorization model in the cloud environment. Users can not only release their own data, but also authorize part or all of their data to other users to release. In such scenario, data is released to the untrustworthy cloud service provider (CSP) [2] by a user who can be called data publisher, and data released by a data publisher may contain both his own data and other contributors' data. Then, if a data requester conducts query over data sets released by one publisher, the query results may consist of multiple contributors' data. To ensure the authenticity and integrity of the query results, all the data contained in the results should be validated. Therefore, in this special setting of cloud environment, a set of safe and efficient query authentication scheme is indispensable.

At present, most scholars focus on validating query over data from single contributor in outsourced database. References [3, 4] present data validation method based on

---

[*] This work is partially supported by National Natural Science Foundation of China No. 61202034, 61232002, and Program for Innovative Research Team of Wuhan, No. 2014070504020237

[**] Corresponding author.

L. Chen et al. (Eds.): APWeb 2014, LNCS 8709, pp. 469–477, 2014.

simple digital signature. References [5-9] describe data validation method based on complex authentication data structure. And references [10-12] introduce data validation method based on probability. In the outsourced data management applications, the digital signature or authentication data structure can only validate the correctness of the publisher's own data. If the query authentication method used in the outsourced database is used to validate the query results in the cloud environment, the contributor needs to establish the corresponding authentication data structure of data authorized to the publisher before the authorization. With more and more authorization, the contributor will face great burden of managing the increasing authentication data structures. Besides, queries on data published by only one publisher may involve authentication data structures of many cloud data distributors, thus leading to additional storage overhead and computational overhead. Therefore, the above methods cannot apply to the cloud environment with multiple data contributors.

For this special data authorization setting in cloud environment, we adopt Merkle Hash Tree (MHT) [13] as the basic authentication data structure (ADS), and combine the data authorization with the update of ADS. Our method needs only one ADS to validate the correctness of query results by merging different users' verification information into the data publisher's ADS, thus solving the problems faced by query result validation in the cloud environment with multiple data contributors.

Our original contributions can be summarized as follows:

- We raise the issue of data authentication under the application environments of multiple data contributors.
- We propose a query authentication scheme which can validate data from multiple contributors on one ADS in the cloud environment.
- We conduct experimental analysis on storage cost and validation efficiency.

The remaining of this paper is organized as follows. We discuss related work on query authentication in Section 2. Our architecture and notations is presented in Section 3. In Section 4, we present the specific method for authenticating query on data from multiple contributors. Section 5 contains experimental evaluation and analysis, and Section 6 concludes the paper.

2   Related Work

There are several notable works that are related to data authentication in outsourced data services, which can be classified into the following three categories.

- **Validation method based on digital signature.** References [3] [4] proposed data authentication methods based on signature chain. Because the signature contains the order of tuples, it can be used to validate the integrity of query result, but may bring large storage cost and high computational overhead.
- **Validation method based on complex authentication data structure.** The basic idea of authentication method based on authentication data structure is to organize data according to certain structure, and thus validating all the data with signature of only part of the data. Reference [5] proposed authentication method based on Merkle Hash Tree (MHT). To make up for the defects of

MHT such as dynamic update maintenance cost and only supporting one-dimensional range access request, researchers put forward various improved methods. Reference [6] created dynamic disk validation data structure Merkle b-tree and Embedded MHT. Reference [7] proposed VKD-tree and VR-tree, and Reference [8] enhanced the efficiency of method in Reference [7]. To support the validation of aggregation function queries, Reference [9] proposed authenticated prefix tree, supporting validation of SUM operation.

- **Validation method based on probability.** Although the above validation methods can provide completely accurate correctness verification, there are limitations on the efficiency and maintenance. Authentication methods based on probability can further improve the verification efficiency, and its main idea is sample verification and cross validation. Researchers mainly put forward the following methods: challenge-response method [10], fake tuple method [11] and dual encryption method [12].

As mentioned above, many researches have been carried out to address the problem of query authentication in cloud computing and other outsourced data management applications. But, to the best of our knowledge, there is not a research to achieve efficient and scalable query authentication over cloud data from multiple data contributors. In our paper, we focus on authenticating query over data from multiple contributors in the cloud environment.

3   Problem Statements and Notations

Figure 1 shows the cloud storage architecture with multiple data contributors, which involves cloud service provider (CSP), data contributor, data publisher and data requester. Data contributor and data publisher are both cloud data owners, data contributor is the one who authorize all or part of his cloud data to data publisher to release, and a cloud data owner can act as data contributor and data publisher at the same time. Therefore, data sets released by a data publisher can contain his own data as well as data authorized by several other data contributors. In this system model, CSP is an untrustworthy service provider, but it still follows our proposed protocol. And data contributors and data publishers are trustworthy data sources and publishers.

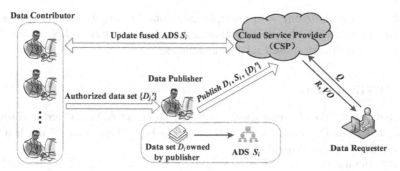

Fig. 1. The cloud storage architecture with multiple data contributors

In the architecture showed in Figure 1, if data publisher U_i wants to publish his own data set D_i to CSP, he will generate an authentication data structure (ADS) S_i according to D_i, and then release D_i and S_i to CSP. Data contributors can authorize all or part of their data to publisher U_i to release, and fuse the authorized data into S_i during the authorization.

If data requester submits a query request over data published by U_i to CSP, CSP will compute the query result R which meets Q, and generate verification object VO from S_i. Finally, R and VO are both returned to data requester, and the data requester can validate the correctness of R with VO locally.

The ADS mentioned above is based on Merkle Hash Tree (MHT). MHT is a binary tree constructed with sorted data, and the root node of the binary tree is signed with digital signature. Our paper is aimed at authenticating cloud data from multiple contributors securely and efficiently. Before describing the solution, we first define some notations as listed in Table 1.

Table 1. Notations

sym-	meaning
U_i	i^{th} user in cloud storage system
D_i	data set owned and released by U_i
$\lvert D_i \rvert$	size of D_i
D_i'	subset of D_i
d_{ij}	j^{th} data in D_i
S_i	ADS corresponding to D_i (MHT)
v_{ij}	j^{th} leaf node of S_i
$sig(ro$	signed root node of S_i
Seq_i	fusion sequence of S_i
$\lvert Seq_i \rvert$	the number of data distributors contained in Seq_i

4   Authenticating Query over Multi-contributor Data

For the cloud environment with multiple data contributors, we put forward a query result validation method based on authentication data structure (ADS) fusion. In this section, we detail the proposed scheme as follows.

4.1   ADS Generation

Before a data publisher U_i releases his own data set D_i, an ADS S_i (Merkle Hash Tree) is generated from D_i, that is, construct a Merkle Hash Tree with all the leaf nodes generated from data contained in D_i.

Firstly, obtain the ordered data sequence $D_i = \{d_{i1}, d_{i2}, ..., d_{in}\}(n=\lvert D_i \rvert)$, and compute the hash value of all the data contained in D_i with hash function, which can be expressed as $h(D_i)=\{ h(d_{i1}), h(d_{i2}), ..., h(d_{in})\}(n=\lvert D_i \rvert)$. Then, create leaf nodes corresponding to every hash value, and $v_{ij} = h(d_{ij})$. Finally, construct a binary tree from the bottom up with two adjacent leaf nodes combined from left to right until the root node $root_i$ is generated, and then U_i signs $root_i$ with its own private key, and releases data D_i and structure S_i with signed root node $sig(root_i)$ to CSP.

4.2   ADS Fusion Mechanism

If data contributor U_j authorizes part of his own data set D_j' to U_i to release, data released by U_i contains his own data set D_i as well as D_j'. In order to validate the correctness of query results with only one ADS, the verification information of D_j' needs to be merged into S_i. Algorithm 1 describes the ADS fusion algorithm based on MHT.

Algorithm 1. ADS Fusion Algorithm
Input: S_i, D_j', Seq_i
Output: updated S_i and Seq_i
1. verify the validity of S_i
2. update the value of leaf nodes with hash value of D_j'
3. update S_i with the updated leaf nodes
4. U_j signs new root node $root_i'$ of updated S_i
5. add U_j to Seq_i
6. upload the updated S_i and Seq_i to CSP

Before updating the value of leaf nodes, the hash value of data contained in D_j' should be computed. And there are two cases when updating the leaf node.

- When $|D_i| \geq |D_j'|$, for ease of presentation, we regard a hash value of data in D_j' as a node, and each node corresponds to a leaf node in S_i from left to right. The value of leaf node v_{in} will be changed as follows.

$$v_{in} = \begin{cases} h(h(d_{in}) \| h(d_{jn}')), & (n \leq |D_j'|) \\ h(d_{in}), & (|D_j'| < n \leq |D_i|) \end{cases} \tag{1}$$

- When $|D_i| < |D_j'|$, we should create $(|D_j'|-|D_i|)$ leaf nodes with value of zero, and each hash value of D_j' corresponds to a leaf node in S_i from left to right. The value of leaf node v_{in} will be changed as follows.

$$v_{in} = \begin{cases} h(h(d_{in}) \| h(d_{jn}')), & (n \leq |D_i|) \\ h(d_{jn}'), & (|D_i| < n \leq |D_j'|) \end{cases} \tag{2}$$

For example, if the data released by U_i contains data sets authorized by U_1, U_2, U_3 and U_4, and $|D_i| > |D_4'| > |D_3'| > |D_2'| > |D_1'|$, $Seq_i = \{U_1, U_2, U_3, U_4\}$, and then the value of leaf node v_{in} can be expressed in the following formula:

$$v_{in} = \begin{cases} h(h(d_{in}) \| h(d_{1n}') \| h(d_{2n}') \| h(d_{3n}') \| h(d_{4n}')), & (n \leq |D_1'|) \\ h(h(d_{in}) \| h(d_{2n}') \| h(d_{3n}') \| h(d_{4n}')), & (|D_1'| < n \leq |D_2'|) \\ h(h(d_{in}) \| h(d_{3n}') \| h(d_{4n}')), & (|D_2'| < n \leq |D_3'|) \\ h(h(d_{in}) \| h(d_{4n}')), & (|D_3'| < n \leq |D_4'|) \\ h(d_{in}), & (|D_4'| < n \leq |D_i|) \end{cases} \tag{3}$$

In the updated ADS S_i, the hash values of internal nodes are modified with the updated leaf nodes according to the discipline to construct MHT. Then, the updated root node $root_i'$ of the fused MHT is signed by the last data contributor U_4 in Seq_i with his private key, and the signed root node is $sig(root_i')$.

4.3   Verification Object Generation

If data requester wants to search information on the data released by U_i, he will send a query request Q on data released by U_i to CSP. Then, CSP computes the query result R which may contain data authorized by many data contributors. To validate the correctness of R, CSP needs to generate verification object VO used to validate the query result R, Algorithm 2 describes the verification object generation algorithm.

Algorithm 2. Verification Object Generation Algorithm
Input: Q, S_i, D_i, { D_j' $|1 \leq j \leq |Seq_i|$}
Output: VO and R
1. for each leaf node in S_i
2.   add data satisfying the query condition Q to R
3.   get hash value of data failing to satisfy Q from S_i, and add them to VO
4. merge VO vertically and horizontally
5. add $sig(root_i')$ to VO
6. return VO and R to data requester

In cloud environment with large amount of data, to reduce the transmission overhead and computation cost on the client side of data requester, CSP needs to simplify VO before returning it to data requester, and the way of simplification is to merge VO vertically and horizontally.

Firstly, CSP merges VO vertically. If data authorized by multiple contributors corresponding to the validation information contained in a leaf node of S_i doesn't satisfy the query condition Q, the data's hash values will be unified as a string, replacing all the hash values constituting the leaf node in VO. For example, a leaf node v_{in} contains the validation information of data owned by U_i, U_1, U_2, U_3, U_4, i.e. $h(d_{in})$, $h(d_{1n}')$, $h(d_{2n}')$, $h(d_{3n}')$, $h(d_{4n}')$. If only d_{2n}' can satisfy the query condition Q, VO will contain $h(d_{in}) \| h(d_{1n}')$ and $h(d_{3n}') \| h(d_{4n}')$, instead of $h(d_{in})$, $h(d_{1n}')$, $h(d_{3n}')$ and $h(d_{4n}')$. If all of d_{in}, d_{1n}', d_{2n}', d_{3n}' and d_{4n}' cannot satisfy the query condition Q, VO will contain the leaf node v_{in}. Then, CSP merges VO horizontally. If VO contains adjacent nodes with the same parent node, replace the child nodes with the parent node until there are no adjacent nodes with the same parent node in VO. VO merged vertically and horizontally are most simplified. When VO is generated, CSP will send VO, R and Seq_i to data requester.

4.4   Query Result Validation

When data requester receives the query results from CSP, he needs to validate the correctness of the query results. Then, both query results R and verification object VO are used to rebuild a Merkle Hash Tree, whose root node value is to be compared with value of the signed root node of data publisher U_i's fused ADS. As the query results R and verification object VO contain data from multiple contributors, the leaf nodes need to be built firstly. Algorithm 3 describes the query result validation algorithm.

Algorithm 3. Query Result Validation Algorithm
Input: R, VO, Seq_i
Output: validation result
1. for each leaf node v_{in}' needed to be recomputed
2.   extract data from R needed to compute v_{in}'
3.   extract data from VO needed to compute v_{in}'
4.   compute v_{in}' with data extracted above according to Seq_i
5. reconstruct MHT with the leaf nodes, and get the root node value $root_s$
6. verify $sig(root_i')$ and get $root_i'$
7. compare $root_s$ with $root_i'$, and output the validation result

If any data contained in the query results is wrong, the value of corresponding leaf node will also be wrong, and thus the root node value $root_s$ of the rebuilt MHT will definitely be different from the real root node value $root_i'$, the cloud storage user will be aware that the query results returned is not correct.

5   Experimental Analysis

Our experiment mainly focuses on the storage space taken by ADS and time taken by query result validation, comparing these two aspects between validation on separated ADSs and validation on fused ADS.

In the experiment, there is a data publisher and four other data contributors who authorize their data to the data publisher to release. Data publisher owns data sets of 10000 files, and the average size of data sets authorized to the data publisher by the four distributors ranges from 1000 files to 10000 files. In the above setting, we will record the storage space taken by ADS and time taken by query result validation, and then conduct comparison and analysis.

The comparison of storage space taken by ADS is shown in figure 2. We can see the storage space of fused ADS is much less than that of separated ADSs. The main reason is that the fused ADS built based on the data publisher's original ADS always has only one root node, and by merging data from different users into a leaf node, the number of internal nodes generated from the leaf nodes keeps the least. However, each of the separated ADSs has a root node, and as the number of leaf nodes equals to that of data, numerous extra internal nodes will be built, which leads to great storage cost.

The comparison of time cost by query result validation on the client side is shown in figure 3. We can see the time cost by query result validation on fused ADS is much less than that on separated ADSs. The main reason is that when the query result is validated on the fused ADS, the client side only needs to do extra hash operation to construct the leaf nodes, but spent much less time to build the internal nodes. Besides, validation on the fused ADS only needs to verify the root node once, but validation on separated ADSs needs to verify multiple times which equals to the number of data distributors. It can be seen that with the growth of the size of data authorized to the data publisher, query result validation on fused ADS becomes increasingly efficient.

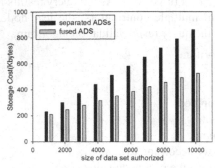
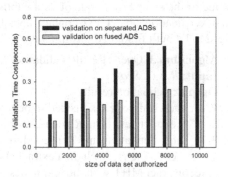

Fig. 2. Comparison of ADS storage cost   **Fig. 3.** Comparison of validation time cost

6   Conclusion

In this paper, we have proposed an efficient query authentication scheme which can validate the correctness of data from multiple contributors on one authentication data structure in the cloud environment. Experimental evaluation shows that our method can authenticate query result containing data from multiple contributors with small storage cost and low computational overhead, and outperform the traditional single-contributor authentication method by a wide margin. Our future work is to optimize the authentication data structure to further improve the efficiency of our validation method.

References

1. Fox, A., Griffith, R., et al.: Above the clouds: A berkeley view of cloudcomputing. Dept. Electrical Eng. and Comput. Sciences, University ofCalifornia, Berkeley, Tech. Rep. UCB/EECS, vol. 28 (2009)
2. Hacigümüs, H., Mehrotra, S., Iyer, B.R.: Providing Database as a Service. In: Proceedings of the 18th International Conference on Data Engineering, pp. 29–40 (2002)
3. Narasimha, M., Tsudik, G.: Authentication of outsourced databases using signature aggregation and chaining. In: Li Lee, M., Tan, K.-L., Wuwongse, V. (eds.) DASFAA 2006. LNCS, vol. 3882, pp. 420–436. Springer, Heidelberg (2006)
4. Pang, H., Jain, A., Ramamritham, K., et al.: Verifying completeness of relational query results in data publishing. In: Proceedings of ACM SIGMOD Conference (SIGMOD 2005), Baltimore, Maryland, USA (2005)
5. Mykletun, E., Narasimha, M., Tsudik, G.: Providing authentication and integrity in outsourced databases using Merkle hash trees. UCI-SCONCE Technical Report[R/OL] (2003), http://sconce.ics.uci.edu/das/MerkleODB.pdf
6. Li, F., Hadjieleftheriouz, M., Kolliosy, G., et al.: Dynamic authenticated index structures for outsourced databases. In: Proceedings of ACM SIGMOD Conference (SIGMOD 2006), Chicago, Illinois, USA (2006)

7. Cheng, W., Pang, H., Tan, K.-L.: Authenticating multi-dimensional query results in data publishing. In: Damiani, E., Liu, P. (eds.) Data and Applications Security 2006. LNCS, vol. 4127, pp. 60–73. Springer, Heidelberg (2006)
8. Yang, Y., Papadopoulos, S., Papadias, D., et al.: Authenticated indexing for outsourced spatial databases. VLDB Journal (2009)
9. Li, F., Hadjieleftheriouz, M., Kolliosy, G., et al.: Authenticated index structures for aggregation queries in outsourced databases, BUCS-TR-2006-011[R] (2006)
10. Sion, R.: Query execution assurance for outsourced databases. In: Proceedings of International Conference on Very Large Data Bases(VLDB 2005), Trondheim, Norway (2005)
11. Xie, M., Wang, H.J., Yin, J., et al.: Integrity auditing of outsourced data. In: Proceedings of International Conference on Very Large Data Bases(VLDB 2007), Vienna, Austria (2007)
12. Wang, H.J., Yin, J., Perng, C., et al.: Dual encryption for query integrity assurance. In: Proceedings of ACM Conference on Information and Knowledge Management (CIKM 2008), Napa Valley, California, USA (2008)
13. Merkle, R.C.: A certified digital signature. In: Brassard, G. (ed.) CRYPTO 1989. LNCS, vol. 435, pp. 218–238. Springer, Heidelberg (1990)

TL: A High Performance Buffer Replacement Strategy for Read-Write Splitting Web Applications

Zhiwen Jiang, Yong Zhang, Jin Wang, Chao Li, and Chunxiao Xing

RIIT, TNList, Department of Computer Science and Technology,
Center for High-speed Railway Technology,
Tsinghua University, Beijing 100084, China
jzw10@mails.tsinghua.edu.cn

Abstract. With the quickly increasing pressure of users' requests, more and more Web applications adopt the read-write splitting to improve the performance, which requires new buffer replacement strategy. Flash memory has emerged as a popular storage media, and we use it to replace hard disk for read-write splitting Web applications. Traditional buffer replacement strategies are suboptimal on flash memory, since flash memory has some distinguished features as out-of-place update and read-write asymmetry. In this paper, we design a flash-aware buffer replacement strategy Tri-List (TL), which emphasizes the I/O asymmetry of flash memory. Unlike other flash-aware buffer replacement policies which are based on LRU method, TL considers both recency and frequency of page requests to make better decision of buffer replacement. Experimental results on both synthetic and benchmarking traces shows that TL has up to 30.3% improvements than state-of-the-art flash-aware buffer management policies.

1   Introduction

With the booming of e-Commerce, Web applications are facing with the challenge of higher pressure than ever. Read-write splitting is an important strategy being adopted in web servers to improve the performance. Buffer also plays an important role in systems to improve the performance by minimizing the access gap between disk and main memory by maintaining some hot data in the main memory. We use flash-based Solid State Drives (SSD) replacing hard disk as to improve the performance.

Traditional buffer management policies take advantage of the temporal locality of page request to reduce the number of disk access [4]. The primary criterion of traditional buffer replacement strategies is maximizing the hit ratio. However, because of the read-write asymmetry, a higher hit ratio doesn't necessarily improve I/O performance on flash memory. So we should use the total I/O cost rather than hit ratio as the primary criterion to evaluate the performance of buffer replacement strategies on flash memory.

However, existing flash-aware buffer replacement strategies have several limitations. To begin with, all of them adopt the LRU (Least Recently Used) method, which evicts the least recently used page. But these strategies fail to take frequency of page request into account. So they cannot make full use of the history information of page request to select victim page for eviction. In read-write splitting Web applications,

L. Chen et al. (Eds.): APWeb 2014, LNCS 8709, pp. 478–484, 2014.
© Springer International Publishing Switzerland 2014

transaction severs usually have access pattern with poor locality. In this case, the performance of LRU method will be suboptimal.

In this paper, we propose a novel buffer replacement strategy *Tri-List* (TL for short) to address the limitations of previous studies. We partition the buffer pool into three parts according to page state (clean/dirty) as well as "hotness" of page request. TL is implemented with low computational overhead. Thus the overall performance of TL can be guaranteed. We perform trace-driven simulation experiments using benchmarking workload. Experimental results show that TL achieves up to 30.3% improvements than state-of-art flash-aware buffer replacement strategies.

The paper is organized as follows: In Section 2 we describe the related work. In Section 3 we introduce the preliminaries of our work. In Section 4, we propose the design of TL in detail. In Section 5 we present the results of performance study. Finally we conclude in Section 6.

2   Related Work

Buffer management has attracted significant attention for several decades. LRU and LFU are two important buffer replacement strategies considering recency and frequency, respectively. FBR [14] is a frequency-based algorithm. LRU-K [11] is a variant of LRU that keeps track of last K references of each page to make decisions about page eviction. It achieves higher hit ratio by considering both frequency and recency. But LRU-K incurs logarithm time complexity. 2Q [6] is a clock-based algorithm that solve this problem. It reaches the same goal of LRU-K with only O (1) time complexity. LIRS [5] is another variant of LRU; it uses a new criterion inter-reference recency to combine recency and frequency of page request.

There are many buffering strategies on flash memory. REF [14] and BPLRU [8] are block-level buffer management policies for embedded system. Flash memory is also used as the extension of buffer pool of database systems [3]. Some flash-based buffer replacement strategies have recently been proposed to improve the I/O performance of database system on flash memory. Such as CFLRU [18] LRUWSR [7], CCFLRU [9], CASA [12] divides the buffer pool into two parts to distinguish clean and dirty pages. The sizes of each pool can be changed adaptively according to different workloads. According to previous studies [1], the access pattern of operation significantly influences the overall I/O performance. CFDC [13] proposes the technique named write clustering to improve the locality of write operation.

[2, 15] have explored partitioning the buffer pool into several regions. DBMIN [2] allocates different parts of buffer pool to different kinds of queries. We adopt the similar idea to partition the buffer pool into different regions to distinguish the infrequent read/write pages from other pages.

3   Preliminaries

Due to the read-write asymmetry of flash memory, hit ratio is not consistent with overall I/O performance. Thus we choose I/O cost as primary criterion in this paper. Specifically, we consider average I/O time per page request. In this way, the I/O cost includes two parts:

the cost of fetching pages into the buffer and the cost of writing dirty pages back to disk. Here we define HR as the hit ratio, C_r/C_w as the average cost of one read/write operation on flash memory, T_r/T_w as the total number of read/write operations and R_d as the portion of dirty pages in all evicted pages. The total I/O cost can be represented as:

$$Cost_{io} = HR * (C_r + C_w * R_d) \tag{1}$$

To represent the read-write asymmetry and then quantify the total I/O cost, we define the asymmetry factor $R = C_w/C_r$. Its value can be estimated according to history information as previous work did [12]. In most cases it is difficult for us to decide the value of R_d in (1). So we estimate the I/O cost using the total times of read and write operations as follows:

$$Cost_{io} = C_r * T_r + C_w * T_w = C_r * (T_r + R * T_w) \tag{2}$$

From (2) we can see that since R varies among different storage devices, it is crucial to make a proper tradeoff between read and write operations instead of giving priority to evict clean pages. Besides, since the access gap between flash disk and memory is smaller than that on hard disk, we also need to avoid complicated data structures with high computational overhead.

4   Implementation of Tri-List

In this section, we will introduce the implementation of TL in detail.

4.1   Overview

In order to solve the problem of LRU based methods, we need to take frequency of page request into consideration. All the frequency-based methods incur logarithm time complexity since they need to compare the value of request time.

The main idea of previous flash-aware buffer replacement strategies is to keep dirty pages in the buffer to reduce the number of write operation. When multiple write operations are performed on a dirty page in the buffer, they will only result in one physical write to flash memory. Similarly, if a page that is written once and never written again in the near future, we call it infrequent write pages. Such a page should not be kept in the buffer for a long time although it is dirty. We should evict it in order to avoid unnecessary extra read operations.

4.2   Data Structure and Algorithms

We implement Tri-List (TL) by dividing the buffer pool into three parts based on the above discussion. TL consists of three lists, denoted as L_1, L_2 and L_3, respectively. All the three lists are managed in a LRU way. List L_1 contains pages that are only requested once. As such pages are just fetched into the buffer, they are clean pages. List L_2 contains two kinds of pages: clean pages that are requested at least two times and dirty pages that are written only once. List L_3 contains dirty pages that are written at least two times. When a dirty page in the second list is written again, it will be moved to the third list. The data structure of TL is shown in Figure 1.

List I

List II

List III

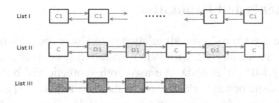

Fig. 1. The Data Structure of TL

The main procedure of reading a page is shown in Algorithm 1. TL uses a hash table to judge whether a page is in the buffer in O (1) time. If a page is hit, TL will adjust the lists according to Algorithm 2. When a buffer miss occurs, TL will choose the least recently used page in L_1 or L_2 as victim according to the number of pages in the two lists, as is shown in Algorithm 3. Then the requested page is fetched into the buffer and the hash table is updated. The procedure of writing a page is similar to that of reading a page. The only difference is that the page needs to be marked as dirty after it is written. The time complexity of Algorithm 1 is O (1).

Algorithm 1 ReadBuffer

Input: the requested page p
Output: the content of page p
1   check whether page p exists in the hash table
2   **if** p is in the buffer **then**
3 | HitAdjustment (p);
4 | **return** the content of p
5   **endif**
6   **if** buffer pool is not full **then**
7 | allocate a free slot for p
8   **else**
9 | page victim = SelectVictim ()
10 | **if** victim is dirty **then**
11 | | write victim out to disk
12 | **endif**
13 | put page p in the slot at the position of page victim
14 **endif**
15 update the hash table
16 **return** the content of p

Algorithm 2 HitAdjust

Input: the hit page p
Parameter: r_3: the largest ratio of L_3, m: buffer size
1   **if** p is in L_1 **then**
2 | move p to the front of L_2
3   **else if** p is in L_2 **then**
4 | **if** the operation performed on p is write and p is dirty
        and the size of $L_3 < r_3 * m$ **then**
5 | | move p to the front of L_3
6 | **else**
7 | | move p to the front of L_2
8 | **endif**
9   **else**
10 | move p to the front of L_3
11 **endif**

Algorithm 2 shows the procedure to deal with buffer hit. If a page in L_1 is hit, it will be moved to L_2. If a dirty page in L_2 is hit and the operation is write, it should be moved to L_3. But the size of list L_3 is limited, if list L_3 is already full, it will be put at the end of L_2. In other cases, the page being hit is just moved to the front of the corresponding list.

Then we discuss about how TL chooses the victim page when buffer miss occurs. Here we need to set a threshold of the largest size of L_1. If the size of L_1 exceeds this threshold, the page at the end of list L_1 will be selected as victim. Otherwise, the page at the end of list L_2 will be selected as victim. This bound is necessary because if the size of list L_1 is too small, pages in list L_1 will be evicted frequently. In this case, list L_1 cannot act well to filer infrequent read pages. Details of discussion about the largest size of L_1 will be shown in Section 5.1.

5   Experiments and Evaluation

In this section, we use trace-driven simulation to evaluate the performance of TL. All the experiments were run on a PC with Win 7 operating system. The storage device was a 128GB Samsung 840 Series SSD. We used both synthetic and benchmarking workloads. The two realistic benchmarking workloads were TPC-C [17] and TATP [16]. To get the page request trace for simulation, we ran each benchmark on PostgreSQL 9.3.1 with default setting (the page size is 8KB). We ran the test for around 3 hours for each benchmark as previous study did [10] and then used the collected traces as the input for simulation test. Details of traces are shown in Table 2.

Table 1. Traces in this experiment

	Database size (GB)	# of referenced	Write ratio
TATP	0.4	2.5	4.8%
TPC-C	2.4	16.8	16.3%

5.1   Discussion

An important issue to ensure the performance is the value of the max size of the list L_1 and L_3. We have found that when the portion of L_3 in the buffer pool, denoted as r_3, is larger than 0.05, the overall performance of TL will deteriorate drastically. So we set r_3 to 0.05. Figure 2 shows the result of changing value of parameter r_1, which denotes the portion of L_1 in the buffer pool, with different buffer sizes under TATP and TPC-C workloads. It is clear that the performance is insensitive to the value of r_1 with all the buffer sizes. Therefore, TL doesn't need parameter tuning and we can set the parameters r_1 and r_3 empirically.

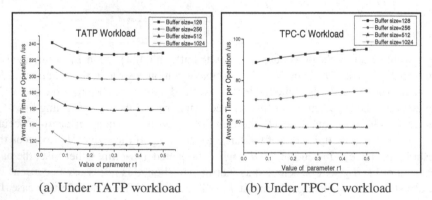

(a) Under TATP workload   (b) Under TPC-C workload

Fig. 2. The result of parameter tuning

5.2   Performance Study

We compare the performance of TL with state-of-art buffer replacement strategies
CFLRU [18], CFDC [13], CASA [12] and LIRS [5]. We don't use LRU as baseline
because all above algorithms outperform LRU as is shown in previous studies. All the
baselines are well tuned according to the references. The window size of CFLRU is set
to 10%; the size of working region of CFDC is set to 40%.

Figure 4 shows the results under TATP and TPC-C benchmarking workload. As is
shown in Figure 4 (a), the performance of each algorithm under TATP workload is
similar to each other. The reason is that the portion of write operation in TATP workload is rather small (only 4.8%). Since all the flash-aware algorithms trade read operations for write operations, the optimization will be limited. In this case, the
disk-oriented algorithm LIRS even outperforms most flash-aware algorithms.

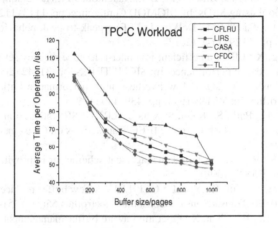

Fig. 3. Result under TPC-C workload

Figure 3 shows the results under TPC-C workload. As we can see from Figure 5, TL
has the best performance. Since TL can evict infrequent write pages by only protecting
the pages that are written more than once in list L_3, compared with TL, LIRS fails to
protect dirty pages to reduce the number of physical writes. Thus, TL outperforms
LIRS.

6   Conclusion

In this paper, we propose a novel buffer replacement strategy TL on flash memory for
read-write splitting Web applications. By dividing the buffer pool into three parts, TL
can take the frequency of page request into account. Besides, compared to other
flash-aware algorithms, TL also avoids extra read operations to guarantee the hit ratio
by distinguishing frequently written pages. Results of experiments under both synthetic
and benchmarking show that TL achieves up to 30.3% improvement than other
state-of-art flash-aware buffer replacement strategies.

Acknowledgement. Our work is supported by National Basic Research Program of China (973 Program) No.2011CB302302, the Support Program of the National '12th Five-Year-Plan' of China under Grant No. 2012AA09A408, Key S&T Projects of Press and Publication under Grant No GXTC-CZ-1015004/02, Tsinghua University Initiative Scientific Research.

References

1. Bouganim, L., Jonsson, B.T., Bonnet, P.: uFlip: Understanding flash IO patterns. In: CIDR (2009)
2. Chou, H.-T., DeWitt, D.J.: An evaluation of buffer management strategies for relational database systems. In: VLDB (1985)
3. Do, J., Zhang, D., Patel, J.M., DeWitt, D.J., Naughton, J.F., Halverson, A.: Turbocharging DBMS buffer pool using SSDs. In: SIGMOD Conference, pp. 1113–1124 (2011)
4. Do, J., Zhang, D., Patel, J.M., DeWitt, D.J.: Fast peak-to-peak behavior with SSD buffer pool. In: ICDE, pp. 1129–1140 (2013)
5. Jiang, S., Zhang, X.: LIRS: an efficient low inter-reference recency set replacement policy to improve buffer cache performance. In: SIGMETRICS, pp. 31–42 (2002)
6. Johnson, T., Shasha, D.: 2Q: A low overhead high performance buffer management replacement algorithm. In: VLDB 1994, pp. 439–450 (1994)
7. Jung, H., Shim, H., Park, S., Kang, S., Cha, J.: LRU-WSR: Integration of LRU and writes sequence reordering for flash memory. IEEE Transactions on Consumer Electronics 54(3), 1215–1223 (2008)
8. Kim, H., Ahn, S.: BPLRU: A buffer management scheme for improving random writes in flash storage. In: FAST (2008)
9. Li, Z., Jin, P., Su, X., Cui, K., Yue, L.: CCF-LRU: A new buffer replacement algorithm for flash memory. IEEE Transactions on Consumer Electronics 55(3), 1351–1359 (2009)
10. Lv, Y., Cui, B., He, B., Chen, X.: Operation-aware buffer management in flash-based systems. In: SIGMOD Conference 2011, pp. 13–24 (2011)
11. O'Neil, E.J., O'Neil, P.E., Weikum, G.: The LRU-K page replacement algorithm for database disk buffering. In: SIGMOD Conference 1993, pp. 297–306 (1993)
12. Ou, Y., Haerder, T.: Clean first or dirty first? A cost-aware self-adaptive buffer replacement policy. In: IDEAS, pp. 7–14 (2010)
13. Ou, Y., Haerder, T., Jin, P.: CFDC: A flash-aware replacement policy for database buffer management. In: DaMoN (2009)
14. Seo, D., Shin, D.: Recently-evicted-first buffer replacement policy for flash storage devices. IEEE Transactions on Consumer Electronics 54(3), 1228–1235 (2008)
15. Robinson, J.T., Devarakonda, M.V.: Data cache management using frequency-based replacement. In: SIGMETRICS, pp. 134–142 (1990)
16. TATP Benchmarking, http://tatpbenchmark.sourceforge.net/
17. TPC-C, http://www.tpc.org/tpc/
18. Park, S.Y., Jung, D., Kang, J.-U., et al.: CFLRU: a replacement algorithm for flash memory. In: CASES, pp. 234–241 (2006)

Nearest Keyword Search on Probabilistic XML Data

Yue Zhao, Ye Yuan, and Guoren Wang

College of Information Science and Engineering, Northeastern University, China
zhaoy0927@163.com

Abstract. This paper pays attention to the nearest keyword (NK) problem on probabilistic XML data (NK-P). NK search occupies an important position in information discovery, information extraction and many other areas. Compared with traditional XML data, it is more expensive to answer NK-P search because of so many possible worlds. NK-P can be seen as an NK problem on many traditional XML documents. For a given node q and a keyword k, an NK-P query returns the node which is nearest to q among all the nodes associated with k in all the possible worlds. NK-P search is not only useful independent operator but also as an important part for keyword search. Firstly, we propose a new NK concept on probabilistic XML data based on possible worlds. Next, we present an indexing algorithm to answer an NK-P query efficiently. Finally, extensive experimental results show that our approach is an effective method on probabilistic XML data, and it could significantly reduce the execution time.

Keywords: NK, NK-P, probabilistic XML data, keyword search, possible world.

1 Introduction

Uncertain data is inherent in information extraction in various web applications, such as sensor networks, social networks and so on. Traditional XML databases allow for the storage and retrieval of large amounts of XML data, but do not make any concessions for probabilistic XML data. We have used probabilistic XML model $PrXML^{\{ind,mux\}}$ [4], which was first discussed in [1], to manage data from information extraction data obtained from the web using a natural language analysis system. In this model, a probabilistic XML document (p-document) is regarded as a labeled tree with two types of nodes, *ordinary* nodes representing the actual data and *distributional* nodes defining the probability distribution for the children nodes. There are two types of distributional nodes, IND means the children nodes are *independent* of each other, while the children of a MUX node are *mutually-exclusive*, it means that at most one child can exist in a random instance document (called a *possible world*). A real number from (0,1] is attached on each edge in the XML tree, representing the conditional probability that the child node will appear under its parent node given the existence of its parent node.

L. Chen et al. (Eds.): APWeb 2014, LNCS 8709, pp. 485–493, 2014.

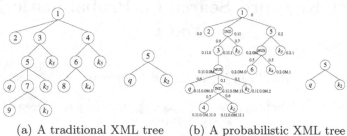

(a) A traditional XML tree   (b) A probabilistic XML tree

Fig. 1. A traditional XML tree and a probabilistic XML tree

NK query is considered as an important information retrieval task, aiming at discovery of the node that is the nearest keyword node of query node. Given an XML tree T, a query node q and a keyword k, an NK query on XML data can return the node that is nearest to q among all the nodes associated with k. Since the significant differences between deterministic XML data and probabilistic XML data, existing NK query methods on deterministic XML data are not suitable for probabilistic XML data. Consider an NK query on the probabilistic XML data in Figure 1(b), the LCA node of q and k_2 is a MUX node. So, for NK search on probabilistic XML data, to naively return the NK nodes as the answers will bring *False Positive Problem*, because the children nodes cannot appear together under a MUX node. To our best knowledge, no existing work pays attention on NK search on probabilistic XML data. In summary, the contributions of this paper are shown as the following:

- This paper is the first work that studies an NK query on Probabilistic XML data (NK-P) to our best knowledge, and we design an algorithm to find NK-P results and calculate the probability without generating any possible worlds.

- Experiments can show that our approach are effective and efficient.

The rest of this paper is organized as following. Section 2 introduces the related work. In Section 3, we describe the problem definition of NK search on probabilistic and elaborate the indexing algorithm of NK-P search. Section 4 reports the experiment results. Section 5 concludes this paper.

2   Related Work

This section introduces related work in two fields: (1) NK semantics on a deterministic XML document; (2) introduce probabilistic XML data and Dewey code.

2.1   NK Semantics on Deterministic XML Data

A deterministic XML document is usually modeled as a labeled tree. We adopt the formalized NK semantics as the work [5]. We introduce some notions first. Define the *length* of a path in T as the number of edges it contains. Denote by

$\| u, v \|$ the length of the path connecting u and v, namely, the distance between two nodes u and v. Let $U(k)$ denote the set of nodes in T that include keyword k. Given a query node q and a keyword k, the result of an NK query is a node $v \in U(k)$ such that

$$\| v, q \| \leq \| u, q \| \quad \forall u \in U(k)$$

Figure 1 (a) shows an example XML tree T. For a query node q and a keyword k, $U(k) = \{k_1, k_2, k_3, k_4, k_5\}$ and node 5 is the result because $\| k_2, q \| = 2 < (\| k_1, q \| = \| k_3, q \| = 3, \| k_5, q \| = 5, \| k_4, q \| = 6)$.

Paper [5] proposed the problem of NK search on XML data. They solved the problem with a novel technique called tree Voronoi partition that gives rise to an indexing scheme with rigorous worst-case performance guarantees.

2.2 Probabilistic XML Data

Probabilistic XML data model $PrXML^{\{ind,mux\}}$ is a popular data model which is used to represent XML data and its uncertain data. A probabilistic XML document defines a probability distribution over a space of deterministic XML documents. In this model, *ordinary* nodes are used to represent the actual data which may appear in a deterministic XML document, in contrast, *distributional* nodes represent the probability distribution of the children nodes which may not appear in a deterministic XML document. If a node is an IND node with n child nodes, it can generate 2^n copies. If it is a MUX node with n child nodes, there are two situations, one is that if the sum of all the exist probability is 1, there are n copies, another is that if the sum is less than 1, we generate $n + 1$ copies.

For example, Figure 2(a) shows an example of an IND node and a MUX node is shown in Figure 1(b).

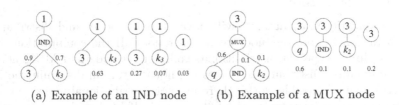

(a) Example of an IND node   (b) Example of a MUX node

Fig. 2. Examples of distributional nodes

2.3 Dewey Code

Dewey code is an effective and efficient way in previous keyword search approaches [2-3]. If using Dewey code, it is easy to find LCA node of any two nodes and determine the relationship between two nodes . If using Dewey code to encode a probabilistic XML document, distributional nodes can not be distinguished with ordinary nodes. So, this paper uses a char "M" or "I" to definite

MUX nodes and IND nodes. If the node is a distributional node, add a char "M" or "I" after the number. Figure 1(b) is a probabilistic XML tree with Dewey code. Because of the type of node is IND, the code is 0.1I.

3   NK-P Search Algorithm

In this section, we provide a new method for an NK query on probabilistic XML data. We start by describing the probability for query, and then introduce the method of an NK query on probabilistic XML data. If we want to capture the NK results on probabilistic XML data, we cannot use existing method on probabilistic XML data, because of the differences between XML data and probabilistic XML data. A wise choice is to retrieve NK-P results by using Dewey code and nodes' probabilities without generating any possible worlds. Next, we will introduce our method.

3.1   NK Semantics on Probabilistic XML Data

In this section, we define NK semantics on probabilistic XML data and compute the results of NK-P with its probability.

We use $lca(u, v)$ to denote the Lowest Common Ancestor of nodes u, v in T(e.g., $lca(q, k_2)$ is node 0.1I.0.0M in Figure 1(b)). We can see that for an NK query, lca node is contained in the path from q to k. Next, we introduce several definitions for NK semantics on probabilistic XML data.

Definition 1: (*P*-distance) *Given a node q in a probabilistic XML tree T_P and a keyword k, the p-distance between q and k is the distance in a possible world which contains q and k. (if q and k are not exist in a possible world at the same time, the p-distance is 0)*

In probabilistic XML data, it will have ordinary nodes and distributional nodes in the path from one node to another node. If the computation of the distance includes types of distributional nodes, IND node and MUX node, it will cause trouble. Distributional nodes are not existing in deterministic XML data, namely, in a possible world, there are not distributional nodes. So, there are three situations is shown as the following: (1) If LCA node of node v_1 and v_2 is a MUX node, set p-distance to 0, because these two nodes can not exist in a possible world at same time. There has not a path from node v_1 to v_2 in any possible worlds. (2) If LCA node is an IND node, we can think of it as an ordinary node. LCA node is an IND node seems that these two nodes could exist in a possible world. (3) If it contains distributional nodes on the path from LCA to leaf node, delete this distributional node and the edge from the distributional node to its child node.

Figure 3 shows an example of P-distance. The path from node 1 to node q has an IND node and a MUX node. The distance cannot consider the edge from the distributional node to its child node, the distance from node 1 to node q is 2.

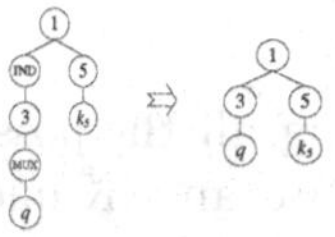

Fig. 3. Example of P-distance

Definition 2: (NK on Probabilistic XML Data). *Given a node q in a probabilistic XML tree T_P and a keyword k, an NK-P query finds the nearest k-neighbor of q, namely, the node having the minimum P-distance to q in T_P.*

The first step of an NK-P query is to find all the minimum P-distance nodes. To find NK-P results, we firstly must ensure that q exists in any possible worlds. Any possible worlds which contains q are the dataset we need. Next, an NK-P query finds NK nodes in the dataset we discussed above. This method is a naive algorithm with too high a cost. We propose a new method to query NK on probabilistic XML data. The specific method is shown in next section.

3.2 NK-P Probability

Given a p-document T_P, a query node q and a keyword k, we define NK-P on T_P as a set of node and probability pair $(v, Pr^G_{NK-P}(k))$. Each node v is a LCA node of q and k in at least one possible world generated by T_P. The probability $Pr^G_{NK-P}(v)$ is the aggregated probability of all possible worlds that have the minimum edges between q and k and node v as their LCA node. The formal definition of $Pr^G_{NK-P}(k)$ is as the following:

$$Pr_{NK-P}(k) = \sum_{i=1}^{m} \{Pr(w_i) \mid NK(k, w_i) = true\}$$

where $NK(k, w_i) = true$ indicates that k is an NK result on the possible world w_i. $Pr(w_i)$ is the existence probability of the possible world w_i. $Pr^G_{NK-P}(k)$ can also be computed as follows:

$$Pr_{NK-P}(k) = Pr(path_{r \to v}) \times Pr(path_{v \to q}) \times Pr(path_{v \to k})$$

where $v = lca(q, k)$.

$$Pr_{NK-P}(k) = Pr(path_{r \to q}) \times Pr(path_{v \to k})$$

We can compute the probability of q and k on probabilistic XML data by above formula. From the above discussion, we know that if we want to compute the probability of an NK result, we must find LCA node of q and k first. In the next section, we mainly focus on how to find out NK-P results.

3.3   NK-P Results

The native algorithm is generating all the possible worlds from a probabilistic XML document. Next, we compute an NK query on each possible world, and the results in all the possible worlds are the results of an NK-P query. But, the native algorithm is not only complex, but also waste times. So, this section illustrates the NK-P search algorithm from q and k, rather than generating any possible worlds.

Under ensuring q exists, the key of an NK-P query is to find suitable keyword nodes that have the minimum P-distance to q. So, d_P and probability are two important factors in our method. Because the result of NK-P has the minimum P-distance, ranking all the d_P is necessary.

q	0.1I.0.0M.0	k_1	0.1I.0.0M.1I.1	0.1I.0.0M	0	0	0
		k_2	0.1I.0.0M.2	0.1I.0.0M	0	0	0
		k_3	0.1I.1	0.1I	2	1	3
		k_4	0.2.0M.1	0	2	2	4
		k_5	0.2.1	0	2	2	4

q	0.1I.0.0M.0	0.9	0.6	k_3	0.1I.1	0.7
				k_4	0.2.0M.1	0.5
				k_5	0.2.1	1

Fig. 4. q and k with P-distance

Our method scans all the keyword inverted lists once. It progressively reads keyword match nodes one by one according to their order from the inverted lists, and compute d_P between q and k. Next, we rank d_P from small to big according to their value in all the keywords lists. The principle is that, when computing the probability of an NK query result, it has retrieved q and k that are descendants of LCA node from all the keyword lists. In another word, the NK probability is determined after the probabilities of q and k have been determined.

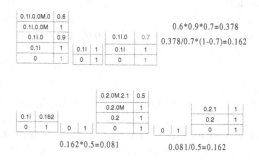

Fig. 5. Stack status on NK-P search

In Figure 1(b), for giving a query q and a keyword k, we can find the node q with Dewey code 0.1I.0.0M.0, and keyword nodes k_1 with Dewey code 0.1I.0.0M.1I.1, k_2 with code 0.1I.0.0M.2, k_3 with code 0.1I.1, k_4 with code 0.2.0M.1 and k_5 with code 0.2.1. The first step is to compute their LCA node, and the P-distance of them. For example, the LCA node of node 0.1I.0.0M.0 and node 0.1I.0.0M.1I.1 is node 0.1I.0.0M that is a MUX node, because this situation is not exist, the Pdistance is 0. The node 0.1I.0.0M.2 has the situation as same as node k_1. Next, the LCA node of node 0.1I.0.0M.0 and node 0.1I.1 is node 0.1I that is an IND node, the P-distance of 0.1I.0.0M.0 and 0.1I is 2 and the P-distance of 0.1I.1 and 0.1I is 1. So, the P-distance from node 0.1I.0.0M.0 to node 0.1I.1 is $2 + 1 = 3$. Node k_4 and k_5 have an ordinary node as their LCA node, the situation is similar to node k_3. The distance is 4.

In addition, we need store the exist probability of the node. If father node is an ordinary node, the probability from it to its children nodes is 1. So, the exist probability of node q should only need storage 0.9 (from 0.1I to 0.1I.0) and 0.6 (from 0.1I.0.0M to 0.1I.0.0M.0).

According to the P-distance, we first select the smallest distance (distance=3) to compute the probability in Figure 4. When distance $=3$, the node 0.1I.1 is the only one node in this distance. Push the node 0.1I.0.0M.0 into stack with the exist probability of node 0.1I.0.0M.0, and push out the probability 0.6 and 0.9 without the LCA node 0.1I. When the node 0.1I.1 is pushed, the probability 0.7 is pushed out, and the probability of NK-P with node 0.1I.1 is $0.6*0.9*0.7 = 0.378$. When we compute distance 4, we need set the exist probability of node 0.1I as $1 - 0.7 = 0.3$(ensure that when distance is 4, the probability do not contain 0.1I.1), and the probability of node 0.1I is set to $(0.378/0.7) * (1 - 0.3) = 0.162$. As pushing the node 0.2.0M.1 into the stack, the NK-P probability of 0.2.0M.1 is $0.162*0.5 = 0.081$. Node 0.2.1 the same with the probability of 0.081. Because node 0.2.1 is existing in all the possible worlds, we need not compute others. In other words, if node v is existing as long as q exists, other keyword match nodes u need not be computed when its d_P satisfy $d_P(v) < d_P(u)$.

q	0	{1I,(0.9)}	0	{0M,(0.6)}	0		{2,0.54}
k_1	0	{1I,(0.9)}	0	{0M,(0.1)}	{1I,(0.6)}	1	{0,(0.6,0.04)}
k_2	0	{1I,(0.9)}	0	{0M,(0.1)}	2		{0,(0.1,0.9)}
k_3	0	{1I,(0.7)}	1				{1,(0.7,0.3)}
k_4	0	2	{0M,(0.5)}	1			{2,(0.5,0.5)}
k_5	0	2	1				{2,(1,0)}

Fig. 6. Probabilities with Dewey code and P-distance of q and k

To compute the d_P between q and k, we should first find out the LCA node between them. $d_P(q \rightarrow k)$ is the sum of two parts, and it is shown as the following:

$$d_P(q \rightarrow k) = d_P(v \rightarrow q) + d_P(v \rightarrow k)$$

Above equation can also be expressed as follows:

$$d_P(q \rightarrow k) = d_P(r \rightarrow q) + d_P(v \rightarrow k) - d_P(r \rightarrow v)$$

where $v = lca(q, k)$. Because $d_P(r \rightarrow q)$ is a constant value, we only need compare the value of $d_P(v \rightarrow k) - d_P(r \rightarrow v)$ between keywords.

In Figure 6, 2 is the d_P between r and q, and 0.54 is the exist probability of q in the first line. For other keyword nodes, the probabilities has two values, and they are the probability from LCA node to keyword node v, another is the probability satisfy that keyword node v do not exist. This probability is used to computer other keyword nodes that whose d_P is more than $v's$. For keyword nodes, the d_P is the value on the path from LCA node to k. So, when computing $d_P = 3$, we only need compute $0.54 * 0.7 = 0.378$. When we compute $d_P = 4$, we need first compute the situation that node k_3 do not exist, that is $0.54 * 0.3 = 0.162$. Next, to compute probability based on 0.162. For node k_4, the probability is $0.162 * 0.5 = 0.081$.

4   Experiments

In this section, the data of an NK-P search on XML data is shown in Table 1. All the algorithms are carried out in a Pentium 4, 2.53 GHZ CPU. We use two datasets, DBLP and XMark.

Table 1. NK-P search for each dataset

Dataset	query	keyword	Dataset	query	keyword
XMARK 1	United States	Gredit	XMARK 2	United States	ship
XMARK 3	ship, Credit	Alexas	XMARK 4	United States	Gredit
DBLP 1	XML	Keyword	DBLP 2	Keyword	Query
DBLP 3	XML	probabilistic	DBLP 4	Keyword	XML

For each XML dataset used, we generate the corresponding probabilistic XML tree, using the same method as used in [4]. This paper controlled the percentage of distributional nodes which is less than 25%. The size of nodes is shown in Table 2.

Table 2. properties of probabilistic XML data

ID	name	size	Ordinary	IND	MUX	ID	name	size	Ordinary	IND	MUX
DOC 1	XMARK 1	10M	170,369	15,740	16,332	DOC 2	XMARK 2	20M	364,285	40,357	37,229
DOC 3	XMARK 3	40M	690,381	75,280	60,771	DOC 4	XMARK 4	80M	1,501,443	160,339	161,553
DOC 5	DBLP 1	20M	358,470	69,553	71,820	DOC 6	DBLP 2	40M	731,001	239,770	227,349
DOC 7	DBLP 3	80M	1,479,230	443,281	403,378	DOC 8	DBLP 4	160M	3,258,890	790,569	770,329

Figure 7 shows the experimental results when we run the queries over Doc 1 to Doc 8. From the results, we can see that compared with possible worlds, the algorithm of NK-P can improve the time efficiency.

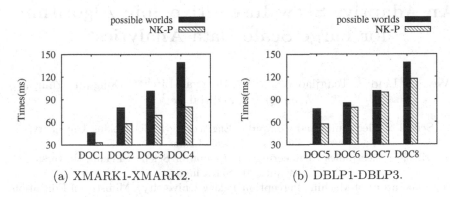

(a) XMARK1-XMARK2.   (b) DBLP1-DBLP3.

Fig. 7. Possible worlds and NK-P

5   Conclusion

[6] is the first work to study keyword search on probabilistic XML data. [5] study NK search on XML data. This paper firstly study on NK search on probabilistic XML data. To our knowledge, this is the first paper studies the NK-P search. This paper presents an indexing algorithm that answers NK-P search efficiently. The experiment shows that our approach performs with higher efficiency.

This paper was supported by the NSFC (Grant No.61025007, 61328202 and 61100024), National Basic Research Program of China (973, Grant No.2011CB302200-G), National High Technology Research and Development 863 Program of China (Grant No.2012AA011004), and the Fundamental Research Funds for the Central Universities (Grant No. N130504006).

References

1. Nierman, A., Jagadish, H.V.: ProTDB: Probabilistic data in xml. In: Proc. of VLDB, pp. 646–657 (2002)
2. Xu, Y., Papakonstantinou, Y.: Efficient Keyword Search for Smallest LCAs in XML Databases. In: Proc. of SIGMOD, pp. 537–538 (2005)
3. Guo, L., Shao, F., Botev, C., Shanmugasundaram, J.: XRANK: Ranked Keyword Search over XML Documents. In: Proc. of SIGMOD, pp. 16–27 (2003)
4. Kimelfeld, B., Kosharovsky, Y., Sagiv, Y.: Query efficiency in probabilistic xml models. In: Proc. of SIGMOD, pp. 701–714 (2008)
5. Tao, Y., Papadopoulos, S., Sheng, C., Stefanidis, K.: Nearest Keyword Search in XML Documents. In: Proc. of SIGMOD (2011)
6. Li, J., Liu, C., Zhou, R., Wang, W.: Top-k Keyword Search over Probabilistic XML Data. In: Proc. of ICDE (2011)

An Adaptive Skew Insensitive Join Algorithm for Large Scale Data Analytics*

Wenjing Liao[1,4], Tengjiao Wang[1,2,4], Hongyan Li[2,3,**], Dongqing Yang[2],
Zhen Qiu[2,3], and Kai Lei[1]

[1] School of Electronics and Computer Engineering(ECE), Peking University,
Shenzhen, 518055, China
[2] School of Electronics Engineering and Computer Science, Peking University,
Beijing, 100871, China
[3] Key Laboratory of Machine Perception(Peking University), Ministry of Education,
Beijing, 100871, China
[4] Key Laboratory of High Confidence Software Technologies(Peking University),
Ministry of Education, Beijing, 100871, China
liaowenjing@sz.pku.edu.cn, {tjwang,dqyang}@pku.edu.cn,
lihy@cis.pku.edu.cn

Abstract. With data explosion in recent years, timely and cost-effective
analytics over large scale data has been a hotspot of data management
research. Join is an important operation in database query. However,
data skew happens naturally in many applications, which will severely
degrade the performance of most join algorithms. To address this problem, this paper introduces an Adaptive Skew Insensitive(ASI) join algorithm to handle with serious data skew. Based on our cost analysis, ASI
join algorithm can adaptively choose the best join algorithm for different inputs. Compared with several state-of-the-art join methods through
adequate experiments, our method achieves significant improvement of
join efficiency dealing with data skew.

Keywords: large-scale, data analytics, join, skew, adaptive.

1 Introduction

With data explosion in recent years, timely and cost-effective analytics over large
scale data has been a hotspot of data management research [1]. Join operation is
essential for many data analysis. For example, in log analytic processing, to get
some useful statistics, an equal join is necessary between log table and reference
tables [2].

However, data skew happens in many practical applications. The well-known
2/8 law demonstrates this phenomenon [3]. On the internet, 20% webpages bring

* This work was supported by Natural Science Foundation of China (No.60973002 and
No.61170003), the National High Technology Research and Development Program
of China (Grant No. 2012AA011002), and MOE-CMCC Research Fund.
** Corresponding author.

L. Chen et al. (Eds.): APWeb 2014, LNCS 8709, pp. 494–502, 2014.

80% of the page view. Data skew will cause load imbalance and degrade system performance. The well-known hash join is vulnerable to data skew [4]. This paper propose a skew insensitive join algorithm for large-scale data analytics.

Traditional parallel RDBMS can hardly handle massive data [5]. Since first introduction [6], the MapReduce framework has become extremely popular due to its simplicity, shielding parallelization details and fault tolerance. Hadoop, the open-source version of MapReduce is a Magnetism, Agility, Depth(MAD) system [7] popular for big data analytics.

Hadoop provides map-side join and reduce-side join [2]. Map-side join, known as broadcast join in parallel RDBMS, only works when one table is small enough to fit in memory. Reduce-side join [8] works well in most situations, but it's vulnerable to data skew and has high network transmission cost in shuffle phase.

There are two difficulties to solve data skew in joins. One is how to avoid load imbalance. Even range partitioning based join algorithms are difficult to guarantee load balance between reducers. The other is how to dynamically choose the best algorithm since sometimes users are not aware of data skew.

This paper proposes Adaptive Skew Insensitive(ASI) join to dynamically handle data skew in large scale data analytics. ASI join won't cause any hot nodes. Based on the cost analysis, ASI join dynamically chooses the best algorithm for different inputs. ASI join works well on current MapReduce framework. Experiments compare the performance of state-of-the-art join algorithms. The results show that ASI join outperforms them in terms of data skewness and execution time.

The rest of the paper is organized as follows. Section 2 discusses related work. Section 3 describes ASI join geography and cost model. Section 4 shows representative experimental results. Section 5 concludes the paper.

2   Related Work

In traditional parallel RDBMS, there has been in-depth research on skew resistant join [9]. However, join is not so well dealt with by MapReduce. Efficiently handling join operations has become a hotspot research. Existing work on MapReduce can be grouped into two categories: (1)Runtime monitoring algorithms, (2)Range partition based algorithms.

MapReduce handles skew using speculative execution [6]. This approach doesn't handle data skew in joins, since the large tasks are not broken up.Some work adopt a runtime monitoring method [10]. Users can set a threshold of maximal data a reducer can process. Once a reducer receives more than the threshold, new arriving data will be processed by a new reducer. Unlike them, our method has much lower network communication cost.

To address data skew, some join algorithms use range partitioning instead of hash partitioning to shuffle data from map to reduce phase [9][11][12]. The goal is to eliminate hot reducers. This method can be very time-consuming due to the prodigious network communication cost during shuffle phase. The performance greatly depends on the result of sampling and range partitioning, which can't always guarantee that records of both inputs are evenly partitioned.

3   Adaptive Skew Insensitive(ASI) Join

Considering an equi-join $L \bowtie_{L.k=R.k} R$, the intuition behind this skew insensitive join algorithm is to deal with the skewed records and non-skewed records differently. In this chapter we first state the problem, then illustrate the geography of ASI join, and propose cost analysis and dynamic execution process.

3.1   Problem Statement

Considering an equi-join $L \bowtie R$ using MapReduce, L and R are too large to fit into memory, so only reduce-side join can be used. If L and R are highly skewed, there will be hot reducers or even out of memory errors. The left of Fig.1 is an example of reduce-side join. DataNode 1-3 represent the data distribution, value a is a popular key in L, and b is a popular key in R. Reduce 1-3 show the workload using hash partition $(h(k) = k \bmod 3 + 1)$. Reducer 2 and 3 become hot nodes and slow down the whole job.

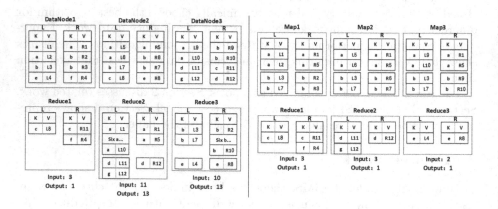

Fig. 1. The nodes' load using reduce-side join and ASI join

3.2   ASI Join Description

Assume that skew in join datasets is detected and the skewed value sets of L and R, represented as S_L and S_R are obtained by sampling, then ASI join will perform map-side join for skewed records and reduce-side join for non-skewed records. The specific approach is described as following: on each mapper we split each of our inputs L^i and R^i into six sets, marked as L^i_{loc}, L^i_{rep}, L^i_{hash}, R^i_{loc}, R^i_{rep}, R^i_{hash}. The basic idea of ASI join plan is illustrated in Fig.2.

L^i_{loc} contains every record of L^i with join value in S_L and is kept locally. R^i_{rep} contains the every record of R^i for any value in S_L. Similarly, R^i_{loc} contains every record of R^i with join value in S_R. L^i_{rep} contains corresponding record of L^i. R^i_{rep} and L^i_{rep} are broadcast to all nodes to join with L^i_{loc} and R^i_{loc} in map phase. L^i_{hash} and R^i_{hash} contain the rest records and are hash partitioned to reducers to be joined.

The right of Fig.1 shows the workload using ASI join under the same data distribution. Records with skewed values are joined in mappers, which greatly reduce the network communication cost between mappers and reducers. Non-skewed records are hash partitioned to reducers and joined there. Apparently there is no hot node and the whole system is more load-balancing.

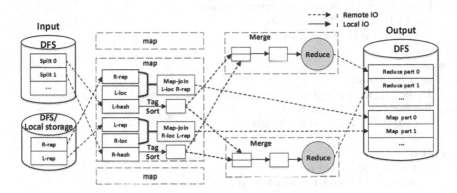

Fig. 2. ASI join: map join for skewed records and reduce join for non-skewed records

When a popular value v appears in both S_L and S_R, we can't broadcast them in both relations. To deal with overlapping skewed values, ASI join plan chooses to include v in only one of S_L and S_R. When the number of skewed records of L times the record size of L is larger than that of R, v will be included in S_L so that the larger skewed records of L are kept locally.

When only L is skewed, S_R is an empty set. L^i and R^i will be split into four sets accordingly: L^i_{loc}, L^i_{hash}, R^i_{rep}, R^i_{hash}. R^i_{rep} is broadcast to join with L^i_{loc}, while reduce-side join is applied to L^i_{hash} and R^i_{hash}. If R_{rep} is too large to fit in memory, it will be read into memory several times. Algorithm 1 is the pseudo code of Skew Insensitive join.

3.3 Cost Analysis

Generally, the CPU cost of join operation is spent on simple comparison, thus, system I/O and network cost dominate the total execution time. Therefore, we build a model based on the analysis of I/O and network cost.

MapReduce framework involves three stages. C_{map}, $C_{shuffle}$ and C_{reduce} represent the time cost of map, shuffle and reduce. The number of reducers is r; the number of nodes is n; x is the percentage of skewed records in L; y is the percentage of matching records in R; $|L|$ and $|R|$ represent the size of L and R. The comparison of map join, reduce join and ASI join is listed in table 1. Sampling time will be explained in experiments.

Algorithm 1. Skew Insensitive Join

1: **Input:**L and R, skewed value sets S_L and S_R
2: Split inputs into six sets:L_{loc},L_{rep},L_{hash},R_{loc},R_{rep},R_{hash}
3: **if** L_{rep} or R_{rep} not exist in local storage **then**
4:     Remotely retrieve L_{rep}, R_{rep} from Distributed Cache
5:     Build HashTable H_L and H_R respectively from L_{rep} and R_{rep}
6: **end if**
7: **Map**(K: null, V: a record from a split of either L or R)
8: **if** v in L_{loc} **then**
9:     Probe H_R with the join key extracted from v
10:     **for** each match r from H_R **do**
11:         Output($null, new\_record(r, v)$)
12:     **end for**
13: **end if**
14: **if** v in R_{loc} **then**
15:     Probe H_L with the join key extracted from v
16:     **for** each match l from H_L **do**
17:         Output($null, new\_record(l, v)$)
18:     **end for**
19: **end if**
20: **if** v in L_{hash},R_{hash} **then**
21:     $join\_key \leftarrow$ Extract the join key from v
22:     $tagged\_record \leftarrow$ Add a tag of either L_{hash} or R_{hash} to v
23:     Output($join\_key, tagged\_record$)
24: **end if**
25: **Reduce**(K': a join key, $list\_r$: records from L_hash and R_hash with join key K')
26: Create buffers B_L and B_R for L_{hash} and R_{hash} respectively
27: **for** each record t in $list\_r$ **do**
28:     Append r to one of the buffers according to its tag
29: **end for**
30: JoinResult = JoinAlgorithm(B_L, B_R)
31: **return** JoinResult

Based on the analysis above, we have a dynamic execution process. If relation L or R is small enough to fit in memory, map join task will be executed. Otherwise, ASI join will sample both inputs to detect data skew. If data skew is detected in one or both relations, Skew Insensitive join will be used to eliminate load imbalance. Reduce-side join will be chosen when join key is uniformly distributed.

Table 1. Cost comparison between map-side join, reduce-side join and ASI join

Algorithms	$Cost_{map}$	$Cost_{shuffle}$	$Cost_{reduce}$
Map-side join	$\lvert L\rvert + n\lvert R\rvert$	0	0
Reduce-side join	$\lvert L\rvert + \lvert R\rvert$	$\lvert L\rvert + \lvert R\rvert$	$x\lvert L\rvert + \frac{(1-x)\lvert L\rvert+\lvert R\rvert}{r}$
ASI join	$\lvert L\rvert + \lvert R\rvert + ny\lvert R\rvert$	$(1-x)\lvert L\rvert + (1-y)\lvert R\rvert$	$\frac{(1-x)\lvert L\rvert+(1-y)\lvert R\rvert}{r}$

4   Experiments

4.1   Testbed and Datasets

All our experiments were run on a 24-nodes cluster. Each node has six Intel(R) Xeon(R) CPU E5645 2.40GHz processors with 16GB of DRAM(SDRAM) and one 500GB SATA disk. The nodes are connected to an HP ProCurve 2650 at a network bandwidth of 100BaseTx-FD. On each node Ubuntu 12.04 LTS, Hadoop 0.20.2, and Java 1.6 are installed. The block size is the default 64MB. The heap memory size is increased to 1024MB. The TPC-H benchmark [13] and following query are used in our experiments:

select * from Customer C, Supplier S where C.Nationkey = S.Nationkey.

There are only 25 unique uniform Nationkey in TPC-H. We increased unique Nationkey to 20000 to highlight skew experiments. To control skewness we randomly choose a portion of data and change Nationkey to one value. In this way it's easy to understand exactly what experiment is being performed and captures the essence of ZipFian distribution [9]. The following SQL will make the skewness of Customer 10%:

update Customer C set C.Nationkey = 1 where random(1,100) ≤ 10.

We respectively generate 1G, 10G, 100G records of CUSTOMER and SUPPLIER and vary the skewness in one or both relations. We compare the performance of Reduce-Side join(RSJ), Hive's skew join(HSJ), Pig's skew join(PSJ) and our ASI join.

4.2   Experimental Results

We first carry out an experiment to show the limitation of map-side join. Fig.3(a) shows the join time is infinite when the small relation gets 100M, which is because the nodes run out of memory while building an in-memory hash table for small relation. So we don't consider map join in experimentation.

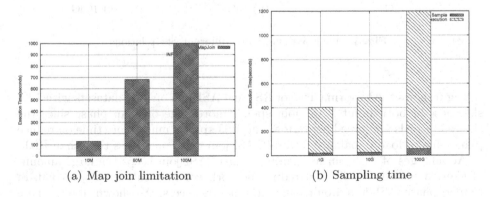

(a) Map join limitation   (b) Sampling time

Fig. 3. Map join limitation and sampling time

We also conduct an experiment to split the sampling time from the whole ASI join time. Fig.3(b) shows the ASI join time when joining two 1G, 10G, 100G datasets with 10% skewness. From which we can see that sampling time only accounts for about five percent of the whole execution time.

We now present the performance comparison of the four algorithms dealing with datasets of different size and skewness. Fig.4 shows the time cost by joining two 1G, 10G, 100G datasets with CUSTOMER having varying skewness. When there is no skew, ASI join takes extra sampling time so reduce-side join is faster. When the skewness increases, the execution time of reduce-side join grows almost linearly because all skewed records are partitioned to one reducer while the execution time of ASI join nearly stays the same. Reduce-side join will run out of memory when the skewness exceeds 10% in Fig.4(b). ASI join can handle more severe skew, so is HSJ and PSJ.

Fig.5 shows the execution time joining with both datasets having varying skewness. ASI join and reduce-side join show the same performance relationship, while PSJ performs worse than Fig.4, which is because Pig's skew join only sample the left input, thus it doesn't handle very well when both inputs are skewed. Hive has optimized the performance by reducing the number of MapReduce jobs and only requires one job while Pig's skewed join is implemented by three jobs, thus Hive has better performance than Pig. Joining 100G relations, PSJ and RSJ will fail when the skewness of both inputs are 5%, so there are only two starting points represent PSJ and RSJ. The performance of ASI join is not affected very much by larger datasets.

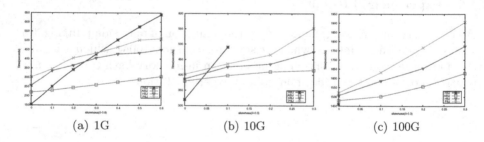

(a) 1G   (b) 10G   (c) 100G

Fig. 4. One input skewed on different size relations

Fig.6 shows the task timelines of RSJ and ASI join on 10G datasets with 10% skewness in both inputs. ASI join spends more time on map phase since the skewed records are joined here. However, RSJ spends much more time on reduce phase due to load imbalance. Overall, ASI join costs much less time than RSJ.

Advantages of ASI join lie mainly in: first, ASI join keeps the large amount of skewed records locally and reduce network communication cost; second, in reduce phase ASI join won't cause any hot reducers. As shown above, these advantages become more obvious as the size and skewness of datasets increase.

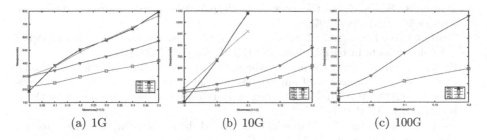

(a) 1G   (b) 10G   (c) 100G

Fig. 5. Two inputs skewed on different size relations

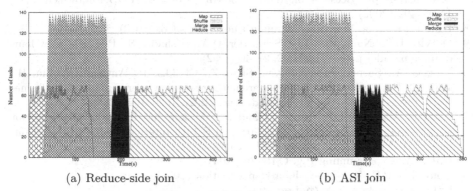

(a) Reduce-side join   (b) ASI join

Fig. 6. 10G Task timelines

5 Conclusion

This paper proposes ASI join algorithm to dynamically handle data skew for large-scale data analytics. We keep the skewed records local and hash join the non-skewed records, which can be applied to any platform to handle skew join. Then we give the cost analysis, based on which ASI join can dynamically chooses the best algorithm for different inputs. ASI join works well on the current MapReduce framework and is of great reference to other high level query languages. Extensive experiment results have proved that ASI join is much more efficient at handling skewed data than state-of-the-art methods.

References

1. Manyika, J., Chui, M., Brown, B., Bughin, J., Dobbs, R., Roxburgh, C., Byers, A.H.: Big data: The next frontier for innovation, competition, and productivity (2011)
2. Blanas, S., Patel, J.M., Ercegovac, V., Rao, J., Shekita, E.J., Tian, Y.: A comparison of join algorithms for log processing in mapreduce. In: Proceedings of the 2010 ACM SIGMOD International Conference on Management of Data, pp. 975–986. ACM (2010)

3. Wilson, R.: Social choice theory without the pareto principle. Journal of Economic Theory 5(3), 478–486 (1972)
4. Walton, C.B., Dale, A.G., Jenevein, R.M.: A taxonomy and performance model of data skew effects in parallel joins. VLDB 91, 537–548 (1991)
5. Pavlo, A., Paulson, E., Rasin, A., Abadi, D.J., DeWitt, D.J., Madden, S., Stonebraker, M.: A comparison of approaches to large-scale data analysis. In: Proceedings of the 2009 ACM SIGMOD International Conference on Management of Data, pp. 165–178. ACM (2009)
6. Dean, J., Ghemawat, S.: Mapreduce: simplified data processing on large clusters. Communications of the ACM 51(1), 107–113 (2008)
7. Cohen, J., Dolan, B., Dunlap, M., Hellerstein, J.M., Welton, C.: Mad skills: new analysis practices for big data. Proceedings of the VLDB Endowment 2(2), 1481–1492 (2009)
8. Lam, C.: Hadoop in action. Manning Publications Co. (2010)
9. DeWitt, D.J., Naughton, J.F., Schneider, D.A., Seshadri, S.: Practical skew handling in parallel joins. VLDB 92, 27–40 (1992)
10. Thusoo, A., Sarma, J.S., Jain, N., Shao, Z., Chakka, P., Anthony, S., Liu, H., Wyckoff, P., Murthy, R.: Hive: a warehousing solution over a map-reduce framework. Proceedings of the VLDB Endowment 2(2), 1626–1629 (2009)
11. Atta, F., Viglas, S.D., Niazi, S.: Sand join–A skew handling join algorithm for google's mapreduce framework. In: 2011 IEEE 14th International Multitopic Conference (INMIC), pp. 170–175. IEEE (2011)
12. Gates, A.: Programming Pig. O'Reilly (2011)
13. Council, T.P.P.: Tpc-h benchmark specification (2008), http://www.tcp.org/hspec.html

A LDA-Based Algorithm for Length-Aware Text Clustering

Xinhuan Chen, Yong Zhang, Yanshen Yin, Chao Li, and Chunxiao Xing

Research Institute of Information Technology,
Tsinghua National Laboratory for Information Science and Technology,
Department of Computer Science and Technology, Tsinghua University, Beijing 100084, China
{xh-chen13,yys12}@mails.tsinghua.edu.cn,
{zhangyong05,li-chao,xingcx}@tsinghua.edu.cn

Abstract. The proliferation of texts in Web presents great challenges on knowledge discovery in text collections. Clustering provides us with a powerful tool to organize the information and recognize the structure of the information. Most text clustering techniques are designed to deal with either long or short texts. However many real-life collections are often made up of both long and short texts, namely mixed length texts. The current text clustering techniques are unsatisfactory, for they don't distinguish the sparseness and high dimension of the mixed length texts. In this paper, we propose a novel approach – *Length-Aware Dual Latent Dirichlet Allocation (ADLDA)*, which is used for clustering the mixed length texts via obtaining auxiliary knowledge from long (short) texts for short (long) texts in the collections. The degree of mutual auxiliary is based on the ratio of long texts and short texts in a corpus. Experimental results on real datasets show our approach achieves superior performance over other state-of-the-art text clustering approaches for mixed length texts.

Keywords: text clustering, topic model, K-means, unsupervised learning.

1 Introduction

The proliferation of texts in Web makes knowledge discovery in text collections become more and more difficult. Clustering has been long recognized as a powerful tool for the task. Text clustering or document clustering has become a hot topic for many years, while text clustering is still faced with several key challenges. Corpora of varying length can contain correlated terms [3], and are high dimensional with respect to words, yet are sparse.

Many successful text clustering techniques [4] have been proposed in the past, but they are designed for and tested on traditional long text corpus such as newswires and blogs. Long texts often span multiple topics and are high dimensional representation. Long texts are by their nature multi-topic and as such the underlying text clustering methods must explicitly focus on modeling and accounting for these topics. Recently, short texts play an important role in various emerging Web applications such as micro-blogging. Short texts do not contain enough terms, it is sparse for text representations. Directly applying the long text clustering methods on short texts often leads to

L. Chen et al. (Eds.): APWeb 2014, LNCS 8709, pp. 503–510, 2014.

poor results [11]. Wang et al. [16] proposed a frequent-term based parallel clustering algorithm specifically designed for short texts.

However, many real datasets are not only composed of long, or short texts, but also texts of mixed length. To the best of our knowledge, little work has been done on texts of mixed length.

Due to the existence of the short texts yet extremely sparse representations, clustering mixed length texts directly bases on the bag of words representation such as TF-IDF can be less than ideal as we would demonstrate in the experiments. On the other hand, if we use some short text clustering algorithms such as MAKM[9] for the mixed length corpus, a lot of long texts information will lost because of dimensionality reduction, which deteriorates the performance of clustering.

In order to deal with clustering of mixed length texts, we present a LDA-based topic model, which can obtain auxiliary knowledge from long (short) texts for short (long) texts in the collections. The process of auxiliary to each other can alleviate the sparseness of the short texts and reduce the dimensions of the long texts in the same collections and thus achieve a balance state between sparseness and dimension. More specifically, the main contributions of this paper include:

- We address the length-aware text clustering. Especially there is rarely specific clustering approach to deal with the mixed length texts in the previous work.
- We propose a novel approach – *Length-Aware Dual Latent Dirichlet Allocation (ADLDA)*, which can adjust the degree of mutual auxiliary based on the length of texts in a corpus. It means that the model can be applied to the length-aware text clustering.
- We have conducted experiments on public datasets. Experimental results show that our algorithm is more robust performance improvement than state-of-the-art text clustering methods.

The rest of the paper is organized as follows: Section 2 reviews related work. Section 3 presents the ADLDA model. Section 4 reports the experimental results. In Section 5, we conclude this paper.

2   Related Work

David el at. [2] did a survey on text clustering, they focused on recent advancements in text clustering separately: long and short texts.

Long texts always discuss multiple topics, this increases the challenge to general purpose text clustering algorithms that try to associate a text with a single topic. A text is made up of smaller topically relevant text blocks, which is the key idea to solve that problem. TextTiling [1] is able to subdivide a text into multi-paragraph, contiguous and disjoint blocks that represent passages, or subtopics. The Segmented Topic Model (STM) [6] extends the LDA model by adding an additional layer in deriving word-topic proportions, modeling the topic structure on a segmented text. Du et al. proposed Sequential LDA (LDSeq) model [7], an extension of STM that addresses the bag of segments text assumption. Clustering long text is not limited to VSM techniques, Ponti et al. [5] described a statistical model for topically segmented documents and provided a clustering strategy for texts modeled this way.

Short text clustering has attracted growing interests in recent years with social networks development. Because of its simplicity and efficiency, the K-means algorithm is accepted and widely used in many different applications. Ma et al. [9] proposed an improved K-means algorithm MAKM (MAFIA-based K-means) for short text clustering, in which the optimized initial centers and number k of clusters can be determined. Mihalcea et al. [13] proposed to measure the similarity of short text snippets by using both corpus-based and knowledge-based measures when acquiring words similarity. Somnath et al.[15] proposed a method of improving the accuracy of clustering short texts by enriching their representation with additional features from Wikipedia. Inspired by the idea of using external data sources, Jin et al. [10] trained topic models on the short texts alongside a collection of auxiliary long texts. They proposed Dual LDA (DLDA) algorithm to distinguish between inconsistent topical structures across domains by correlating the simultaneous training of two LDA models.

Our topic model is similar to DLDA, both of them train two LDA models simultaneously. However in our model long texts and short texts are mutual auxiliary on the whole collections, we don't need external datasets. In the other hand, the proposed model can adaptively determine hyper-parameter γ instead setting it manually.

3   Length-Aware Dual Latent Dirichlet Allocation (ADLDA)

To define the problem of length-aware text clustering, we first define some notations. Table 1 reports some main notations used throughout this paper.

Table 1. Main notations

Symbol	Description	Symbol	Description
c	long(l) or short(s) text collections	$\mathcal{W}$	set of mixed length texts
p	corpus partition point	r	ratio of long texts to short texts in a corpus
K^l	number of topics of long texts	K^s	number of topics of short texts
K	total number of topics	γ^c	the Beta prior parameter
α, β	Dirichlet prior parameters	θ, Φ, π	distribution parameters
z	word-topic assignments	x	binary switch
w	observed words	m, n	subscript of text and word
M^c	number of texts in a collection	N^c	number of words in a text

In this section, we develop a novel approach based on topic model to discover some latent auxiliary knowledge that can more effectively capture the semantic relationships between texts. If short and long texts have the same authors, it could be unreasonable to assume that the topical structure of the two domains is mostly consistent, as done in several previous works [10,12,14]. While our long texts is in the same corpus with short texts, not from external data collections, and our goal is to improve the clustering accuracy of mixed length text.

In following sections, we first put forward the ADLDA, which extends the LDA [8] model to deal with length-aware text clustering based on topical knowledge between long and short texts. And then we describe the process of parameters estimation. Finally, we use hidden topics of corpus to do clustering.

3.1   Length-Aware Dual Latent Dirichlet Allocation Model

ADLDA is based on LDA model, it can obtain auxiliary knowledge from long (short) texts for short (long) texts clustering by training two LDA models. Unlike previous work, ADLDA can adaptively adjust the degree of auxiliary based on the radio of long texts to short texts in the corpus. The hyper-parameter γ is used to represent the degree of auxiliary, and different from the parameter specified in advance in the DLDA model [10].

The ADLDA model can restrict that a text is generated using auxiliary and its own topics. We can use a text dependent binary-switch variable [10] for choosing between the two types of topics when generating the text. This mechanism makes the model automatically to capture whether a text should be more related to the auxiliary collection.

The generative process is shown in table 2, and a graphical representation of the ADLDA is shown in Fig. 2.

Table 2. The generation process of ADLDA

— For each long text topic, draw a Dirichlet distribution over words, $\Phi_z^l \sim Dirichlet(\beta)$

— For each short text topic, draw a Dirichlet distribution over words, $\Phi_z^s \sim Dirichlet(\beta)$

— For each collection $c \in \{ long(l), short(s) \}$, each text d in collection c , select a topic from the distribution over topics, $\theta_d^c \sim Dirichlet(\alpha)$, draw a binomial distribution over long text topics versus short text topics, $\pi_d^c \sim Beta(\gamma^c)$

 • For each word w_d^n in text d, draw a binary switch $x_d^n \sim Binomial(\pi_d^c)$, if $x_d^n = long$, select a long text topic $z_d^n \sim Multinomial(\theta_d^l)$, else $x_d^n = short$, select a short text topic $z_d^n \sim Multinomial(\theta_d^s)$

  ○ draw a word $w_d^n \sim Multinomial(\Phi_{z_d^n}^{x_d^n})$

Under the ADLDA model, there is a binomial distribution over long text topics versus short text topics x_d^n with Beta prior γ^c.

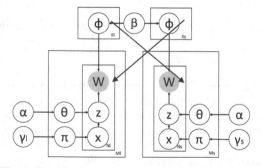

Fig. 1. Graphical representation of the ADLDA model

3.2   Parameters Estimation with Gibbs Sampling

Given the hype-parameters, we can gain the joint distribution of all visible and hidden variables:

$$p(w, z, x, \pi, \theta, \Phi \mid \alpha, \beta, \gamma) =$$
$$p\left(w_{m,n}^c \mid \varphi_{z_{m,n}^x} \right) p\left(z_{m,n} \mid \theta_m \right) p\left(x_{m,n} \mid \pi_m \right) p(\Phi \mid \beta) p(\theta_m \mid \alpha) p(\pi_m \mid \gamma^c) \qquad (1)$$

The probability of a word $w_{m,n}^c$ can be obtained by integrating out π, θ, Φ:

$$p(w \mid \alpha, \beta, \gamma) = \iiint p(\Phi \mid \beta) p(\theta_m \mid \alpha) p(\pi_m \mid \tilde{a}^c) p\left(w_{m,n}^c \mid Ö, è_m, ð_m \right) dÖdè_m dð_m$$

$$(2)$$

Finally, the likelihood of the whole data set is:

$$p(\mathcal{W} \mid á, â, ã) = \prod_{m=1}^{Ml} \prod_{n=1}^{Nl} p(w_{m,n}^l \mid á, â, ã^l) \prod_{m=1}^{Ms} \prod_{n=1}^{Ns} p(w_{m,n}^s \mid á, â, ã^s) \qquad (3)$$

Note that the inference and learning algorithms of the basic LDA model can be easily applied to ADLDA model, because the ADLDA extends the basic model structure and change certain setting of the hyper-parameters. To estimate the latent parameters, we perform approximate inference with Gibbs Sampling, a kind of Markov Chain Monte Carlo (MCMC) algorithm, we can get the following updating rules.

For long text collection topics $z^l \in \{1, \dots, K^l\}$,

$$p(x_i = x, z_i = z^l \mid w_i = w, x_{\neg i}, z_{\neg i}^l, w_{\neg i}, á, â, ã) \propto$$
$$\frac{n_{w,\neg i}^{l,z} + â}{\sum_{n=1}^{N}\left(n_{n,\neg i}^{l,z} + â_n\right)} \frac{n_{d,\neg i}^{l,z} + á}{\sum_{k=1}^{K^l}\left(n_{d,\neg i}^{l,k} + á_k\right)} \left(n_{d,x,\neg i}^l + ã_x^c\right) \qquad (4)$$

For short text collection topics $z^s \in \{1, \dots, K^s\}$,

$$p(x_i = x, z_i = z^s \mid w_i = w, x_{\neg i}, z_{\neg i}^s, w_{\neg i}, á, â, ã) \propto$$
$$\frac{n_{w,\neg i}^{s,z} + â}{\sum_{n=1}^{N}\left(n_{n,\neg i}^{s,z} + â_n\right)} \frac{n_{d,\neg i}^{s,z} + á}{\sum_{k=1}^{K^s}\left(n_{d,\neg i}^{s,k} + á_k\right)} \left(n_{d,x,\neg i}^s + ã_x^c\right) \qquad (5)$$

For a topic z, its probability is calculated as:

$$p(z_i = z^c \mid w_i = w, x_{\neg i}, z_{\neg i}^c, w_{\neg i}, \alpha, \beta, \gamma) = Random[p(x_i = l, z_i^c = z \mid w_i =$$
$$w, x_{\neg i}, z_{\neg i}^c, w_{\neg i}, \alpha, \beta, \gamma), p(x_i = s, z_i^c = z \mid w_i = w, x_{\neg i}, z_{\neg i}^c, w_{\neg i}, \alpha, \beta, \gamma)] \qquad (6)$$

$n_{w,\neg i}^{l,z}$ and $n_{w,\neg i}^{s,z}$ are the numbers of times a term w assigned to a long text topic and short text topic z respectively. $n_{d,\neg i}^{l,z}$ is the number of a word in a document d of long text collection assigned to a topic z, while $n_{d,\neg i}^{s,z}$ is for short text collection, $n_{d,x,\neg i}^l$ and $n_{d,x,\neg i}^s$ denote the numbers of times a word of long text and short text collection assigned to $x \in \{long(l), short(s)\}$ text topics, respectively. Subscript $\neg i$ represents that the i-th word is excluded from the computation. Finally, the probability of a topic z can be obtained by *random* function.

3.3   Clustering Using Hidden Topics

After estimating the model parameters for all texts in the corpus, we normalize the scale of each feature of a text d by $è_d$ as:

$$f_d = \left[\frac{è_{d,1}^l}{\sum_i è_{i,1}^l}, \cdots, \frac{è_{d,K^l}^l}{\sum_i è_{i,K^l}^l}, \frac{è_{d,1}^s}{\sum_i è_{i,1}^s}, \cdots, \frac{è_{d,K^s}^s}{\sum_i è_{i,K^s}^s} \right] \tag{7}$$

This can reduce the importance of some topics that are overly general in most of texts but lack the discriminative power.

Then we apply the traditional clustering methods on the topic based representations for the text collections. We use K-means to cluster the new representation, which achieves better results, as we demonstrate in the experiments.

4   Experimental Results

4.1   Dataset

In order to evaluate the proposed ADLDA, we conducted experiments on two data-sets. Both datasets are from UseNet news articles (20 Newsgroups[1]) with carefully selected by category. The dataset 1 contains the most of long texts, with the matching the dataset 2 contains the most of short texts. The popular micro-blogging services such as Twitter and Sina Microblog restrict the text length to be less than 140 characters, which can be served as the reference of short text length bound. Table 3 shows the distribution of the datasets.

Table 3. The distribution of datasets

	Rec.sport. hockey	Sci. crypt	Sci. med	Soc. religio. chirstian	Short	Long	Radio[2]	Total
Dataset1	999	990	990	1199	1722	2456	41.21%	4178
	Comp. hardware	Rec. autos	Rec. baseball	Sci.space	Short	Long	Radio	Total
Dataset2	961	990	994	987	2747	1185	69.86%	3932

4.2   Comparison Result

In the experiments on the two datasets, we used *precision, recall, F1*[3] value as the evaluation criterion. They have been widely used in the domain of information retrieval.

---

[1] http://people.csail.mit.edu/jrennie/20Newsgroups/
[2] The proportion of short texts in corpus.
  The partition length of two datasets is set as 140 characters.
[3] http://en.wikipedia.org/wiki/F1_score

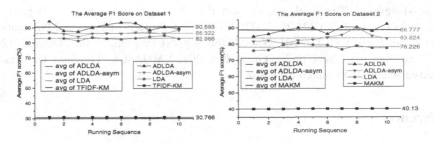

Fig. 2. The average F1 score comparisons in different methods

We compared some standard clustering algorithms with our ADLDA:

- TFIDF-KM, we use K-means with TF-IDF representation as CLUTO [4] do.
- LDA, we learn a LDA from the whole text collection and directly cluster with the θ learned.
- MAKM [9], is a text clustering algorithm for the dataset with the most of short texts.
- ADLDA-asymmetric, we just use long texts to help short texts, the learning process is asymmetrical. It can demonstrate whether mutual auxiliary of the ADLDA has superior performance.

If we only do clustering for short texts of a mixed length text collection and are given parameters in advance, the DLDA becomes a special case of the ADLDA, so we don't choose the DLDA as a baseline. We ran the TFIDF-KM, LDA, ADLDA and ADLDA-asymmetric 10 times on dataset 1, and ran the MAKM, LDA, ADLDA and ADLDA-asymmetric on dataset 2. The number of clustering is set to the actual number of categories in datasets. The results are reported below.

Fig.2. shows the comparisons of average F1 scores among the different methods on two datasets. The larger the F1 score is, the higher the quality of the clustering is.

As expected, our method ADLDA outperformed all the other baseline methods on both datasets. Due to the high dimensionality and sparseness of the representation in a corpus, directly clustering the mixed length texts using the bag of words representation has the poorest performance, which demonstrates the benefit of using topic model to gain low dimensional representation of the text collections. Both variations of the ADLDA model beat the LDA algorithm, for the ADLDA is better than directly clustering. In the other hand, the ADLDA is slightly better than the ADLDA-asymmetric, which shows that mutual auxiliary has superior performance.

5   Conclusion

In this paper, we propose an improved LDA model (ADLDA) for length-aware text clustering. This model splits the texts into two subsets - short text subset and long text subset, then does clustering via obtaining auxiliary knowledge from long (short) texts for short (long) texts in the collections. The ADLDA can adaptively determine hyper-parameter γ instead of setting it manually. The experimental results show that the ADLDA outperforms state-of-the-art long and short text clustering approaches for mixed length texts.

Acknowledgment. This work was supported by National Basic Research Program of China (973 Program) No.2011CB302302, Key S&T Projects of Press and Publication under Grant No GXTC-CZ-1015004/02, the Support Program of the National '12th Five-Year-Plan' of China under Grant No. 2012AA09A408, Tsinghua University Initiative Scientific Research Program.

References

1. Hearst, M.A.: TextTiling: Segmenting text into multi-paragraph subtopic passages. Computational Linguistics 23(1), 33–64 (1997)
2. Tagarelli, A., Karypis, G.: Document Clustering: The Next Frontier. Data Clustering: Algorithms and Applications 305 (2013)
3. Charu, C.A., ChengXiang, Z.: A survey of text clustering algorithms. In: Mining Text Data, pp. 77–128. Springer US (2012)
4. Karypis, G.: CLUTO-a clustering toolkit. Minnesota Univ. Minneapolis Dept. of Computer Science (2002)
5. Ponti, G., Tagarelli, A., Karypis, G.: A statistical model for topically segmented documents. In: Elomaa, T., Hollmén, J., Mannila, H. (eds.) DS 2011. LNCS, vol. 6926, pp. 247–261. Springer, Heidelberg (2011)
6. Du, L., Buntine, W.L., Jin, H.: A segmented topic model based on the two-parameter Poisson-Dirichlet process. Machine Learning 81(1), 5–19 (2010)
7. Du, L., Buntine, W.L., Jin, H.: Sequential latent dirichlet allocation: Discover underlying topic structures within a document. In: ICDM, pp. 148–157. IEEE (2010)
8. Blei, D.M., Ng, A.Y., Jordan, M.I.: Latent dirichlet allocation[J]. The Journal of Machine Learning Research 3, 993–1022 (2003)
9. Ma, P., Zhang, Y.: MAKM: A MAFIA-Based k-Means Algorithm for Short Text in Social Networks. In: Meng, W., Feng, L., Bressan, S., Winiwarter, W., Song, W. (eds.) DASFAA 2013, Part II. LNCS, vol. 7826, pp. 210–218. Springer, Heidelberg (2013)
10. Jin, O., Liu, N.N., Zhao, K., et al.: Transferring topical knowledge from auxiliary long texts for short text clustering. In: Proceedings of the CIKM, pp. 775–784. ACM (2011)
11. Xuan-Hieu, P., Dieu-Thu, L., et al.: Learning to classify short and sparse text & web with hidden topics from large-scale data collections. In: Proceeding of the WWW, pp. 91–100. ACM (2008)
12. Xuan-Hieu, P., Cam-Tu, N., Dieu-Thu, L., et al.: A hidden topic-based framework towards building applications with short web documents. IEEE Transactions on Knowledge and Data Engineering 27 (2010)
13. Mihalcea, R., Corley, C., Strapparava, C.: Corpus-based and knowledge-based measures of text semantic similarity. In: Proceedings of the AAAI, pp. 775–780. AAAI Press (2006)
14. Xue, G.R., Dai, W., Yang, Q., et al.: Topic-bridged PLSA for cross-domain text classification. In: Proceedings of the SIGIR, pp. 627–634. ACM (2008)
15. Banerjee, S., Ramanathan, K., Gupta, A.: Clustering short texts using wikipedia. In: Proceedings of the SIGIR, pp. 787–788. ACM (2007)
16. Wang, Y., Jia, Y., Yang, S.: Short documents clustering in very large text databases. In: Feng, L., Wang, G., Zeng, C., Huang, R. (eds.) WISE 2006 Workshops. LNCS, vol. 4256, pp. 83–93. Springer, Heidelberg (2006)

Semi-supervised Nonnegative Matrix Factorization for Microblog Clustering Based on Term Correlation

Huifang Ma, Meihuizi Jia, YaKai Shi, and Zhanjun Hao

College of Computer Science and Engineering, Northwest Normal University,
Gansu Lanzhou 730070, China
mahuifang@yeah.net

Abstract. Clustering microblogs is very important in many web applications. In this paper, we propose a semi-supervised Nonnegative Matrix Factorization clustering method based on term correlation. The key idea is to explore term correlation data, which well captures the semantic information for term weighting. We then formulate microblog clustering problem as a non-negative matrix factorization using word-level constraints. Empirical study of real-world dataset shows the superior performance of our framework in handling noisy and short microblogs.

Keywords: Semi-supervised Clustering, Microblogs, Term correlation matrix, Nonnegative Matrix Factorization.

1 Introduction

Clustering microblog is of great use for analyzing such up-to-date and tremendous amount of information[1,2]. An intuitive way for clustering microblogs is through Non-negative Matrix Factorization (NMF)[3], which has already been successfully applied to document clustering. However, experiments on short texts, such as microblogs, Q&A documents and news titles, suggest unsatisfactory performance of NMF. One of the possible reasons is that compared with documents, microblogs are in general much shorter, nosier, and sparser. Therefore, clustering such kind of sparse and noisy data can be challenging.

Researchers have presented various ways to aid the clustering process for microblog. Some researchers[4] introduce semi-supervised priors and explore the effects on accuracy of clustering. They try to enrich the representation of a microblog using additional semantics.

In this paper, however, we take advantage of term correlation to enrich the semantics of microblog internally. At first, term similarity based on term-term information is calculated. And then, a non-negative matrix factorization embedded with word-level constraint is performed to obtain clustering results. Experiments performed on microblog dataset demonstrate the superior performance of the proposed method.

The outline of this paper is as follows: Section 2 presents details of our approach. The experiments and results are given in Section 3. We conclude our paper in Section 4.

L. Chen et al. (Eds.): APWeb 2014, LNCS 8709, pp. 511–516, 2014.
© Springer International Publishing Switzerland 2014

2   Our Approach

2.1   Generation of Prior Knowledge

Generally speaking, estimating the relation between terms takes advantage of co-occurrence information, which is based on the assumption that two terms are similar if they frequently co-occur in the same document. A term can then be represented by a term co-occurrence vector, rather than the document vector. Cheng et al. [5] proposed a coupled term-term relation model for document representation, which considers both the intra-relation and inter-relation between a pair of terms.

Likewise, in this paper, we consider both the co-occurrence and dependency of terms to capture the underlying relationship between terms. The co-occurrence of two terms can be quantified by using positive point mutual information (PPMI) while the dependency of terms can be formalized by their interaction with all the link terms.

The weight of co-occurrence between terms t_i and t_j in one document can be defined as:

$$W_{ij} = PPMI(t_i, t_j) = \max(\log \frac{P(t_i, t_j)}{P(t_i)P(t_j)}, 0) \tag{1}$$

Probabilities $P(x)$ and $P(x,y)$ are estimated by counting the number of observations of x and co-occurrence of x and y in a corpus respectively, and normalizing by the size of the corpus

$$P(t_i, t_j) = \frac{n(t_i, t_j)}{\sum_{kl} n(t_k, t_l)}, P(t_i) = \frac{\sum_j n(t_i, t_j)}{\sum_{kl} n(t_k, t_l)} \tag{2}$$

The direct dependency weight between t_i and t_j is referred as $D\text{-}Dep(t_i, t_j)$, where each term is represented by a term co-occurrence vector, We then apply the common vector-similarity measures, like cosine coefficient to compute the $D\text{-}Dep(t_i, tj)$ between any two terms.

The indirect dependency between two terms t_i and t_j by their interaction with the link term t_k can be defined as:

$$I - Dep(t_i, t_j \mid k) = \min(D - Dep(t_i, t_j), D - Dep(t_i, t_j)) \tag{3}$$

We then define the indirect dependency between two terms t_i and t_j by their interaction with all the link terms as:

$$I - Dep(t_i, t_j) = \frac{1}{k} \sum_k Dep(t_i, t_j \mid k) \tag{4}$$

Given a pair of terms t_i and t_j, the co-relation between t_i and t_j can be defined as

$$w(i, j) = \begin{cases} 1 & i = j \\ \alpha * D - Dep(t_i, t_j) + (1 - \alpha) * I - Dep(t_i, t_j) & otherwise \end{cases} \tag{5}$$

When $w(i,j)$ is beyond a certain predefined threshold, these two words are considered to be in the same cluster. Likewise, when it below a predefined threshold, they are considered to be in two different clusters.

Supervision is then provided as two sets of pair-wise constraints of terms. The *must-link* document pairs are encoded as a symmetric matrix A whose diagonal entries all equal to one and the *cannot-link* pairs as another matrix B.

2.2   Algorithm Description

In the proposed model, we perform the corresponding NMF algorithm[6]. Introducing orthogonality constraint leads to rigorous clustering interpretation. The simultaneous row/column clustering can be solved by optimizing

$$J = \min_{F \geq 0, S \geq 0, G \geq 0} \left\| X - FSG^T \right\|_F^2 + Tr(-\beta GAG^T + \gamma GBG^T) \tag{6}$$

The Frobenius norm is often used to measure the error between the original T matrix X and its low rank approximation FSG.

Algorithm 1.   The overall procedure of our approach

Input : *Word-Microblog matrix X, number of word clusters k_1, number of microblog clusters k_2, must-link document pairs A_{ml} and cannot-link document pairs B_{cl}.*

Output : F, S, G.

1. Initialize F, S and G with non-negative values ;

2. Construct *must-link* matrix A and *cannot- link* matrix B;

3. Iterate for each k_1 and k_2 until convergence

$$F_{ik} = F_{ik} \sqrt{\frac{(XGS^T + \beta AF)_{ik}}{(F(SGG^T S^T + \lambda) + \gamma BF)_{ik}}}$$

$$S_{ik} = S_{ik} \sqrt{\frac{(F^T XG)_{ik}}{(F^T FSG^T G)_{ik}}}$$

$$G_{jk} = G_{jk} \sqrt{\frac{(X^T FS)_{jk}}{(GG^T X^T FS)_{jk}}}$$

The correctness and convergence of our algorithm has already been proved [6].

3   Experiments and Results

3.1   Dataset and Performance Metrics

We conducted experiments on the dataset that has been used in [8]. To evaluate the performance of our algorithm, we use three popular measures for clustering [9]: purity, adjusted random index (ARI), and normalized mutual information (NMI).

3.2   Experimental Results

The experiments include two parts: 1) Overall evaluation of our model by comparing with that of other algorithms; 2) Experiments Using Pair-wise Relations.

Experiments Using Prior Knowledge
We denote our method utilizing prior knowledge as TNMF-CP (Tri-Factor Nonnegative Matrix Factorization Clustering with Prior knowledge). Four classical document clustering methods: K-means, Information-Theoretic Co-clustering, which is referred to as IT-Co-clustering[10], Tri-Factor Nonnegative Matrix Factorization (TNMF_E) with the Euclidean distance based cost function and Tri-Factor Nonnegative Matrix Factorization (TNMF_I) denotes the NMF with the generalized I-divergence. All these above methods do not make use of knowledge in the word space. In this experiment, our method takes advantage of different threshold values and we show our result with the best performance with the corresponding threshold.

To give these algorithms some advantage, we set the number of clusters equal to the real number of all the document clusters. Figure 1 shows the experimental results on our dataset using purity, ARI and NMI as the performance measure. All the experimental results are obtained by averaging 20 runs.

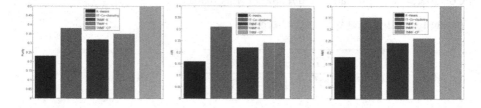

Fig. 1. Purity, ARI, and NMI results on our datasets

Figure 1 shows the experimental comparisons. We can see that our method TNMF-CP can greatly enhance the clustering results by benefitting from the prior knowledge. It achieves the highest performance for all evaluation criteria on the dataset. This means that our model is able to generate significantly better results by quickly learning from these pair-wise constraints.

Effect of Pair-Wise Constraints
In order to illustrate the impact of prior constraints on the performance of clustering, we conduct experiments using different values of parameter α on the experimental

data sets. Figure 2 shows the performance. In this figure, purity, ARI, and NMI scores are used to depict the performance of our proposed approach, varying along with the value of parameter α (from 0.1 to 0.9 with increment 0.1) for each dataset.

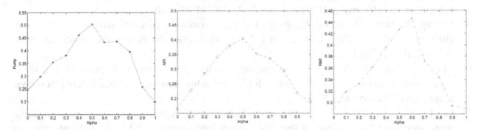

Fig. 2. Purity, ARI, and NMI results with different α for generation of pairwise word relations

Figure 2 illustrates several results. First, the performance of our model is greater than that of either model in isolation, indicating that both the intra and inter relation among words do indeed corroborate each other. Second, the increase in all judging criteria is robust across a wide range of mixing proportions. All these demonstrate that the inter-relation has great impact on the performance of microblog clustering. Besides, we observe that the best performance with the different value of α on different evaluation metrics. Therefore, it's essential to optimize the setting of α when the application requires higher clustering accuracy. In summary, the experimental results match favorably with our hypotheses and encouraged us to further explore the reasons.

4   Conclusions and Future Work

In this paper, we explore the performance of a term correlation based semi-supervised clustering approach for microblog posts. Given the short nature of the posts and no background knowledge source, both intra and inter relations among terms are explored. Therefore, to overcome the challenges of microblogs, semi-supervised priors are introduced into NMF framework. Our evaluations demonstrated the effectiveness of the proposed method for clustering short texts. Nevertheless, microblogs (and possibly other short texts as well) offer several other priors that we have not yet discussed or explored. Future work aims at finding proper ways of adding different priors.

Acknowledgement. This work is supported by the National Natural Science Foundation of China (No., 61363058, 61163039), Research Foundation of Education Department of Gansu Province (No. 2013A-016).

References

1. Lee, C.H.: Mining spatio-temporal information on microblogging streams using a density-based online clustering method. Expert Systems with Applications 39(10), 9623–9641 (2012)
2. Yan, X., Guo, J., Liu, S., et al.: Clustering short text using ncut-weighted non-negative matrix factorization. In: Proceedings of the 21st ACM International Conference on Information and Knowledge Management, pp. 2259–2262. ACM (2012)

3. Lee, D.D., Seung, H.S.: Algorithms for non-negative matrix factorization. In: Advances in Neural Information Processing Systems, pp. 556–562 (2000)
4. Banerjee, S., Ramanathan, K., Gupta, A.: Clustering short texts using wikipedia. In: Proceedings of the 30th Annual International ACM SIGIR Conference on Research and Development in Information Retrieval, pp. 787–788. ACM (2007)
5. Cheng, X., Miao, D., Wang, C., et al.: Coupled term-term relation analysis for document clustering. In: The 2013 International Joint Conference on Neural Networks (IJCNN), pp. 1–8. IEEE (2013)
6. Ma, H., Zhao, W., Shi, Z.: A nonnegative matrix factorization framework for semi-supervised document clustering with dual constraints. Knowledge and Information Systems 36(3), 629–651 (2013)
7. Li, T., Ding, C., Zhang, Y., et al.: Knowledge transformation from word space to document space. In: Proceedings of the 31st Annual International ACM SIGIR Conference on Research and Development in Information Retrieval, pp. 187–194. ACM (2008)
8. Ma, H., Wang, B., Li, N.: A Novel Online Event Analysis Framework for Micro-blog Based on Incremental Topic Modeling. In: 2012 13th ACIS International Conference on Software Engineering, Artificial Intelligence, Networking and Parallel & Distributed Computing (SNPD), pp. 73–76. IEEE (2012)
9. Manning, C.D., Raghavan, P., Schütze, H.: Introduction to information retrieval. Cambridge university press, Cambridge (2008)
10. Dhillon, I.S., Mallela, S., Modha, D.S.: Information-theoretic co-clustering. In: Proceedings of the Ninth ACM SIGKDD International Conference on Knowledge Discovery and Data Mining, pp. 89–98. ACM (2003)

Users' Behavior Session: Integrate Passive Feedback into Microblog Recommendation[*]

Xiao Lu[1,2], Peng Li[3], Shuxin Wang[1,2], and Bin Wang[1]

[1] Institute of Computing Technology, Chinese Academy of Sciences,
Beijing, P.R. China
[2] University of Chinese Academy of Sciences, Beijing, P.R. China
[3] Institute of Information Engineering, Chinese Academy of Sciences,
Beijing, P.R. China
{luxiao,wangbin,wangshuxin}@ict.ac.cn,
lipeng@iie.ac.cn

Abstract. As one of the most popular social networks, microblog has been an important way for people to obtain information, meanwhile, the information overload problem is getting worse, which makes microblog recommendation become very important. Moreover, traditional recommendation methods cannot offer a good solution to this problem for the timeliness of microblog. Many researchers have make contributes to this problem, based on kinds of information, including users' interest, the history of users' behavior, and social relationships. However, most of these methods only use the positive feedbacks in users' behavior and treat these feedbacks independently. We consider that users' behavior should be persistent in a particular time range, which we called the activity session, then we define the passive feedbacks in sessions, and propose various contextual features for the activity session, and integrate these features to microblog recommendation by using both positive and passive feedbacks. Experimental results based on the real data of Sina Weibo show that, compared with the current popular recommendation methods, our method can achieve better performance.

1 Introduction

With the development of social networks, microblog has become one of the most popular Internet applications in recent years, and the information overload problem is getting worse along with the increase of users..

As we know, users' behavior can reflect their preferences. In traditional information retrieval area, users' feedbacks fetched from their browsing behaviors have been treated as useful information to optimize the effectiveness of system. These behaviors contain not only click, but also read, stick. By using browsing model, search engines could judge what users like and what they don't like.

---

[*] This work is supported by the Strategic Priority Research Program of Chinese Academy of Sciences under Grant No. XDA06030200.

L. Chen et al. (Eds.): APWeb 2014, LNCS 8709, pp. 517–524, 2014.

Inspired by this opinion, we assume that in recommendation system, it is necessary to find out not only users' positive feedbacks, but also their passive feedbacks. By comparing these passive feedbacks with positive feedbacks, we can predict users' preferences more accurately. It's difficult to fetch passive feedbacks directly, because users rarely tag what they don't like. However, while in microblog, users' browsing behavior provides the possibility to find out what they don't like – they retweet a small amount of what they've read, so the unretweeted contents could be seemed as passive feedbacks.

The remainder of this paper is organized as follows. In Section 2, we introduce related works. In Section 3, we define the users' behavior session in microblog, and indicate the restricted browsing data which users could receive during each session. Section 4 describe the pair-wise collaborative ranking method, and introduce the inner session features and session contextual features incorporated in our model. We present the detailed experimental results in Section 5 and finally conclude the paper in Section 6.

2   Related Works

Collaborative filtering is one of the most popular techniques for recommendation, and can be categorized to memory-based methods and model-based methods[6]. The users-based[7] and item-based[8] algorithms are common memory-based methods. Different from memory-based methods, model-based methods train the parameters by machine learning, and could relieve the data sparsity problem to a certain extent. The Single Value Decomposition[9] (SVD)   algorithm is one of the most popular models.

With the development of social networks, many social recommendation methods have been investigated. Konstas et al. [10] proposed a random walk model RWR to integrate friendship and social tags. Ma et al. [11] proposed two social regularization methods which constrain the matrix factorization objective function with user social regularization terms. On this basis, Mohsen et al. [12] further proposed SocialMF model, which introduce the propagation of user trust relationship, the feature vector of each user is dependent on the feature vector of his direct neighbors.

However, most of these methods only use the user-item dyads data with explicit user actions while the context dyads are typically treated missing values. Yang et al. [13] describe a similar method to our approach, they take into account the contexts in which user decisions are made, and propose two competitive models to integrate these context. Different from this work, our approach is proposed in microblog senior, in which users' behavior session is not defined, we propose the method to fetch out users' behavior context, and integrate them into feature-based matrix factorization model by distinguishing the positive feedbacks and passive feedbacks.

3   Users' Browsing Behavior in Microblog

3.1   Session Definition

In this paper, we consider users' consistent behaviors in microblog to form a *session*. During one session, users would keep browsing microblogs and do some activities casually, such as posting, commenting or retweeting. However, only these activities could be observed, users' browsing behavior could be seemed as "silent" interaction [1], and for this reason, it's difficult to identify the time point when users leave to stop browsing.

We assume that users' activities should be relatively close in time during the same session, and the users who haven't make any activities for a long time should be considered already left, so we propose *"maximum interval"* to split users' visible activities, and choose 30 minutes to be the threshold, if the interval between two activities exceed this threshold, they should be seem to be in two different sessions.

Assumption: *For microblogs which users have read but choose not to retweet or comment, we assume these microblogs can provide passive feedbacks which are useful to indicate what users don't like.*

It's worth noting that all the positive and passive feedbacks are restricted in independent sessions. To find out the passive feedback microblogs, we need to identify what users have read during each session.

Firstly, we suppose that users wouldn't read duplicate contents which they've examined before. Thus, we consider that contents which users read during current session should not exceed the time point of the last session. And then, because the last activity of current session is sign of users' leaving, so we can generate users' restricted reading range by the end time point of the last session and current session. This method is shown in figure 1:

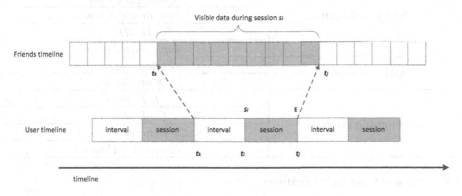

Fig. 1. Users' restricted browsing data during session

Through the above method, we identify what users could receive during each session, and then, we can obtain the passive feedbacks by excluding these positive feedbacks in session. This is practical under the hypothesis that users would examine all contents they received during each session.

3.2   Feature-Based Matrix Factorization

Matrix Factorization models have been popular in recommendation, Chen[3] propose a feature-based matrix factorization model, in which explicit features are integrated as a linear regression term:

$$\tilde{r}_{u,i} = \bar{r} + b_u + b_i + \sum_j b_j \gamma_j + q_i^T \cdot p_u \tag{1}$$

Where γ_j is an explicit feature, and b_j is the weight parameter for this feature. In this paper, we use feature-based MF model, and train this model by pair-wise learning method with using positive and passive feedbacks in each session. Similar to Chen[4], we use maximization of log-likelihood to estimate parameters, the loss function could be described as follow:

$$\mathcal{L} = \min \sum\nolimits_{<u,s,k,h> \in \mathcal{T}} ln\left(1 + e^{-(r_{u,k} - r_{u,j})}\right) + \lambda \cdot \|\alpha_i\|^2 \qquad (2)$$

Where α_i denotes parameters in this model, this is the regularization term to avoid over fitting.

3.3   Inner Session Features

Inner session features are supposed to distinguish different contents in the same session. In microblog, there are plenty of features in content, many studies[4,5] have make effort s on this problem, we choose some useful features as follows:

Table 1. Inner Session Features

	Retweet Count
	Comment Count
Content-based Features	*Length of Content*
	TF-IDF
	Topic Distribution
Author Features	*Follower Count*
	Fans Count
	Is Friends
Relationship Features	*Co-Follower*
	Co-Retweeted Count
	Interaction Count

3.4   Session Contextual Features

It is known that users' historical activities can reflect their preferences, and affect their new activities. We measure this relevance with the topic similarity between the current activity and historical activities, and compute it by using symmetric Kullback-Leibler (KL) divergence.

In this paper, we choose 4 time range to examine the topic similarity:

- **last day:** the last day's activities are the most close to current activity, which could describe some momentary interests of users.
- **last week:** a relative longer time range than one day, which could be useful to identify users' new focusing interest.
- **last month:** a quite long time range, which could describe users' long interest without too much old data.
- **all:** describe users' all interests.

Through these four time range definition, we can get four contextual features of sessions, each feature has a weight value expressed by their topic KL divergences.

4   Experiments

4.1   Experimental Setting

We use the dataset proposed by Zhang et al. [11], which is crawled from Sina Weibo[1], the most popular social network website in China. We filter some active users as our experimental subjects, the filter criteria are shown in Table 2:

Table 2. User filter criteria

fans	200~10000
follows	100~1000
co-follows	50~500
post records (including original and forwards)	1000~10000
post records in crawled dataset	>0

Following the criteria, we choose 538 users and 26271 followers, and make all posts of them as the total experimental dataset.

Then we split these dataset into different sessions by the time point of users' activities including posting and retweeting. It is worth noting that, if there is no retweet activity in one session, then we cannot judge whether users have read any content in this session, which make the session useless to do training or test, therefore, we only keep sessions which have at least one retweet activity.

After that, we split the dataset into training dataset and test dataset based on sessions' timeline. We keep the last 1/5 sessions as test dataset, and others as training dataset.

In this paper, we make microblog recommendation by using ranking-based method, and their relevances are considered to be binary in our scenario. We user P@n, MAP, NDCG@n and MRR to evaluate our approach. We also perform a significance test using Wilconxon signed rank test (p<0.05).

4.2   Methods Comparison

Comparison among Overall Data and Restricted Data

We want to inspect the effect of passive feedbacks in restricted sessions, so we choose some classic recommendation methods - ItemCF and Feature-based SVD (called FSVD) to make comparison.

It is worth noting that all results are measured in sessions, the test dataset has been sorted by time and split into different sessions, therefore, for ItemCF and FSVD

---

[1] http://www.weibo.com

which are trained on overall data, we need to firstly train models on non-split training dataset, and then test them in split session data. On the other side, for rFSVD, both of training and test data have been split already, so we can train models and measure results directly on these data.

During the training process, we use 5-fold cross validation to search parameters. For FSVD, we choose 50 as the latent factor dimensionality.

All of these results are shown in Table 3, "*" indicates statistically significant improvements on FSVD ($p < 0.05$ using Wilconxon test).

Table 3. Results comparison among overall data and restricted data

	ItemCF	FSVD	rFSVD
P@5	0.0532	0.0917	0.2578*
P@10	0.0319	0.0604	0.2203*
P@20	0.0128	0.0514	0.1517*
P@50	0.0086	0.0283	0.1201*
NDCG@5	0.0812	0.1205	0.2101*
NDCG@10	0.0492	0.1053	0.1854*
NDCG@20	0.0175	0.0782	0.1677*
NDCG@50	0.0096	0.0531	0.1215*
MAP	0.1127	0.1789	0.4628*
MRR	0.1321	0.1102	0.3927*

The results in Table 3 show that ItemCF performs badly, the possible reason is data sparsity in microblog is very serious, which make it difficult to compute similar items. In comparison, FSVD make a little progress, for its large number of features and latent factors. However, rFSVD can significantly outperform ItemCF and FSVD in all metrics, such as being up to 1.59 times on MAP and 2.56 times on MRR over FSVD. This could indicate that passive feedbacks can be useful to improve the effect of recommendation.

Comparison among Different Methods

In this part, we add a classic pair-wise learning models – RankSVM as comparison method, to examine the validity of our method. It's close to our approach, we employ the explicit features proposed in this paper. To examine the effect of data restriction, we firstly train and test RankSVM on ono-restrict data, then we train and test it on restrict data, called it as "rRankSVM" to underline its training on restricted data.

As shown in Figure 2, we measure these models' results in P@n and NDCG@n, and choose positions at 5, 10, 20, 50.

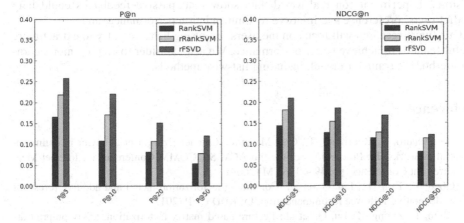

Fig. 2. P@n and NDCG@n comparison among models

Table 4. MAP and MRR among models

	RankSVM	rRankSVM	rFSVD
MAP	0.2786	0.3705*	0.4628**
MRR	0.2031	0.3515*	0.3927**

Table 4 shows the exactly results in MAP and MRR, "*" indicates statistically significant improvements on RankSVM, "**" indicates statistically significant improvements on rRankSVM.

From Figure 2 and Table 4, we can see that rRankSVM performs better than RankSVM in all P@n and NDCG@n, which could indicate that in RankSVM the good results on global may not fit well in local sessions. And further, rFSVD performs better than rRankSVM in all metrics, the reason of this effect maybe its latent factors in rFSVD model.

In addition, when rRankSVM compared with RankSVM, both of them have used passive feedbacks and same features, however, RankSVM is trained on non-split dataset, which means its training pairs are formed by global positive and passive feedbacks, by contrast, rRankSVM is only trained on pairs formed in exactly one session. From the results shown in Table 3, we can see that rRankSVM significantly outperforms RankSVM, which make 33% improvement on MAP and 73% improvement on MRR. The main reason for this effect could be that, global pairs construct all positive and passive feedbacks which could introduce more uncertain factors, for example, if two microblogs of the global pair are generated on large-interval time points, user cannot read them to make a choice, so it's meaningless to predict preference among them.

5   Conclusion and Future Work

In this paper, we propose a new approach to make microblog recommendation by using users' passive feedbacks, and we restrict training process into users' behavior sessions. Experiments on real-world data show that, passive feedbacks could help predict users' preference and improve recommendation performance, and

Our future research will focus on the users' browsing behaviors, try to extract more useful features to achieve better performance. We also consider to employ more learning methods to train our model, including list-wise methods.

References

1. Benevenuto, F., Rodrigues, T., Cha, M., et al.: Characterizing user behavior in online social networks. In: Proceedings of the 9th ACM SIGCOMM Conference on Internet Measurement Conference, pp. 49–62. ACM (2009)
2. Chen, T., Tang, L., Liu, Q., et al.: Combining factorization model and additive forest for collaborative followee recommendation. In: KDD CUP (2012)
3. Chen, T., Zheng, Z., Lu, Q., et al.: Feature-based matrix factorization. arXiv preprint arXiv:1109.2271 (2011)
4. Chen, K., Chen, T., Zheng, G., et al.: Collaborative personalized tweet recommendation. In: Proceedings of the 35th International ACM SIGIR Conference on Research and Development in Information Retrieval, pp. 661–670. ACM (2012)
5. Yang, L., Sun, T., Zhang, M., et al.: We know what@ you# tag: does the dual role affect hashtag adoption? In: Proceedings of the 21st International Conference on World Wide Web, pp. 261–270. ACM (2012)
6. Su, X., Khoshgoftaar, T.M.: A survey of collaborative filtering techniques. Advances in Artificial Intelligence 2009, 4 (2009)
7. Resnick, P., Iacovou, N., Suchak, M., et al.: GroupLens: an open architecture for collaborative filtering of netnews. In: Proceedings of the 1994 ACM Conference on Computer Supported Cooperative Work, pp. 175–186. ACM (1994)
8. Sarwar, B., Karypis, G., Konstan, J., et al.: Item-based collaborative filtering recommendation algorithms. In: Proceedings of the 10th International Conference on World Wide Web, pp. 285–295. ACM (2001)
9. Paterek, A.: Improving regularized singular value decomposition for collaborative filtering. In: Proceedings of KDD CUP and Workshop, pp. 5–8 (2007)
10. Konstas, I., Stathopoulos, V., Jose, J.M.: On social networks and collaborative recommendation. In: Proceedings of the 32nd International ACM SIGIR Conference on Research and Development in Information Retrieval, pp. 195–202. ACM (July 2009)
11. Ma, H., Yang, H., Lyu, M.R., King, I.: Sorec: social recommendation using probabilistic matrix factorization. In: Proceedings of the 17th ACM Conference on Information and Knowledge Management, pp. 931–940. ACM (October 2008)
12. Jamali, M., Ester, M.: A matrix factorization technique with trust propagation for recommendation in social networks. In: Proceedings of the Fourth ACM Conference on Recommender Systems, pp. 135–142. ACM (September 2010)
13. Yang, S.H., Long, B., Smola, A.J., et al.: Collaborative competitive filtering: learning recommender using context of user choice. In: Proceedings of the 34th International ACM SIGIR Conference on Research and Development in Information Retrieval, pp. 295–304. ACM (2011)

Towards Efficient Path Query on Social Network with Hybrid RDF Management*

Lei Gai, Wei Chen**, Zhichao Xu, Changhe Qiu, and Tengjiao Wang

School of Electronic Engineering and Computer Science,
Peking University, Beijing, China
{lei.gai,pekingchenwei,zhchxu,chhqiu,tjwang}@pku.edu.cn

Abstract. The scalability and flexibility of Resource Description Framework(RDF) model make it ideally suited for representing Online Social Networks(OSN). One basic operation in OSN is to find chains of relations, such as k-Hop friends. Property path query in SPARQL can express this type of operation, but its implementation suffers from performance problem considering the ever growing data size and complexity of OSN.

In this paper, we present a main memory/disk based hybrid RDF data management framework for efficient property path query. This hybrid framework realizes an efficient in-memory algebra operator for property path query using graph traversal, and estimates the cost of this operator to cooperate with existing cost-based optimization. Experiments on benchmark and real dataset demonstrated that our approach achieves a good tradeoff between data load expense and online query performance.

1 Introduction

In the age of Web 2.0, OSN have gained pervasive interests in both research communities and industries. There is a trend to model OSN using Semantic Web technologies, especially the vocabularies from FOAF[1] and SIOC[2] project. RDF, originally designed for the Semantic Web, have been wildly adopted for representing such kind of linked data. SPARQL[3] as the de-facto RDF query language is used for Basic Graph Pattern(BGP) query with bounded or unbounded variables. The scalable graph representation and flexible query capability make RDF model suited for large-scale complex OSN management and analysis.

Figure 1 illustrated a snippet of large social graph representing relations between four users and three User Generated Contents(UGC). Query which *Find pair of users in a path of friend relationship which user2 has a job and like the documents created by user1* is expressed in SPARQL as:

---

* This research is supported by the National High Technology Research and Development Program of China (Grant No. 2012AA011002), Natural Science Foundation of China (Grant No. 61300003), Specialized Research Fund for the Doctoral Program of Higher Education(Grant No. 20130001120001).
** Corresponding author.
[1] http://www.foaf-project.org/
[2] http://rdfs.org/sioc/spec/
[3] http://www.w3.org/TR/rdf-sparql-query/

L. Chen et al. (Eds.): APWeb 2014, LNCS 8709, pp. 525–532, 2014.

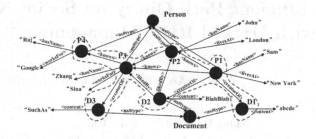

Fig. 1. Examples for a fraction of social network

```
SELECT DISTINCT ?user1, ?user2 WHERE {
    ?user1 knows* ?user2 .
    ?user1 creatorOf ?doc1 .
    ?user2 worksFor ?organization .
    ?doc1 likedBy ?user2 }
```

For RDF graph in Figure 1, this query returns the result set $R(q) = \{<P1, P3>\}$. The pattern *?user1 knows* ?user2* states the path consist of zero or more *knows* predicates, it is a property path query pattern.

Challenges. Path queries are of common interest in OSN analysis for discover complex relations among entities. Despite the scalability and flexibility provided by RDF model, Path queries performs poorly and lack of efficient implementation in existing RDF management. Current researches in graph analysis domain are mainly based on pre-constructed reachability indices. Building such indices are both time and memory consuming, especially when dealing with large complex graph. From RDF management point of view, due to costly join for triple pattern matching, there lacks efficient implementation of property path query. Although property path query is recommended by newest SPARQL 1.1 standard, to the best of our knowledge Jena[4], Virtuoso[5] and Sesame[6] are the only three off-the-shelf RDF stores that support standardized path query. They all suffer from performance problems when dealing with path query on large-scale data.

Overview of Our Approach. Our approach is motivated by three observations. First, current off-the-shelf RDF store performs well only on join-based star queries. Second, the search space of property path query is restricted to triples representing relations among entities. Third, due to the rich semantics in OSN, most triples are for entities attributes not for relations. Based on these observations, we argue that manage graph topology-related triples into main memory is feasible, and this will greatly enhance the online query performance of property path related sophisticate SPARQL queries. We propose a hybrid framework that has in-memory management of graph topology-related RDF data along with

---

[4] https://jena.apache.org/
[5] http://virtuoso.openlinksw.com/
[6] http://www.openrdf.org/

disk-based Jena TDB[7] native triple store. In our approach, while loading and indexing triples into TDB, graph topology-related triples are identified and duplicated in main memory. For an online query, we implement a graph traversal based algebra operators for property path pattern, which is more efficient than traditional join-based operator.

Contributions. We summarized our contribution in this paper as:

1. We propose a main memory/disk based hybrid framework for efficient property path query. While leverage the functionality of existing well-established RDF store for BGP query, it specialized in property path pattern query through manage graph topology related data in main memory.
2. We present an algebra operator for property path pattern query. Its realization based on in-memory graph traversal instead of costly join. Using the characteristics of OSN, heuristics for estimating the execution cost of this operator is given that can be used for cost-base optimization.

Organization of the Paper. The rest of the paper is organized as follows. Section 2 presents the basic design of our hybrid RDF management framework. Section 3 shows the evaluation results. We conclude in Section 5.

2   Hybrid RDF Data Management

Given vocabulary $\Sigma = V_E \cup V_A \cup E_{EE} \cup E_{EA} \cup L_E \cup L_A$ defined in Table 2, an OSN is represented as a triple set $T_{OSN} = T_G \cup T_A$, where the graph-topology set $T_G \subseteq V_E \times L_E \times V_E$ holds triples representing social entities and relations among them, and the attributes set $T_A \subseteq V_E \times L_A \times V_A$ holds triples representing attributes and theirs relations to social entities.

Table 1. Notations for social graph representation

Notations	Refers to the set of	Instance of Figure 1
V_E	Nodes for social entities.	$\{P1, D1, \ldots\}$
V_A	Nodes for attributes values.	$\{"John", "London", "abcde", \ldots\}$
E_{EE}	Edges among V_E.	$\{(P1, P2), (P1, D1), \ldots\}$
E_{EA}	Edges between V_E and V_A.	$\{(P1, "Sam"), (D1, "abcde"), \ldots\}$
L_E	Labels for E_{EE}.	$\{< knows >, < likeBy >, \ldots\}$
L_A	Labels for E_{EA}.	$\{< hasName >, < ns\#type >, \ldots\}$

2.1   Architectural Design

In this paper, we focus on efficient implementation of property path query. Consider that path query only related to Triples in T_G (In Figure 1, T_G is represented as dashline-encircled part), one direct motivation is that manage T_G in memory

---

[7] https://svn.apache.org/repos/asf/jena/

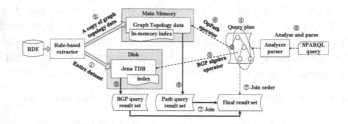

Fig. 2. Hybird RDF management architecture of our approach

will greatly enhance the overall query performance. Based on this motivation, we implement a hybrid RDF data management architecture that manage different query-prone data respectively. This architecture is shown in Figure 2.

Our approach can be thought as a plugin component which override the functionality of corresponding part in TDB. At data loading stage, $\forall t_i \in T_{OSN}$ is loaded into Jena TDB (step ① in Figure 2). At the same time, $\exists t_i \in T_G$ is filtered out based on two kinds of rules:

1. The type of *Objects*. If *Objects* for t_i is a literal, then $t_i \in T_A$.
2. The semantic meaning of *Predicate*. Such as *foaf:knows* defined in FOAF project which state the relation that *Subject User* know *Object User*.

T_G is stored in main memory with subject index(PSO) for forward traversal and object index(POS)for backward traversal(step ②).These indices can be constructed incrementally when topology-related data is extracted and loaded into main memory.

When an online query is submitted, SPARQL parser translates query strings into patterns based on standard abstract syntax tree recommended by W3C (step ③). Analyzer translates these patterns into predefined SPARQL algebra operators and construct execution plan (step ④).An algebra operator generates designated result set from given input (step ⑤). In our approach we implemented a special operator named *OpPath* which only uses in-memory data as input. If a query string in *WHERE* clause is analyzed as property path pattern, *OpPath* operator is added to the query plan. (step ⑥) We explain the design of *OpPath* operator in detail in Section 2.2. Result set of algebra operator is joined to get the final result set. The join order of operators is optimized using cost and selectivity estimation (step ⑦).

2.2 Property Path Algebra Operator

Definition 1 (*OpPath* Operator). *OpPath is a ternary algebra operator that can be defined as $OpPath(O,S,P_P)$. $S,O \subseteq V_{EE}$ can be either bounded or unbounded variables, $|S| = s$, $|O| = o$. P_P is a regular pattern expression defining the property path. $OpPath(O,S,P_P)$ operator find existing path from set S to set O, and return all triple sets that each paths is consist of as result set.*

Based on research [9] which have testified that graph explorations is extremely efficient and more easy to implement than costly joins, the *OpPath* operator is realized as in-memory Breadth-First Search(BFS). The *OpPath* operator has time complexity $O(|V_E| + |E_{EE}|)$ and space complexity $O(|T_G|)$. It is much less than tradition nested-loop join that has time complexity $O(|V_E| \cdot |E_{EE}|)$.

The cost of *OpPath* operator is the cardinality of result set $R(q)$ for path query pattern q. Existing researches such as G-SPARQL [7] using predefined heuristics which always take $|R(q)|$ as the largest, this is far from optimal. Sparqling Kleene [2] using pre-computed reachability path indices which affects data load efficiency. We consider three factors that affects $|R(q)|$, the average nodes out-degree, the path length l and the pathes that fits for the given pattern. In our approach, we leverages the graph generation model [4] which expects the average out-degree as $d_{out} = |V_{EE}|^{1-\ln c}, 1 < c \leq 2$. We also assumes that nodes in T_G has the same probability of being added to the path, thus the modifying factor of out-degree follows the binomial distribution. For all considerations above, $|R(q)|$ can be approximately estimated as:

$$|R_q| = s \cdot o \cdot \sum_{i=1}^{l}(|V_{EE}|^{(1-\ln c)\cdot i} \cdot (\sum_{i=1}^{l}\frac{l!}{i!(l-i)!} \cdot p^i \cdot (1-p)^{l-i})) \qquad (1)$$

where $p = \frac{|E_{EE}|-|V_{EE}|}{|V_{EE}|}$. $|V_{EE}|$ and $|E_{EE}|$ can be got from the metadata in RDF store. We performs preliminary testing to measure the accuracy of Equation 1 with real all-pair cardinality of dataset in Table 2. For SNIB T_G with average $d_{out} = 12$, $c = 1.75$, *relative error* $= \frac{max(real\ cardinality, estimate\ cardinality)}{min(real\ cardinality, estimate\ cardinality)} -$ 1 is about 27%. For DBLP T_G with $d_{out} = 7$, $c = 1.81$, and *error* $= 32\%$. This preliminary testing shows that the heuristic defined in Equation 1 is with acceptable cardinality estimation error.

3   Evaluation

We used one machine with Debian 7.4 in 64-bit Linux kernel, two Intel Xeon E5-2640 2.0GHz processor and 64 GB RAM for our evaluation. Our approach is compared with Jena(version 2.11.1), Sesame(version 2.7.10) and competitive research G-SPARQL [8]. Jena implements path query based on join while Sesame is based on graph traversal. We also implements our approach with no cost estimation and treats path query as the most costly(denoted as *NoCE*). All evaluations were done 10 times and the results are the averages.

We adopted two datasets, the Social Network Intelligence Benchmark (SNIB)[8] as synthetic dataset, and DBLP as real dataset, all in RDF N-Triples format[9]. SNIB dataset is generated using S3G2 [6]. Considering G-SPARQL uses ACM digital library dataset which is not publicly available, we uses the DBLP dataset

---

[8] Social Network Intelligence Benchmark(SNIB),
   http://www.w3.org/wiki/Social_Network_Intelligence_BenchMark/
[9] http://www.w3.org/TR/n-triples/

instead[10]. Statistics of datasets are shown in Table 2. The DBLP dataset has approximately the same characteristics as the *Large Graph Size* experiment in G-SPARQL.

Table 2. Statistics for SNIB and DBLP datasets

Dataset	Vertices($|V_{EE}|$)	Edges ($|E_{EE}|$)	Attributes ($|T_A|$)	$|T_G|/|T_{OSN}|$
SNIB	566,472	2,001,333	7,273,177	26%
DBLP	900,440	2,243,827	9,363,166	25%

For offline data loading time and memory expenses, we compare our approach with four competitors, Sesame and Jena in-memory store which store and index data only in memory, Sesame native store and Jena TDB which use disk as triple storage. Results of data loading time is represented in Figure 3(a),and disk usage in Figure 3(b), memory usage in Figure3(c). For our approach only load graph topological data into main memory, it need fewer memory than that of Jena and Sesame in-memory store, but with a little overhead of the data loading time.

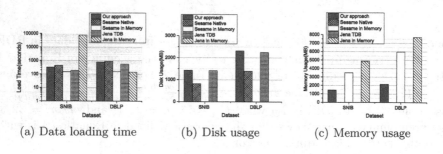

(a) Data loading time   (b) Disk usage   (c) Memory usage

Fig. 3. Offline performance evaluation

For online query performance, in SNIB benchmark only $Q3$ and $Q5$ are path query related, while for DBLP we chosen 7 out of total 12 queries in G-SPARQL experiments(denoted as Q_g). In order for comparison, we had to rewrite these queries on DBLP dataset. Figure 4(a) shows that our approach achieved the best performance for SNIB $Q3$. As for SNIB $Q5$, the 3-HOP which expressed in UNION clause is explicitly parsed into six joins. This causes an expensive join expenses. Results in Figure 4(b) show that our approach works better than G-SPARQL(got directly from the *Large Graph Size* result in [7]), while *NoCE* has approximately the same performance as that of G-SPARQL. This shows that cost estimation for optimal join order can enhance the overall query performance.

---

[10] DBLP dataset can be download from http://sw.deri.org/ aharth/2004/07/dblp/ dblp-2006-02-06.rdf. Same as stated in G-SPARQL, we manually created the co-author relationships between author nodes, which originally recorded as $< creator >$ tag in raw dataset.

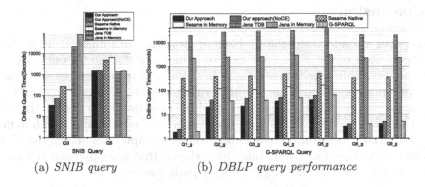

(a) *SNIB query*   (b) *DBLP query performance*

Fig. 4. Online Query Performance

4   Related Works

Most existing RDF stores uses a relational model to manage data, either in a traditional RDBMS or using a native triple store. They all processes SPARQL queries as sets of join operations using disk-based indices, which are costly for sophisticated joins. Some researches have focused on compressing and managing RDFs in main memory, Trinity RDF [9] is the most prominent among them. It uses graph exploration instead of join operations and greatly boosts SPARQL query performance. But manages all data in memory is not trivial, distributed shared memory increases the complexity for maintenance.

From graph analysis perspective, Property path can be viewed as the label-constraint reachability problem on labeled graph. Though reachability on graph is a further investigated problem, few literatures [1, 10] considered its usage in property graph, which is more common in nature. These researches are mainly focus on building reachability indices in advance, which is time or space consuming and not adequate for large-scale data management.

Besides Jena and Sesame, several frameworks and prototypes have been proposed for path queries [2, 3, 7]. BRAHMS [3] only supports query on paths with predefined length. Sparqling Kleene [2] realizes join based on pre-constructed reachability indices which are space consuming. Our work is mainly motivated by G-SPARQL [7] which use the same hybrid storage and manage graph topological data in memory. Our work different from G-SPARQL in that, first, we are not design a new query language but uses standard SPARQL 1.1 instead, this makes our work more general. Second, G-SPARQL uses index-free pointer-based data structure to representing the graph topological data in memory, in order to suit for most graph algorithms. Our work only cares about path patterns which BFS algorithm is used to answer such reachability queries. We build simple indices only for facilitating BFS.

5   Conclusion

In this paper we addressed the problem of property path query in RDF data, presented a step towards incorporation of in-memory storage. In our approach we are not trying to invent new wheels, but managed to combine existing effective approaches as well as some technical enhancements. Contrast to traditional RDF management and graph query method, we used in-memory graph traversal instead of costly join to realize path query operator, used simple graph indices other than RDF permutation indices and complex graph reachability indices for efficient graph traversal. Evaluations have shown that our approach is feasible and efficient for process SPARQL property path queries.

References

1. Fan, W., Li, J., Ma, S., Tang, N., Wu, Y.: Adding Regular Expressions to Graph Reachability and Pattern Queries. In: 2011 IEEE 27th International Conference on Data Engineering (ICDE), pp. 39–50. IEEE (2011)
2. Gubichev, A., Bedathur, S.J., Seufert, S.: Sparqling Kleene: Fast Property Paths in RDF-3X. In: First International Workshop on Graph Data Management Experiences and Systems, p. 14. ACM (2013)
3. Janik, M., Kochut, K.: BRAHMS: A WorkBench RDF Store and High Performance Memory System for Semantic Association Discovery. In: Gil, Y., Motta, E., Benjamins, V.R., Musen, M.A. (eds.) ISWC 2005. LNCS, vol. 3729, pp. 431–445. Springer, Heidelberg (2005)
4. Leskovec, J., Kleinberg, J., Faloutsos, C.: Graph Evolution: Densification and Shrinking Diameters. ACM Transactions on Knowledge Discovery from Data (TKDD) 1(1) (2007)
5. Neumann, T., Weikum, G.: RDF-3X: A RISC-style Engine for RDF. Proceedings of the VLDB Endowment 1(1), 647–659 (2008)
6. Pham, M.-D., Boncz, P., Erling, O.: S3G2: A Scalable Structure-Correlated Social Graph Generator. In: Nambiar, R., Poess, M. (eds.) TPCTC 2012. LNCS, vol. 7755, pp. 156–172. Springer, Heidelberg (2013)
7. Sakr, S., Elnikety, S., He, Y.: G-SPARQL: A Hybrid Engine for Querying Large Attributed Graphs. In: Proceedings of the 21st ACM International Conference on Information and Knowledge Management, pp. 335–344. ACM (2012)
8. Stocker, M., Seaborne, A., Bernstein, A., Kiefer, C., Reynolds, D.: SPARQL Basic Graph Pattern Optimization Using Selectivity Estimation. In: Proceedings of the 17th International Conference on World Wide Web, pp. 595–604. ACM (2008)
9. Zeng, K., Yang, J., Wang, H., Shao, B., Wang, Z.: A Distributed Graph Engine for Web Scale RDF Data. In: Proceedings of the 39th International Conference on Very Large Data Bases, pp. 265–276. VLDB Endowment (2013)
10. Zou, L., Xu, K., Yu, J.X., Chen, L., Xiao, Y., Zhao, D.: Efficient Processing of Label-constraint Reachability Queries in Large Graphs. Information Systems 40, 47–66 (2014)

Discovery of Unique Column Combinations
with Hadoop

Shupeng Han, Xiangrui Cai, Chao Wang, Haiwei Zhang*, and Yanlong Wen

College of Computer and Control Engineering, Nankai University,
94 Weijin Road, Tianjin, P.R. China 300071
{hansp,caixr,wangc,zhanghw,wenyl}@dbis.nankai.edu.cn

Abstract. A unique column combination is one important kind of structural information in relations. From a data management perspective, discovering unique column combinations is a crucial step in understanding and utilizing the data. It will benefit data modeling, data integration, anomaly detection, query optimization and indexing. Nevertheless, discovering all unique column combinations is a NP-hard problem. Therefore, efficiency is a tremendous challenge.

In this paper, we propose *MRUCC*, which is an efficient algorithm to discover unique column combinations in large-scale data sets on Hadoop. Existing algorithms mainly focus on datasets of normal size, which cannot be adapted to large data sets. In contrast, we discover unique column combinations in parallel and implement *MRUCC* on Hadoop. Furthermore, we use column-based and row-based pruning to improve efficiency. Finally, we compare *MRUCC* with state-of-the-art approaches using both real and synthetic data sets. The experiment shows that *MRUCC* has a better performance.

Keywords: unique column combination, MRUCC, pruning, Hadoop.

1   Introduction

A unique column combination is one important kind of structural information in relations. A unique refers to a column or a column combination whose values uniquely identify a tuple in the collection. In other words, no two rows in a unique have identical values. Discovering uniques is a crucial step in many areas of modern data management, but the uniques are often incomplete in complex and large-scale data set. Since uniques represent a lot of valuable information, DBAs and developers are eager for an effective unique discovery method. However, it is impractical to manually detect all uniques in a large and complex data set. Thus, discovering uniques automatically and efficiently is very important in practice.

We focus on the discovery of non-redundant uniques instead of all unique column combinations. The non-redundant unique is a minimal column combination whose subsets are not uniques. It is worth noting that a column combination is

---

* Corresponding author.

L. Chen et al. (Eds.): APWeb 2014, LNCS 8709, pp. 533–541, 2014.
© Springer International Publishing Switzerland 2014

a unique as long as one of its subsets is unique. Discovery of all unique combinations is especially difficult, because the combination number increases exponentially as attributes increase. *Gunopulos et al.*[1] pointed out that discovering a non-redundant unique is an NP-hard problem.

This paper proposes a parallel algorithm *MRUCC* (MapReduce based Unique Column Combination detection) for automatical discovery of non-redundant unique. There are two basic ideas behind *MRUCC*. We detect uniques that include the same number of columns in parallel. For example, we detect column combinations {A,B} and {A,C} simultaneously after verifying {A}, {B} and {C}. In addition, we use both column-based and row-based pruning to improve efficiency. Our pruning rules are: (1)if column combination {A} is a unique, any combination including {A} is a redundant unique; (2)if the count of identical tuples projected on {A} is 1, then we can ignore this tuple when verify the column combinations including {A}. We implement our algorithm on Hadoop. The experiments on both real and synthetic data sets show that *MRUCC* is better than other state-of-art approaches.

In general, we make three contributions.

1. To the best of our knowledge, we are the first to propose a parallel algorithm to discover unique column combinations on Hadoop. With the help of Hadoop, we can deal with large-scale data sets. Furthermore, our algorithm has a good scalability which is easily expanded to large-scale cluster.
2. We utilize column-based and row-based pruning techniques to accelerate our algorithm.
3. We demonstrate the efficiency of *MRUCC* on real and synthetic data sets.

The remainder of this paper is organized as follows. In section 2, We review the related work. Then we discuss two important pruning techniques in section 3. Section 4 contains the description of the *MRUCC* algorithm. Section 5 shows the results of an empirical evaluation of *MRUCC*. At last, we conclude this paper in section 6.

2   Related Work

Currently, only a few of research work aimed to solve unique discovery problem for its complexity. [2,3,4,5] are devoted to detecting uniques of single column, instead of composite uniques. Most existing work can only be used for small-scale data sets due to the limitation of CPU and memory capacity. In general, there are two different kinds of solutions: column-based and row-based.

BruteForce is a column-based algorithm. It needs to traverse all column combinations of a relational table, and verifies each of them by the method of 'projection and count'. Then it removes redundant combinations and eventually gets all non-redundant uniques. In conclusion, the *BruteForce* algorithm consists of two phases: a unique verification phase and a redundancy removal phase. Assuming that a data table has 50 attributes, thus there is $2^{50} - 1$ column combinations altogether to be verified. Therefore, *BruteForce* can only be used for small-scale data set with a few columns.

The typical row-based algorithm is $GORDIAN$[6], which is based on the intuition that non-uniques can be detected without traversing all rows in a table. $GORDIAN$ firstly reorganizes the data table as a prefix-tree to fit into memory, and computes maximal non-uniques by traversing the prefix-tree. Then, it computes minimal uniques from maximal non-uniques. However, it needs the prefix-tree to be fully loaded into memory, which is difficult when the data set is very large. What's more, generating minimal uniques from maximal non-uniques is also the bottleneck of $GORDIAN$.

HCA[7] is an algorithm based on bottom-up apriori technique. HCA uses an efficient candidate generation strategy and applies statistical pruning with value histograms. Besides, it takes advantage of functional dependencies and combines the maximal non-unique discovery with HCA. However, there is no optimization with regard to early identification of non-uniques in a row-based manner as HCA is based on histograms and value-counting.

3   Pruning Methods of Unique Discovery

In section 3, we introduce two important pruning methods used in $MRUCC$, which improve the efficiency of unique discovery. Column-based pruning is designed to prune unique candidates. Row-based pruning can be used to accelerate the verification of a column combination.

In order to verify a column combination, we need to project the data table onto this combination and get a new table S. It proves that combination K is a unique only if there is no duplicate tuples in S.

3.1   Basic Concepts

Unique column combinations are sets of columns of a relational database that fulfill the uniqueness constraint. Uniqueness of a column combination K within a table can be defined as follows[7]:

Definition 1. Unique *Given a relational database schema* $R = \{C_1, C_2, ..., C_m\}$ *with columns* C_i *and instance* $r \subseteq C_1 \times ... C_m$, *a column combination* $K \subseteq R$ *is a unique iff* $\forall t_1, t_2 \in r : (t_1 \neq t_2) \Rightarrow (t_1[K] \neq t_2[K])$.

Minimality is an important property of unique. Minimal uniques are uniques of which no strict subsets hold the property.

Definition 2. Minimal Unique *An unique* $K \subseteq R$ *is minimal, iff* $\forall K' \subset K : (\exists t1, t2 \in R : (t1[K'] = t2[K']) \wedge (t1 \neq t2))$.

3.2   Column-Based Pruning

If both K and K' are uniques of schema R, and $K \subset K'$, then we remark K' as the redundancy of K. As shown in Figure 1, a schema R has 4 columns a, b, c, d and its uniques are $\{b\}$ and $\{a, c\}$. If we use $BruteForce$ algorithm to find all non-redundant uniques, we need to verify all combinations in the column combination

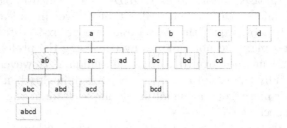

Fig. 1. Column combination tree(CC-Tree)

tree(CC-Tree for short), which has 15 candidates altogether. Heuristically, we can apply column-based pruning to avoid unnecessary verification. For example, we should check every column combination showed in figure 1 in breadth-first order. After confirming that $\{b\}$ is a unique, we can omit the verification of $\{b, c\}$, $\{b, d\}$ and $\{b, c, d\}$ since that they are all redundancies of $\{b\}$. With column-based pruning, it only takes seven verification to find all non-redundant uniques rather than 15 times. The benefits of column-based pruning get more considerable when the table has more attributes.

3.3 Row-Based Pruning

Row-based pruning is used to shrink computational cost of verifying a column combination. Recall that we verify candidates in bread-first order(Figure 1). If a tuple appears only once in the projection of a column combination K, we can ignore this tuple when verify the subtree of K. For example, when we verify column combination {Major} showed in Table 1, we can obtain that {Major} is not a unique. Next it needs to verify combinations that are constituted by {Major} and another attribute, namely {Major,Name}, {Major,Grade} and {Major,StudentID}.

Table 1. Data set sample

Name	Major	Grade	StudentID
Lucy	Computer	freshman	1210368
John	Math	freshman	1210422
Lucy	English	Junior	1010232
Lucy	Computer	Sophomore	1110223

There is only one record whose value is *Math* in the projection on {Major}, so there must be only one record whose *Major* is *Math* in the projection on {Major,Name}, {Major,Grade} and {Major,StudentID}. It is obvious that the second tuple will not affect the verification of these three column combinations, and the same as the third tuple. Therefore, we can prune the data table by removing the tuples that appear only once in the projection and we get a and smaller table shown in Table 2.

Table 2. Pruned data set

Name	Major	Grade	StudentID
Lucy	Computer	freshman	1210368
Lucy	Computer	Sophomore	1110223

4   MRUCC Algorithm

In this section, we introduce our unique discovery algorithm *MRUCC*. It is proposed to deal with large-scale data set on Hadoop with column-based and row-based pruning.

The core of *MRUCC* algorithm is to verify all column combinations located in the same layer of the CC-tree simultaneously. Assume that *MRUCC* is to verify the column combination set of $\{C_1, C_2, ... C_n\}$. Firstly it traverses this set and checks redundancy for each combination C_i. If C_i is not redundant, *MRUCC* adds C_i into a set named *CandidateList*, which is used to maintain combinations that need further verification. Otherwise, if C_i is a redundant unique, all the descendant nodes of C_i will be pruned. After traversing, all combinations in *CandidateList* will be verified simultaneously. If C_i is a unique, *MRUCC* would add C_i into *Unique-Set* and prune its subtree. Then, *MRUCC* processes next level of the CC-Tree.

The *MRUCC* algorithm(Algorithm 1) takes *ContextInfoList* as its input. *ContextInfoList* is a list constituted by *ContextInfo* objects, which is a data structure used to build candidate column combinations. *MRCheck* is a unique verification algorithm that contains a *Mapper* class and a *Reducer* class. The former is responsible for the projection of each column combination, and the latter is in charge of aggregation. We materialize the new table after row-based pruning, in order to accelerate the verification of subtree.

Consider a data table with four attributes a, b, c and d, where {b} and {a,c} constitute its *Unique-Set*. The corresponding CC-Tree is shown in Figure 1. The *MRUCC* algorithm first finds uniques from the first layer of CC-Tree: it checks redundancy of {a}, {b}, {c}, {d} and finds that all of them are not redundant, so it sends these four candidates to *MRCheck* for unique verification. Then it prunes the subtree of {b} since candidate {b} is a unique. Next, the algorithm is processed to the second layer of the CC-Tree, where column combinations are {a,b}, {a,c}, {a,d}, {c,d}. Combination {b,c} and {b,d} are not be processed because they have been pruned before. Since {a,b} is redundant for {b}, the *MRUCC* prunes its subtree analogously. It then passes {a,c}, {a,d}, {c,d} to *MRUCC* and finds that {a,c} is a key, so it performs pruning similarly. At last, the algorithm is processed to the third layer of the CC-tree and it comes to the end since no combinations left in this layer.

Algorithm 1. MRUCC

Input: *ContextInfoList*
Output: Unique collection *UniqueSet*
 1: **if** *ContextInfoList* is null **then**
 2:    **return** *UniqueSet*
 3: **end if**
 4: **for** each *info* in *ContextInfoList* **do**
 5:    Construct *Candidate* using *info* and insert it into *CandidateList*;
 6: **end for**
 7: **if** *CandidateList* is not null **then**
 8:    Invoke *MRCheck(CandidateList)* for unique verification concurrently
 9: **end if**
10: clear *ContextInfoList*;
11: **for all** *Candidate* ∈ *CandidateList* **do**
12:    **if** *Candidate* is a unique **then**
13:       Insert *Candidate* into *UniqueSet*
14:    **else**
15:       Construct new *ContextInfo* node and insert it into *ContextInfoList*
16:    **end if**
17: **end for**
18: invoke *MRUCC(ContextInfoList)*

---

5 Experiment

We use a series of experiments to demonstrate that *MRUCC* has better performance than the state-of-art algorithms on large scale data set. In addition, it also proves that *MRUCC* algorithm has a good scalability.

5.1 Setup

Cluster: Our Hadoop environment has totally 6 nodes: one master and 5 slaves.

Data Sets: We use one synthetic and two real-world data sets in our experiments. TPC-E is a data set which is used to simulate the OLTP workload of a brokerage firm. *FinancialData* and *MovieLens* are real-word data sets. The former is from the economic field while the latter is from the film industry. The statistics of each data set are shown in Table 3.

Table 3. Statistics of data sets

Data Set	Table	Avg Col	Max Col	Avg Row	Max Row
TPC-E	32	6	24	19285770	207407310
FinancialData	8	7	16	134288	1056320
MovieLens	12	6	15	130084	855599

5.2   Scaling the Number of Columns

In this section we run $MRUCC$ and $GORDIAN$ on data sets with different column numbers to compare their run time with the same computer. To thoroughly evaluate their performances, different column numbers and different data set sizes are utilized. The experimental results are reported in Figure 2, Figure 3 and Figure 4 respectively. The cost of $GORDIAN$ increases exponentially with the growth of column number, while the curve of $MRUCC$ is relatively flat. In addition, $MRUCC$ has a better performance when the data set gets lager, which proves that $MRUCC$ is efficient.

5.3   Scaling the Number of Rows

To analyze the effect of row number, we run $MRUCC$, $BruteForce$ and $GORDIAN$ on data sets with different size on a single computer. Figure 5 shows the execution time of these three algorithms.

As can be seen from Figure 5 that the cost of the $MRUCC$ increases nearly in a linear fashion as the data set size grows. Besides, $MRUCC$ is much better than $BruteForce$ all the time. When the data size is small, $GORDIAN$ has a better performance than $MRUCC$, since the parallel overhead account for a large percentage; but when the size gets larger, $MRUCC$ is superior to $GORDIAN$. In conclusion, $MRUCC$ algorithm is more suitable for dealing with large data sets.

5.4   Speed-Up Ratio of Cluster

Speedup ratio is an important criterion to measure the performance of parallel algorithms. The speedup ratio is defined as $S = T_s/T_p$, where T_s is the serialize execution time and T_p denotes the run time of parallel algorithm with p nodes. In this section, we randomly select $1/64, 1/32, 1/16, 1/8, 1/4, 1/2$, and the entirety of a 6GB data table as the sample sets. Then we evaluate speed-up ratio with these sets on different number of nodes. As shown in Figure 6, the $MRUCC$ algorithm increases in a linear fashion when the data set is large, which proves that $MRUCC$ has a good speedup ratio.

5.5   Expansion Rate of Cluster

Expansion rate, which is defined as $E = S/P$, is used to assess the utilization of cluster. S is the speedup ratio, while P denotes node number. Figure 7 shows that $MRUCC$ has a good scalability. The expansion rate is gradually decreased with the growth of node number, since the cost of communication between nodes increases. As the number of nodes grows, the expansion rate curve becomes smooth gradually. It can give full play to its computing ability for each node when the data size is large.

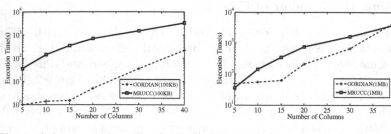

Fig. 2. Column number effect(100KB)   **Fig. 3.** Column number effect(1MB)

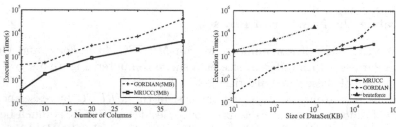

Fig. 4. Column number effect(5MB)   **Fig. 5.** Row number effect

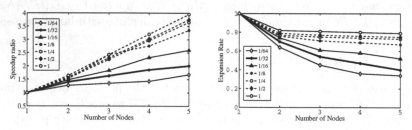

Fig. 6. Speed-up ratio   **Fig. 7.** Expansion rate

6   Conclusion

A unique is the basis of understanding a data table, but it is often incomplete in large data set. This paper proposes a distributed non-redundant unique discovery method named *MRUCC*, which is based on Hadoop platform. Additionally, We use column-based as well as row-based pruning to improve its efficiency.

There are some works to be done in future. Firstly, we can cache intermediate results of *MRUCC* to avoid unnecessary I/O cost. Furthermore, we can apply data partitioning to find as many non-uniques as possible on these subsets, so as to improve column-based pruning.

Acknowledgments. This work is supported by NSF of China under Grant No. 61170184, and Tianjin Municipal Science and Technology Commission under Grant No. 13ZCZDGX02200, 13ZCZDGX01098, 13JCQNJC0100 and 14JC-QNJC00200.

References

1. Gunopulos, D., Khardon, R., Mannila, H., Saluja, S., Toivonen, H., Sharma, R.S.: Discovering all most specific sentences. ACM Trans. Database Syst. 28(2), 140–174 (2003)
2. Brown, P., Haas, P.J., Myllymaki, J., Pirahesh, H., Reinwald, B., Sismanis, Y.: Toward automated large-scale information integration and discovery. In: Härder, T., Lehner, W., et al. (eds.) Data Management in a Connected World. LNCS, vol. 3551, pp. 161–180. Springer, Heidelberg (2005)
3. Bell, S., Brockhausen, P.: Discovery of constraints and data dependencies in databases. In: Lavrač, N., Wrobel, S. (eds.) ECML 1995. LNCS, vol. 912, pp. 267–270. Springer, Heidelberg (1995)
4. Kivinen, J., Mannila, H.: Approximate dependency inference from relations. Theoret. Comput. Sci. 149, 129–149 (1995)
5. Petit, J.-M., Toumani, F., Boulicaut, J.-F., Kouloumdjian, J.: Towards the reverse engineering of renormalized relational databases. In: Proc. ICDE, pp. 218–227 (1996)
6. Sismanis, Y., et al.: GORDIAN: efficient and scalable discovery of composite keys. In: Proceedings of the 32nd International Conference on Very Large Data Bases. VLDB Endowment (2006)
7. Abedjan, Z., Naumann, F.: Advancing the discovery of unique column combinations. In: Proceedings of the 20th ACM International Conference on Information and Knowledge Management. ACM (2011)
8. Adelfio, M.D., Samet, H.: Schema extraction for tabular data on the web. Proceedings of the VLDB Endowment 6(6), 421–432 (2013)
9. Janga, P., Davis, K.C.: Schema extraction and integration of heterogeneous XML document collections. In: Cuzzocrea, A., Maabout, S. (eds.) MEDI 2013. LNCS, vol. 8216, pp. 176–187. Springer, Heidelberg (2013)

Efficient Processing Node Proximity
via Random Walk with Restart

Bingqing Lv[1], Weiren Yu[2], Liping Wang[1], and Julie A. McCann[2]

[1] Software Engineering Institute, East China Normal University, Shanghai, China
[2] Department of Computing, Imperial College London, London, UK
lvbingqings@gmail.com, {weiren.yu,jamm}@imperial.ac.uk,
lipingwang@sei.ecnu.edu.cn

Abstract. Graph is a useful tool to model complicated data structures. One important task in graph analysis is assessing node proximity based on graph topology. Recently, Random Walk with Restart (RWR) tends to pop up as a promising measure of node proximity, due to its proliferative applications in *e.g.* recommender systems, and image segmentation. However, the best-known algorithm for computing RWR resorts to a large LU matrix factorization on an *entire* graph, which is cost-inhibitive. In this paper, we propose hybrid techniques to efficiently compute RWR. First, a novel divide-and-conquer paradigm is designed, aiming to convert the large LU decomposition into small triangular matrix operations recursively on several partitioned subgraphs. Then, on every subgraph, a "sparse accelerator" is devised to further reduce the time of RWR without any sacrifice in accuracy. Our experimental results on real and synthetic datasets show that our approach outperforms the baseline algorithms by at least one constant factor without loss of exactness.

1 Introduction

Finding proximities between objects based on graph topology is an important task in web data management. It has a wide range of applications, *e.g.* nearest neighbor search, image segmentation, and collaborative filtering. With the growing quantities of complex structured data, many fundamental problems have been naturally arising in graph analysis: How closely connected are two nodes in a graph? How to efficiently assess the closeness between two nodes?

To tackle these questions, recent years have witnessed growing attention to node-to-node proximities (*e.g.* [5,6,4,8,10,11,9]). Among them, Random Walk with Restart (RWR) has become a very popular one, which is originally patented by Tong *et al.* [5]. RWR is a PageRank-like node proximity based on a random surfer model. In comparison with other relevance measures, RWR has the following two benefits [5]: (1) it can globally capture the entire topology of a graph; (2) its proximity values can be used for ranking objects with respects to a certain query, as opposed to PageRank that is query-independent.

Prior Approaches. However, existing methods to compute RWR are less desirable. To the best of our knowledge, there exist two noteworthy methods for

L. Chen et al. (Eds.): APWeb 2014, LNCS 8709, pp. 542–549, 2014.

RWR computation: Tong *et al.* [5] developed a closed form of RWR, converting the computation of RWR into a matrix inversion problem, which requires $O(n^3)$ time for assessing all RWR proximities for n^2 pairs of nodes in a graph. Very recently, for top-K search, Fujiwara *et al.* [1] has proposed an excellent algorithm called k-dash, which can be regarded as the state-of-the-art one for computing RWR. Unfortunately, their strategy involves a large LU matrix decomposition over an *entire* graph, which is still time-consuming. Therefore, it is very imperative to devise novel techniques for accelerating RWR computation.

Our Contributions. In this paper, hybrid optimization techniques are proposed for optimizing RWR computation. Different to the framework of [1] that performs large LU decomposition on an *entire* graph, we utilize a novel divide-and-conquer method, with the aim to convert large LU decomposition into small triangular matrix operations on some partitioned subgraphs in a recursive manner. This enables a substantial improvement on the computational time of RWR. Besides, we take advantage of the sparsity of triangular matrix multiplications with a node prioritizing strategy, and apply a fast matrix multiplication algorithm, to further accelerate RWR computation. Finally, we conduct extensive experiments on real and synthetic datasets to verify the high efficiency of our proposed algorithms against other baselines.

Organization. The rest of this paper is structured as follows. Section 2 revisits the related work. Section 3 overviews the background of RWR. Section 4 proposes our divide-and-conquer method, k-LU-RWR, for RWR acceleration, followed by some improved strategies in Section 4.3. Experiment results are reported in Section 5. Section 6 concludes the paper.

2   Related Work

RWR has been widely accepted as a useful measure of node proximity based on graph topology since the pioneering work of Tong *et al.* [5]. In that work, a singular vector decomposition (SVD) based algorithm, B_LIN, was also proposed for computing RWR, by taking advantage of block structure of a graph. However, this method still involves an matrix inversion on very dense matrices, which is rather expensive, requiring cubic time in the number of nodes.

Later, Fujiwara *et al.* [1] proposed a fast top-K search based on RWR proximities. Their algorithm involves two strategies: first, they deployed a large LU decomposition on an *entire* graph for computing RWR; second, they used BFS tree estimation and devised a pruning technique to skip unnecessary scanning of nodes for top-K results. However, after LU decomposition, matrix inversions of **L** and **U** on the *entire* graph are still costly. In contrast, our work deploys a divide-and-conquer method to invert **L** and **U** recursively on small subgraphs, therefore achieving high computational efficiency.

Most recently, Yu *et al.* [7] have developed an incremental algorithm that supports link incremental updates for RWR on dynamical graphs. In comparison, our work focuses on efficient computations of RWR on static graphs.

3   Preliminaries

Notations. Table 1 lists the notations used throughout this paper.

Table 1. Symbols and Definitions

Symbols	Definitions
n	total number of nodes in a graph
c	restarting probability, $0 \leq c \leq 1$
$\mathbf{A} = [a_{i,j}]$	column-normalized adjacency matrix
$\boldsymbol{p}_i = [p_{i,j}]$	$n \times 1$ RWR vector for query i, with $p_{i,j}$ the proximity of node j $w.r.t.$ i
$\mathbf{W}$	$\mathbf{W} := \mathbf{I} - (1 - c)\mathbf{A}$
$\boldsymbol{v}_i$	$n \times 1$ vector, whose i^{th} element is 1, and 0 otherwise
$\mathbf{L}$	lower triangular matrix
$\mathbf{U}$	upper triangular matrix
$\mathbf{I}$	identity matrix

RWR Overview. The formal definition of RWR is as follows [5]:

$$\boldsymbol{p}_i = c\mathbf{A}\boldsymbol{p}_i + (1 - c)\boldsymbol{v}_i. \tag{1}$$

Intuitively, Equation (1) suggests that a random particle starts to walk from a given query node i, and the particle iteratively transmits to its neighbor with the transition possibility in proportion to the edge weight between them. At each step, it has a probability c to return to the original node i until it reaches a steady state. The element $p_{i,j}$ in vector $\boldsymbol{p}_i$ refers to the probability of the particle finally stays at node j.

Based on Equation (1), we have the following closed-form of $\boldsymbol{p}_i$:

$$\boldsymbol{p}_i = (1 - c)(\mathbf{I} - c\mathbf{A})^{-1}\boldsymbol{v}_i = (1 - c)\mathbf{W}^{-1}\boldsymbol{v}_i. \tag{2}$$

The straightforward way of solving $\boldsymbol{p}_i$ in Equation (1) is to adopt an iterative paradigm: $\boldsymbol{p}_i^{(k+1)} = c\mathbf{A}\boldsymbol{p}_i^{(k)} + (1 - c)\boldsymbol{v}_i$, where $\boldsymbol{p}_i^{(k)}$ is the k-th iterative RWR vector $w.r.t.$ query node i. There are two stopping criteria for this iterative method: one is, given a threshold ϵ, to check whether the norm of the difference of two consecutive iterative RWR vectors is below ϵ, $i.e.$, $\|\boldsymbol{p}_i^{(k+1)} - \boldsymbol{p}_i^{(k)}\| \leq \epsilon$; the other is, given the total number of iterations K, to check whether the number of iterations increasingly reaches K. However, both of these criteria may sacrifice a little accuracy, as compared with non-iterative methods. Therefore, in this paper our optimization techniques for RWR are based on non-iterative framework.

LU Factorization. Regarding the non-iterative methods for RWR, LU decomposition is the best-known method, which is based on a closed-form of $\boldsymbol{p}_i$, as shown in Equation (2). However, directly calculating $\mathbf{W}^{-1}$ requires high computation time as the inversion matrix could be dense even though $\mathbf{W}$ is sparse in most cases. To deal with this problem, we take advantage of the Crout's algorithm [2] to do LU decomposition. Consequently, we can compute the inversions of $\mathbf{L}$ and $\mathbf{U}$ instead, namely, $\mathbf{W}^{-1} = \mathbf{U}^{-1}\mathbf{L}^{-1}$.

Algorithm 1. k-LU-RWR Algorithm

Input:
    A : the normalized adjacency matrix
    n : total number of nodes
    i : query node
    c : restarting probability
    k : partitioning times
Output:
    p_i: ranking vector of node i
1: Compute $\mathbf{W} = \mathbf{I} - c\mathbf{A}$
2: Do LU decomposition for $\mathbf{W} = \mathbf{LU}$ according to Crout's algorithm
3: $\mathbf{L}^{-1} = recInvLU(\mathbf{L}, n, k)$
4: $\mathbf{U}^{-1} = recInvLU(\mathbf{U}, n, k)$
5: $p_i = (1-c)\mathbf{U}^{-1}\mathbf{L}^{-1}v_i$
6: **return** p_i

---

4 Our Solution

4.1 A Divide-and-Conquer Strategy for RWR

To meet the challenges raised by RWR, we propose an algorithm named k-LU-RWR shown in Algorithm 1. In consideration of Equation (2), we precompute and store $\mathbf{W}^{-1}$ offline which is from step 1 to step 4 in the algorithm. When a query node i comes, we simply calculate the proximities p_i online by only two multiplication operations of matrix-vector according to step 5.

Now let us concentrate on step 3 and step 4. As we have decided in Section 3, we take advantage of LU decomposition on $\mathbf{W}$. However, directly utilizing LU decomposition still requires to compute inversion matrices for both $\mathbf{L}$ and $\mathbf{U}$, so we apply following optimization strategies. We partition $\mathbf{L}$ and $\mathbf{U}$ into four parts, as presented in Figure 1. After that, we compute the matrix inversions of $\mathbf{L}$ and $\mathbf{U}$ according to Equation (3). Specifically, we do matrix inversions on $\mathbf{L}_{1,1}$, $\mathbf{L}_{2,2}$, $\mathbf{U}_{1,1}$ and $\mathbf{U}_{2,2}$, referred to as *triangle inversion*, and matrix multiplications on $\mathbf{L}_{2,1}$, $\mathbf{U}_{1,2}$ part, referred to as *rectangle multiplication*. When finished, we merge the block matrices into $\mathbf{L}^{-1}$ and $\mathbf{U}^{-1}$.

$$\mathbf{L}^{-1} = \begin{bmatrix} \mathbf{L}_{1,1}^{-1} & 0 \\ -\mathbf{L}_{2,2}^{-1}\mathbf{L}_{2,1}\mathbf{L}_{1,1}^{-1} & \mathbf{L}_{2,2}^{-1} \end{bmatrix} \quad \mathbf{U}^{-1} = \begin{bmatrix} \mathbf{U}_{1,1}^{-1} & -\mathbf{U}_{1,1}^{-1}\mathbf{U}_{1,2}\mathbf{U}_{2,2}^{-1} \\ 0 & \mathbf{U}_{2,2}^{-1} \end{bmatrix} \quad (3)$$

From Figure 1, it is clear that $\mathbf{L}_{1,1}$, $\mathbf{L}_{2,2}$ remain to be lower triangular matrices, and $\mathbf{U}_{1,1}$, $\mathbf{U}_{1,2}$ remain to be upper triangular matrices. This inspires us to do the partition and inversion procedures recursively, as represented in Figure 2. So we further devise a recursive algorithm recInvLU in Algorithm 2 to calculate triangle matrix inversions in step 3 and step 4 of Algorithm 1.

4.2 Time Complexity of k-LU-RWR

In the pre-computation stage, i.e. step 1 to step 4, the main time cost includes LU decomposition and matrix inversion. In LU decomposition part, we adopt

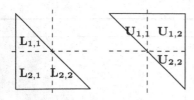
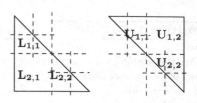

Fig. 1. L and U Partitions   **Fig. 2.** Recursive L and U Partitions

---

Algorithm 2. recInvLU($\mathbf{M}$, n, k)

Input:
    $\mathbf{M}$: the lower or upper triangular matrix after LU factorization
    n : size of matrix $\mathbf{M}$
    k : partitioning times
Output:
    $\mathbf{M}^{-1}$: the inversion matrix of $\mathbf{M}$
 1: **if** $k = 0$ **then**
 2:    $\mathbf{M}^{-1} = inverse(\mathbf{M})$
 3:    **return** $\mathbf{M}^{-1}$
 4: **else**
 5:    Partition $\mathbf{M}$ into $\mathbf{M}_{1,1}$, $\mathbf{M}_{1,2}$, $\mathbf{M}_{2,1}$, and $\mathbf{M}_{2,2}$
 6:    $\mathbf{M}_{1,1}^{-1}$=recInvLU($\mathbf{M}_{1,1}, \lfloor \frac{n}{2} \rfloor, k - 1$)
 7:    $\mathbf{M}_{2,2}^{-1}$=recInvLU($\mathbf{M}_{2,2}, \lceil \frac{n}{2} \rceil, k - 1$)
 8:    **if** $\mathbf{M}$ is lower triangular matrix **then**
 9:       $\mathbf{M}_{2,1}^{-1} = -\mathbf{M}_{2,2}^{-1}\mathbf{M}_{2,1}\mathbf{M}_{1,1}^{-1}$
10:      Merge $\mathbf{M}_{1,1}^{-1}$, $\mathbf{M}_{2,2}^{-1}$ and $\mathbf{M}_{2,1}^{-1}$ into $\mathbf{M}^{-1}$
11:    **else**
12:       $\mathbf{M}_{1,2}^{-1} = -\mathbf{M}_{1,1}^{-1}\mathbf{M}_{1,2}\mathbf{M}_{2,2}^{-1}$
13:      Merge $\mathbf{M}_{1,1}^{-1}$, $\mathbf{M}_{2,2}^{-1}$ and $\mathbf{M}_{1,2}^{-1}$ into $\mathbf{M}^{-1}$
14:    **end if**
15: **end if**

Crout's algorithm, whose theoretical time complexity is $O(n^3)$. Similarly, in the inversion part, if we inverse $\mathbf{L}$ and $\mathbf{U}$ directly, the time complexity is $O(n^3)$ too. However, we applied partitioning strategy and the time complexity is given by Equation (4), where $T(MM(\frac{n}{2}))$ represents the cost of *rectangle multiplication* part in Algorithm 2.

$$T(recInvLU(n)) = 2T(recInvLU(\frac{n}{2})) + 2T(MM(\frac{n}{2}))$$

$$= n\log(n) + 2T(MM(\frac{n}{2})) \qquad (4)$$

In the query stage, we simply do two multiplications of matrix-vector. For this reason, the query response is nearly real-time.

4.3 Further Improvement of k-LU-RWR

From Equation (4), we know that the time of RWR mainly depends on the matrix multiplications. A straightforward implementation of the matrix multiplications needs cubic time in the number of nodes. We now introduce two enhanced versions for accelerating the matrix multiplications: (1) We can adopt sparse matrix storage data structure. Since the adjacency matrix $\mathbf{A}$ is often sparse, we can use the reordering strategy [1] to keep the sparsity of LU decomposition. This reordering strategy has a good performance in practice. However, when matrices are becoming dense, the worst case time is still $O(n^3)$. (2) We can also apply Strassen's algorithm [3] to reduce the time of the matrix multiplications to $O(n^{\log_2 7})$. Combining these two methods together, it requires $O(n^{\log_2 7})$ time in total for computing RWR, while eliminating unnecessary multiplications by filtering zero entries.

5   Performance Evaluation

5.1   Experiments Settings

We set the restart probability $c = 0.9$, as previously used in [5].

We conduct a set of experiments on the value of partition times k, to see how it effects on the experiment performance. To verify the effect of the reorder strategy, we also do experiments on k-LU-RWR without reorder procedure called Un-LU-RWR, compared with k-LU-RWR. The ratio of the number of nonzero entries in L^{-1} and U^{-1} to the edges in matrices is introduced to indicate the time and storage costs we preserve. Moreover, the proposed algorithm is compared with NB_LIN [5] and k-dash [1] in terms of pre-computation time to show the efficiency of our algorithm. In k-dash, we compute proximities of top-n nodes for fair comparison. Besides, we do experiments to show the high response time on queries of k-LU-RWR.

We use real and synthetic datasets. All experiments were conducted on the machine with 2.5GHz CPU and 4.00GB main memory. Our algorithms are implemented in C++. The details of datasets are listed in Table 2.

Table 2. Datasets

Datasets	Number of nodes	Number of edges	Type
bcsstk25	$\approx 15K$	$\approx 252K$	real
bcsstk31	$\approx 36K$	$\approx 1,181K$	binary
bauru5727	$\approx 40K$	$\approx 145K$	binary
crystm03	$\approx 25K$	$\approx 584K$	real
pcrystk03	$\approx 25K$	$\approx 1,751K$	binary
synthetic10000	$10k$	$200k$	real
synthetic15000	$15k$	$250k$	real
synthetic20000	$20k$	$1000k$	real

5.2   Experiment Results

We first conduct experiments on how the value of k influences on the efficiency of k-LU-RWR. The results are shown in Figure 3. When k varies from 0 to 10, we see the time costs decrease gradually on both real datasets and synthetic

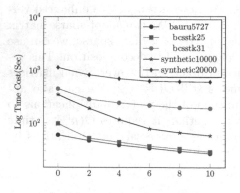

Fig. 3. Different k values of k-LU-RWR

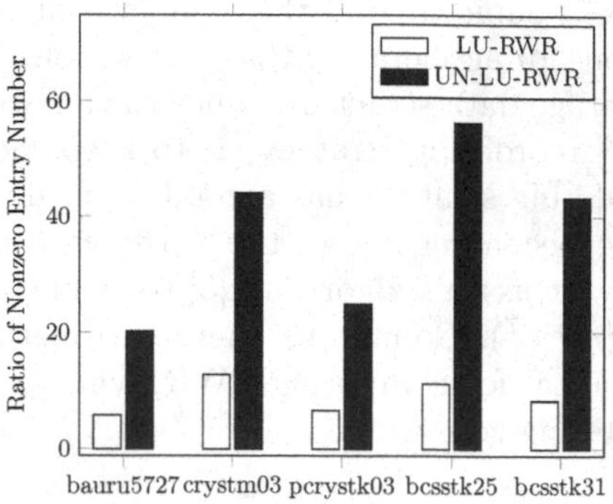

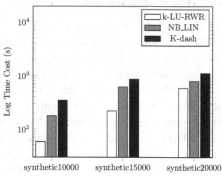

Fig. 4. Effect of Reorder Strategy

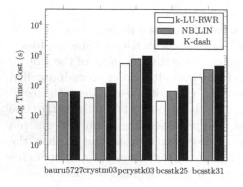

Fig. 5. Pre-computation Cost on RealData

Fig. 6. Pre-computation Cost on SyntheticData

datasets. For the case $k = 0$, we directly calculate the inversions of **L** and **U** without partition technique. When k increases, the falling speeds differ on each dataset due to the different architectures, but the performance changes little when k grows to a certain degree. When $k = 10$, it preserves about 50% pre-computation cost with regard to $k = 0$.

To demonstrate the sparsity of matrices after applying Reorder strategy, we show the ratio of non-zero element numbers to matrix edges in Figure 4. From the figure, we can see almost 70% storage costs are saved by reordering the elements. It also indicates the storages and computation costs we saved by adopting Reorder strategy and sparse storage.

We compare pre-computation costs between k-LU-RWR, NB_LIN and k-dash. The results on real datasets are shown in Figure 5 and the results on synthetic datasets are shown in Figure 6. Figure 5 demonstrates that our algorithm preserves about 50% pre-computation w.r.t NB_LIN and about 70% pre-computation w.r.t k-dash. Figure 6 shows our algorithm saves over 50% pre-computation cost w.r.t NB_LIN and k-dash. There are mainly two reasons for the enhancements:

(1) our algorithm adopts the idea of divide and conquer and takes advantage of a sparse manner so that it skips unnecessary calculations by ignoring zero entries; (2) by utilizing a fast matrix multiplication algorithm Strassen's Algorithm we saved one multiplication operation in each iteration by partitioning k times and reduce the time complexity.

We also do experiments to verify the efficiency of the query stage, in which we perform two matrix-vector multiplications. The query time on each datasets is a few hundred milliseconds, as expected.

6   Conclusion

This paper addressed the problem of efficiently computing RWR proximities based on graph topology. We first devised a divide-and-conquer paradigm to recursively do LU factorization over small subgraphs. Then, by taking advantage of sparsity of triangular matrix structure, we further accelerated RWR computation via fast matrix multiplication. Finally, we conducted extensive empirical results using real and synthetic dataset, showing the superiority of our proposed algorithm against the baselines in terms of computational time.

Acknowledgement. The work is supported by NSFC61232006, NSFC61021004.

References

1. Fujiwara, Y., Nakatsuji, M., Onizuka, M., Kitsuregawa, M.: Fast and exact top-k search for Random Walk with Restart. PVLDB 5, 442–453 (2012)
2. Press, W.H.: Numerical recipes 3rd edition: The art of scientific computing. Cambridge university press (2007)
3. Strassen, V.: Gaussian elimination is not optimal. Numerische Mathematik 13(4), 354–356 (1969)
4. Sun, Y., Han, J., Yan, X., Yu, P.S., Wu, T.: PathSim: Meta path-based top-k similarity search in heterogeneous information networks. PVLDB 4, 992–1003 (2011)
5. Tong, H., Faloutsos, C., Pan, J.-Y.: Fast Random Walk with Restart and its applications. In: ICDM, pp. 613–622 (2006)
6. Yu, W., Le, J., Lin, X., Zhang, W.: On the efficiency of estimating penetrating rank on large graphs. In: Ailamaki, A., Bowers, S. (eds.) SSDBM 2012. LNCS, vol. 7338, pp. 231–249. Springer, Heidelberg (2012)
7. Yu, W., Lin, X.: IRWR: Incremental Random Walk with Restart. In: SIGIR, pp. 1017–1020 (2013)
8. Yu, W., Lin, X., Zhang, W.: Towards efficient SimRank computation on large networks. In: ICDE, pp. 601–612 (2013)
9. Yu, W., Lin, X., Zhang, W.: Fast incremental SimRank on link-evolving graphs. In: ICDE, pp. 304–315 (2014)
10. Yu, W., Lin, X., Zhang, W., Chang, L., Pei, J.: More is simpler: Effectively and efficiently assessing node-pair similarities based on hyperlinks. PVLDB 7(1), 13–24 (2013)
11. Yu, W., Lin, X., Zhang, W., Zhang, Y., Le, J.: SimFusion+: Extending simfusion towards efficient estimation on large and dynamic networks. In: SIGIR, pp. 365–374 (2012)

LCAD: A Correlation Based Abnormal Pattern Detection Approach for Large Amount of Monitor Data

Jianwei Ding[1,2], Yingbo Liu[2], Li Zhang[2], and Jianmin Wang[2]

[1] Department of Computer Science and Technology, Tsinghua University, China
[2] Institute of Information System & Engineering, School of Software, Tsinghua University, China
dingjw09@mails.tsinghua.edu.cn,
{csliuyb,lizhang}@mail.tsinghua.edu.cn,
jimwang@tsinghua.edu.cn

Abstract. The last decade has witnessed tremendous growths of *Internet of Things*(IoT). Numerous condition monitoring systems(CMS) are widely applied to monitor equipments simultaneously. With the help of CMS, a large variety of monitor data from a large number of equipments can be collected in a very short time. However, it is a non-trivial task to take full advantage of such large amounts of monitor data in the context of anomaly detection. In this paper, we propose an approach called Latent Correlation based Anomaly Detection(LCAD) that can quickly detect potential anomalies from a large amount of monitor data, which posits that abnormal ones are a small portion in a mass of similar individuals. Instead of focusing on each single monitor data series, we identify the abnormal pattern by modeling the latent correlation among multiple correlative monitor data series using the Latent Correlation Probabilistic Model(LCPM), a probabilistic distribution model which can help to detect anomalies depending on their relations with LCPM. In order to validate our approach, we conduct experiments on the real-world datasets and the experimental results show that when facing a large amount of correlative monitor data series LCAD has a better performance as compared to the previous anomaly detection approaches.

Keywords: Anomaly Detection, Monitor Data, Condition Monitoring System.

1 Introduction

Nowadays, with the rapid development of *the Internet of Things*(IoT)[1,4] technology, *condition monitoring systems*(CMS) have been widely applied to monitor varieties of equipments. For example, *KOMTRAX*[1] and *IEM*[2] both are well-known CMS, which monitor equipments through the Internet, GPS and so on. By means of CMS, a wide variety of monitor data from a large number of equipments are widely collected within a very short period of time, e.g., the data size of monitor data from equipments collected by *IEM* exceeding $30G$ in a normal workday. If we can detect potential anomalies from these monitor data efficiently, it will enhance the efficiency of maintenance task scheduling, reduce the loss of failing and improve the design of equipments.

---

[1] *KOMTRAX*: http://www.komatsuamerica.com/komtrax
[2] *IEM*: http://www.sanygroup.com/group/en-us/

L. Chen et al. (Eds.): APWeb 2014, LNCS 8709, pp. 550–558, 2014.

Unlike most of the previous studies on anomaly detection, we focus on the latent relations of multiple correlative monitor data series but not each single monitor data series. For instance, there are two sensors in an equipment, which collect the engine temperature and the engine speed respectively. Since the engine temperature varies along with the variation of the engine speed, there exists a relation between the two corresponding monitor data series. During the normal work time this relation varies within a normal range. When anomalies occur, this relation may exceed the normal range. We define this relation as *Latent Correlation*, which depicts dependencies among multiple correlative monitor data series.

However, based on the latent correlation of correlative monitor data series, detecting potential anomalies from a large amount of monitor data faces a set of challenges. First, *during design and manufacture phases, most of potential anomalies of equipments in real work circumstances are not easily foreseen and identified.* For example, in the field of construction machinery, there are a variety of unforeseen issues like illegal operations and poor working circumstances, which lead to all kinds of anomalies that are not identified in the design phase. Furthermore, we analyze more than 5000 real maintenance records from one kind of construction machinery and confirm that most of equipments' anomalies are indeed not recorded or identified. Second, *the amount of monitor data is too large to quickly detect anomalies.* As it is not easy to foresee what kind of anomaly will happen on the equipment in real work circumstances, CMS have to collect a vast variety of monitor data as much as possible. This blind collection strategy makes the volume of collected monitor data increase dramatically. For example, our experimental datasets are collected from less than 300 equipments over a half year period, which have more than $50,000,000$ records.

In this paper, we address the above challenges by positing that abnormal ones are a small portion in a large number of similar individuals. We present Latent Correlation based Anomaly Detection(LCAD) that can quickly detect potential anomalies from a large amount of monitor data. In LCAD, we use Latent Correlation Vector(LCV) to represent the latent correlation among multiple correlative monitor data series. Thus we model these LCVs using Latent Correlation Probabilistic Model(LCPM), a probabilistic distribution model which depicts the probabilistic distribution of LCVs. Based on the LCPM, we can detect anomalies according to their relations with the LCPM. The anomalies detected by LCAD are defined as *Abnormal Patterns*. In order to validate our approach, we conduct experiments on real-world datasets and the experimental results illustrate that LCAD outperforms the previous approaches when facing a large amount of correlative monitor data series.

We believe that this paper mainly makes three contributions as. Firstly, we define the relation of multiple correlative monitor data series as the latent correlation. Furthermore, we formulate the latent correlation as the LCV, which depicts the pairwise relations of these monitor data series. Secondly, based on LCVs of multiple correlative monitor data series, we model these LCVs using LCPM, a probabilistic distribution model which depicts the variation range of LCVs. Thirdly, based on LCPM, we present LCAD, an anomaly detection approach which can quickly detect abnormal patterns from a large amount of monitor data.

The rest of this paper is organized as follows. Section 2 reviews the related work. In Section 3 we talk about the details of LCAD. Section 4 shows the results of experiments to validate our approach. Section 5 gives a summary about this study.

2   Related Work

Most of the previous studies on anomaly detection(also called outlier detection) focused on individual time series. Figure 1 illustrates a hierarchy of individual time series for anomaly detection in the literature. There are mainly four categories in taxonomy: (1) *Classification based*. Classification based anomaly detection consists of rules based[10], neural networks based[8,7] and SVM based[13]. (2) *Nearest neighbor based*. Nearest neighbor based anomaly detection consists of density based[2] and distance based[12,14]. (3) *Cluster based*. Cluster based anomaly detection like FindOut[15] and CBLOF[6], which assumes that normal data records belong to large and dense clusters while anomalies do not belong to any of the clusters or form very small clusters. (4) *Statistical*. Eskin et al.[5] also used stochastic distribution to detect anomalies depending on their relations with this model.

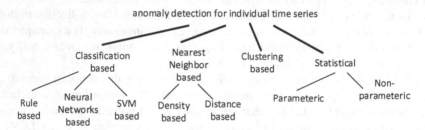

Fig. 1. A hierarchy of individual time series for anomaly detection in the literature

There are some existing methods proposed for anomaly detection of multiple time series. Zhang[16] et al. detected abnormal trend evolution from multiple data streams. However, it could not manage a large amount of time series, e.g. the monitor data series in this paper. Papadimitriou[11] et al. proposed SPIRIT that is a streaming pattern discovery approach in multiple time series data streams. Chan[3] et al. proposed box modeling for multiple training series. Although both approaches are able to efficiently mine multiple homogeneous time series, they are not suitable to directly mine multiple correlative time series in different dimensions. For instance, there are two categories of time series: one represents the engine temperature(temperature series) and the other time series represents the engine revolving speed(revolving series). Since the engine temperature rises with the increase of the engine revolving speed, there exists a latent positive correlation between the two time series. However, the above methods such as SPIRIT just model multiple temperature series or revolving series and lose sight of the latent correlation between two time series. Generally, existing works can not well address anomaly detection for multiple time series based on a large amount of correlative time series.

3   LCAD: Our Anomaly Detection Approach

Latent Correlation based Anomaly Detection(LCAD) focuses on the latent correlation among multiple correlative monitor data series. For definiteness and without loss of generality, we first give some notations to help us explain our anomaly approach LCAD. Given there is a number of equipments of the same category denoted as $\mathcal{E} = \{E_1, E_2, ..., E_M\}$, where E_m represents an equipment. For the equipment E_m, there exist a sequence of sensors denoted as $\mathcal{S} = \{S_1, S_2, ..., S_K\}$, intended to monitor different components of equipments that produce K categories of monitor data series denoted as $\mathcal{W}^m = \{W_1^m, W_2^m, ..., W_K^m\}$. Specially $W_k^m = \{v_k^m(1), v_k^m(2), ..., v_k^m(N)\}$ represents a monitor data series corresponding to the k-th sensor of the m-th equipment, where $v_k^m(n)$ is denoted as the collected values at time T_n.

3.1   Segmentation of Monitor Data Series

Definition 1 (Work Cycle Series). *A **work cycle** of equipment E_m is a complete work process, a complete usage of the equipment which is from the starting up to the shutdown of the equipment. A **work cycle series** is a segment of monitor data series in a work cycle, which is corresponding to a work cycle of an equipment. Illustrated in Figure 2, there are three work cycles shown in a monitor data series(values collected with lines). Hence, this monitor data series consists of three work cycle series.*

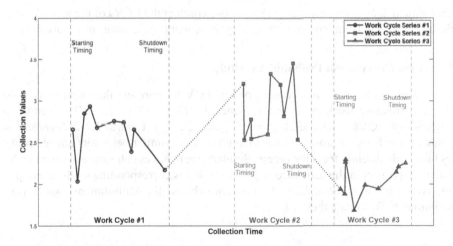

Fig. 2. Illustration of work cycle series

Since different equipments are operated in different work circumstances, the monitor data series collected from different equipments are entirely different. As a consequence, it is not suitable to compare the monitor data series along all the collection time directly. However, no matter what kind of work circumstances and operations, the work cycle series is more suitable for comparisons than the original monitor data series because work cycle series have similar behaviors in a work cycle in spite of different equipments.

3.2 Latent Correlation Extraction

Given there are a number of work cycle series in a work cycle denoted as $\mathcal{D} = \{D_1, D_2, ..., D_K\}$ where D_k means a work cycle series of one sensor denoted as $D_k = \{v_1^k, v_2^k, ..., v_T^k\}$. For K correlative work cycle series, we define a Latent Correlation Matrix(LCM) to represent the latent correlations of work cycle series. We denote the LCM of K work cycle series as $\mathcal{LCM} = \{C_{ij}\}_{KK}$, where the element C_{ij} means the Latent Correlation Parameter(LCP) between the i-th work cycle series D_i and j-th work cycle series D_j, hence the LCP is calculated as follows:

$$C_{ij} = \frac{\sum_{n=1}^{T}(v_n^i - \overline{v^i})(v_n^j - \overline{v^j})}{T-1} \tag{1}$$

In Formula 1, $\overline{v^i} = \frac{\sum_{n=1}^{T} v_n^i}{T}$ and $\overline{v^j} = \frac{\sum_{n=1}^{T} v_n^j}{T}$. Since the LCM is a symmetric matrix, where if $i \neq j$, the LCP C_{ij} is the covariance of the i-th work cycle series and the j-th work cycle series, if $i = j$, the LCP C_{ij}(diagonal element) is the variance. In order to ease the difficulty of modeling, we compress the LCM to the Latent Correlation Vector(LCV) denoted as $\mathcal{LCV} = \{\lambda_1, \lambda_2, ..., \lambda_K\}$ illustrated as Formula 2. The element λ_k of LCV is the k-th eigenvalue of LCM.

$$\mathcal{U} - \lambda_k \mathcal{LCM} = 0 \tag{2}$$

In formula 2, $\mathcal{U}$ is an unit matrix. Hence, we conduct the LCVs of these work cycle series to depict the latent correlations among these work cycle series in a work cycle.

3.3 Latent Correlation Probabilistic Model

In each work cycle, there are a corresponding LCV to represent the latent correlation of these correlative work cycle series. Hence, let $\mathcal{LCV}_1, \mathcal{LCV}_2, ..., \mathcal{LCV}_M$ denote as a sequence of LCVs, where $\mathcal{LCV}_m = \{\lambda_1^m, \lambda_2^m, ..., \lambda_T^m\}$. *Central Limit Theorem*[3] in statistic also tells us that most similar individuals have similar behaviors and abnormal ones behave differently from the others. Similarly there is a conclusion: abnormal LCVs are a small portion in the sequence of LCVs, which is corresponding to abnormal patterns. According to *Central Limit Theorem*, we choose the Multidimensional Normal Distribution to formulate these LCVs.

$$(\mathcal{LCV}_1, \mathcal{LCV}_2, ..., \mathcal{LCV}_M) \sim \mathcal{N}(x|\Sigma, \mu) = \frac{1}{(2\pi)^{\frac{M}{2}}|\Sigma|^{\frac{1}{2}}} e^{-\frac{(x-\mu)^T \Sigma^{-1}(x-\mu)}{2}} \tag{3}$$

In Formula 3, Σ and μ represent the covariance matrix and the average vector of the multivariate gaussian distribution respectively, which determine the LCPM of this sequence of LCVs. We apply the maximum likelihood estimation(MLE) to calculate these parameters.

---

[3] http://en.wikipedia.org/wiki/Central_Limit_Theorem

3.4 Abnormal Pattern Detection

Based on the LCPM, we define **Abnormal Pattern Detection Function**(APDF) of the LCVs denoted as follows:

$$\mathcal{D}\left(LCV;\Sigma,\mu,\alpha\right) = \begin{cases} 1, & \text{if } c_{w,s} > \mu + \alpha\Sigma \text{ or } c_{w,s} < \mu - \alpha\Sigma \\ 0, & \text{if } \mu - \alpha\Sigma \leq c_{w,s} \leq \mu + \alpha\Sigma \end{cases} \tag{4}$$

In the APDF, parameters Σ and μ mean the covariance matrix and the average vector of LCPM calculated as shown in Formula 3. In the experiment the parameter α is equal to 3. The input of APDF is an LCV or a sequence of LCVs. The output of APDF is a boolean value, 1 means that the input LCV is an anomaly corresponding to an abnormal pattern of equipments and 0 means the input LCV is normal.

4 Experimental Evaluation

4.1 Data Preparation

We conduct experiments on real-world datasets which come from a Chinese well-known construction machinery manufacturer. The original datasets contains three sub-datasets, corresponding to the three main components of pump concrete trucks: pumping system(**Pump-sys**), cantilever system(**Can-sys**) and underpan system(**Under-sys**) of pump concrete trucks. The statistics of the three sub-datasets from pump concrete trucks are shown in Table 1.

Table 1. The statistics of three sub-datasets collected from pump concrete trucks

Sub-dataset	Number of monitor data records	Number of monitor data series categories	Number of work cycles	Number of work cycle series
Pump-sys	35,807,982	177	32,632	5,775,864
Can-sys	11,456,724	136	32,632	4,437,952
Under-sys	5,572,806	63	32,632	2,055,816
total	**52,837,512**	**376**	**32,632**	**12,269,632**

As shown in Table 1, we apply $52, 837, 512$ monitor data records to the real experiments collected from 279 pump concrete trucks. There are 376 sensors in each equipment that produce 376 monitor data series over half a year period. Furthermore, there are $12, 269, 632$ work cycle series($32, 632$ work cycle multiplies 376 types of monitor data series.). The three sub-datasets **Pump-sys, Can-sys** and **Under-sys** have $5, 775, 864, 4, 437, 952$ and $2, 055, 816$ work cycle series respectively. Each sub-datasets has its corresponding LCPM, as there are too much parameters, we will not illustrate the three LCPMs in the experiment.

4.2   Baselines and Evaluation Methodology

Baselines. We consider our proposed LCPM for anomaly detection on the three sub-datasets: **Pump-sys,Can-sys** and **Under-sys**. Actually there are not relative approaches for anomaly detection, LCPM focuses on a sequence of work cycle series but the previous focus on one single work cycle series. In the experiments we compare our proposed LCPM with three baseline approaches: (1) *Local Outlier Factor (LOF) approach[2]*. For each work cycle series $D_k = \{v_1^k, v_2^k, ..., v_T^k\}$, compute $LOF(D_k)$ as ratio of average local reachability density of D_k k-nearest neighbors and local reachability density of this work cycle series. (2) *Connectivity Outlier Factor approach[14]*. For each work cycle series $D_k = \{v_1^k, v_2^k, ..., v_T^k\}$, calculate $COF(D_k)$ to identify outliers as points whose neighborhoods is sparser than the neighborhoods of their neighbors. (3) *Cluster based Local Outlier Factor (CBLOF)[9]*. For each work cycle series $D_k = \{v_1^k, v_2^k, ..., v_T^k\}$, we use squeezer clustering algorithm to conduct clustering and determine CBLOF for each work cycle series measured by both the size of the cluster and the distance to the cluster.

Evaluation Metrics. We evaluate the prediction performance of the above algorithms using 3 metrics: Recall (detection rate), Precision and AUC(area under the ROC curve). Generally, Recall measures the ratio between the number of correctly detected anomalies and the total number of anomalies, Precision measures the ratio between the number of correctly detected anomalies and the total number of detected anomalies, and AUC measures the tradeoff between Recall and Precision.

4.3   Experimental Results and Analysis

We present the evaluation results in Table 2. As highlighted in bold, latent correlation anomaly detection(LCAD) consistently outperforms other approaches on most sub-datasets and most metrics. The performances of LCAD far exceeds that of the other approaches on most metrics, demonstrating the importance and effectiveness of latent correlations among condition data series in LCAD and extracting the latent correlation vector in LCPM.

Table 2. The performance of various approaches on the three sub-datasets

Dataset	Metric	LOF	COF	CBLOF	LCAD
Pump-sys	Recall	0.420	0.527	0.505	**0.721**
	Precision	0.469	0.601	0.532	**0.623**
	AUC	0.536	0.761	0.659	**0.854**
Can-sys	Recall	0.559	0.517	0.542	**0.819**
	Precision	0.583	0.681	**0.702**	0.697
	AUC	0.633	0.598	0.721	**0.783**
Under-sys	Recall	0.542	0.452	**0.821**	0.819
	Precision	0.461	0.574	0.583	**0.791**
	AUC	0.514	0.563	0.639	**0.684**

LOF is a nearest neighbor approach based on the reachability distance, another work which calculates the local reachability density to determine the LOF of data records. COF almost achieves better performances as compared to LOF, which is based on the average chain distance. Furthermore, CBLOF outperforms than the two KNN approaches LOF and COF on **Can-sys** and **Under-sys**, which is a cluster approach for anomaly detection based on LOF. However, it fails on **Pump-sys** because data are sparse and distances between any two data records may become quite similar in high dimensional spaces.

Though the precision ratio of LCPM on **Can-sys** is 0.005 less than that of CBLOF, the recall ratio and AUC of LCPM both are much higher than that of CBLOF. There are similar experimental results on **Under-sys**. As a whole, LCAD is not only accurate but also stable than others. This convinces us that the latent relation among work cycle series can help detect more potential anomalies.

4.4 Implementation and Discussion

In real detecting circumstances, there are two ways to implement LCAD: offline detection and online detection. *Offline detection* focuses on the pre-existing monitor data and ignores the real time incremental monitor data. It detects all the monitor data in batch at regular intervals. This paper's experiments are based on offline detection. *Online detection* focuses on the real time monitor data only. It detects the real-time incremental monitor data in real time. We have also applied this type of detection method in a real CMS.

5 Summary

Quickly detecting potential anomalies from a large amount of monitor data is very important for us to better know the working condition of equipments. In this paper, we model the latent correlations of monitor data using LCPM, a probabilistic distribution which assumes that abnormal ones are a small portion in most of similar individuals. Based on LCPM, we proposed LCAD, an anomaly detection approach which can quickly detect potential anomalies from a large amount of monitor data. Our approach achieves promising performances in experimental studies, which leads us to draw the conclusion that our proposed LCAD indeed detect more potential anomalies as compared to the previous approaches.

Our future work mainly includes the model selection, the model training and the conduction experiments on different datasets. Furthermore, the further analysis of the abnormal patterns detected by LCAD is also an interesting question.

References

1. Atzori, L., Iera, A., Morabito, G.: The internet of things: A survey. Computer Networks 54(15), 2787–2805 (2010)
2. Breunig, M.M., Kriegel, H.-P., Ng, R.T., Sander, J.: Lof: identifying density-based local outliers. ACM Sigmod Record 29, 93–104 (2000)

3. Chan, P.K., Mahoney, M.V.: Modeling multiple time series for anomaly detection. In: Fifth IEEE International Conference on Data Mining, p. 8. IEEE (2005)
4. Dutton, W.H.: The internet of things. Available at SSRN (2013)
5. Eskin, E.: Anomaly detection over noisy data using learned probability distributions. In: Proceedings of the International Conference on Machine Learning (2000)
6. Eskin, E., Arnold, A., Prerau, M., Portnoy, L., Stolfo, S.: A geometric framework for unsupervised anomaly detection. In: Applications of Data Mining in Computer Security, pp. 77–101. Springer (2002)
7. González, F.A., Dasgupta, D.: Anomaly detection using real-valued negative selection. Genetic Programming and Evolvable Machines 4(4), 383–403 (2003)
8. Hawkins, S., He, H., Williams, G.J., Baxter, R.A.: Outlier detection using replicator neural networks. In: Kambayashi, Y., Winiwarter, W., Arikawa, M. (eds.) DaWaK 2002. LNCS, vol. 2454, pp. 170–180. Springer, Heidelberg (2002)
9. He, Z., Xu, X., Deng, S.: Discovering cluster-based local outliers. Pattern Recognition Letters 24(9), 1641–1650 (2003)
10. Otey, M.E., Ghoting, A., Parthasarathy, S.: Fast distributed outlier detection in mixed-attribute data sets. Data Mining and Knowledge Discovery 12(2-3), 203–228 (2006)
11. Papadimitriou, S., Sun, J., Faloutsos, C.: Streaming pattern discovery in multiple time-series. In: Proceedings of the 31st International Conference on Very Large Data Bases, pp. 697–708. VLDB Endowment (2005)
12. Ramaswamy, S., Rastogi, R., Shim, K.: Efficient algorithms for mining outliers from large data sets. ACM SIGMOD Record 29, 427–438 (2000)
13. Steinwart, I.: Consistency of support vector machines and other regularized kernel classifiers. IEEE Transactions on Information Theory 51(1), 128–142 (2005)
14. Tang, J., Chen, Z., Fu, A., Cheung, D.: A robust outlier detection scheme for large data sets. In: Proceedings of the 6th Pacific-Asia Conference on Knowledge Discovery and Data Mining, pp. 535–548 (2002)
15. Yu, D., Sheikholeslami, G., Zhang, A.: Findout: finding outliers in very large datasets. Knowledge and Information Systems 4(4), 387–412 (2002)
16. Zhang, C., Weng, N., Chang, J., Zhou, A.: Detecting abnormal trend evolution over multiple data streams. In: Li, Q., Feng, L., Pei, J., Wang, S.X., Zhou, X., Zhu, Q.-M. (eds.) APWeb/WAIM 2009. LNCS, vol. 5446, pp. 285–296. Springer, Heidelberg (2009)

Cost-Based Optimization
of Logical Partitions for a Query Workload
in a Hadoop Data Warehouse

Shu Peng[1], Jun Gu[1], X. Sean Wang[1], Weixiong Rao[2], Min Yang[1], and Yu Cao[3]

[1] Shanghai Key Laboratory of Intelligent Information Processing,
School of Computer Science, Fudan University, Shanghai, China
{pengshu,gujun,xywangCS,m_yang}@fudan.edu.cn
[2] School of Software Engineering, Tongji University, Shanghai, China
rweixiong@gmail.com
[3] EMC Labs, Tsinghua Science Park, Beijing, China
yu.cao@emc.com

Abstract. Recently, Hadoop has become a common programming framework for big data analysis on a cluster of commodity machines. To optimize queries on a large amount of data managed by the Hadoop Distributed File System (HDFS), it is particularly important to optimize the reading of the data. Previous works either designed file formats to cluster data belonging to the same column, or proposed to place correlated data onto the same physical nodes. In query-workload aware situation, a possible optimization strategy is to place data that may not be used by the same query into different logical partitions so that not every partition is needed for a query, while physically distribute the data in each partition evenly across the compute nodes. This paper proposes a condition-based partitioning scheme to implement this optimization strategy. Experiments show that the proposed scheme not only reduces the I/O cost, but also maintains the workload of the compute nodes balanced across the cluster.

Keywords: Hadoop, Data Analysis, Data Partition, Query Workload, Cost-based Optimization.

1 Introduction

Over the past few years, Hadoop [1] has been widely used for data mining and data analysis due to its two advantages. First, the Hadoop parallel programming framework allows users to comfortably write MapReduce [4] jobs on a big cluster of commodity machines. Second, with the help of Hadoop distributed file system (HDFS) to distribute input files across the clustered machines, the MapReduce jobs can then process local file chunks with very low communication cost.

The main processing mode in using HDFS to evaluate queries is to scan the entire data. For an efficient use of the cluster of machines, the HDFS splits large data files into data blocks and then distributes the blocks randomly and evenly

L. Chen et al. (Eds.): APWeb 2014, LNCS 8709, pp. 559–567, 2014.

across the machines. This policy can balance the workload of the machines when the scan is done. When all the data needs to be scanned, this is indeed a very effective method.

Optimization over the above basic scanning method has been introduced in the literature, especially for data in a relational table form. RCFile [7] was designed as a data format that stores the column-wise compressed data in order to reduce the I/O cost. However, often a query does not need to use all the data in a data file. For example, a select-project query may only need to access a small portion of the rows and a few of the columns in a relation. A general approach in the literature (e.g. CoHadoop [5]) is to put the data needed by the same query onto the same physical machines to reduce data shuffling. However, this approach may lead to unbalanced workload across the cluster, reducing the efficiency of the whole cluster.

In this paper, we propose a novel approach, namely a condition based partition scheme (CPS). The main idea of CPS is to analyze the query workload and then to place correlated data into the same logical partitions, and each logical partition is instead physically stored in clustered machines. Here, "correlated data" means the data that are used by the same query. In detail, by analysing the queries, we divide correlated rows of input tables into the logical partitions. When the raw table data is uploaded to HDFS, the HDFS policy then still randomly and evenly distributes the data across the cluster, without incurring unbalanced workload across the cluster. When the queries are processed, only those logical partitions needed by the queries are accessed. In this way, we can avoid the full scan of the whole input data and access only the needed partitions, and yet do not introduce any imbalance in processing tasks among the cluster nodes. Consequently, the CPS greatly optimizes the query processing time.

In summary, in this paper, we make the following contributions:

1. We introduce a logical partitioning approach to avoid full scan of data, yet to keep the physical workload balanced across the cluster.
2. We design a method that does the logical partitioning correctly and automatically in an optimized manner, given a query workload.
3. We design a prototype to implement (based on Hive [2]) the logically partitioning scheme so that only the related partitions are scanned without changing Hadoop internals.
4. We conduct experiments to compare the implemented prototype with the state of art approaches, using the benchmark data from TPC-H [3]. The experimental results show that our prototype implementation outperforms RCFile by 20% to 40% on query processing time.

The rest of the paper is organized as follows. First we introduce the background and motivation of our work in Section 2 and Section 3, respectively. Next, we present the design of our partitioning scheme in Section 4. After that, we evaluate the performance of the developed prototype in Section 5, and review the related works in Section 6. Finally Section 7 concludes the paper.

2   Background

To provide a technical background of this paper, we give an overview of two systems, namely Hadoop and Hive, and an important concept used in this paper: logical partition.

2.1   Hadoop and Hive

The Hadoop system mainly contains two components, namely HDFS and MapReduce. Before processing the input files, Hadoop needs to distribute the files randomly and evenly across a cluster of commodity machines. The files are then maintained on HDFS with data blocks of 64 MB by default. Next, to initiate a data query task, Hadoop starts map tasks (mappers) and reduce tasks (reducers) concurrently on the clustered machines. The mappers sequentially read the input files from HDFS with each data block as a unit and shuffle the intermediate results to the reducers. When the jobs are finished, the reducers write the output back to HDFS.

To support queries, Hive provided an open-source data warehousing solution atop Hadoop. To process the queries written by an SQL alike declarative language, Hive compiles the queries into MapReduce jobs that are executed by Hadoop. Besides, Hive provides commands and third party application interfaces, such that users can execute queries in a flexible way.

2.2   Logical Partition

Hive supports the concept of logical partition. That is, for a given table, the data belonging to the same logical partition is placed into one directory on HDFS. However, the files are physically distributed onto multiple nodes in a cluster. For example, Hive uploads the table raw files onto HDFS by executing MapReduce jobs, and then splits the raw files into N partitions. Next, the N partitions are evenly placed onto M datanodes of a Hadoop cluster.

3   Motivation

For a given table T in data warehouse, in the simplest case, we assume that only one selection query refers to T. We can directly select all rows from T satisfying the query condition into a partition, and let all remaining rows into another partition. Intuitively, by treating the query condition as a sub-range R in the universe U, the partitioning scheme is to separate the universe U into the sub-range R and the opposite $U \setminus R$.

In the general case, there instead could exist multiple queries referring to the table T. As an example of the general case, three following queries refer to the table *Lineitem* in the TPC-H [3] benchmark (we will use the queries throughout this paper).

```
Q1: SELECT l_returnflag, count(1),  sum(l_extendedprice*(1-l_discount))
    FROM Lineitem
    WHERE l_shipdate>'1997-09-02'
    GROUP BY l_returnflag;

Q2: SELECT sum(l_extendedprice*l_discount) as revenue
    FROM Lineitem
    WHERE l_shipdate >= '1994-01-01' AND l_shipdate < '1995-01-01' AND
          l_discount >= 0.05 AND l_discount <= 0.07;

Q3: SELECT l_shipmode, count(1)
    FROM Lineitem
    WHERE l_shipmode = 'MAIL' OR l_shipmode = 'SHIP'
    GROUP BY l_shipmode;
```

Given the general case, the key of the proposed partitioning scheme is to generate a best partition plan with the minimal query processing time. Therefore, we may independently consider each of the queries, and then follow the above simplest case (with only one query) to partition the input table T. However, the approach could lead to too many partitions and MapReduce jobs during processing queries and still cannot guarantee the minimal query processing time.

To this end, we need to carefully find a best way to partition the table T for the minimal query processing time. Here, we will define a *partition plan* that is used to partition T (Section 4.1). Given multiple queries, each of the queries might involve an associated plan to partition the table T, and the whole queries involve the various combinations of such plans (Sections 4.2). Consequently, based on a cost model, we find the best one with the least cost among all possible candidates for the minimal processing time (Section 4.3).

4 Design of CPS Partitioning Scheme

4.1 Definition of Partition Plan

For a given table T with schema T^s, we consider a set of queries over T. Such queries involve the number n of query conditions θ_i with $1 \le i \le n$. Based on such n conditions, we then define a partition plan $P = \{p_1, p_2, ..., p_n\}$ if and only if the conditions θ_i associated with p_i satisfies the requirement $\theta_1 \vee \theta_2 \vee ... \vee \theta_n = True$. In general, partition p_i is determined by an associated condition θ_i, such that the data of p_i satisfies the condition $\theta_i = True$. When p_i are ready, to process a query having multiple conditions, we will consider only those partitions corresponding to such conditions for query evaluation.

Based on the three queries Q_1, Q_2 and Q_3, we give an example of a valid partition plan in Table 1. Just for simplicity, we only consider the predicate conditions referring to the attribute *l_shipdate*. As shown in this table, each partition has an unique ID, and the data in each of the partitions is determined by selecting the rows from *Lineitem* satisfying the associated conditions.

Table 1. Example of Partition Plan for *Lineitem*

UID	Associated Conditions
0	*l_shipdate* < '1994-01-01'
1	*l_shipdate* ≥ '1994-01-01' and *l_shipdate* < '1995-01-01'
2	*l_shipdate* ≥ '1995-01-01' and *l_shipdate* ≤ '1997-09-02'
3	*l_shipdate* > '1997-09-02'

4.2 Generate Candidate Plans

We note that the query conditions could involve disjunctive and (or) conjunctive forms of individual predicates. Thus, we need to transform the disjunctive and (or) conjunctive combinations of such predicates. The purpose of such transformations is to simply the query combinations and meanwhile should not falsely miss any query results needed by the queries (and thus should correctly answer the queries without falsely missing any results).

With equivalent transformations in logical theory, we can transform query conditions into their the major conjunctive normal form (CNF), and each element in CNF refers to one attribute. Based on all such elements, we then use the algorithm in Section 4.2 to generate the candidates of partition plans.

Before transforming the predict conditions in queries, we first formally define the *candidate partition plan* as follows. For the table schema T^s, the candidate partition plan about an attribute a contains all selective conditions involving a and their corresponding negative conditions. To avoid overlapping conditions, a candidate plan satisfies $\forall \theta_i, \theta_j \in \Theta, \theta_i \wedge \theta_j = \emptyset$.

Next, we consider the following typical data warehouse query, and would like to find out all the candidate plans.

$$SELECT \; \mathcal{A} \; FROM \; T \; WHERE \; \mathcal{P}$$

where $\mathcal{A}$ denotes an aggregate function over attributes of table T, and $\mathcal{P}$ denotes a set of predicates in the query conditions. Denote $\pi(\mathcal{P})$ to be the attributes appearing in the conditions. For each query in given workload, we can extract the attributes set and union all the sets to figure out the attributes appearing in the queries. Then, for every attribute, we combine the query conditions refer to it. Finally, we figure out a candidate plan for each attribute as shown in Table 2.

4.3 Cost Model of Partition Plan

In this section, we give a cost model to measure the cost of each plan. Consider table $T = (a_1, a_2, ..., a_k)$ where a_i with $1 \leq i \leq k$ is the i-th attribute of T and $M(T)$ is the size of T. Suppose we have a candidate plan $P = \{p_1, p_2, ..., p_n\}$ determined by attribute a and the corresponding condition set $\phi_T^a = \{\theta_1, \theta_2, ..., \theta_n\}$. Denote $r(\theta)$ is the selective ratio of T, when filtering T according to θ. Then, the size of the i-th partition of table T is

$$S(T, i) = r(\theta_i) \times M(T) \tag{1}$$

Table 2. Candidate Partition Plans of Demo Workload

Attribute	UID	Corresponding Condition
l_shipdate	0	l_shipdate > '1997-09-02'
	1	l_shipdate <= '1997-09-02' AND l_shipdate >= '1995-01-01'
	2	l_shipdate >= '1994-01-01' AND l_shipdate < '1995-01-01'
	3	l_shipdate < '1994-01-01'
l_discount	0	l_discount < 0.05
	1	l_discount >= 0.05 AND l_discount <= 0.07
	2	l_discount > 0.07
l_shipmode	0	l_shipmode = 'MAIL'
	1	l_shipmode = 'SHIP'
	2	l_shipmode <> 'MAIL' AND l_shipmode <> 'SHIP'

Next, we use the function $f(T, i, q)$ to determine whether or not the i-th partition is hit by q, where $\pi(q)$ is the set of attributes in *where* clause of q and c_q is the where clause of q:

$$f(T, i, q) = \begin{cases} 1, & a \notin \pi(q) \\ 1, & c_q \cap \theta_i \neq \emptyset \\ 0, & \text{otherwise} \end{cases} \quad (2)$$

In addition, if aggregation operations existing in query, there incurs two MapReduce jobs to figure out query result, the first one executes selection operation and the other one processes its result for aggregation. We accumulates the input size and use function $g(q)$ to determine whether q having aggregations:

$$g(q) = \begin{cases} 1 + r(q), & \text{if } q \text{ contains aggregation functions} \\ 1, & \text{otherwise} \end{cases} \quad (3)$$

Then, given the query set $Q(T)$ contains all the queries refer to T in current workload, the cost of fetching input data of T is

$$C(T) = \sum_{\forall q \in Q} \sum_{1 \leq i \leq n} S(T, i) \times g(q) \times f(T, i, q) \quad (4)$$

With the above cost model, we then can calculate the cost of each candidate plan, and the one with the least cost is chosen as the final plan.

5   Experiments

We evaluate the performance of CPS on three aspects: (i) the usefulness of our cost model, (ii) the advantages of CPS over previous works.

We conduct our experiments on a Hadoop cluster with one master node and 5 slave nodes. Each node has the same hardware and software configuration with 64-bit Linux and 750 GB hard disk. We implement CPS service atop Hadoop

1.2.1 and Hive 0.11.0. Each mapper/reducer task uses 1024 MB memory and the block size is 64 MB by default. We use dbgen in TPC-H to generate the synthetic dataset and the scale factor is 30.

5.1   Usefulness of the Proposed Cost Model

In section 4.1, we generate 3 candidate partition plans for table *Lineitem*. Next, for each of these plans, we first use the cost model to compute the theoretical cost, and next compute the empirical results based on our experiments. Instead of precisely computing the theoretical cost, we alternatively use the size of the data used by the plans. Denote M to be the total size of an input table, and $r \cdot M$ then indicates the size of the data used by a plan to process the query.

In Table 3, for each of the candidate plans with respect to the rows *l_shipdate*, *l_discount* and *l_shipmode*, the 2nd - 4th columns indicate the data size used by each query from Q_1 to Q_3 (because of aggregation, the ratio of input size to table size maybe larger than 1), and the 5th column sums the data size. The rightmost column instead gives the real query time of executing all three queries. Though the result given by the proposed cost modal does not precisely indicate the absolute cost of each candidate plan, this table does verify that the empirical value (i.e., the real query time) is roughly consistent with the theoretical value computed by the cost model (i.e., the total cost in the 5-th column).

Table 3. Comparison with Theory Cost Values

Key Attribute	Q1	Q2	Q3	Total Value	Execution Time(s)
l_shipdate	$0.33 \cdot M$	$0.15 \cdot M$	$1.39 \cdot M$	$1.87 \cdot M$	101
l_discount	$1.17 \cdot M$	$0.07 \cdot M$	$1.39 \cdot M$	$2.63 \cdot M$	125
l_shipmode	$1.17 \cdot M$	$1 \cdot M$	$0.78 \cdot M$	$2.95 \cdot M$	141

5.2   Comparison between CPS and Previous Works

In this experiment, we compare CPS with two alternative approaches (a special file format RCFile and physically clustering). In detail, we first use RCFile as the typical example of optimize the design of file format. Second, we purposely move the data blocks belonging to the same (logical) partitions onto the same physical nodes, such that we emulate the physical clustering approach (CoHadoop). Finally, we combine the two techniques (the RCFile and the CPS partitioning scheme) together in order to provide the utmost performance. In this experiment, we extract 12 selection queries[1] about table *Lineitem* in TPC-H and processing queries on those tables. Based on these approaches, we conduct the experiment by 10 times and then measure the average processing time given in Figure 1(a).

---

[1] We choose all the selections about *Lineitem*, including the selections in *Join* query by ignoring the operations on other tables.

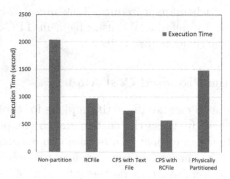

Fig. 1. Comparison of Different Optimization Policy

As shown in this figure, the case without any partition obviously uses the longest time. Next, compared with RCFile, the CPS partition scheme saves about 20% time. The physical clustering method has the longer execution time than RCFile does. Instead, the combination of the two techniques (i.e., RCFile and CPS) can achieve the best result by saving around 40% time. This experiment clearly verifies the advantages of CPS over the previous works, and in particular, the combination of CPS and RCFile achieves the best result among all approaches.

6   Related Work

First, CoHadoop extended Hadoop by placing data blocks (and their replicas) of correlated files onto the same data nodes. In this way, the correlated files can be accessed locally inside the same machine, and the network traffic is reduced. Unfortunately, this approach could lead to unbalanced workloads in clustered machines, in case that the correlated data is associated with very high (or very low) volume size. Different from CoHadoop, some previous works specially designed file formats to optimize Hadoop query processing time. The typical examples of such works include *CFile*, [6] and *RCFile*. *CFile* supported a column-wise file format based on the entire file level, while *RCFile* was an in-block column-wise storage. The column-store allowed faster query processing time by less I/O cost. However, these data formats do not cluster semantically related data together.

7   Conclusion

In this paper, we proposed a new partition scheme, CPS, to optimize query processing, based on the Hive data warehouse and the Hadoop distributed file system. Our experimental results have successfully verified that the CPS scheme can improve the performance of query processing over the state of the art methods. As future work, we will extend our partition scheme to support more complex query conditions, such as those having multiple attributes conditions, and the query operators like *Join* and *Order By*.

References

1. Hadoop, http://hadoop.apache.org/
2. Hive, http://hive.apache.org/
3. TPC-H, Benchmark Specification, http://www.tpc.org/tpch/
4. Dean, J., Ghemawat, S.: MapReduce: simplified data processing on large clusters. Commun. ACM 51(1), 107–113 (2008)
5. Eltabakh, M.Y., Tian, Y., Zcan, F., Gemulla, R., Krettek, A., McPherson, J.: CoHadoop: flexible data placement and its exploitation in Hadoop. Proc. VLDB Endow. 4(9), 575–585 (2011)
6. Lin, Y., Agrawal, D., Chen, C., Ooi, B.C., Wu, S.: Llama: leveraging columnar storage for scalable join processing in the MapReduce framework. In: SIGMOD Conference, pp. 961–972. ACM, New York (2011)
7. He, Y., Lee, R., Huai, Y., Shao, Z., Jain, N., Zhang, X., Xu, Z.: RCFile: A fast and space-efficient data placement structure in MapReduce-based warehouse systems. In: ICDE Conference, pp. 1199–1208 (2011)

DPMFNeg: A Dynamically Integrated Model for Collaborative Filtering

Wenlong Yang, Jun Ma, Shanshan Huang, and Tongfeng Yang

School of Computer Science and Technology, Shandong University,
250101 Jinan, China
{yangwenlonghi,yangtongfeng}@gmail.com, majun@sdu.edu.cn,
huangshanshansdu@163.com

Abstract. Collaborative Filtering (CF) techniques are the mostly applied methods in real world recommender systems. There are two typical types of CF, which are memory-based and model-based CF algorithms. However, these two CF methods in fact pay attention to different parts of ratings data. Memory-based CF methods are adept at finding local similar users, while model-based CF algorithms emphasize achieving global optimization. In this paper, we integrate a neighborhood approach and Probabilistic Matrix Factorization (PMF) into a hybrid CF model, DPMFNeg, which combines the advantages of memory-based and model-based CF algorithms. We explore the performance of our method on two test datasets – MoiveLens-100K and MoiveLens-1M. The results show that DPMFNeg performs better than other methods on those datasets in terms of MAE and RMSE.

Keywords: Collaborative filtering, Recommender Systems, Neighborhood Approach, Probabilistic Matrix Factorization.

1 Introduction

With the vigorous development of electronic commerce, a huge amount of commodity information is produced for consumers. In fact, it is not trivial to offer consumers with appropriate choices. *Recommender systems* have attracted a lot of attention to solve the information overload problem. Many related recommendation techniques have been researched in fields of information retrieval [1,2], machine learning [3] and data mining [4].

Recommender Systems actively present to users a list of items such as films, music, books, news and so on, which the users may be interested in. Typically, the known techniques of recommender systems can be categorized as *Collaborative Filtering* (CF) [5,6] and content-based filtering [7]. CF algorithms are based on the assumption that if users have rated similar items or have similar behaviors, activities or preferences, they will rate or act on other items similarly [5]. Meanwhile, researchers also face several challenges that pose danger [8], which are mainly data sparsity, scalability, diversity and so forth. Some hybrid recommender systems [9,10] are studied with unifying advantages of CF and content-based filtering, which may have better performance and improvements.

L. Chen et al. (Eds.): APWeb 2014, LNCS 8709, pp. 568–575, 2014.

For two categories of CF, memory-based and model-based algorithms can be mutually complementary in some way to take advantages of two methods. However, integrated CF algorithms are simply researched by far, and most of them are only combined with the fixed coefficients. We observe that memory-based methods need significant relationship and model-based algorithms always ignore strong correlations, so we propose a dynamically integrated CF model that individually combines the memory-based and the model-based algorithms. We study our method with explicit ratings on on two datasets and the experimental results show that it outperforms other state-of-the-art algorithms.

2 Related Work

2.1 Neighborhood Approaches

The most representative of memory-based CF methods, neighborhood approaches [11,12] still enjoy a huge amount of popularity. Neighborhood-based CF computes similarity between users or items, and then uses the weighted sum of ratings or simple weighted average to make predictions based on the similarity values. We adopt Pearson Correlation Coefficient (PCC) [13] as similarity function, denoted by $Sim(u, v)$, which is defined as:

$$Sim(u, v) = \frac{\sum\limits_{i \in I_{u,v}} (r_{u,i} - \bar{r}_u)(r_{v,i} - \bar{r}_v)}{\sqrt{\sum\limits_{i \in I_{u,v}} (r_{u,i} - \bar{r}_u)^2 \sum\limits_{i \in I_{u,v}} (r_{v,i} - \bar{r}_v)^2}} \tag{1}$$

where $r_{u,i}$ is the score rated by user u for item i, $\bar{r}_u$ represents the average of ratings by user u and $I_{u,v}$ is the set of items that co-related by both user u and user v. To predict $r_{u,i}$, the user-based neighborhood approach firstly need choose the top-k most similar users, and then $r_{u,i}$ is calculated by the formula:

$$\hat{r}_{u,i} = \bar{r}_u + \frac{\sum\limits_{v \in N_u^k} Sim(u, v)(r_{v,i} - \bar{r}_v)}{\sum\limits_{v \in N_u^k} Sim(u, v)}, \tag{2}$$

where N_u^k is the set of top-k users which are the most similar to u.

2.2 Probabilistic Matrix Factorization

In [3], Salakhutdinov et al. presented a probabilistic linear model, named as Probabilistic Matrix Factorization (PMF). PMF seeks to obtain two low-rank matrices, P and Q, for the user-item rating matrix R. It assumed that attitudes or preferences of a user are determined by a small number of features. A d-dimensional column feature vector of use u or item i is respectively denoted as p_u and q_i. The rating $r_{u,i}$ can be formulated as follows:

$$\hat{r}_{u,i} = r_m + p_u^T q_i, \tag{3}$$

where r_m is a global offset value. The user and item latent factors can be learned by minimizing the sum of squared errors for objective function:

$$L = \min_{P,Q} \frac{1}{2} \sum_{u \in R} \sum_{i \in I_u} (r_{u,i} - (r_m + p_u q_i))^2 + \frac{\lambda_p}{2} \|P\|_F^2 + \frac{\lambda_q}{2} \|Q\|_F^2, \qquad (4)$$

where I_u is set of items rated by u, the parameters λ_p and λ_q are regularization coefficients to prevent the over-fitting , and $\|\bullet\|$ is the Frobenius norm of matrix.

Adopting a stochastic gradient descent technique using observed ratings data, the following parameters updating rules are gotten to learn latent factors p_u, q_i:

$$p_u \leftarrow p_u - \eta_1(\lambda_p p_u - \Delta_{u,i} q_i),$$
$$q_i \leftarrow q_i - \eta_2(\lambda_q q_i - \Delta_{u,i} p_u), \qquad (5)$$
$$\Delta_{u,i} = r_{u,i} - (r_m + p_u q_i),$$

where the parameters η_1 and η_2 are learning rates to control convergence steps.

3   Our Dynamically Integrated CF Model

In above-mentioned section, we have introduced neighborhood approaches and PMF algorithm in detail. Despite the fact that neighborhood models and PMF method have made a great success in collaborative filtering, the two algorithms have their own disadvantages in the real world application. Neighborhood models need to compute similarities between users based on their co-rated items, which often ignores the vast majority of ratings by some users and can not capture the totality of weak signals encompassed in all of a users ratings [4]. The drawback of PMF is poor at detecting strong associations among closely related items, whereas neighborhood model makes better. Hybrid models for neighborhood approaches and latent factor models may be able to get better performance.

In [4], Koren has proposed a hybrid CF model that combined neighborhood and latent factor model, which showed that it improves the prediction accuracy by capturing the advantages of two models. In this paper, the regularized loss function of simplified hybrid model can be formulated as:

$$L = \min_{P,Q} \frac{1}{2} \sum_{u \in R} \sum_{i \in I_u} (r_{u,i} - (\frac{1}{2} r_{N(u,i)} + \frac{1}{2}(r_m + p_u^T q_i)))^2$$
$$+ \frac{\lambda_p}{2} \|P\|_F^2 + \frac{\lambda_q}{2} \|Q\|_F^2, \qquad (6)$$

In above hybrid model, Koren just simply integrated a neighborhood model and latent factor method. That is, the tradeoff parameters of predicted ratings for two approaches are fixed as the constant with coequal form. Due to the difference of values rated by each user, like a user may have few or many ratings, or he (she) has diverse or focused interests, the prediction accuracy of neighborhood model and latent factor method should be diverse for each user. In our opinion, since the two algorithms pay attention to different parts of ratings data and

every user has their own features, the two methods should have varying degrees
of improvement for each user. In consequence of above motivations, we propose a
dynamically integrated model to predict ratings, which combines a neighborhood
approach and latent factor method with the adaptive trade-off parameters. We
call it DPMFNeg, in which we use PMF as latent factor model. Because our focus
is on the user, so we assume that the effect of user-based neighborhood approach
and PMF algorithm are different for each user. Namely, each user has of ones
own trade-off parameters for two methods. The predicted rating for dynamically
integrated model can be combined with Equation 2 and 3, and then its formula
can be defined as:

$$\hat{r}_{u,i} = \alpha_u r_{N(u,i)} + \beta_u (r_m + p_u^T q_i), \tag{7}$$

where α_u and β_u are tradeoff coefficients to control the neighborhood model and
PMF, $r_{N(u,i)}$ is the predicted rating of user-based neighborhood model.

In our proposed method DPMFNeg, our model can be solved by the regularized least squares problem, which is defined as follows:

$$L = \min_{P,Q,\alpha,\beta} \frac{1}{2} \sum_{u \in R} \sum_{i \in I_u} \left(r_{u,i} - \left(\alpha_u r_{N(u,i)} + \beta_u (r_m + p_u^T q_i) \right) \right)^2$$
$$+ \frac{\lambda_p}{2} \|P\|_F^2 + \frac{\lambda_q}{2} \|Q\|_F^2 + \frac{\lambda_\alpha}{2} \|\alpha\|_F^2 + \frac{\lambda_\beta}{2} \|\beta\|_F^2 , \tag{8}$$

where α_u and β_u are trade-off parameters for user u, λ_p and λ_q are regularization
parameters respectively for user and item latent factors, λ_α and λ_β are also
regularization parameters of uses trade-off coefficients.

Model parameters for Equation 8 can be learned by moving in the opposite
direction of the gradient, and learning rules are updated by:

$$p_u \leftarrow p_u - \eta_1(\lambda_p p_u - \Delta_{u,i} q_i),$$
$$q_i \leftarrow q_i - \eta_2(\lambda_q q_i - \Delta_{u,i} p_u),$$
$$\alpha_u \leftarrow \alpha_u - \eta_3(\lambda_\alpha \alpha_u - \Delta_{u,i} r_{N(u,i)}),$$
$$\beta_u \leftarrow \beta_u - \eta_4(\lambda_\beta \beta_u - \Delta_{u,i}(r_m + p_u^T q_i)), \tag{9}$$

where η_1, η_2, η_3 and η_4 are all learning rates to update parameters.

4   Experiments

In this section, we conduct a series of experiments to evaluate our proposed
method DPMFNeg and compare it to some existing approaches on two Movie-
Lens datasets.

4.1   Datasets

The MoiveLens datasets are publicly available in GroupLens[1]. We use MovieLens-
100K and MoiveLens-1M to evaluate our proposed method, which are respectively denoted as ML100K and MoiveLens-1M. The detailed statistics of the
datasets are displayed in Table 1.

---

[1] http://www.grouplens.org/datasets/movielens/

Table 1. Statistics of datasets for MoiveLens-100k and MoiveLens-1M

Dataset	# of Ratings	# of Users	# of Items	Avg # of rating/suser	Sparseness (%)
ML100K	10,0000	943	1682	3.5299	93.7
ML1M	1,000,209	6040	3706	3.5816	95.5

4.2 Evaluation Metrics

In order to measure the prediction accuracy of our experiments, we employ Mean Absolute Error (MAE) and Root Mean Square Error (RMSE) as evaluation metrics. MAE, is the average of absolute errors, and the definition is given as:

$$MAE = \frac{1}{|R_{test}|} \sum_{(u,i) \in R_{test}} |r_{u,i} - \hat{r}_{u,i}|,$$

where R_{test} is the set of the whole user-item pairs in the test dataset. And RMSE is defined as:

$$RMSE = \sqrt{\frac{1}{|R_{test}|} \sum_{(u,i) \in R_{test}} (r_{u,i} - \hat{r}_{u,i})^2},$$

From the definition, we can know that smaller values of MAE and RMSE indicate better prediction accuracy.

4.3 Methodology

In the experiments, we use differently split training dataset and test dataset to evaluate the algorithms. For the ML100K dataset, we use 90% of ratings as train dataset, and the remaining as the test dataset. We also split up ML1M into training and test set in percentage of 90, 80, 60 and 30 accordingly, which are respectively to train models and predict the missing values. And the number of neighbors is set as 50. For two datasets, ML100K and ML1M, we set regularization parameter for all methods as 0.01 in order to avoid over-fitting.

To evaluate the performance of DPMFNeg, we compare our proposed methods with several following methods:

- **UserAvg:** This method uses the average rating of each user to predict the ratings in the test dataset.
- **ItemAvg:** Similar to UserAvg. This method uses the average rating of each item to predict the rating for the items in the test dataset.
- **Neighbor:** This method computes the similarity between users by PCC and selects the nearest neighbors to predict the missing values.
- **PMF:** As a state-of-art rating-oriented CF method, PMF is proposed in [3]. It uses the rating matrix to predict the missing ratings, which is equivalent to DPMFNeg when α_u is set to zeros and β_u is set to one.
- **HybCF:** This approach is a simply integrated CF algorithm, which was proposed in [4]. It is equivalent to DPMFNeg when α_u and β_u is set to one-half for the loss function.

4.4   Impact of Dynamic Parameters α_u and β_u

In this subsection, we investigate the impact of dynamic parameters α_u and β_u on the performance of our proposed DPMFNeg model. The parameters α_u and β_u of the DPMFNeg balance the weight of the users own characteristics on neighborhood approach and PMF method. In above subsection mentioned, the DPMFNeg is equivalent to PMF if the trade parameters $\alpha_u = 0$ and $\beta_u = 1$. And when $\alpha_u = 1$ and $\beta_u = 0$, the DPMFNeg can be regard as neighborhood method, because the loss of function can be directly calculated. HybCF method is also the special case of the DPMFNeg when Neighbor and PMF are integrated with equality. Figure 1 show the influence of dynamic parameters α_u and β_u in their different situations, i.e., RMSE and MAE here. We can see that dynamic parameters can improve the performance of predicting accuracy, because they are learned to adapt to every user by DPMFNeg.

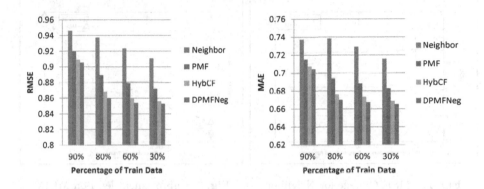

Fig. 1. Impact of various situations of α_u and β_u in ML1M

4.5   Performance Comparison

This subsection presents the results of our experiments which made on ML100K and ML1M datasets, and then we analyze the results concretely in various aspects. Table 2 shows the details of MAE and RMSE for our proposed method DPMFNeg and compared approaches.

We firstly tested whether the number of neighbors for user-based neighborhood model has a heavy influence on methods. Figure 2 shows that the changes of RMSE are very small for neighborhood model on ML100K and ML1M datasets when number of neighbors is greater than 20, so we set the number of neighbors for user-based neighborhood approach, simple hybrid model and DPMFNeg as 50 to predict the missing value in the test datasets.

From the results on the ML100K as shown in the upper part of Table 2, we can see that the performance of DPMFNeg is better than the other methods both on MAE and RMSE. HybCF achieves large improvement than other baseline methods, and it indicates that hybrid model can improve the accuracy in prediction. And in the results, our proposed method DPMF++ outperforms HybCF. Due

Table 2. Results of DPMFNeg and other apprpches on ML100K and ML1M

Data	Train	Metrics	UserAvg	ItemAvg	Neighbor	PMF	HybCF	DPMFNeg
ML100K	90%	MAE	0.8326	0.8354	0.7558	0.7595	0.7486	**0.7395**
		RMSE	1.0431	1.0414	0.9720	0.9651	0.9492	**0.9445**
ML1M	90%	MAE	0.8285	0.7817	0.7043	0.6700	0.6675	**0.6654**
		RMSE	1.0349	0.9807	0.9055	0.8601	0.8538	**0.8528**
	80%	MAE	0.8302	0.7821	0.7074	0.6762	0.6734	**0.6688**
		RMSE	1.0367	0.9794	0.9092	0.8682	0.8605	**0.8558**
	60%	MAE	0.8303	0.7832	0.7154	0.6934	0.6884	**0.6827**
		RMSE	1.0375	0.9808	0.9197	0.8892	0.8791	**0.8720**
	30%	MAE	0.8345	0.7857	0.7373	0.7383	0.7293	**0.7156**
		RMSE	1.0427	0.9844	0.9460	0.9373	0.9234	**0.9107**

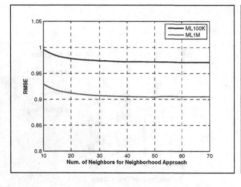

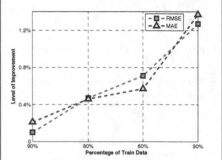

Fig. 2. RMSE Change for Neighbor   **Fig. 3.** Improvement level on ML1M

to the fact that DPMFNeg integrates memory-based method and model-based model, it can be applicable to small dataset. The lower part of Table 2 displays the results of our experiments on ML1M dataset. It shows that our methods can generate better results than other state-of-the-art CF algorithms on four kinds of train data and test data, which are all split from ML1M in different percentages. HybCF also mostly performs better than other methods, and yet the results of DPMFNeg are better than those of HybCF, which is similar to that on ML100K. The observations suggest that our method can better take advantages of two methods than simple hybrid CF. We also analyze the raised level for ML1M. And in Figure 3, it shows that along with the decrease of training data, our method DPMFNeg improves more compared with the best results of other methods.

5   Conclusions

In this paper, we focus on the hybrid Collaborative Filtering problems which are rarely studied in the literature before. Based on the motivation that two types of CF pay attention to different parts of ratings data and they can be mutually complementary, we propose a dynamically integrated CF model called DPMFNeg, which combines a neighborhood approach and Probabilistic Matrix Factorization with the adaptive trade-off parameters on the user-oriented. We also experimentally test the recommendation performance of DPMFNeg. The results show that our method outperforms the other state-of-the-art methods in terms of MAE and RMSE and performance improvements are consistent with respect to various datasets.

Acknowledgments. This work is supported by the Natural Science Foundation of China (61272240, 60970047, 61103151, 71301086), the Doctoral Fund of Ministry of Education of China (20110131110028), the Natural Science foundation of Shandong province (ZR2012FM037) and the Excellent Middle-Aged and Youth Scientists of Shandong Province (BS2012DX017).

References

1. Hofmann, T.: Collaborative filtering via gaussian probabilistic latent semantic analysis. In: ACM SIGIR, pp. 259–266. ACM (2003)
2. Zhang, Y., Koren, J.: Efficient bayesian hierarchical user modeling for recommendation system. In: ACM SIGIR, pp. 47–54. ACM (2007)
3. Mnih, A., Salakhutdinov, R.: Probabilistic matrix factorization. In: Advances in Neural Information Processing Systems, pp. 1257–1264 (2007)
4. Koren, Y.: Factorization meets the neighborhood: a multifaceted collaborative filtering model. In: ACM SIGKDD, pp. 426–434. ACM (2008)
5. Goldberg, D., Nichols, D., Oki, B.M., Terry, D.: Using collaborative filtering to weave an information tapestry. Communications of the ACM 35(12), 61–70 (1992)
6. Ekstrand, M.D., Riedl, J.T., Konstan, J.A.: Collaborative filtering recommender systems. Now Publishers Inc. (2011)
7. Balabanović, M., Shoham, Y.: Fab: content-based, collaborative recommendation. Communications of the ACM 40(3), 66–72 (1997)
8. Lü, L., Medo, M., Yeung, C.H., Zhang, Y.-C., Zhang, Z.-K., Zhou, T.: Recommender systems. Physics Reports 519(1), 1–49 (2012)
9. Basilico, J., Hofmann, T.: Unifying collaborative and content-based filtering. In: The Twenty-first International Conference on Machine Learning, vol. 9. ACM (2004)
10. Burke, R.: Hybrid recommender systems: Survey and experiments. User Modeling and User-adapted Interaction 12(4), 331–370 (2002)
11. Delgado, J., Ishii, N.: Memory-based weighted majority prediction. In: SIGIR Workshop Recomm. Syst. Citeseer (1999)
12. Linden, G., Smith, B., York, J.: Amazon. com recommendations: Item-to-item collaborative filtering. IEEE Internet Computing 7(1), 76–80 (2003)
13. Breese, J.S., Heckerman, D., Kadie, C.: Empirical analysis of predictive algorithms for collaborative filtering. In: Proceedings of the Fourteenth Conference on Uncertainty in Artificial intelligence, pp. 43–52. Morgan Kaufmann Publishers Inc. (1998)

A Consistency-Based Dimensionality Reduction Algorithm in Incomplete Data

Wenbin Qian[1,2], Wenhao Shu[3,*], and Yinglong Wang[1]

[1] School of Software, Jiangxi Agricultural University, Nanchang, China
[2] Beijing Key Laboratory of Knowledge Engineering for Materials Science, University of Science and Technology Beijing, China
[3] School of Computer and Information Technology, Beijing Jiaotong University, Beijing, China
qianwenbin1027@126.com, 11112084@bjtu.edu.cn

Abstract. Feature selection employed for dimensionality reduction is an essential preprocessing task to guarantee high accuracy and efficiency of data analysis in practical applications. This paper proposes a consistency-based feature selection method for dimensionality reduction in incomplete data. The computational efficiency of the proposed feature selection method is improved by proposing a quick algorithm of computing the positive region based on the sorting and label techniques. Compared with the state-of-the-art feature selection methods, the proposed feature selection algorithm achieves less computational time for dimensionality reduction in incomplete data by the experimental results.

Keywords: Dimensionality reduction, Consistency criterion, Incomplete data, Feature selection, Rough sets.

1 Introduction

Handling high-dimensional data represents one of the most challenging problems for learning. Given numbers of features, it is observed that the inclusion of irrelevant and redundant features will deteriorate the performance of learning algorithms both in speed and prediction accuracy. Feature selection is an effective way for dimensionality reduction in knowledge discovery and data mining applications. It aims to select a subset of the most useful features that produces the same results as the original entire set of features [2,6,7]. As a result, the data set quality and data analysis may improve through feature selection.

According to whether combining a machine learning algorithm to evaluate the feature subset, the feature selection methods can be divided into three categories: wrapper, filter and embedded methods [6]. The embedded method mainly combine the advantages of wrapper method and filter method. Compared with the wrapper method, the filter method has much lower computational complexity. Thus we mainly focus on the filter method. It is noteworthy that among the filter methods, rough set-based feature selection provides a systematic theoretic

---

* Corresponding author.

L. Chen et al. (Eds.): APWeb 2014, LNCS 8709, pp. 576–583, 2014.

framework [1, 3], which does not attempt to maximize the class separateness but rather attempts to retain the discernible ability of original feature set for the object set. The main advantage of rough set theory is that it requires no human subjective input other than the given information themselves.

Most existing rough set-based feature selection approaches rely on the complete data, i.e., the data sets without missing data. In fact, it is common to meet with the data sets with missing feature values in real-world tasks [3-5, 7-9]. Here we introduce some representative feature selection algorithms in the context of incomplete data. Meng [4] studied the relationships of several types of feature selection from a theoretical framework in the inconsistent incomplete data. From the viewpoint of discernibility matrix, Qian [5] presented two approximation feature selections to obtain relative feature subsets in an inconsistent incomplete data. However, the construction of discernibility matrices is time-consuming. From the viewpoint of information entropy, Sun [7] developed a rough entropy-based feature selection algorithm in the incomplete data. Dai [3, 8] provided the conditional entropy measure to evaluate the uncertainty in the incomplete data, and they presented the conditional entropy-based feature selection to select a feature subset. However, some possible rules can be extracted from the incomplete data after feature selection. Above all, to improve the efficiency of feature selection from the incomplete data sets, we will develop an efficient consistency-based feature selection algorithm in incomplete data. The key step in the consistency-based feature selection methods is to compute the positive region.

The remainder of this paper is organized as follows. In Section 2, some preliminary concepts are briefly reviewed. In Section 3, an effective method of computing the positive region is provided. In Section 4, a consistency-based feature selection algorithm in incomplete data is developed. In Section 5, the experiments are conducted to demonstrate the efficiency of the proposed algorithm. Finally, Section 6 concludes the paper.

2 Preliminaries

In this section, we briefly review the basic concepts about rough set theory, which can be found in [1, 3-5, 7-9]. In addition, some definitions involved in this paper are introduced.

Rough set-based data analysis starts from a data table, also called information system. If condition features and decision features in an information system are distinguished, it is called a decision system. Let $S = (U, C, D, V, f)$ be an incomplete decision system, where U is a non-empty set of objects, C is a non-empty set of condition features and D is a decision feature set with $C \cap D = \emptyset$; $V = V_C \cup V_D$, where V_C is the set of condition feature values and V_D is the set of decision feature values; f is a mapping function from $U \times (C \cup D)$ to V. For $P \subseteq C$, a tolerance relation T_P is defined as follows: $T_P = \{(x, y) | \forall a \in P, f(x, a) = f(y, a) \vee f(x, a) = * \vee f(y, a) = *\}$. For $\forall x \in U$, $T_P(x)$ can denote the maximal set of objects which are possibly indiscernible by P with object x. i.e., $T_P(x) = \{y \in U | T_P(x, y)\}$. The tolerance classes induced by P is defined as

$U//T_P = \{T_P(x)|x \in U\}$. For $X \subseteq U$, the lower and upper approximations of X with respect to P are defined as follows, respectively. $\underline{T_P}(X) = \{x|T_P(x) \subseteq X\}$ and $\overline{T_P}(X) = \{x|T_P(x) \cap X \neq \emptyset\}$. The lower approximation is called the positive region, that is $POS_P(X) = \underline{T_P}(X)$. The objects in $\underline{T_P}(X)$ belong to X certainly.

Definition 1. *Let* $S = (U, C, D, V, f)$ *be an incomplete decision system, for any* $P \subseteq C$, $a \in C - P$, *the significance measure of feature a is defined as* $sig(a, P, D) = |POS_P(D) - POS_{P-\{a\}}(D)|$.

From Definition 1, the feature with most significance measure can be selected in the process of feature selection.

Definition 2. *Given an incomplete decision system* $S = (U, C, D, V, f)$, *for any* $P \subseteq C$, *if* $POS_P(D) = POS_C(D)$ *and* $POS_P(D) \neq POS_{P'}(D)$ *for any* $P' \subseteq P$, *then* P *is a selected feature subset of the incomplete decision system.*

From Definition 2, the selected feature subset keeps the consistency of the incomplete decision system unchanged. In what follows, we give the definition involved in the design process of the algorithm for computing the positive region in incomplete data.

Definition 3. *Let* $S = (U, C, D, V, f)$ *be an incomplete decision system, for* $P = \{a_1, a_2, \cdots, a_s\} \subseteq C$, *suppose the missing feature value of feature* a_s *is a special known feature value different from other feature values in the system, a partition induced by* P *is defined as* $U/P = \{E_1^P, E_2^P, \cdots, E_k^P, E_{k+1}^P, \cdots, E_{k+l}^P\}$, *where* $E_i^P = [x]_P = \{y \in U|\forall a \in P - \{a_s\}, f(x, a) = f(y, a) \wedge f(x, a_s) = f(y, a_s) \neq *\}(1 \leq i \leq k)$, *and* $E_j^P = [x]_P = \{y \in U|\forall a \in P - \{a_s\}, f(x, a) = f(y, a) \wedge f(x, a_s) = f(y, a_s) = *\}(k + 1 \leq i \leq k + l)$.

3   Computing the Positive Region in Incomplete Data

In this section, we develop an efficient algorithm for computing the positive region in incomplete data.

In Algorithm 1, the key step of computing positive region is to compute the tolerance classes. if the feature value of an object is missing, then the tolerance class of the object is equal to the previous tolerance class, which does not need to recompute. In such case, we can use the label technique to find out the previous results such that the time is saved. In addition, if the feature value of an object is not missing, the tolerance classes of the object can be expressed as the union set of some equivalence classes. In such case, we can use the radix sorting technique to compute directly such that the computation is simple.

Time Complexity Analysis. The time complexity of Steps 2-9 is $O(|U|)$, the time complexity of Steps 10-20 is $O(|t|) + O(m|T_P|)$, where t is the number of represented items, m is the maximal cardinality of the tolerance class generated by the missing objects,where $|m| \ll |U|$. $|T_P|$ is the cardinality of the generated tolerance class under feature set P, in the worst case, $|T_P|$ is equal to $|U|$. The time complexity of Steps 21-26 is $O(m|U|)$, the time complexity of Steps 27-32 is

---

Algorithm 1. Computing the positive region in incomplete data

---

Input: An incomplete decision system $S = (U, C, D, V, f)$, $U = \{x_1, x_2, \cdots, x_n\}$, $C = \{c_1, c_2, \cdots, c_r\}$;

Output: positive region $POS_C(D)$.

1. Initialize $P = \emptyset$, $POS_C(D) = \emptyset$, $i = 1$, $flag = 1$;
2. Allocate and collect the objects U by the radix sorting;
3. Let the objects sequence by Step 2 be $x_1', x_2', \cdots, x_n'$;
4.   let $P = P \cup \{c_i\}$; $t = 1$; $E_t^P = \{x_1'\}$;
5.   **for** $(j = 2; j \leq n; j ++)$
6.   if the value of x_j' is equal to the value of x_{j-1}' under feature c_i
7.   then $E_t^P = E_t^P \cup \{x_j'\}$ and $x_j'.flag = t$;
8.   else let $t = t + 1$, $E_t^P = \{x_j'\}$ and $x_j'.flag = E_t^P.flag = t$;
9.   **endfor**
10. Initialize the static arrays $a[t]$ and $m = 0$;
11.   **for** $(v = 1; v \leq t; v ++)$
12.   let $T_v^P = E_v^P$; and take out the first object from the E_v^P,
13.   if the value of the object is equal to * under feature c_i
14.   then store the object into the arrays $a[m]$ and $m ++$;
15.   **end for**
16.   **for** $(j = 1; j \leq m; j ++)$
17.   for $(k = 1; k \leq |T_P|; k ++)$
18.   if $(a[j].flag == T_k^{P-\{c_i\}}.flag)$
19.   then save the subscript k to $a[j]$;
20.   **end for**
21. // Calculate the corresponding tolerance classes under P
22.   if $E_v^P \subseteq T_k^{P-\{c_i\}} \wedge E_{v+1} \subseteq T_k^{P-\{c_i\}} (1 \leq v \leq t; v \neq k)$
23.   then use $S(v, v+1)$ to save this symmetric sequence;
24.   if $E_v^P \subseteq T_w^P(t - m + 1 \leq w \leq t)$ then $T_v^P = T_v^P \cup E_w^P$;
25.   if E_v^P and E_{v+1}^P exist the symmetric sequence $S(v, v+1)$
26.   then $T_v^P - T_v^P \cup E_{v+1}^P$ and $T_{v+1}^P = T_{v+1}^P \cup E_v^P$;
27. //Update the labels for all the elements in the tolerance classes
28. Let $U//T_C = \emptyset$;
29.   **for** $(k = 1; k \leq t; k ++)$
30.   if $\forall x_j' \in E_k^P$, then $x_j'.flag = k$ and $T_k^P.flag = k$;
31. $U//T_C = U//T_C \cup T_k^P$;
32.   **end for**
33. Let $i = i + 1$;
34.   if $i \leq r$, then turn to Step 2;
35. For each tolerance class $T_C(x_i) \in U//T_C (1 \leq i \leq n)$
36. **If** the decision feature values are the same in $T_C(x_i)$
37.   then $POS_C(D) = POS_C(D) \cup x_i$;
38. **End if**

End

$O(|U| + |t|)$. The time complexity of Steps 35-38 is $O(\sum_{i=1}^{n} |x_i||T_P(x_i)|) < O(t|U|)$, where t is the number of represented items. Therefore, the time complexity of computing the positive region is $O(m|U||C|)$.

4 A Consistency-Based Dimensionality Reduction Algorithm

In this section, a consistency-based dimensionality reduction algorithm is developed by the forward greedy search strategy in incomplete data. At first, some indispensable features that cannot be deleted from the whole feature set are selected, and then a forward greedy feature selection approach takes a feature with the most significance into the feature subset in each loop until this subset satisfies the stopping condition, finally, some possible redundant features can be deleted from the whole feature subset.

Algorithm 2. A consistency-based dimensionality reduction algorithm

---

Input: An incomplete decision system $S = (U, C, D, V, f)$, where $C = \{c_1, c_2, \ldots, c_r\}$;
Output: A selected feature subset Red.
Begin

1. Initialize $Red = \emptyset$;
2. Calculate $POS_C(D)$; // According to Algorithm 1
3. **For** $i = 1$ to r **do**
4.   calculate $sig_(c_i, C, D)$;
5.   if $sig_(c_i, C, D) > 0$, then $Red = Red \cup \{c_i\}$;
6. **End for**
7. for $\forall c_i \in C - Red$, construct a descending sequence by $sig_(c_i, Red \cup \{c_i\}, D)$, and record the result by $\{c'_1, c'_2, \ldots, c'_{|C-Red|}\}$;
8. Let $P = Red$;
9. **While** $POS_P(D) \neq POS_C(D)$ **do**
10.   for $j = 1$ to $|C - P|$ **do**
11.   select $P = P \cup \{c'_j\}$ and compute $POS_P(D)$;
12. **End while**
13. **For** each $p \in P$ **do**
14.   compute $sig_(p, P, D)$;
15.   if $sig_(p, P, D) = 0$, then $P = P - \{p\}$;
16. **End for**
17. $Red = P$, return Red.

End

Time Complexity Analysis. Step 2 is to compute the positive region, the time complexity is $O(m|U||C|)$. Steps 3-6 are to add some indispensable features, the time complexity is $O(m|U||C|^2)$. Step 7 is to construct a descending sequence of the remaining features, the time complexity is $O(m|U||C - P|)$. Step 9-12 are to add the most significance features to the selected feature subset, the time complexity is $O(m|U||C - P|)$, Step 13-16 are to delete some redundant features from the selected feature subset, the time complexity is $O(m|U||P|)$. Therefore, the time complexity of Algorithm 2 is $O(m|U||C|^2)$. where m is the maximal cardinality of the tolerance class generated by the missing objects.

5   Experimental Analysis

In this section, to test and verify the efficiency of the proposed feature selection algorithm, four real-life data sets are downloaded from UCI Database [10]. The data sets are described in Table 1. All the data sets are the incomplete data sets. For the numerical features, we employ the data tool Rosetta [11] to transform them into categorical ones. All the experiments are run on a PC with Windows XP, Core2, CPU E7400 and 2GB memory. Algorithms are coded in C++ and the software being used is Microsoft Visual 2008.

Table 1. The description of incomplete data sets

Data sets	Objects	Features	Classes
Audiology	226	69	24
Soybean-large	307	35	19
Mammographic	961	5	2
Mushroom	8124	22	2

In what follows, we compare the proposed feature selection algorithm with other three algorithms in terms of the size of feature subset and computational time. For convenience, we denote the proposed feature selection algorithm as PFS, the discernibility function-based feature selection algorithm mentioned in [5] as DFS, the feature selection algorithm with the traditional method of computing positive region as TFS and a rough entropy-based feature selection algorithm in [7] as RFS. Table 2 records the comparative results of the feature subset size.

Table 2. The size of feature subsets of the four algorithms

Data sets	Original features	PFS	DFS	TFS	RFS
Audiology	69	15	16	15	14
Soybean-large	35	10	12	10	11
Mammographic	5	5	5	5	5
Mushroom	22	5	6	5	7

From Table 2, we can see that the size of feature subset of Algorithm PFS is smaller or equal than the other three algorithms in most of the data sets. Take the Soybean-large data set for example, PFS selects 10 features, which is the same as that of TFS. DFS and RFS obtain 12 and 11 features, respectively. Obviously, PFS selects fewer features than both DFS and RFS. The possible reason is that PFS deletes the redundant features from the selected result, but DFS and RFS do not have this behavior. The results indicate that PFS can effectively reduce the dimensionality in incomplete data.

To distinguish the computational time, each data set is divided into 10 parts of equal size. The first part is viewed as the first data set, the combination of the first part and the second part is viewed as the second data set, the combination of the second part and the third part is viewed as the third data set and so on. Fig.1 displays the computational time of the four algorithms versus the size of data sets. The x-coordinate pertains to the size of the data sets, while the y-coordinate gives the computational time, which is expressed as seconds.

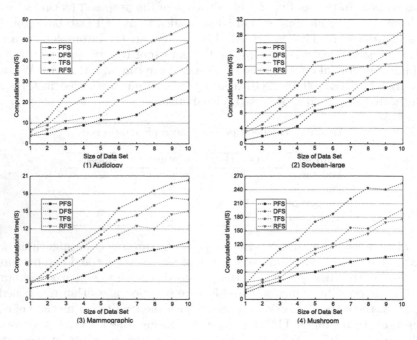

Fig. 1. Computational time of the four algorithms versus the size of different data sets

It is clear from Fig.1 that the curves of the four feature selection algorithms increases with the increase of the size of the data set. However, this relationship is not strictly monotonic. Take the Mammographic data set as an example, the computational time of the RFS algorithm decreases from the fifth data set to the sixth data set, and the computational time of the TFS algorithm decreases from the ninth data set to the tenth data set. The same phenomenon can be observed in other data sets. The underlying reason is that different numbers of features are selected. In additon, there is an obvious difference that PFS runs faster than the other three algorithms. And the difference becomes larger and larger when the size of the data set increases. Take the Mushroom data set as an example, the computational time of PFS is about 94s at the tenth data set, while the computational time of DFS, TFS and RFS is about 259s, 197s and 175s. The reason is that our proposed algorithm for computing the tolerance classes is faster than the traditional method, thus PFS has less time than TFS for feature selection. Also, we can observe that the worst algorithm is DFS, the possible reason is that the Boolean operation for the discernibility matrix is time-consuming. Comparing PFS and RFS, PFS can select a feature subset in much shorter time than RFS. The computation of the tolerance classes takes less time in PFS than that in RFS, and the computation of rough entropy in RFS takes more time than that of positive region in PFS.

From the experimental results, it should be stressed that the proposed algorithm is more efficient than the existing feature selection algorithms for dimensionality reduction, especially for the incomplete data.

6   Conclusions

In real-world data sets, it often happened that the feature values of an object set are missing. Although there are some feature selection algorithms to deal with such data sets, they are usually not computationally costless. The main reason is that computing the tolerance classes is time-consuming. In this paper, we firstly provided an effective method of computing the tolerance classes and positive region, and then we developed a consistency-based dimensionality reduction algorithm, the experiments are conducted on UCI data sets. The results demonstrate the proposed algorithm has less computational time for dimensionality reduction comparing the state-of-the-art methods.

Acknowledgments. This work was supported by the Innovation Funds of Excellence Doctor of Beijing Jiaotong University (No.2014YJS040), the Natural Science Foundation of Jiangxi Province(No.20132BAB201045).

References

1. Pawlak, Z., Skowron, A.: Rough sets: some extensions. Information Sciences 177(1), 28–40 (2007)
2. Zhu, X.F., Huang, Z., Yang, Y., et al.: Self-taught dimensionality reduction on the high-dimensional small-sized data. Pattern Recognition 46(1), 215–229 (2013)
3. Dai, J.H., Wang, W.T., Xu, Q.: An uncertainty measure for incomplete decision tables and its applications. IEEE Transactions on Cybernetics 43(4), 1277–1289 (2013)
4. Meng, Z.Q., Shi, Z.Z.: Extended rough set-based attribute reduction in inconsistent incomplete decision systems. Information Sciences 204, 44–69 (2012)
5. Qian, Y.H., Liang, J.Y., Li, D.Y.: Approximation reduction in inconsistent incomplete decision tables. Knowledge-Based Systems 23(5), 427–433 (2010)
6. Guyon, I., Elisseeff, A.: An introduction to variable feature selection. Journal of Machine Learning Research 3, 1157–1182 (2003)
7. Sun, L., Xu, J.C.: Feature selection using rough entropy-based uncertainty measures in incomplete decision systems. Knowledge-Based Systems 36, 206–216 (2012)
8. Dai, J., Xu, Q.: Approximations and uncertainty measures in incomplete information systems. Information Sciences 198(1), 62–80 (2012)
9. Qian, Y.H., Liang, J.Y., Pedrycz, W., et al.: An efficient accelerator for attribute reduction from incomplete data in rough set framework. Pattern Recognition 44(8), 1658–1670 (2011)
10. UCI Dataset, http://www.ics.uci.edu/~mlearn/MLRepository.html
11. http://www.lcb.uu.se/tools/rosetta/index.php

An Efficient Method
for Topic-Aware Influence Maximization

Yaping Chu[1], Xianghui Zhao[2], Sitong Liu[1], Jianhua Feng[1], Jin Yi[2],
and Hui Liu[2]

[1] Department of Computer Science, Tsinghua University, Beijing, China
[2] China Information Technology Security Evaluation Center, Beijing, China
{cyp11,liu-st10}@mails.tsinghua.edu.cn, fengjh@tsinghua.edu.cn,
{zhaoxh,yijin,liuhui}@itsec.gov.cn

Abstract. Influence maximization aims to identify k nodes from a network such that the expected number of activated nodes by these k nodes is maximized, which is an important problem in viral marketing and has been extensively studied by the industrial and academic communities. We observe that the influence strength between users is diverse on different topics in real-world applications and the topic information plays a significant role in the influence maximization problem. In this paper, we study the topic-aware influence maximization problem. We propose a greedy algorithm with $1 - 1/e$ approximate ratio. Extensive experiments on real datasets show that our method efficiently and effectively finds k nodes on the given topics and outperforms state-of-the-art algorithms.

1 Introduction

Among all the marketing channels, word-of-mouth marketing (a.k.a. viral marketing) has been widely accepted as people are more likely to believe the information obtained from their friends[1], and viral marketing has become as the most effective marketing strategy. Along with the increasing popularity of social networks, they provide opportunities for enabling online viral marketing.

In this paper, we study the problem of *"influence maximization"*[2], especially the topic-aware influence maximization problem, which aims to identify k nodes to maximize the influence on the given topics. This problem is proposed by Barbieri et. al. [3]. However it has two limitations. First, it only considers a single topic. Second, it focuses on how to define the topic-aware influences and does not provide effective algorithms to identify the k nodes.

To summarize, we make the following contributions. (1) We study the topic-aware influence maximization problem and devise an efficient algorithm. (2) We propose effective techniques to estimate the influence bound and utilize the bound to do pruning. We also incorporate the topics into our pruning technique to further improve the pruning power. (3) We have conducted extensive experiments on real datasets and the results show that our method achieves high performance and significantly outperforms state-of-the-art algorithms.

L. Chen et al. (Eds.): APWeb 2014, LNCS 8709, pp. 584–592, 2014.

Paper Organization. We formulate the problem in Section 2. Section 3 introduces the parameter assignments and the algorithm model and Section 4 illustrates the algorithm. We show the experimental studies in section 5. Related works are reviewed in Section 6. We conclude in Section 7.

2 Preliminaries

In this section, we first introduce the propagation model, and then formulate the problem of topic-aware influence maximization.

2.1 Independent Cascade(IC) Model

Given a network $G(V, E)$, for each edge $(u, v) \in E$, $p_{(u,v)}(0 \leq p_{(u,v)} \leq 1)$ is the influence propagation probability from u to v. There are different models to compute the probability. Independent cascade (IC) model [4,5,6] is the representative and widely used influence diffusion model. In the IC model, a node has two states: active or inactive. The active node is either an initial activated node (called "seed") or activated by its in-neighbours, while the inactive state means the node has not yet had a chance to be activated by its in-neighbours. Formally, the IC model in graph G works in an inductive way. At the initial stage 0, a seed set $S \in V$ is selected to start the spread. Let A_t denote the set of activated nodes at stage t and $A_0 = S$. At stage $t + 1$, each node u in A_t has only one chance to active its out-neighbours $v \notin \bigcup_{i=0}^{t} A_i$ with probability $p_{(u,v)}$. The process terminates until $A_{t+1} = \varnothing$. The nodes influenced by S are denoted as $\sigma(S)$, where $\sigma(S) = \bigcup_{i=0}^{n} A_i$ and $A_{n+1} = \varnothing$.

2.2 Problem Formulation

Formally, consider a query $Q = (Z, k)$ with a query topic set $Z = \{z_1, z_2, \cdots, z_n\}$ where $z_i(1 \leq i \leq n)$ is a topic. Let V_Z denote the nodes that have interest in any topics in Z. The influence maximization on topic set is to find a node set S with k nodes to maximize the influence in V_Z. The nodes influenced by S are called the *influence spread*. Accordingly, the influence spread of S on Z is denoted as $\sigma(S, Z)$, and the topic-aware influence maximization is defined as definition 1.

Definition 1 (Topic-Aware Influence Maximization). *Given a directed graph $G = (V, E)$ and a query $Q = (Z, k)$, the topic-aware influence maximization problem aims to find a k-node set S such that for any k-node set $\mathcal{K} \subseteq V$, $\sigma(S, Z) \geq \sigma(\mathcal{K}, Z)$. S is called the seed set and node in S is called a seed.*

The topic-aware influence maximization problem can be proved to be NP-hard by a reduction from the influence maximization problem[4] and computing the exact topic-aware influence spread can be proved to be #P-hard by a reduction from the influence spread problem[5].

3   Topic-Aware Influence Model

In this section, we first introduce how to assign propagation probability on topics, and then introduce the tree-based algorithm model.

3.1   Topic-Aware Propagation Probability

In propagation network, an edges's weight (i.e., propagation probability) is the probability a node influences another. In previous works[5,2,7], propagation probability is defined either by the predefined constants or the reverse of the in-degree. While each user has different interests on different topics. Formally, each node $v \in V$ has a T-dimensional topic distributions $\theta_v \in \mathbb{R}^T$ and $\theta_{v|z_i}$ represents the probability of v on topic z_i. $\sum_{i=1}^{T} \theta_{v|z_i} = 1$.

We combine the topic distribution and influence weight to compute the propagation probability between nodes on different topics, as shown in Formular 1:

$$p_{(u,v)|Z} = \frac{1}{|Z|} \cdot \sum_{z_i \in Z} \frac{w_{(u,v)} \cdot \theta_{u|z_i} \cdot \theta_{v|z_i}}{\sum_{j \in IN_v} (w_{(j,v)} \cdot \theta_{j|z_i} \cdot \theta_{v|z_i})} = \frac{1}{|Z|} \cdot \sum_{z_i \in Z} \frac{w_{(u,v)} \cdot \theta_{u|z_i}}{\sum_{j \in IN_v} (w_{(j,v)} \cdot \theta_{j|z_i})} \tag{1}$$

In Equation 1, IN_v is the in-neighbours of v, and $w_{(u,v)}$ is the original weight between u and v. The influence from u to v on topic set Z equals to the percentage that u has taken among the overall influence of v's neighbours to v. We normalize the result by dividing the number of topic.

3.2   Tree-Based Approximate Model

In this paper, we extend the tree-based algorithm proposed in [5] to approximate the influence spread on topic.

Given a network $G = (V, E)$ and a topic set Z, the propagation probability of path $\mathcal{P} = (u = n_1, n_2, \cdots, v = n_m)$ is denoted by $p(\mathcal{P}|Z)$ where $p(\mathcal{P}|Z)$ is computed as $p(\mathcal{P}|Z) = \prod_{i=1}^{m-1} p_{(n_i,n_{i+1})|Z}$. Formally, we denote $\text{MPP}_{(u,v)|Z}$ as the path with maximum propagation probability from u to v on topic set Z.

Given a node set S, the influence of S to node v can not be simply added up, because the paths with maximum influence probability from each $u \in S$ to v may have intersection. To address this problem, we treat node v as the root, and construct a tree by combing the path from each $u \in S$ to v with $\text{MPP}_{(u,v)|Z}$ as the weight. The influence of S to v on topic set Z can be computed as:

$$\text{MPP}_{(S,v)|Z} = \begin{cases} 1 & v \in S \\ 1 - \prod_{c \in \mathcal{C}_v} 1 - \text{MPP}_{(S,c)|Z} \cdot \text{MPP}_{(c,v)|Z} & v \notin S \end{cases} \tag{2}$$

Where $\mathcal{C}_v$ is the children of v in the tree, and when $v \in S$, $\text{MPP}_{(S,v)|Z} = 1$. According to equation 2, $\sigma(S, Z)$ can be approximately computed as below:

$$\sigma(S, Z) = \sum_{v \in V | \theta_{v|Z} > 0} \text{MPP}_{(S,v)|Z} \tag{3}$$

Since $\sigma(S, Z)$ is submodular and monotone[5], and it satisfies the *"diminishing marginal utility"*[1] law. By exploiting this law, a simple greedy algorithm can be used to find k nodes that maximize the influence on the given topic set Z. However this method is expensive and experimental studies in Section 5 show that it needs more than 15 hours to find top-100 nodes on a small-scale network. We introduce an efficient method on this problem in Section 4.

4   Algorithm Design

In this section, we introduce two strategies to reduce the size of candidate nodes and propose an optimized algorithm to accelerate the seed selection.

4.1   Candidate Seeds Selection

We introduce two strategies to reduce the candidate set (denoted as $\mathcal{C}$, which contains all the possible seeds) as much as possible.

We use a predefined threshold ϑ to differentiate the influence strength between nodes, i.e., given a topic set Z, if $MPP_{(u,v)|Z} < \vartheta$, u has weak influence to v on topic set Z, and if for each $v \in V \backslash u$, $MPP_{(u,v)|Z} < \vartheta$, then u is an insignificant node, and u won't be chosen into $\mathcal{C}$.

Let $I_{u|Z} = \{v | MPP_{(u,v)|Z} > \vartheta, \theta_{v|Z} > 0\}$ denote a set of nodes that influenced by u on Z, and $\dot{I}_{u|Z} = \{v | MPP_{(v,u)|Z} > \vartheta, \theta_{u|Z} > 0\}$ denote a set of nodes that influence u on Z, and u can be added to $\mathcal{C}$ only when $|I_{u|Z}| > 0$.

Moreover, topic distribution can be used to select candidate nodes. Variable $\eta(0 \leq \eta \leq 1)$ is used to differentiate the topic strength. That is if $\sum_{i=1}^{n} \theta_{u|z_i} > \eta$, u is a candidate node.

4.2   Seed Selection Optimization

To avoid redundant calculation, we use an upper bound to select the next seed without recalculating the influence of all nodes that have co-influence with the selected ones.

We use a max-heap(denoted as $\mathcal{H}$) to maintain the remainder candidate nodes. For each node u, we record its *id*, *gain* and *status*, where *id* means node's identifier, and *gain* is its marginal benefit, *status* records the state when its *gain* value has been recalculated.

Given node u and v, if $|I_{u|Z} \bigcap I_{v|Z}| = 0$, they have no co-influenced nodes, otherwise, they co-influence the node in $I_{u|Z} \bigcap I_{v|Z}$. Since it is costly to compute $\sigma(u \cup v, Z)$, we use an upper bound to approximately compute it.

Considering two node u and v, if they independently influence node s:
$$MPP_{(u\cup v,s)|Z} = 1 - (1 - MPP_{(u,s)|Z}) \cdot (1 - MPP_{(v,s)|Z}), \text{ otherwise:}$$
$$MPP_{(u\cup v,s)|Z} \leq 1 - (1 - MPP_{(u,s)|Z}) \cdot (1 - MPP_{(v,s)|Z})$$

---

[1] http://en.wikipedia.org/wiki/Diminishing_marginal_utility#Diminishing_marginal_utility

We use the condition independence assumption as the upper bound to approximately calculate their influence spread, denoted as $\hat{\sigma}(u \cup v, Z)$:

$$\hat{\sigma}(u \cup v, Z) = \sum_{s \in V | \theta_{s|Z} > 0} (1 - (1 - MPP_{(u,s)|Z}) \cdot (1 - MPP_{(v,s)|Z})) \qquad (4)$$

Given a seed set S, the upper bound of marginal benefit of u on topic set Z based on S can be approximately computed as:

$$\widehat{gain}(u|Z) = \hat{\sigma}(S \cup u, Z) - \sigma(S, Z) \qquad (5)$$

Algorithm 1. $\widehat{gain}(u|Z)$

---

1 $\widehat{gain}(u \mid Z) \leftarrow 0$
2 **for** $v \in I_{u|Z}$ **do**
3 $\quad$ **if** $v \notin \mathcal{M}$ **then**
4 $\quad\quad \lfloor \ \widehat{gain}(u \mid Z) + = MPP_{(u,v)|Z};$
5 $\quad$ **else**
6 $\quad\quad \lfloor \ \widehat{gain}(u \mid Z) + = MPP_{(u,v)|Z} \cdot (1 - \mathcal{M}[v]) + \mathcal{M}[v];$

7 **return** $\widehat{gain}(u \mid Z);$

To compute the marginal benefit of u based on S, the co-influence of each node in $I_{u|Z} \cap I_{S|Z}$ has to be recomputed, therefore for some nodes in $I_{S|Z}$, its co-influence will be still repeatedly computed in the same round. To avoid the redundant computation, a map $\mathcal{M}$ is used to cache the nodes influenced by S(as the key) and its co-influence value by S(as the value) on topic set Z. Thus for a candidate node u, its $gain$ can be calculated as Algorithm 1.

In Algorithm 1, $\mathcal{M}[v]$ caches the co-influence of v influenced by the selected seeds. If v has already been influenced by S, the co-influence of a new node u to v based on S can be deduced from equation 5 as shown in line 6.

By using the bounds, we describe the seed selection as follow. For each iteration, we take the top element of heap $\mathcal{H}$, if its $status$ equals to 0 (indicates it is the original value and hasn't been selected as candidate seed), we set its $gain$ as computed in Algorithm 1, and update the $status$ as 1; if its $status$ equals to 1, we update its $gain$ according to equation 3 and set $status$ as 2; if its $status$ equals to 2, we pop it out and add it to S and terminate this iteration. The full algorithm is illustrated as algorithm 2 (we call it *"Heat"* for short, since it uses max *Hea*p and *T*ree structure to obtain the seeds).

We pre-compute the propagation probability on the given query topic set Z and the $MPP_{(u,v)|Z}$ for each pair of nodes in the network via a Dijkstra shortest-path algorithm. We first select the candidate nodes according to the topic threshold η(line 1), and the $I_{v|Z}$ and $\hat{I}_{v|Z}$ for each node v can be obtained based on the threshold of ϑ(line 2). The max-heap $\mathcal{H}$ is built based on the original influence spread of each node(line 4), and for each turn, we get the top element

---

Algorithm 2. Heat algorithm

Input: $G(V, E)$: graph; (Z,k):query topic set and integer; ϑ: threshold of path
  propagation probability; η: threshold of topic probability;
Output: S:k nodes set

1 select node with $\theta_{v|Z} > \eta$ as candidate nodes set $\mathcal{C}$
2 pre-compute $I_{v|Z}$ and $\hat{I}_{v|Z}$ for each $v \in \mathcal{C}$ limited by ϑ
3 initialize seeds set $S = \varnothing$ and map $\mathcal{M} = \varnothing$
4 build $\mathcal{H}$ based on $\sigma(v, Z)$ for $v \in \mathcal{C}$
5 **for** $i \leftarrow 1$ **to** k **do**
6   **while** $\mathcal{H} \neq \varnothing$ **do**
7          $u = \mathcal{H}.top()$;
8   **if** $I_{u|Z} \cap \mathcal{M}.keySet() == \varnothing$ **then**
9              $S = S \cup u$;
10   **else**
11   **if** $u.status == 0$ **then**
12   update $u.gain = \widehat{gain}(u|Z)$; $u.status = 1$
13   **if** $u.status == 1$ **then**
14   update $u.gain = gain(u|Z)$; $u.status = 2$
15   **else**
16                 $\mathcal{H}.pop()$;
17                 $S = S \cup u$;
18             $\mathcal{H}.adjust()$;
19   update $\mathcal{M}$;
20 **return** S

---

of $\mathcal{H}$(line 7), if the node u has no interaction with map $\mathcal{M}$(line 8), we add u to S and update map $\mathcal{M}$; otherwise, according to its status, we decide whether to update its *gain* value(line 11- 13) or pop it out(line 15). This process terminates until k seeds selected.

5 Experimental Study

In this section, we report our experimental studies, we compare our algorithm with the state-of-the-art algorithms PMIA and MIA[5]. Besides, we also run the exact greedy algorithm improved by CELF[6] on the film dataset, which took more than 15 hours to find the top-100 IM seeds, while our method took only 3.12 seconds on average. For the influence spread, our method(*6970.772*) was only 2.82% lower than it(*7173.53*). Since the exact greedy algorithm is much slower than our method, we omit it in the figures.

5.1 Datasets

Experiments are conducted on two real datasets: "DBLP", a citation network, the topic distributions of each node are discovered by using the author topic model[8], and the original weight of edge is the cite frequency; another one is a film dataset, which was used in[9], we use the way in[9] to assign the topic distribution, and the original weight is the link frequency. The propagation probabilities of the two datasets are computed according to part 3.1. Both of the two datasets are directed graph, details of datasets are shown in Table 1.

Table 1. DataSets

Data sets	#Vertices	#Edges	AvgD	MaxD
DBLP	1,031,579	10,717,572	59.86	8,304
Film	8,748	125,336	14.32	725

5.2   Evaluating Different Algorithms

All the algorithms use 2000 Monte Carlo simulations to estimate its influence spread. In Figure 1 we fix threshold ϑ to evaluate the influence spread under different k, and in Figure 2 we fix k to evaluate the influence spread under different ϑ. The experiments show that our algorithm has similar influence spread with MIA, and higher than PMIA. And with the increase of k or decrease of ϑ , the influence spread will increase. Since the bigger ϑ is, the more candidate nodes will be reduced. And the elapsed time will be reduced as shown in Figure 4(a).

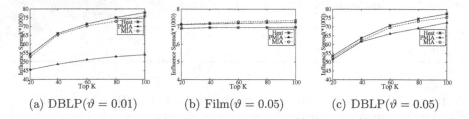

(a) DBLP($\vartheta = 0.01$)   (b) Film($\vartheta = 0.05$)   (c) DBLP($\vartheta = 0.05$)

Fig. 1. Influence Spread on Top-k

In Figure 3 we fix ϑ and compare the elapsed time under different k. In Figure 4 we fix k and compare the elapsed time under different ϑ. The results indicate that our algorithm significantly outperforms PMIA and MIA. For example, in Figure 3(a) we set ϑ as 0.01, when k is 20, our algorithm took 1.55 seconds while PMIA took 324.83 seconds and MIA took 355.26 seconds, which means that our method is more than 200 times than PMIA and MIA. Besides, our method scales well along the network size grows, that's because our method avoids redundant calculation by caching the pre-computed results.

6   Related Works

Influence Maximization. The influence maximization problem was proposed in[2,10]. Kempe et. al.[4] proved the influence maximization problem is NP-hard, and a greedy algorithm approximated $1 - 1/e$ ratio of the optimal solution.

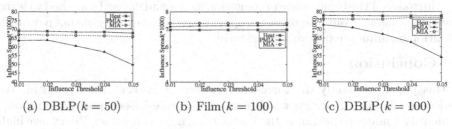

(a) DBLP($k = 50$)   (b) Film($k = 100$)   (c) DBLP($k = 100$)

Fig. 2. Influence Spread on different ϑ

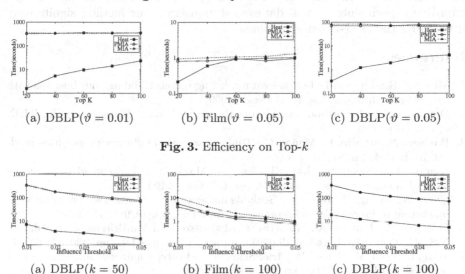

(a) DBLP($\vartheta = 0.01$)   (b) Film($\vartheta = 0.05$)   (c) DBLP($\vartheta = 0.05$)

Fig. 3. Efficiency on Top-k

(a) DBLP($k = 50$)   (b) Film($k = 100$)   (c) DBLP($k = 100$)

Fig. 4. Efficiency on different ϑ

Kimura et al.[10] proposed the shortest path to estimate the influence spread. Leskovec et al.[6] used "lazy-forward" algorithm which faster than the greedy algorithms. Chen et al.[11] used the property of the independent cascade model; Wang et al. [12] broke the whole social network into several communities; and Chen et al.[5] used the local arborescence to estimate the influence of nodes. Kim et al.[13] proposed independent path algorithm for the IC model and Jung et al.[7] proposed linear equations to approximate the real influence, Tang et al.[14] studied the IM problem by taking the relationship into consideration.

Topic-Aware Influence Analysis. To the best of our knowledge, only few papers have studied the social influence from the topic perspective[9],[15],[16],[17],[3]. Tang et al.[9] used the factor graph to learn user-to-user topic-wise influence strength. Lu liu et al.[15] proposed a probabilistic model to learn topic-wise influence strength, Lin et al.[16] studied the joint modeling of influence and topics by adopting textual models. Weng et al.[17] analyzed the topic-aware influence on twitter. None of works mentioned above except[3] studied the influence maximization on topic. Barbieri et al.[3] studied the influence maximization on topic-aware, they introduced the topic-aware propagation model and devised a method to learn model parameters from a log of past propagations, however, they did not pay much attention on influence maximization study.

7   Conclusion

In this paper, we study the *topic-aware influence maximization* problem. We devise an efficient algorithm which extends the tree-based approximate model to identify k nodes to maximize the influence on a given topic set. To achieve high performance, we further introduce two strategies to reduce the candidate nodes. Extensive experiments on real datasets demonstrate our method significantly outperforms the state-of-art algorithms.

References

1. Misner, I.R.: The word's best known marketing secret: Building your business with word-of-mouth marketing. Bard Press (1999)
2. Domingos, P., Richardson, M.: Mining the network value of customers. In: KDD, pp. 57–66 (2001)
3. Barbieri, N., Bonchi, F., Manco, G.: Topic-aware social influence propagation models. In: ICDM, pp. 81–90 (2012)
4. Kempe, D., Kleinberg, J.M., Tardos, É.: Maximizing the spread of influence through a social network. In: KDD, pp. 137–146 (2003)
5. Chen, W., Wang, C., Wang, Y.: Scalable influence maximization for prevalent viral marketing in large-scale social networks. In: KDD, pp. 1029–1038 (2010)
6. Leskovec, J., Krause, A., Guestrin, C., Faloutsos, C., VanBriesen, J.M., Glance, N.S.: Cost-effective outbreak detection in networks. In: KDD, pp. 420–429 (2007)
7. Jung, K., Heo, W., Chen, W.: Irie: Scalable and robust influence maximization in social networks. In: ICDM, pp. 918–923 (2012)
8. Rosen-Zvi, M., Griffiths, T.L., Steyvers, M., Smyth, P.: The author-topic model for authors and documents. In: UAI, pp. 487–494 (2004)
9. Tang, J., Sun, J., Wang, C., Yang, Z.: Social influence analysis in large-scale networks. In: KDD, pp. 807–816 (2009)
10. Richardson, M., Domingos, P.: Mining knowledge-sharing sites for viral marketing. In: KDD, pp. 61–70 (2002)
11. Chen, W., Wang, Y., Yang, S.: Efficient influence maximization in social networks. In: KDD, pp. 199–208 (2009)
12. Wang, Y., Cong, G., et al.: Community-based greedy algorithm for mining top-k influential nodes in mobile social networks. In: KDD, pp. 1039–1048 (2010)
13. Kim, J., Kim, S.K., Yu, H.: Scalable and parallelizable processing of influence maximization for large-scale social networks. In: ICDE, pp. 266–277 (2013)
14. Tang, S., Yuan, J., Mao, X., Li, X.Y., Chen, W., Dai, G.: Relationship classification in large scale online social networks and its impact on information propagation. In: INFOCOM, pp. 2291–2299 (2011)
15. Liu, L., Tang, J., Han, J., Jiang, M., Yang, S.: Mining topic-level influence in heterogeneous networks. In: CIKM, pp. 199–208 (2010)
16. Lin, C.X., Mei, Q., Han, J., Jiang, Y., Danilevsky, M.: The joint inference of topic diffusion and evolution in social communities. In: ICDM, pp. 378–387 (2011)
17. Weng, J., Lim, E.P., Jiang, J., He, Q.: Twitterrank: finding topic-sensitive influential twitterers. In: WSDM, pp. 261–270 (2010)

Efficient Frequent Itemset Mining
from Dense Data Streams

Alfredo Cuzzocrea[1], Fan Jiang[2], Wookey Lee[3], and Carson K. Leung[2],*

[1] ICAR-CNR & University of Calabria, Rende (CS), Italy
[2] University of Manitoba, Winnipeg, MB, Canada
[3] Inha University, Incheon, South Korea
cuzzocrea@si.deis.unical.it, kleung@cs.umanitoba.ca, trinity@inha.ac.kr

Abstract. Due to advances in technology, high volumes of valuable data
can be produced at high velocity in many real-life applications. Hence,
efficient data mining techniques for discovering implicit, previously unknown, and potentially useful *frequent itemsets* from data streams are
in demand. Many existing stream mining algorithms capture important
stream data and assume that the captured data can fit into main memory. However, problems arise when the available memory is so limited
that such an assumption does not hold. In this paper, we present a data
structure to capture important data from the streams onto the disk. In
addition, we present two algorithms—which use this data structure—to
mine frequent itemsets from these dense (or sparse) data streams.

1 Introduction and Related Works

Data mining (e.g., classification [1,15], pattern mining [8,9,19,23], social network
mining [26,27,28]) aims to discover implicit, previously unknown and potentially
useful knowledge from data. Numerous studies [7,17,22] have been proposed for
the research problem of frequent itemset mining from traditional large static
databases (DBs). To improve efficiency, the FP-growth algorithm [13] uses an
extended prefix-tree structure called *Frequent Pattern tree* (*FP-tree*) to capture
the contents of transaction DBs in memory. Although there are some works [3,12]
that use disk-based structures for mining, they mostly mine frequent itemsets
from *static* DBs. As a preview, we mine frequent itemsets from *dynamic* data
streams.

The automation of measurements and data collection, together with the increasing development and usage of a large number of sensors, has produced
streams of valuable data in many real-life application areas. In order to be able
to make sense of the streaming data (e.g., detect outliers from streams [6,11]),
stream mining algorithms are needed [14,20,24,25]. When compared with the
mining from traditional *static* DBs, mining from *dynamic* data streams is observed to be more challenging [4,18] because data streams are continuous and
unbounded. Once the streams flow through, we lose them. Hence, we need some

---

* Corresponding author.

L. Chen et al. (Eds.): APWeb 2014, LNCS 8709, pp. 593–601, 2014.
© Springer International Publishing Switzerland 2014

data structures to capture the important contents of the streams. Moreover, as data in the streams are not necessarily uniformly distributed, their distributions are usually changing with time. A currently infrequent itemset may become frequent in the future, and vice versa. Hence, we must be careful not to prune infrequent itemsets too early; otherwise, we may not be able to get complete information such as frequencies of certain itemsets (as it is impossible to retract those pruned itemsets).

To efficiently mine frequent itemsets from data streams, *approximate* algorithms (e.g., FP-streaming [10]) may find some infrequent itemsets or miss frequency information of some frequent itemsets (i.e., some false positives and some false negatives). To avoid false positives or false negatives, an *exact* algorithm mines truly frequent itemsets by (i) constructing a *Data Stream Tree* (*DSTree*) [21] to capture contents of the streaming data in memory and then (ii) recursively building local FP-trees for projected DBs (containing subsets of streaming data) based on the information extracted from the DSTree. This algorithm runs well when the global DSTree and subsequent local FP-trees fit into main memory.

To handle situations where not all local FP-trees can fit into memory, one can construct a *Data Stream Projected tree* (*DSP-tree*) [16] for the projected DB of every frequent singleton $\{x\}$. As all frequent k-itemsets containing x can then be mined from that tree, it avoids the recursive construction of local FP-trees for all α-projected DB (where k-itemset $\alpha \supseteq \{x\}$ for all $k \geq 1$).

Along this direction, to handle situations where the global DSTree cannot fit into memory, an *on-disk* data structure called *Data Stream Table* (*DSTable*) [5] can be built. Mining with such a DSTable performs well for very sparse streaming data when not too much information needs to be captured in the DSTable.

As streams of high-volume data can be generated at high velocity, efficient data structures and algorithms for mining frequent itemsets with limited memory are in demand. In this paper, we present a simple yet powerful on-disk data structure—called *Data Stream Matrix* (*DSMatrix*)—for capturing and maintaining relevant data found in dense data streams. This structure is designed for *stream mining* of *frequent itemsets* with sliding window models. It captures the contents of relevant transactions in the streams. When the streams flow through, a fixed-size window (i.e., a window containing the interesting portion of the streams—usually, recent data) slides and our structure is properly updated. Although we design the DSMatrix for dense data streams in limited memory environments, this on-disk data structure can also be used as an alternative to (i) the DSTree for stream mining in environments with sufficient memory and/or (ii) DSTable for mining very sparse data streams.

The remainder of this paper is organized as follows. Section 2 introduces our DSMatrix for capturing important information from data streams. Sections 3 and 4 describe the use of the DSMatrix in mining frequent itemsets horizontally and vertically. Section 5 shows evaluation results. Finally, conclusions are presented in Section 6.

2   Data Stream Matrix (DSMatrix)

Given a dense stream of uncertain data with a limited memory environment, we propose an on-disk *Data Stream Matrix* (*DSMatrix*) structure to capture important contents of transactions in all batches of the streaming data within the current sliding window. Specifically, the DSMatrix is a two-dimensional binary matrix, which represents the presence of an item x in transaction t_i by a "1" in the matrix entry (Row x, Column t_i) and the absence of an item y from transaction t_j by a "0" in the matrix entry (Row y, Column t_j). With this binary representation of items in each transaction, each column in the DSMatrix captures a transaction. Each column in the DSMatrix can be considered as a bit vector.

Our DSMatrix is so flexible that it is applicable to different stream processing models. For instance, (i) when using the *landmark model*, DSMatrix just captures the contents of all transactions after the "landmark". Alternatively, (ii) when using the *sliding window model*, DSMatrix captures the *boundary information*. By keeping track of the boundary that marks the end of each batch of streaming data, when the window slides, transactions in the older batches can be easily removed and transactions in the newer batches can be easily added. Note that, as the same boundaries are applied for all rows representing all m domain items, the amount of boundary information that needs to be kept does not directly depend on the number of transactions (or the number of columns in the DSMatrix). The amount of the kept boundary information is proportional to the number of batches, and each batch can be of equal or variable size. Similarly, (iii) when using the *time fading model*, DSMatrix captures the same *boundary information* as in the sliding window model. The only difference is that extra work is required to incorporate the fading factor in the computation of the support of itemsets when using the time fading model.

Example 1. Consider two recent batches of transactions in a dense data stream as shown in Fig. 1(a). Fig. 1(b) shows how our DSMatrix captures (i) contents of these w=2 batches of transactions and (ii) their associated boundary information when using a sliding window or time fading model with a window size w=2 batches. For example, Column 1 shows a transaction containing a, c, d & f.

Batch	Transaction
	$t_1 = \{a, c, d, f\}$
Batch 1	$t_2 = \{a, d, e, f\}$
	$t_3 = \{a, b, c\}$
	$t_4 = \{a, c, f\}$
Batch 2	$t_5 = \{a, c, d, f\}$
	$t_6 = \{b, c, d\}$

Row	Content	
a	1 1 1	1 1 0
b	0 0 1	0 0 1
c	1 0 1	1 1 1
d	1 1 0	0 1 1
e	0 1 0	0 0 0
f	1 1 0	1 1 0
Boundaries	Columns 3, 6	

(a) Dense data stream   (b) Our DSMatrix

Fig. 1. Our DSMatrix captures important contents from a dense data stream

The boundary information reveals that (i) the first batch (starts from Column 1 and) ends in Column 3 and (ii) the second batch (starts from Column 3+1=4 and) ends in Column 6. □

3 Horizontal Stream Mining with the DSMatrix

When data streams flow through, our DSMatrix is constantly updated so that the mining can be "delayed" until it is needed. To find frequent itemsets from the updated DSMatrix, we propose *a tree-based horizontal mining algorithm*. It first extracts relevant transactions from the DSMatrix to form a local tree for the $\{x\}$-projected DB for every frequent singleton $\{x\}$. Each node in such a local tree contains (i) an item x and (ii) a counter. The value of this counter is initially set to the support of x on that tree path and is decremented during the mining process until it reaches 0 (cf. value remains unchanged in the FP-tree). From the tree for the $\{x\}$-projected DB, we get every frequent k-itemset ($\{x\} \cup \alpha$) by traversing the path from leaf node y to the root (where α is formed by some items along that path). If this k-itemset ($\{x\} \cup \alpha$) has not been generated, its support is set to the value of the counter of node y; otherwise, its support is incremented by the value of the counter of node y. After examining node y, counters along the path from y to the root are decremented by the value of the counter of y. Any node with a zero counter can be pruned. See Example 2.

Example 2. Continue Example 1 with user-specified *minsup* threshold $= 2$. We start the tree-based horizontal mining process by computing the support of the $m=6$ domain items, and find that all except e are frequent. Then, we form the $\{f\}$-projected DB. For every column in Row f with a value "1" (i.e., Columns 1, 2, 4 & 5), we extract its column upwards. Specifically, we extract $\{a, c, d, f\}$ from Column 1. We also extract $\{a, d, e, f\}$, $\{a, c, f\}$ & $\{a, c, d, f\}$ from Columns 2, 4 & 5, respectively. All these form the $\{f\}$-projected DB, from which a local tree can be built as shown in Fig. 2(a). From this tree, we traverse the left path $\langle a{:}4, c{:}3, d{:}2 \rangle$ to form (i) 2-itemsets $\{a, f\}$, $\{c, f\}$ & $\{d, f\}$, (ii) 3-itemsets $\{a, c, f\}$, $\{a, d, f\}$ & $\{c, d, f\}$, and (iii) 4-itemset $\{a, c, d, f\}$. The support of these four itemsets are set to 2 (the value in the counter for d), and the counters of every node in this tree path are decremented by the same value to become $\langle a{:}2, c{:}1, d{:}0 \rangle$ (where the zero-counter node d can then be pruned). Based on this path, we form (i) 2-itemsets $\{a, f\}$ & $\{c, f\}$ and (ii) 3-itemset $\{a, c, f\}$. As they have previously

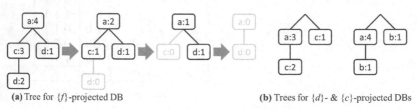

(a) Tree for $\{f\}$-projected DB   (b) Trees for $\{d\}$- & $\{c\}$-projected DBs

Fig. 2. Local trees for $\{f\}$-, $\{d\}$- and $\{c\}$-projected DBs

been formed, their support are incremented by 1 (the current value in the counter for c) to become 2+1=3. Again, the counters of every node in this tree path are decremented by the same value to become $\langle a{:}1, c{:}0\rangle$ (where the zero-counter node c can be pruned). Afterwards, we traverse the right path $\langle a{:}1, d{:}1\rangle$ to form (i) 2-itemsets $\{a, f\}$ & $\{d, f\}$ and (ii) 3-itemset $\{a, d, f\}$. As these three itemsets exist, their support values are incremented by 1. The counters of nodes a and d in this right path are then decremented by 1 to become $\langle a{:}0, d{:}0\rangle$ (where both zero-counter nodes a & d can be pruned). To summarize, we find from $\{f\}$-projected DB the following itemsets with their support: $\{a, f\}$:2+1+1=4, $\{c, f\}$:2+1=3, $\{d, f\}$:2+1=3, $\{a, c, f\}$:2+1=3, $\{a, d, f\}$:2+1=3, $\{c, d, f\}$:2 & $\{a, c, d, f\}$:2. Similar procedures can be applied to the remaining four frequent domain items a, b, c & d to find frequent k-itemsets containing these items. $\square$

4   Vertical Mining with the DSMatrix

Given that the data captured in our DSMatrix can be considered as a collection of bit vectors, the DSMatrix is also applicable for *vertical mining*. To mine frequent 1-itemsets, we examine each row (representing a domain item). The *row sum* (i.e., total number of 1s) gives the support of the item represented by that row. Once the frequent 1-itemsets are found, we *intersect the bit vectors* for two items. If the row sum of the resulting intersection $\geq$ *minsup*, then we find a frequent 2-itemset. We repeat these steps by intersecting two bit vectors of frequent patterns to find frequent itemsets of higher cardinality.

Example 3. Revisit Example 2. We start the vertical mining by first computing the row sum for each row (i.e., for each domain item). As a result, we find that items a, b, c, d & f are frequent with support 5, 2, 5, 4 & 4, respectively. Afterwards, we intersect the bit vector of a (i.e., Row a) with any one of the remaining four bit vectors to find frequent 2-itemsets $\{a, c\}$:4, $\{a, d\}$:3 & $\{a, f\}$:4 because (i) the intersection of $\vec{a}$ and $\vec{c}$ gives a bit vector 101110, (ii) the intersection of $\vec{a}$ and $\vec{d}$ gives a bit vector 110010, and (iii) the intersection of $\vec{a}$ and $\vec{f}$ gives a bit vector 110110. Next, we intersect (i) $\vec{ac}$ with $\vec{ad}$, (ii) $\vec{ac}$ with $\vec{af}$ and (iii) $\vec{ad}$ with $\vec{af}$ to find frequent 3-itemsets $\{a, c, d\}$:2, $\{a, c, f\}$:3 and $\{a, d, f\}$:3. We also intersect $\vec{acd}$ with $\vec{acf}$ to find frequent 4-itemset $\{a, c, d, f\}$:2. These are all frequent k-itemsets containing item a. Similar procedures can be applied to the remaining four frequent domain items b, c, d & f to find frequent k-itemsets containing these items. $\square$

5   Evaluation Results

Analytical Results. Similar to mining with the DSTree [21] or DSTable [5], mining with our DSMatrix also uses a "delayed" mode for mining. So, the actual mining of frequent itemsets is delayed until it is needed to find frequent itemsets. Hence, for S=1000 batches, we only need to build a single global DSMatrix on the disk and update it 995 ($= S{-}w = 1000{-}5$) times. Afterwards, we have an updated DSMatrix capturing the 996th to the 1000th batches.

In terms of main memory space, the DSTree [21] is an in-memory structure. In contrast, as both the DSTable [5] and our DSMatrix are *on-disk* structures, they do not take up memory space.

In terms of disk space, the DSTable [5] requires $64N$ bits (for 32-bit integer representation) for storing the item ID and its corresponding "next" pointer for the N entries in the DSTable (i.e., a total of N occurrences of any domain items). In contrast, as our DSMatrix consists of m rows (one row for each domain item) and n columns (one column for each transaction), it requires only $m \times n$ bits. For dense data streams, N is approaching $m \times n$. This implies that the DSTable requires close to 64 times more than the amount of disk space required by our DSMatrix. For sparse data streams, the DSTable still requires more disk space than our DSMatrix (unless the data density in streams is lower than 1.6%).

Mining with the DSTree [21] requires the construction of the in-memory global DSTree and all subsequent in-memory local trees in memory. The number of nodes in the DSTree can be as large as the number of item occurrences in the data stream. Mining with the DSTable [5] requires the construction of the on-disk global DSTable, but all subsequent local trees need to be in memory. The number of nodes in the DSTable can be as large as the number of item occurrences in the data stream. In contrast, mining with our DSMatrix does not require any construction of global tree in memory. The DSMatrix is stored on disk. Moreover, as the DSMatrix is a binary matrix, the amount of required disk space is substantially lower than that for the DSTable. Horizontal mining with our DSMatrix builds at most m local trees (one for each projected DB containing frequent itemsets); vertical mining with our DSMatrix intersects at most 2^m pairs of bit vectors (though usually much fewer than 2^m pairs of bit vectors).

Experimental Results. We used many different databases including IBM synthetic data, real-life DBs from the UC Irvine Machine Learning Depository (e.g., connect4 data) as well as those from the Frequent Itemset Mining Implementation (FIMI) Dataset Repository. IBM synthetic data are generated by the program developed at IBM Almaden Research Centre [2]. The data contain many records with an average transaction length of 10 items, and a domain of 1000 items. We set each batch to be 0.1M transactions and the window size w=5 batches. All experiments were run in a time-sharing environment in a 1 GHz machine. The reported figures are based on the average of multiple runs. Runtime includes CPU and I/Os; it includes the time for both tree construction and frequent itemset mining steps. In the experiments, we mainly evaluated the accuracy and efficiency of our DSMatrix.

In the first experiment, we measured the accuracy of the three mining options: (i) ⟨global DSTree, local trees⟩, (ii) ⟨global DSTable, local trees⟩, and (iii) ⟨global DSMatrix, local trees⟩ options. Experimental results show that mining with any of these three options give the same mining results.

While these three mining options found the same frequent patterns, their performance varied. In the second and third experiments, we measured the space and time efficiency of our proposed DSTable and DSMatrix. Results show that the DSTree option required the largest main memory space as it stores one global

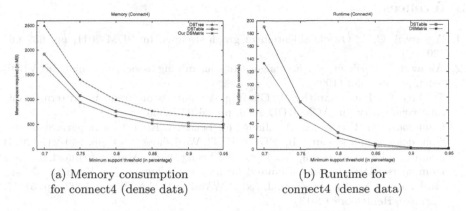

(a) Memory consumption
for connect4 (dense data)

(b) Runtime for
connect4 (dense data)

Fig. 3. Experimental results of our DSMatrix

DSTree and multiple local FP-trees in main memory. The DSTable option required less space as the global DSTable is a disk-based structure. The DSMatrix option required the *smallest* memory space because our proposed DSMatrix is a disk-based structure and it is a *binary* matrix. See Fig. 3(a).

Runtime performance of the three options also varied. When compared with the DSTree, both the DSTable and DSMatrix options just took slightly longer. This is because they both need to read from disk whereas the former two just read from main memory. See Fig. 3(b). It is important to note that reading from disk would be a *logical choice* in a limited main memory environment.

Moreover, we performed some additional experiments. In the fourth experiment, we tested with the effect of *minsup*. As shown in Fig. 3(b), the runtime decreased when *minsup* increased. In the fifth experiment, we tested scalability with the number of transactions. The results show that mining with our DSMatrix was scalable.

We repeated the above experiments on other dense as well as sparse datasets.

6 Conclusions

This paper provides users with (i) a simple yet powerful on-disk structure (DSMatrix) for capturing important information of dense data streams when memory space is limited, (ii) a tree-based horizontal mining algorithm that extracts information from our DSMatrix to find frequent itemsets, and (iii) a vertical mining algorithm that intersects the "bit vectors" stored in our DSMatrix to find frequent itemsets. Analytical and experimental evaluation show the contributions of DSMatrix in frequent itemset mining from dense data streams.

Acknowledgement. This research project is partially supported by (i) NSERC (Canada) and University of Manitoba, as well as (ii) DAPA (South Korea) under the contract UD110006MD.

References

1. Aggarwal, C.C.: On classification of graph streams. In: SDM 2011, pp. 652–663 (2011)
2. Agrawal, R., Srikant, R.: Fast algorithms for mining association rules. In: VLDB 1994, pp. 487–499 (1994)
3. Buehrer, G., Parthasarathy, S., Ghoting, A.: Out-of-core frequent pattern mining on a commodity. In: ACM KDD 2006, pp. 86–95 (2006)
4. Cameron, J.J., Cuzzocrea, A., Jiang, F., Leung, C.K.: Frequent pattern mining from dense graph streams. In: EDBT/ICDT Workshops 2014, pp. 240–247 (2014)
5. Cameron, J.J., Cuzzocrea, A., Jiang, F., Leung, C.K.: Mining frequent itemsets from sparse data streams in limited memory environments. In: Wang, J., Xiong, H., Ishikawa, Y., Xu, J., Zhou, J. (eds.) WAIM 2013. LNCS, vol. 7923, pp. 51–57. Springer, Heidelberg (2013)
6. Cao, K., Han, D., Wang, G., Hu, Y., Yuan, Y.: An algorithm for outlier detection on uncertain data stream. In: Ishikawa, Y., Li, J., Wang, W., Zhang, R., Zhang, W. (eds.) APWeb 2013. LNCS, vol. 7808, pp. 449–460. Springer, Heidelberg (2013)
7. Chiu, D.Y., Wu, Y.H., Chen, A.: Efficient frequent sequence mining by a dynamic strategy switching algorithm. VLDB J. 18(1), 303–327 (2009)
8. Cuzzocrea, A., Leung, C.K., MacKinnon, R.K.: Mining constrained frequent itemsets from distributed uncertain data. FGCS 37, 117–126 (2014)
9. Fariha, A., Ahmed, C.F., Leung, C.K.-S., Abdullah, S.M., Cao, L.: Mining frequent patterns from human interactions in meetings using directed acyclic graphs. In: Pei, J., Tseng, V.S., Cao, L., Motoda, H., Xu, G. (eds.) PAKDD 2013, Part I. LNCS, vol. 7818, pp. 38–49. Springer, Heidelberg (2013)
10. Giannella, C., Han, J., Pei, J., Yan, X., Yu, P.S.: Mining frequent patterns in data streams at multiple time granularities. In: Data Mining: Next Generation Challenges and Future Directions, ch. 6 (2004)
11. Gong, X., Qian, W., Qin, S., Zhou, A.: Fractal based anomaly detection over data streams. In: Ishikawa, Y., Li, J., Wang, W., Zhang, R., Zhang, W. (eds.) APWeb 2013. LNCS, vol. 7808, pp. 550–562. Springer, Heidelberg (2013)
12. Grahne, G., Zhu, J.: Mining frequent itemsets from secondary memory. In: IEEE ICDM 2004, pp. 91–98 (2004)
13. Han, J., Pei, J., Yin, Y.: Mining frequent patterns without candidate generation.In: ACM SIGMOD 2000, pp. 1–12 (2000)
14. Jin, R., Agrawal, G.: An algorithm for in-core frequent itemset mining on streaming data. In: IEEE ICDM 2005, pp. 210–217 (2005)
15. Lee, W., Song, J.J., Leung, C.K.-S.: Categorical data skyline using classification tree. In: Du, X., Fan, W., Wang, J., Peng, Z., Sharaf, M.A. (eds.) APWeb 2011. LNCS, vol. 6612, pp. 181–187. Springer, Heidelberg (2011)
16. Leung, C.K.-S., Brajczuk, D.A.: Efficient mining of frequent itemsets from data streams. In: Gray, A., Jeffery, K., Shao, J. (eds.) BNCOD 2008. LNCS, vol. 5071, pp. 2–14. Springer, Heidelberg (2008)
17. Leung, C.K.S., Carmichael, C.L., Johnstone, P., Yuen, D.S.H.-C.: Interactive visual analytics of databases and frequent sets. IJIRR 3(4), 120–140 (2013)
18. Leung, C.K.-S., Cuzzocrea, A., Jiang, F.: Discovering frequent patterns from uncertain data streams with time-fading and landmark models. TLDKS VIII, 174–196 (2013)

19. Leung, C.K.-S., Hayduk, Y.: Mining frequent patterns from uncertain data with MapReduce for Big data analytics. In: Meng, W., Feng, L., Bressan, S., Winiwarter, W., Song, W. (eds.) DASFAA 2013, Part I. LNCS, vol. 7825, pp. 440–455. Springer, Heidelberg (2013)

20. Leung, C.K.-S., Jiang, F.: Frequent itemset mining of uncertain data streams using the damped window model. In: ACM SAC 2011, pp. 950–955 (2011)

21. Leung, C.K.-S., Khan, Q.I.: DSTree: a tree structure for the mining of frequent sets from data streams. In: IEEE ICDM 2006, pp. 928–932 (2006)

22. Leung, C.K.-S., Khan, Q.I., Li, Z., Hoque, T.: CanTree: a canonical-order tree for incremental frequent-pattern mining. KAIS 11(3), 287–311 (2007)

23. Leung, C.K.-S., Tanbeer, S.K.: PUF-tree: a compact tree structure for frequent pattern mining of uncertain data. In: Pei, J., Tseng, V.S., Cao, L., Motoda, H., Xu, G. (eds.) PAKDD 2013, Part I. LNCS, vol. 7818, pp. 13–25. Springer, Heidelberg (2013)

24. Papapetrou, O., Garofalakis, M., Deligiannakis, A.: Sketch-based querying of distributed sliding-window data streams. In: VLDB 2012, pp. 992–1003 (2012)

25. Rao, W., Chen, L., Chen, S., Tarkoma, S.: Evaluating continuous top-k queries over document streams. WWW 17(1), 59–83 (2014)

26. Tanbeer, S.K., Leung, C.K.-S.: Finding diverse friends in social networks. In: Ishikawa, Y., Li, J., Wang, W., Zhang, R., Zhang, W. (eds.) APWeb 2013. LNCS, vol. 7808, pp. 301–309. Springer, Heidelberg (2013)

27. Xu, B., Deng, L., Jia, Y., Zhou, B., Han, Y.: Social circle analysis on ego-network based on context frequent pattern mining. In: ICIMCS 2013, pp. 139–144 (2013)

28. Zhou, X., Chen, L.: Event detection over twitter social media streams. VLDB J. 23(3), 381–400 (2014)

A Frequent Term-Based Multiple Clustering Approach for Text Documents

Hai-Tao Zheng, Hao Chen, and Shu-Qin Gong

Tsinghua-Southampton Web Science Laboratory
Graduate School at Shenzhen, Tsinghua University Shenzhen, China
zheng.haitao@sz.tsinghua.edu.cn,
{jerrychen1990,gongshuqin90}@gmail.com

Abstract. With the boom of web and social network, the amount of generated text data has increased enormously. On one hand, although text clustering methods are applicable to classify text data and facilitate data mining work such as information retrieval and recommendation, inadequate aspects are still evident. Especially, most existing text clustering methods provide either a hard partitioned or a hierarchical result, which cannot describe the data from various perspectives. On the other hand, multiple clustering approaches, which are proposed to classify data with various perspectives, meet several challenges such as high time complexity and incomprehensible results while applied to text documents. In this paper, we propose a frequent term-based multiple clustering approach for text documents. Our approach classifies text documents with various perspectives and provides a semantic explanation for each cluster. Through a series of experiments, we prove that our method is more scalable and provides more comprehensible results than traditional multiple clustering methods such as OSCLU and ASCLU while applied to text documents. In addition, we also found that our approach achieves a better clustering quality than existing text clustering approaches like FTC.

Keywords: Multiple clustering, Frequent term, Text documents.

1 Introduction

Data mining in database provides data owners with new information and patterns in their data. Clustering is a traditional data mining task for automatically grouping data. However, groups may be hidden in different perspectives of the data. An item may belong to different groups with different perspectives. Traditional clustering approaches only provide either a hard partitioned result or a hierarchical result. In these clustering results, an item can only belong to one group. To discover hidden groups in various perspectives, we need to apply multiple clustering approaches. Multiple clustering methods can assign one item to different groups with respect to different perspectives. Generally speaking, multiple clustering approaches have to deal with two challenges including high time complexity and redundant result.

L. Chen et al. (Eds.): APWeb 2014, LNCS 8709, pp. 602–609, 2014.

On the other hand, as the web continues to grow rapidly, huge number of text documents have been generated. To organize and do data mining work on these text documents, text clustering becomes a very important application of clustering algorithms. However, compared to other applications of clustering, three major challenges including high dimensionality, large data and incomprehensible results should be addressed for text clustering:

Although applying a multiple clustering approach to text documents can help us significantly while doing text mining tasks, to our best knowledge there is no existing feasible multiple clustering approach for text documents since now. The high dimensionality of text documents makes multiple clustering approaches not scalable while applied to text documents. In this paper, we propose the first feasible multiple clustering approach for text documents called FTMTC(frequent term-based multiple text clustering approach). FTMTC represents a cluster with a set of terms to deal with the high dimensionality challenge. We also introduce WordNet[1] to improve the quality of redundancy removal process.

This paper is structured as follows: We review existing text clustering and multiple clustering approaches in section 2. In section 3, we introduce a series of notations to define the problem we are going to solve. We describe details of FTMTC with sequence charts in section4. Then, we prove our approach is feasible and outstanding with a series of experiments in section 5. Finally, we make a conclusion and introduce our future work in section 6.

2   Related Work

2.1   Multiple Clustering Approaches

The main difference between multiple clustering approaches and traditional clustering approaches is that multiple clustering's result contains clusters discovered with various perspectives. Clusters in multiple clustering result can overlap to each other while clusters in traditional clustering result can't. Traditional multiple clustering approaches tend to generate a quite large amount of clusters. The result contains a lot of redundant clusters. OSCLU[2] is a recent proposed non-redundant multiple clustering approach, which is based on the idea that a pair of clusters which share more than a certain amount of overlapped dimensions and items should be regarded as similar to each other. ASCLU[3] applies OSCLU to an alternative clustering way.

2.2   Text Clustering Approaches

Most text clustering approaches rely on a *vector-space model*, in which, each text document d is represented by a vector of frequencies of all terms: $d = (tf_1, tf_2, \ldots, tf_m)$. Based on this model, standard clustering approaches like k-means[4] can be applied to text documents directly. But they can't handel the high dimensional and incomprehensible result challenges well.

In this paper, we propose a multiple clustering solution for text documents based on frequent term model. This model can help us get avoid of the high dimensionality challenge of text documents.

3 Problem Definition

For consistent notations in the following sections, we define some notations here. First of all, we make a formal definition of our problem: Given a set of text documents $DS = \{d_1, d_2, \ldots, d_m\}$ as input, let $T_{all} = \{t_1, t_2, \ldots, t_k\}$ denote all the terms that appear in DS and $T(d)$ denote terms that appear in d. Our target is to generate a set of clusters $R = \{C_1, C_2, \ldots, C_n\}$. In this procedure, three main challenges need to be addressed:

Challenge 1: Incomprehensible Results: Traditional clustering results do not provide explanations for clusters. To give each cluster a explanation, we associate each cluster in R with a term set. To associate terms with documents, we introduce the following definitions: As document d contains a set of terms, a term t can also "cover" a set of documents. We define the set of documents in DS that contain term t as $Cover(t)$:

$$Cover(t) = \{d \in DS | t \in T(d)\} \tag{1}$$

The "cover" of a term set $T = \{t_1, t_2, \ldots, t_k\}$ is defined as the intersection of all terms in T:

$$Cover(T) = \bigcap_{i=1}^{k} Cover(t_i) \tag{2}$$

So, if $Cover(T)$ is the documents grouped by a cluster, T will give an explanation for the cluster.

Challenge 2 High Dimensional Data: To deal with the high dimensional challenge, we control the number of term sets that are associated to clusters. We only associate frequent term sets to clusters. We can judge whether a term set T is a frequent set with $Cover(T)$, we define the set of all frequent term sets as $FTS(DS)$:

$$FTS(DS) = \{T \subseteq T_{all} || Cover(T)| \geq \alpha * |DS|\} \tag{3}$$

Where α is the threshold of frequent term set. So, a cluster is composed with a frequent term set T as explanation and a document set D as members.

$$C = (T, D) \tag{4}$$

Where $T \in FTS(DS)$ and $D = Cover(T)$.

Challenge 3 Redundant Clustering Results: To prevent a redundant clustering result, the size of R should be reasonable. Each cluster in R should bring novel information. We will introduce a cluster picking algorithm in section 4 to handle this challenge.

4 Frequent-Term Based Multiple Text Clustering Approach

Based on the notations above, we propose a multiple clustering approach for text documents called FTMTC(Frequent-term based multiple text clustering). Generally speaking, FTMTC is composed of three steps as shown in Fig. 1:

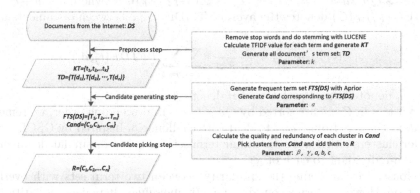

Fig. 1. Sequence diagram of FTMTC

4.1 Preprocess Step

To preprocess the document data, we conduct several steps including stop words removing, stemming and indexing. First of all, a stop word list[1] is employed to remove the stop words. Secondly, we apply Poter stemming algorithm for word stemming. To process the document efficiently, we apply a tool named Lucene to build index files for the documents.

For an efficient algorithm, we extract k important words from T_{all} as key terms. The key term set is noted as KT. Since nouns with high TFIDF value tend to be representative in general, we pick nouns with high TFIDF from T_{all} and add them to KT.

4.2 Candidate Generating Step

In this step, we generate $FTS(DS)$ with Aprior algorithm[5] algorithm. For each T in $FTS(DS)$, we build a corresponding cluster $C = (T, Cover(T))$ and add it to the candidate set $Cand$. Since term sets with more terms tend to cover less documents than those with less terms, we set the document coverage threshold as follows: Assuming that α is the threshold of frequent term set with one term, the threshold of a frequent term set with N terms will be $\alpha \times 0.9^{(N-1)}$

4.3 Candidate Picking Step

In this step, we pick clusters from $Cand$ and add them to the result set R gradually. First of all, we rank clusters in $Cand$ based on clusters' quality. Generally speaking, clusters with large number of documents or terms tend to have high quality. Besides, if the terms are closely related to the documents, the cluster's quality is high. We judge the relationship between terms and documents with average TFIDF value. Therefore, we define the the quality of a cluster

---
[1] http://www.ranks.nl/stopwords

$C(T, D)$ as $Quality(C) = |D|^a \times |T|^b \times AVG_{TFIDF}(C)^c$. where $a + b + c = 1$ and $AVG_{TFIDF}(C)$ denotes the average TFIDF value between documents and terms.

$$AVG_{TFIDF}(C) = \frac{1}{m \times n} * \sum_{i=1}^{m} \sum_{j=1}^{n} TFIDF(t_j, d_i) \tag{5}$$

Where m denotes the size of D and n denotes the size of T

As clusters in $Cand$ are sorted by $Quality(C)$ in descending order, we remove redundant clusters from $Cand$ to deal with challenge 3. Inspired by OSCLU, we consider clusters either have dissimilar term sets or group dissimilar documents to be non-redundant to each other.

Obviously we can define the similarity between two term sets with overlap percentage. However, terms contain semantic meanings. It makes similarity between term sets more complex than similarity between mathematic vectors. For example, term set {"USA", "president", "history"} and term set {"America", "chairman", "past"} share no term, but they do represent similar concepts.

To adapt the redundancy definition to text clustering, we introduce WordNet as external knowledge. WordNet is a lexical database which can be used to calculate the similarity between two terms. We use Jiang and Conrath's word similarity algorithm JNC[6] to judge the similarity between terms. We define semantic similarity between two term sets $T = \{t_1, t_2, \ldots, t_n\}$ and $\hat{T} = \{\hat{t_1}, \hat{t_2}, \ldots, \hat{t_m}\}$ as $Similarity(T, \hat{T})$:

$$Similarity(T, \hat{T}) = \frac{1}{2n} \times \sum_{i=1}^{n} \max_{\hat{t_j} \in \hat{T}} JNC(t_i, \hat{t_j}) + \frac{1}{2m} \times \sum_{i=1}^{m} \max_{t_j \in T} JNC(\hat{t_i}, t_j) \tag{6}$$

With a similarity threshold β, we can get a group of clusters in R that are similar to a given cluster C. The similar group of $C(T, D)$ in R with threshold β is defined as:

$$SimGroup_\beta(C, R) = \{C_i \in R \backslash C | Similarity(T, T_i) \geq \beta\} \tag{7}$$

Although C has similar term set with clusters in $SimGroup_\beta(C, R)$, if C groups dissimilar documents, we also consider C as non-redundant to clusters in R. Given a cluster set $CS = \{C_1, C_2, \ldots, C_n\}$, we define the coverage of CS's document as $Coverage(CS) = \bigcup_{i=1}^{n} D_i$, where D_i denotes the document set of C_i

At last, we define an interest value $Interest(C, R)$ to judge whether C is novel to R. Given a threshold γ, we add C to R if $Interest(C, R)$ is larger than γ. Since we already sort $Cand$ with regard to cluster's quality by descending order, it's obvious that our algorithm is a greedy algorithm and thus can maximize the summation of clusters' qualities under the premise that R is none-redundant. We define the interest of $C = (T, D)$ to R as $Interest(C, R)$:

$$Interest(C, R) = \frac{|D \backslash Coverage(SimGroup_\beta(C, R))|}{|D|} \tag{8}$$

5 Experiments

5.1 Experiment Setup

To build a multi-label data set, we download 4505 biography pages from Wikipedia with two different perspectives. The biography pages are downloaded from four country categories and three occupation categories.

We measure clustering results with three aspects. First of all, we list the clustering result to prove it covers categories with different perspectives in section 5.2. Secondly, we evaluate the scalability of our algorithm in section 5.3. At last, in section 5.4, we evaluate the quality of clustering result with multiple clustering evaluation measurements introduced in [7], including purity, entropy and F1-value.

5.2 Experiment Result

Table 1 shows the result of FTMTC. It handles Challenge 1 and Challenge 2 well. The term set associated to a cluster explains the cluster's topic well. We mark categories in nationality perspective with black font and mark categories in occupation perspective with normal font. We found the result covers every known category in two perspectives. Besides, we are glad to see that FTMTC also can discover clusters we do not know in advance like "War" and detailed category like "Swim". We mark them with italics font.

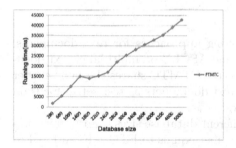

Fig. 2. FTMTC's scalability   **Fig. 3.** running time Vs size

5.3 Scalability Evaluation

Multiple clustering approaches that are based on term vector model's running time grows fast as the database grows. Since FTMTC applies similar redundancy removal process with OSCLU and ASCLU, we compare FTMTC with OSCLU, ASCLU and FTC. We do experiments as the database's size grows from 100 to 5000 (add 200 documents each time). Each time, we run the clustering algorithms ten times and calculate the average running time. From Fig.2 and Fig.3, we can see that FTMTC and FTC's running time grows linearly as the database's size grows while OSCLU and ASCLU's running time grows exponentially. It's obvious that FTMTC outperforms OSCLU and ASCLU with regard to scalability.

Table 1. Clustering result

ID	Term list	Size	Category
1	[aquatics,champion,Europe,olympics,swim]	169	Athlete, *Swim*
2	[China,football,league]	298	**China**, Athlete, *Football*
3	[football,league,France,nation,team]	217	**France**, Athlete, *Football*
4	[Olympics,swim]	331	Athlete, *Swim*
5	[France,Paris]	741	**France**
6	[cup,football,Germany,nation,team]	149	**Germany**, Athlete, *Football*
7	[China]	858	**China**
8	[news,publisher]	875	Writer
9	[basketball,champion,coach,season]	129	Athlete, *Basketball*
10	[Germany]	916	**Germany**
11	[writer,Europe]	992	Writer
12	[America,gold,summer]	468	**USA**, Athlete
13	[election,party,state]	153	Politician
14	[book,publisher]	329	Writer
15	[California]	329	**USA**
16	[Shanghai]	258	**China**
17	[man]	879	*Man*
18	[mayor,Paris]	268	**France**, Politician
19	[president]	384	Politician
20	[war]	266	*War*

5.4   Clustering Quality Evaluation

Since there is no existing multiple clustering approaches for text documents, we compare FTMTC with FTC, OSCLU and ASCLU on multi-label text documents. We choose FTC as the baseline because FTMTC shares the same cluster definition with it. We choose multi-label text documents as test set to focus on discovering clusters in various perspectives.

We compare clustering quality with different database sizes. . For a fair comparison, we set the FTMTC's key word number equals to FTC's. From Fig.4 to Fig.6 we can see that FTMTC can obviously outperform FTC with regard to purity, F1 value and entropy.

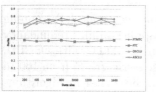 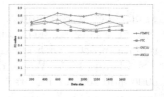

Fig. 4. Purity vs size   **Fig. 5.** Entropy vs size   **Fig. 6.** F1 value vs size

6 Conclusion and Future Work

In this paper, we propose a feasible multiple clustering approach for text documents based on a frequent term model. We also introduce WordNet as external knowledge to help removing results' redundancy. With a series of experiments, we prove that FTMTC can provide an understandable clustering result which contains clusters in various perspectives. FTMTC can also excavate hidden and more detailed clusters, which helps many tasks of data mining. With comparison, we prove that FTMTC is more scalable than traditional multiple clustering approaches and achieves a better clustering result than FTC while applied to multi-label text documents. In the future, we will exploit more external knowledge, such as Cyc Ontology[2] and Wikipedia[3], to improve our clustering results.

Acknowledgments. This research is supported by the 863 project of China (2013AA013300), National Natural Science Foundation of China (Grant No. 61375054) and Tsinghua University Initiative Scientific Research Program(20131089256).

References

1. Miller, G.A.: Wordnet: a lexical database for english. Communications of the ACM 38(11), 39–41 (1995)
2. Günnemann, S., Müller, E., Färber, I., Seidl, T.: Detection of orthogonal concepts in subspaces of high dimensional data. In: Proceedings of the 18th ACM Conference on Information and Knowledge Management, pp. 1317–1326. ACM (2009)
3. Günnemann, S., Färber, I., Müller, E., Seidl, T.: Asclu: Alternative subspace clustering. In: MultiClust at KDD. Citeseer (2010)
4. Kanungo, T., Mount, D.M., Netanyahu, N.S., Piatko, C.D., Silverman, R., Wu, A.Y.: An efficient k-means clustering algorithm: Analysis and implementation. IEEE Transactions on Pattern Analysis and Machine Intelligence 24(7), 881–892 (2002)
5. Agrawal, R., Ramakrishnan, Srikant, o.: Fast algorithms for mining association rules. In: Proc. 20th Int. Conf. Very Large Data Bases, VLDB, vol. 1215, pp. 487–499 (1994)
6. Jiang, J.J., Conrath, D.W.: Semantic similarity based on corpus statistics and lexical taxonomy. arXiv preprint cmp-lg/9709008 (1997)
7. Müller, E., Günnemann, S., Assent, I., Seidl, T.: Evaluating clustering in subspace projections of high dimensional data. Proceedings of the VLDB Endowment 2(1), 1270–1281 (2009)

---

[2] http://www.cyc.com/
[3] https://www.wikipedia.org/

What to Tag Your Microblog: Hashtag Recommendation Based on Topic Analysis and Collaborative Filtering

Yuan Wang[1], Jishi Qu[2], Jie Liu[1,3,*], Jimeng Chen[1], and Yalou Huang[1,2]

[1] College of Computer and Control Engineering, Nankai University, Tianjin, 300071
[2] College of Software, Nankai University, Tianjin, 300071
[3] Information Technology Research Base of Civil Aviation Administration of China,
Civil Aviation University of China, Tianjin, 300071
{yayaniuzi23,2120120447,jeanchen}@mail.nankai.edu.cn,
{jliu,huangyl}@nankai.edu.cn

Abstract. Hashtags are often utilized as metadata tags to mark messages for user-defined topics in a microblogging environment. However, difficulties in providing or selecting appropriate hashtags often force users giving up using them. In this paper, we propose a personalized method for hashtag recommendation that combines advantages of both topical information and collaborative intelligence. On one hand, we characterize the topic relevance of hashtags to posts based on content models. On the other hand, we predict an active user's hashtag usage preference in a collaborative filtering manner. Overall, we recommend hashtags by relevant scores for a specific microblog posted by a specific user. Experimental results show that our model is an effective solution for hashtag suggestion (MRR is around 96%) which outperforms the state-of-the-art methods.

Keywords: Hashtag Recommendation, Topic Analysis, Collaborative Filtering, Social Network Mining.

1 Introduction

Microblogging platforms have become an important information source for late-breaking news and hot topics[1]. To bring an order to the big and chaotic world of microblogging, users adopt *hashtags* to mark key points of their messages. However, difficulties in providing or selecting appropriate hashtags often force users to give up using them. Researches[2, 3] report that only a few users (much less than 20%) add hashtags actively. In fact, it would be quite helpful to recommend hashtags. Existing recommendation methods can be roughly divided into two kinds: content-based methods[2–7] and collaborative filtering methods[8]. The former techniques achieve success by measuring content relevance between a tweet and hashtags, while the latter further consider user preference based on collaborative filtering. But, a single microblog is too short to capture the accurate topic semantics and user preference[9]. How to combine effective topic understanding and user preference modeling for hashtag recommendation is a challenging task.

---

* Corresponding author.

L. Chen et al. (Eds.): APWeb 2014, LNCS 8709, pp. 610–618, 2014.

To solve the problems mentioned above, we propose a collaborative hashtag recommendation method that leverages 1) global content information for modeling topical semantics of messages (topic relevance model) and 2) users' preference background from other like-minded users (user preference model). We summarize our contributions as follows. First, we introduce a novel filtering method that integrates topic semantic dependency and hashtag usage preference from users seamlessly. Second, we prove that information integration contributes to content topical discrimination of microblogs and enhances semantic understanding of hashtags. Third, we explore and discuss three kinds of user preference on hashtag selection and adoption. Finally, we verify our model on a real data set collected from microblogging platforms. The experimental results indicate that our model significantly improves recommendation precision (MRR is around 96%), and outperforms the state-of-the-art methods.

The rest of our paper is organized as follows. We discuss related work in Section 2. Section 3 introduces a clear definition of hashtag recommendation task and shows details of the recommendation process based on topic analysis and user preference modeling. We present experiments and empirical analysis of our models in Section 4. Finally, conclusions are given in Section 5.

2 Related Work

Many researchers have realized the value and significance of hashtags, and study how to help users to select hashtags more efficiently (hashtag recommendation). The proposed practical strategies can be roughly divided into two categories: content-based methods[2–7] and collaborative filtering methods[8]. Content-based methods take different techniques to build semantic bridges between hashtags and messages, such as the TFIDF scheme[2], Bayes rules[3], WordNet similarity information with the Euclidean distance metric[4] and topic translation methods[5–7]. Collaborative filtering mechanism is a traditional technique for recommending[10], where Kywe[8] combines hashtags of similar users and similar messages to propose a more personalized set of tags to meet both user preference and content information.

Currently, content analysis approaches are dominant strategies for this problem. But short and unconstrained texts suffer from sparseness of co-occurrence words. For man-made hashtags, user preference is one of the decisive factors for message description. Drawing on the experience of predecessors, we take advantages of both local (the current microblog content and the user) and global (hashtag-related content and like-minded users' usage preference) information.

3 Proposed Method

In this section, we introduce our recommendation strategy in details.

3.1 A Framework of Our Hashtag Recommendation Model

Let $U = \{u_i\}_{i=1}^{l}$, $D = \{d_i\}_{i=1}^{n}$, $T = \{t_i\}_{i=1}^{v}$, $H = \{h_i\}_{i=1}^{m}$ be a set of users, messages, terms and hashtags that have appeared in datasets separately. A common microblog d posted by user u contains a set of hashtags $\mathbf{h}_d$. We represent a post d as a "bag of words"

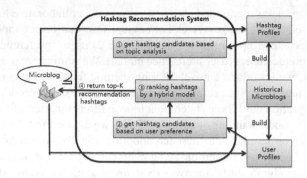

Fig. 1. The Framework of Hashtag Recommendation

with term frequency $d = \{n_{d,i}\}_{i=1}^{v}$. The task of hashtag recommendation is to output a set of semantic related hashtags H_{rec} according to a specific microblog d posted by a specific user u. The framework of our model is shown in Fig. 1.

For a given microblog, recommendation is based on two kinds of off-line processed profiles: hashtag profiles (constructed by using content of all previous messages containing a specific hashtag) and user profiles (constructed for each user, including all messages a specific user has posted). The computation framework of recommendation follows the steps below. Firstly, we get hashtag candidates based on topic analysis between hashtag profiles and the current microblog (①, details in Section 3.2). Secondly, we get hashtag candidates according to user preference and collaborative filtering techniques (②, details in Section 3.3). Thirdly, we recommend hashtags from two candidate sets by a hybrid function (③, details in Section 3.4). Finally, we return the top-K results to users (④).

3.2   Topic Semantic Modeling

A hashtag shows us topic information in messages, thus it's vital to model topic semantic relevance between a post and hashtags when recommending. Due to short and casual texts, we notice that modeling topic relevance information from a single post probably captures weak semantic description, not the topic representation. In fact, aggregated messages give us more accurate and comprehensive topic illustration of high quality[9, 11]. So we collect all microblogs containing a specific hashtag h together as its profile, denoted as $D_h = \{n_{h,i}\}_{i=1}^{v}$, where $n_{h,i}$ is the number of term i in hashtag h's profile. So, each hashtag is a distribution vector over terms from related messages. Different distributions reflect different topic semantic information of hashtags. The accumulative representation for each hashtag makes themes more clearly, enhances semantic signal and decreases the risk of concept or key point drift.

Hence, we measure semantic relevancy score by using the cosine similarity between the input message d and the hashtag profile $\|D_h\|$:

$$p(h|d) = \frac{D_h \cdot d}{\|D_h\| \cdot \|d\|} \tag{1}$$

In the aspect of content, we get hashtag candidates with semantic relevancy scores. Each hashtag's profile can be constructed independently, so it's easy to be implemented in parallel and processed in linear time.

3.3 User Preference Modeling

User preference shows personal characteristics when selecting and adopting hashtags. Users' historical behaviors reflect degree of their interests. In this part, we focus on selecting hashtags based on user profiles under an improved collaborative filtering scheme. Due to the concept of user interest groups, we mine near neighbors for discovering a specific user's hashtag preference.

We construct each user profile with one's historical microblogs. And then we take three user interest description matrices M for user representation, where each row m_i represents the interest vector of user i. M^{CT}, M^{HT}, M^{TK} are a content representation matrix, a hashtag representation matrix and a topic representation matrix respectively, where $m_{u,i}^{CT}$, $m_{u,i}^{HT}$, $m_{u,i}^{TK}$ refer to number of term i, frequency of hashtag i, probability distribution of topic i for user u based on information in user profiles respectively. The topic distribution is trained by a famous topic model called Latent Dirichlet Allocation (LDA)[12] with words in user u's profile. For lack of space, topic model parameter estimation method is not stated here (see more detailed derivation in [13]).

With user interest description matrices mentioned above, we can easily apply a common measurement to find like-minded users. Here we calculate user pair-wise similarity by using the cosine value between their representation vectors:

$$sim(u_i, u) = \frac{m_{u_i} \cdot m_u}{\|m_{u_i}\| \cdot \|m_u\|}. \tag{2}$$

We further represent relationships between users and hashtags under one extension of collaborative filtering schema to find hashtags that are right up their alley. The preference for hashtags with users' interest group considered is represented as $p(h|u)$:

$$p(h|u) = \frac{\overline{n_u} + \kappa \sum_{i=1}^{k} sim(u_i, u)(n_{u_i,h} - \overline{n_{u_i}})}{\|H_u\|}, \tag{3}$$

where $\kappa = \frac{1}{\sum_{i=1}^{k} sim(u_i, u)}$ is a normalization factor, H_u is referred as the set of hashtags that are used by user u, $n_{u,h}$ is frequency of hashtag h used by user u, $\overline{n_u}$ is average hashtag usage times of user u. Until now, we complete predicting user preference on hashtags, and get a set of hashtag candidates with user preference degree.

3.4 Fusion Strategy of Topic Relevance and User Preference

As the methods mentioned above, we have already achieved content topic relevance via topic semantic analysis, denoted as $p(h|d)$, and user preference via considering user interest groups, denoted as $p(h|u)$. The two scores are both probability value between 0 and 1. The higher the value is, the more relevance the message and hashtag are.

We apply a linear combination between semantic relations and user preference relations, marked as "Function-based Hybrid Model". For a specific post written by a specific user, the score for a hashtag h is:

$$Score(h|u,d) = \lambda \cdot p(h|d) + (1 - \lambda) \cdot p(h|u), \qquad (4)$$

where λ is a balance factor for two parts. It represents how great content information has impact on the final score. So far, the hybrid model integrates topic bias of content and user preference, which is more suitable and feasible for users to adopt the recommendation.

4 Experimental Results and Discussions

4.1 Data Collection

Our data is drawn from a large snapshot of microblogs generated from August 26th, 2009 to February 9th, 2012 by Chinese users in Sina-Weibo (http://weibo.com). After removing microblogs with no hashtags, we get 21,992 posts, 2,179 relevant users and 3,762 distinct hashtags. The average length of one post is 30.34.

We divide our data set into a training set (21,742 posts) and a testing set (250 posts). The training set is used for constructing user profiles and hashtag profiles. For evaluation, we randomly sample 250 original microblogs as our testing set, posted by 23 users, marked with 106 distinct hashtags, containing 53.48 available characters on average.

4.2 Evaluation Metrics and Comparison Models

For each microblog, we consider the rate of accurate recommendation and position related evaluation metrics. We choose *Precision*, *Top-k Accuracy*, *At-k Accuracy* and *MRR* to measure the performance of our model. In the testing microblogs, the hashtags actually used by users serve as our ground truth.

Precision is a positive predictive value, percentage of correctly hashtags among all hashtags recommended by the model. *Top-k Accuracy* is percentage of microblogs correctly marked by at least one of the top k hashtags in the recommended list. *At-k Accuracy* is percentage of microblogs correctly marked by the kth hashtags in the recommended list. *MRR* stands for Mean Reciprocal Rank. The reciprocal rank of a post response is the multiplicative inverse of the rank of the first correct hashtag. The Mean Reciprocal Rank is the average reciprocal rank of all microblogs in testing sets.

In the following sections, we abbreviate our model "Function-based Hybrid Model" to *FHM*. We compare FHM with two state-of-the-art hashtag recommendation models (Content-based Collaborative Filtering[2] (*CCF*) and Majority Vote-based Hybrid Model[8] (*MVHM*)) and one classical User-based Collaborative Filtering model (*UCF*) on the same microblogs collection. Here, MVHM is a hybrid model.

4.3 Experimental Results

We firstly compare FHM with three other recommendation models, and then go through two major components of the model, recommendation based on topic semantic and recommendation based on user preference, respectively.

Table 1. Comparison of MRR between Recommendation Methods

Method	CCF	UCF	MVHM	FHM
MRR	65.77%	32.09%	79.28%	**96.56%**

(1) Personalized Hashtag Recommendation Model

For each model, we find optimal parameters by the way of grid search. In CCF, we take TFIDF hashtag profiles to describe hashtags, use M^{HT} as the user interest description matrix, and choose 1-nearest neighbor for calculating user hashtag preference. We set balance factor λ as 0.5, which allows us to best leverage topic semantic relevance and user preference. For MVHM, we set the number of nearest neighbors as 1 and the number of similar microblogs as 10.

The MRR of four models is shown in the Table 1. From Table 1, We can draw the following conclusions. (1) Both hybrid models, MVHM and FHM, outperform the single component models CCF and UCF respectively. (2) Our model with aggregated hashtag topic semantic modeling and user near neighbor relevancy modeling achieves the best performance. Fig. 2 depicts performance of four methods on three position-related evaluation metrics at position from 1 to 10. It obviously shows that our model has more notable advantages at the top of the recommendation list and achieves the highest accuracy at position 1.

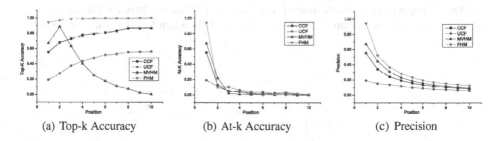

(a) Top-k Accuracy   (b) At-k Accuracy   (c) Precision

Fig. 2. Recommendation Results of Four Methods

(2) Hashtag Recommendation Based on Topic Semantic

In this part, we discuss two weighing ways of describing profiles (TF and TFIDF) and two ways of constructing hashtag profiles (MB and HtPro). Here, MB denotes taking a single microblog as its hashtag profile just like [2] does. While, HtPro denotes using all historical microblogs containing the same hashtag as profiles as Section 3.2 describes. We suggest hashtags by their Cosine relevance scores to get the recommendation list. According to different representation methods (TF, TFIDF) and different similarity metrics (MB, HtPro), we get four content-based recommendation methods. Meanwhile, our method is TFIDF_HtPro, and CCF[2] can be denoted as TFIDF_MB. The results are shown in Table 2.

Table 2. Recommendation Results Using Semantic Topic Modeling

Method	MRR	Top-k Accuracy			
		1	3	5	7
TF_MB	0.343	0.308	0.344	0.372	0.4
TFIDF_MB (CCF)	0.536	0.484	0.556	0.588	0.62
TF_HtPro	0.435	0.368	0.464	0.516	0.564
TFIDF_HtPro (Ours)	**0.658**	**0.552**	**0.728**	**0.792**	**0.832**

From Table 2, we have following observations. (1) TFIDF representation models outperform the TF representation models. (2) HtPro models further improve the performance of MB models. (3) Our TFIDF_HtPro model can successfully boost other semantic analysis methods, with a MRR of 65.77%.

(3) Hashtag Recommendation Based on User Preference

In this part, we evaluate how different user representation matrices fulfil the task of hashtag recommendation. We determine near neighbors by three user information matrices: content representation matrix (CT), hashtag representation matrix (HT) and topic representation matrix (TK). The results are shown in Fig. 3. As Fig. 3 shows, information from the nearest neighbors has contributed to hashtag recommendation. We have got the highest MRR when considering the nearest neighbor. The position of the first accurate recommendation moves backwards as the number of nearest neighbor increases. Especially, content description shows a preference bias for this task. As to topic interest representation, we can get a better MRR when latent number of topics is 50 or 400.

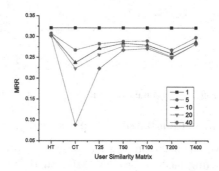

Fig. 3. Results Based on User Preference (different color for different number of neighbors)

5   Conclusions

This paper studies how to recommend appropriate hashtags for a specific microblog written by a specific user. The recommend strategy characterizes topic semantic by global content information and considers usage preference by the local user interest group. Besides, our fusion model (named FHM) can seamlessly associate these two factors for recommending. The results demonstrate that our proposed method outperforms the state-of-the-art approaches with a large margin.

Our work can directly provide at least two benefits. For microbloggers, it helps them to join topic discussion, to promote interaction activities and to make microblogs easier to retrieve. For researchers, credible complementary hashtags for microblogs can promote researches in social media, such as topic detection and tracking, text classification, community detection and etc. Under our framework, we will further introduce explicit social relations for users' interest group modeling and explore generative topic modeling techniques for modeling relevance between a short message and hashtags.

Acknowledgments. This research is supported by the National Natural Science Foundation of China (No. 61105049 and No. 61300166), Open Project Foundation of Information Technology Research Base of Civil Aviation Administration of China (No. CAAC-ITRB-201303 and No. CAAC-ITRB-201204), Science and Technology Planning Project of Tianjin, China (No. 13ZCZDGX01098) and Tianjin Research Program of Application Foundation and Advanced Technology (No. 14JCQNJC00600).

References

1. Huang, J., Thornton, K.M., Efthimiadis, E.N.: Conversational tagging in twitter. In: Proceedings of the 21st ACM Conference on Hypertext and Hypermedia, HT 2010, pp. 173–178. ACM, New York (2010)
2. Zangerle, E., Gassler, W., Specht, G.: Using tag recommendations to homogenize folksonomies in microblogging environments. In: Datta, A., Shulman, S., Zheng, B., Lin, S.-D., Sun, A., Lim, E.-P. (eds.) SocInfo 2011. LNCS, vol. 6984, pp. 113–126. Springer, Heidelberg (2011)
3. Mazzia, A., Juett, J.: Suggesting hashtags on twitter. Technical report (2009)
4. Li, T., Wu, Y., Zhang, Y.: Twitter hash tag prediction algorithm. In: Proceedings of the 2011 International Conference on Internet Computing, ICOMP 2011 (2011)
5. Godin, F., Slavkovikj, V., De Neve, W., Schrauwen, B., Van de Walle, R.: Using topic models for twitter hashtag recommendation. In: Proceedings of the 22nd International Conference on World Wide Web Companion, WWW 2013 Companion, pp. 593–596. International World Wide Web Conferences Steering Committee, Republic and Canton of Geneva (2013)
6. Ding, Z., Zhang, Q., Huang, X.: Automatic hashtag recommendation for microblogs using topic-specific translation model. In: Proceedings of the 24th International Conference on Computational Linguistics, COLING 2012 Poster, pp. 265–274 (2012)
7. Ding, Z., Qiu, X., Zhang, Q., Huang, X.: Learning topical translation model for microblog hashtag suggestion. In: Proceedings of the Twenty-Third International Joint Conference on Artificial Intelligence, IJCAI 2013, pp. 2078–2084. AAAI Press (2013)
8. Kywe, S.M., Hoang, T.-A., Lim, E.-P., Zhu, F.: On recommending hashtags in twitter networks. In: Aberer, K., Flache, A., Jager, W., Liu, L., Tang, J., Guéret, C. (eds.) SocInfo 2012. LNCS, vol. 7710, pp. 337–350. Springer, Heidelberg (2012)
9. Hong, L., Davison, B.D.: Empirical study of topic modeling in twitter. In: Proceedings of the First Workshop on Social Media Analytics, SOMA 2010, pp. 80–88. ACM, New York (2010)
10. Herlocker, J.L., Konstan, J.A., Borchers, A., Riedl, J.: An algorithmic framework for performing collaborative filtering. In: Proceedings of the 22nd Annual International ACM

SIGIR Conference on Research and Development in Information Retrieval, SIGIR 1999, pp. 230–237. ACM, New York (1999)

11. Mehrotra, R., Sanner, S., Buntine, W., Xie, L.: Improving lda topic models for microblogs via tweet pooling and automatic labeling. In: Proceedings of the 36th International ACM SIGIR Conference on Research and Development in Information Retrieval, SIGIR 2013, pp. 889–892. ACM, New York (2013)

12. Blei, D.M., Ng, A.Y., Jordan, M.I.: Latent dirichlet allocation. J. Mach. Learn. Res. 3, 993–1022 (2003)

13. Griffiths, T.: Gibbs sampling in the generative model of Latent Dirichlet Allocation. Technical report, Stanford University (2002)

Trust Discounting and Trust Fusion in Online Social Networks

Yao Ma, Hongwei Lu, Zaobin Gan*, and Xiao Ma

Huazhong University of Science and Technology, Wuhan 430074, China
mayaobox@qq.com, {luhw,zgan,cindyma}@hust.edu.cn

Abstract. Discounting and fusing trust is a fundamental work in trust inference. Existing trust discounting operators are mainly based on the structure balance theory but ignoring the distribution of the balanced triads, and the trust fusion operator for dependent opinions is also not practical. In order to solve these issues, we propose an adaptive trust discounting operator based on the structure balance theory taking into account the distribution regularities of the balanced transitive triads. An partial dependent trust fusion operator is also given to deal with recommenders' conflicting judgements on the same observations. Comparative experiments show that the proposed trust discounting and fusion operators can yield better trust inference accuracy than existing ones.

Keywords: trust discounting operator, trust fusion operator, trust inference, online social network.

1 Introduction

Trust plays a very important role in the Online Social Network (OSN) and E-commerce applications, especially when the user encounters unfamiliar people or products. Epinions.com is a such consumer reviews web site that helps users make informed buying decisions by the *Web of Trust*. Trust inference based on trust transitivity considers that people's trust can be relayed along the trust propagation paths with the consistent trust scope. How to accurately discount and fuse the user's trust along these paths emerges as a question.

Most existing trust discounting operators [1,5,2] actually utilize the structure balance theory principles, under the assumption that the triangle relationships in the social network are all balanced. However, the triads in the real world are not all balanced and it may lead to inaccurate trust discounting. The fusion of independent and dependent trust are discussed in [5]. However, the recommenders' conflicts on observations are not distinguishable during the trust fusion operation for dependent opinions in practice, because the observations are already discounted in the previous trust discounting. In order to solve these issues, we first illustrate the distribution regularities of the balanced triads and propose the adaptive trust discounting operator. Then, the situation that different recommenders have conflicting judgements on the same observations is discussed

---

* Corresponding author.

L. Chen et al. (Eds.): APWeb 2014, LNCS 8709, pp. 619–626, 2014.

and the partial dependent trust fusion operator is proposed to fuse the trust opinions in a practical way.

2   Related Work

The research on trust discounting and trust fusion attracts much attention. Golbeck [1] proposed TidalTrust to personalize applications through integration of inferred trust. The indirect trust is deduced by a weighted sum of the witnesses' trusts about the target, taking the source user's trusts about the witnesses as the weights. Jøsang et al. [5] analyzed different trust discounting operators and fusion operators with the subjective logic. The trust fusion operator for dependent and independent opinions are also proposed to deduce the opinion of a user combination about the target user. But the shared observations can not be distinguishable in the trust fusion, which leads to the trust fusion operator unpractical. Based on the subjective logic, Hang et al. [2] proposed the Concatenation, Aggregation and Selection operators to propagate and fuse trust in social networks. The trust discounting operations mentioned above are mainly consistent with the structure balance theory under the assumption that all triads are balanced, but they ignore that triads are not all balanced in fact.

There are also novel trust operators based on other theories. Victor et al. [10,9] built a trust model based on bilattice theory and proposed different trust score propagation and aggregation operators with t-norms and t-conorms. Zhang et al. [11] considered that the trust evaluation is similar to the physical measurement, which increases the measurement accuracy by combining different measurement methods, or repeating the measurement. They also proposed the trust metrics and trust operators to propagate and aggregate trust based on measurement theory and error propagation theory.

3   Trust Discounting and Fusion Operators

This paper follows Jøsang's work [5] to model trust with the *subjective logic* and discusses the trust discounting operator and the trust fusion operator for the *trust opinions*.

3.1   Structure Balance Based Adaptive Trust Discounting

The structure balance theory [3] considers that balanced triads are more plausible and prevalent than the unbalanced triads in social networks. The transitive triad cases t_1, t_2, t_5 and t_6 (shown in Fig.1) are investigated in [7], because they are consistent with the intuition of recommendation. Based on the structure balance theory, we can derive A's relationship with X by the recommender B and the dashed relation in t_1 can be derived as a positive relation, according to the principle 1) "the friend of my friend is also my friend". The rest cases correspond with the principles 2) "the enemy of my friend is my enemy", 3) "the friend of my enemy is my enemy" and 4) "the enemy of my enemy is my friend" respectively.

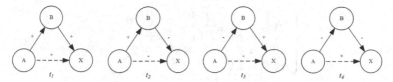

Fig. 1. Edge sign prediction cases in balanced transitive triads

However, the triads are not all balanced in reality and there is a negative correlation between the distribution of the Balanced Transitive Triad Percentage (BTTP) and the edge uncertainties of the triads [7]. According to the statistics, nearly half of the transitive triads for t_2, t_5 and t_6 cases are not balanced, which means that for example the enemy of my friend is probably my friend. Without any priori knowledge of the distribution of the balanced transitive triads, the existing trust discounting operators are risking the misuse of the structure balance theory for t_2, t_5 and t_6 cases at the probability nearly 50%.

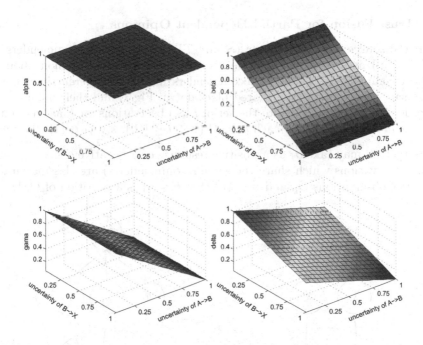

Fig. 2. Distributions of the balance confidence factors

Definition 1. *Adaptive Trust Discounting Operator*
Let A, B and X be three users, the trust opinions of A and B about the competence of B and X be expressed as ω_B^A and ω_X^B. The adaptive trust discounted opinion of A on X can be denoted as $\omega_X^{A:B} = \omega_B^A \otimes \omega_X^B = (b_X^{A:B}, d_X^{A:B}, u_X^{A:B}, a_X^{A:B})$ that

$$\begin{cases} b_X^{A:B} = r_X^{A:B}/(r_X^{A:B} + s_X^{A:B} + 2) \\ d_X^{A:B} = s_X^{A:B}/(r_X^{A:B} + s_X^{A:B} + 2) \\ u_X^{A:B} = 2/(r_X^{A:B} + s_X^{A:B} + 2) \\ a_X^{A:B} = a_X^B \end{cases} \qquad (1)$$

where the number of the deduced A's observations about X can be

$$\begin{cases} r_X^{A:B} = \alpha(b_B^A + a_B^A u_B^A)r_X^B + \beta(d_B^A + (1 - a_B^A)u_B^A)s_X^B \\ s_X^{A:B} = \gamma(b_B^A + a_B^A u_B^A)s_X^B + \delta(d_B^A + (1 - a_B^A)u_B^A)r_X^B \end{cases} \qquad (2)$$

here α, β, γ and δ are the balance confidence factors of the t_1, t_6, t_2 and t_5.

The distributions of the balance confidence factors are obtained by building linear planes ($\alpha = 1$, $\beta = 1 - 0.5u_B^A - 0.5u_X^B$, $\gamma = 1 - u_X^B$ and $\delta = 1 - u_B^A$, shown in Fig.2) to approach the surfaces of BTTP distribution shown in [7]. For the given three users (A, B and X), the balance confidence factors vary according to the edge uncertainties (u_B^A and u_X^B) and the proposed ATD operator adjusts the utilization rate of the mentioned principles for the four cases.

3.2   Trust Fusion for Partial Dependent Opinions

Given the source and target user (S and T) and multiple recommenders R_i ($1 \le i \le m$) as shown in Fig.3, we want to infer S's trust opinion about T by the recommenders. Different recommenders may have different judgements on the same observation (the shared black dot in Fig.3) and their opinions are called dependent opinions. Note the set of R_i's observations on T as $O(R_i)$ and $\bigcup_{1 \le i \le m} O(R_i) = O$. Thus, for each $o_j \in O$ ($1 \le j \le |O|$), $s_i(o_j) \in \{1, -1\}$ which means that R_i may take o_j as a positive response or a negative one.

The observations which share the same recommender(s) are classified into a new set of observations O_k' and $\pi = \{O_k'|1 \le k \le p\}$ is a partition of O, here p

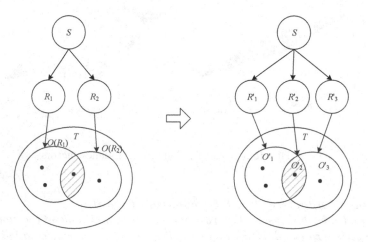

Fig. 3. Trust Fusion for Partial Dependent Opinions

is the number of the observation sets. Then each O'_k is assigned with a *virtual recommender* R'_k. For the set of observations that share only one recommender, there is no conflicting judgements on observations and the source user's opinion about the corresponding virtual recommender is identical to his opinion about the recommender. For the example in Fig.3, $\omega^S_{R'_1} = \omega^S_{R_1}$. While, for the set of observations O'_k that share multiple recommenders $\{R^*_i | 1 \leq i \leq n\}$ here n is the number of the shared recommenders, the source user's opinion about the corresponding virtual recommender R'_k, i.e. $\omega^S_{R'_k}$, can be obtained by

$$
\begin{cases}
b^S_{R'_k} = \sum_{1 \leq i \leq n} (c^S_{R_i} b^S_{R^*_i} / \sum_{1 \leq i \leq n} c^S_{R^*_i}) \\
d^S_{R'_k} = \sum_{1 \leq i \leq n} (c^S_{R_i} d^S_{R^*_i} / \sum_{1 \leq i \leq n} c^S_{R^*_i}) \\
u^S_{R'_k} = 1 - b^S_{R'_k} - d^S_{R'_k} \\
a^S_{R'_k} = \sum_{1 \leq i \leq n} (c^S_{R_i} a^S_{R^*_i} / \sum_{1 \leq i \leq n} c^S_{R^*_i})
\end{cases}
\tag{3}
$$

where $c^S_{R_i}$ is S's confidence about the recommender R^*_i and can be set as: 1) $c^S_{R^*_i} = b^S_{R^*_i}$ or 2) $c^S_{R^*_i} = 1 - u^S_{R^*_i}$. Considering the example in Fig.3, $\omega^S_{R'_2}$ is obtained by the weighted average opinion of $\omega^S_{R_1}$ and $\omega^S_{R_2}$. Furthermore, the number of the virtual recommender's observations about the target can be

$$
\begin{cases}
r^{R'_k}_T = |\{o_j | \sum_{1 \leq i \leq n} c^S_{R_i} s_i(o_j) \geq 0, o_j \in O'_k\}| \\
s^{R'_k}_T = |\{o_j | \sum_{1 \leq i \leq n} c^S_{R_i} s_i(o_j) < 0, o_j \in O'_k\}|
\end{cases}
\tag{4}
$$

and the corresponding opinion $\omega^{R'_k}_T$ can be obtained by Eq.(1).

Definition 2. *Partial Dependent Trust Fusion Operator*
Let S and T be the source and target users, $\{R_i\}(1 \leq i \leq m)$ be the set of recommenders who have direct observations $O(R_i)$ about T with conflicting judgements and the opinion of S about recommender R_i be $\omega^S_{R_i} = (b^S_{R_i}, d^S_{R_i}, u^S_{R_i}, a^S_{R_i})$. The partial dependent trust fused opinion of S about T by recommenders $\{R_i\}$ can be denoted as $\omega^{S:\{R_i\}}_T = \omega^{S:R'_1}_T \oplus \ldots \oplus \omega^{S:R'_k}_T$. Here, $\{R'_k\}(1 \leq k \leq p)$ is the set of virtual recommenders and $\oplus$ is the Consensus Operator for Independent Opinions in [5].

The PDTF operator first regards the recommenders who share the same observation set as a virtual recommender. Then, the source user's trust opinion about the virtual recommenders and the virtual recommenders' trust opinions about the target user are obtained and concatenated by the trust discounting operator. Finally, the virtual recommenders share no observations and the trust opinions of the source user about the target user via multiple virtual recommenders are fused as independent trust opinions.

4   Experiments and Analysis

Comparative experiments are carried on the Epinions data set [8] to demonstrate the superiority of the proposed trust discounting and fusion operators over the representative existing work (Jøsang [4,5], Hang [2], Zhang [11] and Victor [10,9]) on trust inference accuracy. The random walk based sampling method [6] is used to scale down the extended Epinions data set (available at trustlet.org) and there are 33036 users who issued 84141 trust and distrust statements.

4.1   Methodology and Metrics

Given a pair of arbitrary users (A and B), we regard the number of the A's ratings on B's articles as the number of observations (noted as $n_{rating} \geq 0$) and compute the mean rating (noted as $m_{rating} \in [1,5]$). For each article written by B, A can rate at most once. Then, $w_B^A = (b_B^A, d_B^A, u_B^A, a_B^A)$ can be obtained by:

$$\begin{cases} b_B^A = (m_{rating} - 1) \cdot (1 - u_B^A)/4 \\ d_B^A = (5 - m_{rating}) \cdot (1 - u_B^A)/4 \\ u_B^A = 2/(2 + n_{rating}) \\ a_B^A = 0.5 \end{cases} \tag{5}$$

2000 edges are randomly chosen from the data set as samples and each edge is associated with the source and target users. The cross validation technique *Leave-one-out* is utilized. We first remove one sample edge and find multiple paths connecting the user pair (total number of the paths found is 230089). Then, 1) infer the source vertex's opinion about the target w' along the trust inference path with different trust discounting operators $\otimes$ by $w_T^{'S} = w_{R_1}^S \otimes w_{R_2}^{R_1} \otimes \cdots \otimes w_S^{R_m}$; 2) given the multiple trust inference paths, the same trust discounting operation but different trust fusion operations $\oplus$ are applied to deduce w' by $w_T^{'S} = w_T^{S:\{path_1\}} \oplus w_T^{S:\{path_2\}} \oplus \cdots \oplus w_T^{S:\{path_n\}}$. Here, each witness is associated with one trust inference path to avoid the mass hysteria [5]. For the both parts, w' is compared with the opinion w mapped by the ground truth (Eq.(5)) in terms of E-error ($E - error(w, w') = |(b + u \cdot a) - (b' + u' \cdot a')|$) and B-error ($B - error(w, w') = |b - b'|$) [2] for trust inference accuracy evaluation.

4.2   Results and Analysis

The overall MAEs (Mean Absolute Errors) of E-error and B-error for the trust inference with different trust operators are given in the Table 1. While, the partial MAEs are plotted from different perspectives for further analysis.

(1) Trust Discounting Operation. Jøsang(o1) (Uncertainty Favouring Discounting operator in [5]), Jøsang(o2) (Opposite Belief Favouring Discounting operator in [5]), Hang (Concatenation operator in [2]), Zhang (Transitive operator

Table 1. Overall MAEs of E-error and B-error for trust discounting and trust fusion

MAE	Jøsang(o1)	Jøsang(o2)	Hang	Zhang	Victor	ATD	
E-error	0.2957	0.3015	0.1902	0.2897	0.2375	**0.1048**	
B-error	0.5833	0.5818	0.3637	0.4574	0.4226	**0.1943**	

MAE	Jøsang& Hang		Zhang	Victor	PDTF(belief)	PDTF(cert.)
E-error	0.1203		0.1375	0.1553	**0.1143**	0.1145
B-error	0.2205		0.2342	0.2738	0.2046	**0.2041**

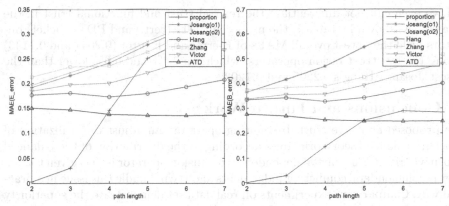

Fig. 4. Partial MAEs of trust discounting versus the trust inference path length

in [11]), Victor (Propagation operator in [9] which shows the best performance) and the proposed ATD operator are compared in terms of MAEs of B-error and E-error. Fig.4 shows that the trust inference with most trust discounting operators becomes inaccurate as the path length increases. However, the B-error and E-error of the proposed ATD are insensitive to the path length and they are the lowest among the six operators. The overall MAEs of B-error and E-error of ATD (0.1943 and 0.1048 shown in Table 1 are also the lowest, which are 46.6% and 44.9% lower than Hang's 0.3637 and 0.1902.

(2) Trust Fusion Operation. Jøsang&Hang (Consensus operator for independent opinions in [5] or Aggregation operator in [2], which are the same), Zhang (Aggregation operator in [11]), Victor ($KAAV_2$ in [9]), PDTF(belief)(taking belief as confidence) and PDTF(cert.)(taking certainty as confidence) are compared in terms of MAEs of B-error and E-error. Fig.5 shows that the deviations of the trust inference float as the number of witness increases. It means that more witnesses do not lead to more accurate trust inference, which is consistent with the phenomenon in [10]. The main reason is that the trust scopes are coarse grained

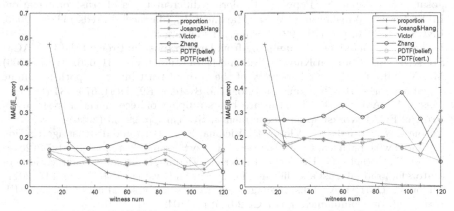

Fig. 5. Partial MAEs of trust fusion versus the number of witnesses

and we even can not differentiate the referral trust and functional trust in the data set. As shown in Table 1, the proposed PDTF(cert.) and PDTF(belief) operators yield the lowest overall MAEs of B-error and E-error (0.2041 and 0.1143) among the five trust fusion operators, which are 7.4% and 5.0% lower than the closest Jøsang&Hang's 0.2205 and 0.1203.

5 Conclusions and Future Work

The proposed adaptive trust discounting operator can adjust the utilization of structure balance theory principles according to the distribution of the balanced transitive triads. The partial dependent trust fusion operator is also given to consider recommenders' conflicting judgements and it can handle this issue in a practical way. Comparative experiments on real data set demonstrate the superiority of the proposed trust operators on trust inference accuracy. For future work, we will discuss how to efficiently apply the trust operators to multiple trust inference path with shared edges and avoid the mass hysteria in the trust aggregation.

Acknowledgment. This research is funded by the National Natural Science Foundation of China under grant No. 61272406 and the Fundamental Research Funds for the Central Universities, HUST: 2013TS101.

References

1. Golbeck, J.: Personalizing applications through integration of inferred trust values in semantic web-based social networks. In: Proc. of the 4th Intl. Semantic Web Conf. (ISWC 2005). pp. 15–28 (2005)
2. Hang, C.W., Wang, Y., Singh, M.P.: Operators for propagating trust and their evaluation in social networks. In: Proc. of the 8th Intl. Conf. on Autonomous Agents and Multiagent System, pp. 1025–1032 (2009)
3. Heider, F.: Attitudes and cognitive organization. The Journal of Psychology 21(1), 107–112 (1946)
4. Jøsang, A., Hayward, R., Pope, S.: Trust network analysis with subjective logic. In: Proc. of the 29th Australasian Computer Science Conf., vol. 48, pp. 85–94. Australian Computer Society (2006)
5. Jøsang, A., Marsh, S., Pope, S.: Exploring different types of trust propagation. In: Stølen, K., Winsborough, W.H., Martinelli, F., Massacci, F. (eds.) iTrust 2006. LNCS, vol. 3986, pp. 179–192. Springer, Heidelberg (2006)
6. Leskovec, J., Faloutsos, C.: Sampling from large graphs. In: Proc. of the 12th ACM SIGKDD Intl. Conf. on Knowl. Disc. and Data Mining, pp. 631–636. ACM (2006)
7. Ma, Y., Lu, H., Gan, Z.: Discovery of the optimal trust inference path for online social networks. IEICE Trans. on Infor. and Systems E97-D(4), 673–684 (2014)
8. Massa, P., Avesani, P.: Trust-aware bootstrapping of recommender system. In: Proc. of ECAI Workshop on Recommender System, pp. 29–33 (2006)
9. Verbiest, N., Cornelis, C., Victor, P., Viedma, E.H.: Trust and distrust aggregation enhanced with path length incorporation. Fuzzy Sets and Systems 202, 61–74 (2012)
10. Victor, P., Cornelis, C., De Cock, M., Herrera Viedma, E.: Practical aggregation operators for gradual trust and distrust. Fuzzy Sets and Systems 184(1), 126–147 (2011)
11. Zhang, P., Durresi, A.: Trust management framework for social networks. In: IEEE Intl. Conf. on Communications (ICC2012), pp. 1042–1047 (2012)

Topic-Based Sentiment Analysis Incorporating User Interactions

Jiayi Wu[1,2], Wei Chen[1,2], Gaoyan Ou[1,2], Tengjiao Wang[1,2], Dongqing Yang[1,2], and Kai Lei[3]

[1] Key Laboratory of High Confidence Software Technologies,
Ministry of Education, Beijing 100871, China
[2] School of Electronics Engineering and Computer Science,
Peking University, Beijing 100871, China
[3] The Shenzhen Key Lab for Cloud Computing Technology and Applications
(SPCCTA), Peking University Shenzhen Graduate School, Shenzhen 518055, China
dotabomber@163.com, {pekingchenwei,tjwang}@pku.edu.cn, ougaoyan@126.com

Abstract. With the popularity of various social media platforms, the number of people who tend to publish their opinions on the internet grows dramatically. Discovering the public sentiment towards new topics and events becomes an important and challenging task in sentiment analysis. Current methods have not considered the effects caused by user interactions, leading to inaccurate topic and sentiment extractions. In this paper, we propose a novel probabilistic generative model (TSIUM) to extract topics and topic-specific sentiments from online comments. We model the effects between online comments to avoid the error caused by user interactions. Experimental results show that the proposed model is able to accurately identify topics and filter spam and outperform other methods in the sentiment classification task, making a great improvement on both topic and sentiment extraction.

Keywords: topic modeling, topic extraction, sentiment analysis, user interaction.

1 Introduction

With the development of web2.0, people are more inclined to publish their comments on social media, such as forums, blogs and microblogs. Users have contributed a plenty of online comments, containing user sentiments towards different topics and events. It is significant and valuable to extract topic and sentiment information from these online comments. The governments can detect the public sentiment toward policies and emergencies, give feedback in time. However, it is also a job with challenges. The huge amount of data makes it impossible to complete this job through manual analysis, and the unstructured data increases the difficulty of the machine analysis.

So far, there are lots of researches on how to extract topic-based sentiment. However, these algorithms regard comments as independent individuals, ignoring the connections among them. In fact, the socialized characteristic of media

L. Chen et al. (Eds.): APWeb 2014, LNCS 8709, pp. 627–635, 2014.

platform makes it easier for users to interact with each other, which will result in more connections.

We list some real comments and the interactions between them in Fig. 1. Red comments represent positive comment, support the policy, while green comments represent negative. Red arrows represent agree with previous comment, while green arrows represent disagree. In such a situation, we find there are some drawbacks in existing methods. First, for example, in comment "Too stupid, this is pure discrimination", the existing methods can not extract the corresponding topics unless considering the interaction to the original news. Second, the normal sentiment polarities positive and negative can not describe the sentiment polarities of comments precisely. This makes the sentiment classification results very inaccurate using existing methods. Therefore, user interaction affects both topics and sentiments extraction, which makes the existing methods no longer applicable.

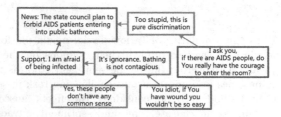

Fig. 1. News comments and the interactions between them

In this paper, we propose a novel probabilistic generative model, called Topic Sentiment Interaction Union Model(TSIUM), to address this problem. There are three key advantages in our models.

- We extract the topic information of comments using the topic information of interactive comments.
- We introduce two special sentiment, AGREEMENT and DISAGREEMENT, to represent the transformation of user sentiment. Agreement and disagreement enrich the sentiment expression, make the model could adapt to complex relations between comments.
- Third, we analyze topic-based sentiments in comments with considering the effects caused by interactions, combine the sentiment polarities in interactive comments and the relations between them. This characteristic makes the proposed model more accurately in topic-based sentiment classification.

The rest of the paper is organized as follows. Section 2 introduces the related work. In section 3, we present our new model. We describes the data sets, experiment settings and the prior information we use in section 4. Section 5 shows our experiment results. Finally, we present the conclusions in Section 6.

2   Related Work

In topic extraction area, the authors in [1,2,3] use frequent-based methods to extract nouns and noun phrases as topic candidates. However, it is difficult for these methods to group related topics together, or extract implicit topics from the unstructured text. Latent topic modeling in [4] has become very popular as a completely unsupervised technique for topic extraction in large document collections. This method can not extract the corresponding topics if the reply comments only contain sentiment words, makes it hard to extract topic information accurately.

In topic-special sentiment extraction area, [5,6,7] applied sequential labeling techniques to extract topics and sentiments from comments. The massive manual work for obtaining labeled training data make these supervised methods unsuitable for the huge number of online comments. [8] introduced sentiment polarities into topic modeling, presented a model called JST which can extract mixture of aspects and different sentiment polarities for products and services. However, this method are unsuitable for news and events because of the sentiment polarity transformation caused by user interactions.

Our proposed model TSIUM modifies the generation process of online comments, considering the effects caused by user interactions, makes a great improvement on both topics and topic-special sentiment extraction.

3   The TSIUM Model

In this section, we will present our proposed model TSIUM. According to our observation, there are two points worthy of our attention in user comments. First, the sentiment of comment do not exist independently, it depends on the comment it reply to and their relationship. However, the existing models only analyze the comments independently, leading to wrong outcome. Second, according to our observation, the reply tweet often omit the topic information, because it has the same topic with the original tweet. We call this characteristic of user interaction as "Topic Consistency". However, the existing models all assume that the comment itself contains the topic information, which is not correct in fact. Therefore, the proposed model should be able to correct the mistakes caused by these two characteristics.

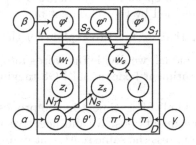

Fig. 2. TSIUM model

The graphical representation of TSIUM is shown in Fig.3. Let D be the number of comments, K be the number of topics, S_1 be the number of normal sentiments (positive, negative) S_2 be the number of special sentiments (agreement and disagreement), and $M = S_1 + S_2$ be the total number of sentiments. Let n_d^t be the number of sentiment words in comment d, n_d^s be the number of topic words in comment d. There are K topic models $\varphi_{k=1\cdots K}^t$. For each topic k, there are S_1 topic-specific normal sentiment models $\varphi_{k,m=1\cdots S_1}^n$. There are S_2 special sentiment models $\varphi_{m=1\cdots S_2}^s$. The variable θ denotes the distribution of topics in comment d, the variable π denotes the distribution of sentiments in comment d. Let d' be the comment that d interacts with, then the variable θ' and π' denotes the distribution of topics and sentiments in comment d'.

The generative process of TSIUM is as follows:

- For each topic $k \in \{1, \ldots, K\}$:
  1. Choose a distribution $\varphi_k^t \sim Dir(\beta_k^t)$
  2. For each normal sentiment $m \in \{1, \ldots, S_2\}$:
     Choose a distribution $\varphi_{k,m}^n \sim Dir(\beta_{k,m}^n)$
- For each special sentiment $m \in \{1, \ldots, S_1\}$:
  Choose a distribution $\varphi_m^s \sim Dir(\beta_m^s)$
- For each comment $d \in \{1, \ldots, D\}$:
  1. Choose a distribution $\theta_{temp} \sim Dir(\alpha)$:
     Create a new distribution θ_d by combining θ_{temp} and $\theta_{d'}'$
  2. Choose a distribution $\pi_{temp} \sim Dir(\gamma)$:
     Create a new distribution π_d by combining π_{temp} and $\pi_{d'}'$
  3. For each topic word $w_{d,i}^t$ where $i \in \{1, \ldots, n_d^t\}$:
     (a) Choose a topic $z_i^t \sim Mult(\theta_d)$
     (b) Choose a word $w_{d,i}^t$ from the distribution φ^t over words defined by the topic z_i^t.
  4. For each sentiment word $w_{d,j}^s$ where $j \in \{1, \ldots, n_d^s\}$:
     (a) Choose a topic $z_j^s \sim Mult(\theta_d)$
     (b) Choose a sentiment label $l_j \sim Mult(\pi_d)$
     (c) If l_i is a normal sentiment, choose a sentiment word $w_{d,j}^s$ from the distribution φ^n over words defined by the topic z_j^s and sentiment l_j. Otherwise, choose a special sentiment word $w_{d,j}^s$ from the distribution φ^s over words defined by the sentiment m_j.

There are some points that we need to explain for this generative process.

- First, in the proposed model, we divide the words into topic words and sentiment words. We use sentiment lexicon and POS tagging to identify the sentiment words.
- Second, we define two kinds of sentiment in the proposed model, normal and special. The normal sentiments positive and negative are topic-sensitive, user use different words to express the same sentiment in different topics. However, the special sentiments agreement and disagreement are not topic-sensitive, according to [9], there are some patterns in agreement and disagreement. Therefore, we choose distributions of all k topics for each normal sentiment s^n, but only choose one distribution for each special sentiment s^s.

- Third, as we considered, the topics and sentiments of the comment are effected by the comment user interacted with. To the best of our knowledge, no existing work deals with this problem in topic modeling. In the proposed model, we introduce the topics distribution θ' and sentiments distribution π' of the interacted comment to reflect this effect. Intuitively, we expect the two distributions θ and θ' are linear correlation, $\theta = p\theta' + (1-p)\theta_{temp}$. The greater p value means better topic consistency, depends on the data set. We also expect $\pi = q\pi' + (1-q)\pi_{temp}$. Approximatively, larger q represents more weight on user interactions, The setting for p and q was determined empirically. We leave the estimation of p and q in a more principled way as future work.

We use collapsed Gibbs Sampling [10] to inference the model. We only show the sampling formulas without detailed derivations because of the space limit. We can estimate the model parameters θ, π, φ^t, φ^n and φ^s as:

$$\theta_{d,k} = \frac{n_{d,k}^t + n_{d,k}^s + \alpha_k}{\sum_{k=1}^{K}(n_{d,k}^t + n_{d,k}^s + \alpha_k)} \tag{1}$$

$$\pi_{d,m} = \frac{n_{d,m}^s + \gamma_m}{\sum_{m=1}^{M}(n_{d,m}^s + \gamma_m)} \tag{2}$$

$$\varphi_{k,v}^t = \frac{n_{k,v}^t + \beta_{k,v}^t}{\sum_{v=1}^{V}(n_{k,v}^t + \beta_{k,v}^t)} \tag{3}$$

$$\varphi_{k,m,v}^n = \frac{n_{k,m,v}^n + \beta_{k,m,v}^n}{\sum_{v=1}^{V}(n_{k,m,v}^n + \beta_{k,m,v}^n)} \tag{4}$$

$$\varphi_{m,v}^s = \frac{n_{m,v}^s + \beta_{m,v}^s}{\sum_{v=1}^{V}(n_{m,v}^s + \beta_{m,v}^s)} \tag{5}$$

$n_{d,k}^t$ is the number of topic words assigned to topic k in review d. $n_{d,k}^s$ is the number of sentiment words assigned to topic k in review d. $n_{d,m}^s$ is the number of sentiment words assigned to sentiment m in review d. Other variables containing n are defined similarly.

4   Experimental Setup

4.1   Data Sets

We evaluate our proposed approach on the two data sets. The news comment data consist of 2000 news comments extracted from Netease News[1] including current affairs, politics, sports and technology. There are about 1400 comments have interactions with other comments by reply. The microblog data extracted from Sina Weibo[2] contains about 4000 microblogs, including the original microblogs, forward microblogs and comments. We labeled 1000 items with topics

---

[1] http://www.163.com/
[2] http://www.weibo.com/

and sentiment polarities for both data sets. We use ICTCLAS[3] for word segmentation and POS tagging.

4.2 Prior Information

We did not introduce any prior knowledge for topic detection. For normal sentiment positive and negative, we use the sentiment lexicon NTUSD[4] to incorporate prior information into TSIUM. The sentiment lexicon is also used to distinguish between topic words and sentiment words. For special sentiment agreement and disagreement, we use some seed words as prior information for agreement, such as "praise", "agree", "support", and we use the question mark and swear words as prior information for disagreement.

4.3 Experiment Settings

In our experiments, the number of topics K is set to be 20, the number of special sentiments $S1$ is set to be 2, the number of normal sentiments $S2$ is set to be 2. We set the Gibbs sampling iterations to be 5000. We fix $\alpha = 50/K$, $\beta = 0.01$, $\gamma = 50/(S1 + S2)$.

5 Experiments

In this section, we evaluate the performances of our proposed models with three experiments. In the first experiment, we show the topics and topic-based sentiments extracted by TSIUM with some qualitative analysis. In the second experiment, we apply a comment-level topic classification task to analyze the topic sensitivity of our models. In the third experiment, we apply a comment-level sentiment classification task to compare our models with several baselines.

5.1 Qualitative Results

In the first experiment, we show some sample topics and topic-specific sentiments extracted by TSIUM by using the Netease News data set. Table 1 lists the top 5 topic words of five topics discovered by TSIUM. For each topic, top 5 positive and top 5 negative sentiment words are also listed.

We can see from Table 1 that TSIUM can extract topics and topic-based sentiments well. The biggest improvement is that the proposed model could automatically adjust the polarity of sentiment words. For example, in topic 1, the word "fear" become positive while it is negative in lexicon. In the comment "Why don't you understand? We just fear to be infected!", "fear" should have labeled this comment negative, but the prior information question mark "?" makes this comment labeled as disagreement. And because this comment is

---

[3] http://www.ictclas.org/
[4] http://nlg.csie.ntu.edu.tw/

a reply to a comment which is disagree with the new policy, we change the sentiment distribution of this comments to very tend to support the policy, makes "fear" become positive words. This characteristic makes the prior information used flexibly based on topic, avoid the error in sentiment classification caused by prior information.

Table 1. Example Topics and Sentiments Extracted by TSIUM

News	TSIUM		
	Topic	Senti(p)	Senti(n)
1. The state council plan to forbid AIDS patients entering into public bathroom (Policy News)	AIDS	infect	discriminate
	patient	fear	infect
	blood	extreme	dangerous
	society	sick	ignorant
	bathroom	dangerous	sick
2. Tsinghua professor: Examination is needed to get Beijing hukou (Policy News)	hukou	low	stupid
	Beijing	rogue	discriminate
	examination	jealous	low
	quality	expel	parochialism
	Shanghai	high	pig
3. Bell join Real Madrid with one hundred million transfer fee (Sports News)	Bale	strong	worthless
	Real	worth	expensive
	Madrid	handsome	weak
	million	reliable	ridiculous
	Ronaldo	powerful	sick
4. 100000 Xiaomi phone 3 all sold out in 86 seconds (Technology News)	phone	cheap	unbelievable
	Xiaomi	domestic	dupe
	marketing	worth	bad
	snag	good	low
	Lei	high	domestic

Table 2. Example Topic Classification Results

Topic	Precision	Recall
Bale	78.0%	86.5%
AIDS Patient	89.5%	97.5%
ALL News	85.7%	95.5%
All News (LDA)	74.2%	77.5%

5.2   Topic Sensitivity

In this section, we present some experiment results to discuss the topic sensitivity of TSIUM. We merged the topic labels based on the similarity between topics. The table 2 shows some example topic classification results using merged topics. The example topics are chosen from table 1, the news names are in short.

The existing LDA model only extract topic information from comment itself, making the result very incomplete. As we can see, compare to LDA, which did not consider the "Topic Consistency" in user interactions, the proposed model greatly improved the precision and recall. That is because the proposed model could distinguish the similar comments of different topics using the "Topic Consistency" in user interactions. The TSIUM adjusts the topic distribution of these comments to their interactive comments, makes the similar comments have different topic distribution. However, LDA could only extract topic information form the words in comments, leading to aggregating these similar comments as a new topic.

5.3 Sentiment Classification

In this section, we present the results of sentiment classification. We compare the performance of our models with lexicon-based method, JST [11] and supervised method [12]. We introduce the two special sentiments to JST, making the new model called JST+ could identify agreement and disagreement. The experimental results for all these methods are shown in Table 3.

As we can see, the Supervised Classification method works not well on both data sets, because it is impossible to obtain a training set containing all of the situations. Compare to JST, JST+ introduce agreement and disagreement, significantly improved the accuracy of sentiment classification on both data sets. This suggests that the agreement and disagreement have a significant impact to the sentiment classification result. The TSIUM consistently outperforms JST+ on both data sets. JST+ could detect the user interactions, but dose not use the user interactions to modify the topic and sentiment distribution of comments, makes them can not avoid the error caused by user interaction on both topic and sentiment. This suggests that we need to not only detect the user interactions, but also use them wisely.

These results show that the TSIUM outperforms other methods very significantly. It can not only detect the user interactions, but also use the information already analyzed to adjust the results, and make a great improvement on both topic and sentiment extractions.

Table 3. Sentiment Classification Results

Method	News Data	Microblog Data
Supervised Classification	55.1%	70.2%
Lexicon-based Method	50.3%	69.5%
JST	55.6%	71.1%
JST+	74.7%	75.4%
TSIUM	80.1%	79.2%

6 Conclusion

In this paper, we proposed a generative model TSIUM to solve the topic-based sentiment analysis problem of online comments. Our model introduced the effects between online comments to avoid the error caused by user interactions. We compared our model against existing approaches using three different experiments. The experiments show that the proposed model greatly improved the accuracy in both topic and sentiment extractions.

Acknowledgments. This research is supported by the National High Technology Research and Development Program of China (Grant No. 2012AA011002), Natural Science Foundation of China (Grant No. 61300003), Research Foundation of China Information Technology Security Evaluation Center (No. CNITSECKY- 2013-018) and Specialized Research Fund for the Doctoral Program of Higher Education (Grant No. 20130001120001).

References

1. Hu, M., Liu, B.: Mining and summarizing customer reviews. In: KDD, pp. 168–177 (2004)
2. Popescu, A.M., Nguyen, B., Etzioni, O.: Opine: Extracting product features and opinions from reviews. In: HLT/EMNLP (2005)
3. Moghaddam, S., Ester, M.: Opinion digger: an unsupervised opinion miner from unstructured product reviews. In: CIKM, pp. 1825–1828 (2010)
4. Blei, D.M., Ng, A.Y., Jordan, M.I.: Latent dirichlet allocation. The Journal of Machine Learning Research 3, 993–1022 (2003)
5. Jin, W., Ho, H.H.: A novel lexicalized hmm-based learning framework for web opinion mining. In: Proceedings of the 26th Annual International Conference on Machine Learning, ICML 2009, pp. 465–472. ACM, New York (2009)
6. Jakob, N., Gurevych, I.: Extracting opinion targets in a single and cross-domain setting with conditional random fields. In: EMNLP, pp. 1035–1045 (2010)
7. Choi, Y., Cardie, C.: Hierarchical sequential learning for extracting opinions and their attributes. In: ACL (Short Papers), pp. 269–274 (2010)
8. Lin, C., He, Y.: Joint sentiment/topic model for sentiment analysis. In: CIKM, pp. 375–384 (2009)
9. Agresti, A.: Modelling patterns of agreement and disagreement. Statistical Methods in Medical Research 1(2), 201–218 (1992)
10. Griffiths, T.L., Steyvers, M.: Finding scientific topics. Proceedings of the National Academy of Sciences of the United States of America 101(suppl.1), 5228–5235 (2004)
11. Jo, Y., Oh, A.H.: Aspect and sentiment unification model for online review analysis. In: WSDM, pp. 815–824 (2011)
12. Denecke, K.: Are sentiwordnet scores suited for multi-domain sentiment classification? In: ICDIM, pp. 33–38 (2009)

Relevance Measure
in Large-Scale Heterogeneous Networks

Xiaofeng Meng, Chuan Shi, Yitong Li, Lei Zhang, and Bin Wu

Beijing University of Posts and Telecommunications, Beijing, China 100876

Abstract. Recently, there is a surge of heterogeneous information network analysis, where network includes multiple types of objects or links. Many data mining tasks have been studied on it, among which similarity measure is a basic and important function. Several similarity measures have been proposed in heterogeneous information network. However, they suffer from high computation and memory demand. In this paper, we propose a novel measure, called AvgSim, which can measure similarity of same or different-typed object pairs in a uniform framework and has some good properties. **AvgSim** value of two objects is evaluated through two random walk processes along the given meta-path and the reverse meta-path, respectively. In addition, we implement AvgSim using MapReduce parallel model in order to enable the application in large-scale networks. Experiments on real data sets verify the effectiveness and efficiency of AvgSim.

Keywords: Heterogeneous information network, Similarity search, Random walk, MapReduce.

1 Introduction

In recent years, heterogeneous information network analysis has become a hot research topic in data mining field. Different from widely used homogeneous networks which include only same-typed objects or links, Heterogeneous Information Network (HIN) organizes the networked data as a network including different-typed objects and links. For example, in the case of bibliographic network, the object types include authors, papers, venues and links between objects correspond to different relations, such as write relation between authors and papers, and citation relation between papers. Fig.1(a) and Fig.1(b) shows two bibliographic information network schemas which are ACM dataset and DBLP dataset. Combination of different-typed objects and links results in more comprehensive structure information and rich semantics information. Thus, heterogeneous information network analysis will mine more interesting patterns.

Many data mining tasks have been exploited in heterogeneous information network, such as clustering [1], classification [2]. Among these data mining tasks, similarity measure is a basic and important function, which evaluate the similarity of object pairs on networks. Although similarity measure on homogeneous

L. Chen et al. (Eds.): APWeb 2014, LNCS 8709, pp. 636–643, 2014.
© Springer International Publishing Switzerland 2014

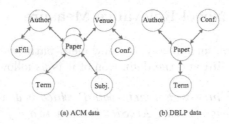

(a) ACM data (b) DBLP data

Fig. 1. Bibliographic network schema

networks have been extensively studied in the past decades, such as PageRank [3] and SimRank [4], the similarity measure in heterogeneous network is just beginning now and several measures have been proposed including PathSim [5], PCRW [6] and HeteSim [7]. All the three methods are based on **Meta-Path** whose definition can be found in the related work [7]. Specially, HeteSim, proposed by Shi et al., has the ability to measure relatedness of objects with the same or different types in a uniform framework. HeteSim has some good properties (e.g., self-maximum and symmetric), and has shown its potential in several data mining tasks. However, we can also find that it has several disadvantages. (1) HeteSim has relatively high computational complexity, in particular, the adoption of path decomposition approach while measuring the relevance on odd-length path further increases complexity of calculation. (2) Besides, HeteSim cannot be extended to large-scale network with massive data, since its calculation process is based on memory computing. Therefore, it is desired to design a new similarity measure, which not only contains some good properties of HeteSim but also overcomes the disadvantages on computation.

In this paper, we propose a new relevance measure method - **AvgSim**, which is a symmetric and uniform measure to evaluate the relevance of same or different-typed objects. Since AvgSim can also measure the relevance of different-typed objects, we use the relevance measure instead of similarity measure in the following section. AvgSim value of two objects is the average of reachable probability under the given path and the reverse path. It guarantees that AvgSim can measure relevance of same or different-typed objects and it has symmetric property. In addition, we take parallelization of this new algorithm on MapReduce in order to eliminate restriction of memory size and deal with massive data more efficiently in practical applications. Experiments on real dataset show that AvgSim can achieve comparative performances with high efficiency and effectiveness, compared with other methods including HeteSim, PathSim and PCRW. Moreover, experiments on large-scale dataset also validate the effectiveness of parallelized AvgSim.

The rest of this paper is organized as follows: Section 2 describes AvgSim in detail. And the method of parallelization of AvgSim is explained in Section 3. Section 4 analyzes performance experiment results of AvgSim to validate its effectiveness and efficiency. And some matrix parallelization experiments are also in this section. Finally we conclude this paper in Section 5.

2 AvgSim: A Novel Relevance Measure

In this section, we will introduce you a new meta-path based relevance measure which is called **AvgSim** and the definition of it is as follows.

Definition 1 *AvgSim: Given a meta-path P which is defined on the composite relation $R = R_1 \circ R_2 \circ \ldots \circ R_l$, AvgSim between two objects s and t (s is the source object and t is the target object) is:*

$$AvgSim(s,t|P) = \frac{1}{2}[RW(s,t|P) + RW(t,s|P^{-1})] \qquad (1)$$

$$RW(s,t|R_1 \circ R_2 \circ \ldots \circ R_l) = \frac{1}{|O(s|R_1)|} \sum_{i=1}^{|O(s|R_1)|} RW(O_i(s|R_1),t|R_2 \circ \ldots \circ R_l) \qquad (2)$$

Equation (1) shows the relevance of source object and target object based on meta-path P is the arithmetic mean value of random walk result from s to t along P and reversed random walk result from t to s along P^{-1}. Equation (2) shows the decomposed step of AvgSim, namely the measure of random walk. The measure takes a random walk step by step from starting point s to end point t along path P using iterative method, where $|O(s|R_1)|$ is the out-neighbors of s based on relation R_1. If there is no out-neighbors of s on R_1, then the relevance value of s and t is 0 because s cannot reach t. We need to calculate random walk probabilities for each out-neighbor of s to t iteratively, and then sum them up. Finally the summation should be normalized by the number of out-neighbors to get average relatedness. The stop sign of iteration is that s meets t at t node along P. In contrast to simple random work method, AvgSim shows its comprehensiveness and the effectiveness reflected in later experiments verifies its advantages.

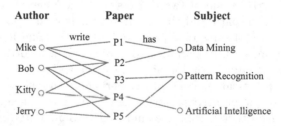

Fig. 2. Heterogeneous relation network example

We take the simple network showed in Fig.2 as an example to calculate the relevance between $Mike$ and the subject $DataMining$ (DM for short) based on path APS ("Author-Paper-Subject").

$$AvgSim(Mike, DM|APS) = \frac{1}{2}[RW(Mike, DM|APS) + RW(DM, Mike|SPA)] \qquad (3)$$

$$RW(Mike, DM|APS) = \frac{1}{|O(Mike|AP)|} \sum_{i=1}^{|O(Mike|AP)|} RW(O_i(Mike|AP), DM|PS) \tag{4}$$

We notice from Fig.2 that $O(Mike|AP) = \{P_1, P_2, P_3\}$, thus we need to calculate relatedness between each out-neighbor of $Mike$ and DM, like $RW(P_1, DM|PS)$.

$$RW(P_1, DM|PS) = \frac{1}{|O(P_1|PS)|} \sum_{i=1}^{|O(P_1|PS)|} RW(O_i(P_1|PS), DM) \tag{5}$$

Since that $O(P_1|PS) = \{DM\}$, out-neighbors of P_1 based on relation PS will meet with DM, thus $RW(P_1, DM|PS) = 1$. Finally, we can easily calculate the relatedness value of random walk from $Mike$ to DM along path APS is $2/3$. Likewise, relatedness value of reverse random walk along path SPA is $2/3$. Thus the relevance value (i.e. AvgSim) between author $Mike$ and subject $DataMining$ is 0.67 ($2/3$).

The example above shows the operation process of AvgSim measuring relevance of two arbitrary objects along a meta-path. Next we will study on how to calculate AvgSim generally **using matrices**.

Given a simple directed meta-path $A \xrightarrow{R} B$, where object A and B are linked though relation R. The relationship between A and B can be expressed by adjacent matrix, denoted as M_{AB}. Two normalized matrix R_{AB} and C_{AB} are generated by normalizing M_{AB} according to row vector and column vector respectively. R_{AB} and C_{AB} are **transition probability matrix** which represent $A \xrightarrow{R} B$ and $B \xrightarrow{R^{-1}} A$ respectively. According to properties of matrix, we can derive relations $R_{AB} = C'_{BA}$ and $C_{AB} = R'_{BA}$, where R'_{AB} is the transpose of R_{AB}.

If we extend the simple meta-path to $P = A_1 \xrightarrow{R_1} A_2 \xrightarrow{R_2} \ldots \xrightarrow{R_l} A_{l+1}$ where R is a composite relation $R = R_1 \circ R_2 \circ \ldots \circ R_l$, then the relationship between A_1 and A_{l+1} is expressed as **reachable probability matrix** which is obtained by computation on the basis of transition probability matrix. The reachable probability matrix of P is defined as $RW_P = R_{A_1 A_2} R_{A_2 A_3} \cdots R_{A_l A_{l+1}}$, where RW suggests RW_P is the random walk relatedness matrix from object A_1 to A_{l+1} along path P.

Then we can rewrite AvgSim using reachable probability matrix according to equation (1) and (2) as follows.

$$AvgSim(A_1, A_{l+1}|P)$$
$$= \frac{1}{2}[RW(A_1, A_{l+1}|P) + RW(A_{l+1}, A_1|P^{-1})] = \frac{1}{2}[RW_P + RW'_{P^{-1}}] \tag{6}$$

Applied relation $C_{AB} = R'_{BA}$, equation (8) is derived below. We notice that the calculation of AvgSim is unified as two chain matrix multiplication of transition probability matrices. The only difference between two chains is the normalization form of original adjacent matrix.

$$AvgSim(A_1, A_{l+1}|P) = \frac{1}{2}[R_{A_1 A_2} R_{A_2 A_3} \cdots R_{A_l A_{l+1}} + (R_{A_{l+1} A_l} R_{A_l A_{l-1}} \cdots R_{A_2 A_1})']$$

$$= \frac{1}{2}[R_{A_1 A_2} R_{A_2 A_3} \cdots R_{A_l A_{l+1}} + C_{A_1 A_2} C_{A_2 A_3} \cdots C_{A_l A_{l+1}}]$$

$$(7)$$

AvgSim can measure relevance of any heterogeneous or homogeneous objects based on symmetrical path (*e.g.APCPA*) or asymmetrical path (*e.g.APS*). Besides, the method has symmetric property, which can be verified easily from the definition equation of AvgSim and the symmetric property has a positive effect on clustering. However, the calculation of AvgSim mainly the chain matrix multiplication is time-consuming and restricted of memory size. In order to apply our algorithm in real large-scale heterogeneous information network, we have to consider how to improve the efficiency of AvgSim.

3   Parallelization of AvgSim

Parallelism is an effective method for processing of massive data and improving algorithm's efficiency. According to the features and application scenarios of AvgSim, we will realize it using parallelization method and the specific steps are as follows.

1. Since the core calculation of AvgSim is the chain matrix multiplication, we firstly change the order of matrix multiplication operations applying Dynamic Programming strategy.

2. After step 1, we turn to focus on single large-scale matrix multiplication and it can be parallelized on Hadoop distributed system using MapReduce programming model.

As we know, different orders of operations in chain matrix multiplication leads to different time of computation. There exists an optimal order of chain matrix multiplication using Dynamic Programming, which consumes the shortest computation time. Thus, we can apply Dynamic Programming to improve the efficiency of parallelized AvgSim. And the parallelization of AvgSim is mainly the parallelization of matrix multiplication after Dynamic Programming process. Here we use "block matrix multiplication"method on MapReduce to transform multiplication of two large matrices into several multiplications of smaller matrices. This method is flexible with selecting dimensions of block matrix according to the configuration of Hadoop cluster and avoids exceeding the memory size.

Applying "block matrix multiplication"iteratively to the chain matrix multiplication which is re-ordered by Dynamic Programming, we can get one of the two reachable probability matrices of AvgSim (e.g., RW_P, which is measured in the given meta-path P), and the other probability matrix (RW'_{P-1}) can be obtained in exactly the same procedure. Finally, the relevance matrix is derived by taking arithmetic mean of these two reachable probability matrices.

4 Experiments

4.1 Data Sets

Two data sets, **DBLP dataset** and **Matrix dataset**, are used in experiments and the previous network schema is shown in Fig. 1(b). In detail, the DBLP dataset contains 14K papers, 14K authors, 20 conferences and 8.9K terms. And we label 20 conferences, 100 papers, and 4057 authors in the dataset with four research areas including database, data mining, information retrieval and artificial intelligence for experiments use. And the Matrix dataset *(40 matrices in total)* contains several artificially generated large-scale sparse square matrices, whose dimensions are 1000×1000, 5000×5000, 10000×10000, 20000×20000, 40000×40000, 80000×80000, 100000×100000 and 150000×150000 respectively. And the sparsity of each matrix includes $0.0001, 0.0003, 0.0005, 0.0007$ and 0.001.

4.2 Performance of AvgSim

Performance on Query Task and Clustering Task. In the query task, we compare the performance of AvgSim with both HeteSim and PCRW though measuring the relevance of heterogeneous objects on DBLP dataset. Based on labels of the dataset, we calculate the AUC (Area Under ROC Curve) score to evaluate the performance of the results which are the related authors ranked by relevance scores for each conference on meta-path CPA. We evaluated 9 out of 20 marked conferences, whose AUC values are shown in Table 1. We notice that AvgSim gets the highest value on 8 conferences, which means AvgSim performs better than other two methods in the query task.

Table 1. AUC values for relevance search of conferences and authors based on CPA path on DBLP dataset

	KDD	ICDM	SDM	SIGMOD	VLDB	ICDE	AAAI	IJCAI	SIGIR
HeteSim	0.8111	0.6752	**0.6132**	0.7662	0.8262	0.7322	0.8110	0.8754	0.9504
PCRW	0.8030	0.6731	0.6068	0.7588	0.8200	0.7263	0.8067	0.8712	0.9390
AvgSim	**0.8117**	**0.6753**	0.6072	**0.7668**	**0.8274**	**0.7286**	**0.8114**	**0.8764**	**0.9525**

Table 2. Clustering accuracy results for path-based relevance measures on DBLP dataset

	Venue NMI	Author NMI	Paper NMI
PathSim	0.8162	0.6725	0.3833
HeteSim	0.7683	0.7288	0.4989
AvgSim	**0.8977**	**0.7556**	**0.5101**

In the clustering task, we compare the performance of AvgSim with both HeteSim and PathSim though measuring the relevance of homogeneous objects on DBLP dataset. We firstly apply three algorithms respectively to derive the relevance matrices on three meta-paths including $CPAPC$, $APCPA$ and $PAPCPAP$. Based on the result matrices and applied Normalized Cut, we perform clustering task and then evaluate the performances on conferences, authors, and papers using NMI criterion (Normalized Mutual Information). The clustering accuracy result is shown in Table 2 and AvgSim gets the highest NMI value in all the three tasks. The results of query task and clustering task suggest that AvgSim performs well in effectiveness.

Performance of Parallelized Matrix Multiplication. All parallelized matrix multiplication experiments are conducted on $Matrix$ dataset in a cluster composed of 7 machines with 4-cores E3-1220 V2 CPUs of 3.10GHz and 32 GB RAM running on RedHat 4 operating system. The experiments will measure several factors affecting block matrix multiplication, including matrix dimensions, matrix sparsity and partition strategy (i.e. dimensions of blocks).

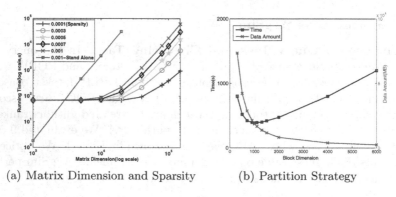

(a) Matrix Dimension and Sparsity   (b) Partition Strategy

Fig. 3. Factors affecting parallelized block matrix multiplication

Fig.3(a) shows the relationship among matrix dimensions, matrix sparsity and running time of parallelized block matrix multiplication together with the comparison between stand-alone and parallelized matrix multiplication. We notice that the larger dimensions or sparsity of matrix are, the more time in matrix multiplication is required. And the stand-alone algorithm costs shorter time for quite small matrix dimension because parallelized algorithm spends lots of time in starting task nodes of Hadoop cluster and resources of cluster are not fully utilized for small amount of calculations. However, efficiency of parallelized algorithm is much better as matrix dimension increasing. Besides, stand-alone algorithm is restricted of memory size for there are no results derived in the last three large-scale matrix multiplications.

Fig.3(b) shows the relationship among running time, intermediate data amount and partition strategy of block matrix multiplication. There are 11 kinds of partition strategies with square block matrix dimensions of 300×300, 500×500, 700×700, 900×900, 1000×1000, 1100×1100, 1300×1300, 1500×1500, 2000×2000, 4000×4000 and 6000×6000 respectively applying in the square matrix with dimension of 100000×100000 and a sparsity of 0.0001 in the experiment. We notice that intermediate data amount of matrix multiplication decrease gradually with the increase of block dimension. In contrast, running time reaches its minimum value at 5-th data point shown in figure. Smaller intermediate data amount results in less disk IO operations and data amount transmitted by shuffle, which also means shorter time and better performance to a certain extent as front several data points reflected. However, excessive large block dimension will reduce the concurrent granularity and increase the amount of calculations for single node, which conversely results in longer time of computation as several data points behind reflected.

In conclusion, appropriate partition strategy and sufficient sizes of cluster greatly affect the efficiency in parallelized block matrix multiplications. Applying parallelization method, AvgSim gains the ability to measure relevance in larger-scale networks with massive data efficiently.

5   Conclusions

In this paper, we introduced a novel algorithm with symmetrical features named AvgSim for measuring relevance of arbitrary objects in heterogeneous information network. In addition, using Dynamic Programming and "block matrix multiplication" methods, parallelized AvgSim is able to be applied to actual large-scale networks. Experiments given in the paper verified the effectiveness and efficiency of AvgSim while measuring the relevance of heterogeneous or homogeneous objects based on meta-paths.

Acknowledgment. This work is supported by the National Key Basic Research and Department(973) Program of China (No.2013CB329603), the National Science Foundation of China (Nos.61375058, and 71231002), the Ministry of Education of China and China Mobile Research Fund (MCM20123021) and the Special Co-construction Project of Beijing Municipal Commission of Education.

References

1. Sun, Y., Han, J., Zhao, P., Yin, Z., Cheng, H., Wu, T.: RankClus: integrating clustering with ranking for heterogeneous information network analysis. In: EDBT, pp. 565–576 (2009)
2. Kong, X., Yu, P.S., Ding, Y., Wild, D.J.: Meta path-based collective classification in heterogeneous information networks. In: CIKM, pp. 1567–1571 (2012)
3. Page, L., Brin, S., Motwani, R., Winograd, T.: The pagerank citation ranking: bringing order to the web. Stanford University Database Group. Technical report (1998)
4. Jeh, G., Widom, J.: SimRank: a measure of structural-context similarity. In: KDD, pp. 538–543 (2002)
5. Sun, Y., Han, J., Yan, X., Yu, P., Wu, T.: Pathsim: meta path-based top-k similarity search in heterogeneous information networks. In: VLDB, pp. 992–1003 (2011)
6. Lao, N., Cohen, W.: Relational retrieval using a combination of path-constrained random walks. Machine Learning 81(1), 53–67 (2010)
7. Shi, C., Kong, X., Huang, Y., Yu, P.S., Wu, B.: HeteSim: A General Framework for Relevance Measure in Heterogeneous Networks. In: CoRR, pp.abs/1309.7393 (2013)

Query Dependent Time-Sensitive Ranking Model for Microblog Search*

Shuxin Wang[1,3], Kai Lu[2], Xiao Lu[1,3], and Bin Wang[3,4]

[1] University of Chinese Academy of Sciences, P.R. China
[2] School of Engineering, University of California, Santa Cruz, USA
[3] Institute of Computing Technology, Chinese Academy of Sciences, P.R. China
[4] Institute of Information Engineering, Chinese Academy of Sciences, P.R. China
{wangshuxin,luxiao,wangbin}@ict.ac.cn, kailu@soe.ucsc.edu

Abstract. Previous works show that one main difference between web search and microblog search is that most microblog queries are time-sensitive. Therefore, many existing works based on one straightforward temporal assumption have tried to incorporate the temporal factors into ranking model to improve the retrieval effectiveness. However, our study show that temporal role in ranking is complicated and hard to be summarized into one straightforward assumption. In addition, temporal influence is different among queries. To address these problems, we propose a query-dependent time-sensitive microblog ranking model, which use learning to rank to combine both temporal and entity evidences into the ranking process as the basic ranking model. In order to leverage the query difference, the k most similar training queries are used to train the ranking model. Experimental results on the public TrecMicroblog2011 data set show that comparing with the existing time-sensitive models, our models can significantly improve the performance of microblog search.

Keywords: Time-sensitive, Query dependent ranking, Microblog search.

1 Introduction

Microblog is a user-generated content system, which allows its users to publish and share short messages. Microblog search has become a hot research topic in recent years. Related works [1] show that microblog search queries are time sensitive. User's motivation of microblog search is time sensitive, whether event searches including keep up with what was happening and understanding trends or real-time information searches. Hence, incorporating temporal information in relevance judgement has been studied by many researchers. Based on different assumptions of temporal role played in ranking, different methods are proposed to incorporate temporal information to the ranking process [6, 7]. However, the

---

* This work is supported by the National Science Foundation of China under Grant No. 61070111 and the Strategic Priority Research Program of Chinese Academy of Sciences under Grant No. XDA06030200.

L. Chen et al. (Eds.): APWeb 2014, LNCS 8709, pp. 644–651, 2014.

temporal influence in ranking of microblog search is very complicated, and hard to be summarized into one simple straightforward assumption.

In this paper, we first analyze the temporal influence over ranking in microblog search, and come up with two important hypotheses. Then, in order to capture the complex pattern of the temporal influence, we propose to employ learning to rank framework to combine both temporal and entity evidences into ranking process. Experimental result shows that time-sensitive learning to rank model improves the retrieval effectiveness. Moreover, in order to leverage the query difference information, the k nearest neighbors with the most similar temporal distribution patterns are found to build a query dependent model. Experimental results show that the query dependent model discriminates different queries in the temporal influence, and achieve the best performance.

2   Related Works

Previous works have tried to incorporate temporal information into the ranking process. An important temporal assumption is how fresh the results are, also known as "the newer the document, the more important", [6] and [8] tried to retrieve not only relevant but also fresh documents. [9] and [7] considered the other important temporal assumption, i.e., the event's peak time point. [7] proposed a method to give more weight to these documents around peak points. [9] tried to combine query expansion on temporal variation with recency in order to improve the retrieval performance. However, these studies have strong assumption on the temporal influence over ranking, which in fact, the influence could be complex, and it's inaccurate to be summarized into one simple assumption.

[10] proposed to use learning to rank for time-sensitive web search, however, there're different specialties in microblog search, and most of their features are not applicable in the microblog search any more.

The problem of the large differences among different queries can be addressed by query dependent ranking approaches. There're different loss functions to be employed to leverage the query difference to improve the retrieval effectiveness, such as query-classification-based approach [11], query clustering-based approach [12] and nearest neighbor-based approach [13]. As for web search, queries can be navigational, informational or transactional [15]. However, the queries in time-sensitive microblog search may have different patterns.

3   Our Methods

In this section, we first analyze the temporal distributions of query relevant documents and pseudo relevant documents, and come up with two hypotheses, which are the cornerstones of this paper, and then introduce our methods.

3.1   Query Temporal Distribution Analysis

We study the queries released by TREC Microblog Track 2011-2012. The corpus consists of microblogs between January 23rd and February 7th 2011, in total 17 days. Given a query, we want to find out the temporal distributions of relevant documents and pseudo relevant documents. Regard ground-truth labeled documents as relevant collection, and the top 500 documents retrieved by the query likelihood model as pseudo relevant collection[1].For a collection, the temporal distribution is computed as follows: Firstly, we divide the relevant documents by different days, then we count the ratio of documents fallen into each day.

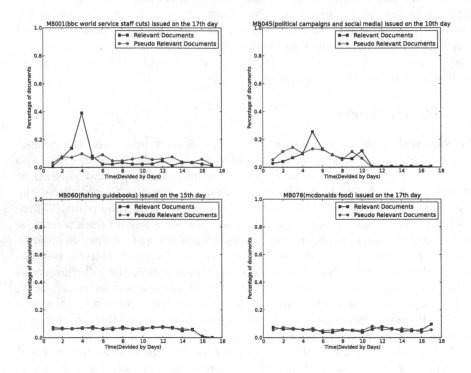

Fig. 1. Temporal Distribution of Queries

To demonstrate the temporal property of microblog, we take four queries used in the TREC 2011 Microblog Track as examples. Temporal distributions are plotted in the Fig. 1 using the method mentioned above.

To interpret this figure, we need to pay attention to the trends of pseudo relevant documents comparing with the relevant documents. We can see in this figure every subfigure's trend of pseudo relevant documents coordinate with relevant documents curve respectively. This phenomenon implies that the temporal feature between pseudo relevant is quite similar. Its obvious that queries may vary in temporal distribution.

---

[1] For the real time ad-hoc queries, the documents returned newer than the time when query is issued are removed.

When the curve of relevant documents is higher than that of the pseudo relevant documents, this means the ranking model should give more weight to the documents at that point. From the figure, we can see every subfigure implies different weighting schema. For query MB001, the document around peak point should be weight more, While for query MB078, the newer document should be weighed more. The situation of MB060 and MB045 are complex situations.

Consider if a querys temporal distribution is similar to the query MB001, it implies the pattern of temporal influence over ranking is the same with MB001. To sum up:

Hypothesis 1. *The temporal features between relevant documents set and pseudo relevant documents set are quite similar. A query can be projected in the temporal feature space of its relevant or pseudo relevant documents set.*

Hypothesis 2. *Temporal influence over ranking is complicated and it's inaccurate to summarize into one straightforward assumption. The temporal influence is different among queries, and similar temporal distribution of query imply similar pattern of temporal influence.*

3.2 Query Temporal Distribution Dependent Ranking Method

Query Dependent Learning to Rank Model. It will be beneficial to combine temporal information into the learning to rank framework. We utilize a simple linear score function which can be adopted to the point-wise, pair-wise or list-wise learning to rank process. In this paper, we use listnet[14] as a basic learning to rank model, the typical list-wise learning to rank model whose loss function is defined by the probability distribution over permutations.

In[13], Geng et al. performed query-dependent ranking using K Nearest Neighbor method. In our study, according to Hypothesis 1, query can be projected into as a temporal distribution. Since the most similar temporal distribution implies the similar impact of temporal information in ranking, k nearest neighbors used to training ranking models would leverage the useful information of similar training queries, and avoid the negative effects from dissimilar ones. The similarity is computed by the distance of two queries' temporal distributions. The distance of two distributions can be computed by Kullback-Leibler Divergence(KLD). Given two arbitrary queries q_i and q_j, The KLD of two queries can be defined as:

$$KLD(q_i, q_j) = \sum_k^n \log \frac{P_{q_i}{}^k}{P_{q_j}{}^k}. \tag{1}$$

where $P_{q_i}{}^k$, $P_{q_j}{}^k$ indicate temporal distribution probability of query q_i, query q_j on kth time unit separately.

For queries in training set, the temporal distribution can be calculated by relevant documents with ground-truth labels. For queries in test set, according to Hypothesis 1, the pseudo relevant documents' distribution is quite similar to relevant documents' for a given query, therefore, pseudo relevant documents' temporal distribution are used to represent this query.

Features. As we know, the quality of features is vital to the learning to rank framework. We divide the features into two categories: the first one is entity related, the other one is temporal related.

Entity based features are aimed at measuring the textual similarity between a query and a document. Since our study focus on time-sensitive problem, we only choose representative entity features. The proposed features include qlSim, tfSim, hashTagSim, senLen and hashTagLen. The qlSim measures the query likelihood probability, which is calculated by $\log(p(Q|M_D))$. The tfSim measures the *tf-idf* similarity of query-document pair in vector space model. hashTagSim measures the similarity between query and hashtags, which is calculated by word Jaccard distance after stemmed. senLen is the length of tweet after removing the hashtags, hasTagLen is the length of hashtags. Among these features, hashTagSim, SenLen and hashTagLen can be computed offline, while the qlSim and tfSim were computed by the retrieval system (E.g., lemur).

Temporal features try to capture temporal influence over ranking. In our work, we extract two types of temporal features. The global features including h, tc, ta and tp indicate the feature extracted from whole collection. While the local features including ti, tde,tai and tpi denote the current document's characteristics.

h indicates whether the temporal distribution is concentrated or uniform. The probability distribution is calculated by the ratio of documents fallen into a time unit. $p(x)^i$ stands for the distribution probability of the ith time unit.

$$h(x) = -\sum_{i=0}^{n} p(x)^i log p(x)^i. \tag{2}$$

ta indicates the average time of the whole collection. td_i stands for the time of document i.

$$ta = \frac{\sum_i^m td_i}{m}. \tag{3}$$

tp is the peak point of whole collection[7], is computed by finding the highest ratio in the distributions of the whole collection in different days. $c(i)$ stands for the count of documents on the ith day.

$$tp = argmax_i\|c(i)\|. \tag{4}$$

tc indicates the newest time of the whole collection.

$$tc = argmax_i td_i. \tag{5}$$

ti measures the time interval between the query and the current document. tq stands for query time.

$$ti = |tq - td_i|. \tag{6}$$

tde is exponential decay to indicate the time decay from the newest document's time stamp to the current document's time stamp. λ is parameter to be tuned.

$$tde = \lambda^{\lambda(tc-td_i)}. \tag{7}$$

The interval between the average time of pseudo relevant documents and the time of current document is defined as tai.

$$tai = |td_i - ta|. \tag{8}$$

The interval between the peak point and the current document's time stamp is defined as thi.

$$thi = |td_i - th|. \tag{9}$$

The combined feature could be meaningful in linear formed score function in learning to rank, this enlarges the dimension of feature space, and make the score function non-linear. We combine ti, tde, tmi, thi with h to a series of new features as $ti * h, tde * h, tai * h, thi * h$.

4 Experiments

To empirically evaluate our proposed hypotheses and approaches, we conduct a series of experiments on public data set TrecMicroblog2011 in this section.

4.1 Experimental Setup

The experimental corpus is distributed by TREC 2011 Microblog Track[2]. After preprocessing(remove the mentions, url information, delete non-english tweets and repost tweets), the documents set size is 9,679,710. The query set contains 110 queries. The evaluation metrics include precision at 30 (P@30) and mean average precision(MAP), the same as in the TREC Microblog Track [2].

In our two approaches, the first one combines a series of our proposed features into the learning to rank framework, which is named as TLTR model. The other one is the query-dependent ranking model(QDLTR). We use the basic query likelyhood model (QLM) as the baseline model, and also evaluate the methods proposed in [6](TLM) and [7] (HTLM-AdaptiveMultiML).

In our experiments, the QLM is smoothed by Jelinek-Mercery, and all the parameters are tuned using 5-fold cross validation one by one based on P@30 metric. The parameters are shown in Tab.1.

Table 1. Parameters in experiments of best performance

Model	Parameter	Description	Value
QL	λ	JK smooth parameter	0.4
TLM	λ	exponential decay parameter	0.3
HTLM-AdaptiveMultiML	α	threshold of peak point	0.1
	λ	exponential decay parameters	0.5
TLTR&QDTLTR	λ	exponential decay parameter	0.8

---

[2] http://sites.google.com/site/microblogtrack/

4.2   Experimental Results

The experimental results are shown in Tab.2. Statistical significant tests are performed using paired T-test at 0.05 level of significance. From the table, we can see that:

Table 2. Experimental Results(The significance of QDLTD compare with QLM is marked as *, and with TLTR is marked as ⋆)

model	MAP	P@30
QLM	0.2283	0.3019
TLM	0.2344	0.2972
HTLM-AdaptiveMulitiML	0.2358	0.3062
TLTR	0.2415	0.3327
QDLTR(K=20)[3]	0.2463**	0.3428**

As a baseline and benchmark of this evaluation, QLM model only measures textual similarity, and performs the worst on both metrics. Then TLM uses recency information as document's prior which ranks the newer documents higher. The results reflect that TLM has a little improvement on the MAP comparing QLM. After leveraging the temporal specialty of microblog, where lots of queries are event-related and the documents around peak point are more favorable. HTLM-AdaptiveMultiML brings positively effect on the P@30 and MAP, while the improvement is still limited. This reflects that the queries in microblog search is time-sensitive and very complex, although incorporating the temporal feature can bring a little improvement, it is limited if we only rely a simple assumption.

Through incorporating a series of features including the temporal features and entity features to the learning to rank framework, we can see that TLTR effectively improves the performance on both of evaluation metrics compared with TLM and HTLM-AdaptiveMultiML. It shows without any assumption of temporal influence, learning to rank is powerful to combine temporal evidence into ranking process.Furthermore, we can see QDLTR shows the best performance on both of evaluation metrics. Comparing with the baseline models, it outperforms QLM by 7.88% on the MAP score. Moreover, it shows even more significant improvement on the P@30 score which increases by 13.55%. Through considering the differences among different queries, the QDLTR model significantly outperforms the other methods.

Through the experiments, we can see that by combining temporal information into ranking can effectively improve retrieval effectiveness, and by further considering the query dependent will have much better performance. Therefore, our two hypotheses are very meaningful in the time-sensitive microblog retrieval tasks.

---

[3]   K is chosen by 5-fold cross validation.

5   Conclusion and Future Work

In this paper, we propose a query dependent learning to rank model to address the time-sensitive problem in microblog search. First, we extract the temporal and entity features from microblogs, and use learning to rank framework to combine these diverse temporal evidences which are able to capture the temporal influence in ranking. Second, to leverage the query difference over time distribution, we employ k-nearest neighbor algorithm to find temporal patterns similar to given query, and use this model to rank the documents for a given query. Experimental results show that our models can significantly improve the retrieval effectiveness of microblog search.

As for future work, there're lots of words in microblog indicates time, such as "yesterday", "last week" and "Jan 5th". These temporal information can also be extracted as temporal evidence used for ranking.

References

1. Teevan, J., Ramage, D., Morris, M.R.: #TwitterSearch: a comparison of microblog search and web search, pp. 35–44 (2011)
2. Ounis, I., Macdonald, C., Lin, J.: Overview of the trec-2011 microblog track. In: Proceeddings of the 20th Text REtrieval Conference (TREC 2011) (2011)
3. Metzler, D., Cai, C.: USC/ISI at TREC 2011: Microblog Track. In: TREC (2011)
4. Miyanishi, T., Okamura, N., Liu, X., Seki, K., Uehara, K.: TREC 2011 Microblog Track Experiments at Kobe University. In: TREC (2011)
5. Zhang, X., He, B., Luo, T., Li, B.: Query-biased learning to rank for real-time twitter search. Presented at the CIKM 2012: Proceedings of the 21st ACM International Conference on Information and Knowledge Management, New York, New York, USA (October 2012)
6. Li, X., Croft, W.B.: Time-based language models, pp. 469–475 (2003)
7. Wei, B., Zhang, S., Li, R., Wang, B.: A Time-Aware Language Model for Microblog Retrieval, trec.nist.gov
8. Efron, M., Golovchinsky, G.: Estimation methods for ranking recent information. In: Proceedings of the 34th International ACM SIGIR Conference on Research and Development in Information Retrieval, pp. 495–504 (2011)
9. Miyanishi, T., Seki, K., Uehara, K.: Combining recency and topic-dependent temporal variation for microblog search. In: Serdyukov, P., Braslavski, P., Kuznetsov, S.O., Kamps, J., Rüger, S., Agichtein, E., Segalovich, I., Yilmaz, E. (eds.) ECIR 2013. LNCS, vol. 7814, pp. 331–343. Springer, Heidelberg (2013)
10. Kanhabua, N., Ng, K.: Learning to rank search results for time-sensitive queries, pp. 2463–2466 (2012)
11. Kang, I.-H., Kim, G.: Query type classification for web document retrieval. ACM, New York (2003)
12. Banerjee, S., Dubey, A., Machchhar, J.: Efficient and accurate local learning for ranking. In: SIGIR Workshop: Learning to Rank for Information Retrieval (2009)
13. Geng, X., Liu, T.-Y., Qin, T., Arnold, A., Li, H., Shum, H.-Y.: Query dependent ranking using K-nearest neighbor. In: SIGIR 2008, pp. 115–122 (2008)
14. Cao, Z., Qin, T., Liu, T.Y., Tsai, M.F., Li, H.: Learning to rank: from pairwise approach to listwise approach. In: Proceedings of the 24th International Conference on Machine Learning (2007)
15. Broder, A.: A taxonomy of web search. ACM SIGIR Forum 36, 3–10 (2002)

A Social Trust Path Recommendation System in Contextual Online Social Networks

Guohao Sun[1], Guanfeng Liu[1], Lei Zhao[1], Jiajie Xu[1],
An Liu[1], and Xiaofang Zhou[1,2]

[1] School of Computer Science and Technology, Soochow University, China
[2] School of Information Technology and Electrical Engineering,
The University of Queensland, Australia
{gfliu,zhaol,xujj,anliu,zxf}@suda.edu.cn

Abstract. Online Social Network (OSN) is becoming increasingly popular and being used as the means for a variety of activities, where trust is one of the most important factors for participants decision making. This demands the evaluation of the trustworthiness between two unknown participants along a certain social path between them in OSNs. This paper presents a social trust path recommendation system which allows a user to find the optimal social trust path between two participants in OSN with the state-of-the-art path selection method. In addition, users could specify their preferences of social contexts including social relationships and social trust between participants and social positions of participants in path selection. This recommendation system provides three types of social trust paths to evaluate the trustworthiness of the unknown participants effectively. i.e., the shortest path, the path with the maximal trust values (denoted as Max T) and the optimal social trust path, which can be used in many applications like to help an employee find potential trustworthy employees or to help a retailer to find trustworthy loyal customers.

Keywords: OSN, trust, social trust path recommendation.

1 Introduction

In recent years, Online Social Network (OSN) has been used in variety of activities, such as employment and CRM systems [1], etc , requiring evaluating the trustworthiness between two unknown participants as trust is one of the most important impact factors for participants decision making [1]. In a Contextual Online Social Network (COSN) [1] depicted in Fig. 1 , each node represents a participant and each link corresponds to real world interactions or online interactions between participants. Some social contexts like social trust ($T \in [0, 1]$) and social intimacy degree ($r \in [0, 1]$) could be computed between two participants to illustrate the intimacy relationship between them. In addition, role impact factor ($Rou \in [0, 1]$) could be computed to illustrate the impact of a participant in a specific domain [1]. As each participant usually interacts with many other participants, multiple paths may exist between two participants (i.e., a source and a target) without any direct link between them, such as the path $A \to B \to C \to E$, and $A \to B \to D \to E$ in Fig. 1. These paths are called social trust paths which can help

L. Chen et al. (Eds.): APWeb 2014, LNCS 8709, pp. 652–656, 2014.
© Springer International Publishing Switzerland 2014

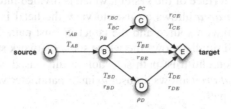

Fig. 1. A contextual online social networks

evaluate the trust between two unknown participants. It is computationally impossible to evaluate the trust based on all the social trust paths as it is an NP-Complete problem [1]. Therefore, it is necessary to select the optimal social trust path that can deliver the most trustworthy trust evaluation result.

In this social trust path recommendation system, we provide three types of social path selection methods. They are (1) the shortest path between a pair of source and target, (2) the path with the maximum T value based on the method proposed in [2], and (3) the optimal social trust path based on the state-of-the-art method proposed in [1] which is based on the Monte Carlo method [3]. This method considers the social contexts like T, r and Rou, and and users' preferences. These three different types of social paths provide different angles of trust path connection, which can effectively help evaluate the trustworthiness of participants.

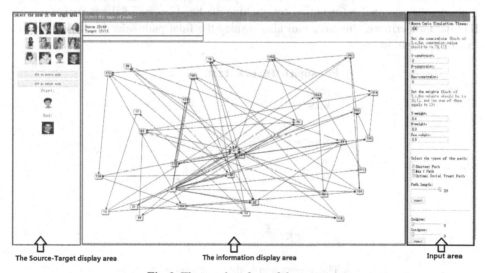

Fig. 2. The user interface of the system

2   System Overview

Our system is based on Struts and Hibernate, and the server runtime is Tomcat 7 and JDK 7. We use MySQL database and Mxgraph[1] to display the social network structure.

---

[1] http://www.mxgraph.com

Fig. 2 shows the user interface of the system, which is divided into three areas: (1) The *Source-Target selection area* allows an user to view the head images of participants and selects two of them as a source and the target in trust path selection. (2) The *information display area* initially shows the whole social network structure and can also display users information and trust path selection results based on different the user's operations. (3) The *input area* allows an user to input parameter values to select different types of social trust path.

2.1   The Source-Target Selection Area

This area mainly shows the information of the participant in the social network. When an user clicks a node from the social network displayed in information display area, the corresponding participant's head image will be added in this area. In addition, users can view the details personal information by clicking the head images, and can add one of them as a source or a target by clicking the corresponding buttons.

2.2   The Information Display Area

When loading the system, initially, this area displays the social network structure as shown in Fig. 1. In addition, by clicking the head image in Source-Target selection area, the detailed personal information of the participant like, node ID, name, age, social position, address and the friends of the participant will be shown in this area. Fig. 3 shows the personal information by clicking the head image of the participant with ID=14. Furthermore, this area can also display the final path selection results as the example shown in Fig. 4.

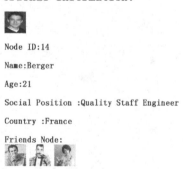

Fig. 3. The information of the participant with ID=14

2.3   Input Area

This area is divided into three parts. The top of the area is for users to set the simulation times of the Monte Carlo method [3] and the multiple end-to-end constraints for T, r and Rou as the requirements of the optimal social trust path selection. For example, an user can set T-constraint$>$ 0.5, r-constraint$>$ 0.05 and Rou-constraint$>$ 0.5 in the domain of *employment* or set r-constraint> 0.4 in the domain of *product introduction*, where T-constraint, r-constraint and Rou-constraint are the constraints of T, r and Rou respectively. In addition, the middle part is a checkbox list, which is used for users to determine which type of path they would like to find. Under the checkbox list, there is a range control for user to control the maximal length of the selected social trust path. Furthermore, at the bottom of the input area, there are two range controls for indegree and outdegree of the social network. This can help users to filter those nodes with small indegree and outdegree, and then select the social trust path in the filtered social network based on their preferences.

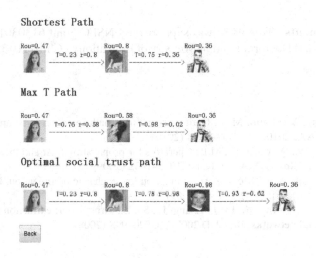

Fig. 4. The three types of social trust paths between ID=18 and ID=41

3 Demo

Users can visit this system via the web link *http://ada.suda.edu.cn:8080/social/*. After opening the user interface, an user could select a source and a target by clicking the nodes from the social network displayed in the information display area, and the corresponding head images will be displayed in the Source-Target area. Then the user can input parameter information to select certain social trust paths based on his/her preferences. The path selection results will be displayed in the information display area. Fig. 4 shows the three different types of social trust paths between a source (ID=18) and the target (ID=41), where T and r values are displayed on path links, and Rou values are displayed on the top of the head images. If $T_{AB} = 0$, it indicates that A completely distrusts B while $T_{AB} = 1$ is just the reverse. $r_{AB} = 0$ indicates that A and B have no social relationship while $r_{AB} = 1$ indicates they have the most intimate social relationship. $Rou_A = 1$ indicates A is a domain expert while $Rou_A = 0$ indicates that A has no knowledge in the domain. All these factor values can be computed by using data mining technique [4].

4 Conclusion

In this paper, we have introduced a novel recommendation system to find the social trust path in COSNs. Our system has provided three main path selection methods for users, i.e., the shortest path, the Max T path and the optimal social trust path. Our system could recommend diverse social trust paths to help users evaluate the trustworthiness of two unknown participants, and can be used in may applications. For example, it can be used in employment systems to help an employer find trustworthy potential employees or be used in CRM systems to help a retailer introduce products to trustworthy loyal customers.

Acknowledgements. This work was supported by NSFC grant 61303019, 61073061 and 61003044, and Doctoral Fund of Ministry of Education of China 20133201120012.

References

1. Liu, G., Wang, Y., Orgun, M.A.: Optimal social trust path selection in complex social networks. In: AAAI 2010, pp. 1397–1398 (2010)
2. Hang, C.-W., Wang, Y., Singh, M.P.: Operators for propagating trust and their evaluation in social networks. In: AAMAS 2009, pp. 1025–1032 (2009)
3. Morton, D., Popova, E.: Monte-carlo simulation for stochastic optimization. In: Encyclopedia of Optimization, pp. 2337–2345 (2009)
4. Tang, J., Zhang, J., Yao, L., Li, J., Zhang, L., Su, Z.: Arnetminer: extraction and mining of academic social networks. In: KDD 2008, pp. 990–998 (2008)

CrowdCleaner: A Data Cleaning System Based on Crowdsourcing

Chen Ye, Hongzhi Wang, Keli Li, Qian Chen, Jianhua Chen,
Jiangduo Song, and Weidong Yuan

School of Computer Science, Harbin Institute of Technology, Harbin, 150000

Abstract. As data in real life is often dirty, data cleaning is a natural way to improve the data quality. However, due to the lack of human knowledge, existing automatic data cleaning systems cannot find the proper values for dirty data. Thus we propose an online data cleaning system CrowdCleaner based on Crowdsourcing. CrowdCleaner provides a friendly interface for users dealing with different data quality problems. In this demonstration, we show the architecture of CrowdCleaner and highlight a few of its key features. We will show the process of the CrowdCleaner to clean data.

Keywords: Data cleaning, crowdsourcing, truth discovery.

1   Introduction

As in many applications, dirty data cause serious problems [5, 6]. Due to its importance, notable research efforts have been made to improve the quality of data. Currently, a natural way to deal with dirty data is data cleaning. Many data cleaning systems have been proposed, such as Potter's Wheel [4], AJAX [3].

A problem of current systems is the lack of sufficient knowledge. In many cases, without knowledge, machine could not tell how to revise the data. Even though expert efforts are involved in the data cleaning for some systems, recruiting experts are expensive for cleaning large data set. Another problem is that some data cleaning methods are difficult to compute, which are NP-hard problems or even non-computable.

Since crowdsourcing [1] integrates the efforts of non-experts and could achieve the goal with low cost, we attempt to clean the data with crowdsourcing to balance the cost and quality of data cleaning. Additionally, with crowdsourcing, some problems that are difficult for machine could be easily solved by human. For example, for automatic approaches, the repairing for inconsistency detected with CFD is NP-Complete [10].

With these advantages, we develop CrowdCleaner which use crowdsourcing to clean data that are difficult to repair with automatic approaches. Comparing with current systems, our system has following benefits.

High Accuracy but Low Costs. CrowdCleaner makes human answer the questions through Crowdsourcing. To reduce the cost and ensure the cleaning quality, we choose a small share of data that are most difficult to be cleaned with automatic methods for crowdsourcing, and choose a few reliable workers.

L. Chen et al. (Eds.): APWeb 2014, LNCS 8709, pp. 657–661, 2014.

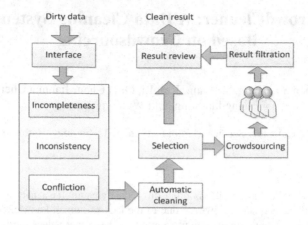

Fig. 1. System architecture

Simpleness. CrowdCleaner uses human to input answers via crowdsourcing to clean data, neither complex machine-calculation nor extra knowledge base is needed.

Flexibility. CrowdCleaner can deal with different data quality problems to meet different requirements of users, such as incompleteness, inconsistency or conflicts.

Friendly User Interface. CrowdCleaner provides users with interfaces to upload the dirty data files and downloaded the cleaning data files according to different data problems. We also design questions forms to make workers answer easily.

The remaining parts of the paper are organized as follows. Section 2 shows the architecture of our system. Section 3 describes the algorithms used in our system CrowdCleaner. Demo scenarios are introduced in the Section 4. We draw conclusions in Section 5.

2   System Architecture

In this section, we introduce the architecture of our system which is shown in Figure 1. We use a flexible architecture to solve different data quality problems. In our system, we can deal with three data quality problems named incompleteness, inconsistency and conflicts which are the most common among data quality problems.

When a user uploads a dirty data file through the user interface, the system scans the data set to check if there exists incompleteness, inconsistency or conflicts. The detection of incompleteness is trivial by scanning all tuples for missing attributes. The inconsistency is detected by rules such as FD and CFD [9]. Conflicts could be found by entity resolution [7].

The dirty records are automatic cleaned preliminarily. An uncertainty is attached for each automatic cleaned tuple to show whether it is reliable. Then according to users' selection and machine's selection in the selection module, crowdsourcing module is invoked to generate questions for workers and send them to the crowdsourcing platform.

Result filtration module generates the final clean results according to the answers from workers. Then combining with the cleaning results of automatic and crowdsourcing cleaning approaches, the results review module show the whole results to users.

3   Data Cleaning Methods

In this section, we will introduce the techniques used in our system. Since error detection and automatic cleaning could be accomplished with existing methods [1, 3, 4, 7, 11], in this section, we focus on crowdsourcing-related techniques.

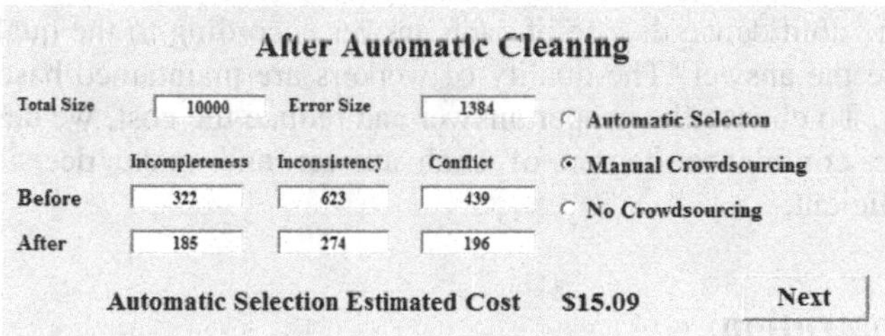

After Automatic Cleaning

Total Size	10000	Error Size	1384	○ Automatic Selecton
	Incompleteness	Inconsistency	Conflict	⊙ Manual Crowdsourcing
Before	322	623	439	○ No Crowdsourcing
After	195	274	196	

Automatic Selection Estimated Cost $15.09   Next

(a)   After automatic cleaning

Manual Crowdsourcing Choices

Task_id	Attribute	Error Type	Cost	Choice	
1	city_name	Incomplete	$0.01	☑	
2	city_history	Inconsistency	$0.03	☑	Estimated Cost
3	city_population	Conflict	$0.01	☐	
4	city_area	Incomplete	$0.01	☐	$0.06
5	city_GDP	Inconsistency	$0.02	☑	
6	city_mayor	Conflict	$0.01	☐	

Back   Select All   Next

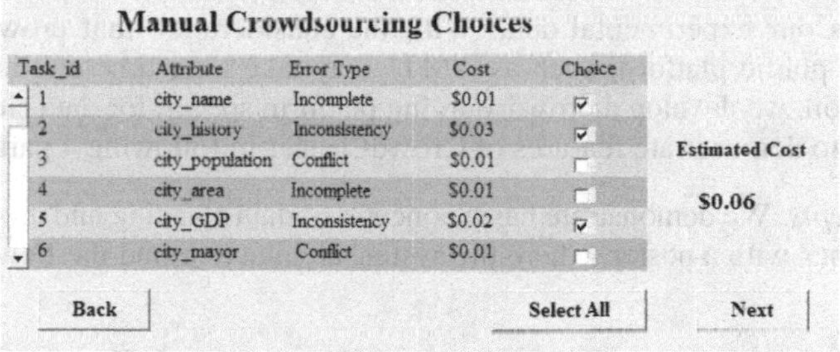

(b)   Manual crowdsourcing choices

Cleaning Results						
File Name	Records	ICM	ICN	COM	Auto	Crowd
city name	1350	55	10	7	59	10
people name	1444	69	15	6	45	12
animals	2651	35	11	8	67	16
school name	4624	34	6	4	23	8
maths history	5242	65	21	4	32	12
movies	6354	344	53	32	432	42

ICM: incompleteness size   ICN: inconsistency size   CON: conflicts size
Auto: automatic cleaning   Crowd: crowdsourcing

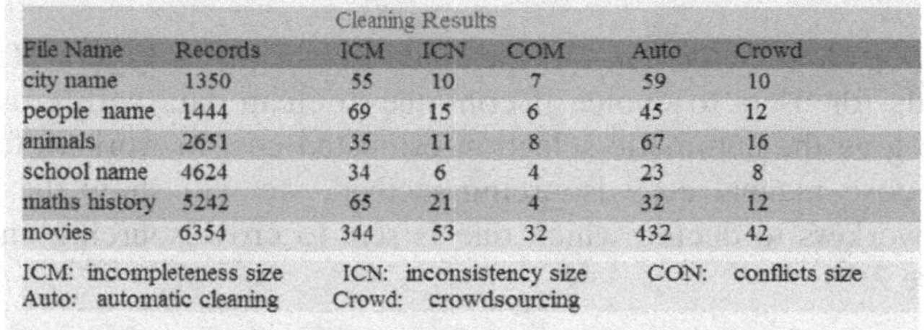

(c)   Result review

Fig. 2. Interfaces of CrowdCleaner

Crowdsourcing Tuple Selection. Since it is costly to send all dirty data for crowdsourcing, we select the records with the most uncertainty in automatic cleaning. For inconsistency and conflicts, we use entropy on the fraction of tuples to calculate the uncertain score of a record [8]. For missing attribute imputation, we compute the uncertainty of the filling value according to the Bayesian network [2] and select the tuples with uncertainty larger than a given threshold.

Question Generation. For missing attribute imputation, we give the candidate value which calculated by automatic method to workers. For inconsistency and conflicts, we provide several candidate options with their frequency of occurrence as a reference, so that workers can achieve enough information to make a choice.

Result Filtration. Answers from different workers are sent to result filtration module. We calculate the confidence degree of each answer according to the quality of workers who provide the answer. The quality of workers are maintained based on history information [8]. To choose the proper answer and reduce the cost, we design a model to evaluate the confidence degree of each answer and make decision once the evidence is sufficient.

4   Demonstration

To demonstrate the features of our system, we download the name clusters of city, animal, school on the web. Since data sources may contain errors or inconsistency, we use them as our experimental data. With the consideration that crowdsourcing the tasks to the public platform such as AMT[1] may take long time and not suitable for demonstration, we develop a crowdsourcing platform special for data cleaning.

We plan to demonstrate features of CrowdCleaner in following 4 parts.

Basic Concepts. We demonstrate basic concepts of data cleaning and crowdsourcing in CrowdCleaner with a poster, where the system architecture and the flow of algorithms are shown.

Standard Data Cleaning. Our system provides users a default interface for data cleaning. CrowdCleaner provides a simple interface to upload the file for cleaning. After cleaning, the user can download the clean results as a flat file.

Crowdsourcing Data Selection. As the interface shown in Figure 2(a), we provide three methods for users to choice if continue to clean data with crowdsourcing. In addition, we give the automatic selection estimated cost to workers for reference. If the users choose manual crowdsourcing method, we will show the detail of dirty records for workers to decide which one is sent to crowdsourcing and estimate the cost in Figure 2(b).

Data Cleaning Result Review. As the interface shown in Figure 2(c), CrowdCleaner provides an interface for the detail of different data problems and the records we have corrected by automatic cleaning or crowdsourcing.

---

[1] https://www.mturk.com/mturk/welcome

5   Conclusion

To deal with the problems of lack of knowledge and computation difficulty in current data cleaning systems, we develop CrowdCleaner, a data cleaning system based on crowdsourcing. The system balances the cost and result quality by selecting a small share of data for crowdsourcing and choosing proper answers from workers. Friendly interfaces are provided by the system to both users and workers. This demonstration will show these features of the system. Further work includes scaling the system for big data and integrating more data quality types in the system such as currency and accuracy.

Acknowledgement. This paper was partially supported by NGFR 973 grant 2012C B316200, NSFC grant 61003046, 61111130189 and NGFR 863 grant 2012AA011004.

References

1. Howe, J.: The rise of crowdsourcing. Wired Magazine 14(6), 1–4 (2006)
2. Jin, L., Wang, H., Gao, H.: Imputation for categorical attributes with probabilistic reasoning. In: Wang, J., Xiong, H., Ishikawa, Y., Xu, J., Zhou, J. (eds.) WAIM 2013. LNCS, vol. 7923, pp. 87–98. Springer, Heidelberg (2013)
3. Galhardas, H., Florescu, D., Shasha, D., Simon, E., Saita, C.-A.: Declarative data cleaning: Language, model, and algorithms. In: VLDB, pp. 371–380 (2001)
4. Raman, V., Hellerstein, J.M.: Potter's wheel: An interactive data cleaning system. In: VLDB, pp. 381–390 (2001)
5. Redman, T.C.: Data: An unfolding quality disaster. Information Management Magazine (August 2004)
6. Shilakes, C., Tylman, J.: Enterprise information portals. Merrill Lynch (1998)
7. Bhattacharya, I., Getoor, L.: Collective entity resolution in relational data. ACM Transactions on Knowledge Discovery from Data (TKDD) 1(1), 5 (2007)
8. Ye, C., Wang, H., Gao, H., Li, J., Xie, H.: Truth discovery based on crowdsourcing. In: Li, F., Li, G., Hwang, S.-w., Yao, B., Zhang, Z. (eds.) WAIM 2014. LNCS, vol. 8485, pp. 453–458. Springer, Heidelberg (2014)
9. Fan, W.: Dependencies revisited for improving data quality. In: PODS, pp. 159–170 (2008)
10. Cong, G., Fan, W., Geerts, F., Jia, X., Ma, S.: Improving Data Quality: Consistency and Accuracy. In: VLDB 2007, pp. 315–326 (2007)
11. Liu, S., Liu, Y., Ni, L.M., et al.: Towards mobility-based clustering. In: Proceedings of the 16th ACM SIGKDD International Conference on Knowledge Discovery and Data Mining, pp. 919–928. ACM (2010)

Prototype System for Visualizing Review Text Using Evaluative Expression Dictionaries

Yuki Tanimoto, Hirotaka Niitsuma, and Manabu Ohta

Graduate School of Natural Science and Technology, Okayama University,
3-1-1 Tsushima-naka, Kita-ku, Okayama, 700-8530, Japan
{tanimoto,ohta}@de.cs.okayama-u.ac.jp,
niitsuma@suri.cs.okayama-u.ac.jp

Abstract. We propose a system that can score online reputation text for a given attribute, e.g., design and portability, in a certain category, e.g., mp3 players and laptops. Additionally, we visualize scored results as an interactive system. The scoring system has evaluative expression dictionaries created in advance using reviews. They comprise evaluative values that determine the attribute-wise polarity of evaluative expressions: good or bad. Our system analyzes online reputation using the evaluative expression dictionaries, and then outputs the scores of the reputation. The system helps users to ascertain a reputation easier than merely by reading through textual information.

Keywords: visualization, review, reputation, evaluative expression dictionary.

1 Introduction

Online reputation in blogs, customer reviews of products, and SNS, such as Twitter, has become an important information source for both potential buyers and sellers. However, it is not realistic to expect someone in a transaction to read all the reputation information because of the rapid growth of its volume. Actually, only the top ranked or latest reputation is used in the buyer decision processes.

This study examines a proposed review visualization system that performs a reputation search and then visualizes the reputation. Many researchers[1,2] have proposed the classification of evaluative expressions into positive or negative ones based on which they calculated the polarity scores of reviews. The difference between our research and other earlier studies is the method of calculating the scores. Our system extracts evaluative expressions from review text and calculates their polarity scores associated with individual evaluative attributes. Few reports in the literature describe direct transformation of evaluative expressions into numerical scores for the respective evaluative attributes, as our system does.

Figure 1 portrays a screenshot of our system, which is still under development. Here, category *mp3* is selected and *ipod* is input as the product name. It is also specified that *10* reviews are retrieved from *local* cached data. The stars beside

L. Chen et al. (Eds.): APWeb 2014, LNCS 8709, pp. 662–665, 2014.

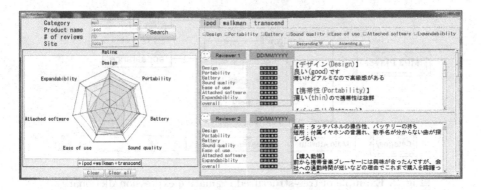

Fig. 1. Screenshot of the review visualization system under development

each review represent the ratings for individual evaluative attributes, which are determined by averaging the weighted polarity scores of evaluative expressions extracted from the review. The radar chart presents the averages of all ratings over analyzed review text for each evaluative attribute. This layout is fairly common among review sites. These ratings indicated by the stars and the radar chart are useful for users to ascertain the reputation quickly. Our research was undertaken to transform review text into appropriate ratings for each evaluative attribute.

2   Proposed System

The proposed system has two parts.

- creation of evaluative expression dictionaries and
- visualization of a textual reputation.

Evaluative expressions are expressions referring to evaluation of items or products. Evaluative expression dictionaries store these expressions. In [3], we provide more details to define evaluative expressions further. Using the dictionaries, our system visualizes a textual reputation. In this section, we first explain the evaluative expression dictionaries. Then we present a method of scoring and visualizing a reputation.

2.1   Evaluative Expression Dictionary

The evaluative expression dictionaries have tree-structured data. The root node represents the category. Other nodes represent evaluative attributes and have evaluative values and polarity scores (Fig. 2). In Fig. 2, the root node is *MP3 Player* and has child nodes *design* and *portability*, which we designate as main attributes. The *design* node has three evaluative values, *good*, *very good* and *not good*. Their respective polarity scores are 0.5, 0.8, and −0.2. The *design* node also has two child nodes: *shape* and *appearance*.

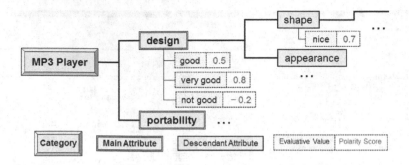

Fig. 2. Example of tree-structured evaluative expression dictionary

Evaluative expression dictionaries such as this are constructed automatically using Japanese reviews in Kakaku.com[5]. We use the Japanese dependency analyzer, CaboCha[4], to parse each review. We defined adjectives and adjective verbs as candidates of the evaluative values and nouns as candidates of the evaluative attributes. For dictionary construction, we first add main attribute nodes as children of the root node. These main attributes are determined at Kakaku.com. We then assign the evaluative values that modify the main attributes to the modified main attribute nodes and calculate their polarity scores using user-posted ratings with reviews. Evaluative attributes which frequently co-occur with a main attribute in the same review text are added to the dictionary tree as child nodes of the main attribute node. The child nodes of the child nodes, i.e., the descendant nodes of the main attribute nodes, are added to the dictionary tree similarly.

2.2   Scoring and Visualizing Reputation

When using our system, users first specify a product by name. Users can also specify the number of reviews to be retrieved and the category. Next, the system collects a set of reviews using Web search service API and analyzes each text. We use the Japanese dependency analyzer, CaboCha, to extract pairs of an evaluative attribute and value from the review text. Then, the system calculates the score of each pair by searching the evaluative expression dictionary for the pair.

Presuming the pair of *design* and *good* is extracted from the review text in Fig. 1, then using the dictionary as shown in Fig. 2, it is possible to assign a score of 0.5 to the pair because the identical pair can be found in the dictionary. However, we also propose calculation of the score of a pair of, say, *design* and *nice*, using the neighboring nodes such as *shape*, which has the same evaluative value of *nice*, because we cannot find the identical pair in the dictionary. When we find more than one *nice* in the descendant nodes of the main attribute node *design*, we average each score, which is weighted in accordance with the length of the path from the node of *design*.

Finally, the averaged scores of the pairs extracted from a review are normalized into five grades corresponding to the number of stars displayed in the GUI of our system as shown in Fig. 1. The average 0.75 is the polarity score for the attribute of *design* if we extract a pair of *design* and *very good* with the score of 0.8 and a pair of *shape* and *nice* with the score of 0.7 in one review text.

3   Demonstration Scenario

In our demo, we show the visualized online reputation of some products such as mp3 players and laptops. The attendees can specify a product name, a category, the number of reviews, and the site to be retrieved with the GUI. Moreover, attendees can browse a visualized result along with retrieved review text. The attendees can select the site from Kakaku.com and local cached data.

4   Conclusion

In this article, we proposed a review visualization system that used our tree-structured evaluative expression dictionaries. Our system can transform textual information of reviews into ratings that are readily comprehensible visually. Moreover, our system helps users to find the reviews of products in which they are interested. Some review sites such as Amazon.com do not give scores for individual attributes. They merely assign an overall score for individual reviews. Our system can calculate attribute-wise scores from review text.

In the current version, the selectable categories for reviews are limited to a few particular domains. Exploring other categories is a main concern. Another concern is the quantitative evaluation of the propriety of the calculated scores, which has been improved constantly.

References

1. Dave, K., Lawrence, S., Pennock, D.M.: Mining the Peanut Gallery: Opinion Extraction and Semantic Classification of Product Reviews. In: Proc. of the 12th International Conference on World Wide Web, pp. 519–528 (2003)
2. Liu, B., Hu, M., Cheng, J.: Opinion Observer: Analyzing and Comparing Opinions on the Web. In: Proc. of the 14th International Conference on World Wide Web, pp. 342–351 (2005)
3. Tanimoto, Y., Ohta, M.: A Proposal of Visualizing Reputation Using Evaluative Expression Dictionaries. In: Proc. of the Fourth International Conference on Ubiquitous Information Management and Communication, pp. 339–346 (2010)
4. CaboCha, http://chasen.org/taku/software/cabocha/
5. Kakaku.com, http://kakaku.com/

MOOD: Moving Objects Outlier Detection

Salman Ahmed Shaikh and Hiroyuki Kitagawa

Graduate School of Systems and Information Engineering, University of Tsukuba
Tennodai, Tsukuba, Ibaraki 305-8573, Japan
salman@kde.cs.tsukuba.ac.jp, kitagawa@cs.tsukuba.ac.jp
http://www.kde.cs.tsukuba.ac.jp/

Abstract. This paper describes and demonstrates MOOD, a system for detecting outliers from moving objects data. In particular, we demonstrate a continuous distance-based outlier detection approach for moving objects' data streams. We assume that the moving objects are uncertain, as the state of a moving object can not be known precisely, and this uncertainty is given by the Gaussian distribution. The MOOD system provides an interface which takes moving objects' states streams and some parameters as input and continuously produces the distance-based outliers along with some graphs comparing the efficiency and accuracy of the underlying algorithms.

Keywords: Outlier Detection, Moving Objects, Uncertain Data, Data Streams.

1 Introduction

Outlier detection is a fundamental problem in data mining. It has applications in many domains including credit card fraud detection, network intrusion detection, environment monitoring, medical sciences, moving objects monitoring etc. Several definitions of outlier have been given in past, but there exists no universally agreed definition. Hawkins [1] defined an outlier as an observation that deviates so much from other observations as to arouse suspicion that it was generated by a different mechanism.

Recently, with the advancement in data collection technologies, e.g., wireless sensor networks (WSN), data arrive continuously and contain certain degree of inherent uncertainty [2]. The causes of uncertainty may include but are not limited to limitation of equipments, inconsistent supply voltage and delay or loss of data in transfer [2]. Detection of outliers from such data is a challenging research problem in data mining. Hence this paper describes and demonstrates the MOOD system, to detect outliers from moving objects' streams, where the moving objects are uncertain and this uncertainty is given by the Gaussian distribution. In addition, the MOOD system generates dynamic graphs comparing the efficiency and accuracy of the underlying algorithms.

The problem of outlier detection on uncertain datasets was first studied by Aggarwal et al. [3]. However, their work was given for static data and cannot handle moving objects data or data streams. In [4], Wang et al. proposed an outlier

L. Chen et al. (Eds.): APWeb 2014, LNCS 8709, pp. 666–669, 2014.

Table 1. State sets

Time	State set	o_1	o_2	...	o_N
t_1	S^1	$\overrightarrow{\mathcal{A}_1^1}$	$\overrightarrow{\mathcal{A}_2^1}$	...	$\overrightarrow{\mathcal{A}_N^1}$
t_2	S^2	$\overrightarrow{\mathcal{A}_1^2}$	$\overrightarrow{\mathcal{A}_2^2}$	...	$\overrightarrow{\mathcal{A}_N^2}$
t_3	S^3	$\overrightarrow{\mathcal{A}_1^3}$	$\overrightarrow{\mathcal{A}_2^3}$	...	$\overrightarrow{\mathcal{A}_N^3}$
$\vdots$	$\vdots$	$\vdots$	$\vdots$	$\vdots$	$\vdots$

detection approach for probabilistic data streams. However, their work focuses on tuple-level uncertainty. In contrast, in this work, attribute level uncertainty is considered.

2   Moving Objects Outlier Detection

This section describes the distance-based outlier detection approach for moving objects' data steams. In this paper, o_i denotes a k-dimensional uncertain object with attributes vector $\overrightarrow{\mathcal{A}_i} = (x_{i1}, ..., x_{ik})$ following the Gaussian distribution with mean $\overrightarrow{\mu_i} = (\mu_{i1}, ..., \mu_{ik})$ and co-variance matrix $\Sigma_i = diag(\sigma_{i1}^2, ..., \sigma_{ik}^2)$. Namely, $\overrightarrow{\mathcal{A}_i}$ is a random variable that follows the Gaussian distribution $\overrightarrow{\mathcal{A}_i} \sim \mathcal{N}(\overrightarrow{\mu_i}, \Sigma_i)$. Assuming that there are N objects whose states may change over time, $S^j = \{\overrightarrow{\mathcal{A}_1^j}, ..., \overrightarrow{\mathcal{A}_N^j}\}$ denotes a state set of N objects at time t_j. Note that the $\overrightarrow{\mu_i^j}$ denotes the observed coordinates (attribute values) of an object o_i at time t_j. Hence streams are the sequences of moving objects' states (locations) generated over time. We assume that the states of all the objects are generated synchronously and the set of states at a timestamp t_j is called a state set S^j as shown in table 1. We now present the definition of distance-based outliers for uncertain data streams, originally proposed in our previous work [6], as follows.

Definition 1. *An uncertain object o_i is a distance-based outlier at time t_j, if the expected number of objects in S^j lying within D-distance of o_i are less than or equal to threshold $\theta = N(1 - p)$, where p is the fraction of objects that lie farther than D-distance of $o_i \in S^j$.*

The straightforward approach to detect outliers from each state set is to use the cell-based approach of uncertain distance-based outlier detection (UDB) for every timestamp, presented in our previous work [5]. However, the duration between two consecutive timestamps is usually very short and the state of all the objects may not change much in this duration. Hence, we proposed an incremental approach of outlier detection (denoted by CUDB in this work), which makes use of outlier detection results obtained from previous state set S^{j-1} at timestamp t_{j-1} to detect outliers in current state set S^j at timestamp t_j [6]. This eliminates the need to process all the objects' states at every timestamp and saves a lot of computation time.

3   The MOOD System Overview

In the following, we present an overview of the MOOD system, its interface and functionalities and the underlying algorithms.

3.1   The MOOD System Interface

The main interface of the MOOD system is shown in Fig. 1. The MOOD system accepts moving objects' streams. In addition, the system takes as input some parameters, as shown in the top-left corner of the MOOD system interface in Fig. 1. These parameters are required by the underlying algorithms for the computation of continuous outliers.

The MOOD system computes outliers for three algorithms. Namely UDB, CUDB and Knorr. In the MOOD system interface, the circles represent the objects at current timestamp while the squares represent the objects in the previous timestamp. The black bordered circles/squares represent the inliers. The red circles/squares represent the outliers identified by both the algorithms (i.e., CUDB and Knorr), while the pink and blue circles/squares represent the outliers identified by only CUDB algorithm and only Knorr algorithm, respectively. Moreover, the movement of objects is represented by green arrows as can be seen from Fig. 1.

3.2   The Underlying Algorithms

The UDB algorithm is proposed in our previous work [5] and can only detects distance-based outliers from uncertain static data. In order to make this algorithm work for continuous moving objects' data or streaming data, the UDB algorithm is executed for every timestamp. The CUDB is an incremental algorithm for distance-based outlier detection from uncertain data streams, proposed in our work [6]. The CUDB makes use of outlier detection results obtained from previous state set S^{j-1} at timestamp t_{j-1} to detect outliers from current state set S^j at timestamp t_j. This eliminates the need to process all the objects' states at every timestamp and saves a lot of computation time. The graph on the top-right corner of the MOOD interface (see Fig. 1) shows the difference in execution times of the UDB and the CUDB algorithms for moving objects data streams.

The Knorr algorithm is proposed by E.M.Knorr et al. [7] for distance-based outlier detection from deterministic static data. In the MOOD system, the Knorr outlier detection algorithm is used as a baseline to compare the accuracy of the CUDB algorithm. The graphs on the mid-right and the bottom-right of the MOOD interface (see Fig. 1) shows the comparison of precision and recall respectively. The precision is defined as the ability of the algorithms to present only true outliers. The recall is defined as the ability of the algorithms to present all true outliers. The precision and recall of the algorithms are measured on the perturbed dataset in the MOOD system. The perturbations are added to simulate the noise in moving objects' data. The perturbed dataset is obtained by adding normal random numbers with zero mean and standard deviation 15 to each of the tuple values of the original dataset.

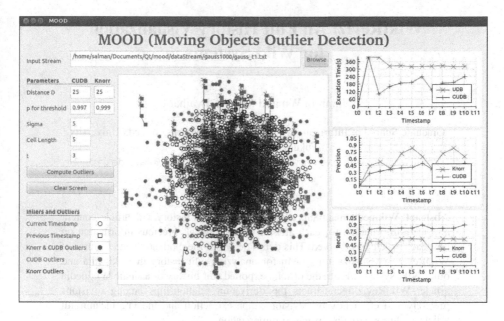

Fig. 1. The MOOD System Interface

Acknowledgements. This research was partly supported by the program "Research and Development on Real World Big Data Integration and Analysis" of the Ministry of Education, Culture, Sports, Science and Technology, Japan.

References

1. Hawkins, D.: Identification of Outliers. Chapman and Hall, London (1980)
2. Sharma, A.B., Golubchik, L., Govindan, R.: Sensor faults: detection methods and prevalence in real-world datasets. ACM Trans. Sens. Netw. 6(3), 23:1–23:39 (2010)
3. Aggarwal, C.C., Yu, P.S.: Outlier detection with uncertain data. In: SIAM ICDM, pp. 483–493 (2008)
4. Wang, B., Xiao, G., Yu, H., Yang, X.: Distance-based outlier detection on uncertain data. In: IEEE 9th ICCIT, pp. 293–298 (2009)
5. Shaikh, S.A., Kitagawa, H.: Efficient Distance-based Outlier Detection on Uncertain Datasets of Gaussian Distribution. In: World Wide Web, pp. 1–28 (2013)
6. Shaikh, S.A., Kitagawa, H.: Continuous Outlier Detection on Uncertain Data Streams. In: Proc. of IEEE 9th ISSNIP (2014)
7. Knorr, E.M., Ng, R.T., Tucakov, V.: Distance-Based Outliers: Algorithms and Applications. The VLDB Journal (2000)

WikiReviz: An Edit History Visualization for Wiki Systems

Jianmin Wu and Mizuho Iwaihara

Graduate School of Information, Production and Systems, Waseda University,
Fukuoka 808-0135, Japan
jianmin.wu@moegi.waseda.jp, iwaihara@waseda.jp

Abstract. Wikipedia maintains a linear record of edit history with article content and meta-information for each article, which conceals precious information on how each article has evolved. This demo describes the motivation and features of WikiReviz, a visualization system for analyzing edit history in Wikipedia and other Wiki systems. From the official exported edit history of a single Wikipedia article, WikiReviz reconstructs the derivation relationships among revisions precisely and efficiently by revision graph extraction and indicate meaningful article evolution progress by edit summarization.

Keywords: Wikipedia, Mass Collaboration, Visualization.

1   Introduction

As a collaborative project, online encyclopedia Wikipedia receives contribution from all over the world [13] and its content is well accepted by those who want reliable social news and knowledge. Guided by the fundamental principle of "Neutral Point of View", Wikipedia articles need plenty of extra editorial efforts other than simply content expanding and fact updating. Users can choose to edit on an existing revision and override the current one or revert to a previous revision. However, there is no explicit mechanism in Wikipedia to trace such derivation relationship among revisions, while the trajectories how such collaboration appears in Wikipedia articles in terms of revisions are valuable for group dynamics and social media research [4]. Also, research exploiting revision history for term weighting [1] requires clean history without astray, which can be accomplished by such trajectories.

Wikipedia and other Wiki systems generally keep all revisions' texts for each article and make the edit history publicly available. The meta-data of the edit history, such as timestamps, contributors, and edit comments are also recorded. We propose WikiReviz to model the article evolution process as *revision graph*. Here ReViz stands for "Revision Visualization". A *revision graph* is a DAG (directed acyclic graph) where each node represents one revision and each directed edge represents a derivation relationship from the origin node to the destination node [6]. Users create a new revision by editing either the current revision, or one of past revisions. Also, a completely new input may replace the current revision. Most existing research

L. Chen et al. (Eds.): APWeb 2014, LNCS 8709, pp. 670–673, 2014.
© Springer International Publishing Switzerland 2014

modeling Wikipedia's revision history choose tree [4][5] or graphs [2] to represent the relationship, but few of them concern about the accuracy.

2   WikiReviz Overview

WikiReviz takes the original XML file of edit history dump as an input, and automatically generates the revision graph with edit summaries in the GraphML format [9]. It is intended for English Wikipedia and other languages that have inter-word separation. WikiReviz is implemented in Java and currently consists of two functional parts: the Revision Graph Extraction [6] Unit, which reconstructs the graph structure from original edit history; and Edit Summarization [7] Unit, where we generate supergram summaries on revision graph.

2.1   Revision Graph Extraction (RGE)

For a given revision r, at least one parent revision r_p should be identified from r's previous revisions, which involves comparison between those revisions. The best candidate is decided by a certain similarity measure as well as the characteristics of Wikipedia editing. In WikiReviz, revisions are split into supergrams, which are maximal-length phrases and retrieved by word transition graph and path contraction. After comparing with others' supergrams, supergram diff score can be computed for each revision pair in the comparison scope. The whole process is shown in Fig. 1.

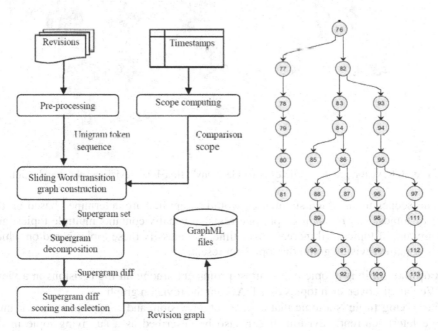

Fig. 1. RGE Process

Fig. 2. Part of result graph "PhpBB", from revision #76 to #113

The output of the RGE part is a GraphML file illustrating the revision graph, which can be viewed by existing software such as yEd graph editor. Fig. 2 shows a part of the graph of article "PhpBB" about an Internet forum package written in the PHP scripting language [8], where each node's id represents a revision number. Since the whole revision graph is too large, we only capture a close look at a small portion of it.

2.2　Edit Summarization

In the process of edit summarization, WikiReviz automatically summarizes contributed contents during a specified edit period in the revision graph of a Wikipedia article, into a group of maximal-length phrases, i.e. supergrams, and attaches to the original revision graph. From the supergram generated in previous RGE part, two supergram selection algorithms, TF-IDF and Extended LDA ranking are developed to pick up representative supergrams.

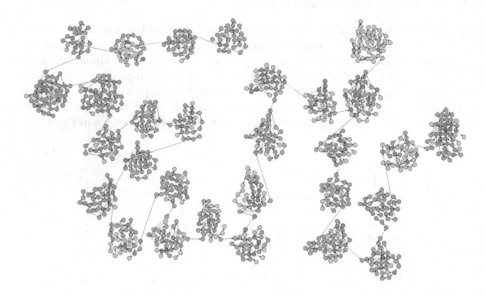

Fig. 3. Revision graph of article "Nazi Germany", first 1000 revisions, compact layout

The scopes upon which summaries would be applied are determined based on the type of topics. In a revision graph, one revision usually contains multiple topics, and the amount of topics will increase over time. We classify these topics based on which context in the revision graph the topics represent:

1. **Popular topic** is a topic that is most prominent among all the revisions in a view. We can discover such topics by LDA from the revision graph.
2. **Surviving topic** is a topic that appears at a revision, and continues to appear until the latest (current) revision. It can also be described as a surviving topic in the mainstream. After a period of edits, certain topics become stable and survive to the latest.

3. **Extinct topic** is a topic that is not surviving to the current revision. The definition of surviving topics is relative to the current revision, so if there are large amount of deletes after the current revision, several topics may be lost and surviving topics can be changed to extinct.

Fig. 3 shows an example, the whole revision graph of the first 1000 revisions of article "Nazi Germany", where scopes are divided by orange nodes. The blue nodes represent revisions that contain the surviving topics and the grey nodes are for extinct topics.

3   Conclusion

In this demo, we describe the motivation and features of our edit history visualization system WikiReviz, with visualization of revision graphs representing evolution processes of Wikipedia articles.

References

1. Aji, A., Wang, Y., Agichtein, E., Gabrilovich, E.: Using the past to score the present: extending term weighting models through revision history analysis. In: CIKM 2010, pp. 629–638. ACM, New York (2010)
2. Keegan, B., Gergle, D., Contractor, N.: Staying in the Loop: Structure and Dynamics of Wikipedia's Breaking News Collaborations. In: WikiSym 2012. ACM, New York (2012)
3. Lih, A.: Wikipedia as participatory journalism: Reliable sources: Metrics for evaluating collaborative media as a news resource. In: Proc. Int. Symp. Online Journalism (2004)
4. Ekstrand, M., Riedl, J.T.: rv you're dumb: identifying discarded work in Wiki article history. In: WikiSym 2009. ACM, New York (2009)
5. Flöck, F., Vrandečić, D., Simperl, E.: Revisiting reverts: accurate revert detection in Wikipedia. In: Proc. Hypertext and Social Media, pp. 3–12. ACM, New York (2012)
6. Wu, J., Iwaihara, M.: Revision graph extraction in Wikipedia based on supergram decomposition. In: Proc. WikiSym 2013(OpenSym 2013), Hongkong (August 2013)
7. Li, B., Wu, J., Iwaihara, M.: Tracking Topics on Revision Graphs of Wikipedia Edit History. In: Li, F., Li, G., Hwang, S.-w., Yao, B., Zhang, Z. (eds.) WAIM 2014. LNCS, vol. 8485, pp. 204–207. Springer, Heidelberg (2014)
8. http://en.wikipedia.org/wiki/PhpBB
9. http://graphml.graphdrawing.org/specification.html

TruthOrRumor: Truth Judgment from Web

Guangze Liu, Hongzhi Wang, ChengHui Chen, and Hong Gao

Harbin Institute of Technology, Harbin, China
{liugzhit,chenchenghui456}@gmail.com,
{wangzh,honggao}@hit.edu.cn

Abstract. Difficulty of truth judgment is the lack of knowledge. Motivated by this, we develop TruthOrRumer, which uses the information from web to judge the truth of a statement. In our system, we make sufficient use of search engines. To increase the accuracy, we also integrate web reliability computation and currency determination in our system. For the convenience for users to input the statement and review the judgment results with reasons, we design elegant interfaces. In this demonstration, we will show how the user interacts with our system and the accuracy of the system.

1   Introduction

The determination of whether a claim is a truth or a rumor has widely applications such as the judgment of the news media's speech, making sure uncertain statements, eliminating the bad impact of false information. Such techniques are called *truth judgment*. Some truth judgment methods have been proposed [1]. A difficulty in truth judgment is the lack of knowledge, especially for the truth judgment on open-field claims.

Since web is a very large knowledge base, it is a promising way to extract the knowledge from web for truth judgment. Web-based truth judgment brings following technical challenges.

(1). The information provided by multiple data sources may conflict. We may see completely different comments in different sites. For example, floods may be said on some blogs in 2012 (the end of the world), while CNN did not report it.

(2). The web may contain out-of-date information, which will misleading the judgment. For example, a news report there will be a hurricane recently, but this is a matter of a month ago. A concert had changed the time, but we still arrive at the old time.

(3). The description of a claim may have various form in different data sources. Due to the difficulty in nature language processing, it is difficult to make the computer recognize the different meanings we speak.

For these challenges, some techniques have been proposed such as a truthfulness determination approach for fact statements [2],[3]. Even though they could judge truths for many cases, they are not usable for many real applications. On one hand, they rely on the evaluation of multiple factors of data sources, which is inefficient in practice. On the other hand, they ignore the currency of information and copying relationship between data sources. For this reason, no end-to-end web-based truth judgment system for open field has been proposed.

L. Chen et al. (Eds.): APWeb 2014, LNCS 8709, pp. 674–678, 2014.

To support practical truth judgment, we develop TruthOrRumer, a web-based truth judgment system. Our system has following features.

(1). In contrast of crawling web pages, we use search engine to obtain sufficient related web pages for truth discovery efficiently. With the support of sufficient web pages, our system gains high accuracy in truth judgment. Additionally, with the help of search engine, our system could judge claims in open fields.

(2). For the effectiveness issues, we consider both reliability and currency of the data sources. We also use the results of truth discovery to evaluate the quality of data sources. Thus, the accuracy of our system keeps on increasing with more usages.

(3). The reasons for truth judgment are shown in our system. With this feature, users could explore the background and related information for the truth judgment. This makes the judgment results more trustable.

(4). We provide a single graphical interface. Even a preliminary user could use the system easily.

This paper is organized as follows. In Section 2, we briefly discuss the system overview to detect the principle. Then, we introduce key techniques in Section 3 before demonstrations are discussed in Section 4. The conclusions are drawn in Section 5.

2   System Overview

The organization of the system is shown in Figure 1. Then we describe these modules are follows.

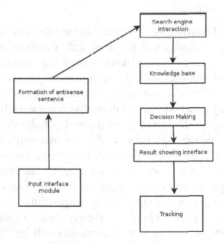

Fig. 1. System Overview

• **Input Interface Module:** This module collects users' input.

• **Formation of Antisense Sentence:** This module the system finds words such as verbs, adjectives, etc and matches thesaurus we established corresponding antonyms. As the result, the antisense statement of the input statement is generated.

• **Search Engine Interaction:** This module utilizes the search engine to obtain search results of the input statement and the antisense statement respectively. After that the system uses the results of our analysis to combine the search terms.

• **Knowledge Base:** To improve efficiency and increase accuracy, we use a knowledge base in the system. Based on the knowledge base, the relevant contents are obtained. We stored knowledge prior that we have to admit. When users use the system, it will first call the knowledge base. If the knowledge base has no relevant content, and then use the Google search engines. The advantage of this system is to improve the speed and accuracy of speech.

• **Decision Making:** This module makes decisions for the truth statement according to the search results. Search results are analysis is to parse the search results to draw the conclusion. The details of this part will be discussed in Section 3.1.

• **Result Showing Interface:** This module shows the judgment results to the users.

• **Tracking:** This module shows users the reasons for the judgment. With this module, users could review the websites that support or oppose the statement to make their own decisions.

3   Web-Based Truth Judgement

In this section, we discuss the techniques used in our system including search result analysis for truth judgment strategy, website weight computation and currency determination.

3.1   Search Results Analysis

The truth could be judged by trivially comparing the numbers of search results of the two statements. Unfortunately, this way will not work well. Consider an example. We believe that the extent of the authority of the well-known large websites comments on something is higher than the level of websites with low authority. However, for a case, with 5 true statement on CNN, but 1000 false statements on tweet, the comparison of search result numbers will draw wrong conclusions. Additionally, if some web sites copy each other, the count of the search result could not show the real popular degree. Thus the analysis takes both the reliability and the copy between data sources into consideration.

We use a weighted voting strategy for truth judgment. To reduce the affects of result numbers, we choose top-n search results for each statement. Then by analyzing the content of the web pages, irrelevant pages are filtered. The votes are from remaining pages. Each page contributes w votes for corresponding statement, where w is the weight of the page. $w=ar+(1-a)c$, where r is the reliability of the website and c is the currency factor. The computation of these parameters will be discussed in Section 3.2 and 3.3, respectively, and a is the reliability importance. a is obtained by learning from history judgment records in period.

3.2   Reliability Computation

We compute the reliability of the web page from two aspects. The first is its accuracy in history record and the second is the copying relationship.

Initially, all websites are assigned the same reliability 0.5, showing the uncertain reliability. Then we store the reliability during truth judgment, the reliability is update according to the results. Then we discuss the strategy. We denote the total numbers of positive and negative judgment in historical records supported by a web site s as T and F, respectively. We use $r=T/(T+F)$ as the reliability of the web set. The reliability of each web site is stored and maintained according to the judgment results.

With the consideration of copying relationship, we revise the techniques in [4] to modify the reliability. The major difference between our approach and that in [4] is that we use historical truth judgment results instead of the results for various tuples.

3.3   The Currency Determination

Clearly, the out-of-date statements will mislead the judgment. For accurate judgment, we propose currency determination techniques. Firstly, based on the web pages obtained from the search engine, we obtain the time stamped t in the priority order of (1) the time stated in the nearest position of the statement, i.e. in the same sentence, paragraph or text fragment with the statement; (2). the time stamp in the web page. Then the currency parameter is computed as b^{t_0-t}, where b is decay factor and fixed as 0.9 in our system, and t_0 is current time stamp.

4   Demonstration

In this section, we will discuss the demonstration of our system.

The welcome interface is shown in Figure 2. As shown in Figure 3, we provide a very elegant interface for users to input the statement.

Fig. 2. Welcoming Interface

Fig. 3. Input Interface

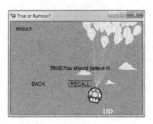

Fig. 4. Feedback Interface

Fig. 5. Tracking Interface

The judgment of the statement is shown as Figure 4. For a better interaction with users, we provide the tracking function to make users review the reasons to make the decision. Figure 5 shows that our system provides the URLs to support users to find a related site.

5   Conclusions and Ongoing Work

Internet provides plenty of information to judge the truth of a statement. To make sufficient use of the information on the web, we develop TruthOrRumer. This system permits a user to input a statement. Then the negative statement of the statement is generated. These two statements are sent to the search engine. From the obtained search results, the truth is determined. To make the judgment accurate, we also take the reliability and the currency into consideration. In this demonstration, we will show the functions and benefits of our system. Our future work includes web-based interface and involving larger knowledge base in our system.

Acknowledgement. This paper was partially supported by NGFR 973 grant 2012C B316200, NSFC grant 61003046, 61111130189 and NGFR 863 grant 2012AA011004.

References

[1] Meng, W., Li, X., Dong, X.L.: Truth Finding on the Deep Web: Is the Prob-lem Solved? Proceedings of the VLDB Endowment 6(2), 97–108 (2012)
[2] Wang, T., Zhu, Q., Wang, S.: Multi-verifier: A Novel Method for Fact Statement Verification. In: Ishikawa, Y., Li, J., Wang, W., Zhang, R., Zhang, W. (eds.) APWeb 2013. LNCS, vol. 7808, pp. 526–537. Springer, Heidelberg (2013)
[3] Wang, T., Zhu, Q., Wang, S.: MFSV: A Truthfulness Determination Approach for Fact Statements. In: Meng, W., Feng, L., Bressan, S., Winiwarter, W., Song, W. (eds.) DASFAA 2013, Part II. LNCS, vol. 7826, pp. 155–163. Springer, Heidelberg (2013)
[4] Dong, X.L., Srivastava, D.: Detecting Clones, Copying and Reuse on the Web. In: ICDE, pp. 1211–1213 (2012)

Author Index